Study Guide to Accompany

INTRODUCTION TO PSYCHOLOGY
EXPLORATION AND APPLICATION

Fifth Edition

by

Dennis Coon
Santa Barbara City College

Prepared by:

Faren Akins

With crossword puzzles prepared by:

David E. Cunningham
IECC-Olney Central College

West Publishing Company
St Paul   New York   Los Angeles   San Francisco

COPYRIGHT © 1989 by WEST PUBLISHING CO.
50 W. Kellogg Boulevard
P.O. Box 64526
St. Paul, MN 55164-1003

Contents

Acknowledgements

The author wishes to thank Dr. Dennis L. Coon for his help in the evaluation and criticism of the *Study Guide*. Thanks also go to Dr. and Mrs. Coon for their friendship and encouragement throughout each phase of this project.

Appreciation is also extended to my West editor for his assistance and positive guidance. The excellent staff at West also deserves praise for their efficiency and reliability.

Finally, I'd like to acknowledge and dedicate this edition to some very special friends—John and Laura, Pete, Teri, and Christopher, and Galon and Jane. Thanks for all your love.

FAREN R. AKINS, PH.D.

Preface

Welcome to the world of psychology, and to the *Study Guide* which accompanies *Introduction to Psychology: Exploration and Application*. It is hoped that this manual will help you in mastering the principles presented in the text and stimulate your interest in the field of psychology.

If you have read the preface to the text, you know that each chapter is designed to help you use the SQ3R method. As discussed in Chapter One's Applications, Dr. Francis Robinson designed the SQ3R approach to help you
    1) select what is important;
    2) understand these ideas quickly;
    3) remember what you have read; and
    4) review effectively for tests.
The *Study Guide* has also been designed to help you use this learning technique.

Each chapter of the *Study Guide* is divided into five sections. The first section (Contents) provides you with an overview of the main topics discussed in the text. Use these headings as a foundation for outlining your own notes and organizing your thoughts. Remember that effective note-taking is an extremely important way for you to learn and remember. When reviewing for tests use the headings as a starting point to quiz yourself about the material in those sections. Remember that self-testing is an excellent way to catch your errors before actually taking in-class tests. As you review each topic, ask yourself, "What could I be asked about this?" Ask as many questions as you can and be sure you can answer them.

The next two sections of the *Study Guide* (Terms and Concepts, Important Individuals) provide you with a listing of key items from the text. These sections are designed to help you *select what is important*. They are listed in the same order as presented in the text and, like "Contents," can also help you check the thoroughness of your notes. When reviewing for exams, a good idea is to make up flashcards using the listed items. When using your flashcards, remember that study beyond "bare mastery" of a topic improves performance on class exams.

The Programmed Review section of each chapter is designed to give you immediate *feedback* on your knowledge of the material in the text. After thoroughly reading the chapter, work through the Programmed Review by writing words or phrases in the blank spaces provided. Then check the Answer Section at the end of each chapter to evaluate your accuracy. It's a good idea to put a check by any items you missed and be sure to give yourself extra practice on those items and the material they discuss. The Programmed Review section provides you with a handy study guide to help you do this. In the parentheses to the left of each question, you'll find the page of the text on which the correct answer to that question appears. You can then easily find pages of the text pertinent to each question in the *Study Guide*.

While the Programmed Review is designed to help you *review effectively for tests,* remember that this is only a study *guide.* Not every detail, example, or question in the text is covered in the Programmed Review. Rather, this section of the *Study Guide* is designed to help you *select what is important* by reviewing the main ideas of each text chapter. As with the other *Study Guide* sections use it as a foundation for notes, evaluation of your understanding, and review of important principles.

The best way to prepare for in-class exams is to test yourself using questions similar to those you might expect to face on actual exams. That is the purpose of the Self-Test section of the *Study Guide.* These questions are written in multiple-choice and true-false format since that is what the majority of college instructors use for introductory classes. (If your instructor uses essay questions you'll want to give special attention to the Survey Questions at the beginning of each main text chapter and to the Questions for Discussion section at the end of each main text chapter.) When you work on the Self-Test items, remember these guidelines for taking tests:

1) Read each statement or question carefully.
2) In the case of multiple-choice items, read each alternative answer carefully.
3) Eliminate certain alternatives.
4) Feel free to change your answers, especially if you feel *very* uncertain of your first answer. When you have strong doubts, your second answer is more likely to be correct.

After you complete the Self-Test items, check your answers with those in the Answer Section at the end of each chapter. Make special note of any items you missed; reread and study the main text pages and the Programmed Review items that relate to that topic. The number of the main text page which answers each Self-Test question appears in the parentheses at the beginning of each question.

A new and enjoyable feature in this edition of the *Study Guide* is a set of crossword puzzles, one for each chapter prepared by David E. Cunningham of IECC-Olney Central College. The puzzles test your knowledge of terminology and emphasize key concepts from the chapters. Answer keys for all the puzzles are found at the end of the *Study Guide.*

While the *Study Guide* and the main text are designed to help you learn, remember that motivation, time management, consistency, and practice are all important. If you need help in any of these areas make use of the Suggestions for Further Reading presented at the end of the text's introduction. Good luck!

Chapter 1

Psychology and Psychologists

CONTENTS

TERMS AND CONCEPTS

psychology
empirical evidence
data
scientific observation
comparative psychology
anthropomorphic fallacy
models
psychometrics
introspection
experimental self-observation
structuralism
functionalism
natural selection
educational psychology
industrial psychology
behaviorism
stimulus-response psychology
conditioned response
behavior modification
Gestalt psychology
psychoanalytic psychology
unconscious
psychoanalysis

neo-Freudians
humanistic psychology
determinism
free will
self-image
self-evaluation
frame of reference
self-actualization
psychobiology
cognitive psychology
basic research
applied research
American Psychological Association (APA)
SQ3R
LISAN
mnemonic
overlearning
pseudo-psychologies
palmistry
phrenology
graphology
astrology
fallacy of positive instances

IMPORTANT INDIVIDUALS

Wilhelm Wundt

Edward B. Titchener

William James

Charles Darwin

John B. Watson

Ivan Pavlov

B. F. Skinner

Christine Ladd-Franklin

Margaret Washburn

Max Wertheimer

Sigmund Freud

Francis Robinson

Franz Gall

PROGRAMMED REVIEW

1. (p. 3)   Psychology is the scientific study of human and animal _____.

2. (p. 3)   Behavior is defined as anything you do. Behavior can be either _____ (visible) or _____ (private or internal).

3. (p. 3)   Facts or information gained through observation and measurement are called _____ evidence.

4. (p. 3)   Whenever possible, psychologists settle differences by collecting _____ (facts or evidence). Psychologists are keenly aware that opinions, or claims made by an "authority," may be wrong.

5. (p. 4)   An example of collecting data to answer questions is provided by psychologists Douglas Kenrick and Steven MacFarlane. They recorded the number of times drivers honked at a stalled car when temperatures ranged from 88 degrees to 116 degrees. They found that the higher temperatures were linked with an _____ in the amount of time spent honking.

6. (p. 4)   Empiricism alone is not enough to make a science. True scientific observation must also be _____. That is, it has to be structured so that observations reveal something about the underlying nature of behavior. They must be carefully planned and recorded.

7. (p. 5)   While psychology is definitely a science, it is a "young" science. Sometimes, psychologists are unable to answer questions because of _____ or _____ concerns. As one example, consider that the study of human sexual response by Masters and Johnson could not be conducted and published earlier in psychology's history because of the prevailing social climate.

8. (p. 6)   More frequently, psychological questions remain unanswered because a suitable _____ _____ does not yet exist. For example, only since the development of the electroencephalograph have researchers been able to objectively determine when a person is dreaming.

9. (p. 6)   As a group, psychologists are interested in the natural laws governing the behavior of any living creature. Indeed, specialists known as _____ psychologists may spend their entire careers comparing the behavior of different species to learn about their similarities and differences.

10. (p. 6)   Attributing human thoughts, feelings, and motives to animals constitutes the _____ _____ and should be avoided because it can lead to false conclusions and cloud our understanding of animal behavior.

11. (p. 7)   Many psychologists use animal research to discover principles in simplified experiments that prove useful for solving human problems. In fact, animals serving as _____ may sometimes provide the only information available on a particular topic.

12. (p. 7)   Psychological knowledge also benefits animals. For example, the successful breeding and care of endangered species in _____ relies on behavioral research. So, too, does the training of guide dogs for the blind.

13. (p. 7)   In general, the goals of psychology are to _____, _____, _____, and _____. Beyond this, psychology's ultimate goal is to gather knowledge for the benefit of humanity.

14. (p. 7)   Useful knowledge begins with accurate _____, or naming and classifying. But understanding behavior is met when we can _____ why an event occurs.

15. (p. 7)   Psychology's third goal is _____. In psychology it is rarely as precise as in the "hard sciences," but often quite useful nonetheless. For example, psychological research predicts that you will suffer less jet lag if you fly _____ early in the day and _____ late in the day.

16. (p. 7)   Prediction is especially important in _____. Specialists in this area use various tests to predict such things as success in school, work, or career.

17. (p. 7)   To most psychologists the fourth goal, _____, simply means altering conditions that influence behavior in predictable ways.

18. (p. 8)   Psychology's past is centuries old because it includes _____, the study of knowledge, reality, and human nature. But, modern psychology's history began only about _____ years ago.

19. (p. 8)   Psychology's history began in 1879 at Leipzig, Germany where the "father" of psychology, _____ _____, created the first psychological laboratory to study conscious experience.

20. (p. 8)   Wundt wondered how sensations, images, and feelings are formed. To find out, he observed and carefully measured _____ of various kinds (lights, sounds, weights).

21. (p. 8)   Wundt combined this scientific measurement with _____ (or "looking inward") and called this approach _____ _____.

22. (p. 8)   Experimental self-observation was a highly developed skill, much like that needed to be a professional wine taster. Wundt's subjects had to make at least _____ practice observations before they were allowed to take part in a real experiment.

23. (p. 8)   Wundt's ideas were carried to the United States by one of his students, _____, who helped launch a school of thought called _____, because they dealt with the structure of mental life.

24. (p. 8)   The structuralists hoped to develop a sort of "mental chemistry" by analyzing

conscious experience into basic _____ or building blocks. They relied greatly upon introspection.

25. (p. 8)   Introspection left much to be desired because introspectionists frequently _____. Still, "looking inward" is a useful part of today's psychology in the study of hypnosis, meditation, drug effects, problem-solving, etc.

26. (p. 9)   _____ _____, an American psychologist, broadened the scope of psychology to include animal behavior, religious experience, and abnormal behavior.

27. (p. 9)   James is interested in how the mind _____ to adapt us to a changing environment, hence the term _____ de- scribing James' school of thought.

28. (p. 9)   The functionalists were particularly influenced by _____ _____ and his theory of evolution.

29. (p. 9)   Darwin showed that animals evolve, through _____ _____, in ways that favor their survival. That is, features which function to adapt animals to their environment are retained in evolution.

30. (p. 9)   The functionalists, then, sought to understand how thought, perceptions, habits, and emotions aid human _____. They wanted to study the mind in use.

31. (p. 9)   Functionalism brought the study of animals into psychology by linking human and animal _____.

32. (p. 9)   Functionalists emphasized that learning improves personal adaptability, and urged psychologists to help improve education. Thus, they helped to foster the development of _____ psychology.

33. (p. 9)   Functionalism also spurred the rise of _____ psychology, a specialty involving the study of people at work.

34. (p. 9)   Functionalism was soon challenged by a new school of thought called _____ or _____ - _____ psychology, led in part by John B. Watson.

35. (p. 9)   Watson objected to introspection and rejected the functionalists' use of mentalistic concepts. Instead, he observed the relationship between _____ (events in the environment) and an animal's _____ to them.

36. (p. 9)   Watson adopted the _____ _____ (a learned reaction to a particular stimulus) as an explanation for most behavior. This concept was originally introduced by Russian physiologist Ivan Pavlov.

37. (p. 10)   One of the best-known and most influential modern behaviorists is _____, who maintains that behavior is shaped and maintained by its _____.

38. (p. 10)   Skinner's emphasis on stimulus-response relationships, and his tendency to ignore thought and subjective experience has led some observers to charge that Skinnerian psychology has "lost consciousness." However, most psychologists would still agree that human behavior is greatly influenced by _____.

39. (p. 10)   The behavioristic approach is responsible for much of what we know today about learning, memory, conditioning, and the proper use of reward and punishment. A very direct descendant of behavioristic thought is _____ _____, a system which uses conditioning principles to treat problems such as overeating, phobias, and childhood misbehavior.

40. (p. 10)   Histories of psychology seldom mention women because men dominated academic life in the late 1800s. Even so, by 1906 in America about one psychologist in every _____ was a woman.

41. (p. 10)   _____ was the first American woman to complete requirements for the doctorate in psychology, in 1882. However, her degree was not awarded due to a university policy that denied women the doctorate.

42. (p. 10)   The first woman to be awarded a Ph.D. in psychology was _____, in 1894.

43. (p. 10)   Today the number of males and females receiving doctoral degrees in psychology is roughly _____. And, in recent years, the number of female psychology graduates at the bachelor's level has far _____ the number of male psychology graduates.

44. (p. 10)   The _____ (meaning form, pattern, or whole) school of thought was founded by Max Wertheimer.

45. (p. 10)   The Gestaltists thought it was a mistake to analyze psychological events into pieces or "elements." Instead, they tried to study experiences as _____.

46. (p. 10)   They emphasized the _____ between elements, such as the notes in a musical score or the qualities of a painting. Their slogan was, "The whole exceeds the sum of its parts."

47. (p. 10)   Many experiences resist analysis that divides them into separate pieces. For this reason, the Gestalt viewpoint remains influential in the study of _____ and _____.

48. (p. 10)   As the mainstream of psychology was becoming more objective, scientific, and experimental, _____ _____, an Austrian physician, was developing a theory of personality known today as _____ psychology.

49. (p. 11)   Freud felt that mental experience was like an iceberg, only part is exposed to view. There are vast areas of _____ thoughts, conflicts, and desires, which cannot be experienced directly.

50. (p. 11)   Because these thoughts are usually of a sexual or aggressive nature they are threatening and therefore _____ (actively held out of consciousness).

51. (p. 11)   Sometimes these thoughts are revealed in dreams, emotions, or _____ _____ (slips of the tongue).

52. (p. 11)   Freud made many contributions to the field of psychology. One of these was his insistence that all thoughts, emotions, and actions are _____ (nothing is an accident).

53. (p. 11)   Another contribution was his emphasis on the importance of _____ in later personality development. Thus the phrase, "the child is father to the man."

54. (p. 11)   Also, Freud developed a method of psychotherapy called _____.

55. (p. 11)   Not long after Freud's rise, some of his students, such as Carl Jung, began to break away from him. These psychologists developed their own theories and became known as _____ - _____.

56. (p. 11)   Today, Freud's ideas have been enlarged, altered, revised, and adapted to the point that few strictly psychoanalytic psychologists are left. However, Freud's legacy is still evident in various _____ approaches to psychology, which emphasize the interplay of internal forces in the personality.

57. (p. 11)   The "third force" in psychology is _____, a relatively recent development. The other two forces are _____ psychology and _____.

58. (p. 11)   Psychologists Carl Rogers, Abraham Maslow, and others developed the humanistic approach to counter the negativity they saw in other views. They are uncomfortable with determinism and in contrast stress _____ _____, the human ability to make choices.

59. (p. 11)   Humanists do admit that past experiences affect personality. However, they also believe that people can freely _____ to live more creative, meaningful, and satisfying lives.

60. (p. 11)   Humanists helped stimulate interest in psychological _____ for love, self-esteem, belonging, self-expression, and creativity. As an example of how important these factors are, they point out that newborn infants who are deprived of human love and emotional warmth may die just as surely as they would if deprived of food.

61. (p. 11)   While humanists collect data and seek evidence to support their ideas, they tend to be less interested in treating psychology as an objective, behavioral science. Instead, they stress the importance of _____ factors.

62. (p. 12)   As examples of such subjective factors, they focus on _____ - _____, which refers to your total perception of yourself, including images of your body, personality, and abilities.

63. (p. 12)   Another important subjective factor is your _____ - _____, which consists of positive and negative feelings you hold toward yourself.

64. (p. 12)   The humanists also stress the concept of your _____ of _____. That is, the mental and emotional perspective you use to judge events.

65. (p. 12)   A unique feature of the humanistic approach is Maslow's description of _____ - _____, the need to develop one's potential fully, to lead a rich and meaningful life, and to become the best person one can become.

66. (p. 12)   Today, several of the traditional schools of thought have given way to a blending of ideas and perspectives. Many psychologists can be described as _____ (drawing from many sources) in their approach.

67. (p. 12)   In addition to the more traditional views within the field, other approaches have recently become increasingly valuable. Due to an explosive growth in knowledge

about how the brain works and its relation to thought, feelings, perception, and abnormal behavior, _____ approaches for understanding behavior have become a major emphasis.

68. (p. 12) A similar trend has occurred for _____ psychology. This approach studies thoughts, expectations, language, perception, problem solving, consciousness, creativity, and other mental processes.

69. (p. 12) Some of the topics now studied by cognitive psychologists were neglected for so many years that psychology can be said to have recently "regained consciousness." _____ models of human thinking have been especially important in spurring recent advances in cognitive psychology.

70. (p. 13) Psychologists usually have a _____ degree or a _____ in psychology; that is, from three to eight years of specialized postgraduate training in psychological theory and research methods.

71. (p. 13) Psychologists interested in human emotional problems and their treatment specialize in _____ or _____ psychology.

72. (p. 13) The practice of counseling was once limited to problems not involving serious _____ _____, such as adjustment at work or school. Recently, however, differences between counseling and clinical psychology are beginning to fade as more counseling psychologists have shifted to doing psychotherapy primarily.

73. (p. 14) To enter the profession of psychology today, you would probably find it necessary to have a doctorate in order to be licensed or to qualify for employment. Most clinical psychologists now have a Ph.D. or a Psy.D. (Doctor of Psychology). The latter is a new degree that emphasizes practical _____ skills rather than research.

74. (p. 14) Psychiatrists are physicians who specialize in abnormal behavior and psychotherapy. They are trained to treat the _____ causes of psychological problems and can prescribe _____.

75. (p. 14) A _____ is a psychologist or psychiatrist extensively trained in the theory and practice of Freudian psychoanalysis.

76. (p. 14) Today, few psychiatrists and almost no psychologists become analysts. Traditional psychoanalysis is _____ and _____ consuming and fewer clients are seeking this form of treatment. In practice, many psychotherapists find that a flexible and eclectic approach is most effective.

77. (p. 14) In many states counselors (such as marriage and family counselors, _____ counselors or _____ counselors) also do mental health work. To be a licensed counselor typically requires a master's degree and supervised counseling experience.

78. (p. 14) To be legally called a _____, a person must now meet a rigorous set of educational requirements. To work as a clinical or counseling psychologist, an individual must have a _____ issued by a state examining board.

79. (p. 14) Psychologists are expected to follow professional codes established by the American Psychological Association (APA) which stress: (1) accurate representation of one's

professional _____ ; (2) _____
in handling of personal information in teaching, practice, or research; and (3) protection of the client's _____ .

80. (p. 14)   Approximately _____ percent of psychologists are clinical or counseling psychologists.
The rest divide into _____ specialties currently recognized by the APA.

81. (p. 15)   Roughly one psychologist out of every ___ is employed full-time at a college or
university where he/she teaches and may also do research, consultation, or therapy.

82. (p. 15)   Psychologists engaged in research may do _____ research, seeking knowledge for the sake of knowledge, or _____ research, in which
immediate uses are planned for the information gained.

83. (p. 15)   Be familiar with the wide range of interests and specialties within the field of
psychology described in Table 1-3 and in the main body of the text. As one example,
a _____ psychologist carries out research on child
development, adult developmental trends and aging; and may do clinical work with
disturbed children or act as a consultant to preschools or programs for the aged.

84. (p. 18)   Over 40 years ago, educator _____ _____
developed a method of combining studying with reading. The technique was called
the _____ method.

85. (p. 18)   The symbols S-Q-R-R-R stand for five steps that can help you understand ideas
quickly, remember more, and review effectively for tests. The letters represent

_____, _____, _____, _____,
and _____ .

86. (p. 18)   Experiments show that using the SQ3R method improves both reading
_____ and _____ .

87. (p. 19)   While the SQ3R method is good for reading, it is also important to understand and
practice how to be an effective note taker. This skill requires _____
listening—the ability to control one's attention to avoid classroom daydreaming.

88. (p. 19)   LISAN is a listening/note-taking plan that involves five steps, each represented by a
letter in the word. The five steps are _____, _____, _____
_____, _____ _____ , and _____-
_____ .

89. (p. 19)   A recent study found that most students do take reasonably good notes and then don't
use them. Instead of waiting until just before exams to review notes, it pays to
review them on a _____ basis.

90. (p. 19)   Making a course interesting means both students and teachers must do their part. As
a student, interest has much to do with your _____ . Students
who believe that success is due to effort and motivation do better in the long run.

91. (p. 19)   To make the most of your study time, work in a quiet, well-lighted area free of
distractions. If possible, you should also have at least one place where you
_____ _____ . In this way, studying will become strongly linked
with a specific place and make it easier to get work done.

92. (p. 20)   Using a large number of relatively short study sessions has been shown to be a more
efficient way to study than to use one or two long periods. Cramming places a

tremendous burden on memory. Therefore, use _____ practice rather than _____ practice when learning information for the first time.

93. (p. 20)   To help in memorizing material for classes, it can be helpful to use a _____—that is, a memory aid. Most link new information to ideas or images that are easy to remember.

94. (p. 20)   A good way to improve test scores is to arrange to take several "practice tests" before the real one in class. Studying should include _____-_____ by use of flashcards, Learning Checks, a study guide, or questions you ask yourself.

95. (p. 20)   In order to avoid underpreparing for exams, make sure to _____— that is, continue studying beyond "bare mastery" of a topic.

96. (p. 20)   It is probably best to approach all tests as if they were _____. Research shows that students who expect multiple-choice questions actually score lower.

97. (p. 20)   A tendency to _____ is almost universal among college students. Studies show that this can include putting off work until the last possible moment, working only under pressure, skipping classes, giving false reasons for late work, and feeling ashamed of last-minute efforts.

98. (p. 20)   Psychologists Jane Burka and Lenora Yuen observe that many students seem to equate performance in school with their _____ _____. By procrastinating, students can blame poor work on a late start, rather than a lack of ability.

99. (p. 20)   _____ is a related problem. If you have high expectations for yourself, you may find it hard to start an assignment and end up with all-or-nothing work habits.

100. (p. 21)   A formal _____ _____ can do much to prevent procrastination and maintain motivation in school. Start by making a chart showing all of the hours in each day of the week. Then fill in committed times, times when you will study for various classes, and add the remaining hours as open or free times.

101. (p. 21)   Many students also find it helpful to set _____ _____ for themselves. If you have trouble staying motivated, it's a good idea to set goals for the semester, the week, the day, and even for single study sessions.

102. (p. 21)   Objective tests evaluate your ability to recognize a correct statement among wrong answers. When taking multiple-choice and true-false items, remember these points: (1) Read the _____ carefully—they may give you good advice or clues for the test. (2) Read _____ of the choices for each question before you make a decision. (3) Read rapidly and _____ items you are uncertain about. (4) Eliminate certain alternatives. (5) Unless there is a penalty for guessing, be sure to answer every question. (6) When you have strong doubts, your _____ answer is more likely to be correct.

103. (p. 21)   When taking essay exams remember these points: (1) Read the question carefully and make sure that you note _____ words. (2) Think about your answer before _____; make a brief list of the points you want to make. (3) Don't pad your answer. Be direct. Make a point and support it. (4) Check your essay for spelling errors, sentence errors, and grammatical errors.

104. (p. 23)   _____ - _____ are dubious and unfounded systems superficially resembling psychology. Many offer a highly developed system that gives the appearance of science, but is actually false.

105. (p. 23)   As one example of pseudo-psychologies, _____ claims that lines in the hand are indicators of personality and a person's future.

106. (p. 23)   Franz _____ popularized _____, the notion that personality traits could be determined by bumps on a person's head.

107. (p. 23)   _____ postulates that personality is revealed by handwriting. This technique is widely used for job placement and advancement in _____ and by at least _____ companies in the United States.

108. (p. 23)   These uses are somewhat distressing to psychologists because studies show that graphologists score close to _____ on careful tests of accuracy in rating personality.

109. (p. 23)   One study has found that graphologists do _____ than untrained college students in rating personality and sales success, based on the handwriting of a group of salespersons.   In another study, graphologists scored no better than _____ at predicting the professions of 40 people.

110. (p. 24)   _____, probably the most popular pseudo-psychology, is based on the assumption that the position of the stars and planets at the time of a person's birth determines personality characteristics and affects behavior.

111. (p. 24)   Astrology seems to work for several reasons. For one, it tends to describe personality in _____ terms, showing a preponderance of flattering traits.

112. (p. 24)   All pseudo-psychologies are subject to the _____ of _____ _____ in which persons remember or notice things that confirm their expectations and forget the rest.

113. (p. 25)   Finally, pseudo-psychologies are stated in such _____ terms that they always have "a little something for everybody." We can call this the P. T. Barnum Effect.

114. (p. 25)   A recent experiment showed that among people given the same personality description, those who had initially provided more detailed information considered their horoscopes to be more _____. Thus, the more "hocus-pocus" to the pseudo-psychology, the more believable the results.

SELF-TEST

1. (p. 3)   Psychology is the scientific study of human and animal _____.
   a. psyche
   b. behavior
   c. physiology
   d. social organization

2. (p. 3)   Psychologists try to be objective in their observations and place special importance on information obtained through
   a. empirical evidence
   b. open communication
   c. professional opinion
   d. reliance on authority

3. (p. 5)   Scientific study of some topics in psychology is not yet possible. Which of the following best explains why?
    a. ethical and practical limitations exist or there is a lack of suitable research methods
    b. in some areas, humans have not yet evolved to the point where behavior can be properly observed and measured
    c. we have everything we need to scientifically study all behavior, but the social climate does not always permit this
    d. most psychologists feel that behavior should not be studied scientifically

4. (p. 6)   Which of the following is an example of an anthropomorphic statement?
    a. Johnny hoped the dog would come to him.
    b. The dog hoped Johnny would come to him.
    c. Johnny looked at the dog.
    d. The dog looked at Johnny.

5. (p. 7)   Which of the following is *not* a goal of psychology?
    a. description of behavior   c. depiction of behavior
    b. prediction of behavior   d. understanding behavior.

6. (p. 7)   Control is an important goal of psychology. For most psychologists, control means
    a. heavy reliance upon rewards rather than punishments
    b. manipulation of behavior by government, educators, scientists, or authorities
    c. altering conditions that influence behavior in predictable ways
    d. explaining why a phenomenon occurs or exists under structured conditions

7. (p. 8)   The goal of Wilhelm Wundt, the "father" of psychology, was
    a. to understand how humans perceive thoughts
    b. to understand how sensations, images, and feelings are formed
    c. to compare animal and human behaviors in functional ways
    d. to explore behavior in an "armchair" fashion using the principles of philosophy

8. (p. 8)   Wundt combined scientific measurement with careful introspection to create an approach he called
    a. experimental structuralism   c. scientific self-actualization
    b. psychoanalysis   d. experimental self-observation

9. (p. 8)   Wundt's student, Edward B. Titchener, helped launch a school of psychology called _____ that sought to analyze conscious experience into basic "elements."
    a. structuralism   c. functionalism
    b. chemical psychology   d. humanism

10. (p. 9)   The functionalist school of thought developed from William James' interest in
    a. how basic elements of behavior function in the mind
    b. how the mind functions to adapt us to a changing environment
    c. how functional relationships exist such that the whole exceeds the sum of its parts
    d. how responses are a function of stimuli

11. (p. 9)   Which of the following is *not* a contribution to psychology made by the functionalists?
    a. introducing the study of animals into psychology
    b. contributing to the development of educational psychology
    c. developing an important form of psychotherapy
    d. spurring the development of industrial psychology

12. (p. 9)   John B. Watson, who helped define the behavioristic viewpoint, relied heavily upon which concept in explaining behavior?

a. consciousness
b. behavior modification

c. conditioned response
d. functional relationships

13. (p. 10)   "In order to understand human behavior we must take into account what the environment does to an organism before and after it responds." This quote defines the position of which of the following?
a. William James
b. Sigmund Freud

c. B. F. Skinner
d. Wilhelm Wundt

14. (p. 10)   The first American woman to be awarded a Ph.D. in psychology in 1894 was
a. Mary Calkins
b. Christine Ladd-Franklin

c. Lillien Martin
d. Margaret Washburn

15. (p. 10)   The slogan, "The whole exceeds the sum of its parts," is associated with which school of thought?
a. functionalism
b. structuralism

c. behaviorism
d. Gestalt

16. (p. 11)   Which of the following is *not* a contribution to psychology made by Sigmund Freud and the psychoanalytic school of thought?
a. insistence that all thoughts, emotions, and actions are determined
b. introducing the study of animals into psychology
c. emphasis on the importance of childhood in later personality development
d. developing a method of psychotherapy

17. (p. 11)   True-False. Humanism is a science interested in humane research with animals.

18. (p. 11)   The humanistic viewpoint emphasizes the importance of
a. free will
b. biological needs

c. unconscious processes
d. behavior determined by the environment

19. (p. 12)   The _____ approach in psychology has provided a new and increasingly important perspective. Here, the emphasis is on the study of thoughts, expectations, language, perception, problem solving, etc.
a. biological
b. cognitive

c. humanistic
d. psychoanalytic

20. (p. 14)   A _____ is trained to treat physical causes of psychological difficulties and can prescribe drugs.
a. psychoanalyst
b. psychiatrist

c. school or child counselor
d. clinical or counseling psychologist

21. (p. 14)   True-False. The majority of psychologists today still practice the theories of Sigmund Freud.

22. (p. 14)   True-False. To practice as a clinical or counseling psychologist, an individual must have a master's degree, two years of full-time supervised experience, and sometimes a license issued by a state examining board.

23. (p. 14)   Psychologists adhere to a professional code established by the APA. Which of the following is *not* a part of the code?
a. protection of the client's welfare
b. accurate representation of one's professional qualifications
c. ensuring availability of services to everyone by charging the same rates regardless of the client's financial or social status
d. confidentiality in handling personal information in teaching, practice, or research

24. (p. 14)   About 50% of psychologists are employed full-time in
         a. private practices   c. research facilities
         b. government projects   d. educational institutions

25. (p. 15)   Who among the following would be most likely to do clinical work with disturbed children, explore aging and adult trends, or act as consultants to preschools or programs for the aged?
         a. social psychologists   c. comparative psychologists
         b. clinical psychologists   d. developmental psychologists

26. (p. 16)   True-False. Social psychologists are primarily interested in studying people in a group setting, or under any circumstance in which social factors play a part.

27. (p. 18)   Which of the following is a method developed by Francis Robinson for learning new information that combines studying with reading?
         a. LISAN   c. APA
         b. SQ3R   d. structuralism

28. (p. 20)   True-False. Massed practice is a better way to learn new material than spaced practice because it allows for more continuous study and therefore less problems with forgetting.

29. (p. 20)   A memory aid that links new information to ideas or images that are easy to remember is called a
         a. learning basic   c. recitation
         b. massing practice   d. mnemonic

30. (p. 20)   Working under pressure, skipping classes, giving false reasons for late work, and feeling ashamed of last-minute efforts may be signs that a student has significant problems with
         a. procrastination   c. overlearning
         b. perfectionism   d. impossibly high self-standards

31. (p. 23)   True-False. Pseudo-psychologies are legitimate subdisciplines within psychology.

32. (p. 23)   The theory that personality is revealed by bumps on the skull was popularized by Franz Gall during the 19th century and is known as
         a. astrology   c. phenomenology
         b. palmistry   d. phrenology

33. (p. 24)   Which of the following is *not* a reason why astrology, phrenology, graphology, and palmistry tend to be dubious, unfounded systems?
         a. They are popular and are practiced by significant numbers of people.
         b. They are subject to the fallacy of positive instances.
         c. Their predictions or descriptions are often stated in desirable terms which encourage uncritical acceptance.
         d. Their predictions or descriptions are often stated in such general terms that they can hardly miss being vaguely accurate.

ANSWERS — PROGRAMMED REVIEW

1. behavior
2. overt; covert
3. empirical

4. data
5. increase
6. systematic

7. ethical; practical
8. research method
9. comparative
10. anthropomorphic fallacy
11. models
12. zoos
13. describe, understand, predict, control
14. description; understanding
15. prediction; east; west
16. psychometrics
17. control
18. philosophy; 100
19. Wilhelm Wundt
20. stimuli
21. introspection; experimental self-observation
22. 10,000
23. Edward B. Titchener; structuralism
24. elements
25. disagreed
26. William James
27. functions; functionalism
28. Charles Darwin
29. natural selection
30. adaptation
31. adaptation
32. educational
33. industrial
34. behaviorism; stimulus-response
35. stimuli; responses
36. conditioned response
37. B. F. Skinner; consequences
38. learning
39. behavior modification
40. 10
41. Christine Ladd-Franklin
42. Margaret Washburn
43. equal; exceeded
44. Gestalt
45. wholes
46. relationship
47. perception; personality
48. Sigmund Freud; psychoanalytic
49. unconscious
50. repressed
51. Freudian slips
52. determined
53. childhood
54. psychoanalysis
55. neo-Freudians
56. psychodynamic
57. humanism; psychodynamic; behaviorism
58. free will
59. choose
60. needs
61. subjective
62. self-image
63. self-evaluation
64. frame of reference
65. self-actualization
66. eclectic
67. biological
68. cognitive
69. Computer
70. master's; doctorate
71. clinical; counseling
72. mental disorder
73. clinical
74. physical; drugs
75. psychoanalyst
76. expensive; time
77. child, school
78. psychologist; license
79. qualifications; confidentiality; welfare
80. 50; 45
81. 3
82. basic; applied
83. developmental
84. Francis Robinson; SQ3R
85. Survey; Question; Read; Recite; Review
86. comprehension; grades
87. active
88. Lead; Ideas; Signal words; Actively listen; Note-taking
89. regular
90. attitude
91. only study
92. spaced; massed
93. mnemonic
94. self-testing
95. overlearn
96. essays
97. procrastinate
98. personal worth
99. Perfectionism
100. time schedule
101. specific goals
102. directions; all; skip; second
103. key; writing
104. Pseudo-psychologies
105. palmistry
106. Gall; phrenology
107. Graphology; Europe; 3,000
108. zero
109. no better; chance
110. Astrology
111. desirable
112. fallacy of positive instances
113. general
114. accurate

ANSWERS — SELF-TEST

1. b	17. False
2. a	18. a
3. a	19. a
4. b	20. b
5. c	21. False
6. c	22. False
7. b	23. c
8. d	24. d
9. a	25. d
10. b	26. True
11. c	27. b
12. c	28. False
13. c	29. d
14. d	30. a
15. d	31. False
16. b	32. d
	33. a

Chapter 2

Research Methods
in Psychology

CONTENTS

Scientific Method—Can a Horse Add?
Naturalistic Observation—Psychology Steps Out!
Correlational Studies—In Search of the Perfect Relationship
The Psychology Experiment—Where Cause Meets Effect
Placebo Effects—Sugar Pills and Salt Water
The Clinical Method—Data by the Case
Survey Method—Here, Have a Sample
Psychology in the News—Notes on Reading the Popular Press
Smile, You're on Candid Camera!—The Ethics of Psychological Research

TERMS AND CONCEPTS

scientific method
hypothesis
operational definition
naturalistic observation
observer bias
correlational studies
correlation
coefficient of correlation
positive correlation
negative correlation
linear relationship
curvilinear relationship
experiment
subjects
experimental group
control group
independent variable
dependent variable
extraneous variable

random assignment
laboratory experiments
field experiments
replication
parascience
placebo
placebo effect
endorphins
single-blind procedure
double-blind procedure
experimenter effect
self-fulfilling prophecy
clinical method
case study
survey method
representative sample
Gallup poll
Harris poll
courtesy bias

IMPORTANT INDIVIDUALS

Jane Goodall
Arnold Gesell
James Bryan
Mary Test

Robert Rosenthal
J. M. Harlow
Barbara Gutek
Phillip Zimbardo

PROGRAMMED REVIEW

1. (p. 29)   To avoid the trap of faulty observation, psychologists use the _____
    _____, defined in its ideal form by five steps:
    1) Observation
    2) Defining a problem
    3) Proposing a hypothesis
    4) Experimentation
    5) Theory formulation

2. (p. 29)   A _____ is a tentative explanation of an event or a behavior,
    clearly stated and testable.

3. (p. 30)   In testing a hypothesis you must specify the exact procedures used to represent the
    concepts within the hypothesis.   You must define the relevant terms using
    _____ definitions.

4. (p. 30)   Operational definitions are important because they allow _____
    concepts to be tested in "real-world" terms. In general, concepts become more useful
    when they have been tested with a variety of operational definitions.

5. (p. 30)   A good example of how to apply the five steps of the scientific method is seen in the
    story of _____ _____, the mathematical wonder horse.

6. (p. 31)   When we actively observe subjects in their natural setting, we are making
    _____ _____.

7. (p. 31)   Jane Goodall has conducted naturalistic observations of chimpanzees and discovered
    that they, like humans, use _____ to obtain some goals.

8. (p. 31)   One of the advantages of naturalistic observation is that the behavior being studied
    has not been tampered with by outside influences. However, a disadvantage is that
    the presence of an _____ may change the behavior of the
    _____.

9. (p. 31)   This problem can be minimized by _____ the observer, as in the work of
    Arnold Gesell who determined at what age children develop certain abilities by
    observing them through one-way vision screens.

10. (p. 31)   A closely related problem is _____ _____ in which observers
    see what they expect to see, or record only selected details. For example, one study
    showed that the ratings teachers gave children differed markedly, depending upon the
    label (learning-disabled, normal, etc.) applied to the child.

11. (p. 32)   Psychologists doing naturalistic studies make a special effort to minimize observer
    bias by keeping _____ _____ of observations.

12. (p. 32)   A _____ study is one that determines the degree to

which two factors of interest (traits, behaviors, events, etc.) vary together in some orderly fashion.

13. (p. 32)   Correlations can be expressed as a _____ of correlation, which is a number that falls between _____ and _____ .

14. (p. 32)   If the coefficient of correlation is _____ or close to it, this indicates a weak or non-existent relationship (such as between shoe size and intelligence).

15. (p. 32)   If the correlation coefficient is +1.00 a perfect _____ correlation exists; if it is –1.00 a perfect _____ correlation has been discovered.

16. (p. 32)   Perfect correlations rarely exist in psychology, most fall between zero and plus or minus one. The closer the correlation coefficient is to +1.00 or –1.00, the _____ the relationship.

17. (p. 32)   In a positive correlation, increases in one measure are matched by _____ in another (or decreases in the first factor are accompanied by _____ in the second). An example is the positive correlation between high school grades and college grades.

18. (p. 32)   In a negative correlation, increases in the first measure are associated with _____ in the second. For example, we might observe such a relationship between air temperature and the activity levels of zoo animals.

19. (p. 32)   Correlational studies help us discover relationships and make useful predictions, but correlation does not demonstrate _____ .

20. (p. 33)   When using correlational studies, psychologists sometimes draw graphs to help clarify the relationship between the measures. Some graphs reveal a _____ (or straight-line) relationship. Other graphs are _____ , consisting of a curved line.

21. (p. 35)   To identify cause-effect relationships, psychologists use a powerful research tool, the _____ .

22. (p. 35)   To perform a psychological experiment, you would:
    1) directly _____ a condition you think might cause changes in a behavior.
    2) create two or more groups of _____ who are treated alike in all ways *except* the condition you are varying.
    3) _____ whether varying the condition had any effect on behavior.

23. (p. 35)   The simplest psychological experiment is based on two groups of _____ , either animals or people.

24. (p. 35)   The two groups used are called the _____ group and the _____ group.

25. (p. 35)   Both groups are treated exactly alike except for one condition, the independent _____ (anything that can change or vary, and which might affect the outcome of the experiment).

26. (p. 35)   There are three essential elements contained in an experiment:
    1) _____ variables, which are conditions altered or varied by the experimenter. They are suspected causes in the experiment.

2) _____ variables, which measure the outcome of the experiment. They are the results of the experiment.

3) _____ variables, which are conditions the researcher wishes
to prevent from affecting the experiment.

27. (p. 35)   The group exposed to the independent variable is called the _____
group; the group not exposed to the independent variable is called the
_____ group.

28. (p. 35)   The control group is needed in an experiment to allow us to compare differences
between the experimental group, which is exposed to the independent variable, with
subjects not exposed to this factor.   Thus, the control group serves as a
_____ of _____ .

29. (p. 35)   The _____ _____ is what is measured in an
experiment.   This measure will be different between the two groups if the
independent variable does have an affect on the experimental group's performance.

30. (p. 36)   Differences in personal characteristics of subjects that might influence the outcome
of an experiment can be controlled by _____ assigning subjects to
the two groups.

31. (p. 36)   Random assignment means that a subject has an _____ chance of being a
member of either the experimental group or the control group.   Random assignment
helps ensure that subject differences are evenly balanced across the two groups.

32. (p. 36)   Any variables, such as sex of the subject, temperature of the testing situation, time
of day, etc. that could influence the behavior of subjects (besides the independent
variable) are called _____ , or outside, variables.   Such
influences can be prevented from affecting the outcome of an experiment by making
all conditions exactly the same for both groups.

33. (p. 37)   Thus, if we have controlled all _____ variables and the
experimental and control groups differ in the value of the _____
variable, changes in the _____ variable can be the only
possible cause.

34. (p. 37)   An alternative to the laboratory experiment is the _____ experiment which
uses the "real world" as a laboratory.   This is illustrated by the work of James Bryan
and Mary Test who tested whether people are more likely to help a person in distress
when they have recently seen someone else being helpful.

35. (p. 37)   The problem of deciding whether or not an independent variable really made enough
difference in the outcome of an experiment to call it meaningful is handled
_____ .

36. (p. 37)   When results are said to be statistically _____ , this
means that the obtained results in a particular experiment would occur very rarely by
chance alone.

37. (p. 37)   For a difference to be considered significant, it usually must be sufficiently large so
that it would occur by chance in less than ___ experiments out of 100.

38. (p. 37)   A key element in the scientific pursuit of truth is the ability to _____
(repeat) observations or experiments.   This is necessary to ensure the scientific
believability of obtained results.

39. (p. 37)   The failure to replicate observations is a major failing of _____ (that which resembles science, but is not truly scientific).

40. (p. 37)   A good example of the failure of replication is Cleve Backster's "experiments" claiming that plants wired to a polygraph respond to music, threats, and other stimuli. When scientists tried to repeat his experiments, using either identical or improved methods, the results were completely _____.

41. (p. 38)   In drug experiments, an accurate test cannot be achieved if the experimental group is given the drug and the control group gets nothing. Without using a _____ (a fake pill or injection) it is impossible to tell if the drug actually affected the dependent variable or if just swallowing a pill did.

42. (p. 38)   As an example of the placebo effect, one study showed that injections of saline solution had _____ percent of the effectiveness of morphine in reducing pain for hospital patients.

43. (p. 38)   Although this effect is not entirely understood, recent experiments relate it to the release of brain chemicals called _____, which are similar to opiate drugs such as morphine.

44. (p. 38)   To control for placebo effects, a psychologist doing drug research could use a _____-_____ arrangement where all subjects get a pill or injection (the experimental group gets the real drug, the control group receives a placebo).

45. (p. 38)   Using this procedure, subjects are *blind* as to whether or not they receive the drug, but the experimenter is not. For added control, researchers use the _____-_____ arrangement where the experimenter also lacks knowledge of who does and does not receive the real drug.

46. (p. 38)   Human subjects are very sensitive to hints from an experimenter about what is expected from them. This may produce the _____ _____, which causes a powerful influence on a subject's behavior.

47. (p. 38)   Robert Rosenthal demonstrated this phenomenon in an experiment where airmen were randomly assigned to one of five math classes and their teachers were told that class members were selected for _____ or _____ levels of ability.

48. (p. 38)   Students in the supposed "high-ability" classes showed substantially more improvement despite the fact that initially the classes were of equal ability. Apparently, the teacher's expectations created a _____-_____ _____.

49. (p. 39)   The clinical method employs _____ _____, which are in-depth studies on all aspects of a single subject.

50. (p. 39)   Case studies may sometimes be thought of as natural clinical tests of the effect of unusual variables. For example, in the remarkable case reported by J. M. Harlow, Phineas Gage suffered an accidental _____ _____, the destruction of frontal brain matter. This resulted in profound personality change.

51. (p. 39)   When Michael Melnick suffered a similar freakish accident over 120 years after Gage, Melnick recovered completely with no sign of lasting ill-effects. These very different reactions to a similar injury show why psychologists prefer controlled

_____ and often use lab _____ for studies of the brain.

52. (p. 40)   Another classic psychology case study is *The Three Faces of Eve.* Eve demonstrated _____ _____ in the form of Eve White, Eve Black, and Jane.

53. (p. 40)   Multiple personality disorders are quite rare. Eve's case was particularly interesting in that over the years, she manifested _____ different personalities.

54. (p. 40)   In the _____ method, a representative sample of people are asked a carefully worded series of questions. This technique can provide an accurate picture of how large segments of the general population feel about current issues, even though only a small percentage of people are polled.

55. (p. 40)   A representative sample means that the same _____ of men, women, white-collar workers, Republicans, Democrats, blacks, and so on, are included in the sample as are found in the population as a whole.

56. (p. 40)   Modern surveys like the _____ and _____ polls are examples of this method.

57. (p. 40)   While the Gallup poll has erred in its election predictions by only _____ percent since 1954, some polls have at times made major blunders.

58. (p. 40)   The Literary Digest predicted that Alfred Landon would defeat Franklin Roosevelt by a landslide, but Roosevelt won overwhelmingly. The sample for the poll was _____ rather than representative, a critical problem for the survey method.

59. (p. 40)   Replies to survey questions are not always accurate or truthful. Many people show a _____ _____, or tendency to give answers that are agreeable and socially acceptable. For example, black persons talking to white interviewers are less likely to admit support for a black candidate. White persons talking to black interviewers are more likely to claim support for black candidates.

60. (p. 40)   Barbara Gutek's assessment of sexual harassment on the job is another example of the use of the survey method. Gutek found that _____ percent of women, but only _____ percent of men had experienced this problem.

61. (p. 41)   A good scientific theory is stated in terms that make it _____. In other words, its concepts and assertions can be put to a test.

62. (p. 42)   When reading psychological claims in the popular press, there are several steps to use in evaluating their truthfulness. One is to be _____. Since psychological reports often have a definite bias, you must be a critical thinker.

63. (p. 42)   This point is illustrated by the critical thinking of Martin Gardner in exploring _____-_____ perception, the supposed ability of people to identify colors and read print while blindfolded.

64. (p. 42)   Another helpful suggestion is to consider the _____ of information. Claims made by an individual or company intent on selling a product often reflect the profit motive more than objective truth.

65. (p. 42)   One factor that should always be considered is, "Was there a _____

group?" It is not always possible to determine if an event or situation really does have a meaningful impact unless there is a frame of reference for comparison.

66. (p. 43) The need for a control group is evident in the study conducted by physicist Bernard Leikind. He investigated whether people really need to learn "_____ programming" in order to walk barefoot on hot coals. He found that student volunteers without special training could do so, because the coals of such beds are light fluffy carbon that transmit little heat when touched.

67. (p. 43) Looking for errors in distinguishing _____ from _____ is also important. As we know, it is dangerous to assume that because two factors correlate, one factor caused the other. Such was the mistake made by the nutritionist quoted as saying that drinking excessive amounts of milk may cause "juvenile delinquency."

68. (p. 43) A fifth suggestion is to distinguish between _____ and _____. What we see does not always support what we think this must mean. Assuming that someone is sad because he or she is crying is an example.

69. (p. 44) Beware of _____, especially those motivated by monetary gains. Courses, programs, or products that claim rapid or immediate gains or success should be suspect.

70. (p. 44) A final tip is to remember that "_____ _____" is no proof. The fact that something appears to be beneficial for one individual does not necessarily mean it will be equally helpful for everyone.

71. (p. 45) Experiments such as those conducted by Phillip Zimbardo to investigate the effects of imprisonment have raised new questions about the _____ of psychological research.

72. (p. 45) One area of ethical concern involves experiments where the true interests of a researcher are concealed by _____. For example, a researcher interested in guilt once falsely led subjects to believe they had broken an expensive piece of machinery. Subjects later asked to sign a petition (almost universally refused by control subjects) signed because of their guilt.

73. (p. 45) A second area of debate concerns the extent to which invasions of _____ should be allowed. For example, Eric Knowles, interested in stress caused by "personal space" invasions, secretly monitored activity in public restrooms.

74. (p. 45) Perhaps the most serious ethical problem is whether experiments may cause _____ _____ as in Stanley Milgram's study of obedience to authority.

75. (p. 45) To ensure appropriate ethics in psychological research, the American Psychological Association has adopted guidelines emphasizing the dignity and welfare of subjects. Also, most college psychology departments have _____ _____ that oversee proposed research.

76. (p. 46) If you become a subject you have a right to expect that your reactions will remain _____; that you will be debriefed about the _____ of the research; that you will receive an _____ of your responses or test results; and that the results of the research project will be made available to you.

SELF-TEST

1. (p. 29)   Which of the following is *not* a step in the ideal use of the scientific method?
   a. observation   c. incubation of ideas
   b. defining a problem   d. theory formulation

2. (p. 30)   True-False. Clever Hans was a horse who seemed to solve difficult math problems.

3. (p. 31)   Research psychologists sometimes actively observe subjects in their native habitats. Such work involves primarily
   a. casual observations   c. experimental manipulations
   b. common sense   d. naturalistic observations

4. (p. 31)   True-False. Jane Goodall used naturalistic observations to study tool-using behavior among chimpanzees in Tanzania.

5. (p. 31)   Which of the following is *not* a disadvantage or limitation to the use of naturalistic observations?
   a. Unless careful, observers may show bias in what they see or record.
   b. The presence of an observer may change the behavior of the observed.
   c. Naturalistic observations only provide descriptions, not explanations.
   d. Behavior being studied has not been altered by outside influences.

6. (p. 32)   True-False. A negative coefficient of correlation means that two events or observations do not systematically vary together since there is no positive relationship.

7. (p. 32)   Which of the following correlations might you expect to obtain if you studied the relationship between shoe size and intelligence?
   a. -1.00   c. +.50
   b. 0   d. +1.00

8. (p. 34)   True-False. The important value of correlational studies is that correlation demonstrates causation.

9. (p. 35)   The two subject groups in an experiment are called the
   a. experimental and control groups
   b. dependent and independent groups
   c. extraneous and random groups
   d. scientific and placebo groups

10. (p. 35)   In an experiment, the variable to which only the experimental group is exposed is called the _____ variable.
   a. dependent   c. independent
   b. extraneous   d. experimental

11. (p. 35)   The _____ variable is what is measured in an experiment to determine the effects of the _____ variable.
   a. dependent, extraneous   c. dependent, independent
   b. independent, dependent   d. independent, extraneous

12. (p. 36)   True-False. Differences in the personal characteristics of subjects that are extraneous to and might influence the outcome of the experiment can be controlled by randomly assigning subjects to the experimental and control groups.

13. (p. 36)   Conditions which vary across experimental and control groups such as sex, intelligence, etc., but which are not of interest in the experiment, are called _____ variables.
    a. independent   c. extraneous
    b. dependent   d. personal

14. (p. 37)   True-False. Field experiments usually do not provide objective, empirical data because they cannot be done in an actual laboratory under highly controlled conditions.

15. (p. 37)   The results of an experiment are said to be statistically significant when statistical procedures show that
    a. differences between the experimental and control groups would occur due to the independent variable at least 50% of the time
    b. differences between the experimental and control groups were very unlikely to have occurred by chance alone
    c. correlations between events are very strong and graphically linear
    d. all extraneous variables have been controlled for, yet measures of the experimental and control group performance are still quite similar

16. (p. 38)   A _____ is a fake pill or injection.
    a. sham   c. neo
    b. pseudo   d. placebo

17. (p. 38)   Placebos can have a tremendous psychological impact, as in the reduction of pain. Recent experiments suggest this effect may be due to the release of brain chemicals called
    a. metamorphins   c. saline
    b. endorphins   d. opiates

18. (p. 38)   What is the procedure used most effectively to control for placebo effects?
    a. randomization   c. controlled subject selection
    b. extraneous analysis   d. double-blind testing

19. (p. 39)   A _____ _____ is an in-depth focus on all aspects of a single subject.
    a. naturalistic observation   c. case study
    b. controlled experiment   d. casual observation

20. (p. 39)   J. M. Harlow offered a classic example of a natural clinical test. He reported the case of Phineas Gage, a victim of an accidental _____.
    a. frontal lobotomy   c. cerebral contusion
    b. cortical ablation   d. anatomical diffusion

21. (p. 40)   The case study of Eve White involved detailed observations regarding
    a. frontal lobotomy   c. sexual conduct
    b. multiple personalities   d. brain functioning

22. (p. 40)   The _____ _____ involves asking a representative sample of people a carefully worded series of questions.
    a. experimental method   c. observational method
    b. clinical method   d. survey method

23. (p. 40)   True-False. Modern surveys, like the Gallup and Harris polls, are frequently inaccurate as in the Landon-Roosevelt election prediction.

24. (p. 40)   True-False. Using the survey method, Barbara Gutek found that women are about twice as likely as men to be the target of sexual comments, gestures, or touching on the job.

25. (p. 42)   Which of the following is *not* a useful suggestion in evaluating coverage of psychological research and theories in popular magazines and daily newspapers?
    a. Be skeptical.   c. Consider the source of information.
    b. Use creative imagination.   d. Beware of oversimplification.

26. (p. 42)   True-False. Individuals who can identify colors and read print while blindfolded are said to have dermo-optical perception. Carefully designed psychological experiments suggest that such abilities exist in a large segment of the population.

27. (p. 43)   True-False. The rate of violent crimes rises and falls with lunar cycles meaning that the moon affects human behavior. This statement fails to distinguish correlation and causation.

28. (p. 45)   True-False. Ethical guidelines for psychological research have been adopted by the American Psychological Association; most college psychology departments have ethics committees that oversee proposed research.

29. (p. 45)   Which of the following is not an issue involved in the ethics of psychological research?
    a. invasion of privacy   c. lasting harm
    b. deception   d. student recruitment for research

30. (p. 45)   True-False. Stanley Milgram's research on obedience to authority, in which subjects believed they inflicted shocks on another person, raises the ethical issue of whether psychological experiments can do lasting harm.

ANSWERS — PROGRAMMED REVIEW

1. scientific method
2. hypothesis
3. operational
4. abstract
5. Clever Hans
6. naturalistic observations
7. tools
8. observer; observed
9. concealing
10. observer bias
11. careful records
12. correlational
13. coefficient; +1.00, -1.00
14. zero
15. positive; negative
16. stronger
17. increases; decreases
18. decreases
19. causation
20. linear; curvilinear
21. experiment
22. vary; subjects; record

23. subjects
24. experimental; control
25. variable
26. Independent; Dependent; Extraneous
27. experimental; control
28. point of reference
29. dependent variable
30. randomly
31. equal
32. extraneous
33. extraneous; dependent; independent
34. field
35. statistically
36. significant
37. 5
38. replicate
39. parascience
40. negative
41. placebo
42. 70
43. endorphins
44. single-blind

45. double-blind
46. experimenter effect
47. high, low
48. self-fulfilling prophecy
49. case studies
50. frontal lobotomy
51. experiments; animals
52. multiple personalities
53. 21
54. survey
55. proportion
56. Gallup, Harris
57. 1.5
58. biased
59. courtesy bias
60. 53; 37

61. falsifiable
62. skeptical
63. dermo-optical
64. source
65. control
66. neurolinguistic
67. correlation, causation
68. observation, inference
69. oversimplifications
70. for example
71. ethics
72. deception
73. privacy
74. lasting harm
75. ethics committees
76. confidential; purpose; interpretation

ANSWERS — SELF-TEST

1. c
2. True
3. d
4. True
5. d
6. False
7. b
8. False
9. a
10. c

11. c
12. True
13. c
14. False
15. b
16. d
17. b
18. d
19. c
20. a

21. b
22. d
23. False
24. True
25. b
26. False
27. True
28. True
29. d
30. True

Chapter 3

The Brain, Biology, and Behavior

CONTENTS

Neurons—Building a "Biocomputer"
A Brief Tour of the Nervous System—Wired for Action
The Cerebral Cortex—My, What a Big Brain You Have!
The Subcortex—At the Core of the (Brain) Matter
The Brain in Perspective—Beyond the Biocomputer
The Endocrine System—Slow but Sure Messenger Service
Handedness—If Your Brain is Right, What's Left?
Electrical Stimulation of the Brain—The Promise and Peril of Brain Control

TERMS AND CONCEPTS

neuron
physiological psychology
dendrites
soma
axon
axon terminals
ions
cell membrane
resting potential
threshold
action potential
ion channels
all-or-nothing event
negative after-potential
myelin
neurotransmitter
synapse
receptor sites
acetylcholine
curare
noradrenaline
neuropeptides
enkephalins
endorphins

nerves
neurilemma
central nervous system (CNS)
peripheral nervous system
somatic system
autonomic system
sympathetic branch
parasympathetic branch
white matter
spinal nerves
cranial nerves
reflex arc
sensory neuron
connector neuron (interneuron)
motor neuron
effector cells
brain-body ratio
cerebral cortex
grey matter
corticalization
positron emission tomography (PET)
hemispheres
corpus callosum
"split brain"

electrode
occipital lobes
tumors
homunculus
parietal lobes
somatosensory area
temporal lobes
primary auditory area
frontal lobes
olfaction
motor cortex
association cortex
neglect
Broca's area
Wernicke's area
aphasia
agnosia (mindblindness)
subcortex
brainstem (hindbrain)
midbrain
forebrain
medulla
cerebellum
reticular formation (RF)
reticular activating system (RAS)
thalamus
hypothalamus
limbic system

hippocampus
pleasure centers
aversive centers
redundancy
plasticity
endocrine system
hormone
pituitary gland
growth hormone
giantism
acromegaly
hypopituitary dwarf
thyroid gland
metabolism
hyperthyroidism
hypothyroidism
adrenaline
adrenal gland
adrenal medulla
adrenal cortex
corticoids
virilism
premature puberty
handedness
lateralization
amygdala
electrical stimulation of the brain (ESB)
electrode implantation

IMPORTANT INDIVIDUALS

Richard J. Haier
Robert Sperry
Michael Gazzaniga

Robert Ornstein
W. R. Hess
Jose Delgado

PROGRAMMED REVIEW

1. (p. 50) The human brain is about the size of a large grapefruit and weighs a little over three pounds. It is composed of some 100 billion nerve cells called _____.

2. (p. 50) Neurons specialize in carrying and processing information. They also activate muscles and glands. Each neuron is linked to as many as _____ others.

3. (p. 51) _____ psychology is the study of how the brain and nervous system relate to behavior.

4. (p. 51) The nervous system is made up of long "chains" of neurons. No two neurons are exactly alike in size and shape, but most have four basic parts. One of these, the _____, look like the roots of a tree and serve as a receiving area for information from other neurons.

5. (p. 51) The _____, or cell body, also accepts incoming information, which it collects and combines.

6. (p. 51) Periodically, the soma sends nerve impulses down a long thin fiber called the _____.

7. (p. 51) Axons may carry messages from the sensory organs to the brain, from the brain to muscles or glands, or from one nerve cell to the next. Most axons branch at their ends to form an array of _____ _____ which connect the neuron to the dendrites and somas of other nerve cells.

8. (p. 51) Nerve cells are filled with and surrounded by electrically charged molecules called _____, especially sodium and potassium.

9. (p. 51) Differing numbers of these ions inside and outside each nerve cell result in a tiny difference in electrical charge across the cell _____ or "skin."

10. (p. 51) In humans, this electrical charge, called a _____ _____, is about 70 millivolts.

11. (p. 51) Messages arriving from other neurons alter the resting potential until it reaches a _____, or trigger point, for firing of about 50 millivolts.

12. (p. 51) Reaching the threshold triggers an _____ _____, or nerve impulse, which then sweeps down the axon.

13. (p. 51) The action potential occurs because tiny tunnels, called _____ _____, pierce the axon membrane.

14. (p. 51) These channels are normally closed by molecular "gates." During an action potential, the gates pop open and allow sodium ions to rush into the axon. This happens first near the _____. Then, as the axon potential moves along, the gates open in sequence down the length of the axon.

15. (p. 51) The existence of a threshold for firing makes the action potential an _____-_____-_____ event: it occurs completely or not at all.

16. (p. 52) After an action potential occurs, the cell's voltage briefly drops below its resting level. This drop is called a _____ _____-_____ and occurs while the neuron is recharging.

17. (p. 52) The negative after-potential is due to an outward flow of _____ ions that occurs while the membrane gates are open. The neuron must recharge after each nerve impulse by shifting ions back across the cell membrane until the resting potential is restored.

18. (p. 52) It takes about one-thousandth of a second for a neuron to fire an impulse and return to its resting level. Thus, a maximum of about 1,000 nerve impulses per second is possible. However, firing rates of one per second to _____ or _____ per second are more typical.

19. (p. 52) The speed of an action potential depends on many factors, including axon size. In small, thin axons, impulses travel at about _____ meters (roughly, eight feet) per second and up to _____ meters per second (about 225 miles per hour) in large axons.

20. (p. 52) The speed of nerve impulses also increases with the presence of _____ which forms a layer of fatty insulation around some axons. This material typically

has small gaps every millimeter or so which allow nerve impulses to move faster by jumping from gap to gap.

21. (p. 53)   The nerve impulse is primarily an electrical event. That is why electrically stimulating the brain affects behavior. In contrast, communication between neurons is _____.

22. (p. 53)   When a nerve impulse reaches the tips of the axon terminals it causes a release of _____.

23. (p. 53)   These potent chemicals cross the _____, the tiny space between two neurons.

24. (p. 53)   Transmitter molecules then attach to special _____ _____ on the dendrites and soma of the next neuron. This process is also how muscles and glands are activated.

25. (p. 53)   Neurotransmitters may _____ the next neuron (move it closer to firing) or _____ it (make it less likely to discharge).

26. (p. 53)   If several "exciting" messages arrive close in time, and they are not canceled by "inhibiting" messages, the neuron reaches its threshold for firing. This means that chemical messages are _____ before a neuron "decides" to send on its all-or-nothing message.

27. (p. 53)   There are now some _____ known or suspected neurotransmitters in the brain including acetylcholine, adrenaline, noradrenaline, serotonin, dopamine, histamine, and various amino acids.

28. (p. 54)   Thousands of drugs may affect mood and behavior by imitating, duplicating, or blocking the actions of neurotransmitters. For example, the drug _____ attaches to receptor sites on muscles, which prevents acetylcholine (a transmitter that normally activates muscles) from reaching the sites. Paralysis occurs as a result.

29. (p. 54)   The mind-altering drug mescaline, which is similar to the neurotransmitter _____, is an example of a drug that imitates a brain transmitter. Similarly, LSD and psilocybin appear to act directly on receptor sites for the neurotransmitter _____.

30. (p. 54)   Recently a new class of brain transmitters called _____, or simply brain peptides, has been discovered. These chemicals seem to regulate the activity of other neurons and in so doing affect memory, pain, emotion, pleasure, mood, hunger, sexual behavior, and other basic processes.

31. (p. 54)   The fact that some neurons have specific receptor sites for opiate drugs such as morphine led scientists to search for natural opiate-like peptides in the brain. Scientists found that the brain produces opiate-like neural regulators called _____ to relieve pain and stress.

32. (p. 54)   Related chemicals called _____ are released by the pituitary gland. These chemicals, along with enkephalins, may help explain phenomena as diverse as "runner's high," the placebo effect, and acupuncture.

33. (p. 54)   When you touch something hot, you jerk your hand away. The neural messages for this action are carried by _____.

At the same time, pain may cause the brain to release enkephalins and endorphins. These chemical regulators reduce the pain so that it is not too disabling.

34. (p. 54)   _____ are bundles of axons and dendrites often whitish in color due to a coating of myelin.

35. (p. 54)   Nerve fibers outside the brain and spinal cord usually have a thin layer of cells called _____, which provide a tunnel through which damaged nerve fibers can grow when repairing themselves.

36. (p. 55)   If damage occurs to neurons within the _____ or _____ _____, generally no regeneration is possible. Damage to these areas may cause permanent loss of function.

37. (p. 55)   Also, if the cell body of a neuron is destroyed, the damage cannot be reversed. For example, this type of damage is the cause of _____, a crippling disease in which the cell bodies of neurons controlling muscles are destroyed.

38. (p. 55)   The _____ nervous system consists of the brain and spinal cord. The _____ nervous system consists of nerves which carry information to and from the CNS.

39. (p. 55)   It seems likely that brain _____ may someday be used to correct a variety of brain diseases and injuries. Recent research does show that brain-damaged rats given brain tissue implants do significantly better on a maze-learning test than those left untreated.

40. (p. 55)   Another grafting experiment showed that a number of human patients with severe _____ disease showed noticeable improvement when dopamine-producing tissue from their adrenal glands was grafted into their brains.

41. (p. 55)   The peripheral system is divided into two subparts: the _____ system which conveys information from the sense organs and the skeletal muscles; and the _____ system which conveys information to and from the internal organs and glands.

42. (p. 56)   The _____ branch of the autonomic nervous system responds during times of danger or emotion to prepare the body for "fight or flight." It arouses the body for action.

43. (p. 56)   The _____ or "sustaining" branch is most active immediately after a stressful or emotional event. Its role is to return the body to a lower level of arousal and to maintain certain vital functions at moderate levels.

44. (p. 57)   If you were to cut through the spinal cord, you would see columns of _____ _____, nervous tissue made up of axons which leave the spinal cord at various points to form peripheral nerves.

45. (p. 57)   There are 30 pairs of _____ _____ leaving the spinal cord and one pair leaving the bottom tip.

46. (p. 57)   These nerves, together with an additional _____ nerves which leave the brain directly (the cranial nerves), place the body in contact with the brain.

47. (p. 57)   Within the spinal cord, the simplest behavior pattern, a _____ _____, can be carried out without any help from the brain.

48. (p. 57)   The reflex arc begins when sensory information is detected by a _____ _____ and a message in the form of an action potential is carried to the spinal cord.

49. (p. 57)   Next, the sensory neuron synapses with an _____, or connector neuron, inside the spinal cord, which in turn activates another connector cell, in this case a _____ _____ that leads back to muscle fibers.

50. (p. 57)   The muscle fibers are made up of _____ cells which contract and move the muscle.

51. (p. 58)   Relative to body size, humans have very large brains. The proportion of brain weight to body weight for humans is _____ to _____ compared, for example, with the 1 to 1000 ratio of elephants or the 1 to 10,000 ratio of sperm whales.

52. (p. 58)   The only creatures that compare well with humans in both brain size and brain-body ratio are dolphins and _____. It is possible that these animals may be as intelligent (or more so) as humans. We already know that dolphins communicate with sounds as complex as our own, but they do not necessarily generate a language as complex. Also, they may use larger portions of their brains for swimming, coordination, and "lower" sensory-motor functions.

53. (p. 58)   The cerebral cortex, which accounts for no less than 70 percent of the neurons in the CNS, covers most of the visible portions of the brain with a mantle of _____ _____ (spongy tissue made up mostly of cell bodies).

54. (p. 58)   Human intellectual superiority appears to be related to _____, an increase in the size and wrinkling of the cortex.

55. (p. 59)   The cortex is composed of two sides, or _____. They are connected by a thick band of fibers called the _____ _____.

56. (p. 59)   The two hemispheres control _____ sides of the body and perform differently on tests of language, perception, music, and other capabilities.

57. (p. 60)   Roger Sperry has studied people who have had a radical form of brain surgery that disconnects the hemispheres: "_____-_____" operations. The result is a person with essentially two brains in one body.

58. (p. 60)   According to folklore, a person with a large head and a high forehead is likely to be intelligent.   But psychologist Richard J. Haier has found that brain _____ probably has more to do with intelligence. He found that people who perform well on mental tests consume less energy than the brains of poor performers.

59. (p. 60)   Haier measured brain activity with a technique called _____ _____ tomography or PET, a scan that records the amount of glucose (sugar) used by brain cells.

60. (p. 60)   On occasion, having two "brains" creates dilemmas like those described by Michael Gazzaniga. However, most split-brain individuals act normally because both halves of the brain have about the same experience at the same time. Also, if any conflict arises, one hemisphere tends to _____ the other.

61. (p. 60)   However, if a dollar sign is flashed to the right brain and a question mark to the left, when "split-brain" patients are asked to draw what they saw using the left hand, they

draw a _____ _____. If asked to point with the right hand to a picture of what the left hand drew, they will point to a _____ _____.

62. (p. 61) The brain divides its work between the two hemispheres. For example, roughly 95 percent of all adults use the _____ brain for speaking, writing, and comprehending language.

63. (p. 61) Also, the left hemisphere is better at _____, judging time and rhythm, and at coordinating complex movements (especially those needed for _____).

64. (p. 61) The right hemisphere is superior at _____ skills such as recognizing visual patterns, faces, and melodies and is also involved in detecting and expressing _____.

65. (p. 61) The right brain is also better at tasks requiring _____, and "manipulo-spatial" skills such as drawing a picture or putting together a puzzle.

66. (p. 61) While activity may focus on one hemisphere, the skills of both sides of the brain are _____ in most activities. This is a fact too often ignored in books which purport to teach you to use the "right brain" to be more creative.

67. (p. 62) In general, the left hemisphere is mainly involved with _____ (breaking information into parts). It also processes information sequentially. The right hemisphere appears to process information simultaneously and _____ (all at once).

68. (p. 62) In addition to hemispheres, the cerebral cortex can be divided into several other areas called _____.

69. (p. 62) To determine the function of each lobe, the cortex can be activated by a small electrified needle or wire called an _____.

70. (p. 63) The functions of the cortex have also been identified by _____ _____ of changes in personality, behavior, or sensory capacity caused by diseases or injury of the brain.

71. (p. 63) The _____ lobes, located at the back of the brain, are the primary visual area of the cortex.

72. (p. 63) Patients with _____ (a growth of cells which interferes with brain activity) in the occipital lobes experience blind spots in areas of the visual field.

73. (p. 63) Visual images are mapped onto the cortex, but the map is greatly distorted. It does not create a TV-like image. It is a classic error to think of the brain in terms of some _____, meaning "little man," that makes decisions or observes incoming information.

74. (p. 64) The _____ lobes are located just above the occipital lobes.

75. (p. 64) Touch, temperature, pressure and other somatic, or bodily sensations are channeled to the _____ area on the parietal lobes.

76. (p. 64) The correspondence between areas of the parietal lobes and parts of the body is not a perfect one. As a map of the sensations, the cortex reflects the _____ of areas, not their size.

77. (p. 64)   The _____ lobes are located on each side of the brain. They are the site where hearing registers.

78. (p. 64)   If we were to stimulate the _____ _____ area of a temporal lobe, our subject would "hear" a series of sounds.

79. (p. 64)   Sound qualities are precisely mapped out on the surface of the cortex. Sounds from top to bottom vary in _____, while stimulation in another direction affects _____.

80. (p. 64)   For most people, the _____ temporal lobe also contains a language "center." Damage to this area can severely limit ability to use language meaningfully.

81. (p. 64)   The _____ lobes perform a mixture of functions. For one thing, _____ (smell) information registers on the underside of these lobes.

82. (p. 64)   The _____ _____, an arch of tissue running over the top of the brain, directs the body's muscles. Like the somatosensory area, it corresponds to the importance of bodily areas, not to their size.

83. (p. 64)   When areas of the frontal lobes are removed, animals lose the ability to judge the passage of _____, to hold the solution to a problem in mind, or to respond to _____ _____ situations.

84. (p. 64)   Damage to the frontal lobes in humans tends to alter personality and decrease _____. Doing intellectual tasks based on reasoning or planning also seems to rely on the frontal lobes. Patients with frontal lobe damage often get "stuck" on such tasks and repeat the same wrong answers.

85. (p. 64)   The _____ _____, all other areas of the brain besides the sensory and motor areas, seems to process and combine information from the various senses.

86. (p. 64)   The association cortex is probably also related to higher mental abilities. The size and relative amount of association cortex _____ strikingly as one ascends the evolutionary scale.

87. (p. 64)   Damage to the right brain often results in paralysis on the _____ side of the body; this situation is reversed for damage to the left brain.

88. (p. 64)   Damage to the right hemisphere may also cause a curious problem called _____. Affected patients pay no attention to the left side of visual space. Often, the patient will not eat food on the left side of a plate and may refuse to acknowledge a paralyzed left arm as his or her own.

89. (p. 64)   Brain injuries may also impair the special abilities of the hemispheres. A person with damage in the _____ brain may lose the ability to speak, read, write, or spell. Yet the same person may remain able to draw or hum with skill.

90. (p. 64)   Persons with right brain damage may get _____ while driving, or they may have difficulty understanding _____ and pictures. Yet they can speak and read as before.

91. (p. 64)   A person with _____ brain damage may not understand what you say, but he or she will pick up your emotional tone. With _____ hemisphere damage,

the person can understand what is said but fails to recognize if it is spoken in an angry or humorous way.

92. (p. 65) Generally, damage to the left hemisphere is more serious. However, if you are an artist, right brain dysfunction may be more problematic. For instance, painters with right brain damage may neglect the left side of the canvas, distort outlines, or portray _____ and _____ subject matter.

93. (p. 65) Injury to cortical areas related to language can cause _____, meaning an impaired ability to use language.

94. (p. 65) Persons with damage in _____ area can read and understand the speech of others, but have great difficulty speaking or writing. Typically, their grammar and pronunciation is poor and their speech is slow and labored.

95. (p. 65) In Wernicke's aphasia, grammar is normal and pronunciation is correct, but the person has problems with the _____ of words. People with such injuries often speak in incredibly roundabout ways to avoid using certain nouns.

96. (p. 65) Brain injury which involves an inability to identify seen objects is called _____ and sometimes referred to as _____.

97. (p. 65) Someone with agnosia might describe or draw a viewed object correctly, yet be unable to name it. This condition is not limited to objects however, for some patients demonstrate _____ _____, the inability to identify familiar persons.

98. (p. 65) Study of facial agnosias shows that a brain area devoted to recognizing others is located on the underside of the _____ _____.

99. (p. 66) Structures below the cerebral cortex are collectively termed the subcortex. They can be divided into three general areas called the _____ or _____, the _____, and the _____.

100. (p. 66) One part of the brainstem, the _____, contains centers important for the reflex control of vital life functions such as heart rate, breathing, and swallowing.

101. (p. 66) Various drugs, diseases, or injuries can interrupt the vital functions of the medulla enough to end or endanger life. That's why a karate chop to the back of the _____, like those depicted in movies, can be extremely dangerous.

102. (p. 66) The other component of the brainstem, the _____, lies at the base of the brain and is closely connected to many areas in the brain and spinal cord.

103. (p. 66) The cerebellum primarily regulates posture, muscle tone, and muscular coordination. It may also play a role in some types of _____.

104. (p. 66) The importance of the cerebellum is indicated by the effects of a crippling disease called _____ _____. This disease first produces tremor, dizziness, and muscular weakness and later affects many responses related to balance and distance judgment.

105. (p. 67) In a space within the medulla and brainstem is a network of fibers and cell bodies called the _____ (RF). It acts as a kind of central clearinghouse for most of the information coming to and from the brain. It

gives priority to some incoming messages while excluding others, basically what we mean by _____, and appears to be responsible for alertness and wakefulness.

106. (p. 67)   Incoming impulses from the sense organs branch into the reticular formation where they form a _____ _____ _____ which bombards the cortex with stimulation, keeping it active and alert.

107. (p. 67)   Destroying the RAS causes animals to enter a _____ resembling sleep. Electrical stimulation of the same area instantly _____ sleeping animals.

108. (p. 68)   The _____ of the forebrain is a football-shaped structure that acts as a final "switching station" for sensory information on its way to the cortex.

109. (p. 68)   Injury to even small areas of the thalamus could cause deafness, blindness, or loss of any of the other senses, except _____.

110. (p. 68)   The _____ of the forebrain is about the size of a thumbnail (in humans) and is a kind of master control center for emotion and many basic motives. It's a sort of "crossroads" that connects with many other areas of the cortex and subcortex.

111. (p. 68)   The hypothalamus acts as a "final path" for many kinds of behavior leaving the brain. It has been implicated in the control of behaviors as diverse as _____, rage, _____ control, _____ release, _____ and drinking, sleep, waking, and emotion.

112. (p. 68)   The hypothalamus, parts of the thalamus, and several structures buried within the cortex form the _____ _____. As a group they share a role in the production of _____ and _____ behavior.

113. (p. 68)   During evolution, the limbic system was the _____ layer of the forebrain to develop. In lower, relatively primitive animals, the limbic system helps organize the appropriate response to stimuli: feeding, fleeing, fighting, or reproduction.

114. (p. 68)   In humans, the link to emotion remains. However, some parts of the limbic system have taken on additional, higher-level functions. For example, the _____, found at the core of the temporal lobes, appears to be linked to memory.

115. (p. 69)   Several reward or "_____" centers have been found in the limbic system, and many in the hypothalamus where they overlap with areas associated with drives such as thirst, sex, and hunger. Rats can be trained to press a bar to receive stimulation of these areas.

116. (p. 69)   In addition, punishment or "_____" areas have been found. When these areas are stimulated, animals show discomfort and will work to turn off the stimulation.

117. (p. 69)   One reason for the brain's great complexity is the fact that it shows tremendous _____, or duplication. This phenomenon yields an impressive capacity for reorganization and recovery after injury.

118. (p. 69)   Children show greater _____ (or flexibility) of brain organization than adults. As examples, children under the age of seven can usually

shift language processing to the right brain when there is severe damage to the left hemisphere. Also, children born without corpus callosums usually can function normally using either hemisphere as adults.

119. (p. 69) The brain is amazingly resilient. In one astounding case, an adult who had the entire _____ hemisphere of his brain removed at age five was able to speak, read, write, and comprehend so well that he maintained a double major in college and has an above average IQ.

120. (p. 69) The nervous system is not the only communication network in the body. The _____ _____ is made up of a number of glands which pour chemicals directly into the bloodstream.

121. (p. 69) These chemicals, called _____, are carried throughout the body where they affect bodily functioning and behavior.

122. (p. 69) Hormones are chemically related to neurotransmitters. Like transmitters, hormones activate cells in the body. To respond, the cells must have _____ _____ for the hormone.

123. (p. 70) The _____ is a small grape-sized structure hanging from the base of the brain. It is important in the regulation of bodily growth.

124. (p. 70) The pituitary secretes _____ hormone that speeds bodily development. If too little is released, a person may remain far smaller than average. Too much growth hormone produces _____.

125. (p. 70) Secretion of too much growth hormone toward the end of the growth period causes excessive growth of the arms, hands, feet, and facial bones. This condition is known as _____.

126. (p. 70) The pituitary also regulates the thyroid, adrenal glands, ovaries, and testes, which in turn regulate reproduction, metabolism, and responses to stress. Because of its many effects, the pituitary is often called the "_____ _____."

127. (p. 70) The _____, which lies directly above the pituitary in the brain directs the activity of the pituitary and provides the major link between the brain and the glandular sytem.

128. (p. 70) The _____ gland consists of tissue found in the neck on each side of the windpipe. It regulates _____ (the rate of energy production and expenditure in the body).

129. (p. 70) The thyroid can have a sizeable effect on personality. A person with an overactive thyroid, termed _____, tends to be thin, tense, excitable, and nervous.

130. (p. 70) An underactive thyroid, _____, in an adult can cause inactivity, sleepiness, slowness, and overweight. In infancy this condition limits development of the nervous system and can cause severe mental retardation.

131. (p. 70) When you are frightened or angry, important changes take place in your body that are brought about by the release of _____ and _____ into the bloodstream.

132. (p. 71) These hormones are produced by the _____ _____ which are located just under the back of the rib cage atop the kidneys.

133. (p. 71) The _____ _____ or inner core of the adrenal glands is the source of adrenaline and noradrenaline.

134. (p. 71) The _____ _____, or outer "bark" of the adrenal glands, produces a second set of important hormones called _____, which regulate salt balance in the body and are related also to the body's ability to resist stress.

135. (p. 71) Corticoids are also a secondary source of sex hormones. Athletes sometimes use _____ _____, a synthetic version of male corticoids, in efforts to promote muscle growth. However, there is no evidence that they improve performance and they may cause voice deepening or baldness in women, and shrinkage of the testicles or breast development in men. For some users they may cause emotional disturbances and near-psychotic reactions.

136. (p. 71) An over-secretion of the adrenal sex hormones can cause _____, in which a woman grows a beard or a man's voice becomes so low it is difficult to understand.

137. (p. 71) Over-secretion of sex hormones in children may cause _____ _____, resulting in full sexual development. Such was the remarkable case of a 5-year-old Peruvian girl who gave birth to a son.

138. (p. 71) Insufficient production of growth hormone can cause children to fall ___ to _____ inches behind agemates in height. As adults, some will be _____ _____ who are perfectly proportioned, but tiny.

139. (p. 71) Dwarfism used to be treated with injections of human growth hormone extracted from the pituitary glands of human cadavers. Now, a _____ growth hormone has become available. Its use should be weighed against various medical and ethical issues.

140. (p. 73) It is not necessarily true that the right brain is dominant in left-handed people. About _____ percent of left-handers produce speech from the right hemisphere, while _____ percent use the left brain.

141. (p. 73) The way a person writes can be a clue to which hemisphere is dominant. Right-handed individuals who write with a straight hand, and lefties who write with a hooked hand, are usually _____-brain dominant for language. Left-handed people who write with their hand below the line, and righties who use a hooked position, are usually _____-brain dominant.

142. (p. 73) Animals such as monkeys show definite hand preferences, split about 50-50 between right and left. Among humans the split is about _____-_____ in favor of right-handedness. This probably reflects the left brain's specialization for language production.

143. (p. 73) Evidence exists that the majority of humans have been right-handed for at least _____ centuries.

144. (p. 73) It was long believed that children don't express clear-cut handedness until they are four or five. But a recent study shows that hand preference for many children is stabilized by _____ months of age, or earlier.

145. (p. 73)   Early preference for handedness underscores the fact that parents should never try to force a left-handed child to use the right hand. It could cause speech or reading problems because handedness is _____.

146. (p. 74)   A recent large-scale study of high school students in California found no differences in _____ _____ between left- and right-handers, and no physical or mental _____ associated with left-handedness.

147. (p. 74)   Since the right hemisphere is superior at imagery and visual abilities, left-handedness may conceivably be more advantageous to those who paint or draw than right-handedness. Interestingly, there are more left-handed _____ than would be expected.

148. (p. 74)   Left-handed individuals are generally less _____, that is, they show less specialization in the two sides of the brain.

149. (p. 74)   In some situations, less lateralization may be an advantage. Individuals who are moderately left-handed or ambidextrous seem to have better than average _____ _____, a basic music skill.

150. (p. 74)   More musicians are _____ than would normally be expected. It's not clear, however, if those who are musically gifted were initially _____ lateralized or if playing music develops both hands, or possibly both sides of the brain.

151. (p. 74)   Math abilities may also benefit from fuller use of the _____ hemisphere. Extremely mathematically gifted students are much more likely to be left handed or ambidextrous than other students are.

152. (p. 74)   The clearest advantage to being left-handed and mildly lateralized comes up when brain injury occurs. Lefties typically experience less _____ loss after damage to either hemisphere and recover more easily.

153. (p. 76)   Direct control over the machinery of the brain is possible through _____ _____ of the brain, abbreviated _____.

154. (p. 76)   ESB begins with _____ _____: the placing of fine steel or platinum electrodes into strategic areas of the brain. By this means, many separate brain sites can be electrically stimulated on command.

155. (p. 76)   An advantage of ESB in exploring brain-behavior connections is that it allows an animal to function normally while the experimenter turns various brain areas on and off. For example, W. R. Hess showed that full-blown _____ could be elicited from cats.

156. (p. 76)   ESB experiments with humans are limited to situations involving extraordinary needs such as the identification of brain areas that are triggering violent outbursts. One part of the limbic system, the _____, is especially associated with anger.

157. (p. 76)   Upon stimulation of the _____ lobes, one patient giggled and expressed enjoyment of the stimulation. Repetition made her flirtatious and forward.

158. (p. 76)   Jose Delgado has conducted animal research which suggests that ESB could not be used to control persons against their will. Monkeys receiving ESB became more

aggressive in direct proportion to their rank in the "_____
_____" of the colony. ESB does not produce random, uncontrollable
aggression.

SELF-TEST

1. (p. 51)   Which of the following is *not* part of a neuron?
a. axon   c. soma
b. effector cells   d. dendrites

2. (p. 51)   The long, thin neural fiber along which nerve impulses travel is the
a. axon   c. dendrite
b. soma   d. synapse

3. (p. 51)   The firing of a nerve impulse down the axon is called a(n)
a. resting potential   c. moving potential
b. action threshold   d. action potential

4. (p. 52)   Which of the following is *not* associated with the firing of a neuron?
a. all-or-nothing event   c. exceeding threshold
b. negative after-potential   d. reticular potential

5. (p. 53)   When a nerve impulse reaches the tips of the axon terminals, it causes a release of
_____ across the _____.
a. myelin, dendrites   c. neurotransmitters, synapse
b. sodium ions, soma   d. adrenaline, arc

6. (p. 53)   True-False. Neurotransmitters may either excite or inhibit an adjoining neuron when
they attach to the receptor sites on the dendrites or soma.

7. (p. 54)   True-False. Drugs like LSD or mescaline imitate the effects of some neurotransmitters, while other drugs like curare block the action of certain neurotransmitters.

8. (p. 54)   Natural relief from pain and stress, the placebo effect, acupuncture, and "runnner's
high" have all been linked with
a. enkephalins and endorphins   c. corticalization
b. myelin and neurilemma   d. corticoids and steroids

9. (p. 54)   Nerve fibers outside the brain and spinal cord usually have a thin layer of cells called
a. myelin   c. neurilemma
b. nuclei   d. soma

10. (p. 55) True-False. The central nervous system is composed of two subparts, the somatic and
autonomic systems.

11. (p. 55) True-False. Implants of healthy dopamine-producing tissue into diseased brain areas
has recently been shown to be helpful in the treatment of Parkinson's disease.

12. (p. 56) The _____ branch of the autonomic nervous system responds during times of
arousal or emotional upheaval to prepare the body for "fight or flight."
a. sympathetic   c. parasympathetic
b. peripheral   d. somatic

13. (p. 57) Which of the following represents the sequence of neuronal travel in a spinal cord
reflex arc?

a. sensory neuron, interneuron, motor neuron, effector cells
b. effector cells, connector neuron, motor neuron, sensory neuron
c. motor neuron, effector cells, sensory neuron, connector neuron
d. sensory neuron, effector cells, interneuron, motor neuron

14. (p. 59)   True-False. In most people, the left side of the brain controls the left side of the body.

15.ʼ (p. 59)   When the corpus callosum is severed, the resulting condition is referred to as
a. "split-brain"   c. spinocerebellar degeneration
b. hypothyroidism   d. hyperthyroidism

16. (p. 61)   Usually, the left hemisphere is superior to the right for which of the following functions?
a. spatial tasks   c. recognition of patterns, faces, and melodies
b. perceptual skills   d. language

17. (p. 63)   The visual area of the brain is the
a. temporal lobes   c. occipital lobes
b. frontal lobes   d. parietal lobes

18. (p. 64)   Touch, temperature, pressure, and other somatic functions are channeled to which area of the brain?
a. temporal lobes   c. occipital lobes
b. frontal lobes   d. parietal lobes

19. (p. 64)   The brain sites in which hearing is registered are the
a. parietal lobes   c. temporal lobes
b. occipital lobes   d. frontal lobes

20. (p. 64)   Which of the following is *not* associated with the temporal lobes?
a. hearing   c. dream-like experiences when stimulated
b. storage of long-term memories   d. olfaction

21. (p. 64)   Olfaction, muscle action, and time judgments are among the functions performed by the
a. temporal lobes   c. frontal lobes
b. hypothalamus   d. brainstem

22. (p. 64)   True-False. All areas of the brain not specifically sensory or motor in function are collectively called the association cortex.

23. (p. 65)   A brain-injured individual who has normal grammar and correct pronunciation, but has problems with the meaning of words is most likely suffering from which of the following?
a. Broca's aphasia   c. Wernicke's aphasia
b. spinocerebellar degeneration   d. agnosia

24. (p. 65)   True-False. Persons with damage in Broca's area can read and understand the speech of others, but may speak in incredibly roundabout ways to avoid using certain nouns.

25. (p. 65)   The condition in which an individual is unable to identify seen objects or even familiar faces is known as
a. Wernicke's aphasia   c. Broca's aphasia
b. agnosticism   d. agnosia

26. (p. 65)   True-False. Persons suffering from facial agnosia can recognize familiar faces they see, but not the voices of the same individuals when heard.

27. (p. 66)   The _____ contains centers important for the reflex control of vital life functions, including heart rate, swallowing and breathing.
    a. reticular formation   c. medulla
    b. cerebellum   d. forebrain

28. (p. 66)   The _____, a part of the hindbrain located at the base of the brain, functions primarily to regulate posture, muscle tone, and muscular coordination.
    a. cerebellum   c. medulla
    b. reticular formation   d. corpus callosum

29. (p. 67)   Which of the following is *not* a function of the reticular formation?
    a. acts as a clearinghouse directing information to and from the brain
    b. responsible for alertness and wakefulness by bombarding the cortex with stimulation
    c. responsible for attention: gives priority to some incoming messages while excluding others
    d. regulates basic drives such as hunger, thirst, and sex

30. (p. 68)   The _____ acts as a final "switching station" by relaying visual, auditory, taste, and touch information to the cortex after undergoing preliminary processing and analysis.
    a. medulla   c. hypothalamus
    b. reticular formation   d. thalamus

31. (p. 68)   The _____ acts as a "final path" for many kinds of behavior leaving the brain and is involved in the control of sex, eating, drinking, sleeping and emotion.
    a. medulla   c. hypothalamus
    b. reticular formation   d. thalamus

32. (p. 68)   The _____ _____ is important in the production of emotion and motivated behavior, including rage, fear, sexual response, and other intense arousal.
    a. limbic system   c. corpus callosum
    b. reticular formation   d. frontal lobe

33. (p. 69)   True-False. Animals can be trained to press a lever in order to deliver electrical stimulation to "pleasure" centers of the brain or to turn off stimulation directed at "aversive" areas of the brain.

34. (p. 69)   True-False. One of the reasons why the brain demonstrates an impressive capacity for reorganization and recovery after injury is that there is so little redundancy in the functions of the brain.

35. (p. 69)   True-False. Plasticity refers to changes in brain functions which result from corticalization.

36. (p. 70)   Which of the following is *not* a function of the pituitary gland?
    a. regulation of emotion and motivated behavior
    b. regulation of bodily growth
    c. regulation of other important glands
    d. regulation of milk production during pregnancy

37. (p. 70)   Which of the following is *not* a condition which can result from inadequate hormonal regulation by the pituitary gland?

a. giantism
b. acromegaly

c. amygdalism
d. dwarfism

38. (p. 70)   Which of the following conditions would *not* be expected to result from inadequate functioning of the thyroid gland?
a. overactivity, thinness, tenseness, excitability, nervousness
b. hearing loss combined with impaired vision and an inability to spatially locate objects
c. underactivity, sleepiness, slowness, and overweight
d. limited development of the nervous system and severe mental retardation

39. (p. 71)   The source of adrenaline and noradrenaline, important when you are frightened or angry, is the
a. thyroid gland
b. adrenal medulla

c. adrenal cortex
d. hypothalamus

40. (p. 71)   The functions of corticoids include which of the following?
a. salt regulation, adjustment to stress, secondary source of sex hormones
b. regulates metabolism and has important implications for personality
c. regulates bodily growth, directs connecting glands, produces milk during pregnancy
d. builds muscles, increases strength, improves performance

41. (p. 71)   Virilism, premature puberty, and powerful cravings for salt are all conditions associated with inadequate functioning of the
a. thyroid gland
b. thalamus

c. pituitary gland
d. adrenal glands

42. (p. 73)   True-False. About a quarter of left-handed people produce speech from the right brain, compared with three percent for right-handed individuals.

43. (p. 73)   The best way to determine hemisphere dominance is to observe
a. eye movements
b. how a person writes

c. agility
d. handedness

44. (p. 73)   Which of the following is *not* true of handedness?
a. About 10 percent of humans are left-handed.
b. Handedness is an hereditary characteristic.
c. Parents should insist that left-handed children become right hand dominant.
d. About 15 percent of lefties use both sides of the brain for language processing.

45. (p. 74)   True-False. The stress of living in a world generally designed for right-handed individuals has an adverse emotional impact on lefties. They are more prone to mental defects than right-handers.

46. (p. 74)   Left-handers are generally less brain lateralized than right-handers, meaning that
a. there is less distinct specialization in the two sides of the brain
b. there is less dependency upon the lateral part of the brain
c. there is less specialization, and thus less plasticity
d. there is more asymmetry in the size and shape of the two hemispheres

47. (p. 74)   Which of the following professionals have a higher percentage of left-handers than would be expected?
a. architects and musicians
b. teachers and scholars

c. athletes and coaches
d. nurses and doctors

48. (p. 76) Electrical stimulation applied to the amygdala can produce
    a. sudden outbursts of anger
    b. giggling and enjoyment of the stimulation
    c. flirtatious and forward behavior
    d. long-forgotten, but vivid memories

49. (p. 76) True-False. Initial stimulation of the temporal lobes can produce giggling; repeated stimulation may produce flirtatious and forward behavior.

50. (p. 77) True-False. ESB can be used to control persons completely against their will in much the same way that it can artificially produce almost all basic behaviors.

ANSWERS — PROGRAMMED REVIEW

1. neurons
2. 10,000
3. Physiological
4. dendrites
5. soma
6. axon
7. axon terminals
8. ions
9. membrane
10. resting potential
11. threshold
12. action potential
13. ion channels
14. soma
15. all-or-nothing
16. negative after-potential
17. potassium
18. 300; 400
19. 2.5; 100
20. myelin
21. molecular
22. neurotransmitters
23. synapse
24. receptor sites
25. excite; inhibit
26. combined
27. 30
28. curare
29. noradrenaline; serotonin
30. neuropeptides
31. enkephalins
32. endorphins
33. neurotransmitters
34. Nerves
35. neurilemma
36. brain; spinal cord
37. polio
38. central; peripheral
39. grafts
40. Parkinson's

41. somatic; autonomic
42. sympathetic
43. parasympathetic
44. white matter
45. spinal nerves
46. 12
47. reflex arc
48. sensory neuron
49. interneuron; motor neuron
50. effector
51. 1 to 60
52. porpoises
53. grey matter
54. corticalization
55. efficiency
56. positron emission
57. hemispheres; corpus callosum
58. opposite
59. split-brain
60. override
61. dollar sign; question mark
62. left
63. math; speech
64. perceptual; emotion
65. visualization
66. combined
67. analysis; holistically
68. lobes
69. electrode
70. clinical studies
71. occipital
72. tumors
73. homunculus
74. parietal
75. somatosensory
76. sensitivity
77. temporal
78. primary auditory
79. pitch; loudness
80. left

81. frontal; olfactory
82. motor cortex
83. time; emotionally unpleasant
84. emotionality
85. association cortex
86. increases
87. left
88. neglect
89. left
90. lost; diagrams
91. left; right
92. bizarre, repulsive
93. aphasia
94. Broca's
95. meaning
96. agnosia; mindblindness
97. facial agnosia
98. occipital lobes
99. brainstem, hindbrain; midbrain, forebrain
100. medulla
101. neck
102. medulla
103. memory
104. spinocerebellar degeneration
105. reticular formation; attention
106. reticular activating system
107. coma; awakens
108. thalamus
109. smell
110. hypothalamus
111. sex; temperature; hormone; eating
112. limbic system; emotion; motivated
113. earliest
114. hippocampus
115. pleasure
116. aversive
117. redundancy
118. plasticity
119. left

120. endocrine system
121. hormones
122. receptor sites
123. pituitary
124. growth; giantism
125. acromegaly
126. master gland
127. hypothalamus
128. thyroid; metabolism
129. hyperthyroidism
130. hypothyroidism
131. adrenaline, noradrenaline
132. adrenal glands
133. adrenal medulla
134. adrenal cortex; corticoids
135. anabolic steroids
136. virilism
137. premature puberty
138. 6; 12; hypopituitary dwarfs
139. synthetic
140. 25; 60
141. left; right
142. 90-10
143. 50
144. 18
145. hereditary
146. school achievement; defects
147. architects
148. lateralized
149. pitch memory
150. ambidextrous; less
151. right
152. language
153. electrical stimulation; ESB
154. brain implantation
155. rage
156. amygdala
157. temporal
158. pecking order

ANSWERS — SELF-TEST

1. b	13. a	25. d	38. b
2. a	14. False	26. False	39. b
3. d	15. a	27. c	40. a
4. d	16. d	28. a	41. d
5. c	17. c	29. d	42. True
6. True	18. d	30. d	43. b
7. True	19. c	31. c	44. c
8. a	20. d	32. a	45. False
9. c	21. c	33. True	46. a
10. False	22. True	34. False	47. a
11. True	23. c	35. False	48. a
12. a	24. False	36. a	49. True
		37. c	50. False

Chapter 4

Sensation and Reality

CONTENTS

General Properties of Sensory Systems—What You See is What You Get
Psychophysics—Taking It to the Limit
Vision—Catching Some Rays
Color Vision—There's More to It than Meets the Eye
Dark Adaptation—Let There Be Light!
Hearing—Good Vibrations
Smell and Taste—The Nose Knows When the Tongue Can't Tell
The Somesthetic Senses—Flying by the Seat of Your Pants
Adaptation, Attention, and Gating—Tuning In and Tuning Out
Controlling Pain—This Won't Hurt a Bit
Sensation in Space—Adapting to an Alien Environment

TERMS AND CONCEPTS

data reduction system
electromagnetic spectrum
transduction
perceptual features
feature detectors
phosphenes
localization of function
sensations
psychophysics
absolute threshold
photon
hertz
perceptual defense
limen
subliminal perception
difference threshold
just noticeable difference (JND)
Weber's law
visible spectrum
hue
saturation

brightness
lens
photoreceptors
retina
cornea
accommodation
hyperopia
myopia
astigmatism
presbyopia
iris
pupil
dilation
constriction
rods
cones
blind spot
fovea
visual acuity
peripheral vision
tunnel vision

trichromatic theory
opponent-process theory
afterimage
visual pigments
color blindness
color weakness
Ishihara test
dark adaptation
rhodopsin
retinal
night blindness
compression
rarefaction
sound waves
frequency
pitch
amplitude
loudness
pinna
eardrum
auditory ossicles
oval window
cochlea
hair cells
frequency theory
place theory
hunter's notch
conduction deafness

nerve deafness
cochlear implants
stimulation deafness
temporary threshold shift
tinnitus
chemical senses
olfaction
gustation
anosmia
lock and key theory
taste bud
somesthetic senses
skin senses
kinesthetic senses
vestibular senses
sensory adaptation
physiological nystagmus
selective attention
sensory gates
acupuncture
beta-endorphin
prepared childbirth training
counterirritation
space adaptation syndrome
otolith organs
semicircular canals
ampulla
sensory conflict theory

IMPORTANT INDIVIDUALS

Jerome Lettvin
John Vokey
Don Read
David Hubel

Torsten Wiesel
Ronald Melzack
Patrick Wall

PROGRAMMED REVIEW

1. (p. 81) Our sensory organs can detect only a limited range of physical energies. They act as a _data reduction system_ system in boiling down floods of information into a select stream of useful data.

2. (p. 81) Using vision as an example, "light" is only a small slice of the _electromagnetic spectrum_ which also includes infrared and ultraviolet light, radio frequencies, television broadcasts, gamma rays, and other energies.

3. (p. 81) Selection of information reduces confusion that would be overwhelming if we were sensitive to all energies. One way our sensory system facilitates selection is the fact that sensory receptors act as biological _transducer_, converting one kind of energy into another.

4. (p. 81) Each sensory receptor is designed to convert only certain kinds of energy into nerve impulses. Also, many sensory systems _analyze_ the environment into important features before sending nerve impulses to the brain.

5. (p. 81) Perceptual _____ features _____ are basic elements of a stimulus pattern, such as line, shapes, edges, spots, or colors. The neural circuits of many sensory systems act as feature detectors. In other words, they are highly attuned to specific stimulus patterns.

6. (p. 81) For example, a frog's eye seems to be especially sensitive to small, dark, moving spots. It seems that the frog's eyes are "wired" to detect bugs flying nearby. Jerome Lettvin has called such sensitivity a "_____-_____."

7. (p. 81) Sensory systems also _____ important features into messages understood by the brain. For example, the eye is only prepared to _____ stimulation, including pressure, into visual features.

8. (p. 81) The concept of sensory coding for the visual system can be demonstrated when you press firmly on your eyelids covering the eye itself. This produces flashes of "light" called _____, even though nothing has really been "seen."

9. (p. 81) The sensations you experience often depend on the area of the brain activated. This is known as _____ of _____.

10. (p. 82) One practical implication of this phenomenon is that it may be possible someday to artificially route visual information to the brain. Another implication is that "seeing" does not take place in the eyes, but rather involves the entire eye-brain system. It is this flow of information from the senses to the brain that we call _____.

11. (p. 82) _____ is the approach whereby changes in physical stimuli are measured and related to psychological sensations, such as loudness, brightness, or taste.

12. (p. 82) If we seek the absolute minimum amount of stimulation necessary for a sensation to occur, we are looking for the _____ _____.

13. (p. 82) Testing for absolute thresholds is a good indication of just how sensitive we are. For example, it takes only _____ photons (the smallest possible particle of light) striking the retina to produce a visual sensation.

14. (p. 82) Humans can hear sounds ranging in pitch from about _____ hertz (vibrations) per second to about _____ hertz.

15. (p. 82) The "silent" dog whistle may produce sounds as high as _____ or _____ thousand hertz, well beyond the range of humans, but still within a dog's range.

16. (p. 83) Absolute thresholds not only vary from person to person, they also vary from time to time for a single person. The type of _____, the state of one's _____ system, and the costs of false "detections" are also factors.

17. (p. 83) Emotional factors are also important. Unpleasant stimuli may raise the threshold for recognition. This effect is called _____ _____ and was first demonstrated in experiments on the recognition of "dirty" and "clean" words.

18. (p. 83) Anytime information is processed below the _____ (threshold or limit) for awareness it is referred to as _____.

19. (p. 83) Subliminal perception was demonstrated in an experiment in which people shown shapes flashed on a screen for one-thousandth second later preferred these shapes

when compared with new ones not presented at the subliminal level. Apparently, the "old" shapes had become _____, and thus more "likable."

20. (p. 83)   Advertising using subliminal stimuli has caused much furor. However, controlled laboratory experiments show that subliminal stimuli are basically weak stimuli and that this approach is largely _____.

21. (p. 83)   When we seek the amount of stimulus change necessary to be perceived as different, we are looking for the _____ _____.

22. (p. 83)   This process involves determining how much stimulus change (increase or decrease) must occur to be _____ _____ _____, abbreviated _____.

23. (p. 83)   _____ _____ states that the amount of change in a stimulus needed to produce a JND is a constant proportion of the original stimulus intensity.

24. (p. 84)   Subliminal perception critics have heatedly charged that spoken messages recorded backward (called "_____") in rock music are perceived unconsciously by listeners.

25. (p. 84)   However, psychologists John Vokey and Don Read found no evidence of conscious or unconscious _____ of meaning when subjects were exposed to a variety of backward sentences. They were also unable to influence subjects' _____ with backward messages.

26. (p. 84)   Proportions for some common judgments determined by Weber's law include: pitch 1/333; weight _____; loudness _____; and taste _____.

27. (p. 84)   Weber's law is really just an approximation because it applies mainly to stimuli in the _____ rather than at the extremities. For other than pure sensory judgments, it is even more approximate.

28. (p. 85)   You are constantly surrounded by electromagnetic radiation which includes light and other energies. The _____ _____ is composed of light with various wavelengths.

29. (p. 85)   The spectrum starts at wavelengths of _____ nanometers (one-billionth of a meter) which produce sensations of purple or violet.

30. (p. 85)   Longer and longer wavelengths of light produce sensations of blue, green, yellow, and orange, until _____ with a wavelength of 700 nm is reached.

31. (p. 85)   As a physical property of light, wavelength corresponds to the psychological experience of _____, or the specific color of a stimulus.

32. (p. 85)   Colors produced by a very narrow band of wavelengths are said to be very _____, or "pure."

33. (p. 85)   A third dimension of vision, _____, corresponds roughly to the amplitude (or height) of light waves.

34. (p. 85)   Several of the basic elements of a camera and the eye are similar. Both have a _____ that focuses an image on a light-sensitive layer at the back of a closed space.

35. (p. 85)   In a camera this layer is the film; in the eye it is a layer of _____ (light-sensitive cells) about the size and thickness of a postage stamp, called the _____.

36. (p. 85)   The eye focuses using multiple processes. For one, the front of the eye has a curved, clear covering called the _____, that bends light rays inward.

37. (p. 85)   Next, the lens, which is elastic, is stretched or thickened by a series of muscles, so that more or less additional bending of light occurs. This process is called _____.

38. (p. 85)   The shape of the eye also affects focusing. If the eye is too short, objects close to the eye cannot be focused and farsightedness or _____ results.

39. (p. 85)   If the eyeball is too long, the image falls short of the retina and objects in the distance cannot be focused, resulting in nearsightedness or _____.

40. (p. 85)   When the cornea or the lens is misshapen, some of the visual field will be focused and some will be fuzzy, a problem called _____.

41. (p. 85)   _____ or "old vision" occurs when the lens becomes less resilient and less able to accommodate, often due to aging.

42. (p. 87)   In front of the lens in both a camera and the eye, there is a mechanism to control the amount of light entering. This mechanism is the diaphragm in a camera; in the eye it is the _____.

43. (p. 87)   The iris is a colored circular muscle that expands and contracts to control the size of the _____, or dark opening at the center of the eye.

44. (p. 88)   The retina can adapt to changing light conditions only very slowly, while the iris can do so very quickly. In dim light the pupils _____ (enlarge) and in bright light they _____ (narrow).

45. (p. 88)   The eye is equipped with two types of receptor cells. One type, called _____, number about 6.5 million in each eye, function in bright light, produce color sensations, and pick up fine details.

46. (p. 88)   Nobel Prize-winning psychobiologists David Hubel and Torsten Wiesel have shown that vision acts more like a computer than a camera. They shone lights of various sizes and shapes on the retina and recorded reactions from _____ _____ in the visual cortex.

47. (p. 88)   They found that many brain cells respond only to lines of a certain width or orientation. Other cells respond only to lines at certain _____, or lines of certain _____, or to lines moving in a particular _____.

48. (p. 89)   In contrast, _____, numbering about 100 million, function in dim light, and are capable of producing only sensations of black or white.

49. (p. 89)   However, the rods are much more _____ to light than cones and therefore mainly responsible for our ability to see in very dim light.

50. (p. 89)   At this point the comparison between the eye and the camera breaks down. The rods and cones point toward the _____ of the eye, away from incoming light.

51. (p. 89)   Also, each eye has a _____ _____ because there are no receptors where the optic nerve leaves the eye.

52. (p. 89)   And last, the eye is constantly in _____, a factor essential for normal vision but which would obviously be disasterous for a camera.

53. (p. 89)   The cup-shaped depression in the middle of the retina, packed with about 50,000 cones, is called the _____.

54. (p. 89)   The large number of cones in the fovea produce great visual _____, or sharpness. Thus, vision is sharpest when an image falls on the fovea and steadily decreases as images are moved to the edge of the retina.

55. (p. 89)   Normal acuity is designated as 20/20 vision: at 20 feet in distance you can distinguish what the average person can see at 20 feet. If vision can be corrected to no better than _____ acuity, a person is considered "legally blind."

56. (p. 89)   Areas outside the fovea also get light. This situation creates a large region of _____ (side) vision.

57. (p. 89)   The rods reach their greatest density about _____ degrees to each side of the fovea and are particularly sensitive to _____.

58. (p. 89)   Those who have lost peripheral vision are said to have _____ vision, a condition much like wearing blinders.

59. (p. 90)   Although the rods give poor acuity, they are many times more responsive to light than are cones. Thus, rods are most important for _____ vision which is best when looking to one side or the other of an object.

60. (p. 90)   In determining the brightest color, we must consider that rods and cones differ. Since cones show maximal color sensitivity to wavelengths in the _____-_____ region of the spectrum, this color range will appear brightest when all colors are tested in the daylight.

61. (p. 90)   Although rods do not produce color, they are most sensitive to _____-_____ lights. Thus, if all colors are tested at night or under other conditions of dim light, this color range will appear brightest.

62. (p. 91)   The _____, or three-color theory of color, holds that there are three types of cones, each with a heightened sensitivity to a specific color: _____, _____, or _____. Other colors are assumed to result from a combination of these three.

63. (p. 91)   However, there appear to be four colors psychologically primary, the original three and _____.

64. (p. 91)   The _____-_____ theory was developed to explain why you can't have a reddish-green or a yellowish-blue.

65. (p. 91)   According to this theory, the visual system analyzes information into "_____-_____" messages for red/green, yellow/blue, black/white. Coding one color in a pair seems to block the opposite message.

66. (p. 91)   According to this theory, fatigue caused by making one response causes an _____ of the opposite color as the system recovers.

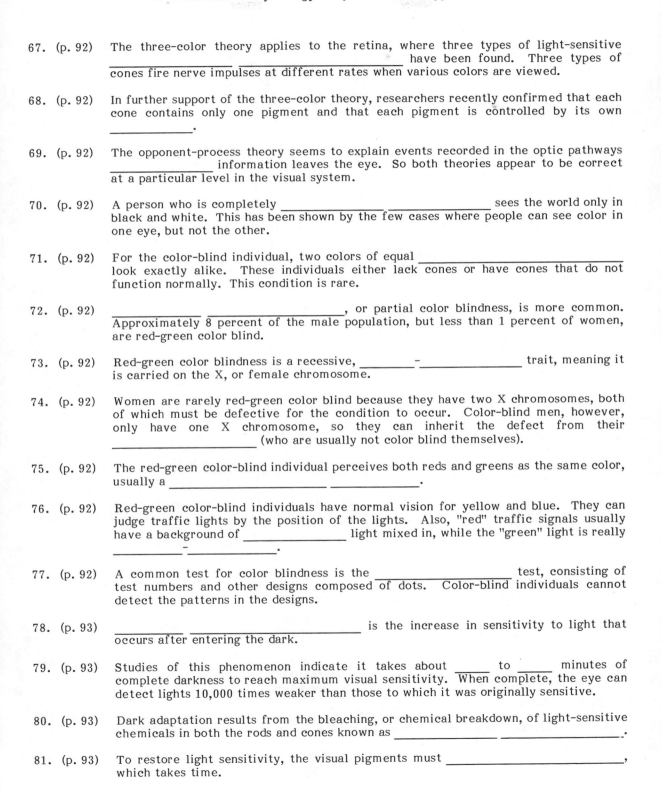

67. (p. 92) The three-color theory applies to the retina, where three types of light-sensitive _____ _____ have been found. Three types of cones fire nerve impulses at different rates when various colors are viewed.

68. (p. 92) In further support of the three-color theory, researchers recently confirmed that each cone contains only one pigment and that each pigment is controlled by its own _____.

69. (p. 92) The opponent-process theory seems to explain events recorded in the optic pathways _____ information leaves the eye. So both theories appear to be correct at a particular level in the visual system.

70. (p. 92) A person who is completely _____ _____ sees the world only in black and white. This has been shown by the few cases where people can see color in one eye, but not the other.

71. (p. 92) For the color-blind individual, two colors of equal _____ look exactly alike. These individuals either lack cones or have cones that do not function normally. This condition is rare.

72. (p. 92) _____ _____, or partial color blindness, is more common. Approximately 8 percent of the male population, but less than 1 percent of women, are red-green color blind.

73. (p. 92) Red-green color blindness is a recessive, _____-_____ trait, meaning it is carried on the X, or female chromosome.

74. (p. 92) Women are rarely red-green color blind because they have two X chromosomes, both of which must be defective for the condition to occur. Color-blind men, however, only have one X chromosome, so they can inherit the defect from their _____ (who are usually not color blind themselves).

75. (p. 92) The red-green color-blind individual perceives both reds and greens as the same color, usually a _____ _____.

76. (p. 92) Red-green color-blind individuals have normal vision for yellow and blue. They can judge traffic lights by the position of the lights. Also, "red" traffic signals usually have a background of _____ light mixed in, while the "green" light is really _____-_____.

77. (p. 92) A common test for color blindness is the _____ test, consisting of test numbers and other designs composed of dots. Color-blind individuals cannot detect the patterns in the designs.

78. (p. 93) _____ _____ is the increase in sensitivity to light that occurs after entering the dark.

79. (p. 93) Studies of this phenomenon indicate it takes about _____ to _____ minutes of complete darkness to reach maximum visual sensitivity. When complete, the eye can detect lights 10,000 times weaker than those to which it was originally sensitive.

80. (p. 93) Dark adaptation results from the bleaching, or chemical breakdown, of light-sensitive chemicals in both the rods and cones known as _____ _____.

81. (p. 93) To restore light sensitivity, the visual pigments must _____, which takes time.

82. (p. 93)   Night vision is due mainly to an increase of the rod pigment _____.

83. (p. 93)   Dark adaptation can be completely wiped out by a few seconds exposure to bright light. Glare recovery normally takes about 20 seconds, but after a few drinks may take _____ to _____ percent longer because alcohol dilates the pupils.

84. (p. 93)   Submarines and airplane cockpits are illuminated with _____ light, since the _____ are insensitive to this color. This provision allows people to perform their duties while dark-adapting.

85. (p. 93)   One of the components of rhodopsin is _____, which the body makes from vitamin A. When too little vitamin A is available, rhodopsin production declines.

86. (p. 95)   A person suffering from vitamin A deficiency may develop _____ _____, where they see normally in bright light (using the cones), but become blind when the rods must function.

87. (p. 96)   Sound travels as a series of invisible waves composed of _____ (peaks) and _____ (valleys).

88. (p. 96)   Any vibrating object will produce _____ _____ by setting air molecules in motion. Other materials, such as fluids or solids, will also carry sound, but sound does not travel in a vacuum.

89. (p. 96)   The frequency of sound waves (the number of waves per second) corresponds to the _____ of a sound. The _____ or height of a sound wave tells how much energy it contains and corresponds to loudness.

90. (p. 96)   What we call the "ear" is only the _____, or visible external portion of the ear that helps funnel and concentrate sounds.

91. (p. 96)   As sound waves are funneled into the ear, they collide with the _____, which is like a tight drumhead within the ear canal.

92. (p. 96)   These sound waves move the eardrum, which in turn causes the vibration of three small bones called the _____ _____.

93. (p. 96)   The third ossicle is attached to a second membrane, or drumhead, called the _____ _____.

94. (p. 96)   As the oval window moves back and forth, it sets up waves in a fluid within the canals of the _____, which is really the organ of hearing.

95. (p. 96)   Waves in the cochlear fluid are detected by tiny _____ _____ which generate nerve impulses to be sent to the brain.

96. (p. 96)   The _____ theory of hearing states that as pitch rises, nerve impulses of the same frequency are fed into the auditory nerve. This explains how sounds up to about 4000 hertz reach the brain.

97. (p. 96)   The _____ theory of hearing applies to higher tones and states that high tones register most strongly at the base of the cochlea (near the oval window).

98. (p. 96)   According to the place theory, lower tones mostly move hair cells near the

_____ _____ of the cochlea. Pitch is therefore signaled by the area of the cochlea most strongly activated.

99. (p. 96)   Place theory explains "_____ _____" so called because hunters sometimes lose hearing in a narrow pitch range. This phenomenon occurs when hair cells are damaged in the area activated by the pitch of gunfire.

100. (p. 97)   There are three types of deafness. _____ _____ occurs when the auditory ossicles are damaged or immobilized by disease or injury.

101. (p. 97)   Conduction deafness reduces the _____ of vibrations to the inner ear and can often be overcome through the use of a _____ _____, a device that makes sounds louder and clearer.

102. (p. 97)   _____ _____ is a hearing loss resulting from damage to the hair cells or auditory nerve. Hearing aids are of no help to a person with this condition because messages cannot reach the brain.

103. (p. 97)   _____ _____ results from exposure to very loud noise that can damage fragile hair cells in the cochlea.

104. (p. 98)   Researchers have recently found that in many cases of "nerve" deafness, the nerve is actually intact. This finding has spurred development of _____ _____ that bypass hair cells and stimulate the auditory nerves directly.

105. (p. 98)   Early implants allowed recipients to hear only _____-_____ sounds. But, newer multi-channel models make use of place theory to separate higher and lower tones. This has allowed some formerly deaf persons to hear human voices and other higher frequency sounds.

106. (p. 98)   Artificial hearing remains crude and not always very effective. In fact, _____ percent of adults who have tried implants have given up on them. However, improvements are sure to come.

107. (p. 98)   As examples, daily exposure to _____ decibels or more may cause permanent hearing loss, short periods of exposure to _____ decibels (as at rock concerts) may cause temporary deafness, and even brief exposure to _____ decibels (jet airplane nearby) can cause permanent deafness.

108. (p. 98)   To prevent permanent hearing loss, you should be particularly wary of any activity that causes a _____ _____ _____, or temporary loss of hearing.

109. (p. 98)   Be aware that decibels are plotted on a _____ scale. This means that every 20 decibels increase the amount of energy in a sound by a factor of 10. Therefore, a rock concert at 120 decibels is not just twice as powerful as a normal voice at 60 decibels. It is actually 1,000 times stronger.

110. (p. 98)   If a ringing sensation known as _____ follows exposure to loud sounds, chances are that hair cells have been damaged.

111. (p. 99)   _____, or smell, is a chemical sense, responding primarily to gaseous substances carried in the air. _____, or taste, is also a chemical sense.

112. (p. 99)   As air enters the nose, it passes over roughly _____ million nerve fibers embedded in the lining of the upper nasal passages. Airborne molecules passing over the exposed fibers trigger nerve signals that are sent to the brain.

113. (p. 99)   _____, or taste, is also a chemical sense. We could survive without taste and smell, but occasionally they do prevent poisonings and daily add pleasure to our lives.

114. (p. 99)   It is still somewhat of a mystery as to how different odors are produced. One hint comes from the condition known as _____ where a sort of "smell blindness" develops for only one odor. This suggests that there are specific receptors for different odors.

115. (p. 99)   It seems that molecules having a particular odor are quite similar in shape. Specific shapes have been identified for _____ (flower-like), _____ (camphor-like), musky, minty, and _____.

116. (p. 99)   This does not mean, however, that there are different olfactory _____ comparable to the three types of cones in vision. Each receptor in the nose is probably sensitive to many molecules or combinations of molecules.

117. (p. 99)   It is currently believed that there are different shaped "holes," or depressions, on the odor receptors. When a molecule matches up with a hole, it produces an odor. This is the essence of the concept known as the _____ and _____ theory.

118. (p. 99)   A recent large-scale test found that _____ of the population cannot smell at all. This can be a significant problem since many anosmics are unable to cook and they may be poisoned by spoiled food.

119. (p. 100) Factors that can cause anosmia include _____, _____, and blows to the head (which may tear the olfactory nerves). Exposure to chemicals such as _____, photo-developing chemicals, and hair-dressing potions can also produce olfactory loss.

120. (p. 100) There are at least four basic taste sensations. We are most sensitive to _____, next to _____, less sensitive to _____, and least sensitive to _____.

121. (p. 100) Flavors are actually more varied and complex than implied by the four taste qualities because we tend to include the sensations of _____, _____, _____, and even pain along with taste.

122. (p. 100) The primary receptors for taste are the _____ _____, located mainly on the top of the tongue, but also at other points in the mouth.

123. (p. 100) Part of the reason people seem to have very different tastes is _____. For example, the chemical PTC tastes bitter to about 70 percent of those tested, and has no taste for the other 30 percent. These tendencies are inherited.

124. (p. 100) Another reason is that taste cells have a life of only several _____. With age, cell replacement rate slows down so the sense of taste diminishes. This is why many foods you disliked in childhood may be more acceptable now.

125. (p. 101) An additional reason for individual differences in taste is the fact that most taste preferences are _____. What you are exposed to and accustomed to will have much to do with your likes and dislikes in foods.

126. (p. 101) Gymnasts launching themselves through a complex routine on the uneven bars rely heavily on the _____ _____, of which there are three.

127. (p. 101) The somesthetic senses include the _____ senses which produce light touch, pressure, pain, cold, and warmth.

128. (p. 101) _____ _____, receptors in the muscles and joints that relay information on body position and movement, are another type of somesthetic sense.

129. (p. 101) Another type of somesthetic sense, the _____ _____, involves receptors in the inner ear that signal balance and are involved in motion sickness.

130. (p. 101) Receptors specialize somewhat in various sensations. However, the surface of the eye, which has only free nerve endings, produces all five sensations. Altogether the skin has about 200,000 nerve endings for _____, 500,000 for touch and pressure, and three million for _____.

131. (p. 101) A _____-_____ touch test can be used to show that sensitivity roughly corresponds to the number of skin receptors in a given area. Generally speaking, important body areas have higher concentrations of receptors and are thus more sensitive.

132. (p. 102) _____ receptors are heavily represented, but do vary in their distribution, averaging about 232 points per square centimeter behind the knee, 184 per centimeter on the buttocks, 60 on the pad of the thumb, and 44 on the tip of the nose.

133. (p. 102) There are actually two kinds of pain. The first type, representing the body's warning system, is carried by _____ nerve fibers. It is sharp, bright, fast, and associated with specific body areas. It also quickly disappears.

134. (p. 102) The second type of pain, representing the body's reminding system, is carried by _____ nerve fibers, is slower, nagging, aching, widespread, and very unpleasant. It gets worse if the stimulus is repeated.

135. (p. 103) The decrease in sensory response that accompanies a constant or unchanging stimulus is called _____ _____.

136. (p. 103) _____ receptors are among the most quickly adapting. When exposed to a constant odor, they send fewer and fewer nerve impulses to the brain until the odor is no longer noticed.

137. (p. 103) Vision does not usually undergo sensory adaptation because the eye normally makes thousands of tiny movements every minute. These movements are caused by tremors in the eye muscles known as _____. It is these movements which shift visual images from one receptor cell to another and prevent adaptation.

138. (p. 103) This phenomenon has been demonstrated by using special equipment designed to follow the exact movements of the eye. When projected geometric designs are stabilized on the _____ they fade within a few seconds.

139. (p. 103) The ability to select, by "tuning in" or "tuning out," what senses we are receiving, is called _____ _____.

140. (p. 104) Selective attention appears to be based on the ability of various brain structures to select and divert incoming sensory messages. Recent evidence suggests that there are _____ _____ that control the flow of incoming nerve impulses to the brain.

141. (p. 104) For example, researchers Ronald Melzack and Patrick Wall have studied "_____ _____" in the spinal cord, and suggest that if the gate is closed by one pain message other messages may not be able to pass through.

142. (p. 104) Pain clinics use this effect by applying a mild _____ _____ to the skin. Such stimulation, at or just below the threshold of pain, can greatly reduce more agonizing pain.

143. (p. 104) This gate theory is an explanation for the effectiveness of the ancient Chinese art of _____. The needles activate small fibers which relay through a "central biasing system" in the brain to close the gates to intense or chronic pain.

144. (p. 104) People undergoing acupuncture often report feelings of light-headedness, relaxation, or euphoria. This effect seems to be due to the body's ability to produce opiate-like chemicals. To combat pain, the brain causes the pituitary gland to release a chemical called _____-_____, which is similar to morphine.

145. (p. 104) Receptor sites for endorphins are found in large numbers in the _____ system and other brain areas associated with pleasure, pain, and emotion.

146. (p. 105) The nervous system makes its own "drugs" to block pain. This relates to the idea of pain gates in that the central biasing system, which closes pain gates in the spinal cord, is highly _____ to morphine and other opiate pain-killers.

147. (p. 105) The "high" often felt by long-distance runners is an example of endorphin's effect. One study showed that after running a mile (a stress which causes the brain to release endorphins), subjects could tolerate pain about _____ percent longer than before.

148. (p. 105) When _____, a drug that blocks the effects of endorphins, was administered to subjects before running a mile, subjects lost their protection from pain.

149. (p. 106) Fear or overall levels of _____ increases pain. That fact explains why the relief of being excused from combat sometimes leaves soldiers insensitive to wounds.

150. (p. 106) Loss of _____ over pain seems to increase pain by increasing anxiety and emotional distress. People who are allowed to regulate, avoid, or _____ a painful stimulus suffer less.

151. (p. 106) Pain can be selectively tuned out to some extent. This fact was illustrated in experiments where subjects reported the _____ pain when distracted by the viewing and description of color slides and the _____ pain when describing their moment to moment reactions to the pain stimulus.

152. (p. 106) The meaning or _____ given a painful stimulus also affects pain. For example, in one experiment it was found that thinking of pain as pleasurable (denying the pain) greatly increased pain tolerance.

153. (p. 106) _____ _____, which emphasizes birth with a minimum of drugs or painkillers, utilizes all four of the factors involved in pain.

154. (p. 106) Natural childbirth techniques reduce pain by an average of about _____ percent. Even so, many women who have had prepared-childbirth training still end up asking for an epidural block because of the very severe pain.

155. (p. 106) In any situation where pain can be anticipated, lowered anxiety may be achieved by making sure that you are fully _____. Be sure you know what will happen or could happen.

156. (p. 106) In other situations, shifting attention away from pain can be aided by focusing on some _____ object. Prior practice in meditation can be a tremendous aid to such attention shifts.

157. (p. 107) Research suggests that distraction through attention shifts works best for mild or brief pain. For chronic or strong pain, _____ is more effective.

158. (p. 107) Physicians have found that intense surface stimulation of the skin can control pain from other parts of the body, and that a brief, mildly painful stimulus can relieve more severe pain. Such procedures, known as _____ are evident when applying ice packs, hot-water bottles, or mustard packs.

159. (p. 108) At least one-half of all astronauts have suffered from _____ _____ or "space sickness"—a type of motion sickness.

160. (p. 108) Like sea sickness, car sickness, and air sickness, its initial signs are _____ and mild _____. However, it usually does not produce the pallor, "cold sweating," and nausea so common on earth.

161. (p. 108) In most types of motion sickness, these signs warn that vomiting is about to occur. But in space, vomiting is usually _____ and _____.

162. (p. 108) The _____ organs are fluid-filled sacs which contain tiny crystals in a soft, gelatine-like mass. The tug of gravity or rapid head movements can cause the mass to shift, which stimulates hair-like receptor cells, allowing us to sense gravity and movement.

163. (p. 108) Another part of the vestibular system are three fluid-filled tubes called the _____ _____.

164. (p. 108) Head movements cause the fluid in the canals to swirl about, which bends a small "flap" called an _____. This bending stimulates hair cells that signal head rotation.

165. (p. 108) The most widely accepted explanation of motion sickness is the _____ _____ theory. It states that dizziness and nausea occur when sensory information from the vestibular system fails to match information received from the eyes and body.

166. (p. 108) The reason why sensory conflict causes nausea may be rooted in evolution. Many _____ disturb the coordination of messages from the vestibular

system, vision, and the body. It may be that we react to sensory conflict by vomiting to expel _____.

167. (p. 109) During _____, the otolith organs send unexpected signals to the brain and head movements are no longer confirmed by the semicircular canals. This can produce sensory conflict.

168. (p. 109) A further problem in space is that few of the messages the brain receives from the vestibular system and kinesthetic receptors agree with a lifetime of past _____.

169. (p. 109) Space sickness usually disappears in two or three days. This adaptation seems to occur because astronauts shift to using _____ cues instead of vestibular information.

170. (p. 109) This same shift can cause "earth sickness." Immediately after returning to earth some astronauts have experienced _____ and _____. All had considerable difficulty in standing with their eyes closed for the first day or two.

171. (p. 109) The most successful medication for motion sickness is _____. Non-prescription "sea sickness" pills also offer some protection. Alcohol and other intoxicating drugs usually make symptoms worse.

172. (p. 109) Soviet cosmonauts have had some success with a system that limits _____ _____ for the first two days in space.

173. (p. 109) To minimize sensory conflict, stay out of the cabin on boats. In cars and airplanes, try closing your eyes. It can help to fixate your eyes on an _____ _____ or look above the horizon at the unmoving sky.

174. (p. 109) If possible, you should _____ _____. The otoliths are less sensitive to vertical movements when you are horizontal, and your head will move less.

175. (p. 109) _____ seems to intensify motion sickness. Try to breathe slowly and deeply since this can be a good focus for attention.

SELF-TEST

1. (p. 81) Which of the following is *not* a factor in the data reduction system of the senses?
   a. transduction of energy into nerve impulses
   b. analysis of environment into important features prior to neural transmission
   c. coding of important environmental features into messages understood by the brain
   d. activation of sensory receptors by the brain to prepare them for transmission

2. (p. 81) True-False. Pressure to the eye produces visual perceptions of stars, checkerboards, and flashes of color called phosphates.

3. (p. 81) The principle that the sensations you experience depend on the area of the brain stimulated is called _____.
   a. Weber's Law   c. nerve impulse transduction
   b. localization of function   d. selective attention

4. (p. 82) True-False. Study of sensory systems shows that seeing takes place in the eyes.

5. (p. 82)   True-False. Psychophysics is the study of how changes in psychological functioning affect stimuli in the brain.

6. (p. 82)   The minimum amount of stimulation necessary for a sensation to occur is called the
a. difference threshold   c. stimulation threshold
b. absolute threshold   d. minimum threshold

7. (p. 82)   Humans can hear sounds ranging from _____ hertz to _____ hertz.
a. 200 – 2,000   c. 20 – 200,000
b. 20 – 20,000   d. 20 – 200

8. (p. 83)   True-False. Absolute thresholds are absolutely the same from person to person.

9. (p. 83)   The fact that subjects take longer to recognize "dirty" rather than "clean" words illustrates which of the following?
a. perceptual vigilance   c. perceptual defense
b. perceptual adaptation   d. subliminal perception

10. (p. 83)   True-False. Subliminal stimuli are unusually effective in commercial advertisements designed to increase product sales.

11. (p. 83)   The principle that the amount of change in a stimulus needed to produce a JND is a constant proportion of the original stimulus intensity is called
a. sensory adaptation   c. opponent-process theory
b. absolute threshold   d. Weber's Law

12. (p. 85)   True-False. The visible spectrum of electromagnetic radiation is made up of light producing a range of color sensations from purple or violet, through blue, green, yellow, and orange, until red is reached.

13. (p. 85)   Which of the following is *not* a dimension of vision?
a. hue   c. saturation
b. brightness   d. pitch

14. (p. 85)   One part of the eye that focuses an image on the retina is the
a. pupil   c. rod
b. cone   d. lens

15. (p. 85)   The process whereby the lens of the eye stretches or thickens due to a series of muscle and ligament adjustments is called _____.
a. facilitation   c. adaptation
b. accommodation   d. acuity

16. (p. 85)   Which of the following is improperly associated?
a. hyperopia, farsightedness   c. myopia, nearsightedness
b. astigmatism, "old vision"   d. presbyopia, farsightedness due to aging

17. (p. 87)   The mechanism of the eye that controls the amount of light entering is the _____.
a. lens   c. diaphragm
b. cornea   d. iris

18. (p. 89)   The receptors of the eye primarily responsible for color vision and seeing fine details are the _____.
a. rods   c. foveas
b. retinas   d. cones

19. (p. 89)   True-False. Visual acuity is best when an image falls on the fovea because of the large number of cones in that part of the retina.

20. (p. 89)   Which of the following is *not* associated with the functioning of the rods of the eye?
   a. sensitive to movement
   b. essential for night vision
   c. less responsive to light than cones
   d. facilitate peripheral vision

21. (p. 90)   True-False. Rods and cones have different maximal color sensitivities. Rods are most sensitive to blue-green lights, while yellowish-green colors appear brightest when cones are tested.

22. (p. 91)   The theory that the visual system analyzes information into "either-or" color messages is known as
   a. the trichromatic theory
   b. the opponent-process theory
   c. the gating theory
   d. Weber's theory

23. (p. 92)   True-False. The trichromatic theory of color vision seems to work at the level of the retina, while the opponent-process theory seems to apply to events recorded in the optic pathways, after information leaves the retina.

24. (p. 92)   Which of the following is *not* true of red-green color blindness?
   a. It occurs in about 1 percent of women and 8 percent of men.
   b. It is a recessive, sex-linked trait.
   c. Red-green color-blind individuals perceive both colors as a yellowish brown.
   d. It is less common than blue-yellow color blindness.

25. (p. 92)   True-False. A common test for measuring farsightedness is the Ishihara test.

26. (p. 93)   The increase in sensitivity to light that occurs when you stay in the dark for some time is called
   a. light enhancement
   b. dark adaptation
   c. dark facilitation
   d. light adaptation

27. (p. 93)   Rhodopsin is
   a. a light-sensitive pigment in the rods important in night vision
   b. an ingredient of vitamin A important in color vision
   c. a visual pigment in the cones sensitive to artificial illumination
   d. an important chemical missing in the eyes of red-green color-blind individuals

28. (p. 93)   True-False. Complete dark adaptation takes about 30 to 35 minutes, but can be completely wiped out by just a few seconds exposure to bright lights, such as the head lights of an approaching car during night driving.

29. (p. 95)   One of the components of rhodopsin is retinal, which the body makes from _____.
   a. vitamin A
   b. vitamin B
   c. vitamin C
   d. vitamin D

30. (p. 96)   Where hearing is concerned, wave frequency corresponds to pitch, while wave amplitude corresponds to
   a. sound
   b. loudness
   c. tone
   d. depth

31. (p. 96)   True-False. What we usually call the ear is really only the pinna or visible external part of the ear.

32. (p. 96) Sound waves travel through the ear and affect the process of hearing through which sequence?
    a. eardrum, auditory ossicles, oval window, cochlea, hair cells
    b. cochlea, eardrum, oval window, auditory ossicles, hair cells
    c. auditory ossicles, oval window, cochlea, eardrum, hair cells
    d. eardrum, oval window, auditory ossicles, cochlea, hair cells

33. (p. 96) True-False. The eardrum is the ultimate receptor for hearing.

34. (p. 97) When the eardrums or ossicles are damaged or immobilized by disease or injury, _____ deafness results.
    a. stimulation   c. impulse
    b. nerve   d. conduction

35. (p. 97) True-False. Hearing aids are of no help to a person with nerve deafness because auditory messages cannot reach the brain due to damage to the hair cells or auditory nerve.

36. (p. 98) Which of the following is *not* a warning signal of stimulation deafness?
    a. temporary threshold shift
    b. perceived temporary reduction in hearing
    c. tinnitus
    d. anosmia

37. (p. 99) Which of the following are chemical senses?
    a. vision, audition   c. gustation, olfaction
    b. skin, vestibular   d. somesthetic, kinesthetic

38. (p. 99) Anosmia refers to
    a. smell blindness for one type of odor
    b. heavily saturated colors
    c. one ingredient of rhodopsin
    d. a distortion of the eye lens

39. (p. 99) The lock and key theory generally appears to explain the process of
    a. gustation   c. olfaction
    b. pain gating   d. psychologically perceived colors

40. (p. 100) The principle organ of taste is the
    a. pinna   c. cochlea
    b. taste bud   d. cornea

41. (p. 100) True-False. You may find as an adult that there are foods you now like which were not preferred as a child. This phenomenon is because of sensory adaptation.

42. (p. 101) Which of the following is *not* a somesthetic sense?
    a. skin senses   c. kinesthetic senses
    b. vestibular senses   d. gustation senses

43. (p. 101) True-False. Skin receptors are about equally sensitive to each of the five different sensations, although they are found in varying concentrations all over the body surface.

44. (p. 102) True-False. The body's warning system for pain involves sharp, bright pain carried by large nerve fibers associated with specific body areas.

45. (p. 103) The fact that you do not notice the smell of cooking fish after you have been in a room for a few minutes, illustrates the phenomenon of
    a. selective functioning   c. function localization
    b. sensory adaptation   d. sensory deprivation

46. (p. 103) True-False. The rods and cones would undergo sensory adaptation were it not for physiological nystagmus, which shifts visual images from one receptor to another.

47. (p. 103) Our ability to tune in on any one of the many sensory messages while excluding others defines the process of
    a. selective attention   c. sensory adaptation
    b. sensory selection   d. selective sensation

48. (p. 104) The presence of sensory gates possibly explains all of the following *except*
    a. selective attention
    b. the effectiveness of acupuncture
    c. sensory adaptation
    d. how one type of pain can cancel another

49. (p. 104) True-False. The study of endorphins suggests that pain and stress may be counteracted by the release of morphine-like substances in the body.

50. (p. 106) Which of the following is *not* a factor that can be used to influence the amount of pain produced by a particular stimulus?
    a. diffusion   c. control
    b. attention   d. interpretation

51. (p. 106) Which of the following would *not* be expected to reduce pain?
    a. counterirritation   c. denying pain
    b. fear of pain   d. meditation

52. (p. 108) A type of motion sickness called _____ has affected at least one-half of all astronauts, producing sudden and unexpected vomiting.
    a. vestibular conflict sickness   c. sensory conflict syndrome
    b. space adaptation syndrome   d. ampulla illness

53. (p. 108) Which of the following is *not* true of sensory conflict theory?
    a. It postulates that space sickness vomiting may be due to an evolutionary link whereby poisons are expelled from the body.
    b. It postulates that during weightlessness conflict between messages sent by the otolith organs and the semicircular canals produces illness.
    c. It postulates that as biological systems adapt to the unusual conditions of space that space sickness should disappear within two or three hours.
    d. All of the above

54. (p. 109) Immediately after returning from space, astronauts have experienced dizziness, nausea, and an inability to stand with eyes closed. This pattern has become known as
    a. space sickness   c. air sickness
    b. space rebound sickness   d. earth sickness

55. (p. 109) True-False. Becoming intoxicated can diminish motion sickness symptoms because alcohol acts as a depressant to numb the effects of sensory conflict.

ANSWERS — PROGRAMMED REVIEW

1. data reduction
2. electromagnetic spectrum
3. transducers
4. analyze
5. Perceptual features
6. bug detector
7. code; code
8. phosphenes
9. localization of function
10. sensation
11. Psychophysics
12. absolute threshold
13. three
14. 20; 20,000
15. 40; 50
16. stimulus; nervous
17. perceptual defense
18. limen; subliminal
19. familiar
20. ineffective
21. difference threshold
22. just noticeably different; JND
23. Weber's law
24. backmasking
25. recognition; behavior
26. 1/50; 1/10; 1/5
27. midrange
28. visible spectrum
29. 400
30. red
31. hue
32. saturated
33. brightness
34. lens
35. photoreceptors; retina
36. cornea
37. accommodation
38. hyperopia
39. myopia
40. astigmatism
41. Presbyopia
42. iris
43. pupil
44. dilate; constrict
45. cones
46. single cells
47. angles; lengths; direction
48. rods
49. sensitive
50. back
51. blind spot
52. motion
53. fovea
54. acuity
55. 20/200
56. peripheral
57. 20; movement
58. tunnel
59. night
60. yellowish-green
61. blue-green
62. trichromatic; red, green, blue
63. yellow
64. opponent-process
65. either-or
66. afterimage
67. visual pigments
68. gene
69. after
70. color blind
71. brightness
72. Color weakness
73. sex-linked
74. mothers
75. yellowish brown
76. yellow; blue-green
77. Ishihara
78. Dark adaptation
79. 30; 35
80. visual pigments
81. recombine
82. rhodopsin
83. 30; 50
84. red; rods
85. retinal
86. night blindness
87. compression; rarefaction
88. sound waves
89. pitch; amplitude
90. pinna
91. eardrum
92. auditory ossicles
93. oval window
94. cochlea
95. hair cells
96. frequency
97. place
98. outer tip
99. hunter's notch
100. Conduction deafness
101. transfer; hearing aid
102. Nerve deafness
103. Stimulation deafness
104. cochlear implants
105. low-frequency
106. 30

107. 85; 120; 150
108. temporary threshold shift
109. logarithmic
110. tinnitus
111. Olfaction
112. 20
113. Gustation
114. anosmia
115. floral; camphor; etherish
116. receptors
117. lock and key
118. 1.2
119. infections, allergies; ammonia
120. bitter; sour; salt; sweet
121. texture, temperature, smell
122. taste buds
123. genetic
124. days
125. acquired
126. somesthetic senses
127. skin
128. Kinesthetic senses
129. vestibular senses
130. temperature; pain
131. two-point
132. Pain
133. large
134. small
135. sensory adaptation
136. Olfactory
137. physiological nystagmus
138. retina
139. selective attention
140. sensory gates
141. pain gates

142. electrical current
143. acupuncture
144. beta-endorphins
145. limbic
146. sensitive
147. 70
148. naloxone
149. anxiety
150. control; control
151. least; greatest
152. interpretation
153. prepared childbirth training
154. 30
155. informed
156. external
157. reinterpretation
158. counterirritation
159. space adaptation syndrome
160. dizziness; disorientation
161. sudden; unexpected
162. otolith
163. semicircular canals
164. ampulla
165. sensory conflict
166. poisons; poison
167. weightlessness
168. experience
169. visual
170. dizziness; nausea
171. scopolamine
172. head movements
173. unmoving point
174. lie down
175. Anxiety

ANSWERS — SELF-TEST

1. d	15. b	29. a	43. False
2. False	16. b	30. b	44. True
3. b	17. d	31. True	45. b
4. False	18. d	32. a	46. True
5. False	19. True	33. False	47. a
6. b	20. c	34. d	48. c
7. b	21. True	35. True	49. True
8. False	22. b	36. d	50. a
9. c	23. True	37. c	51. b
10. False	24. d	38. a	52. b
11. d	25. False	39. c	53. c
12. True	26. b	40. b	54. d
13. d	27. a	41. False	55. False
14. d	28. True	42. d	

Chapter 5

Perceiving the World

CONTENTS

TERMS AND CONCEPTS

perception
size constancy
shape constancy
brightness constancy
figure-ground organization
reversible figures
nearness
similarity
continuation (continuity)
closure
contiguity
illusory figures
camouflage figures
perceptual hypothesis
ambiguous stimuli
impossible figures
depth perception
nativists
empiricists
visual cliff
depth perception
depth cues
monocular cues

binocular cues
accommodation
convergence
retinal disparity
stereoscopic vision
random dot stereograms
pictorial depth cues
linear perspective
relative size
light and shadow
overlap (interposition)
texture gradients
aerial perspective
relative motion (motion parallax)
moon illusion
apparent distance hypothesis
percentual habits
Ames Room
inverted vision
stimulus context
frame of reference
adaptation level
illusion

hallucination	perceptual categories
stroboscopic movement	weapon focus
Müller-Lyer illusion	reality testing
size-distance invariance	extrasensory perception (ESP)
attention	parapsychology
selective attention	psi phenomenon
divided attention	clairvoyance
habituation	telepathy
orientation response (OR)	precognition
bottom-up processing	prophetic dreams
top-down processing	psychokinesis
perceptual expectancy	Zener cards
tachistoscope	

IMPORTANT INDIVIDUALS

Richard Gregory	Norman Mackworth
Jane Gwiazada	Geoffrey Loftus
Bela Julesz	Jerome Bruner
William Hudson	Sidney Jourard
Colin Blakemore	Abraham Maslow
Graham Cooper	J. B. Rhine

PROGRAMMED REVIEW

1. (p. 112) The process of assembling sensations into a usable mental representation of the world is called _____.

2. (p. 113) Newly sighted persons do not immediately recognize their environment, but rather must _____ to identify objects, to read clocks, numbers and letters, and to judge sizes and distances.

3. (p. 113) The fact that the perceived size of an object remains the same even though the size of its retinal image changes is called _____ _____.

4. (p. 113) Some perceptions, like seeing a line on a piece of paper, are so basic they seem to be _____ (inborn). But much perception is _____, or based on prior experience.

5. (p. 113) For example, one researcher showed that a jungle-dwelling _____ had limited size constancy. Since he had no past experience with seeing objects far away, a buffalo in the distance looked like an insect.

6. (p. 113) _____ _____ refers to the fact that objects are perceived as having the same form even though the retinal image of the object changes with the angle at which the object is viewed.

7. (p. 113) _____ _____ refers to the fact that under changing lighting conditions the same object reflects different total amounts of light, and yet the psychological brightness of the object does not change.

8. (p. 113) This principle is true because the _____ of light reflected by an object is still the same, relative to other objects in the environment, under any lighting conditions.

9. (p. 115) The simplest organization is to group some sensations into an object or "thing" that stands out against some plainer background. This process is called _____-_____ organization.

10. (p. 115) It is probably _____ since it is the first perceptual ability to emerge when a cataract patient regains sight. Such was the case for Mr. S. B. as described by Richard Gregory.

11. (p. 115) In normal figure-ground perception only one figure is seen. However, in _____ _____ figure and ground can be switched.

12. (p. 115) Gestalt psychologists have studied extensively what causes the formation of a "figure." According to their studies, the principles that bring order to your perceptions include:
    1) Stimuli that are _____ each other tend to be grouped together.
    2) Stimuli that are _____ in size, shape, color, or form tend to be grouped together.
    3) Perceptions tend toward simplicity and _____.
    4) The tendency to complete a figure so that it has a consistent overall form is known as _____.

13. (p. 116) The principle of closure is evidenced through the use of _____ figures. Even young children can identify the implied shapes seen in such forms.

14. (p. 116) The principle of _____, or nearness in time and space, is often responsible for the perception that one thing has caused another. For example, knocking on your head while knocking on a wooden table (out of sight) gives the perception that the head is made of wood.

15. (p. 116) Other factors which greatly affect perceptual organization include learning and past experience. While the normal person could easily solve _____ patterns (those that break up figure-ground organization), individuals like Mr. S. B. would be at a total loss.

16. (p. 116) A meaningful pattern represents a _____ _____, or guess, held until the evidence contradicts it. Pre-existing ideas and expectations actively guide our interpretation of sensations.

17. (p. 116) The active nature of perceptual organization is perhaps most apparent in the case of _____ _____ (patterns allowing more than one interpretation). For example, clouds can be perceptually organized to resemble many shapes and scenes.

18. (p. 116) In some instances, a stimulus may present such a conflict that perceptual organization becomes impossible. For example, the tendency to make a three-dimensional object out of a drawing is frustrated by the "three-pronged widget"—an _____ figure.

19. (p. 117) Humans almost always appear to understand lines that represent the _____ of surfaces. We also have no problem with a single line used to depict the _____ edges of a narrow object. However, we do not easily recognize lines that show color boundaries on the surface of an object. This was demonstrated in studies with the Songe tribe of New Guinea.

20. (p. 118) _____ _____ is the ability to see three-dimensional space and to accurately estimate distance.

21. (p. 118) Some psychologists, called "_____," hold that depth perception is inborn. Others, called "_____," view it as learned. Most likely, it involves elements of both positions.

22. (p. 118) Some evidence regarding depth perception comes from work with the _____ _____, a table covered with glass. On one side, a checkered surface lies directly beneath the glass, while on the other side, the surface is four feet below the glass.

23. (p. 118) Using this device, 6- to 14-month-old infants were placed in the middle and given the choice of crawling to the "shallow" or the "deep" side. The majority chose the _____ side and most refused the _____ side even when their mothers tried to call them towards it.

24. (p. 118) Psychologist Jane Gwiazada has expanded this work by testing babies with goggles that make some designs stand out three-dimensionally, while others remain flat. Recognition of "3-D" designs occurs at age ___ months.

25. (p. 118) As soon as infants become active crawlers, they refuse to cross the deep side of the visual cliff. When babies accidentally crawl off tables or beds, this is most likely due to a lack of _____ than to an inability to see depth.

26. (p. 118) _____ _____ are features of the environment, or messages from the body, that supply information about distance and space.

27. (p. 119) Depth cues that will function using only one eye are referred to as _____ cues; those requiring both eyes are called _____ cues.

28. (p. 119) Muscular cues come from within the body. One such cue is _____, which refers to the ability of the eye lens to bend more to focus objects close to the eye than those at a distance.

29. (p. 119) However, accommodation, a monocular depth cue, contributes little to depth perception beyond _____ feet.

30. (p. 119) A second bodily cue for depth is _____. This binocular depth cue stems from the fact that when you look at something 50 feet or less in distance, your eyes must turn in to focus the object.

31. (p. 119) Both accommodation and convergence provide depth cues based on the relationship between muscle sensations and distance. The former relies on muscles which support the _____, the latter on muscles attached to the _____.

32. (p. 119) The most basic source of depth perception is _____ _____, in which each eye receives a slightly different view of the world. It is also a binocular cue.

33. (p. 119) When the images seen by both eyes are _____ into one overall image, a powerful sensation of depth occurs. This is the principle behind _____ movies where two cameras film a scene from slightly different angles.

34. (p. 119) In such 3-D movies, the two separate films are then simultaneously projected on a screen while the audience wears glasses that filter out one of the images to each eye. This duplicates normal _____ _____.

35. (p. 119) Three-dimensional space is woven from countless tiny differences between what the right and left eyes see. This effect is demonstrated by random dot stereograms created by Bela Julesz to show how sensitive the brain is to any _____ of information from the eyes.

36. (p. 120) _____ depth cues refer to cues that work on a flat surface to reproduce depth. They contain much of the information present when a person looks at a real three-dimensional scene.

37. (p. 120) One such pictorial depth cue is _____ _____, which refers to the apparent convergence of parallel lines in the environment.

38. (p. 120) If artists wish to depict two objects of the same size at different distances, they make the more distant object smaller. Thus, they use _____ _____ to reproduce depth.

39. (p. 121) Most objects in the environment are lighted in such a way as to create definite patterns of _____ and _____. Appropriate use of these qualities can give a two-dimensional design a three-dimensional feeling.

40. (p. 121) _____ or interposition describes a depth cue caused by one object partially blocking the view of another.

41. (p. 121) If you are standing in the middle of a cobblestone street, the street looks coarse near your feet but the _____ of the stones gets smaller and finer as you look off into the distance. This gradual decrease in fine detail refers to a texture _____.

42. (p. 121) Smog, fog, dust and haze add to the apparent depth of an object. Objects seen at a distance tend to be hazy, washed-out in color, and lacking in detail due to _____ _____.

43. (p. 121) Relative motion, also known as _____ _____, can be seen by looking out a window and moving your head from side to side. Objects near to you seem to move more than objects in the distance.

44. (p. 122) Pictorial depth cues do appear to require learning. William Hudson has tested members of remote tribes who are unfamiliar with these cues. They see simplified drawings as _____-_____ designs.

45. (p. 122) The moon illusion refers to the fact that the moon looks _____ when it is low in the sky than when it is overhead.

46. (p. 122) This illusion occurs because the _____ _____ of the moon is greater when it is on the horizon and seen behind houses, trees, etc.

47. (p. 122) The moon illusion is best explained by the _____ _____ _____, which states that if two objects form identical images, but one is more distant, the more distant object must be larger.

48. (p. 122) The moon illusion is directly related to changes in _____. Extra depth cues near the horizon cause the eyes to focus on a more distant point than they do when you look overhead. Such changes appear to provide the brain with a "yardstick" for judging the size of images, including the moon.

49. (p. 123) Learning may affect perception through ingrained patterns of organization and attention, referred to as _____ _____.

50. (p. 124) Perceptual habits may become so ingrained that they lead us to distort or misperceive a stimulus. For example, in the Ames Room, the left corner is further from the viewer than the right. This makes a person standing in the left corner look very _____, whereas one standing in the right corner looks very _____.

51. (p. 124) Perceptual habits seem to program the brain for sensitivity to important environmental features. For example, Colin Blakemore and Graham Cooper found that kittens raised in rooms with _____ stripes could jump onto a chair, but bumped into chairs when walking on the floor. Likewise, "_____" cats easily avoided chair legs but missed when trying to jump onto chairs.

52. (p. 124) Other experiments show that for such animals there is a decrease in _____ _____ tuned to the missing features.

53. (p. 125) The question of whether an adult can adapt to a completely new perceptual world is addressed by experiments involving _____ _____, where special glasses turn the world upside down and reverse objects from right to left.

54. (p. 125) At first, even the simplest tasks are incredibly difficult. Eventually, human inverted vision subjects do adapt (unlike _____ who swim in circles and rarely adapt when their eyes are surgically turned upside down).

55. (p. 125) Throughout the period that subjects wore their goggles, their visual images remained upside down. But, subjects learned to perform most routine activities and some were able to drive cars and fly airplanes. Such a high degree of adaptation is related to superior human _____ abilities.

56. (p. 125) _____ _____ in a new visual world (as with inverted vision) seems to be a key in adaptation. Subjects who walked on their own adapted more quickly than subjects pushed around in a wheeled cart.

57. (p. 125) An important factor affecting perception is the external _____ in which a stimulus is judged. For example, a man six feet in height looks tall when surrounded by others of medium height and short among professional basketball players.

58. (p. 126) In addition to external contexts, we all have an internal _____ of _____, or standard by which stimuli are judged.

59. (p. 126) Your own personal "medium point" is called your _____ _____. It determines how heavy you judge a particular weight to be when given no artificial standard with which to compare it.

60. (p. 126) Perceptual learning is responsible for a number of _____ in which length, position, motion, curvature, or direction is consistently misjudged.

61. (p. 126) While illusions distort stimuli that actually exist, people who are _____ perceive objects or events that have no external reality (like hearing "voices" that are not there).

62. (p. 126) The illusion of _____ _____ is responsible for putting the "motion" in motion pictures. Movies project a series of rapid "snapshots" on the screen giving the sense of normal motion.

63. (p. 127) The familiar _____-_____ illusion illustrates how perceptual habits and past experience combine to produce illusions. In this illusion, a horizontal line with "arrowheads" appears _____ than a horizontal line with "Vs" on each end.

64. (p. 127) Richard Gregory uses the concept of _____-_____ _____ to explain this illusion. The V-tipped line looks farther away than the arrowhead-tipped line, so you compensate by seeing the V-tipped line as larger.

65. (p. 127) The South African _____ who live in a "round" world typically do not experience the Müller-Lyer illusion because they have had little previous experience with straight lines. At most, he or she sees the V-shaped line as slightly longer than the other.

66. (p. 128) The first stage of perception is _____, the selection of incoming stimuli.

67. (p. 128) _____ attention refers to the fact that we give some messages priority and put others on hold. Think of this concept as a sort of bottleneck or narrowing in the information channel linking the senses to perception. When one message enters the bottleneck, it seems to prevent others from passing through.

68. (p. 128) _____ attention often arises from our limited capacity for processing information. Overload may occur because at any moment we must split our mental effort among tasks, each of which required more or less attention.

69. (p. 128) Very _____ stimuli are attention getting. That is, stimuli that are brighter, louder, or larger tend to capture attention.

70. (p. 128) A dripping faucet at night makes little noise by normal standards, but because of _____ it may become as attention-getting as a single sound many times louder.

71. (p. 128) Attention is also frequently related to contrast or _____ in stimulation. For example, Norman Mackworth and Geoffrey Loftus found that people who look at commonplace drawings with unusual elements focus first and longest on the unexpected parts.

72. (p. 128) Change, contrast, and incongruity are perhaps the most basic sources of attention. We quickly _____ (respond less) to predictable and unchanging stimuli.

73. (p. 128) Messages arriving at the brain are selected by attention. Then the body makes an _____ _____ (OR) characterized by enlarged pupils, brain wave changes, a short pause in breathing, increased blood flow to the head, and turning to face the stimulus.

74. (p. 128) When a stimulus is repeated without change, the OR _____, or decreases. For example, when an album becomes "old," a whole side may play without your really hearing it.

75. (p. 129) Advertisers take advantage of two motives, _____ and _____, in gaining your attention.

76. (p. 129) Motives may alter what is perceived, as in the supposed study of the dating practices

of male college students. Subjects who read a more sexually-arousing passage rated potential female blind dates as _____ _____.

77. (p. 129) An emotional stimulus can shift attention away from other information. Jewish subjects shown quickly-flashed pictures did not recognize symbols at the edge of the figures as well when the central item was an emotional symbol like a _____.

78. (p. 129) Perception seems to proceed to two major ways. In _____-_____, we analyze information starting at the "bottom" with small units (features) and build upward into a complete perception.

79. (p. 129) A second major means by which perception proceeds is _____-_____ processing. In this case, preexisting knowledge is used to rapidly organize features into a meaningful whole.

80. (p. 129) In perception, past experiences, motives, context, or suggestion may create a _____ _____ that sets you to perceive in a certain way.

81. (p. 130) Many perceptual expectancies are created by _____. In one experiment, students perceived a guest lecturer as unhappy and irritable when previously given the suggestion that the lecturer was "cold." Those who got a "warm" description responded positively.

82. (p. 130) Psychologist Jerome Bruner believes that perceptual learning builds up a set of mental _____.

83. (p. 130) Bruner demonstrated this by using a _____ to flash pictures of cards on a screen. Subjects often misperceived the cards that did not fit their expectations.

84. (p. 131) Perceptual categories have a strong impact on our perception of others. For example, psychotherapists told that a man was a job applicant described him as "realistic," "sincere," and "pleasant." When told he was a _____ _____, others described him as "defensive," "dependent," and "impulsive."

85. (p. 132) Most perceptions, such as our impression that the sun "sets" rather than the earth revolving backwards, reflect our active and creative _____ of events. We see what we believe.

86. (p. 132) The highly subjective quality of perception can be a liability, particularly in eyewitness testimony. Recent experiments show that a person's confidence in his or her testimony has almost no bearing on its _____.

87. (p. 132) In addition, misleading questions about what a person saw can greatly _____ eyewitness accuracy.

88. (p. 132) In one court case, a police officer testified that he saw the black defendant shoot the victim as both stood in a doorway 120 feet away. Measurements made by a psychologist demonstrated that identification under such conditions was _____.

89. (p. 132) Perception rarely provides an "instant replay" of events. Of 84 pilots who saw a DC-10 airline crash, _____ said the landing gear was up and _____ said it was down.

90. (p. 132) The same type of inaccuracies were reported when "eyewitness" subjects were interviewed following a staged attack on a college professor. The total accuracy score for the group tested was _____ percent of the maximum possible.

91. (p. 132) A recent experiment found that eyewitness accuracy was virtually the _____ for witnessing a crime as it was for being a victim. Jurors who place more weight on the testimony of victims may be making a serious mistake.

92. (p. 132) In many crimes, victims fall prey to _____ _____. They fix their entire attention on the weapon and fail to perceive details of appearance, dress, or other clues to identify the attacker.

93. (p. 132) Psychologist Sidney Jourard offers a suggestion to help individuals increase the accuracy of their perceptions. By _____ _____, we can obtain additional information as a check on our perceptions. This may be as simple as asking what someone thinks or feels.

94. (p. 133) Abraham Maslow has studied people who are especially alive, open, aware, and mentally happy. He found their perceptual styles marked by 1) immersion in the _____; 2) a lack of _____-_____; 3) freedom from selecting, criticizing, or evaluating; and 4) a general "surrender" to the experience.

95. (p. 133) Zen masters fail to show _____ to repeated stimuli. They show dishabituation in that they perceive objects as vividly after seeing them 500 times as they did the first time.

96. (p. 134) _____ _____ (ESP) is the purported ability to perceive events in ways that cannot be explained by accepted perceptual principles.

97. (p. 134) _____ is the study of ESP and other _____ phenomena, or events that seem to defy accepted scientific laws.

98. (p. 134) Three areas of parapsychological investigation can be distinguished. One area deals with _____, the ability to perceive events or gain information in ways that appear unaffected by distance or normal physical barriers.

99. (p. 134) Another area entails the study of _____, the extra sensory perception of another person's thoughts.

100. (p. 134) A third area involves researching _____, the ability to perceive or accurately predict future events.

101. (p. 134) Precognition may take the form of _____ _____ which foretell the future.

102. (p. 134) A fourth area deals with _____, the ability to exert influence over inanimate objects by "will power."

103. (p. 134) The difficulty of excluding _____ makes natural ESP occurrences less conclusive than they might be.

104. (p. 134) If by coincidence a "hunch" proves to be correct, it may be reinterpreted as a _____, or case of clairvoyance. If it is not confirmed, it is simply forgotten.

105. (p. 134) The formal study of psi events owes much to the late _____ who established the first parapsychological laboratory at Duke University.

106. (p. 134) Rhine tried to study ESP objectively. Many of his early experiments made use of _____ cards.

107. (p. 134) For example, in a typical test of _____ subjects tried to guess the symbols on the cards as they were turned up from a shuffled deck.

108. (p. 134) Unfortunately, some of Rhine's most dramatic early experiments used badly printed Zener cards that allowed the symbols to show faintly on the back. It is also very easy to cheat, by marking with a _____, or by noting marks on the cards caused by normal use.

109. (p. 135) Also, there is evidence that the experimenter knew which card was correct and unconsciously gave subjects cues with their _____, _____ gestures, or _____ movements.

110. (p. 135) While many reports supporting the existence of psi abilities have been published in parapsychological journals in the past ten years, psychologists remain skeptical. In part, this is due to fraud which continues to plague the field. _____, who was former director of Rhine's laboratory, was caught faking records, as have some others who got positive results.

111. (p. 135) A major criticism of psi research focuses on the inconsistency of psi abilities. It is rare for a subject to maintain psi ability over any sustained period. ESP researchers consider this "_____ _____" an indication that parapsychological skills are very fragile and unpredictable.

112. (p. 135) Critics argue that subjects who only temporarily score above chance have just received credit for a _____ of _____.

113. (p. 135) Many of the most spectacular findings in parapsychology simply cannot be _____ (repeated). More importantly, improvements in _____ _____ usually result in fewer positive results.

114. (p. 135) Believers in ESP such as ex-astronaut Edgar Mitchell feel that the scientist's own mental processes may influence the phenomenon he or she is observing. Scientists who are true skeptics may _____ _____ the psychic subject.

115. (p. 136) If psychic phenomena do occur, they cannot be controlled by entertainers such as Uri Geller. As Professor Ray Hyman has pointed out, tests conducted on Geller were fraught with "incredible sloppiness." As one example, original reports of Geller's ability to reproduce sealed drawings failed to mention that there was a _____ in the _____ between the two rooms which allowed him to hear discussions of the pictures being drawn.

116. (p. 136) Also unreported was the fact that Geller's friend _____ _____ was present at every test and frequently acted as Geller's accomplice in trickery.

SELF-TEST

1. (p. 112) _____ is the process of assembling sensations into a usable mental representation of the world.

a. Learning   c. Perception
b. Conditioning   d. Motivation

2. (p. 113) An airplane in the distance appears very small, yet we know it has not shrunk. This exemplifies _____ _____, the perceived size of an object remains the same even though the size of its retinal image changes.
a. perceived equality   c. retinal disparity
b. size constancy   d. distance invariance

3. (p. 113) Shape constancy is the principle whereby
a. an object appears to have the same shape from whichever eye it is viewed
b. an object appears to have the same shape from any angle it is viewed
c. an object appears to change shape constantly from any angle it is viewed
d. an object appears to have the same shape no matter what the lighting conditions

4. (p. 113) The principle of brightness constancy reflects the fact that objects always
a. reflect the same relative proportion of light
b. appear equally bright under all lighting conditions
c. appear brighter when constantly illuminated
d. appear darker when constantly illuminated

5. (p. 115) The simplest perceptual ability is _____. It is probably inborn since it is the first perceptual ability to appear when a cataract patient regains sight.
a. closure   c. size constancy
b. size-distance invariance   d. figure-ground organization

6. (p. 116) Which of the following is *not* a factor that facilitates the organization of sensations into a figure?
a. nearness   c. similarity
b. continuity   d. disparity

7. (p. 116) True-False. In addition to nearness, similarity, continuity, closure, and contiguity, learning and past experience greatly affect perceptual organization.

8. (p. 118) True-False. Infants and newborn animals do not show evidence of depth perception; it is an acquired trait.

9. (p. 118) The visual cliff is
a. a device used in measuring depth perception
b. the point on the visible spectrum where our vision begins to decline
c. a mechanism in the eyeball that facilitates depth perception
d. a pictorial representation of how the angles of objects determine our perception of distance

10. (p. 119) All of the following are muscular cues that facilitate depth perception *except*
a. interposition   c. retinal disparity
b. convergence   d. accommodation

11. (p. 119) True-False. Convergence, the most important bodily cue for depth perception, is a binocular cue based on the fusion of images received by the eyes.

12. (p. 119) Which of the following is most closely associated with the concept of retinal disparity?
a. inverted vision, synesthesia
b. random dot stereograms, 3-D movies

c. moon illusion, Müller-Lyer illusion
d. stroboscope, motion parallax

13. (p. 120) Which pictorial depth cue refers to the apparent convergence of parallel lines in the environment?
a. convergency
b. linear perspective
c. aerial perspective
d. interposition

14. (p. 120) Which of the following is *not* a pictorial depth cue?
a. interposition
b. texture gradients
c. accommodation
d. aerial perspective

15. (p. 121) True-False. Movies, television, and cartoon animation rely heavily upon motion parallax to produce visual depth.

16. (p. 122) True-False. The moon illusion refers to the fact that the moon appears larger when viewed on the horizon despite the fact that it is actually farther away than when overhead.

17. (p. 122) If two objects form identical images, but one is more distant, the more distant object must be larger. This principle is known as _____ and is exemplified by the _____.
a. shape constancy; Ames Room.
b. size constancy; three-pronged widget impossible figure
c. brightness constancy; Müller-Lyer illusion
d. apparent distance hypothesis; moon illusion

18. (p. 123) Learning affects perception through established patterns of organization and attention referred to as
a. perceptual constancies
b. sensory reconstructions
c. perceptual habits
d. sensory constancies

19. (p. 124) True-False. Perceptual learning seems to program the brain for sensitivity to important features of the environment.

20. (p. 125) Inverted vision experiments with humans have shown that
a. with time, humans can learn to function normally with completely different visual cues
b. perceptual habits are so ingrained that humans never learn to adapt to different cues
c. we are like most animals in that we do adapt to the differences almost immediately
d. basic physiology can be modified so that when the goggles are removed, we do not recover

21. (p. 125) The fact that you appear shorter, when standing among professional basketball players, than when you are standing with classmates, demonstrates
a. perceptual expectancy
b. adaptation level
c. stimulus context
d. relative size

22. (p. 126) Adaptation level refers to
a. how quickly a given individual can adapt to changing environmental conditions (such as inverted vision)
b. your own personal "medium" point or frame of reference in judging size, weight, age, etc.

    c. how perceptual learning influences our perception of external contexts

    d. the perceptual plateau that is reached once an individual has habituated to a repetitive stimulus

23. (p. 126) Perceptual learning is responsible for a number of _____ in which length, position, motion, curvature, or direction is consistently misjudged.

    a. habits   c. hallucinations

    b. inversions   d. illusions

24. (p. 126) Which of the following is *not* an illusion?

    a. stroboscopic movement   c. moon illusion

    b. Müller-Lyer illusion   d. hearing voices that do not exist

25. (p. 127) True-False. While past experience is quite important in contributing to illusions, some illusions appear to be inborn. For example, African Zulus exposed to the Müller-Lyer illusion experience the illusion immediately, although never before exposed to it.

26. (p. 128) Which of the following is *not* a factor which captures attention?

    a. very intense stimuli   c. repetitious stimuli

    b. constant, unchanging stimuli   d. contrast or change in stimulation

27. (p. 128) A(n) _____ is characterized by enlarged pupils, brain wave changes, a short pause in breathing, and increased blood flow to the head.

    a. orientation response   c. perceptual expectancy

    b. habituated response   d. synesthesia

28. (p. 128) True-False. When a stimulus is repeated without change, the OR increases or dishabituates.

29. (p. 129) Motives play a role in attention and may affect perception. Which of the following is *not* a true statement exemplifying this principle?

    a. Advertisers take advantage of sex and anxiety to merchandise a wide range of products.

    b. One experiment showed that students reading a sexually arousing passage rated potential blind dates more attractive.

    c. Members of a Jewish organization showed increased recognition for symbols at the edge of a figure when the central item was an "emotional" stimulus.

    d. Fans of opposing sports teams often act as if they had seen two completely different games.

30. (p. 129) Perception seems to proceed in two major ways. One of these organizations, _____, involves using preexisting knowledge to rapidly organize features into a meaningful whole.

    a. bottom-up processing   c. perceptual expectancy

    b. selective attention   d. top-down processing

31. (p. 130) Jerome Bruner found in his research on perceptual expectancies that subjects misperceived cards that did not fit their expectations. He believes that perceptual learning builds up a set of mental _____.

    a. categories   c. constancies

    b. illusions   d. cues

32. (p. 132) Which of the following is *not* a true statement with regard to witness testimony?

    a. A person's confidence in his or her testimony has almost no bearing on its accuracy.

    b. Eyewitness accuracy is virtually the same for witnessing a crime as it is for being a victim.

    c. Psychologists are gradually convincing lawyers, judges, and police officers of the fallibility of eyewitness testimony.

    d. Victims of crimes are more likely to be accurate in their testimony of the crime than are on-looking eyewitnesses.

33. (p. 132) Weapon focus refers to the fact that
    a. victims usually focus their attention more on the identities of people holding weapons than on those who do not
    b. victims often fix their entire attention on the weapon and fail to perceive clues to the identity of the assailant
    c. eyewitnesses are often so frightened that they focus more on their own feelings than on the details of the situation, such as the weapons involved
    d. victim perceptions are often distorted; when focused on weapons they are often uncertain whether it was a knife, gun, or other object

34. (p. 132) True-False. Frequent reality testing may be required to maintain personal objectivity.

35. (p. 133) Abraham Maslow felt that some people are unusually accurate in perceptions of themselves and others. Which of the following is *not* a characteristic of the perceptual style of such people?
    a. freedom from selecting, criticizing, or evaluating
    b. general "surrender" to experience
    c. lack of self-consciousness
    d. immersion in the future

36. (p. 133) True-False. Zen masters show greater levels of habituation than most individuals.

37. (p. 134) The study of psychic or psi phenomena is called
    a. psichology   c. magic
    b. demonology   d. parapsychology

38. (p. 134) The ability to perceive events or gain information in ways that appear unaffected by distance or normal physical barriers is called
    a. telepathy   c. precognition
    b. clairvoyance   d. psychokinesis

39. (p. 134) The ability to read someone else's mind is called
    a. psychokinesis   c. clairvoyance
    b. telepathy   d. precognition

40. (p. 134) _____ refers to the ability to exert influence over inanimate objects by will power.
    a. Telepathy   c. Precognition
    b. Clairvoyance   d. Psychokinesis

41. (p. 134) True-False. Factors such as coincidence, statistics and consistency must be considered when investigating extrasensory skills.

42. (p. 134) _____ established the first parapsychological laboratory and made use of Zener cards in an effort to make the study of psi phenomena more objective.
    a. Edgar Mitchell   c. Sidney Jourard
    b. J. B. Rhine   d. Abraham Maslow

43. (p. 136) True-False. Skeptics and serious researchers in ESP both agree that if psychic phenomena do occur, they cannot be controlled well enough to be used by entertainers such as Uri Geller.

ANSWERS — PROGRAMMED REVIEW

1. perception
2. learn
3. size constancy
4. native; empirical
5. Pygmy
6. Shape constancy
7. Brightness constancy
8. proportion
9. figure-ground
10. inborn
11. reversible figures
12. near; similar; continuity; closure
13. illusory
14. continuity
15. camouflage
16. perceptual hypothesis
17. ambiguous stimuli
18. impossible
19. edges; parallel
20. Depth perception
21. nativists; empiricists
22. visual cliff
23. shallow; deep
24. 4
25. coordination
26. Depth cues
27. monocular; binocular
28. accommodation
29. 4
30. convergence
31. lens; eyeball
32. retinal disparity
33. fused; 3-D
34. stereoscopic vision
35. mismatch
36. Pictorial
37. linear perspective
38. relative size
39. light, shadow
40. Overlap
41. texture; gradient
42. aerial perspective
43. motion parallax
44. two-dimensional
45. larger
46. apparent distance
47. apparent distance hypothesis
48. accommodation

49. perceptual habits
50. small; large
51. horizontal; vertical
52. brain cells
53. inverted vision
54. goldfish
55. learning
56. Active movement
57. context
58. frame of reference
59. adaptation level
60. illusions
61. hallucinating
62. stroboscopic movement
63. Müller-Lyer; shorter
64. size-distance invariance
65. Zulus
66. attention
67. Selective
68. Divided
69. intense
70. repetition
71. change
72. habituate
73. orientation response
74. habituates
75. anxiety, sex
76. more attractive
77. swastika
78. bottom-up
79. top-down
80. perceptual expectancy
81. suggestion
82. categories
83. tachistoscope
84. mental patient
85. reconstruction
86. accuracy
87. decrease
88. improbable
89. 42; 42
90. 25
91. same
92. weapon focus
93. reality testing
94. present; self-consciousness
95. habituation
96. Extrasensory perception

97. Parapsychology; psi
98. clairvoyance
99. telepathy
100. precognition
101. prophetic dreams
102. psychokinesis
103. coincidence
104. premonition
105. J. B. Rhine
106. Zener

107. clairvoyance
108. fingernail
109. eyes; facial; lip
110. Walter J. Levy
111. decline effect
112. run of luck
113. replicated; research methods
114. turn off
115. hole in the wall
116. Shipi Stang

ANSWERS — SELF-TEST

1.	c	23.	d
2.	b	24.	d
3.	b	25.	False
4.	a	26.	b
5.	d	27.	a
6.	d	28.	False
7.	True	29.	c
8.	False	30.	d
9.	a	31.	a
10.	a	32.	d
11.	False	33.	b
12.	b	34.	True
13.	b	35.	d
14.	c	36.	False
15.	True	37.	d
16.	False	38.	b
17.	d	39.	b
18.	c	40.	d
19.	True	41.	True
20.	a	42.	b
21.	c	43.	True
22.	b		

Chapter 6

States of Consciousness

CONTENTS

TERMS AND CONCEPTS

consciousness
waking consciousness
altered states of consciousness (ASC)
innate biological rhythm
microsleep
sleep-deprivation psychosis
long sleepers
short sleepers
sleep patterns
stages of sleep
electroencephalograph (EEG)
beta brain waves
alpha brain waves
hypnic jerk
myoclonus
sleep spindles
delta brain waves

deep sleep
rapid eye movement
REM sleep
NREM sleep
somnambulist
sleeptalking
nightmares
night terrors
narcolepsy
cataplexy
insomnia
sedatives
drug-dependency insomnia
tryptophan
sleep apnea
hypersomnia
Sudden Infant Death Syndroms (SIDS)

REM rebound effect
REM myth
wish fulfillment
dream symbols
activation-synthesis hopothesis
hypnosis
mesmerize
animal magnetism
hypnotic susceptibility
Stanford Hypnotic Susceptibility Scale
basic suggestion effect
dissociation
hidden observer
sensory deprivation
hypnogogic images
theta waves
REST
psychoactive drugs
physical dependence (addiction)
withdrawal symptoms
drug tolerance
psychological dependence
patterns of drug abuse
stimulants
amphetamines
Dexedrine
Methedrine

Benzedrine
amphetamine psychosis
cocaine
caffeine
caffeinism
nicotine
carcinogens
depressants
barbiturates
sedatives
drug interaction
Seconal
Tuinal
Methaqualone (Quaalude, Sopor, Parest)
alcohol
detoxification
marijuana
hashish
Cannabis sativa
tetrahydrocannabinol (THC)
hallucinogen
dream processes
condensation
displacement
symbolization
secondary elaboration
lucid dream

IMPORTANT INDIVIDUALS

Peter Tripp
John Lilly
Wilse Webb
Randy Gardner
Nathaniel Kleitman
Eugene Aserinsky
William Dement
Calvin Hall
Sigmund Freud
Allan Hobson
Robert McCarley
Franz Mesmer
James Braid
Ernest Hilgard

T. X. Barber
D. O. Hebb
Peter Suedfeld
Stanley Schachter
Roger Vogler
Wayne Bartz
Herman Friedman
Rosalind Cartwright
Ann Faraday
Fritz Perls
Gordon Globus
Stephen La Berge
Thomas Szasz

PROGRAMMED REVIEW

1. (p. 139) After 100 hours without sleep, New York disc-jockey Peter Tripp began to
    _____. After 170 hours his brain waves looked like
    those of _____, his memory was poor, and he struggled with even simple
    thoughts and problems. By 200 hours, Tripp could not distinguish between waking
    nightmares, hallucination, and reality.

2. (p. 139) In John Lilly's womb tank experiments, he created an unusual sensory deprivation environment. Subjects wore darkened goggles and floated naked in a tank of body-temperature water. Cut off from all sensations, subjects often lose track of _____ and find it hard to concentrate. Some subjects also experience strange alterations in consciousness.

3. (p. 140) To be conscious means to be aware. _____ consists of all the sensations, perceptions, memories, and feelings that you are aware of at any given instant.

4. (p. 140) We spend most of our lives in ordinary _____ consciousness, which is organized, meaningful, and clear. It is perceived as real, and it is marked by a familiar sense of time and place.

5. (p. 140) Altered states of consciousness (ASCs) related to fatigue, delirium, hypnosis, meditation, drugs, and ecstasy differ significantly from what might be considered normal. They represent a distinct change in the _____ and _____ of mental functioning.

6. (p. 140) ASCs typically differ from normal waking consciousness with regard to: perceptions, emotions, _____, time sense, thinking, feelings of self-control, and _____.

7. (p. 140) Contrary to common belief, we are not totally unresponsive during sleep. Experiments show that you are more likely to awaken if your _____ is spoken, instead of another. Likewise, a sleeping mother may ignore a jet rumbling by overhead, but wake at the slightest whimper of her child.

8. (p. 140) In one experiment, subjects learned to avoid an _____ _____ by touching a switch each time a tone sounded. Eventually, they could do it without waking.

9. (p. 141) Sleep expert Wilse Webb considers sleep an innate biological rhythm. While flexible, it has limits. Animals surgically prevented from sleeping fall into a _____ and _____ after several days.

10. (p. 141) Webb tried vigorously to teach animals to eliminate sleep, but sleep won out. After periods of forced wakefulness, Webb's animals began to engage in _____, a brief shift in brain activity to patterns normally found in sleep.

11. (p. 141) The world record for continuous wakefulness is held by Randy Gardner who went _____ days without sleep. He needed only 14 hours of sleep to recover.

12. (p. 141) Most symptoms of sleep deprivation, as with Randy Gardner, are removed by a _____ night of sleep.

13. (p. 141) The costs of sleep loss are partly determined by _____ and _____. For example, Randy Gardner remained coherent to the end of his vigil, whereas Peter Tripp's behavior became quite bizarre.

14. (p. 141) Most persons show no impairment on _____ mental tasks after two days without sleep. But most grow _____, and their ability to pay attention, remain vigilant, and follow simple routine _____.

15. (p. 141) With mild to moderate sleep deprivation, what usually suffers most is low-level, boring, _____-_____ tasks.

16. (p. 141) From these results, Webb concluded that moderate sleep loss does not diminish thinking or memory, but rather the _____ to _____.

17. (p. 141) Longer periods without sleep occasionally produce a temporary _____-_____ _____ like that experienced by Peter Tripp.

18. (p. 141) Common elements of sleep-deprivation psychosis include confusion and _____, _____ (false or distorted beliefs), and hallucinations.

19. (p. 141) "Crazy" behavior such as Tripp's is less common than once thought. Hallucinations and delusions, if they occur at all, are never evident before ___ hours without sleep.

20. (p. 141) The most common reactions to extended sleep loss are inattention, staring, trembling _____, drooping _____, and an increased sensitivity to _____.

21. (p. 141) Rhythms of sleep and waking are so steady that they continue for many days even when clocks and light-dark cycles are eliminated. Under such conditions, humans eventually shift to a rhythm that averages _____ hours, not 22.

22. (p. 141) Individuals who can sleep only a few hours each night are rare. Only _____ percent of the population averages 5 hours or less of sleep per night, while the majority sleep on a 7- to 8-hour-per-night schedule.

23. (p. 141) The restorative function of sleep may be reflected in two types of sleepers: _____ sleepers tend to be daytime "worriers," while _____ sleepers are typically "non-worriers." People who worry may need more rest each night.

24. (p. 141) As people age they usually sleep less. People over the age of 50 average _____ hours of sleep a night.

25. (p. 141) In contrast, infants spend up to _____ hours a day sleeping, usually in _____ to _____ hour cycles.

26. (p. 142) Shortened sleep periods are not effective, because people often can't get to sleep when the cycle calls for it. A more promising possibility is to adapt to longer than normal days. Such days can be tailored to match natural sleep patterns, which show a ratio of _____ to _____ between time awake and time asleep.

27. (p. 142) One study showed that _____-hour "days" work for some people. Unfortunately, subjects did poorly on longer 36-hour cycles (24 awake and 12 asleep) because they couldn't use the entire 12 hour sleep period.

28. (p. 142) Early concepts of sleep hypothesized that some substance caused by _____ accumulated in the bloodstream causing sleep. But studies of _____ _____ (individuals whose bodies are joined at birth) show this is false.

29. (p. 142) During extended wakefulness, a sleep-promoting chemical collects in the _____ and _____ _____, not in the blood.

30. (p. 142) If this substance is extracted from one animal and injected into another, the second

animal will _____. Unfortunately, this does not explain many other aspects of sleep.

31. (p. 143) Sleep is actively generated by several important structures in the brain: the _____; _____ _____; and a "sleep center" in the _____.

32. (p. 143) Rather than "shutting down" during sleep, the brain changes the _____ of its activity, not the amount.

33. (p. 143) The changes that come with sleep can be measured through the use of the _____, abbreviated _____.

34. (p. 143) When a person is awake and alert, the EEG shows a pattern of _____, _____ waves called _____; immediately before sleep and when one is relaxed a pattern of _____ and _____ waves called _____ is observed.

35. (p. 143) As you close your eyes and begin to fall asleep, your breathing becomes slow and regular, your pulse rate slows, and body temperature drops. As you lose consciousness and enter _____ sleep, your heart rate slows even more.

36. (p. 143) During Stage 1 sleep, breathing becomes more irregular and the muscles of your body relax. This sometimes triggers a reflex contraction called a _____ jerk, which is quite normal.

37. (p. 143) Muscle spasms in the legs that occur later, during sleep itself, are called _____. This problem causes about _____ to _____ percent of all cases of insomnia.

38. (p. 143) In Stage 1 sleep, the EEG is made up mainly of _____, _____ waves with some alpha. Persons awakened at this time may or may not say they were asleep.

39. (p. 144) During Stage 2 sleep, the EEG begins to show short bursts of activity called _____ _____.

40. (p. 144) Sleep spindles seem to mark the true boundary of sleep. Within ___ minutes after they appear, the majority of subjects who are awakened report that they were asleep.

41. (p. 144) Stage 3 sleep is characterized by the appearance of a new brain wave called _____, which is very _____ and _____.

42. (p. 144) The final stage, also called _____ _____, is characterized by almost completely pure _____ brain waves. The sleeper eventually returns to Stage 1 (through Stages 3 and 2) with further shifts occurring throughout the night.

43. (p. 144) _____ _____ _____ or REMs are strongly associated with dreaming. Roughly _____ percent of awakenings made when REMs are present produce reports of dreams.

44. (p. 144) The two most basic states of sleep now appear to be _____ sleep with its associated dreaming and _____-_____ sleep, abbreviated _____ which occurs during Stages 2, 3, and 4.

45. (p. 144) NREM sleep is dream-free about _____ percent of the time. Dreams that do occur are less detailed and less vivid than ones experienced during REM.

46. (p. 144)   NREM sleep helps us recover from _____. It increases with _____ or physical exertion.

47. (p. 144)   REM sleep totals about _____ hours per night, but may become more pronounced when stress or emotionally charged events occur during the day.

48. (p. 144)   During REM sleep, the heart beats _____ and blood pressure and breathing _____.

49. (p. 145)   Males usually have an _____, and _____ blood flow increases in females, even if the dream is not erotic. When an erotic dream does occur, evidence of sexual arousal _____.

50. (p. 145)   During REM sleep, the body becomes quite still. Changing positions takes place _____ REM periods.

51. (p. 145)   Sleepwalkers, or _____, usually have their eyes open, can negotiate obstacles, descend stairways, and climb trees, but a blank face, lack of recognition, and shuffling feet show they are still asleep.

52. (p. 145)   Children of sleeptalkers and sleepwalkers are likely to have the same problems, which suggests that these sleep disturbances are at least partially _____.

53. (p. 145)   A parent who finds a child sleepwalking should gently guide the child back to bed. Awakening a sleepwalker does _____ _____, but it is not necessary and the sleepwalker often resists.

54. (p. 145)   It was long supposed that sleepwalkers are acting out dream events, but somnambulism actually occurs during NREM Stages ___ and ___.

55. (p. 145)   Sleeptalking occurs during _____ stages of sleep, and appears to be an outlet for NREM "thinking."

56. (p. 145)   A nightmare is simply a bad dream (usually brief) that takes place during _____ sleep. The person awakens and remembers the dream in complete detail.

57. (p. 145)   _____ _____ are severely frightening dreams where the sleeper experiences blind panic and may hallucinate. Such experiences occur during Stage ___ sleep.

58. (p. 145)   Such attacks may last _____ or _____ minutes during which the victim may sit up, get out of bed, or run around the room. When over, the person awakens drenched in perspiration, but has only a vague memory of the terror itself.

59. (p. 146)   Night terrors are most common during _____, although they may occur at other ages as well.

60. (p. 146)   _____ is the dramatic sleep problem characterized by sudden, repeated, and irresistible "sleep attacks," when the person falls asleep for a few minutes to a few hours while standing, talking, or even driving. Emotional excitement, especially laughter, commonly triggers this problem.

61. (p. 146)   Most of these victims also suffer from _____, a sudden temporary paralysis of the muscles leading to complete body collapse.

62. (p. 146) The EEGs of narcoleptics indicate that during attacks, they fall directly into _____ sleep, which produces immediate sleep and muscle paralysis.

63. (p. 146) Narcolepsy is quite rare and appears to be _____ as confirmed by breeding narcoleptic dogs. For humans there is no cure, but _____ drugs may diminish attacks.

64. (p. 146) About 32 percent of adult Americans suffer from _____, the inability to sleep, awakening too early, frequent nighttime awakenings, or some combination. Fifteen to twenty percent have a serious or chronic problem.

65. (p. 146) Non-prescription sleeping pills have little or no sleep-inducing effect. Even worse are prescription _____ (usually barbiturates) which decrease both Stage ___ and _____ sleep and thereby reduce sleep quality.

66. (p. 146) An additional problem with prescription sedatives is that a drug tolerance rapidly builds so that the initial dosage becomes ineffective leading to "sleeping pill junkies" and _____-_____ insomnia.

67. (p. 146) Withdrawal from sleeping medications may produce terrible _____ and rebound insomnia, which often drive the user back to dependency.

68. (p. 146) A new drug called _____ appears to be effective for some cases of insomnia. However, even this pharmaceutical has drawbacks, and it too can cause rebound insomnia on the first few nights after it is withdrawn.

69. (p. 146) Temporary insomnia usually involves a cycle of physical arousal from worry, stress, or excitement which interferes with sleep, causing _____ and anger which causes more arousal, and so on.

70. (p. 146) One way to beat temporary insomnia is to avoid _____ it. Get up and do something useful or satisfying.

71. (p. 147) Some insomniacs have been found to have a drop in _____ during the night. This result can be avoided by having a small snack before sleeping.

72. (p. 147) Also, it has been discovered that the amino acid _____ helps put people to sleep. This substance can be found in a glass of milk and in certain other items.

73. (p. 147) Treatment for chronic insomnia usually begins with training in _____ techniques, stimulus control procedures, and establishing a regular routine.

74. (p. 147) _____ _____ strategies are also helpful. For example, patients are told to strictly avoid doing anything other than sleeping when they go to bed. In this way, only sleeping becomes associated with retiring.

75. (p. 147) Many insomniacs have scattered sleep habits. For these people, adopting a _____ _____ (getting up and going to sleep at exactly the same time each day) helps establish a firm body rhythm and greatly improves sleep.

76. (p. 147) When you suffer from insomnia, there are several things you can do to help. Avoid _____ such as coffee or cigarettes. Remember too that alcohol impairs sleep quality.

77. (p. 147)   Schedule time in the _____ to write down worries
                or concerns and what you will do about them the next day.

78. (p. 147)   Learn a physical or mental strategy for relaxing such as _____
                muscle relaxation, _____, or blotting out worries with
                calming images. Very light evening exercise may be helpful.

79. (p. 147)   To implement stimulus control principles in the treatment of insomnia, be sure to:
                (1) go to bed only when you are feeling _____; (2) avoid _____;
                (3) awaken at the same time each morning; (4) avoid _____
                activities in bed; (5) always leave the bedroom if sleep has not occurred within _____
                minutes; (6) do something else when you are upset about not being able to sleep.

80. (p. 147)   To remove the pressure of trying to get to sleep, use _____
                intention. That is, try to keep your eyes open (in the dark) and stay awake as long as
                possible. This will allow sleep to overtake you unexpectedly and lower performance
                anxiety.

81. (p. 147)   A person who snores loudly, with short silences and loud gasps or snorts, may suffer
                from _____ _____.

82. (p. 147)   In sleep apnea, breathing stops for periods of _____ seconds to _____ minutes until
                need for oxygen becomes intense and the person awakens slightly and gulps in air,
                then returns to sleep until breathing again stops.

83. (p. 147)   This cycle is repeated hundreds of times a night and is associated with complaints of
                daytime sleepiness known as _____.

84. (p. 147)   Some apnea occurs because the _____ stops sending signals to the diaphragm
                to maintain breathing.   Another cause is blockage of the upper _____
                _____.

85. (p. 147)   Sleep apnea is especially dangerous in infancy, when it is suspected as one cause of
                "crib death" or _____ _____ _____ _____,
                abbreviated _____.

86. (p. 147)   SIDS is the most frequent cause of death for infants under ____ year of age. Typically,
                a slightly premature baby with a mild cold or infection dies during sleep.

87. (p. 148)   Doctors think that some cases of SIDS are caused by apnea due to immature breathing
                centers in the _____. Others suspect a defect that stalls the
                _____ during sleep.

88. (p. 148)   Sometimes it appears that direct blockage of the nose is responsible. These cases
                may be linked to babies who remain _____ when breathing is blocked.

89. (p. 148)   Babies at risk for SIDS must be carefully watched for the first ____ months of life. To
                aid parents in this task, a special monitor may be used which sounds an alarm when
                breathing or pulse becomes weak.

90. (p. 148)   Some warning signs for SIDS include: (1) the mother is a _____
                or _____; (2) the baby is premature, (3) the baby has an unusual
                _____-_____ cry; (4) the baby engages in "snoring," breath-
                holding, or frequent awakening at night; (5) the baby breathes mainly through an
                _____ _____; (6) the baby remains passive when its face rolls into
                a pillow or blanket.

91. (p. 148) When researchers _____ _____ and _____ discovered REM sleep in 1952, they ushered in a "Golden Era" of dream inquiry.

92. (p. 148) Most people dream _____ or _____ times a night, but not all people remember their dreams.

93. (p. 148) Dreams are usually spaced about _____ minutes apart, with each succeeding dream lasting a little longer.

94. (p. 148) The first dream of the evening lasts about _____ minutes; the last averages _____ minutes and may last as long as _____ minutes (in real time).

95. (p. 148) William Dement has shown that when subjects are deprived of REM sleep, they show an _____ tendency to dream. To prevent dreaming, Dement found that he had to wake subjects _____ or _____ times by the fifth night.

96. (p. 148) When subjects were finally allowed to sleep without interruption, they dreamed extra amounts. This is called the REM _____ effect.

97. (p. 148) This phenomenon explains why alcoholics often have horrible nightmares after they quit drinking. Alcohol _____ REM sleep and sets up a powerful rebound effect when it is withdrawn.

98. (p. 148) While deprived of dream sleep, Dement's subjects complained of _____ _____, difficulty in _____, and feelings of _____ during the day.

99. (p. 148) For a time these and similar results led to widespread belief that a person would go crazy if permanently kept from dreaming. This belief is now called the _____ _____.

100. (p. 148) Recent experiments indicate that missing out on any particular sleep stage can cause a rebound for that stage. Also, daytime disturbances are generally related to the _____ _____ of sleep lost, not the type of sleep lost.

101. (p. 149) Dream sleep may provide stimulation necessary for brain development. Newborn babies spend about _____ percent of their sleeping time in REM sleep, while premature infants get up to _____ percent REM.

102. (p. 149) By age five, when the nervous system is more mature, REM stabilizes at _____ percent, about the same as for an adult.

103. (p. 149) In adulthood, REM sleep may help restore brain _____ needed for learning and memory. Also, dreams may help integrate _____ learned during the day, prevent _____ _____ during sleep, and aid the processing of emotional events.

104. (p. 149) Calvin Hall, a noted authority on dreams, has collected and analyzed over 10,000 dreams. He found that most dreams are extensions of _____ _____.

105. (p. 149) The usual dream involves familiar settings, people, and actions. About _____ of the recorded dreams had sexual elements with dreams of flying, floating, and falling less frequently occurring.

106. (p. 149)   Unpleasant emotions such as fear, anger, and sadness are _____ frequent in dreams than pleasant emotions.

107. (p. 149)   The dreams of men and women in our culture seem to reflect traditional _____ _____. Women's dreams are more _____, less _____, less focused on sexual themes, more often indoors, and more often about home and family. Also, women are more often pursued or endangered in their dreams.

108. (p. 149)   _____ characters appear more in the dreams of both sexes, but for men they are more likely to be rivals or antagonists. Men dream more of men than women do.

109. (p. 149)   Upon analyzing his own dreams, Freud felt that many represented _____ _____. However, there is evidence against this since volunteers experiencing prolonged starvation showed no particular increase in dreams about food and eating.

110. (p. 150)   Freud's response to this result probably would have been that not all wish fulfillment is so direct. One of his key insights is that dreams represent thoughts expressed in _____ or pictures, rather than in words.

111. (p. 150)   Freud believed that the conscience relaxes during sleep, allowing dreams to express unconscious desires and conflicts in disguised _____ _____.
For instance, death might be symbolized by a journey, children by small animals, or sexual intercourse by horseback riding or dancing.

112. (p. 150)   A radically different view of dreaming is offered by Allan Hobson and Robert McCarley. Their approach is called the _____-_____ _____.

113. (p. 150)   The activation-synthesis hypothesis states that cells in the "sleep center" of the _____ are activated during REM sleep. These cells arouse nearby cells that control eye movements, balance, etc. Messages from these cells are blocked from reaching the body, but continue to reach higher brain areas which interpret the incoming information by searching stored _____ and manufacturing a dream.

114. (p. 150)   This approach seems to explain dreams where chases, flying, or floating are central, but most psychologists continue to believe that dreams have _____ _____.

115. (p. 151)   _____ is an altered state of consciousness, characterized by narrowed attention and an increased openness to suggestion.

116. (p. 151)   Interest in hypnosis began in the 1700s with _____ _____, who believed he could cure disease by passing _____ over the body of an afflicted person.

117. (p. 151)   While Mesmer (whose name is the basis for the term mesmerize) enjoyed quite a following for a short time, his theories of _____ _____ were soon rejected and he was branded a quack and a fraud.

118. (p. 151)   The term hypnosis was coined later by _____ _____ to refer to the sleep-like trance. Today we know that hypnosis is not sleep, since _____ recordings made during hypnosis are similar to those obtained when a person is awake.

119. (p. 151) Approximately _____ out of ten people can be hypnotized, but only _____ out of ten will be good hypnotic subjects.

120. (p. 151) Hypnotic suggestibility can be measured by making a series of suggestions to subjects and recording the number of suggestions to which they respond. A typical hypnotic test is the _____ _____ _____ Scale.

121. (p. 152) There are many hypnotic routines. Common factors in all techniques are that they encourage a person to: (1) focus _____ on what is being said; (2) relax and feel _____; (3) "let go" and accept _____ easily; and (4) to use vivid _____.

122. (p. 152) In deeper stages of hypnosis, "reality testing" may be relaxed so that a partial suspension of normal "_____ _____" is achieved. But at first, one must cooperate willingly in order to become hypnotized.

123. (p. 152) Many theorists believe that all hypnosis is really _____-_____ and that the hypnotist simply serves as a guide to help the subject achieve a state that could be reached alone.

124. (p. 152) During hypnosis you might experience mild feelings of _____, sinking, anesthesia, or _____ from your body. However, in all but the deepest stages of hypnosis, people remain aware of what is going on.

125. (p. 152) A key element in hypnosis is the _____ _____ effect. Hypnotized persons feel that suggested actions or experience are automatic.

126. (p. 152) Hypnosis often produces a _____ or "split" in awareness. For example, Ernest Hilgard told hypnotized subjects to feel no pain when they plunged their hands into icewater. When asked if they felt pain, subjects reported none. When asked if any part of their minds felt pain, many wrote that they did.

127. (p. 152) Hilgard has referred to this later part as the _____ _____— it is aware of pain but remains in the background.

128. (p. 152) Hypnosis has no more effect on physical strength than instructions that encourage subjects to make their best effort. It does not produce _____ acts of strength.

129. (p. 152) There is some evidence that hypnosis can enhance memory. However, it also frequently increases the number of _____ _____. Because of this, many states now bar persons who have been hypnotized from testifying in court cases.

130. (p. 152) Hypnosis can relieve _____. Therefore, it can be especially useful in situations where pharmaceuticals cannot be used, or are ineffective.

131. (p. 152) As an example of the usefulness of hypnosis in relieving pain, it can be successfully used to control _____ _____ pain where amputees sometimes experience recurring pains which feel as if they come from the missing limb.

132. (p. 152) Through hypnosis, subjects have been "_____" to childhood. Doubt is cast on this possibility by the fact that such persons continue to use knowledge they could only have learned as adults.

133. (p. 152)   Hypnotic suggestions concerning _____ seem to be among the most effective. It is possible to alter color vision, hearing sensitivity, time sense, perception of illusions, etc.

134. (p. 153)   Generally, hypnosis seems to have greatest value as a tool for inducing _____, as a means of controlling _____ (in dentistry and childbirth), as an aid to maintaining _____ (to study, diet, quit smoking, etc.), and as an adjunct to other forms of psychological therapy and counseling.

135. (p. 153)   In general, hypnosis is better at changing _____ _____ than at modifying behavior, such as smoking or overeating. Hypnotic effects are useful, but seldom amazing.

136. (p. 153)   Authority T. X. Barber says that stage hypnotists make use of several factors excluding legitimate hypnosis to perform their act. For example, they employ _____ _____: On stage, people are unusually cooperative because they don't want to ruin the act.

137. (p. 153)   Stage hypnotists are careful to select _____ subjects. Participants must volunteer thus ensuring that they are relatively uninhibited. They are hypnotized as a group and anyone who does not succumb is eliminated.

138. (p. 153)   The hypnosis label _____. Once a person is labeled as hypnotized he or she can "perform" without fear of embarrassment.

139. (p. 153)   The stage hypnotist acts as a "_____." Audience response to participants encourages their antics so that all the "hypnotist" need do is guide the action.

140. (p. 153)   And finally, stage hypnotists use _____. Much like magicians, they rely on deception to convince the audience of their abilities.

141. (p. 154)   _____ _____ refers to any major reduction in external stimulation. It has been one of the most frequently used means of altering consciousness.

142. (p. 154)   Under such conditions of reduced or monotonous stimulation, people tend to experience lapses in _____, bizarre _____, and perceptual distortions.

143. (p. 154)   D. O. Hebb studied volunteers paid to lie on their backs in a small cubicle. They wore darkened goggles, and gloves and cardboard cuffs restricted touch. A constant hissing noise masked all sounds. Under such conditions, few subjects could take more than ___ or ___ days without "pushing the panic button."

144. (p. 154)   The most consistent disturbances after sensory deprivation are a distortion of _____, heightened visual _____, slower _____, and a brief warping of visual lines and space. Some participants in early experiments also reported strange and vivid images.

145. (p. 154)   We now know that true hallucinations are rare during sensory deprivation. The fanciful, dreamlike visions that sometimes do occur are actually _____ _____, similar to those that may occur just before you fall asleep.

146. (p. 154)   Hypnogogic images may be vivid and surprising, but they are rarely mistaken for real

objects.   Such images are apparently linked to an increase in the number of _____ waves produced by the brain.

147. (p. 154)   These brainwaves, in the ___- to ___-cycles-per-second range, are usually recorded just before sleep. Sensory deprivation also increases their occurrence.

148. (p. 154)   One of the most consistent after-effects of sensory deprivation is increased _____ acuity. Some people report using this effect to aid creative thinking.

149. (p. 154)   While most people find prolonged sensory deprivation stressful and aversive, brief periods of restricted sensation are very relaxing and can produce a large drop in blood _____, muscle _____, and other signs of stress. It is one of the surest ways to induce deep relaxation.

150. (p. 155)   Peter Suedfeld has found that sensory deprivation can help people change habitual behaviors. For example, of subjects exposed to standard anti-smoking messages combined with sensory deprivation, _____ percent less were smoking three months later when compared with controls.

151. (p. 155)   Another study found similar prolonged benefits for people in a _____-_____ program based on using Suedfeld's REST technique—restricted environmental stimulation therapy.

152. (p. 155)   Suedfeld's technique makes use of tape recorded suggestions played to subjects while they are isolated in a flotation tank.   Deep _____ and mental confusion leading to the _____ of belief systems may make it easier to produce lasting changes.

153. (p. 155)   The   surest   way   to   alter   human   consciousness   is   to   administer   a _____ _____. Such substances are capable of altering attention, memory, judgment, time sense, self-control, emotion, and perception.

154. (p. 155)   Most   psychoactive   drugs   can   be   placed   on   a   scale   ranging   from _____ to _____.

155. (p. 158)   Drug dependence falls into two broad categories. When a person compulsively uses a drug to maintain bodily comfort a _____ dependence, commonly referred to as _____, exists.

156. (p. 158)   Addiction occurs most often with drugs that cause _____ _____—painful or even agonizing reactions that take place when the drug is withheld.

157. (p. 158)   Addiction is often accompanied by a drug _____, the need to take larger and larger doses to achieve the same effects initially supplied by smaller doses.

158. (p. 158)   A _____ _____ is said to exist when an individual feels that a drug is necessary to maintain emotional or psychological well-being. Usually this is based on an intense craving for the drug and its rewarding qualities.

159. (p. 158)   Psychological dependence may affect a drug user as powerfully as physical addiction does. This is why some psychologists prefer to define addiction more broadly as any

_____ habit pattern. By this definition, a person who has lost control over his or her drug use, for whatever reason, is addicted.

160. (p. 158)   The psychoactive drugs most associated with physical dependence are: heroin, morphine, codeine, methadone, barbiturates, alcohol, amphetamines and tobacco. All can lead to _____ _____ .

161. (p. 158)   Drug-taking behavior can be classified as: (1) _____ , short-term use motivated by curiosity; (2) _____ , occasional social use considered pleasurable by participants; (3) _____ , used to cope with a specific problem such as boredom or staying awake for night work; (4) _____ , daily use having elements of dependence; or (5) _____ , intense use and extreme dependence.

162. (p. 158)   Amphetamines form a large group of synthetic stimulants. Drugs commonly available in this group are _____ , _____ , and _____ .

163. (p. 158)   Amphetamines were once widely prescribed by doctors to aid _____ _____ or to combat _____ _____ . Both practices are now discouraged because of drug dependency problems.

164. (p. 158)   Amphetamines rapidly produce a _____ _____ , with abusers taking ever larger quantities of pills or switching to injections directly into the bloodstream to maintain the desired effect.

165. (p. 159)   Amphetamine use poses many dangers. To stay high, the abuser must take more of the drug as the body's tolerance grows. Higher doses can cause _____ , _____ , high blood _____ , life-threatening heart _____ and crippling strokes.

166. (p. 159)   Amphetamines speed the expenditure of _____ _____ . They do not magically supply energy.

167. (p. 159)   The aftereffects of an amphetamine high may include _____ , _____ , terrifying nightmares, confusion, and uncontrolled irritation and _____ .

168. (p. 159)   Repeatedly overextending one's body with stimulants may lead to considerable _____ loss, sores and non-healing _____ , brittle _____ , tooth-grinding, chronic chest _____ , _____ disease, a variety of _____ disorders, and in some cases _____ hemorrhage.

169. (p. 159)   Amphetamines can cause a loss of contact with reality known as _____ _____ . Affected users feel threatened and suffer from paranoid delusions that someone is out to get them. Acting on these delusions, the speed-freak may become violent, resulting in self-injury or injury to others.

170. (p. 159)   Cocaine is a powerful central nervous system stimulant derived from the leaves of the coca plant. Its subjective effects are sensations of _____ , _____ , well-being, power, and boundless energy.

171. (p. 159)   Until 1906 when the Pure _____ and _____ Act was passed, Coca-Cola

contained cocaine (since replaced by caffeine), as did dozens of non-prescription potions and cure-alls.

172. (p. 159) Cocaine is becoming one of the most widely abused drugs. An estimated ___ to ___ million Americans use it at least once a month, and an estimated 30 million have tried it.

173. (p. 159) Cocaine and amphetamines are very similar in their effects on the central nervous system. At high dosages the main difference is that amphetamine effects may last _____ _____, while cocaine effects last only about _____ to _____ minutes.

174. (p. 159) Many scientists are beginning to think that cocaine is addicting. However, there is little evidence that _____ _____ occur when a person stops taking the drug. On the other hand, many users report powerful cravings when they try to stop using it.

175. (p. 159) Cocaine users show little _____-term tolerance. But, _____-term tolerance is common. That is, later doses have less and less impact during a drug-taking session.

176. (p. 159) Many authorities now regard cocaine as one of the most dangerous drugs in use today. Even casual or first-time users run a risk because cocaine can cause _____, heart _____, or a stroke.

177. (p. 159) Rats and monkeys given free access to cocaine find it irresistible, some to the point of dying of _____ from self-administered overdoses.

178. (p. 159) Cocaine increases activity in brain pathways sensitive to the chemical messengers _____ and _____. One arouses the brain, while an increase in the other can produce a "rush" of pleasure.

179. (p. 159) Because of the powerfully rewarding effects of cocaine, there is a high risk of becoming a dependent and compulsive abuser. Many authorities estimate that if cocaine were cheaper, ___ out of 10 users would progress to compulsive use. In fact, rock cocaine (or "crack"), which is cheaper, appears to be producing very high abuse rates among those who try it.

180. (p. 159) A survey of 500 cocaine abusers found that complaints about the drug included anxiety, irritability, _____ thoughts, insomnia, headaches, _____ problems, tremors, _____, and many more.

181. (p. 159) Serious signs of cocaine abuse include: (1) _____ use—when it is available, you can't say "no" to it. (2) Loss of _____ — once you have had some cocaine, you keep using it until you are exhausted or the cocaine is gone. (3) Disregarding _____—you use cocaine no matter what happens or how serious the cost.

182. (p. 160) The most frequently used psychoactive drug in the U.S. is _____, a substance that stimulates the brain by blocking chemicals which normally inhibit or slow nerve activity.

183. (p. 160) Caffeine in doses as small as 100 to 200 milligrams has an effect. Psychologically, caffeine suppresses _____ or drowsiness, and increases feelings of _____.

184. (p. 160) It is common to think of _____ as the major source of caffeine, but it is also found in tea, soft drinks, chocolate, cocoa, and over two thousand non-prescription drugs.

185. (p. 160) Serious abuse of caffeine is known as _____. People with this condition commonly drink 15 to 20 cups of coffee a day and may suffer increased health risks.

186. (p. 160) Caffeine encourages the development of breast _____ in women, and may contribute to insomnia, _____ problems, _____ problems, and high blood pressure.

187. (p. 160) Health authorities urge pregnant women to give up caffeine entirely because of a suspected link between caffeine and _____ _____. A possible link between caffeine and _____ has also been detected.

188. (p. 160) Next to caffeine, _____, found mainly in tobacco, is the most widely used psychoactive drug.

189. (p. 160) In large doses nicotine causes stomach pain, _____ and diarrhea, cold sweats, _____, confusion, and tremors.

190. (p. 160) In very large doses nicotine may cause _____, respiratory failure, and _____.

191. (p. 161) For a non-smoker, 50-75 milligrams of nicotine could be lethal. In contrast, a heavy smoker may inhale 40 cigarettes a day without feeling ill. This difference indicates that regular smokers build a _____ for nicotine.

192. (p. 161) A 1988 report by the United States Surgeon General concluded that nicotine is addicting. Withdrawal may cause _____, _____, cramps, insomnia, _____ upset, irritability, and a sharp craving for cigarettes.

193. (p. 161) These symptoms may last from ___ to ___ weeks and may be worse than heroin withdrawal. Indeed, relapse patterns are nearly identical for alcoholics, heroin addicts, cocaine abusers, and smokers who try to quit.

194. (p. 161) A burning cigarette releases more than 6,800 different chemicals. Many of these, including nicotine, are potent _____, cancer-causing substances.

195. (p. 161) _____ - _____ percent of lung cancers among men and ____ percent among women are caused by smoking. Altogether smoking is responsible for about one-third of all cancer deaths in the U.S.

196. (p. 161) Users of smokeless tobacco run a ___ to ___ times higher risk of developing oral cancer. Smokeless tobacco also causes shrinkage of the _____, contributes to _____ disease, and probably is as addicting as cigarettes.

197. (p. 161) Most smokers claim that smoking helps them concentrate, feel sociable, or calm down. However, psychologist Stanley Schachter asserts that smokers only smoke to prevent _____.

198. (p. 161) Schachter has shown that smoking does not improve mood or performance, but that heavy smokers who are _____ of nicotine feel and perform worse than non-smokers.

199. (p. 161) Also, smokers adjust their smoking to keep bodily levels of nicotine _____. Thus when smokers are given lighter cigarettes or when they are under stress (which speeds removal of nicotine) they smoke more.

200. (p. 161) Schachter's work shows that smokers who cut down are in a constant state of _____ causing irritability and discomfort without really ending smoking.

201. (p. 162) Smokers who switch to lighter cigarettes often smoke more and thus may expose themselves to more _____-_____ substances than before.

202. (p. 162) Barbiturates are _____ drugs that produce a general depression of activity in the brain. They are used medically to calm patients or to induce sleep.

203. (p. 162) In mild doses, barbiturates have an effect similar to _____ intoxication, but an overdose of barbiturates can cause _____ or _____.

204. (p. 162) Barbiturates taken with alcohol are particularly dangerous as the combined effects of the two drugs are multiplied by a _____ _____ (one drug enhances the effect of another).

205. (p. 162) Barbiturates may be taken in excessive amounts because increasing consumption makes users uninhibited or forgetful. An overdose first causes unconsciousness and then so severely depresses brain centers controlling _____ and _____ that death results.

206. (p. 162) The most frequently abused downers are short-acting barbiturates such as _____ and _____ and the non-barbiturate _____ (Quaadlude, Sopor, and Parest are its trade names).

207. (p. 162) These drugs seem to be preferred because they take effect quickly and the rush of intoxication only lasts from ___ to ___ hours. Like the other depressants, repeated use can cause a physical dependence and emotional depression.

208. (p. 162) Alcohol is not a stimulant, but instead is a _____ which in small amounts produces relaxation, euphoria, and diminishes inhibition, but in larger amounts can impair brain functioning to the point of unconsciousness.

209. (p. 162) Alcohol is not an _____, usually it impairs sexual performance particularly in males.

210. (p. 162) In America, alcohol is used by over _____ million people, _____ to _____ million of whom have a serious drinking problem.

211. (p. 162) A recent national survey found that _____ percent of college students are heavy drinkers. Among college males, the figure was _____ percent.

212. (p. 162) There are several phases involved in the progression of a social drinker to a problem drinker. Four danger signs that signal excessive dependence during the initial phase are: _____ consumption; _____ drinking; _____ behavior; and _____.

213. (p. 163)   During the second phase (crucial phase) there is usually control over when and where a first drink is taken, but one drink starts a _____ _____.

214. (p. 163)   Finally, at the _____ phase, the alcoholic drinks compulsively and continuously.

215. (p. 164)   Psychologists Roger Vogler and Wayne Bartz have studied the amount of alcohol per hour that can be consumed to maintain a level which makes you feel good. As long as blood alcohol remains below a level of about _____ people feel relaxed, euphoric, and sociable.

216. (p. 164)   At blood alcohol levels above 0.05, drinkers may go from moderately intoxicated to thoroughly drunk. Later, as blood alcohol begins to _____, those who over-drink become sick and miserable.

217. (p. 164)   Treatment for alcoholism begins by sobering the person up and cutting off the supply. This procedure is referred to as _____ and fre-quently produces all the symptoms of drug withdrawal.

218. (p. 164)   The next step is to try to restore the alcoholic's _____ through food, vitamins, and medical care.

219. (p. 164)   And finally the alcoholic may be treated with _____, _____, or psychotherapy.

220. (p. 164)   One mutual-help approach that has been fairly successful in treating alcoholics is _____ _____, which functions on the prem-ise that it takes a former alcoholic to understand and help a current alcoholic.

221. (p. 165)   One study has shown that of those who remain in AA over one year, _____ percent get through the following year without a drink.

222. (p. 165)   The National Institute of Drug Abuse has found that one out of every _____ Americans has tried marijuana at least once. More than _____ million Americans may be regular users.

223. (p. 165)   Marijuana and hashish are derived from the hemp plant _____ _____ containing the active chemical _____ (abbreviated THC), a mild hallucinogen.

224. (p. 165)   While there have been no overdose deaths from marijuana, it cannot be considered harmless. One issue is that THC accumulates in the body's fatty tissues, especially in the _____ and _____ organs.

225. (p. 165)   Studies of long-term heavy users of marijuana in Jamaica, Greece, and Costa Rica have failed to find evidence of _____ dependence. Its potential for abuse, therefore, lies primarily in the realm of psychological dependence, not addiction.

226. (p. 165)   Marijuana's typical psychological effects are: a sense of _____ or well-being, _____, altered _____ sense and percep-tual distortions. Marijuana also impairs short-term _____ and slows _____.

227. (p. 165)   Although marijuana intoxication is relatively subtle by comparison to a drug such as alcohol, it is still extremely _____ to drive a car or operate machinery while high.

228. (p. 166)   Marijuana has been charged with causing brain _____, _____ damage, loss of _____, and a reduction in the body's natural immunity to diseases. Each of these effects has been criticized for being based on poorly done or inconclusive research.

229. (p. 166)   Major studies in Jamaica, Greece, and Costa Rica failed to find any serious _____ problems or _____ impairment in long-term marijuana users.

230. (p. 166)   There are several liabilities associated with marijuana. As is true of alcohol, some adults become highly _____ on marijuana. Frequent use of any psychoactive drug can seriously impair mental, physical, and emotional development.

231. (p. 166)   Several potential risks have been identified for marijuana usage. In regular users it causes chronic _____ and pre-_____ changes in lung cells.

232. (p. 166)   A recent study by Swiss researchers found that marijuana smoke contains _____ percent more cancer-causing hydrocarbons than does tobacco smoke. Some doctors estimate that smoking several "joints" a week is the equivalent of smoking a dozen cigarettes a day.

233. (p. 166)   Other researchers have found that smokers of only a few joints a day have as much microscopic damage to the cells lining the _____ as smokers of more than a pack of cigarettes a day.

234. (p. 166)   Marijuana temporarily lowers _____ production in males and may produce reproductive abnormalities. This effect could be a problem for a marginally fertile man who wants to have a family.

235. (p. 166)   In experiments with female monkeys, THC causes abnormal _____ _____ and disrupts ovulation. Other animal studies have shown it causes a higher rate of _____ and can reach the fetus. The effect on human females is as yet unclear, but marijuana should be avoided during pregnancy.

236. (p. 166)   Researcher Herman Friedman has produced direct evidence that THC can suppress the body's _____ _____, possibly increasing the risk of disease.

237. (p. 167)   Freud identified four dream processes which help disguise hidden meanings of dreams. In the first, called _____, a single character in a dream represents several people at once.

238. (p. 167)   A second means of disguising dream content is _____. The most important emotions of a dream may be redirected toward safe or seemingly unimportant images.

239. (p. 167)   A third process is _____. Freud believed that dreams usually express symbolic images, rather than being literal in meaning.

240. (p. 167)   A process called _____ _____ is the fourth method by which the meaning of dreams is disguised. This process refers to the tendency to reorganize a dream when remembering it.

241. (p. 167) Dream theorist _____ _____ thinks of dreams as plays and the dreamer as a playwright. He feels much can be learned by simply considering the setting, cast, plot, and emotions portrayed in a dream.

242. (p. 167) Rosalind Cartwright suggests that one's everyday dream life can be a source of varied experience and personal enrichment. Emphasis is placed on the overall _____ _____ of the dream as a clue to its meaning.

243. (p. 167) Ann Faraday thinks of dreams as messages from yourself to yourself. She believes in the value of studying one's own dreams and suggests the following techniques to "catch a dream:"
      1) Before retiring, plan to _____ your dreams.
      2) If possible, arrange to awaken _____.
      3) If you rarely remember your dreams, set an alarm clock to wake you up earlier.
      4) Upon awakening, review the images with your _____ _____.
      5) Make your first _____ with your eyes closed.
      6) Review the dream again and record as many additional details as possible.
      7) Keep a permanent "dream diary."
      8) Remember that a number of drugs _____ dreaming.

244. (p. 168) _____ _____ feels that dreams are a special message about what is missing in our lives. They are a means of filling in gaps in personal experience.

245. (p. 168) An approach that Perls found helpful in understanding a dream is to "take the part of" each of the characters and objects in the dream. It is also revealing to set up dialogues between people or objects in the dream, especially those that stand in _____ to one another.

246. (p. 168) The dream state is one of reduced _____, and may be helpful in _____ _____ that require a fresh point of view. Certainly individuals such as Otto Loewi, to whom the idea for a breakthrough experiment leading to the Nobel Prize came in a dream, have found them to be of value in the production of creative solutions.

247. (p. 168) During a _____ dream, the dreamer "wakes" within an ordinary dream and feels capable of normal thought and action. Such dreamers know they are dreaming, but feel fully conscious within the dream world.

248. (p. 168) _____ _____ showed that lucid dreaming and voluntary action in dreams are possible by training lucid dreamers to make prearranged signs when they became aware they were dreaming.

249. (p. 169) La Berge found he could greatly increase lucid dreaming with this routine:
      1) When you awaken, _____ your dream.
      2) Next engage in 10 or 15 minutes of any activity requiring full _____.
      3) Then while lying in bed and returning to sleep, say to yourself, "Next time I'm dreaming, I want to remember I'm dreaming."
      4) Finally, visualize yourself lying in bed asleep, while in the dream just rehearsed, and simultaneously picture yourself realizing you are dreaming.

250. (p. 170) The best predictors of adolescent drug use and abuse are _____ drug use, _____ drug use, delinquency, parental maladjustment, poor _____-_____, social nonconformity, and stressful life changes.

251. (p. 170)　For many young people, drug abuse is just one part of a general pattern of problem behavior. This may be why drug intervention programs that teach _____ _____ have been relatively successful.

252. (p. 170)　A combination of immediate pleasure and delayed punishment allows abusers to feel good on demand. As a result, drug taking can become _____.

253. (p. 170)　Closely related to a drug's actual effects are users' beliefs and expectations about drugs. For example, one study found that heavy drinkers expect far more _____ effects and fewer _____ consequences from drinking alcohol than light drinkers do.

254. (p. 170)　There is a widespread tendency to think of drugs as a magic way to produce good feelings by avoiding, minimizing, or escaping negative situations. Some observers believe that drug use is so deeply ingrained in modern society that we are addicted to _____.

255. (p. 170)　Some observers feel that the medical profession, well meaning but misguided, unnecessarily encourages legal drug use. Many _____ and _____ problems of living are now being redefined as medical problems, to be solved by physicians with prescription pads.

256. (p. 170)　Drug abuse and drug-related problems once restricted to certain subcultures and the urban poor have spread widely. For example, one recent survey found that nearly _____ percent of doctors under age 40 admitted that they use marijuana or cocaine to get high with friends.

257. (p. 171)　Psychiatrist Thomas Szasz and *Consumer Reports* have independently taken the position that current drug regulations encourage a black market, organized crime, disrespect for the law, and adulterated drugs. They believe it is futile for the government to "legislate _____."

258. (p. 171)　Although billions of dollars have been spent on drug enforcement, there has been an _____ in the overall level of drug use in the United States. Given this, some experts believe prevention through education and early intervention is the answer to drug problems.

SELF-TEST

1. (p. 140)　Mental states related to fatigue, delirium, hypnosis, meditation, drugs, and ecstasy are referred to as _____ states of consciousness.
   a. altered　　　　　　　　　　c. extrasensory
   b. distorted　　　　　　　　　d. psi

2. (p. 141)　_____ is a brief shift in brain activity to patterns normally found in sleep.
   a. Minisleep　　　　　　　　　c. Brain sleep
   b. EEG sleep　　　　　　　　　d. Microsleep

3. (p. 141)　True-False. The experiences of Peter Tripp and Randy Gardner demonstrate that a person must sleep at least 8 hours for each 24 hours of sleep deprivation to regain normal functioning.

4. (p. 141)　True-False. Moderate sleep loss affects motivation and influences performance of low-level, boring tasks much more than complex mental tasks.

5. (p. 141) Extremely long periods without sleep can produce sleep-deprivation psychosis. Which of the following is *not* a common element of this reaction?
      a. confusion   c. delusions
      b. illusions   d. hallucinations

6. (p. 141) True-False. The average sleep time for adults is 8 hours, but the actual sleep time needed by various individuals may vary greatly from this average.

7. (p. 141) Which age group averages the least sleep per night?
      a. young infants   c. adults
      b. adolescents   d. elderly adults

8. (p. 143) Which of the following is *not* an area of the brain actively involved in generating sleep?
      a. pituitary gland   c. hypothalamus
      b. reticular formation   d. brainstem

9. (p. 143) Which of the following pairings of brain waves and state of consciousness is *not* an accurate association?
      a. beta brain waves — relaxed state or just prior to sleep
      b. delta brain waves — deep sleep
      c. beta brain waves — awake and alert state
      d. alpha brain waves — relaxed state or just prior to sleep

10. (p. 144) Which of the following is strongly associated with dreaming?
      a. REMs   c. Stage 2 sleep
      b. NREMs   d. Stage 3 sleep

11. (p. 145) True-False. Sleepwalking and sleeptalking occur during dream periods, as if the person is acting out dreams.

12. (p. 145) True-False. Night terrors are more intense, but basically similar to nightmares; they both occur during REM sleep.

13. (p. 146) Which of the following is *not* a sleep disorder?
      a. microsleep   c. insomnia
      b. narcolepsy   d. apnea

14. (p. 146) True-False. Drug-dependency insomnia may result from drug tolerance to prescription sedatives.

15. (p. 147) Which of the following is *not* an effective technique for reducing insomnia problems?
      a. Drink a glass of milk or eat something containing tryptophan.
      b. Establish your own schedule of sleeping—sleep when you want to, not on a fixed routine.
      c. Avoid fighting it—get up and do something useful or satisfying.
      d. Establish the pattern of only sleeping in bed.

16. (p. 147) Some doctors think SIDS is caused by
      a. narcolepsy   c. cataplexy
      b. night terrors   d. apnea

17. (p. 148) About how many dreams do you have each night?
      a. 1 or 2   c. 4 or 5
      b. 3 or 4   d. 6 or 7

18. (p. 148) True-False. Dreams may seem to take hours, but actually occur in a flash.

19. (p. 148) When finally allowed to dream following periods of dream sleep deprivation, people will dream extra amounts. This reaction is known as
    a. the REM myth
    b. paradoxical sleep
    c. the REM rebound effect
    d. displacement effect

20. (p. 149) Which of the following is *not* a possible function of REM sleep?
    a. provide stimulation for infant brain development
    b. process emotional events
    c. reduce sleep-inducing chemicals in the blood
    d. restore the brain's chemical balance

21. (p. 149) True-False. Unpleasant emotions such as fear, anger, and sadness are more frequent in dreams than pleasant emotions.

22. (p. 149) Which of the following is more characteristic of men's dreams, compared with women's dreams?
    a. men are more often pursued or endangered
    b. men dream more of men than women do
    c. men's dreams are more emotional
    d. men's dreams are more often indoors

23. (p. 149) True-False. Sigmund Freud believed that many dreams represent wish fulfillment of repressed or unconscious desires or conflicts.

24. (p. 150) The activation-synthesis hypothesis proposed by Hobson and McCarley postulates that dreams
    a. represent a way of filling in gaps in personal experience
    b. are a meaningless carry-over of waking thoughts or the result of indigestion
    c. are manufactured by the brain as a means of interpreting incoming information from cells aroused by "sleep center" cells in the brainstem
    d. represent a message from yourself to yourself that can be of value to understand and study

25. (p. 151) Which of the following statements is *not* true of hypnosis?
    a. Approximately 8 out of 10 people can be hypnotized, but only about 4 out of 10 are good hypnotic subjects.
    b. Hypnosis is not sleep, since brain wave recordings made during hypnosis are similar to those obtained when a person is awake.
    c. Many theorists feel hypnosis is really self-hypnosis guided by a hypnotist.
    d. Hypnosis is an altered state of consciousness, characterized by expansive attention and a decreased openness to suggestion.

26. (p. 151) True-False. The term hypnosis was coined by Franz Mesmer as an extention of his theories of animal magnetism.

27. (p. 152) Effective techniques of hypnotic induction have in common all but one of the factors below. Which does *not* apply?
    a. encouraging subjects to focus attention on what is being said
    b. decreasing imagination so as to focus on the hypnotist's instructions and control
    c. inducing relaxation and tiredness
    d. helping a person to "let go" and accept suggestions easily

28. (p. 152) Which of the following is true of human abilities under hypnosis?
    a. Hypnotic suggestions can be used to so convince subjects of their strength that

they can perform superhuman acts.
b. Hypnosis is helpful in the relief of pain; particularly where chemical painkillers cannot be used.
c. Memory can be improved dramatically.
d. Hypnotic suggestions concerning sensations seem to be at best mildly effective.

29. (p. 153) Stage hypnotists make use of tricks, deception, waking suggestibility, and _____, to perform their act.
a. disinhibition of subjects labeled hypnotized
b. psi abilities
c. easily hypnotized subjects
d. the same effective techniques used by non-stage hypnotists

30. (p. 154) Which of the following is *not* an effect reported by subjects in experiments of sensory deprivation?
a. loss of time boundaries
b. increased concentration
c. inability to tolerate reduced stimulation for more than two or three days
d. a variety of perceptual changes

31. (p. 154) Subjects severely deprived of sensory information while floating in a tank of water experience _____ similar to those that occur when one is falling asleep.
a. hypnogogic images   c. hallucinations
b. sleep distortions   d. subliminal perception

32. (p. 155) True-False. Peter Suedfeld has found that sensory deprivation can be used to help people quit smoking.

33. (p. 158) Which of the following is *not* associated with drug addiction?
a. physical dependence   c. drug tolerance
b. relaxation response   d. withdrawal symptoms

34. (p. 158) When drugs are used to cope with a specific problem such as boredom or staying awake for night work, such drug-taking behavior is classified as
a. recreational   c. situational
b. intensive   d. compulsive

35. (p. 158) Dexedrine, Methedrine, and Benzedrine are all drugs from a large group of synthetic stimulants collectively referred to as
a. speed   c. barbiturates
b. amphetamines   d. hallucinogens

36. (p. 159) Repeated use of which drug may lead to weight loss, ulcers, hypertension, liver disease, and/or cerebral hemorrhage?
a. barbiturates   c. alcohol
b. hallucinogens   d. amphetamines

37. (p. 159) True-False. Amphetamines and cocaine are so much alike in their effect on central nervous system functioning, experienced users cannot tell them apart.

38. (p. 159) True-False. Cocaine is one of the most rewarding of all known chemicals.

39. (p. 159) Which of the following is *not* true of cocaine usage?
a. Some scientists believe it may be physically addictive.
b. Drug tolerance never develops.

    c. Physical and emotional depression may follow a high.

    d. Even first-time users may risk convulsions, heart attack, or a stroke.

40. (p. 160) _____ is the most frequently used psychoactive drug in America.
    a. Nicotine   c. Marijuana
    b. Alcohol   d. Caffeine

41. (p. 160) True-False. Tea, cocoa, soft drinks, and chocolate drinks are all good alternatives to coffee because they contain no caffeine.

42. (p. 160) Which of the following is *not* true of caffeine?
    a. It encourages the development of breast cysts in women.
    b. It may contribute to lung problems.
    c. It can stimulate high blood pressure.
    d. It may contribute to stomach problems.

43. (p. 161) True-False. A burning cigarette releases more than 6,800 different chemicals.

44. (p. 161) Which statistic is *not* associated with tobacco usage in the U.S.?
    a. Cigarette smoking is the cause of 97% of lung cancer deaths among men.
    b. Smoking is responsible for about one-third of all cancer deaths.
    c. Users of smokeless tobacco actually run a lower risk of developing oral cancer.
    d. Cigarette smoking is the cause of 74% of lung cancer deaths among women.

45. (p. 161) True-False. Psychologist Stanley Schachter believes it is better to cut down smoking gradually or switch to lighter cigarettes rather than suddenly quitting because quitting abruptly can place the body under tremendous physical stress.

46. (p. 162) The combined effects of two drugs may be multiplied by a _____ _____.
    a. dosage excess   c. drug intolerance
    b. drug interaction   d. drug narcosis

47. (p. 162) An overdose of _____ first causes unconsciousness and then so severely depresses activity in brain centers controlling heartbeat and respiration that death results.
    a. amphetamines   c. barbiturates
    b. marijuana   d. cocaine

48. (p. 162) Which of the following is *not* a frequently abused "downer?"
    a. Seconal   c. Tuinal
    b. Tetrahydrocannabinol   d. Parest

49. (p. 162) True-False. Alcohol is a stimulant used by over 140 million Americans.

50. (p. 162) Which of the following does *not* signal excessive dependence on alcohol?
    a. morning drinking   c. regretted behavior
    b. blackouts   d. increased feelings of control over the drug

51. (p. 164) Treatment for alcoholism does *not* include which of the following?
    a. detoxification
    b. restoring physical health
    c. use of tranquilizers, antidepressants, and psychotherapy
    d. gradual reduction of alcohol intake

52. (p. 165) Which of the following is *not* true of marijuana usage in the U.S.?
    a. About 40 to 50 million Americans consider themselves regular users of marijuana.

       b. The psychoactive ingredient in marijuana is tetrahydrocannabinol.
       c. Marijuana's potential for abuse lies primarily in the realm of psychological dependence.
       d. The drug's typical effects include relaxation, altered time sense, slowed reflexes, and perceptual distortions.

53. (p. 166) True-False. A strong research base exists to support claims that marijuana causes brain damage, genetic damage, loss of motivation, and a reduction in the body's natural immunity to diseases.

54. (p. 166) The National Academy of Sciences concluded in 1982 that all of the following are long-term health risks associated with marijuana usage *except*
       a. lowered sperm production in males
       b. chronic bronchitis and pre-cancerous changes in lung cells
       c. possible gynecological problems such as abnormal menstrual cycles and increased miscarriages
       d. brain damage, genetic damage, and possible reductions in disease immunity

55. (p. 167) Which of the following is *not* a Freudian dream process which disguises the meaning of consciously remembered dreams?
       a. symbolization   c. condensation
       b. displacement   d. archetype images

56. (p. 168) Which of the following pairs of dream theorists and dream theories is incorrect?
       a. Cartwright — dreams are feeling statements
       b. Hobson — dreams are messages from yourself to yourself
       c. Hall — dreams are plays and dreamers are playwrights
       d. Perls — dreams are special messages about what is missing in our lives

57. (p. 168) True-False. Scientists such as Loewi have used dreams to solve problems of major importance, thus demonstrating the potential value of dreams for the production of creative solutions.

58. (p. 168) During a _____ _____ the dreamer "wakes" within an ordinary dream and feels capable of normal thought and action.
       a. lucid dream   c. secondary elaboration
       b. REM period   d. paradoxical sleep

59. (p. 170) Which of the following may be a factor in our society's increased use and dependence upon drugs?
       a. our society's apparent belief that everyone should be able to will themselves to be calm, cheerful, thin, industrious, and creative
       b. marketing and advertising campaigns directed to encourage overuse of drugs
       c. physicians rely more than ever upon the use of drugs to deal with a range of problems
       d. all of the above

60. (p. 171) True-False. Psychiatrist Thomas Szasz believes that current attempts to "legislate morality" through drug regulation encourages a black market, organized crime, and disrespect for the law.

61. (p. 171) True-False. Thanks to the billions of dollars spent on drug enforcement, the overall level of drug use by young adults in the United States has declined. Stricter laws and heavier penalties do work quite effectively.

ANSWERS — PROGRAMMED REVIEW

1. hallucinate; sleep
2. time
3. Consciousness
4. waking
5. quality, patterning
6. memory; suggestibility
7. name
8. electric shock
9. coma; die
10. microsleep
11. 11
12. single
13. age, personality
14. complex; irritable; declines
15. self-motivated
16. will to continue
17. sleep-deprivation psychosis
18. disorientation; delusions
19. 60
20. hands; eyelids; pain
21. 25
22. 8
23. long; short
24. 6
25. 20; 2; 4
26. two to one
27. 28
28. fatigue; Siamese twins
29. brain; spinal cord
30. sleep
31. hypothalamus; reticular formation; brainstem
32. pattern
33. electroencephalograph; EEG
34. small, fast; beta; larger, slower; alpha
35. light
36. hypnic
37. myoclonus; 15; 20
38. small, irregular
39. sleep spindles
40. 4
41. delta; large, slow
42. deep sleep; delta
43. Rapid eye movements; 85
44. REM; non-REM; NREM
45. 90
46. fatigue; exercise
47. 1½
48. irregularly; waver
49. erection; genital; increases
50. between
51. somnambulists
52. hereditary
53. no harm
54. 3, 4
55. NREM
56. REM
57. Night terrors; 4
58. 15; 20
59. childhood
60. Narcolepsy
61. cataplexy
62. REM
63. hereditary; stimulant
64. 40; insomnia
65. sedatives; 4; REM
66. drug-dependency
67. nightmares
68. triazolam
69. frustration
70. fighting
71. blood sugar
72. tryptophan
73. relaxation
74. Stimulus control
75. regular schedule
76. stimulants
77. early evening
78. progressive; meditation
79. sleepy; naps; nonsleep; 10
80. paradoxical
81. sleep apnea
82. 20; two
83. hypersomnia
84. brain; air passages
85. Sudden Infant Death Syndrome; SIDS
86. 1
87. brainstem; heart
88. passive
89. 6
90. teenager, smoker; high-pitched; open mouth
91. Nathaniel Kleitman, Eugene Aserinsky
92. 4, 5
93. 90
94. 10; 30; 50
95. increased; 20; 30
96. rebound
97. suppresses
98. memory lapses; concentrating; anxiety
99. REM myth
100. total amount
101. 50; 75
102. 20
103. chemicals; information; sensory deprivation

104. everyday experience
105. half
106. more
107. sex roles; emotional; aggressive
108. Male
109. wish fulfillment
110. images
111. dream symbols
112. activation-synthesis hypothesis
113. brainstem; memories
114. deeper meaning
115. Hypnosis
116. Franz Mesmer; magnets
117. animal magnetism
118. James Braid; EEG
119. 8; 4
120. Stanford Hypnotic Susceptibility
121. attention; tired; suggestions; imagination
122. will power
123. self-hypnosis
124. floating; separation
125. basic suggestion
126. dissociation
127. hidden observer
128. superhuman
129. false memories
130. pain
131. phantom limb
132. regressed
133. sensations
134. relaxation; pain; motivation
135. subjective experience
136. waking suggestibility
137. responsive
138. disinhibits
139. director
140. tricks
141. Sensory deprivation
142. awareness; sensation
143. 2; 3
144. colors; illusions; reactions
145. hypnogogic images
146. theta
147. 4; 7
148. sensory
149. pressure; tension
150. 40
151. weight-loss
152. relaxation; unfreezing
153. psychoactive drug
154. stimulation, depression
155. physical; addiction
156. withdrawal symptoms
157. tolerance
158. psychological dependence

159. compulsive
160. psychological dependence
161. experimental; recreational; situational; intensive; compulsive
162. Dexedrine, Methedrine, Benzedrine
163. weight loss; mild depression
164. drug tolerance
165. nausea, vomiting; pressure; arrhythmias
166. bodily resources
167. fatigue; depression; aggression
168. weight; ulcers; fingernails; infections; liver; hypertensive; cerebral
169. amphetamine psychosis
170. alertness, euphoria
171. Food; Drug
172. 4, 5
173. several hours; 15; 30
174. withdrawal symptoms
175. long; short
176. convulsions; attack
177. convulsions
178. dopamine, noradrenaline
179. 9
180. paranoid; interpersonal; nausea
181. Compulsive; control; consequences
182. caffeine
183. fatigue; alertness
184. coffee
185. caffeinism
186. cysts; stomach, heart
187. birth defects; miscarriages
188. nicotine
189. vomiting; dizziness
190. convulsions, death
191. tolerance
192. headaches, sweating; digestive
193. 2; 6
194. carcinogens
195. Ninety-seven; 74
196. 4; 6; gums; heart
197. withdrawal
198. deprived
199. constant
200. withdrawal
201. cancer-causing
202. sedative
203. alcohol; coma, death
204. drug interaction
205. heartbeat, respiration
206. Seconal, Tuinal; Methaqualone
207. 2; 4
208. depressant
209. aphrodisiac
210. 140; 14; 18
211. 17; 25

212. increased; morning; regretted; blackouts
213. chain reaction
214. chronic
215. 0.05
216. fall
217. detoxification
218. health
219. tranquilizers, antidepressants
220. Alcoholics Anonymous
221. 81
222. three; 18
223. Cannabis sativa; tetrahydrocannabinol
224. brain; reproductive
225. physical
226. euphoria; relaxation; time; memory; learning
227. hazardous
228. damage; genetic; motivation
229. health; mental
230. dependent
231. bronchitis; cancerous
232. 50
233. airways
234. sperm
235. menstrual cycles; miscarriages

236. immune system
237. condensation
238. displacement
239. symbolization
240. secondary elaboration
241. Calvin Hall
242. emotional tone
243. remember; gradually; eyes closed; dream record; suppress
244. Fritz Perls
245. opposition
246. inhibition; solving problems
247. lucid
248. Stephen La Berge
249. memorize; wakefulness
250. peer; parental; self-esteem
251. social skills
252. compulsive
253. positive; negative
254. addiction
255. psychological; social
256. 40
257. morality
258. increase

ANSWERS — SELF-TEST

1. a
2. d
3. False
4. True
5. b
6. True
7. d
8. a
9. a
10. a
11. False
12. False
13. a
14. True
15. b
16. d
17. c
18. False
19. c
20. c
21. True
22. b
23. True
24. c
25. d
26. False
27. b
28. b
29. a
30. b
31. a
32. True
33. b
34. c
35. b
36. d
37. True
38. True
39. b
40. d
41. False
42. b
43. True
44. c
45. False
46. b
47. c
48. b
49. False
50. d
51. d
52. a
53. False
54. d
55. d
56. b
57. True
58. a
59. d
60. True
61. False

Chapter 7

Conditioning and Learning I

CONTENTS

TERMS AND CONCEPTS

fixed action pattern (FAP)
innate behaviors
reflex
instincts
species specific behavior
learning
reinforcement
antecedents
consequences
classical conditioning (respondent conditioning)
operant conditioning (instrumental conditioning)
neutral stimulus (NS)
conditioned stimulus (CS)
unconditioned stimulus (US)
unconditioned response (UR)
conditioned response (CR)
acquisition
higher order conditioning
extinction
spontaneous recovery
stimulus generalization
stimulus discrimination

phobia
conditioned emotional response (CER)
desensitization
vicarious conditioning (secondhand conditioning)
prepared fear theory
law of effect
operant reinforcer
voluntary responses
conditioning chamber (Skinner box)
response contingent
shaping
successive approximations
primary reinforcer
biological constraints
instinctive drift
intra-cranial stimulation (ICS)
secondary reinforcer
tokens
generalized reinforcer
Premack principle
prepotent responses
delay of reinforcement

response chaining
superstitious behavior
schedules of reinforcement
continuous reinforcement
partial reinforcement
partial reinforcement effect
fixed ratio (FR)

variable ratio (VR)
fixed interval (FI)
variable interval (VI)
stimulus control
discriminative stimuli (S+, S-)
behavioral contracting

IMPORTANT INDIVIDUALS

Ivan Pavlov
Martin Seligman
Edward L. Thorndike
B. F. Skinner
Keller Breland

Marion Breland
David Premack
Melissa Bowerman
Paul Graubard
Harry Rosenberg

PROGRAMMED REVIEW

1. (p. 177) Weaver birds raised in total isolation for several generations can still tie a special knot for nesting at the first opportunity. This phenomenon is an example of a _____ _____ _____, abbreviated _____.

2. (p. 177) FAPs are instinctual chains of movements found in all members of a species. Like other _____ (inborn) behaviors they help prepare animals to meet major needs in their lives.

3. (p. 177) A simpler innate behavior is a _____, such as blinking when your eyelashes are touched. More complicated behaviors, such as the maternal instinct in lower animals, combine this innate behavior and FAPs.

4. (p. 177) Humans have reflexes, but most psychologists reject the idea that people have _____.

5. (p. 177) To qualify as instinctual, a behavior must be complex, unlearned, and _____ _____ (it occurs in almost all members of a species).

6. (p. 177) _____ is formally defined as a relatively permanent change in behavior due to reinforcement. This definition excludes changes caused by motivation, fatigue, maturation, disease, injury, or drugs.

7. (p. 177) Merely repeating a response may not produce learning. In conditioning some type of _____ must be present. This term refers to any event which increases the chances that a response will be made again.

8. (p. 178) Events before a response are called _____. Events that follow a response are called _____. An understanding of learning requires that careful attention be given to the "before and after" aspects of the situation.

9. (p. 178) In _____ conditioning, all the "action" occurs before a response. Learning involves an association between antecedent events. A stimulus that does not produce a response is associated with one that does. Learning is evident when the new stimulus also begins to elicit the response.

10. (p. 178) _____ conditioning involves learning affected by consequences. Each time a response is made, it may be followed by reinforcement, punishment, or nothing. These results determine whether or not a response is likely to be made again.

11. (p. 178) At the beginning of the twentieth century, Russian physiologist _____ _____ discovered and began to research the concept of classical conditioning (also known as _____ conditioning).

12. (p. 178) In his experiments, Pavlov found that dogs salivated to the sound of a bell consistently rung before meat powder was given them. The bell starts out as a _____ stimulus, abbreviated _____, because it is a stimulus that does not evoke a response.

13. (p. 179) In time, the bell becomes a _____ stimulus, abbreviated _____, because it is a stimulus to which the dog has learned to respond.

14. (p. 179) The meat powder is called an _____ stimulus, abbreviated _____, because the dog does not have to learn to respond to it.

15. (p. 179) Unconditioned stimuli typically produce "built in" reflex responses called _____ (non-learned) responses, abbreviated _____. In Pavlov's experiment, this was salivation.

16. (p. 179) When the bell alone causes salivation, the response can no longer be called a simple reflex. Instead, it is a _____ (learned) _____, abbreviated _____.

17. (p. 179) Applying these terms to the effects of the shower and flushing toilet described in the chapter "Preview" we get the following:
_____ response = reflex jump from the hot water
_____ stimulus = pain caused by the hot water
_____ stimulus = sound of a flushing toilet

18. (p. 179) During _____, or training, a conditioned response must be reinforced, or strengthened.

19. (p. 179) In classical conditioning, reinforcement occurs when the _____ _____ is followed by, or paired with, an _____ _____.

20. (p. 179) Conditioning will be most rapid if the US follows immediately after the CS. With most reflexes, for conditioning to occur the optimal delay between CS and US is from ____ second to ____ seconds.

21. (p. 180) In _____ _____ conditioning, a well-learned CS is used to reinforce further learning. Through this procedure, learning can be extended one or more steps beyond the original conditioned stimulus.

22. (p. 180) Many _____ try to use higher order conditioning by pairing images associated with good feelings with pictures of their products. The hope is that you will learn to feel good when you see their products.

23. (p. 180) If the US never again follows the CS, conditioning will _____. We say that the CR has been _____ (or suppressed).

24. (p. 180) Thus, classical conditioning can be weakened by removing reinforcement. This process is called _____.

25. (p. 180) The next day following extinction, presentation of the conditioned stimulus may initially elicit a response, a reaction called _____ _____.

26. (p. 180) Because of spontaneous recovery, several _____ sessions may be necessary to completely reverse learning.

27. (p. 180) Once a subject is conditioned to respond to a particular conditioned stimulus, other stimuli similar to the CS may elicit (bring forth) a response. This effect is called _____ _____.

28. (p. 180) For instance, a child accidentally burned by matches may also show a healthy fear of flames produced by lighters, fireplaces, stoves, etc. Generalization tends to extend the effects of learning to _____ _____ and similar situations.

29. (p. 180) Stimulus generalization does have limits. There is a gradual decrease in generalization as test stimuli become _____ like the original CS.

30. (p. 181) Using the example of a child conditioned to salivate to a bell paired with lemon juice, suppose that we occasionally sound a buzzer instead of the bell, but never follow it with the US. At first, the buzzer produces salivation due to _____.

31. (p. 181) But after the buzzer has been presented several more times, the child ceases to respond to it. The child has now learned to _____, or respond differently to the bell and the buzzer.

32. (p. 181) This process of _____ discrimination is a common and important element of learning. For example, most children quickly learn to discriminate voice qualities associated with pain from those associated with praise or affection.

33. (p. 181) In its simplest form, classical conditioning depends on responses called _____, dependable, inborn stimulus-and-response connections. Withdrawal of various parts of the body in response to pain would be one example.

34. (p. 181) Simple conditioning of human reflexes is a common occurrence. Of greater importance, perhaps, are more subtle kinds of conditioning involving complex emotional or "gut" responses. For instance, if your face reddened as a child, you may blush now as an adult when you are embarrassed or ashamed. Many such _____, autonomic nervous system responses, are linked with new stimuli and situations by classical conditioning.

35. (p. 181) Another common example of such conditioning is a _____—a fear that persists even when no realistic danger exists.

36. (p. 181) Reactions of fear to animals, water, heights, and so forth are called _____ _____ _____, abbreviated _____. They may be broadened into phobias by stimulus generalization.

37. (p. 181) Fortunately, phobias can be extinguished. In a therapy technique called _____, learning principles are used to extinguish or counter-condition phobias, fears, or anxieties.

38. (p. 182)   People can be conditioned to give an emotional response to a light, merely by watching another person get an electric shock each time the light comes on. Children can learn to fear thunder by watching their parents. These are examples of _____ classical conditioning.

39. (p. 182)   Vicarious conditioning probably plays a part in _____ reactions to many situations including attitudes toward certain types of food, political parties, minority groups, and so forth.

40. (p. 183)   Many of our likes, dislikes, and fears are acquired as CERs. For example, when colored geometric shapes were paired with the theme music from the movie Star Wars, college students gave _____ ratings to those shapes than to ones associated with silence.

41. (p. 183)   Through classical conditioning, it is possible to learn to fear or dislike just about anything. But Martin Seligman's _____ _____ theory holds that we are prepared by evolution to readily develop fears to certain stimuli, such as snakes and spiders.

42. (p. 183)   According to Seligman's theory, such stimuli posed dangers earlier in human history and through _____ _____ have become highly effective conditioning stimuli.

43. (p. 184)   _____ conditioning concerns how we learn to associate responses with their consequences. The basic principle behind this is quite simple: acts followed by _____ tend to be repeated.

44. (p. 184)   Pioneer learning theorist Edward L. Thorndike called this the _____ of _____. According to Thorndike, learning is strengthened each time a response is followed by a satisfying state of affairs.

45. (p. 184)   While classical conditioning is passive and involuntary, in operant conditioning the learner actively "operates on" the environment. Thus, operant conditioning refers mainly to learning _____ responses.

46. (p. 184)   "_____" do not always increase responding and are therefore not always the same as reinforcers. If you give licorice candy to a child as a "_____" for good behavior it will work only if the child likes licorice.

47. (p. 184)   Psychologists therefore define an _____ _____ as any event that increases the probability of a response.

48. (p. 184)   Most laboratory research on operant conditioning takes place in some form of _____ _____ also called a "Skinner box." It is usually a cagelike chamber with bare walls except for a metal lever and a tray from which food pellets may be dispensed.

49. (p. 184)   This simplified environment increases the chances that subjects will make the response we are interested in rewarding. Hunger also ensures that animals will be motivated to seek food and to actively _____, or give off, a variety of responses.

50. (p. 184)   In operant conditioning _____ is used to alter the frequency of responses, or to mold them into new patterns or habits.

51. (p. 185) To be effective, operant reinforcement must be _____
_____. That is, reinforcement is given only when a
desired response is made.

52. (p. 185) This principle was demonstrated in a study on changing deviant behaviors performed
by children in a special classroom. When reinforcement was given only for good
behavior (made response contingent), disruptive actions _____
rapidly.

53. (p. 185) When we reward responses that come closer and closer to the final desired pattern,
the process is called _____.

54. (p. 185) The basic principle of shaping is that gradual or _____
_____ to the desired response are rewarded.

55. (p. 186) At one time, psychologists assumed that almost any voluntary response could be
taught by operant conditioning. However, it has become clear that animals,
especially, will learn some responses much more easily than others. This suggests
that there are a number of _____
_____, or limits, to learning.

56. (p. 186) Two psychologists, Keller and Marion _____, have found many
examples of learning limitations in their business of training animals for television
shows, zoo displays, and amusement parks.

57. (p. 186) As one example, they found it nearly impossible to condition a raccoon to place coins
in a piggy-bank. Instead, the animal repeatedly rubbed the coins together (an innate
food-washing response). They called this problem _____
_____: learned responses tend to "drift" toward innate ones.

58. (p. 186) If a learned response is not reinforced, it gradually drops out of an organism's behavior. Such a process is called _____, just as in classical
conditioning.

59. (p. 187) If a rat is removed from a Skinner box and allowed to rest after bar pressing is extinguished, he will begin pressing the bar when returned to the Skinner box. This brief
return of an operant response following extinction is called _____
_____.

60. (p. 187) _____ reinforcers are unlearned rewards that apply almost universally
to a species. They are usually biological in nature and produce comfort or end discomfort, such as _____, _____ or _____.

61. (p. 187) Rats wired for pleasurable intra-cranial stimulation (an unusual form of primary
reinforcement) will bar press _____ of times per hour for 15 to 20
hours before collapsing. They will ignore _____, _____ and sex in favor
of bar pressing.

62. (p. 187) _____ reinforcers are learned reinforcers, such as money, praise,
attention, approval, success, affection, and grades. Reinforcers of this type become
rewards through association with primary reinforcers.

63. (p. 188) This effect can be shown experimentally by associating bar pressing, food, and a tone.
Once learned, rats transferred to a new test chamber will bar press to receive a
_____ even when food is unavailable.

64. (p. 188) Secondary reinforcers may also gain their value more directly when they can be exchanged for primary reward. For example, _____ can be used with chimpanzees to reinforce behavior.

65. (p. 188) One problem with primary reinforcers is that people and animals receiving them quickly _____ (meaning they are fully satisfied or have reduced desire).

66. (p. 188) A major advantage of _____ is that they do not lose their reinforcing value as quickly as do primary reinforcers. They are particularly useful in work with troubled children, adolescents, adults in special programs, and in the education of the mentally retarded.

67. (p. 188) When a secondary reinforcer has become largely independent of its connection to primary reinforcers, it is called a _____ reinforcer.

68. (p. 188) For example, chimps working for tokens also tended to _____ them, even when hungry. For humans, money is a similar example of a generalized reinforcer.

69. (p. 188) One way to discover what will serve as a reinforcer is to apply the _____ _____: Any high-frequency (or "_____") response can be used to reinforce a low-frequency response.

70. (p. 188) If TV watching is a high-frequency response and studying is infrequent, TV watching can be used as a _____ to increase the frequency of studying.

71. (p. 189) Reinforcement has its greatest effect on learning when the time lapse between a response and the reward is _____. Reward is most effective when given _____ after the response.

72. (p. 189) Operant conditioning experiments with rats show that when reward follows responding by 50 seconds, very little occurs. When food delivery follows a bar press by more than _____ minutes, no learning occurs.

73. (p. 189) Humans are less affected by delay of reinforcement because they are able to _____ future reward. Also, a single reward can often maintain a long _____ of responses.

74. (p. 189) A simple example of _____ _____ is provided by Barnabus, a rat trained to perform a long series of complex behaviors.

75. (p. 190) When behaviors develop as a result of reinforcement, but actually have nothing to do with bringing about reinforcement, they are called _____ behaviors.

76. (p. 190) These behaviors develop because a reward will reinforce not only the last response that precedes it, but also other responses occurring shortly before the reward is given. Such responses tend to persist because they _____ to pay off.

77. (p. 190) As an example, if pigeons initially trained to key peck for food then have food delivered at _____ intervals (independent of responding) they will still make thousands of responses during a 20 minute period.

78. (p. 191) When rewards are given in particular patterns, the patterns are called _____ of _____.

79. (p. 191) _____ _____ means that a reinforcer follows every response.

80. (p. 191) Reinforcement which does not follow every response is called _____
_____.

81. (p. 191) Partial reinforcement while acquiring a response makes the response very resistant to
_____. This effect is called the _____ _____
effect and applies to both classical and instrumental conditioning.

82. (p. 191) One reason for this effect is that acquisition on a schedule of partial reward includes
long periods of nonreward. This fact makes it harder to discriminate between
conditions of _____ and _____.

83. (p. 191) If we follow every third, fourth, fifth, or other number of responses with reinforcement, the reinforcement schedule is _____ _____.

84. (p. 191) A fixed ratio schedule where every third response is rewarded would be symbolized
_____.

85. (p. 191) The most prominent characteristic of FR schedules is that they produce very
_____ rates of responding.

86. (p. 192) An example is illustrated when factory or farm workers are paid on a
_____ basis. When a fixed number of items must be produced for a
set amount of pay, work output is high.

87. (p. 192) If subjects receive reward every fourth response *on the average,* the schedule of reinforcement is _____ _____, which is symbolized _____.

88. (p. 192) Variable ratio schedules also produce high response rates. VR schedules tend to
produce _____ resistance to extinction than FR schedules. Playing
a slot machine is an example of behavior maintained by a VR schedule.

89. (p. 192) If reinforcement is given for the first correct response made after a fixed amount of
time has passed, the reward pattern is called _____
_____, abbreviated _____.

90. (p. 192) FI schedules produce _____ response rates characterized by spurts of
_____ mixed with periods of _____.

91. (p. 192) Having a paper due in a class every two weeks is one illustration of an FI schedule.
Immediately after turning in a paper, your work probably drops to _____ until
the next due date draws near.

92. (p. 192) When subjects are given reinforcement for the first correct response made after a
variable amount of time has passed, the schedule is _____
_____, abbreviated _____.

93. (p. 192) For example, a VI-30 sec. schedule means that reinforcement is available after an
interval that _____ 30 seconds duration.

94. (p. 192) VI schedules produce _____, _____ rates of response and tremendous
_____ to _____.

95. (p. 193) When you dial a phone number and get a busy signal, reward (getting through) is on a
_____ schedule. People usually dial repeatedly until getting a connection.

96. (p. 193) Responses that are reinforced in a particular situation tend to come under the control of stimuli present during conditioning. This process is called _____ _____. A child who learns to ask for candy when her mother is in a good mood (but not at other times) is an example of this principle.

97. (p. 193) Psychologists symbolize a stimulus that precedes reinforced responses as an _____. Discriminative stimuli that precede unrewarded responses are symbolized as _____.

98. (p. 193) Responses followed by reinforcement tend to be made again when the stimuli that preceded them are present. As a result, similar stimuli also tend to bring forth a response. This process is called _____.

99. (p. 193) A good example of generalization is the way children use _____ _____. One child studied by psychologist Melissa Bowerman first used the word "snow" for several white objects.

100. (p. 194) Stimulus discrimination is illustrated by "sniffer" dogs trained to locate drugs and explosives. Since these dogs are reinforced only for approaching contraband, contraband becomes a _____ stimulus.

101. (p. 196) One of the most common mistakes people make with pets is beating them if they do not come when called. Calling the animals then becomes a _____ _____ for fear and withdrawal.

102. (p. 196) An effective alternative is to give a distinctive call during feeding so that the call becomes a _____ _____ for reward (food).

103. (p. 196) One reason why dogs often beg at the table is that they occasionally have been rewarded for doing so. Thus, they have been rewarded on a _____ schedule, which is very _____ to _____.

104. (p. 196) Conditioning in business often focuses on reinforcement schedules. For example, productivity (and often satisfaction) has been shown to increase when a _____ _____ (or piecework) schedule is used instead of a _____ _____ (or straight salary) schedule.

105. (p. 196) The most widely used business adaptation of schedules of reinforcement is a combination of _____ _____ rewards and _____ _____ reinforcements.

106. (p. 196) For example, in one study clerks given a chance to earn paid time off by meeting minimum standards for selling and stock work showed a significant _____ in performance compared with a control group's behavior which remained the same.

107. (p. 197) _____ and approval from parents is a very powerful reinforcer for children. Parents may knowingly reinforce _____ _____-seeking in children by ignoring them when they are quiet or are playing constructively.

108. (p. 197) In helping teach a child not to engage in negative attention-seeking behavior (such as tantrums), the key is _____.

109. (p. 197) Attention and operant conditioning procedures can be used to accomplish such feats as controlling the position that a teacher lectures from and, more constructively,

helping socially outcast students better relate to others, as in the work of _____ _____ and _____ _____ .

110. (p. 198) In 1948, B. F. Skinner published *Walden Two*, a utopian novel about a model communi-ty based on _____ _____ .

111. (p. 198) One "operant community" organized at the University of Kansas has been quite suc-cessful. Here, college students have taken part in an _____ _____ _____ in which work sharing is strongly reinforced.

112. (p. 199) To increase the frequency of any behavior, several steps can be suggested. First, choose a _____ behavior; that is, identify what you want to change.

113. (p. 199) Then, record a _____ so you'll know how much time you currently spend performing the target behavior.

114. (p. 199) Next, establish _____ . Make them realistic and set them daily so that they add up to a weekly total.

115. (p. 199) You also need to choose _____ that you can reward yourself with for making your daily goals.

116. (p. 199) Be sure to _____ your progress. Keeping accurate records of the amount of time spent each day on the desired activity can help.

117. (p. 199) Finally, _____ successes. If you meet your daily goal, collect your reward. But be honest and skip the reward if you fall short. Do the same for your weekly goal.

118. (p. 199) The   key   to   any   self-management   program   is   accurate   _____ _____ . This fact was demonstrated by an investigation in which students who recorded their study time and graphed their study behavior earned better grades than those who did no recording, even though no rewards were offered.

119. (p. 199) In a _____ _____ , you state a specific goal to be achieved and the rewards you will receive for completion, along with the privileges you will forfeit or punishments you must accept if you fail to complete the goal. It should be signed by you and someone with whom you are close.

SELF-TEST

1. (p. 177) A fixed action pattern can be defined as
    a. an instinctual chain of movements found in all members of a species
    b. a chain of responses learned through classical conditioning
    c. the pattern of responding usually observed when using fixed ratio schedules of reinforcement
    d. a type of conditioned response observed when certain conditioned stimuli are present

2. (p. 177) Which of the following is *not* a quality of instinctual behaviors?
    a. complex   c. unlearned
    b. spontaneous   d. species specific

3.   (p. 177) _____ is a relatively permanent change in behavior due to reinforcement.
a. Instinct   c. Learning
b. FAP   d. Memory

A young child is bitten by a particular dog and later fears all dogs, but not all animals.   Answer Questions 4-9 with reference to this event.

4.   (p. 179) What is the unconditioned stimulus?
a. pain from being bitten   c. seeing or being near any animal
b. seeing or being near a dog   d. fear of any dog

5.   (p. 179) What is the conditioned stimulus?
a. pain from being bitten   c. seeing or being near any animal
b. seeing or being near a dog   d. fear of any dog

6.   (p. 179) What is the conditioned response?
a. pain from being bitten   c. seeing or being near any animal
b. seeing or being near a dog   d. fear of any dog

7.   (p. 180) The child's fear of all dogs illustrates
a. stimulus generalization   c. stimulus discrimination
b. spontaneous recovery   d. vicarious conditioning

8.   (p. 181) The child's fear of all dogs, but not all animals, illustrates
a. stimulus generalization   c. stimulus discrimination
b. successive approximation   d. resistance to extinction

9.   (p. 181) The child's fear of dogs illustrates a(n)
a. instinct   c. spontaneous recovery
b. conditioned emotional response   d. fixed action pattern

10. (p. 179) Pavlov's dogs salivated to the presence of the meat powder because
a. they had learned to do so prior to the experiment
b. they associated the meat powder with the presentation of the bell
c. it was a naturally elicited, reflex response
d. that was what Pavlov wanted them to do

11. (p. 179) During acquisition, a conditioned response must be reinforced. In classical conditioning, reinforcement occurs when the CS is followed by a
a. US   c. UR
b. CR   d. FAP

12. (p. 180) After acquisition, if the CS is never again followed by the US, the CR will be inhibited. This process is called
a. reinforcement   c. desensitization
b. generalization   d. extinction

13. (p. 180) If on the next day following extinction, the CS is again presented, a response may occur. This reaction is called
a. reinforcement   c. vicarious conditioning
b. spontaneous recovery   d. emitted responding

14. (p. 181) A _____ is a fear which persists even when no realistic danger exists. Many are thought to be learned through classical conditioning.
a. phobia   c. conditioned unemotional response
b. reflex   d. fixed action pattern

15. (p. 182)   Children who learn to fear thunder by watching their parents have undergone
         a. vicarious extinction   c. conditioned acquisition
         b. spontaneous conditioning   d. vicarious conditioning

16. (p. 184)   Classical conditioning involves _____, while instrumental conditioning involves
         _____.
         a. voluntary behaviors, learned reflexes
         b. learned reflexes, voluntary behaviors
         c. freely paced trials, individual learning trials
         d. stimulus generalization, stimulus discrimination

17. (p. 185)   Reinforcing successive approximations to the desired act, defines the basic principle of
         a. vicarious conditioning   c. reinforcement scheduling
         b. shaping   d. stimulus control

18. (p. 186)   True-False. Instinctive drift refers to the use of partial schedules to produce long
         chains of behavior.

19. (p. 186)   The fact that honey bees can only learn the location of their hives in the morning is
         an example of
         a. biological constraints on learning
         b. stimulus discrimination and generalization
         c. extinction and spontaneous recovery
         d. classical conditioning in the "real world"

20. (p. 186)   True-False. Extinction and spontaneous recovery are phenomena that occur in both
         classical and instrumental conditioning.

21. (p. 187)   Food, water, and sex are all examples of _____ reinforcers.
         a. secondary   c. stimulatory
         b. primary   d. generalized

22. (p. 187)   Which of the following are examples of secondary reinforcers?
         a. praise, attention, affection, grades
         b. food, water, sex
         c. stimulation of brain pleasure centers, money, sex
         d. pain, discomfort, fear

23. (p. 188)   One problem with primary reinforcers is that subjects receiving them may satiate
         quickly. A valuable alternative is to use
         a. punishment   c. tokens
         b. delayed reinforcement   d. food, water, or sex

24. (p. 188)   Which of the following defines a generalized reinforcer?
         a. primary reinforcers that are effective across a general species population
         b. secondary reinforcers that facilitate stimulus generalization in operant condition-
             ing experiments
         c. secondary reinforcers that have become independent of their connection with
             primary reinforcers
         d. any reinforcer that is effective across a wide (generalized) class of stimuli

25. (p. 188)   The Premack principle refers to the fact that
         a. animals will bar press for electrical stimulation of brain pleasure centers while
             ignoring food, water, or sex
         b. punishment normally only suppresses a response, it does not extinguish it

c. in order for reinforcement to be effective it must be made contingent upon responding

d. prepotent responses can be used to reinforce low-frequency responses

26. (p. 189) True-False. The longer the interval between a response and a reward, the greater the learning, since subjects have more time to think about the response.

27. (p. 190) True-False. A reward will reinforce only the last response which precedes it. This phenomenon is the principle behind superstitious behavior.

28. (p. 191) Schedules of partial reinforcement, as contrasted with continuous reinforcement, produce
    a. equally fast learning
    b. more rapid shaping
    c. more rewards per time
    d. slower extinction

29. (p. 191) Which of the following is *not* true of the partial reinforcement effect?
    a. It occurs when acquisition of a response is reinforced on a continuous basis.
    b. It refers to the fact that partial reinforcement makes a response very resistant to extinction.
    c. Acquisition on a partial schedule makes it harder to discriminate between conditions of reward and extinction.
    d. For many people, gambling often involves the partial reinforcement effect.

30. (p. 192) Which schedule produces slow, steady of responding?
    a. FI
    b. FR
    c. VR
    d. VI

31. (p. 192) On an FI-10 sec. schedule, how is reward dispensed?
    a. The first response following an average interval of 10 seconds duration is reinforced.
    b. Reward follows every time the subject responds continuously for 10 seconds.
    c. During the first 10 second interval of each minute period, reward is available on a continuous basis.
    d. The first correct response following the passage of a 10 second interval is reinforced.

32. (p. 192) Which of the following characterizes responding on an FI schedule?
    a. extremely high rates of responding
    b. low rates of responding, but high resistance to extinction
    c. slow, steady rates of responding
    d. moderate response rates marked by bursts of activity mixed with periods of inactivity

33. (p. 193) True-False. Stimulus control refers to the fact that stimuli that precede a rewarded response tend to influence when and where the response will occur in the future.

34. (p. 193) Which of the following is *not* associated with both classical and instrumental conditioning?
    a. discrimination
    b. extinction
    c. learned reflexes
    d. generalization

35. (p. 196) Beating a dog that come when called makes calling the animal a(n) _____ for fear and withdrawal.
    a. conditioned stimulus
    b. unconditioned stimulus
    c. instrumental reinforcer
    d. conditioned emotional response

36. (p. 196) Paying employees on a piecework basis is basically the same as which schedule of reinforcement?
    a. FI
    b. VI
    c. VR
    d. FR

37. (p. 197) The key principle in using rewards to modify behavior is
    a. developing rapport with the subject
    b. consistency in giving and withholding rewards
    c. not letting the subject know that they are being manipulated
    d. giving rewards when it is most convenient for the experimenter

38. (p. 198) University of Kansas students participated in an experimental living project which emphasized
    a. interpersonal compatibility
    b. use of rewards to increase studying
    c. worksharing
    d. existence unencumbered by responsibilities

39. (p. 199) True-False. Recording study time may be necessary before you can reward progress, but keeping records alone has no effect on behavior.

40. (p. 199) A _____ _____ involves a written agreement outlining a specific behavior to be changed and the rewards and punishments to be applied.
    a. token economy
    b. behavioral contract
    c. behavior therapy
    d. systematic record

ANSWERS — PROGRAMMED REVIEW

1. fixed action pattern; FAP
2. innate
3. reflex
4. instincts
5. species specific
6. Learning
7. reinforcement
8. antecedents; consequences
9. classical
10. Operant
11. Ivan Pavlov; respondent
12. neutral; NS
13. conditioned; CS
14. unconditioned; US
15. unconditioned; UR
16. conditioned response; CR
17. unconditioned; unconditioned; conditioned
18. acquisition
19. conditioned stimulus; unconditioned stimulus
20. $\frac{1}{2}$; 5
21. higher order
22. advertisers
23. extinguish; inhibited
24. extinction
25. spontaneous recovery
26. extinction
27. stimulus generalization
28. new settings
29. less
30. generalization
31. discriminate
32. stimulus
33. reflexes
34. involuntary
35. phobia
36. conditioned emotional responses; CERs
37. desensitization
38. vicarious
39. emotional
40. higher
41. prepared fear
42. natural selection
43. Operant; reinforcement
44. law of effect
45. voluntary
46. Rewards; reward
47. operant reinforcer
48. conditioning chamber
49. emit
50. reinforcement
51. declined

52. response contingent
53. shaping
54. successive approximations
55. biological constraints
56. Breland
57. instinctive drift
58. extinction
59. spontaneous recovery
60. Primary; food, water, sex
61. thousands; food, water
62. Secondary
63. tone
64. tokens
65. satiate
66. tokens
67. generalized
68. hoard
69. Premack principle; prepotent
70. reinforcer
71. short; immediately
72. $1\frac{1}{2}$
73. anticipate; chain
74. response chaining
75. superstitious
76. appear
77. random
78. schedules of reinforcement
79. Continuous reinforcement
80. partial reinforcement
81. extinction; partial reinforcement
82. reinforcement, extinction
83. fixed ratio
84. FR-3
85. high

86. piecework
87. variable ratio; VR-4
88. greater
89. fixed interval; FI
90. moderate; activity; inactivity
91. zero
92. variable interval; VI
93. averages
94. slow, steady; resistance to extinction
95. VI
96. stimulus control
97. S+, S-
98. generalization
99. new words
100. discriminative
101. conditioned stimulus
102. discriminative stimulus
103. partial; resistant to extinction
104. fixed ratio; fixed interval
105. fixed interval; fixed ratio
106. improvement
107. Attention; negative attention
108. consistency
109. Paul Graubard, Harry Rosenberg
110. behavioral engineering
111. Experimental Living Project
112. target
113. baseline
114. goals
115. reinforcers
116. record
117. reward
118. record keeping
119. behavioral contract

ANSWERS — SELF-TEST

1. a
2. b
3. c
4. a
5. b
6. d
7. a
8. c
9. b
10. c
11. a
12. d
13. b
14. a
15. d
16. b
17. b
18. False
19. a
20. True
21. b
22. a
23. c
24. c
25. d
26. False
27. False
28. d
29. a
30. d
31. d
32. d
33. True
34. c
35. a
36. d
37. b
38. c
39. False
40. b

Chapter 8

Conditioning and Learning II

CONTENTS

TERMS AND CONCEPTS

two-factor learning
informational view
expectancies
feedback (knowledge of results or KR)
programmed instruction
computer-assisted instruction (CAI)
branching program
drill and practice
instructional games
educational simulations
positive reinforcement
negative reinforcement
punishment
response cost
escape learning
avoidance learning
cognitive learning

cognitive map
latent learning
rote learning
discovery learning
modeling (observational learning)
biofeedback
alpha brain waves
electroencephalograph (EEG)
motor skill
motor program
mental practice
spaced practice
massed practice
transfer of training
positive transfer
negative transfer
negative practice

IMPORTANT INDIVIDUALS

Robert Rescorla
Albert Bandura
Tannis Williams
Elmer Green
Alyce Green

Joseph Kamiya
Rowell Huesmann
Neil Malamuth
Victor Cline

PROGRAMMED REVIEW

1. (p. 203) Video games often promote rapid learning. Such games provide two key elements that underlie learning: a _____ environment and _____. The same dynamic applies to many other learning situations.

2. (p. 204) _____-_____ learning refers to the fact that in the "real world" classical and operant conditioning are often intertwined.

3. (p. 204) An ice cream truck approaches with its bell ringing continuously; a boy runs to the truck, buys an ice cream, and eats it, salivating as he does. In this learning situation, _____ _____ is demonstrated because each time the ice cream truck approaches, the boy will salivate when he hears the bell.

4. (p. 204) Also, the bell is a _____ _____ signaling that reward is available if certain responses are made.

5. (p. 204) _____ _____ is demonstrated when the boy hears the bell, runs to the truck, then buys and eats the ice cream.

6. (p. 204) The boy's _____ responses are altered by classical conditioning while his _____ behavior is shaped by operant conditioning.

7. (p. 204) At one time psychologists considered conditioning a mechanical "stamping in" of responses. Now many think of learning in terms of _____ _____.

8. (p. 204) According to this informational view, learning creates mental _____ (or expectations) about events which, once acquired, alter behavior.

9. (p. 204) Researcher Robert Rescorla explains classical conditioning this way: Because the CS consistently precedes the US, it _____ the US. When the CS is present, the brain _____ the US to follow and prepares the body to respond.

10. (p. 204) The CS gives valuable _____ about the US before the US appears. Pavlovian conditioning is not a "stupid" process that links any two stimuli that happen to occur together. Rather, conditioning occurs as we seek _____ about the world.

11. (p. 204) In operant conditioning we learn to _____ that a certain response will have a certain effect at certain times. Reward tells a person or animal which response was right and discriminative stimuli tell what response to make to get a reinforcer.

12. (p. 204) The _____ value of information helps explain why much human learning occurs without obvious reinforcement by food, water, and the like. Humans readily learn responses that merely have a desired effect or that bring a goal closer.

13. (p. 205) Particularly important to human learning is the value of _____, information about what effect a response has had.

14. (p. 205) Increasing feedback (also called _____ of _____, abbreviated _____) generally leads to faster learning or improved performance.

15. (p. 205) There are numerous ways to apply feedback. For example, tape-recorded feedback can be very helpful. Videotapes are often useful in sports, but are most helpful when a skilled coach directs attention to _____ _____.

16. (p. 205) Feedback is valuable in education too. Feedback is most effective when it is _____, _____, and detailed.

17. (p. 205) Recently, operant learning and feedback have been combined in two interesting ways. One of these is _____ _____, which gives information to students in a format that requires precise answers about information as it is presented.

18. (p. 205) This arrangement supplies frequent feedback to keep learners from practicing _____. It also has the advantage of letting students work at their own _____.

19. (p. 205) In _____-_____ instruction, abbreviated _____, a computer transmits lessons to a display screen while the student responds by typing answers.

20. (p. 205) The computer can provide immediate feedback and can analyze each answer. This capacity allows use of a _____ _____ in which additional information and questions are given when an error is made.

21. (p. 205) The newest CAI programs, which use _____ _____ programs, can even give hints about why an answer was wrong and what is needed to correct it.

22. (p. 205) Elementary school children seem to do especially well with a "computer tutor" due to the rapid feedback and individualized pacing. Among adults, CAI has been found to speed training in the _____ and in _____.

23. (p. 205) CAI also accelerates learning for various _____ subjects (although the final level of skill or knowledge is no higher than that gained by conventional methods).

24. (p. 206) The simplest computerized instruction consists of self-paced _____ and _____. In this format, students answer questions similar to those found in printed workbooks. This has the advantage of instantly providing correct answers.

25. (p. 206) Higher-level CAI programs include _____ _____ which use stories, competition with a partner, sound effects, and game-like graphics to increase interest and motivation.

26. (p. 206) CAI programs also include _____ _____ where students face problems in an imaginary situation or "microworld" through which they can learn basic principles for a variety of subjects.

27. (p. 207) _____ reinforcement occurs when pleasant or desirable consequences follow a response. This increases responding.

28. (p. 207) _____ reinforcement occurs when a response causes the removal of an unpleasant event. This also increases responding.

29. (p. 207) Often positive and negative reinforcement combine. If you are uncomfortably hungry, eating a meal is reinforced by the good-tasting food (_____ reinforcement) and by an end to nagging hunger (_____ reinforcement.

30. (p. 207) _____ is any event that follows a response and decreases its likelihood of occurring again. Thus, this process is different from that of negative reinforcement which tends to increase responding.

31. (p. 207) Punishment can involve either the addition of a negative event or removal of a reinforcer or positive state of affairs. The second type of punishment is called _____ _____ and is exemplified by parents who "ground" their teenage children for misbehavior.

32. (p. 208) Psychologists have learned that the effectiveness of punishment depends greatly on its _____, _____, and _____.

33. (p. 208) Punishment is most effective when it occurs while a response is being made, or _____ afterward and when it is given each time a response occurs.

34. (p. 208) _____ punishment can be extremely effective in stopping behavior. More often, however, punishment only temporarily _____ a response.

35. (p. 208) If the punished behavior is still reinforced, it will usually _____, especially if only mild punishment is used.

36. (p. 208) This effect has been shown experimentally with rats slapped on the paws while bar pressing during extinction. Compared with rats not punished, those whose paws were slapped temporarily _____ responding but their responding did not _____ more rapidly.

37. (p. 208) However, intense punishment may _____ _____ a response. For instance, animals severely punished while eating may never eat again.

38. (p. 208) Three tools useful in controlling simple learning are:
    1) _____, which strengthens a response;
    2) _____-_____, which causes a response to extinguish; and
    3) _____, which suppresses a response.

39. (p. 208) These tools work best in combination. Punishment used without reinforcement is less effective, because punishment only tells a person or an animal that a response was "_____"; it provides no alternative. It does not teach new behaviors.

40. (p. 208) In a situation that poses immediate danger, punishment is most effective when it produces responses _____ with the undesirable response.

41. (p. 209) When punishment is necessary to manage the behavior of an animal, child, or even another adult, keep these tips in mind:
    1) Don't use punishment at all if you can discourage misbehavior in other ways.
    2) Apply punishment during or _____ after misbehavior.
    3) Use the _____ punishment necessary to suppress misbehavior.
    4) Be consistent.
    5) Expect _____ from a punished person.
    6) Punish with kindness and respect.

42. (p. 209)   The basic problem with punishment is that it is usually _____. As a result, people and situations associated with punishment may also be feared or resented.

43. (p. 210)   _____ learning reflects the operation of negative reinforcement. If a dog is placed in a two-compartment cage and shocked in one of the compartments, it will quickly learn to jump to the second compartment to escape the shock.

44. (p. 210)   If a buzzer is sounded ten seconds before the shock is turned on, the animal will learn to jump before the shock begins. This response is known as _____ learning.

45. (p. 210)   Psychologists have theorized that avoidance involves two-factor learning. An animal first learns to feel fear in the presence of the buzzer (a form of _____ _____). Then, leaping from the compartment is rewarded by negative reinforcement in the form of a reduction in fear (a process involving _____ _____).

46. (p. 210)   When drivers learn to fasten their seat belts in order to stop the unpleasant buzzer features in new automobiles, this is an example of _____ conditioning.

47. (p. 210)   _____ conditioning is evident when a driver learns to buckle up before the buzzer sounds.

48. (p. 210)   Once avoidance is learned, it is very _____. This can be explained in informational terms given that once the dog has learned to expect that the buzzer is followed by shock, if the dog leaves before the shock would normally occur, it gets no new information to change the expectancy.

49. (p. 210)   In any situation involving frequent punishment, desires to escape and avoid are activated. For example, children who run away from punishing parents (_____), may soon learn to lie about their behavior (_____).

50. (p. 210)   Punishment can greatly increase _____. Researchers have shown that animals consistently react to pain by attacking whomever or whatever else is around.

51. (p. 210)   Punishment may produce _____, which in turn leads to increased _____. For example, one study found that boys severely punished for aggression at home frequently were aggressive at school.

52. (p. 211)   Humans can anticipate future reward or punishment and react accordingly. For example, extinction of a fear response to electric shock occurs almost _____ when subjects are told the shock will not occur again.

53. (p. 211)   Human learning usually includes a large _____, or mental, dimension, being affected by expectations, information, perceptions, mental images, etc.

54. (p. 211)   Cognitive learning, then, refers to understanding, knowing, anticipating, or otherwise making use of higher mental processes, and extends into the realms of _____, _____, problem solving, and _____.

55. (p. 211)   A _____ _____ is an internal representation of relationships that acts as a guide in gaining an overall mental picture of some stimulus complex.

This principle applies when you must detour or take a new route while driving in a familiar area.

56. (p. 211)   Animals are capable of cognitive learning as well. One experiment showed that chimpanzees permitted to watch fruit being hidden in different places could later return and collect about _____ pieces of fruit each.

57. (p. 211)   Cognitive maps also apply to other kinds of knowledge. For instance, students develop a "map" of psychology while reading a textbook. This may be why students sometimes find it helpful to draw _____ of how they envision concepts fitting together.

58. (p. 211)   Cognitive learning is closely related to _____ (hidden) _____ where learning sometimes occurs with no obvious reinforcement at all. For example, rats allowed to explore a maze without reinforcement show no learning, but when later given food they perform as well as rats rewarded all along.

59. (p. 211)   Learning in this situation may be related to satisfying curiosity or ending boredom. In humans, this phenomenon is probably related to higher level abilities such as _____ future reward.

60. (p. 212)   Much of what is meant by cognitive learning is summarized by the word _____. Specific skills are learned that can be applied to new situations.

61. (p. 212)   Although ideas can be learned through _____ (repetition and memorization), many psychologists believe that learning is more lasting when people use _____ learning where skills are gained by insight and understanding.

62. (p. 212)   As an example, one experiment showed that students taught to calculate the area of a parallelogram by modifying it into a triangle were _____ _____ to solve unusual problems than were students who simply memorized a rule.

63. (p. 213)   Albert Bandura has studied learning through imitation, which is often called _____ learning or _____.

64. (p. 213)   Modeling can be used to: (1) learn new _____; (2) learn to carry out or avoid previously learned responses, depending on what happens to the model for doing the same things; or (3) learn a _____ _____ that can be applied to various situations.

65. (p. 213)   For observational learning to occur, several things must take place. The learner must pay _____ to the model and _____ what was done. Then the learner must be able to _____ the learned behavior.

66. (p. 213)   Also, if a model is _____ or _____, the learner is more likely to imitate the behavior.

67. (p. 213)   This principle is also the case for models who are _____, _____, _____ or high in status.

68. (p. 213)   Once a new response is learned through modeling, normal _____ determines if it will be repeated thereafter.

69. (p. 214) This phenomenon was demonstrated in a classic experiment where children saw models displaying aggression toward a blow-up doll. When later frustrated and allowed to play with the doll, most imitated the attack. A cartoon was only _____ less effective in encouraging aggression than a live model or a filmed model.

70. (p. 214) Research shows that when parents tell a child to do one thing, but model a completely different response, children tend to imitate what the parents _____, and not what they _____.

71. (p. 214) There is reason to believe that television can serve as a model for observational learning. It may teach new antisocial actions and _____ dangerous impulses that viewers already have.

72. (p. 214) Many TV programs give the message that violence is normal, acceptable behavior. For some people, this message can lower _____ against acting out hostile feelings.

73. (p. 214) Disinhibition may even extend to _____-_____ impulses. There is evidence that after a television soap opera character commits suicide, real suicides increase among viewers.

74. (p. 214) TV also presents viewers with a distorted image of minorities, women, sex, alcohol, and authority figures. For example, stable, happy marriages are rarely portrayed on TV. Soap operas average _____ mentions of sexual intercourse per hour. Most workers shown are authority figures.

75. (p. 215) Televised violence is even more disturbing. There are about _____ hours of violence per week. _____-_____ percent of all programs contain violence, averaging 5.2 aggressive acts per hour.

76. (p. 215) More gunshots are fired in one evening of TV than in one year in a medium-sized American city. _____-_____ percent of these shots fail to hit their targets, which makes it seem like violence typically does not end in bloodshed.

77. (p. 215) Also disturbing is the finding that more than _____ of all music videos contain violence, and more than three-fourths of these violent videos include sexual imagery.

78. (p. 215) TV lawmen more often than not contribute to violence rather than prevent it. Murder, robbery, kidnapping, and assault comprise _____ percent of TV crimes.

79. (p. 215) The distortions and stereotypes of "TV land" are cause for concern, especially considering that over _____ percent of all United States households contain a TV. Also, average TV viewing in America now exceeds ____ hours per day.

80. (p. 216) Tannis Williams recently studied residents of a town in northwestern Canada before TV arrived and again two years later. Her research revealed reading development among children _____ when TV was introduced.

81. (p. 216) This natural experiment showed that children's scores on tests of creativity _____. Also, children's perceptions of sex roles became more _____.

82. (p. 216) Williams' study also demonstrated that there was a significant _____ in both verbal and physical aggression for both boys and girls regardless of whether they were high or low in aggression before they began watching TV.

83. (p. 216) Examples of "involuntary" functions which yoga and Zen masters can control include heart _____, _____ pressure, _____ consumption, and temperature of parts of the body.

84. (p. 216) These involuntary functions can now be self-controlled using _____, the application of the general principle of feedback to the control of bodily responses.

85. (p. 217) When you are given feedback, you can repeat successful responses, even if they are subtle. Biofeedback promotes learning by converting bodily processes into a clear signal that provides _____ about correct responses.

86. (p. 217) Biofeedback holds promise as a way to treat _____ problems (illnesses caused mainly by stress or psychological factors).

87. (p. 217) For example, Elmer and Alyce Green have had success in training people to prevent _____ using biofeedback to redirect blood flow away from the head to the extremities.

88. (p. 217) Early successes with biofeedback led many to predict it would be a cure for a long list of ailments. In reality it has proven useful for a more limited set of problems including:
1) relief of muscle-tension headaches and migraine headaches;
2) lowering blood _____ and alleviating irregular heart rhythms;
3) some control of _____ seizures.

89. (p. 217) Questions still remain about the value of biofeedback. Many of the benefits reported may simply reflect _____ _____.

90. (p. 217) Also, the method simply acts as a "mirror" to help a person perform tasks involving _____-_____. Although it can help people make desired changes in their behavior, it does not do anything by itself.

91. (p. 217) Biofeedback has special promise for the rehabilitation of people suffering from _____ damage, _____ disorders, and stroke. For example, Neal Miller has reported on the use of biofeedback to help a child regain use of a paralyzed hand.

92. (p. 217) Alpha waves are one of several distinctive patterns of brain activity that can be recorded with the _____, abbreviated _____.

93. (p. 217) Joseph Kamiya developed a technique whereby subjects are signaled by a _____ or _____ whenever they produce alpha waves.

94. (p. 217) Subjects in early alpha-control experiments reported that high levels of alpha were linked with sensations of _____, _____, passive alertness, or peaceful images.

95. (p. 217) More recently, serious questions have been raised about the use of alpha training to promote deep relaxation. Research has shown that for some people increased alpha output is the product of relaxation; but for others, it occurs at times of _____.

96. (p. 217) Low-cost home "alpha-feedback" machines are so inaccurate that many users are actually listening to _____ _____ from their house wiring rather than their own brain waves.

97. (p. 217) A _____ skill is a series of actions molded into a smooth and efficient performance. Typing, walking, and driving a car are examples.

98. (p. 218) Many such skills begin as simple response chains. However, as skills improve we typically develop _____ _____ for them—mental plans or models of what a skilled movement should be like.

99. (p. 218) Walking is a good example. We use feedback from the body and senses to compare our actions to an internal standard or program. Such monitoring, plus rapid _____, is what allows us to walk on varied surfaces.

100. (p. 218) Eventually skills become _____, or nearly automatic. This ability frees higher brain centers to make decisions and attend to other information.

101. (p. 218) The following points should be kept in mind for optimal skill learning:
    1) Begin by observing and imitating a _____ _____.
    2) Learn _____ _____ to back up motor learning.
    3) Practice should be as _____ as possible so that artificial cues and responses do not become a part of the skill.
    4) Get feedback. Someone experienced should direct attention to correct responses when they occur.
    5) It is better to practice _____ _____ than to break the task into artificial parts.
    6) Learn to evaluate and analyze your own performance.

102. (p. 219) Research has shown that merely thinking about or imagining a skilled performance can aid learning. This technique is called _____ _____.

103. (p. 219) Although mental practice is better than no practice at all, it is still not better than _____ practice. Also, the more familiar you are with a skill, the _____ mental rehearsal helps.

104. (p. 219) Since performance improves after a short rest, motor learning proceeds most efficiently using _____ practice rather than _____ practice.

105. (p. 219) Also, there is evidence that in the long run, new skills learned with _____ practice are retained better than those learned by _____ practice.

106. (p. 219) In the _____ _____ method the beginning skier learns on short, easily managed skis, and moves to progressively longer skis as skill is developed. This example illustrates transfer of training.

107. (p. 219) The graduated length method is specifically an example of _____ transfer, where mastery of one task aids mastery of a second task.

108. (p. 219) In _____ _____, skills developed in one situation conflict with those required for mastery of a new task. Learning to back a car with a trailer attached is a good example.

109. (p. 219) Negative transfer occurs _____ often than positive transfer and it is usually brief. It is most likely to occur when a _____ response must be made to an _____ stimulus.

110. (p. 221) There are several techniques which you can use to break a bad habit. The place to begin is by discovering what is _____ the habit and remove, avoid, or delay the _____.

111. (p. 221) Another suggestion is to try to get the same reinforcement with _____ responses. For example, instead of being rewarded with peace and quiet for yelling at her children, a young mother might achieve the same rewards by reinforcing the children when they are quiet and playing constructively.

112. (p. 221) Another way to control the habit is to avoid or narrow down _____ that elicit the habit. To help reduce smoking, remove ashtrays, matches, and extra cigarettes. Also, try smoking only in one place, such as an uninteresting room at home.

113. (p. 222) Another strategy for controlling antecedents is to break _____ _____ that precede an undesired behavior. The key idea is to scramble the chain of events that leads up to the undesired response.

114. (p. 222) Making an _____ _____ in the presence of stimuli that usually precede the bad habit can also be useful. Persons who bite their nails in particular situations could learn to put their hands in their pockets, chew gum, comb their hair, etc.

115. (p. 222) Use _____ _____, that is, deliberately repeat a bad habit until it becomes boring, painful, or produces fatigue, to associate a bad habit with discomfort.

116. (p. 222) Utilizing _____ is one of the most direct of all approaches to changing bad habits. For example, a study of families asked to write down and post the numbers shown on their electric meter each day showed that they greatly reduced their energy use.

117. (p. 223) If you would like to break a bad habit, pay close attention to _____, the _____ itself, and the _____ that follow the behavior. Be familiar with the general plan, provided in this chapter, for breaking a bad habit.

118. (p. 224) Hundreds of studies involving over 10,000 children all point to the conclusion that if large groups of children watch a great deal of televised violence, they will be more prone to behave _____.

119. (p. 224) Children may learn new aggressive actions by watching violent behavior, or they may learn that violence is "okay." Younger children may simply remember that when TV heroes were bothered, they aggressed. TV dramas tend to give the message that violence leads to _____ and _____.

120. (p. 224) Psychologists Rowell Huesmann and Neil Malamuth believe that habitual aggression is mostly learned during the first _____ years of life. By then, aggression becomes a set style of behavior that is very hard to change.

121. (p. 224) Not only does TV encourage violence, it may also lower _____ to violent acts. Victor Cline found that among groups of boys shown a brutal and bloody fight scene, those boys who averaged 42 hours per week of TV viewing showed much less emotion compared to those boys who watched little or no TV.

122. (p. 224) In another study, college men saw five R-rated slasher films that depicted violence against women. The men consistently reported _____ levels of anxiety when viewing the last film as compared with the first.

123. (p. 224) Televised violence can make aggression more likely, but it does not "cause" it to occur. Many factors affect the chances that hostile thoughts will be translated into

actions.   Among children, one such factor is the extent to which a child
_____ with aggressive characters.

124. (p. 225) TV can also be a _____ model. Over 150 research reports evaluating the impact of educational programs such as "Sesame Street" and "The Electric Company" have been positive.

125. (p. 225) TV can be an effective model for "prosocial" attitudes and responses. Over 200 studies have shown that prosocial behavior on TV increases prosocial behavior by viewers. As one example, children in one experiment who watched a TV program that emphasized helping were _____ _____ than others to help a puppy in distress even when it meant skipping a chance to win prizes.

126. (p. 225) Children typically model _____ TV viewing habits, and they are guided by their reactions to programs. Be familiar with the TV guides provided for parents in this chapter.

SELF-TEST

1. (p. 204) True-False. In the "real world" operant and classical conditioning often occur together.

2. (p. 204) True-False. The information processing view of conditioning holds that a response is "stamped in" during conditioning.

3. (p. 204) The information processing view of learning stresses that learning creates _____ about events that alter behavior.
   a. predictions
   b. instincts
   c. expectancies
   d. consistencies

4. (p. 205) Which of the following is *not* directly involved in learning?
   a. KR
   b. practice
   c. reinforcement
   d. instinct

5. (p. 205) Which of the following is *not* a factor in programmed instruction?
   a. analyzes each answer and uses branching programs
   b. breaks learning into a series of small steps
   c. provides constant feedback to correct errors
   d. requires precise answers about information as it is presented

6. (p. 206) The simplest CAI consists of
   a. instructional games
   b. branch programming
   c. educational simulations
   d. self-paced drill and practice

7. (p. 207) _____ _____ increases responding by ending discomfort.
   a. Positive punishment
   b. Negative reinforcement
   c. Negative punishment
   d. Positive reinforcement

8. (p. 207) Which of the following is *not* true of punishment?
   a. Severe punishment can be extremely effective in stopping behavior.
   b. The effectiveness of punishment depends greatly on its timing, consistency, and intensity.
   c. Responses suppressed by mild punishment often reappear later.
   d. Punishment is best delayed until well after an undesirable behavior has occurred.

9. (p. 208)   Which of the following conditions would *not* enhance the effectiveness of punishment?
    a. punishment given on a partial schedule so that resistance to extinction is high
    b. use of rewards to reinforce other responses while punishing the undesirable response
    c. punishment that produces responses incompatible with the undesired response
    d. punishment applied during or immediately after the undesired response

10. (p. 209)   Which of the following is *not* true of the use of punishment?
    a. People and situations associated with punishment also tend to become aversive.
    b. Aversive stimuli associated with punishment encourage escape and avoidance learning.
    c. Weak punishment typically overwhelms the effects of even strong reinforcers.
    d. Punishment can greatly increase aggression.

11. (p. 210)   Escape and avoidance learning are maintained by
    a. positive reinforcement   c. generalized reinforcement
    b. primary reinforcement   d. negative reinforcement

12. (p. 210)   True-False.   Children who receive a lot of physical punishment from parents or teachers tend to be well disciplined, good students who respect and like authority figures.

13. (p. 211)   When humans or animals develop an overall mental picture of a stimulus complex (such as a town or a maze) it is referred to as
    a. superstitious behavior   c. a cognitive map
    b. observational learning   d. response chaining

14. (p. 211)   When no obvious reinforcement is available, yet learning occurs, we are probably speaking of the type of cognitive learning known as
    a. avoidance learning   c. motor skill learning
    b. latent learning   d. learning to learn

15. (p. 212)   In _____ learning, skills are acquired by insight and understanding.
    a. rote   c. discovery
    b. latent   d. generalized

16. (p. 213)   Which of the following does *not* tend to facilitate observational learning?
    a. model is rewarded for observed responses
    b. model is engaged in constructive activities rather than violent ones
    c. model is high in status
    d. model is attractive, rewarding, or admired

17. (p. 214)   True-False. In many situations modeling is more effective than verbal instruction.

18. (p. 214)   Which of the following is *not* true about television?
    a. Television may disinhibit dangerous impulses that viewers already have.
    b. Most victims on TV are single women, young boys, or nonwhites.
    c. Eighty-one percent of all programs contain violence.
    d. Music videos can be especially prosocial because only a small number of them contain violence.

19. (p. 217)   Biofeedback has been shown to be at least somewhat helpful in the treatment of all of the following *except*
    a. retinal blindness   c. epileptic seizures
    b. migraine headaches   d. high blood pressure

20. (p. 217) One unanswered question regarding biofeedback is whether many of the benefits reported may simply reflect
    a. latent learning
    b. placebo effects
    c. transfer of training
    d. general relaxation

21. (p. 217) Brain wave patterns can be recorded using an _____ machine.
    a. EKG
    b. EMG
    c. EEG
    d. EGG

22. (p. 218) Motor skills usually first develop as response chains, but later are guided by mental models called
    a. automated images
    b. overlearned engrams
    c. motor programs
    d. cognitive habits

23. (p. 218) Which of the following would *not* be expected to optimize skill learning?
    a. learning verbal rules to back up motor learning
    b. using mental practice to refine motor programs
    c. using negative practice to decrease knowledge of results
    d. practicing the task in natural units rather than artificial parts

24. (p. 219) Which of the following is *not* true about how the pattern of practice and rest periods affect learning and performance?
    a. Improvement in performance of a motor skill is most rapid when spaced practice is used.
    b. Massed practice lowers performance during training.
    c. In the long run, skills learned with massed practice are retained better than those learned by spaced practice.
    d. Both massed and spaced practice produce similar amounts of learning after a short break in training.

25. (p. 219) Learning to balance and turn on a bicycle should make it easier for you to learn riding a motorcycle. This fact is an example of
    a. learning to learn
    b. negative transfer
    c. motor programming
    d. positive transfer

26. (p. 219) When mastery of one task adversely affects the acquisition of a new task, this is known as
    a. learning set
    b. positive transfer
    c. negative transfer
    d. negative practice

27. (p. 221) When trying to break a bad habit, which of the following is *not* recommended?
    a. Remove, avoid, or delay what is reinforcing the habit.
    b. Increase the number of cues that elicit the bad habit to help remind you to stop.
    c. Make an incompatible response in the presence of stimuli that usually precede the bad habit.
    d. Seek the same reinforcement from new responses.

28. (p. 222) When you deliberately repeat a bad habit until it becomes boring, painful, or produces fatigue, so as to break the habit, the technique is called _____ _____.
    a. habit reversal
    b. negative practice
    c. modified punishment
    d. negative repetition

29. (p. 224) True-False. Hundreds of studies have concluded that children who watch a great deal of television violence are more prone to behave aggressively.

30. (p. 224) In addition to encouraging imitation of violence, television also adds to tendencies toward aggression by
    a. reducing emotional sensitivity to violence
    b. stimulating frustration among viewers
    c. romanticizing competition
    d. increasing the number of outlets for hostilities

31. (p. 225) Television can be a force for prosocial attitudes and responses. This was demonstrated by one study in which
    a. children punished for watching violent shows became less violent and more helpful
    b. children watching a program that emphasized helping were more willing to assist an animal in distress
    c. children told they would be given prizes for helping other children were more likely to do so after viewing violent programs
    d. none of the above

ANSWERS — PROGRAMMED REVIEW

1. responsive; information
2. Two-factor
3. classical conditioning
4. discriminative stimulus
5. Operant conditioning
6. involuntary; voluntary
7. information processing
8. expectancies
9. predicts; expects
10. information; information
11. expect
12. adaptive
13. feedback
14. knowledge of results; KR
15. key details
16. frequent; immediate
17. programmed instruction
18. errors; pace
19. computer-assisted; CAI
20. branching program
21. artificial intelligence
22. military; business
23. college
24. drill and practice
25. instructional games
26. educational simulations
27. Positive
28. Negative
29. positive; negative
30. Punishment
31. response cost
32. timing, consistency, intensity
33. immediately
34. Severe; suppresses
35. reappear
36. slowed; extinguish

37. permanently suppress
38. reinforcement; non-reinforcement; punishment
39. wrong
40. incompatible
41. immediately; minimum; anger
42. aversive
43. Escape
44. avoidance
45. classical conditioning; operant learning
46. escape
47. Avoidance
48. persistent
49. escape; avoidance
50. aggression
51. frustration; aggression
52. immediately
53. cognitive
54. memory, thinking; language
55. cognitive map
56. 12
57. pictures
58. latent learning
59. anticipating
60. understanding
61. rote; discovery
62. better able
63. observational; modeling
64. responses; general rule
65. attention; remember; reproduce
66. successful; rewarded
67. attractive, rewarding, admired
68. reinforcement
69. slightly
70. do; say
71. disinhibit

72. inhibitions
73. self-destructive
74. 1.5
75. 188; Eighty-one
76. Eighty-five
77. half
78. 85
79. 99; 7
80. declined
81. dropped; stereotyped
82. increase
83. rate; blood; oxygen
84. biofeedback
85. information
86. psychosomatic
87. migraine headaches
88. pressure; epileptic
89. general relaxation
90. self-regulation
91. nerve; muscular
92. electroencephalograph; EEG
93. tone, light
94. pleasure, relaxation
95. heightened arousal
96. electrical noise
97. motor
98. motor programs
99. corrections

100. automated
101. skilled model; verbal rules; lifelike; natural units
102. mental practice
103. actual; more
104. spaced; massed
105. spaced; massed
106. graduated length
107. positive
108. negative transfer
109. less; new; old
110. reinforcing; reinforcement
111. new
112. cues
113. response chains
114. incompatible response
115. negative practice
116. feedback
117. antecedents; response; consequences
118. aggressively
119. success; popularity
120. 10
121. sensitivity
122. lower
123. identifies
124. positive
125. more willing
126. parents'

ANSWERS — SELF-TEST

1. True
2. False
3. c
4. d
5. a
6. d
7. b
8. d
9. a
10. c
11. d

12. False
13. c
14. b
15. c
16. b
17. True
18. d
19. a
20. d
21. c

22. c
23. c
24. c
25. d
26. c
27. b
28. b
29. True
30. a
31. b

Chapter 9

Memory

CONTENTS

TERMS AND CONCEPTS

memory
encoding
storage
retrieval
sensory memory
icon
echo
short-term memory (STM)
working memory
long-term memory (LTM)
digit-span test
chunks of information
recoding
rehearsal
constructive processing
pseudo-memories
memory structure
network model
tip-of-the-tongue state
feeling-of-knowing reactions
memory tasks
recall

verbatim memory
recognition
distractors
false positive
relearning
savings score
redintegration
eidetic imagery
internal images
nonsense syllables
curve of forgetting
memory traces
memory decay
disuse
cue-dependent forgetting
state dependent learning
interference
retroactive interference
proactive interference
repression
suppression
flashbulb memories

retrograde amnesia
anterograde amnesia
consolidation
electroconvulsive shock (ECS)
hippocampus
engram
progressive part method

cognitive interview
mnemonics
keyword method
procedural memory (skill memory)
fact memory
semantic memory
episodic memory

IMPORTANT INDIVIDUALS

George Miller
Wilder Penfield
Elizabeth Loftus
Geoffrey Loftus
A. R. Luria
William Chase
Anders Ericsson

Herman Ebbinghaus
Roger Brown
James Kulik
Brenda Milner
Karl Lashley
Eric Kandel
R. Edward Geiselman
Ron Fisher

PROGRAMMED REVIEW

1. (p. 229) _____ is an active system that receives, stores, organizes, alters, and recovers information.

2. (p. 229) In some ways, memory acts like a computer. Information to be recorded is first _____, or changed into a usable form, then _____, or held in the system.

3. (p. 229) To be used, memories must be _____, or taken out of storage. In order to "remember" something all three of these processes must occur.

4. (p. 229) To be stored for a long time, information must pass through three stages of memory. Incoming information first enters _____ memory, where an exact copy of what is seen or heard is held.

5. (p. 229) If the information is seen, an _____, or image, persists for about $\frac{1}{2}$ second afterward. Hearing is held as a brief _____ in sensory memory, lasting as long as 2 seconds.

6. (p. 229) _____ _____ determines what information moves from sensory memory to the second memory system.

7. (p. 229) This second system is called _____-_____ memory, abbreviated _____. Memories are also brief here, but longer than sensory memories.

8. (p. 229) Short-term memories can be stored as images, but more often they are encoded by _____, especially in remembering words and letters.

9. (p. 230) Short-term memory acts as a _____ storehouse for _____ amounts of information. Unless the information is important it is quickly removed from STM and forever lost.

10. (p. 230) While STM prevents our minds from being cluttered with trivia, it also provides a _____ _____ where we do much of our thinking, like dialing a phone number, remembering a shopping list, and the like.

11. (p. 230) STM is severely affected by any _____ or _____. You've probably experienced this when dialing a phone number, getting a busy signal, and not remembering the number when you try to redial.

12. (p. 230) Information that is important or meaningful is transferred to the third memory system called _____-_____ memory, abbreviated _____.

13. (p. 230) LTM acts as a _____ storehouse for information and appears to have almost _____ capacity to store information.

14. (p. 230) Information in LTM is stored on the basis of _____ and _____, not by sound as in STM.

15. (p. 230) When new information enters STM it is related to knowledge stored in LTM. This gives the new information _____ and makes it easier to store in LTM.

16. (p. 231) In studying short-term memory, George Miller found that we can normally retain about _____ _____ of information, the "magic number" for memory.

17. (p. 231) This number was determined through his use of the _____-_____ test in which subjects must remember a series of numbers.

18. (p. 232) Humans can retain more than seven individual bits (or single "pieces") of information by converting them into _____ of information. Through this process we combine several individual units into one "stack" of information.

19. (p. 232) Chunking _____ information into larger units. Most often it does so by taking advantage of units that already have meaning in LTM. For example, one memory experiment found that subjects remembered best when the letters used were read as familiar meaningful chunks such as TV, IBM, USN, and YMCA than when unconnected letters were employed.

20. (p. 232) Short-term memory traces appear to weaken and disappear very rapidly, but can be prolonged by _____, mentally repeating the information.

21. (p. 232) One experiment showed that when rehearsal is prevented, as little as _____ seconds after presentation of a stimulus, subjects could not recall the stimulus.

22. (p. 232) In Wilder Penfield's research, patients whose brains were electrically stimulated seemed to have _____ _____ of long-forgotten events.

23. (p. 233) This finding led Penfield to claim that all memories are absolutely permanent. However, this claim is exaggerated because many events never get past _____-_____ memory.

24. (p. 233) Also, brain stimulation only produces memory-like experiences in about _____ percent of cases. Most reports are more like dreams, and many are clearly fictional.

25. (p. 233) Memory experts Elizabeth and Geoffrey Loftus conclude that there is little evidence that long-term memories are absolutely permanent. Rather, it is more accurate to say that they are _____ permanent, or long-lasting.

26. (p. 233) There is another reason to doubt Penfield's claim. As new long-term memories are

formed, older memories are often updated, changed, lost, or revised. This process is called _____ _____.

27. (p. 233)   Research shows that gaps in memory may be filled in by logic, guesses, or new information. It is possible to have _____ _____ (or false memories) for things that never happened.

28. (p. 234)   News stories often give the impression that hypnosis can be used to help recall lost or blocked memories. However, recent research has shown that a hypnotized person is more likely than normal to use _____ to fill in gaps in memory.

29. (p. 234)   When hypnotized subjects are given _____ information, they tend to weave it into their memories. Also, "leading" questions asked during hypnosis can alter memories.

30. (p. 234)   A further problem with the use of hypnosis in reviving memories is that even when a memory is completely false, the hypnotized person's confidence in it can be _____.

31. (p. 234)   Hypnosis increases false memories more than it does true ones. For instance, subjects in one experiment were able to slightly improve their memory scores under hypnosis, but _____ percent of their new memories were incorrect.

32. (p. 233)   Long-term memory may record one _____ separate bits of information in a lifetime.

33. (p. 234)   Long-term memories appear to be highly organized. The _____, or arrangement, of this organization may be based on rules, images, categories, symbols, similarity, formal meaning, or personal meaning.

34. (p. 234)   The _____ _____ of memory proposed by Collins and Quillian hypothesizes that LTM is organized as a network of linked ideas. When ideas are farther apart, it takes a longer chain of associations to connect them.

35. (p. 235)   The experience of having an answer or a memory just out of reach is sometimes called the _____-____-_____-_____ state.

36. (p. 235)   One study illustrating partial memory showed that students were often able to accurately guess the first and last letter and even the number of syllables of the word they were trying to remember. They were also able to give words that sounded like or meant the same as the defined word. This illustrates that memory is not an _____-____-_____ event.

37. (p. 235)   A related finding is that people can often tell beforehand if they are likely to remember something. This ability is based on a state called the _____ of _____. Such reactions are easy to observe on television game shows, where they occur just before contestants are allowed to answer.

38. (p. 235)   There are three commonly used memory _____ employed to measure memory.

39. (p. 235)   To _____ means to supply or reproduce important facts and information. Tests of this type usually require _____ (word-for-word) memory.

40. (p. 235) A type of recall is required when you take an _____ examination, or when you memorize a poem until you can recite it without looking.

41. (p. 236) The order in which information is memorized has an effect on recall because of the _____ _____ effect. The greatest number of errors occurs for items in the middle of a list.

42. (p. 236) The last items in a list appear to be remembered best because they are still in _____. The first items are also remembered because they entered an "empty" short-term memory where they could be _____.

43. (p. 236) A multiple-choice examination is based on a testing procedure called _____. It is a more sensitive measure of memory than recall.

44. (p. 236) Recognition memory can be amazingly accurate. Subjects shown 2560 photographs and then asked to pick those they had seen from each of 280 pairs of pictures could do so with _____ to _____ percent accuracy.

45. (p. 236) Recognition is usually _____ to recall. This fact explains why police departments use photographs or a lineup to identify criminal suspects.

46. (p. 236) While recognition is usually superior, it depends greatly on the kind of _____ used. These elements are false items included along with an item to be recognized.

47. (p. 236) If the distractors are very similar to the correct item, memory may be poor. A reverse problem sometimes occurs when only one choice looks like it could be correct. This fact can produce a _____ _____, or false sense of recognition.

48. (p. 237) For example, witnesses describing a criminal as black, tall, or young might make a _____ _____ if the lineup only includes one suspect who is black among whites, tall among short individuals, or young among older persons.

49. (p. 237) In a classic memory experiment, a Greek passage was read daily to a young child. Years later, the child could recall nothing, but could memorize the same passage _____ percent faster than others of equal difficulty.

50. (p. 237) Thus, testing memory by _____ shows a savings in the time or effort necessary to remaster previously learned material.

51. (p. 237) Relearning is measured by a _____ _____. For example, if you memorize a list in 60 minutes and much later cannot recall any of it, but can relearn it in 45 minutes, your savings is 25 percent (15 divided by 60 times 100).

52. (p. 237) When an entire past experience is reconstructed from one small recollection, this is called _____.

53. (p. 237) It usually involves _____ _____ rather than formal learning.

54. (p. 237) _____ _____, known informally as photographic memory, occurs when a person has visual images clear enough to be scanned or retained for at least 30 seconds after viewing a picture.

55. (p. 237) Eidetic imagery is most often observed in childhood. About _____ children out of a hundred can give detailed descriptions of pictures they have viewed for only seconds.

56. (p. 237) Eidetic imagery appears to disappear with age. This change is no great loss, as the majority of eidetic memorizers have no better _____-_____ memory than average.

57. (p. 238) Eidetic memory depends on images projected on a surface in front of a person. A second type of "photographic" memory occurs in people who have very vivid _____ _____.

58. (p. 238) Such was the case of Mr. S, reported by A.R. Luria, who had a completely photographic memory. Unfortunately, Mr. S remembered so much that he could not separate what was _____ from what was _____.

59. (p. 239) Another case of exceptional memory has been studied by William Chase and Anders Ericsson. Their subject, Steve, practiced memorizing longer lists of digits until he was able to remember around _____ digits.

60. (p. 239) Steve relied on other associations, such as ages or dates, to chunk digits. But his short-term memory did not improve, nor was he able to memorize more than seven _____.

61. (p. 239) Chase and Ericsson believe Steve's performance shows that exceptional memory may be merely a _____ extension of normal memory. However, in the case of Mr. S, this hypothesis is open to debate since he could memorize strings of digits, meaningless consonants, mathematical formulas, and poems in foreign languages.

62. (p. 240) In a series of famous early experiments, Herman Ebbinghaus learned long lists of _____ _____, meaningless three letter words like GEX or WOJ.

63. (p. 240) Ebbinghaus used nonsense syllables to prevent being swayed by prior learning. By waiting various amounts of time before testing his memory, he constructed a _____ of _____.

64. (p. 240) The curve shows that forgetting is _____ at first and then is followed by a slow decline.

65. (p. 240) The Ebbinghaus curve shows that less than _____ percent of nonsense syllables were remembered after only two days had passed. However, forgetting is not lost nearly as quickly for meaningful information.

66. (p. 240) For example, tests show that students of Spanish forget an average of _____ percent of their vocabulary during the first three years after they stop studying. After this early decline, however, little more forgetting occurs during the next 20 years.

67. (p. 241) The most obvious reason for forgetting is also the most commonly overlooked. In many cases we forget because we never _____ (formed a memory of) the information in the first place. This is illustrated by Nickerson and Adams' experiments in which it was found that very few students could accurately draw a penny or even recognize a drawing of a real one among fakes.

68. (p. 241) One view of why forgetting occurs says that _____ _____ (changes in nerve cells or brain activity) fade or decay over a period of time.

69. (p. 241)   Such decay seems to apply to the loss of sensory memories and to STM and has appeal as an explanation for long-term forgetting. Perhaps long-term memory traces fade from _____ and eventually become so weak they cannot be retrieved.

70. (p. 241)   Reasons exist to question this view. One is the seemingly forgotten memories recovered through _____. Another is that disuse fails to explain why some unused memories fade and others are carried for life.

71. (p. 241)   A third contradiction is revealed by those elderly people who have vivid memories of trivial and long-forgotten events from the _____, while _____ memories are fading.

72. (p. 241)   There appear to be several additional possibilities that explain LTM forgetting. One emphasizes that many memories appear to be available but not accessible, because _____ present at the time of learning are no longer present when the time comes to retrieve information.

73. (p. 241)   In theory, memory will be best if you study in the _____ _____ where you will be tested. Since this is often impossible, it may be wise to vary your study environment so that memories are not tied too strongly to a particular place.

74. (p. 242)   The bodily state that exists during learning can be a strong cue for later memory. For this reason, information learned under the influence of a drug is best remembered when the drugged state occurs again. This effect is known as _____ _____ _____.

75. (p. 242)   A similar effect applies to _____ states. For instance, Gordon Bower found that people who learned a list of words while in a particular mood recalled the list better when experiencing that same mood.

76. (p. 242)   Another aspect of forgetting is demonstrated in an experiment in which one group of college students learned lists of nonsense syllables, then slept for eight hours and were retested. They performed better than a second group that remained awake for eight hours. This difference is based on the fact that new learning can _____ with previous learning.

77. (p. 242)   In another supporting experiment, subjects were asked to memorize new lists of words only to be remembered until the next day. Subjects who learned only one list recalled _____ percent, while those who learned 20 lists (one each day) were only able to recall _____ percent of the last list one day later.

78. (p. 243)   The sleeping college students remembered more because _____ interference was held to a minimum. This term refers to the tendency for new learning to inhibit retrieval of old learning.

79. (p. 243)   Retroactive interference is demonstrated by this arrangement:
Experimental group: Learn A   Learn B   Test A
Control group: Learn A   _____   Test A
When the experimental group does not remember as much when tested on Task A as the control group, retroactive interference has occurred.

80. (p. 243)   A second basic type of interference is _____ _____.
It is demonstrated when experimental subjects in this arrangement remember less of Task B than controls:
Experimental group: Learn A   Learn B   Test B
Control group: Rest   Learn B   Test B

81. (p. 244)   Many people find that they tend to remember happy, positive events better than disappointments and irritations. A clinical psychologists would call this tendency _____, or motivated forgetting. In it, painful, threatening, or embarrassing memories are actively held out of consciousness by forces within one's personality.

82. (p. 244)   Repression can be distinguished from _____, a conscious attempt to put something out of mind.

83. (p. 244)   By not thinking about something unpleasant, you have merely suppressed a memory. Clinicians consider true repression an _____ event. When a memory is repressed, we are unaware that forgetting has even occurred.

84. (p. 244)   We have much evidence of the existence of repression, but do not understand why some traumatic events are frozen in memory at times of personal tragedy, accident, or other significant events. Psychologists Roger Brown and James Kulik refer to these as _____ _____.

85. (p. 244)   One reason such memories can be so vivid is that the hormones _____ and _____, which have been shown to enhance memory formation, are secreted during times of emotion or stress.

86. (p. 244)   Not all flashbulb memories are negative. In general, vivid memories are most likely when an event is _____, important, or _____.

87. (p. 244)   A head injury may cause a "gap" in memories preceding the accident. This effect is called _____ _____.

88. (p. 244)   In contrast, _____ amnesia involves forgetting events that occur after an injury or trauma.

89. (p. 244)   Retrograde amnesia can be understood by recognizing that transferring memories from short-term storage to long-term storage takes a certain amount of time. The process is called _____.

90. (p. 244)   Support for the notion of memory consolidation comes from work showing that a mild electric shock to the brain, known as _____ _____ and abbreviated _____, can prevent consolidation.

91. (p. 245)   For example, rats given a painful _____ for stepping off a platform would continue to step off if ECS was used to block consolidation immediately after each learning experience.

92. (p. 245)   ECS has been employed as a psychiatric treatment for severe _____ in humans. Used in this way, electroshock therapy also causes memory loss.

93. (p. 245)   If enough time is allowed to pass between learning and ECS, the memory is unaffected, apparently because consolidation is already complete. This is why people with head injuries usually only lose memories from _____ before the accident, while older memories remain intact.

94. (p. 245)   In controlled dosages, various drugs can speed up consolidation, although they do not directly increase memory. These drugs include metrazol, strychnine, _____, _____, and _____.

95. (p. 245) However, if the dosage of a stimulant drug is too high by even a small amount, memory will be _____.

96. (p. 245) Memory losses are common when a person overindulges in _____. Blackouts may cause loss of memory for a few minutes to several hours.

97. (p. 245) Such losses appear to result because alcohol impairs _____ and _____ of memories. Research makes it clear that studying while drunk is an excellent way to lower test scores.

98. (p. 245) An area of the brain of particular importance to memory is the _____. This structure, buried deep within the brain, seems to act as a sort of "switching station" between short-term and long-term memory.

99. (p. 245) Humans who have had the hippocampus damaged show a striking inability to store _____ _____, as in the case reported by Brenda Milner. Her patient suffered from anterograde amnesia and, therefore, lived eternally in the present.

100. (p. 245) At one time researchers sought to discover where in particular memory is stored in the brain. For instance, Karl Lashley, a pioneering brain researcher, began in the 1920s to search for an _____, or memory trace.

101. (p. 245) Lashley taught animals to run mazes and then removed parts of their brains to see how memory of the maze changed. He discovered that it mattered little which part of the cortex was removed. Only the _____ removed correlated to memory loss.

102. (p. 245) There is now extensive evidence that learning alters the electrical activity, structure, and chemistry of the brain. For example Eric Kandel has found that learning in the marine snail *Aplysia* occurs when certain nerve cells in a circuit alter the amount of _____ chemicals they release.

103. (p. 246) Such changes essentially determine which circuits get strengthened and which become weaker. Others have shown that an increase in _____ _____ for transmitter chemicals occurs during learning.

104. (p. 246) Several suggestions can be made for improving memory. One of these emphasizes the importance of _____ or knowledge of results.

105. (p. 246) Feedback can help you check to see if you are learning and can help identify material that needs extra practice. A prime means of providing feedback is _____, repeating to yourself what you have learned.

106. (p. 247) One experiment illustrating this point showed that the best memory score was earned by students who spent _____ percent of their time reciting and only _____ percent reading.

107. (p. 247) Numerous studies have shown that memory is greatly improved by _____, that is, study continued beyond bare mastery.

108. (p. 247) Another suggestion is to boil down paragraphs to one or two important terms or ideas. Such careful and _____ marking of a text makes memorization more manageable.

109. (p. 247) _____ practice is generally superior to _____ practice. By scheduling your time into brief study sessions, you maximize your study skills.

110. (p. 247) _____ class notes can be extremely helpful. In fact, outlining your outlines so that the organization of ideas becomes clearer and simpler can also help.

111. (p. 247) It is generally better to practice whole packages of information rather than smaller parts. Try to study the largest _____ amount of information possible at one time.

112. (p. 247) For very long or complex material, try the _____ _____ method: Break a learning task into short sections, first study part "A," then parts "A" and "B," then "A," "B," and "C," and so forth.

113. (p. 247) Whenever you must learn something in order, remember the _____ _____ effect and give special attention to items in the _____ of the list, since they are most easily forgotten.

114. (p. 247) Remember that _____ after study reduces interference. Also, include ample breaks between subjects.

115. (p. 247) _____ shortly before an exam to cut down the time during which you must remember details. However, hold the amount of new information you try to memorize to a minimum, as it will confuse you and interfere with what you already know.

116. (p. 248) Remember that the best _____ cues for remembering are those that were present during encoding. You should elaborate information as you learn and form images that include the new information, and relate it to knowledge you already have.

117. (p. 248) This principle is demonstrated by one study where students were asked to give three words closely related in meaning to each of 600 words they were later asked to recall. They correctly recalled _____ percent of the original word list when the words supplied by the students were used as cues to jog memory.

118. (p. 248) Successful recall is usually the result of a planned _____ of memory. For example, one study found that students were most likely to recall a name that eluded them if they made use of partial information.

119. (p. 248) R. Edward Geiselman and Ron Risher have developed a technique called the _____ _____ to help police detectives jog the memory of eyewitnesses.

120. (p. 248) Cognitive interviewing is a good example of how active probing often helps improve recall. When used properly, it produces _____ percent more correct information than standard questioning.

121. (p. 248) There are four simple steps you can use when searching for a "lost" memory. First, say or write down _____ you can remember that relates to the information you are seeking.

122. (p. 248) Secondly, try to recall events of information in different _____. Let your memories flow out backward or start with whatever impressed you the most.

123. (p. 248) As a third step, recall from different _____. Review

events by mentally standing in a different place. Try to view information as another person would remember it.

124. (p. 248) And finally, mentally put yourself back in the situation where you learned the information. Try to mentally recreate the _____ _____ or relive the event. As you do, include sounds, smells, details of weather, nearby objects, other people present, etc.

125. (p. 250) _____ refers to any kind of memory system or aid.

126. (p. 250) Mnemonic techniques are effective alternatives to rote learning, as demonstrated by many studies. One experiment showed that subjects using mnemonics remembered an average of _____ items from a 100 item list, while those using simple or rote learning remembered an average of _____.

127. (p. 250) There are several basic principles of mnemonics. One is to use _____ _____, since visual memory is usually superior to verbal memory.

128. (p. 250) Another aid is to make things _____, since this technique facilitates the transfer of information from short-term to long-term memory.

129. (p. 250) Along with this, try to make information _____ by connecting it with information already stored in LTM.

130. (p. 250) Finally, try to form _____, _____, or exaggerated mental associations, since connecting two ideas, terms, or images in this way increases the likelihood you will remember them later.

131. (p. 250) Mnemonics can be used to avoid rote memorization. As one example, use the _____ method. To remember that pajaro means bird in Spanish, visualize a parked car full of birds.

132. (p. 251) Mnemonics are not a complete substitute for normal memory. They are not likely to be helpful unless you make extensive use of _____. Mnemonics can be thought of as a built-in hint in your memory.

133. (p. 251) There are three mnemonic techniques which can be used to help remember things in order. One of them is to _____ a _____. Connecting one item to the next can be quite useful for lists of twenty or more items.

134. (p. 251) Another suggestion is to take a _____ _____. By mentally "placing" objects or ideas along a familiar path, you can later retrace your steps mentally to remember the items.

135. (p. 251) A third tool is to use a _____. As an example, the first letter or syllable of words or ideas can be formed into another word which can serve as a reminder of the order you wish to remember.

136. (p. 252) Many psychologists have concluded that long-term memories fall into at least two categories. One of these, _____ memory (or "_____" memory), includes basic conditioned responses and response chains like those involved in typing, solving a puzzle, etc.

137. (p. 252) It is likely that skill memories register in "lower" brain areas, especially the _____, and that they appeared early in the evolution of the brain.

138. (p. 252) The second category of long-term memories is sometimes called _____ memory. It is the ability to learn specific information such as names, faces, words, dates, or ideas.

139. (p. 252) Most of our factual knowledge about the world is almost totally immune to forgetting. Such facts make up a part of LTM called _____ _____.

140. (p. 252) Semantic memory has no connection to time or places. In contrast, _____ _____ is autobiographical; it records life events in time sequences.

141. (p. 252) In general, episodic memories are more easily _____ than semantic memories because new information constantly pours into the system. (Flashbulb memories are an exception.)

SELF-TEST

1. (p. 229) The memory system that stores information as icons or echoes is
   a. long-term memory   c. working memory
   b. short-term memory   d. sensory memory

2. (p. 229) Which of the following is *not* true of short-term memory?
   a. Most often memories are encoded on the basis of meaning and importance.
   b. Information that is lost from STM is gone forever.
   c. STM is brief, easily interrupted, and limited in capacity.
   d. It provides a working memory where we do most of our thinking.

3. (p. 230) Two weeks after memorizing a list of words you try to remember the word "wheat" and can't. You are more likely to say _____ because of the way in which memories are encoded in LTM.
   a. heat   c. grain
   b. what   d. brown

4. (p. 231) Which of the following is a test used to measure STM?
   a. Ishihara   c. digit-span
   b. recoding   d. relearning

5. (p. 231) George Miller has shown that humans can normally retain about how many bits of information in STM?
   a. 3   c. 13
   b. 7   d. 4 for numbers, 8 for words

6. (p. 232) The process of _____ allows us to organize information into larger, meaningful units so that greater STM storage is possible.
   a. rehearsing   c. construction
   b. encoding   d. chunking

7. (p. 232) A good way to keep information in STM or to increase the chances of transfer to LTM is through
   a. frequent retrieval   c. repression
   b. rehearsal   d. consolidation

8. (p. 233) True-False. There is little evidence that long-term memories are absolutely permanent; rather they are only relatively permanent, or long lasting.

9. (p. 233) One example of constructive processing is
    a. pseudo-memories   c. consolidation
    b. eidetic imagery   d. mental scripts

10. (p. 234) Which of the following is not true of the relationship between hypnosis and memory?
    a. Hypnosis decreases false memories more than it does true ones.
    b. A hypnotized person is more likely than normal to use imagination to fill in gaps in memory.
    c. "Leading" questions asked during hypnosis can alter memories.
    d. When hypnotized subjects are given false information, they tend to weave it into their memories.

11. (p. 234) True-False. According to the network model proposed by Collins and Quillian, LTM is organized such that when ideas are "farther" apart, it takes a shorter chain of associations to connect them.

12. (p. 235) True-False. While people used to think that partial memory existed, we now know that you either remember something or you don't.

13. (p. 236) The serial position effect indicates that the most easily forgotten material in a sequence is
    a. the first part   c. the middle part
    b. the last part   d. not the items *per se*, but their order

14. (p. 236) Which of the following is *not* true of recognition?
    a. It is a more sensitive testing procedure than recall.
    b. Recognition yields a savings score based on the number of items initially identified correctly.
    c. Recognition can be greatly influenced by the presence of distractors.
    d. Exams involving multiple choice are an example of the recognition procedure.

15. (p. 237) When a person is tested by relearning, how do we know a memory still exists?
    a. through the use of a savings score
    b. through the use of essay tests
    c. through the use of multiple-choice tests
    d. because one memory can serve as a cue to trigger another

16. (p. 237) When you smell a perfume that triggers a reconstructive memory, you are experiencing
    a. recall   c. relearning
    b. recognition   d. redintegration

17. (p. 237) True-False. The incidence of eidetic imagery is much greater among adults than children since adults have had more opportunity to develop memory skills.

18. (p. 237) Which of the following is *not* true of "photographic memory?"
    a. It may involve eidetic images projected on a surface out in front of a person.
    b. It may involve vivid internal images.
    c. Complete "photographic memory," as in the case of Mr. S, may be more a liability than an asset.
    d. The majority of eidetic memorizers have much better than average long-term memory.

19. (p. 240) Ebbinghaus conducted a famous set of experiments to
    a. develop a mnemonic system
    b. study relearning by teaching Greek passages to his child

        c. develop a curve of forgetting
        d. discover flashbulb memories

20. (p. 240) True-False. We forget relatively more information long periods after it has been learned than after short periods.

21. (p. 241) Which of the following facts supports the view that some forgetting occurs through decay or disuse of memories?
        a. Recovery of seemingly forgotten memories may occur through redintegration.
        b. Some memories fade away and others are carried for life.
        c. Among elderly people, recent memories may fade, while long past memories remain vivid.
        d. None of the above.

22. (p. 242) Which of the following is *not* a factor in forgetting?
        a. Cues present at the time of learning may not be available at the time of retrieval.
        b. New learning may interfere with memories of previously learned material.
        c. Previously learned material may interfere with the recall of new material.
        d. Through suppression, unpleasant memories may be held out of consciousness by forces within one's personality.

23. (p. 243) True-False. If on the same night, you cram for a psychology exam and then cram for a biology exam, memory for biology may be reduced due to proactive interference, while memory for psychology may suffer from retroactive interference.

24. (p. 244) True-False. Flashbulb memories are relatively short-lived memory traces that result from intense stimuli such as the temporary white images you see when a flashbulb is operated.

25. (p. 244) True-False. A person suffering from retrograde amnesia can learn new information, but has great difficulty remembering events prior to whatever caused the amnesia.

26. (p. 245) The process of consolidation refers to
        a. how information gets into short-term memory
        b. how information in long-term memory is recalled
        c. how information in short-term memory is recalled
        d. how information is transferred from STM to LTM

27. (p. 245) Which of the following can be used to retard or prevent consolidation?
        a. amphetamines   c. caffeine
        b. ECS   d. nicotine

28. (p. 245) Damage to which area of the brain may result in a striking inability to store new memories?
        a. hypothalamus   c. amygdala
        b. hippocampus   d. cerebellum

29. (p. 247) Which of the following is *not* a useful aid to increasing memory?
        a. recitation   c. organization
        b. underlearning   d. knowledge of results

30. (p. 247) Which of the following will *not* tend to increase your ability to retain information in memory?
        a. using spaced versus massed practice to improve concentration
        b. studying the largest meaningful amount of information possible at one time

    c. learning in a novel environment to heighten your attention
    d. trying to sleep after study if possible, and using ample breaks between subjects

31. (p. 248) Which of the following is *not* true of the cognitive interview?
    a. This technique was designed by Geiselman and Fisher to help police detectives jog the memory of eyewitnesses.
    b. There are four steps involved, including the idea that you should say or write down everything you can remember that relates to the information you are seeking.
    c. One of the steps involved in this technique is the notion of trying to recall information from different viewpoints.
    d. The cognitive interview produces 85 percent more correct information than standard questioning when used properly.

32. (p. 250) Mnemonics are
    a. memory traces linked with changes in RNA
    b. an example of the network model of LTM
    c. lasting images that are frozen in memory at times of personal tragedy
    d. memory systems or aids

33. (p. 250) Which of the following is *not* a basic principle of mnemonics?
    a. make things familiar
    b. form bizarre or unusual mental associations
    c. focus on words or verbal memories
    d. make things meaningful

34. (p. 252) Which of the following is *not* a true statement with respect to procedural memory?
    a. It includes basic conditioned responses and response chains.
    b. This is the memory that a person with amnesia lacks.
    c. It is registered in "lower" brain areas.
    d. It can be fully expressed only as actions.

35. (p. 252) Episodic memory refers to
    a. occasions when one part of a larger memory will trigger thoughts of previous life episodes
    b. transient memories which usually decay before transfer into LTM
    c. the mental dictionary or encyclopedia of basic knowledge stored in LTM
    d. the autobiographical part of LTM which records life events involving times or places

ANSWERS — PROGRAMMED REVIEW

1. Memory
2. encoded; stored
3. retrieved
4. sensory
5. icon; echo
6. Selective attention
7. short-term; STM
8. sound
9. temporary; small
10. working memory
11. interruption, interference
12. long-term; LTM
13. permanent; limitless
14. meaning, importance
15. meaning
16. seven bits
17. digit-span
18. chunks
19. recodes
20. rehearsal
21. 18
22. vivid memories
23. short-term
24. three
25. relatively
26. constructive processing

27. pseudo-memories
28. imagination
29. false
30. unshakable
31. 80
32. quadrillion
33. structure
34. network model
35. tip-of-the-tongue
36. all-or-nothing
37. feeling of knowing
38. tasks
39. recall; verbatim
40. essay
41. serial position
42. STM; rehearsed
43. recognition
44. 85; 95
45. superior
46. distractors
47. false positive
48. false identification
49. 25
50. relearning
51. savings score
52. redintegration
53. personal experience
54. Eidetic imagery
55. eight
56. long-term
57. internal images
58. important, trivial
59. 80
60. consonants
61. learned
62. nonsense syllables
63. curve of forgetting
64. rapid
65. 30
66. 30
67. encoded
68. memory traces
69. disuse
70. redintegration
71. past; recent
72. cues
73. same room
74. state dependent learning
75. emotional
76. interfere
77. 80;15
78. retroactive
79. Rest
80. proactive interference
81. repression

82. suppression
83. unconscious
84. flashbulb memories
85. adrenaline; ACTH
86. surprising, emotional
87. retrograde amnesia
88. anterograde
89. consolidation
90. electroconvulsive shock; ECS
91. shock
92. depression
93. immediately
94. nicotine, caffeine, amphetamines
95. disrupted
96. alcohol
97. encoding; consolidation
98. hippocampus
99. new memories
100. engram
101. amount
102. transmitter
103. receptor sites
104. feedback
105. recitation
106. 80; 20
107. overlearning
108. selective
109. Spaced; massed
110. Organizing
111. meaningful
112. progressive part
113. serial position; middle
114. sleep
115. review
116. cues
117. 90
118. search
119. cognitive interview
120. 35
121. everything
122. orders
123. viewpoints
124. learning environment
125. Mnemonics
126. 72; 28
127. mental pictures
128. meaningful
129. familiar
130. bizarre, unusual
131. keyword
132. images
133. form a chain
134. mental walk
135. system
136. procedural; skill

137. cerebellum
138. fact
139. semantic memory
140. episodic memory
141. forgotten

ANSWERS — SELF-TEST

1.	d	19.	c
2.	a	20.	False
3.	c	21.	d
4.	c	22.	d
5.	b	23.	True
6.	d	24.	False
7.	b	25.	True
8.	True	26.	d
9.	a	27.	b
10.	a	28.	b
11.	False	29.	b
12.	False	30.	c
13.	c	31.	d
14.	b	32.	d
15.	a	33.	c
16.	d	34.	b
17.	False	35.	d
18.	d		

Chapter 10

Cognition and Creativity

CONTENTS

TERMS AND CONCEPTS

thinking (cognition)
cognitive psychology
delayed response problems
insight
multiple-stick problem
mental imagery
synesthesia
stored images
created images
muscular imagery
kinesthetic sensations
micromovements
concepts
concept formation
conjunctive concept
relational concept
disjunctive concept
prototypes
denotative meaning
connotative meaning
semantic differential
semantics

symbols
phonemes
morphemes
grammar
syntax
transformation rules
American Sign Language (ASL)
conditional relationships
mechanical solutions
trial-and-error (rote) problem solving
solutions by understanding
random search strategy
heuristic
ideal problem solving
selective encoding
selective combination
selective comparison
fixation
functional fixedness
inductive thinking
deductive thinking
logical thinking

illogical thinking
fluency
flexibility
originality
divergent thinking
convergent thinking
Unusual Uses Test
Consequences Test
Anagrams Test
stages of creative thought
representativeness

base rate
problem framing
mental set
syllogism
all-or-nothing thinking
stereotypes
brainstorming
cross-stimulation effect
artificial intelligence
computer simulations
expert systems

IMPORTANT INDIVIDUALS

Shakuntala Devi
Wolfgang Köhler
David Premack
Donald Griffin
Stephen Kosslyn
Jerome Bruner
Charles Osgood
Noam Chomsky
Beatrice Gardner
Allen Gardner
Penny Patterson

Roger Fouts
Debbi Fouts
Karl Duncker
John Bransford
Robert Sternberg
Janet Davidson
Jerome Singer
Donald MacKinnon
Daniel Kahneman
Amos Tversky
Kemal Ebcioglu

PROGRAMMED REVIEW

1. (p. 257) Thinking or _____ refers to the mental manipulation of images, concepts, words, rules, symbols, and percepts.

2. (p. 257) The challenge of studying thinking is similar to figuring out how a computer works by repeatedly asking, "I wonder what would happen if I did this?" In _____ psychology the "computer" is the brain, and thinking is the "programming" we seek to understand.

3. (p. 257) The incredibly complex thinking of humans is demonstrated in the remarkable feats of Shakuntala Devi. She holds the "world record" for mental calculation having once multiplied two _____ digit numbers in her head, giving the answer in 28 seconds.

4. (p. 257) In its most basic form, thinking is the _____ _____ of a problem or situation.

5. (p. 257) Animals   demonstrate   internal   representation   in   _____ _____ problems. For example, a hungry animal allowed to watch as food is hidden under one of three goal boxes can usually pick the correct one if the choice can be made without too long a delay.

6. (p. 257) Wolfgang Köhler felt that the problem solving observed in chimpanzees revealed a capacity for _____, a sudden reorganization of the elements of a problem whereby the solution becomes evident.

7. (p. 257) One of Köhler's subjects, Sultan, was given a _____-_____ problem. Sultan had to use one stick to retrieve a second, slightly-longer stick, which

could be used to retrieve an even longer stick which would reach a banana placed out of reach.

8. (p. 258) David Premack has provided additional evidence of insightful problem solving by a chimp. Premack showed a chimpanzee a videotape of an actor jumping below a bunch of bananas. The chimp was then shown several photographs and chose one of the actor _____ onto a _____.

9. (p. 258) Evidence that animals are capable of intelligent thought is supported by the following findings:
    1) Monkeys can learn to select, from among three objects, the one that _____ from the other two;
    2) When sugar water is moved farther from a bee hive each day, the bees begin to look for the new location _____ the water is moved;
    3) Pigeons can learn to select photographs of humans from among various pictures;
    4) A chimpanzee can recognize itself in a _____.

10. (p. 258) To verify animal thinking, Donald Griffin suggests that we must observe behavior that is _____ and _____ to changing circumstances. Thinking is implied by actions that appear to be planned with an awareness of likely results.

11. (p. 258) As one example, sea _____ select suitably sized rocks and use them to hammer shellfish loose for eating. They then use the rock to open the shell.

12. (p. 258) Such examples have been challenged. For instance, Epstein, Lanza, and Skinner have conditioned pigeons to duplicate seemingly insightful behavior. David Premack, however, replies that the pigeons only achieved the _____ of thinking, because their behavior was strongly guided by reinforcement.

13. (p. 258) The basic units of thought include images, muscular responses, concepts, and language or symbols. Grandmaster chess player Miguel Najdorf uses several of these when simultaneously playing 45 chess games while _____.

14. (p. 259) A survey of 500 people found that _____ percent have visual imagery and _____ percent auditory imagery. Over _____ percent had imagery that included movement, touch, taste, smell, and pain.

15. (p. 259) When we speak of images we are usually referring to a mental "_____." But as the results of this survey show, images may involve the other senses as well.

16. (p. 259) Some people experience a rare form of imagery called _____ in which images cross normal sensory barriers. For instance, hearing music may induce a burst of colors or tastes as well as sounds.

17. (p. 259) Stephen Kosslyn discovered that mental images are not _____, like photographs. Instead they can be moved about as needed.

18. (p. 260) _____ images can be used in problem solving to bring prior experience to bear. To generate more original solutions, _____ images may be used.

19. (p. 261) Recent research indicates that people who have good imaging ability also tend to score higher on tests of _____. Thus, an artist may completely picture a proposed sculpture before beginning work.

20. (p. 260) Stephen Kosslyn found that the _____ an image is, the harder it is to "see" its details. To apply this to problem solving, try forming over-sized images of things you want to think about.

21. (p. 260) It is surprising to note that we think with our bodies as well as our heads. Jerome Bruner believes that we often represent things in a kind of _____ _____ created by actions or implicit actions.

22. (p. 260) A great deal of information is contained in _____ sensa-tions (sensations from the muscles and joints). As one talks, these sensations help structure the flow of ideas.

23. (p. 260) One of the reasons thinking can be hard work is that it is accompanied by muscular tension and _____ throughout the body.

24. (p. 260) This fact has been demonstrated in one classic study where a subject was asked to imagine that he was hitting a nail with a hammer. As he did, there was a clearly discernible burst of activity in the muscles of his unmoving _____.

25. (p. 260) A concept is a word or idea that represents a _____ of objects or events. They allow us to think more _____, free from distracting details.

26. (p. 260) Concept _____ is the process by which we classify information into meaningful categories. At its most basic, this phenomenon involves experience with _____ and _____ instances of the concept.

27. (p. 260) Adults are more likely to acquire concepts by learning or formulating _____. This process is generally more efficient than exposure to examples.

28. (p. 261) Several general types of concepts have been identified. A _____ _____ refers to a class of objects having one or more features in common.

29. (p. 261) Conjunctive concepts are sometimes called "_____" concepts because to belong to the concept class, an item must have "this feature, and this feature, and this feature." For example, "motorcycles" have wheels, engines, and handle bars.

30. (p. 261) _____ concepts classify objects on the basis of their relation-ship to something else, or by the relationship between features of an object. Examples include "large," "above," "left," and "north."

31. (p. 261) _____ _____ refer to objects that have at least one of several possible features. They possess an either-or quality. For example, a "strike" is either a swing or a miss or a pitch down the middle, or a foul ball.

32. (p. 261) Most people do not picture a list of features when thinking of a concept. Rather, they think in terms of _____, or ideal models.

33. (p. 261) Reliance on prototypes suggests that not all instances of a concept are equally _____. That fact explains why concept identification becomes difficult when there is no prototype for comparison.

34. (p. 261) Generally speaking, concepts have two types of meaning. The _____ meaning of a word or concept is its explicit definition. The _____ meaning is its emotional or personal meaning.

35. (p. 261) Charles Osgood has used the _____ _____ to measure connotative meaning. He found that when words or concepts are rated on a series of scales, most of their connotative meaning boils down to the dimensions: _____-_____, _____-_____ and _____-_____.

36. (p. 262) While thought can take place without language, most thought does lean heavily on language because it allows us to _____ the world into easily manipulated _____.

37. (p. 262) Study of the meaning of words and language is called _____. It is here that the connection between language and thought becomes most evident.

38. (p. 263) True language must provide _____ which can be used to stand for objects and ideas.

39. (p. 263) The symbols we call words are built out of _____, the basic speech sounds, and _____, speech sounds collected into meaningful units.

40. (p. 263) A second requirement of true language is that it have a _____, or set of rules for the combination of sounds into words and words into sentences.

41. (p. 263) One part of grammar is known as _____, rules pertaining to word order in sentences.

42. (p. 263) Rather than concentrating on the "surface" of language as does traditional grammar, linguist Noam Chomsky has emphasized _____ rules that allow us to change core ideas into a variety of sentences.

43. (p. 263) The third, and perhaps most essential, characteristic of language is that it is _____. It can be used to produce new possibilities or to generate new ideas.

44. (p. 264) While animals do communicate, it is quite limited. Animal communication seems to lack the _____ quality of human language.

45. (p. 264) Early experiments involving attempts to teach chimpanzees to talk were a failure. Even after six years of intensive training, one subject named Vicki could only say _____ words.

46. (p. 264) The first major breakthrough in this area came from the work of Beatrice and Allen Gardner who used a combination of operant conditioning and imitation to teach Washoe to use _____ _____ abbreviated _____, a set of hand gestures used by the deaf.

47. (p. 264) Washoe now has a vocabulary of about _____ signs and can construct _____-word sentences.

48. (p. 264) Some critics are skeptical of Washoe's haphazard arrangement of words. An answer to this criticism has come from the work of Premack, who taught Sarah to use _____ words consisting of _____ _____ arranged on a magnetized board.

49. (p. 264) Sarah has been required to use proper word order in answering questions, labeling things "same" or "different," classifying things by color, shape, and size, and constructing _____ sentences.

50. (p. 264)   One of Sarah's most outstanding achievements is use of sentences involving
_____ _____. For example, "If
Sarah take apple, then Mary give Sarah chocolate."

51. (p. 265)   Other primates have been taught language as well. For example, Penny Patterson has
taught a young gorilla named Koko to use over _____ signs.

52. (p. 265)   Patterson regards conversations held about _____ events and _____ a
strong indication of Koko's comprehension.

53. (p. 265)   Several psychologists have recently expressed doubt that apes can really use language. For one thing, the chimps rarely "speak" without _____.

54. (p. 265)   Also, many of their seemingly original sentences turn out to be responses to questions
or _____ of signs made by the teacher.

55. (p. 265)   Further, it often appears that the apes are simply performing chains of
_____ _____ to get food or other rewards.

56. (p. 265)   Roger and Debbi Fouts have recently countered such criticism. An analysis they
performed of some 6000 conversations between chimps showed that only ___ percent
had anything to do with food. Also, they have videotaped conversations between
chimps that took place when no humans were present to _____ them.

57. (p. 265)   A number of different approaches to thinking and reasoning in problem solving can be
identified. _____ solutions may be achieved by trial and error,
or by _____. Such problem solving is inefficient when more than a few alternative solutions exist.

58. (p. 265)   When a solution is achieved by rote, we mean that thinking is guided by a learned set
of _____.

59. (p. 265)   Many problems are unsolvable by mechanical means or by the use of habitual modes
of thought. In this case a higher level of thinking based on _____
is necessary.

60. (p. 265)   This fact is demonstrated in the classic studies of Karl Duncker. He studied the
problem-solving process of students and discovered two phases. First, the student had
to discover the _____ _____ of a correct
solution. The second stage was marked by _____ (workable)
_____ from which a specific solution was selected.

61. (p. 266)   Solving problems often requires a strategy. If the number of alternatives is small, a
_____ _____ strategy may work. This is an example of
trial-and-error problem solving in which all possibilities are tried.

62. (p. 266)   A _____ or problem-solving strategy reduces the number of
alternatives that a thinker must consider. For example, try to identify how the
current state of affairs differs from the desired goal. Then find steps that will
reduce the difference.

63. (p. 266)   Another heuristic is to try working _____ from the desired goal
to the starting point or current state. Other examples are discussed in your text that
you should remember.

64. (p. 266)   Perhaps the most valuable heuristic of all is having a _____ thinking

strategy. John Bransford has developed one based on five steps that can lead to effective problem solving.

65. (p. 266) To apply Bransford's "IDEAL" strategy you should _____ the problem, _____ it clearly, and then _____ possible solutions and relevant knowledge. Next, you must _____ by trying a possible solution or hypothesis. Finally, you should _____ at the results and learn from them.

66. (p. 267) You may be headed for a mistake if an insight is not _____. As an example, one study rated how "warm" (close to an answer) students felt while solving insight problems. Students who had insights usually jumped directly from "cold" to the correct answer. Those who _____ felt "warmer," and then "very warm," usually gave wrong answers.

67. (p. 267) Robert Sternberg and Janet Davidson have hypothesized that insight involves three abilities. The first is _____ _____, which refers to the ability to select information that is relevant to a problem while ignoring that which is not.

68. (p. 267) _____ _____ also produces insights by bringing together seemingly unrelated bits of useful information.

69. (p. 267) A third source of insights is _____ _____, which is the ability to compare new problems to old information or to problems already solved.

70. (p. 267) The ease with which a solution is achieved in problem solving is related to a variety of factors. A very important barrier to problem solving is _____, the tendency to get hung up on inappropriate solutions or to become blind to other alternatives.

71. (p. 267) A prime example of this tendency is _____ _____, the inability to see new uses (functions) for familiar objects, or for objects that have been used in a particular way.

72. (p. 267) Karl Duncker found functional fixedness to be a problem when experimental subjects were asked to mount a candle on a vertical board using a variety of common objects. When the objects were presented in boxes, solution was difficult because the boxes were seen as _____, rather than items necessary to complete the task.

73. (p. 268) There are several other blocks that prevent creative thinking. One of these, _____ barriers, refers to inhibition and fear of making a fool of oneself, fear of making a mistake, inability to tolerate ambiguity, and/or excessive self-criticism.

74. (p. 268) _____ barriers refer to values which hold that fantasy is a waste of time; playfulness is for children; reason, logic, and numbers are good, and/or feelings, intuitions, pleasure, and humor are bad or have no place in problem solving.

75. (p. 268) _____ barriers include conventions about uses (functional fixedness), meanings, possibilities, and taboos.

76. (p. 268) _____ barriers are habits leading to a failure to identify important elements of a problem.

77. (p. 269)   Creative thinking involves more than mechanical, insightful, or understanding modes of thinking. We must also add _____ thinking (going from specific facts or observations to general principles) or _____ thinking (going from general principles to specific situations).

78. (p. 269)   Thinking may also be _____ thinking (proceeding from given information to new conclusions on the basis of explicit rules) or _____ thinking (intuitive, associative, or personal).

79. (p. 269)   _____ is defined as the total number of suggestions to a problem you can produce.

80. (p. 269)   _____ is defined as the number of times you shift from one class of possible uses to another.

81. (p. 269)   _____ refers to how novel or unusual your suggestions in solving a problem are.

82. (p. 269)   By totaling the number of times you showed fluency, flexibility, and originality, we could rate the creativity of your thinking. Speaking more generally, we would be rating your capacity for _____ thinking.

83. (p. 269)   Psychologist Jerome Singer has found that most people daydream sometime each day. Two of the most common daydream "plots" are the _____ _____ and the _____ _____ themes.

84. (p. 269)   Daydreams often fill a need for _____ when a person performs a routine or monotonous task and they improve the ability to delay immediate _____ so that future goals can be achieved.

85. (p. 269)   Fantasy can be a valuable outlet for _____ impulses. Studies confirm that discharging hostility in fantasy can reduce the impulse to behave aggressively.

86. (p. 269)   Perhaps the greatest value of fantasy is its contribution to _____, to which it is directly linked.

87. (p. 269)   For most people, fantasy and daydreaming are associated with positive _____ adjustment, lower levels of _____, and greater mental flexibility or creativity.

88. (p. 269)   _____ thinking is the most widely used measure of creative problem solving. It is the process by which many possibilities are developed from one starting place.

89. (p. 269)   In routine problem solving, there is one correct answer, and the problem is to find it. This leads to _____ thought where lines of thought converge on the correct answer.

90. (p. 269)   There are several tests of divergent thinking. In the _____ _____ a person is asked to think of as many uses for an object as possible.

91. (p. 269)   In the _____ _____ the object is to answer questions phrased in "what-if" form, where the subject tries to list as many reactions as possible.

92. (p. 269)   In the _____ _____ subjects are given a word like "creativity" and asked to make as many new words as possible by rearranging the letters.

93. (p. 270)   Tests of divergent thinking apparently tap something quite different from intelligence. Generally there is _____ _____ between such tests and IQ test scores.

94. (p. 270)   Creativity is more than divergent thinking. To be creative, problem solutions must be more than novel, unusual, or original. They must also be _____ or _____, and must meet the demands of the problem.

95. (p. 270)   A good summary of the sequence of events in creative thinking proposes five stages. The first step is _____, where the problem must be defined and important dimensions identified.

96. (p. 270)   _____ is next, where individuals saturate themselves with as much information pertaining to the problem as possible.

97. (p. 270)   The third stage, _____, involves a period during which all attempted solutions will have proven futile, and the person leaves the problem "cooking" in the background.

98. (p. 270)   The stage of incubation is often ended by a rapid insight or series of insights which mark the fourth stage referred to as _____.

99. (p. 270)   The final step, _____, is to test and critically evaluate the solution obtained during the stage of illumination. If the solution proves faulty, the thinker reverts to the stage of _____.

100. (p. 271) Psychologist David MacKinnon has discovered several important factors about creative people. First, while most creative people have above average IQ, there was _____ _____ in average IQ between highly creative and less creative people in the same field.

101. (p. 271) Creative people have a greater than average range of _____ and _____, and they are more fluent in combining ideas from different sources.

102. (p. 271) The creative person has an _____ to experience, and shows a relative lack of inhibition about thoughts, feelings, and fantasies.

103. (p. 271) Creative people enjoy _____ _____, ideas, concepts, and possibilities. Their creative work is an end in itself.

104. (p. 271) Highly creative people value _____ and have a preference for _____. They are nonconforming in their work, but otherwise are not particularly unusual or bizarre.

105. (p. 272) We often make decisions on the basis of _____, rather than by logic. Doing so may provide quick answers, but it can also be misleading and sometimes disastrous.

106. (p. 272) Daniel Kahneman and Amos Tversky have studied how people make decisions in uncertain situations. They have found that human judgment is often seriously _____.

107. (p. 272) One error in thinking they have pointed out is the intuitive error called
_____. That is, a choice that
seems to be representative of what we already know is given greater weight.

108. (p. 272) A second common error in judgment involves ignoring the _____ _____,
or underlying probability of an event. In many high-risk situations, ignoring this
factor is the same as thinking you are an exception to the rule.

109. (p. 273) Kahneman and Tversky found that the way a problem is stated, or _____,
affects decisions. People often give different answers to the same problem posed in
slightly different ways.

110. (p. 274) There are several factors which can contribute to difficulties in thinking and problem
solving. One of these factors is the limiting effects of a _____ _____.

111. (p. 275) Another major thinking difficulty focuses on the process of _____
reasoning.

112. (p. 275) This process can be demonstrated in simple sequences involving a set of premises
(assumptions) and a conclusion in the format known as a _____.

113. (p. 275) A syllogism can be evaluated for the _____ of its reasoning and for
the _____ of its conclusion.

114. (p. 275) Another very basic source of thinking errors is oversimplification. In the first type,
_____-_____-_____ thinking, things are classified as absolutely
right or wrong, good or bad, or in other ways that prevent appreciation of the complexity of most life problems.

115. (p. 275) The other type of oversimplification, thinking in terms of _____,
is particularly troublesome when human relationships are involved.

116. (p. 275) Several suggestions can be offered as to how to begin increasing creativity. One of
these is to define the problem _____. Whenever possible, enlarge the
definition of problems for which you seek creative solutions.

117. (p. 276) A variety of experiments show that people make more original, spontaneous, and
imaginative responses when exposed to others (models) doing the same thing, so
create the _____ _____.

118. (p. 276) Trying to hurry or force a problem solution may simply encourage fixation on a dead-
end, so always allow time for _____.

119. (p. 276) Creativity requires divergent thinking, so remember to seek _____
_____. Attempt to shift your mental "prospecting" to new areas.

120. (p. 276) Edward de Bono suggests a technique to help with this process. He recommends that
you _____ look up words in the dictionary and _____ each
to the problem.

121. (p. 276) Representing a problem in a variety of ways is often the key to solution. One way to
do this is to look for _____.

122. (p. 276) Various studies suggest that people are most likely to be creative when they are free
to play with ideas and solutions without having to worry about being

_____. Especially in the first stages of creative thinking, it is important to avoid _____ your efforts.

123. (p. 277) _____ is an alternative approach to enhancing creativity that involves keeping production and criticism of ideas completely separate.

124. (p. 277) As ideas are freely generated an interesting _____-_____ effect takes place, in which one participant's ideas trigger ideas for others.

125. (p. 277) The four basic rules for successful brainstorming are:
   1) _____ of an idea is absolutely barred;
   2) _____ or combination with other ideas is encouraged;
   3) _____ of ideas is sought; and
   4) _____, remote, or wild ideas are sought.

126. (p. 277) As an aid to the brainstorming method, a creativity checklist is suggested. The key terms here include:
   1) Redefine
   2) _____   6) _____
   3) _____   7) _____
   4) _____   8) _____
   5) Minify   9) Combine

127. (p. 278) In 1988, Kemal Ebcioglu devised a computer program that writes harmonies remarkably similar to Bach's. Ebcioglu employed 350 rules that govern the harmonization process to produce a program that displays what is known as
_____ _____.

128. (p. 278) Artificial intelligence (AI) refers to computer programs capable of doing things that require intelligence when done by people. AI is based on the fact that many tasks can be reduced to a set of _____ applied to a body of _____.

129. (p. 278) Increasingly, cognitive psychologists are using AI as a research tool in two basic ways. In _____ _____, programs are used as analogs to human behavior, especially problem solving. The computer acts as a "laboratory" for testing models of cognition.

130. (p. 278) _____ are programs that display advanced knowledge of a specific topic or skill. Such programs have been created to predict the weather, to analyze geologic formations, to diagnose disease, etc.

131. (p. 278) Working with AI has helped especially to clarify differences between novices and experts. Research on chess masters, for example, shows that their skills are based on specific organized _____ and acquired _____.

132. (p. 278) Becoming a star performer does not come from some general strengthening of the mind or from better memory. Master players have superior ability to recognize _____ that suggest what lines of play should be explored next.

133. (p. 278) Expertise also allows more _____ processing, or fast, fairly effortless thinking based on experience with similar problems. This frees attention and "space" in short-term memory that can be used to work on the problem.

134. (p. 278) Experts in one area do not automatically become better _____ _____ elsewhere. Nor do they become generally smarter.

135. (p. 279) Likewise, expert systems are very adept with a narrow range of problem solving, but they are "idiots" at everything else. They process information without regard for the _____ of actions, which might be disastrous in unanticipated situations.

SELF-TEST

1. (p. 257) Of the following, which are problems that can be used to demonstrate representational thought in animals?
   a. delayed response problems   c. Consequences Test
   b. response deprivation tasks   d. Anagrams Test

2. (p. 257) Köhler tested insight among chimpanzees using
   a. delayed response problems   c. items from the Unusual Uses Test
   b. multiple-stick problems   d. the Consequences Test

3. (p. 259) Of the following, which is *not* an internal representation you use in thinking?
   a. language   c. images
   b. muscular responses   d. photographs

4. (p. 259) The ability to experience a given sensation in a totally different physical dimension is called
   a. kinesthesia   c. anesthesia
   b. synesthesia   d. euthanasia

5. (p. 260) Which of the following is *not* a type of imagery that can be used in problem solving?
   a. stored images   c. transformational imagery
   b. muscular imagery   d. created images

6. (p. 260) True-False. We often think with our bodies as well as our heads; that is, we often represent things in a kind of muscular imagery created by implicit actions.

7. (p. 260) Which of the following is *not* true of concept formation?
   a. In early childhood, much concept formation involves experience with positive and negative instances of the concept.
   b. Rule learning in concept formation is generally less efficient than exposure to examples.
   c. Concept formation is the process whereby we classify information into meaningful categories.
   d. As adults, we are more likely to acquire concepts by learning or formulating rules.

8. (p. 261) True-False. Conjunctive concepts refer to a class of objects having one or more features in common.

9. (p. 261) _____ concepts refer to objects that have at least one of several possible features.
   a. Conjunctive   c. Relational
   b. Disjunctive   d. Conditional

10. (p. 261) "Left," "above," "north," and "up" are all examples of what type of concept?
    a. conjunctive   c. disjunctive
    b. relational   d. conditional

11. (p. 261) True-False. Most people tend to think of concepts in terms of prototypes since all instances of a concept are considered equally representative.

12. (p. 261) The explicit definition of a word or concept is its
    a. denotative meaning
    b. connotative meaning
    c. semantic differential
    d. derogatory meaning

13. (p. 261) The connotative meaning of words can be measured using
    a. Osgood's Inventory
    b. the Consequence Test
    c. the Denotative Scale
    d. the semantic differential

14. (p. 263) The basic speech sounds built into words are called
    a. symbols
    b. phonemes
    c. grammar
    d. morphemes

15. (p. 263) Speech sounds collected into meaningful units are called
    a. symbols
    b. phonemes
    c. grammar
    d. morphemes

16. (p. 263) Of the following, which is *not* a requirement that defines true language?
    a. productivity
    b. symbols
    c. grammar
    d. simplicity

17. (p. 263) True-False. One part of grammar, known as semantics, refers to rules pertaining to word order in sentences.

18. (p. 263) Noam Chomsky has argued that we do not learn all sentences we might ever utter, but rather we actively and creatively generate them by applying
    a. transformation rules
    b. syntax
    c. divergent thinking
    d. semantics

19. (p. 264) Which of the following is *not* true of language learning in primates?
    a. The first breakthrough came with the learning of ASL by Washoe.
    b. One of the most outstanding achievements of Sarah was her use of sentences involving conditional relationships.
    c. Koko is another language-using chimp trained to communicate by pressing buttons on a computer keyboard.
    d. Viki, a chimp taught to speak, could only say four words after six years of intensive training.

20. (p. 265) Which of the following is *not* a criticism that has been leveled against the interpretation that primates actually use and understand true language?
    a. The primates rarely "speak" without prompting.
    b. Their vocabularies are quite small and they cannot master important features such as proper word order.
    c. Many of their seemingly original sentences turn out to be imitations of signs made by their trainer.
    d. It often appears they are simply performing instrumental responses to get food.

21. (p. 265) Which of the following is *not* true of problem solving?
    a. Problem solving by understanding involves first understanding the general properties of a correct solution and then selecting a correct solution from a number of functional solutions.
    b. Solution by insight occurs when an answer suddenly appears after a period of unsuccessful thought.
    c. Mechanical problem solving may be achieved by trial and error but is quite inefficient when more than a few alternative solutions exist.
    d. When solution is achieved by rote, we mean that thinking has proceeded erratically until insight is achieved.

22. (p. 266) Problem-solving strategies that reduce the number of alternatives that a thinker must consider are called
    a. random searches
    b. heuristics
    c. idea problem solving
    d. insights

23. (p. 267) Which of the following is *not* an ability involved in solving problems that require insight as detailed by Sternberg and Davidson?
    a. selective attention
    b. selective combination
    c. selective comparison
    d. selective encoding

24. (p. 267) True-False. The point at which a useful idea or insight becomes set in one's mind is known as fixation.

25. (p. 268) Values which hold that fantasy is a waste of time, playfulness is for children only, or feelings, intuitions, pleasure, and humor have no place in problem solving all define _____ barriers to creative thinking.
    a. perceptual
    b. emotional
    c. cultural
    d. learned

26. (p. 269) Which of the following definitions regarding thinking is *not* true?
    a. Constructive thinking involves going from specific facts or observations to general principles.
    b. Thinking that is intuitive, associative, or personal is referred to as illogical.
    c. Deductive thinking involves going from general principles to specific situations.
    d. Logical thinking is thought which proceeds from given information to new conclusions on the basis of explicit rules.

27. (p. 269) Creative thinking involves all of the following *except*
    a. fluency
    b. flexibility
    c. fixation
    d. originality

28. (p. 269) Which of the following is *not* a benefit of daydreaming?
    a. It contributes to creativity.
    b. It can be a valuable outlet for frustrated impulses.
    c. Fantasies can act as a substitute source of gratification during times of deprivation.
    d. It facilitates other types of more concrete or realistic thinking.

29. (p. 269) Of the following, which is *not* a test of divergent thinking?
    a. Anagrams Test
    b. Unusual Uses Test
    c. Consequences Test
    d. Semantic Differential Test

30. (p. 270) Which of the following sequences best describes the process of creative thinking?
    a. preparation, orientation, illumination, incubation, verification
    b. orientation, preparation, verification, illumination, incubation
    c. preparation, incubation, orientation, illumination, verification
    d. orientation, preparation, incubation, illumination, verification

31. (p. 271) Which of the following is *not* true of creative persons according to Donald MacKinnon?
    a. Creative people are usually talented in only one area; they have an average range of knowledge or interests.
    b. Creative people show a relative lack of inhibition about their thoughts, feelings, and fantasies.
    c. They do not have particularly unusual personalities.

    d. They tend to be interested in truth, form, and beauty rather than in recognition or success.

32. (p. 271) True-False. Most creative individuals have above average IQ, but not all above average IQ individuals are necessarily creative.

33. (p. 272) Which of the following is *not* a problem of intuition and problem solving as discussed by Kahneman and Tversky?
    a. The way in which problems are framed can affect the answers people give, even for problems identical in content.
    b. People do not always carefully consider the base rate of events.
    c. People do not always ignore probabilities in high risk situations. It's hard for them to believe they can be the exception to the rule.
    d. People demonstrate an intuitive error called representativeness.

34. (p. 274) Which of the following is *not* a difficulty in thinking and problem solving?
    a. rigid mental set   c. oversimplification
    b. disjunctive conceptual thinking   d. problems with logic

35. (p. 275) The format for presenting simple sequences of logical thought involving premises and a conclusion is known as a(n)
    a. syntax   c. syllogism
    b. semantic   d. anagram

36. (p. 276) Which of the following is *not* a good suggestion for enhancing creativity?
    a. allow time for incubation
    b. seek varied input
    c. develop a narrow, but consistent chain of thoughts
    d. look for analogies

37. (p. 277) Which of the following is *not* a basic rule for successful brainstorming?
    a. Cross-stimulation through criticism is necessary.
    b. Unusual, remote, or wild ideas are sought.
    c. Modification or combination with other ideas is encouraged.
    d. Quantity of ideas is sought.

38. (p. 278) Which of the following is *not* a true statement about artificial intelligence?
    a. AI refers to computer programs capable of doing things that require intelligence when done by people.
    b. AI is based on the fact that many tasks cannot be reduced to a set of rules, instead intuition and insight (intelligence) are needed.
    c. AI will play an increasingly visible role in cognitive research and in our lives, but is not likely to soon replace human involvement.
    d. AI is valuable in situations where speed, vast memory, and persistence are required.

39. (p. 278) Expert systems are
    a. programs that emulate human behavior and provide models of how we think.
    b. adept across a broad range of problem solving.
    c. potentially disastrous in unanticipated situations because they cannot anticipate an infinite number of possible events.
    d. unable to provide more automatic processing because such a precise set of rules must be followed.

ANSWERS — PROGRAMMED REVIEW

1. cognition
2. cognitive
3. 18
4. internal representation
5. delayed response
6. insight
7. multiple-stick
8. stepping; chair
9. differs; before; mirror
10. versatile; appropriate
11. otters
12. appearance
13. blindfolded
14. 97; 92; 50
15. picture
16. synesthesia
17. flat
18. Stored; created
19. creativity
20. smaller
21. muscular imagery
22. kinesthetic
23. micromovements
24. arm
25. class; abstractly
26. formation; positive, negative
27. rules
28. conjunctive concept
29. and
30. Relational
31. Disjunctive concepts
32. prototypes
33. representative
34. denotative; connotative
35. semantic differential; good-bad, strong-weak, active-passive
36. encode; symbols
37. semantics
38. symbols
39. phonemes; morphemes
40. grammar
41. syntax
42. transformation
43. productive
44. productive
45. four
46. American Sign Language; ASL
47. 240; six
48. 130; plastic chips
49. compound
50. conditional relationships
51. 300
52. past; feelings

53. prompting
54. imitation
55. instrumental responses
56. 5; cue
57. Mechanical; rote
58. rules
59. understanding
60. general properties; functional solutions
61. random search
62. heuristic
63. backward
64. general
65. identify; define; explore; act; look
66. rapid; gradually
67. selective encoding
68. Selective combination
69. selective comparison
70. fixation
71. functional fixedness
72. containers
73. emotional
74. Cultural
75. Learned
76. Perceptual
77. inductive; deductive
78. logical; illogical
79. Fluency
80. Flexibility
81. Originality
82. divergent
83. conquering hero; suffering martyr
84. stimulation; gratification
85. frustrated
86. creativity
87. emotional; aggression
88. Divergent
89. convergent
90. Unusual Uses Test
91. Consequences Test
92. Anagrams Test
93. little correlation
94. useful, meaningful
95. orientation
96. Preparation
97. incubation
98. illumination
99. verification; incubation
100. no difference
101. knowledge, interests
102. openness
103. symbolic thought
104. independence; complexity
105. intuition

106. flawed
107. representativeness
108. base rate
109. framed
110. mental set
111. logical
112. syllogism
113. validity; truth
114. all-or-nothing
115. stereotypes
116. broadly
117. right atmosphere
118. incubation
119. varied input
120. randomly; relate
121. analogies

122. evaluated; criticizing
123. Brainstorming
124. cross-stimulation
125. Criticism; Modification; Quantity; Unusual
126. Adapt; Modify; Magnify; Substitute; Rearrange; Reverse
127. artificial intelligence
128. rules; information
129. computer simulations
130. Expert systems
131. knowledge; strategies
132. patterns
133. automatic
134. problem solvers
135. meaning

ANSWERS — SELF-TEST

1. a
2. b
3. d
4. b
5. c
6. True
7. b
8. True
9. b
10. b
11. False
12. a
13. d
14. b
15. d
16. d
17. False
18. a
19. c
20. b

21. d
22. b
23. a
24. False
25. c
26. a
27. c
28. d
29. d
30. d
31. a
32. True
33. c
34. b
35. c
36. c
37. a
38. b
39. c

Chapter 11

Motivation

CONTENTS

TERMS AND CONCEPTS

motivation
need-drive-response-goal-need reduction
incentive value
primary motives
stimulus motives
learned (secondary) motives
homeostasis
hypoglycemia
hypothalamus
feeding system
ventromedial hypothalamus
satiety system
lateral hypothalamus
set point
weight cycling
metabolic rate
taste aversion
bait shyness
self-selection feeding
extracellular thirst
intracellular thirst
episodic drive
estrus
estrogen
Coolidge Effect

sensory deprivation
arousal
arousal theory
Sensation-Seeking Scale (SSS)
inverted U function
Yerkes-Dodson law
circadian rhythms
jet lag
shift work
biorhythm theory
opponent-process theory
social motives
need for achievement (nAch)
need for power
fear of success
hierarchy of human needs
basic needs
growth needs
meta-needs
instrinsic motivation
extrinsic motivation
behavioral dieting
anorexia nervosa
bulimia (binge-purge syndrome)

IMPORTANT INDIVIDUALS

Cannon and Washburn
Judith Rodin
Albert Stunkard
Marvin Zuckerman
Richard Soloman

David McClelland
Benjamin Bloom
Abraham Maslow
Janet Polivy
Peter Herman

PROGRAMMED REVIEW

1. (p. 283) _____ "refers to the dynamics of behavior, the process of initiating, sustaining, and directing activities of the organism."

2. (p. 283) In developing a model of motivation, we may begin with a _____, the starting point of many motivated activities.

3. (p. 283) Needs cause a psychological state or feeling called a _____ to develop.

4. (p. 283) Drives activate a _____ (or a series of actions) designed to attain a _____ that will relieve the need.

5. (p. 283) Relieving the need temporarily ends the motivational sequence. This may be referred to as _____ _____.

6. (p. 283) We need both "drive" and "need" to discuss motivation because the _____ of these two is not always the same. If you begin fasting, your bodily need for food increases daily, but you would probably find yourself less "hungry" the seventh day compared to the first.

7. (p. 283) Motivated behavior can be energized by the "pull" of _____ _____ as well as by the "push" of internal needs.

8. (p. 283) The "pull" exerted by a goal is called its _____ _____. Very desirable goals (strawberry pie) may motivate behavior in the absence of internal need, while undesirable goals (live grubs) may be rejected even though they might meet the internal need.

9. (p. 284) In most instances it is helpful to recognize that actions are energized by both internal needs and external incentives, and that a strong state of _____ may make a less attractive _____ into a desirable goal.

10. (p. 284) For the purpose of study, motives can be divided into three major categories. The first, referred to as _____ _____, are innate motives based on biological needs which must be met for survival.

11. (p. 284) The most important primary motives are hunger, _____, _____ avoidance, and needs for air, _____, elimination of wastes, and regulation of body _____.

12. (p. 284) _____ _____ are related to a second category of needs. Like the primary motives, they appear to be _____, but they are not necessary for mere survival of the organism.

13. (p. 284) Their purpose seems to be to provide useful information about the environment and stimulation to the nervous system.   The stimulus motives include: activity,

_____, _____, _____, and
physical _____.

14. (p. 284) The third category, _____ or _____ motives,
accounts for the great diversity of human activities.

15. (p. 284) The most important secondary motives are related to acquired needs for power,
affiliation, _____, _____, _____, and
achievement.

16. (p. 284) The important motives of _____ and _____ also appear to
be subject to learning.

17. (p. 285) Biological drives are essential because they maintain bodily equilibrium or
_____ (meaning standing steady, or steady state).

18. (p. 285) The body constantly attempts to maintain itself at an ideal level through automatic
reactions that correct deviations. Homeostatic mechanisms are similar in operation
to a _____ set at a particular temperature.

19. (p. 285) When you feel hungry you probably associate a desire for food with sensations from
your stomach. This idea led _____ and _____ to investi-
gate whether contractions of an empty stomach cause hunger.

20. (p. 285) Washburn trained himself to swallow a toy balloon which could be inflated through an
attached tube so that stomach contractions could be recorded. They found that when
Washburn's stomach contracted, he felt "_____ _____."

21. (p. 286) While it is true that eating is limited when the stomach is _____
(full), it can be shown conclusively that the stomach is not essential for experiencing
hunger. For one thing, cutting the _____ _____ from the
stomach (so that stomach sensations can no longer be felt) does not abolish hunger.

22. (p. 286) Also, people who have had their stomachs removed surgically continue to feel hungry
and eat regularly. This fact leads us to believe that some _____ factor
must be the cause of hunger.

23. (p. 286) One important factor in hunger appears to be the level of _____ in the blood.
For example, if insulin is injected in a human it produces
_____ (low blood sugar) and stimulates feelings of hunger
and stomach contractions.

24. (p. 286) It now appears that the _____ may be responsible for hunger since it
responds to a lack of bodily "fuel" by sending nerve impulses to the brain that trigger
eating.

25. (p. 286) When you are hungry, many brain areas are affected, so no single "hunger center"
exists. However, one area of importance is the _____,
a small structure near the base of the brain.

26. (p. 286) Cells in the hypothalamus are sensitive to levels of sugar (and perhaps other
substances) in the blood. The hypothalamus also receives messages from the
_____ and the _____ which all combine to produce
hunger.

27. (p. 286)   One area of the hypothalamus seems to be part of a feeding system in the brain—the
_____ hypothalamus (meaning it is located at the
sides of the hypothalamus).

28. (p. 286)   If the lateral hypothalamus is activated electrically, even a well-fed animal will
immediately begin _____. If this same area is destroyed, the animal
will refuse to eat and will _____ if not force-fed.

29. (p. 287)   A second area within the hypothalamus seems to be part of a satiety system—the
_____ hypothalamus (meaning it is found on the bottom of the
hypothalamus).

30. (p. 287)   If the ventromedial hypothalamus is destroyed, dramatic overeating results. Normal-
sized rats weighing about 180 grams will balloon up to weights of _____ grams
or more and become so totally obese that they can barely move.

31. (p. 287)   While it is clear that the hypothalamus plays a role in hunger, there are no simple
"hunger control centers." The effects of damage to the hypothalamus, for example,
may simply reflect the fact that a large amount of _____ and
_____ activity passes through this area.

32. (p. 287)   There is more to hunger than "start" and "stop" systems in the brain. Recent evidence suggests that _____ stored in the body also influences hunger.

33. (p. 287)   The body acts as if there is a _____ _____ for the proportion of body
fat it maintains. When your body goes below this level, you are likely to feel hungry
most of the time.

34. (p. 287)   People do appear to have different set points, partially _____ and
partially determined by _____ feeding patterns.

35. (p. 287)   Adopted children whose birth _____ are overweight are much more
likely to be overweight themselves. This shows that a person's genes greatly
influence adult weight.

36. (p. 287)   The set point may be lastingly altered when a child is overfed. If a weight problem
begins in childhood, the person will, as an adult, have _____ fat cells and
_____ fat cells in the body.

37. (p. 287)   If the person does not become overweight until adulthood, his or her fat cells will be
_____, but their number will not increase.

38. (p. 287)   The sight or aroma of food often makes people want to eat, even when they do not
feel hungry. Such observations suggest that many people are sensitive to
_____ _____ for eating.

39. (p. 287)   For those sensitive to the wide variety of signs and signals linked with food, eating is
more likely when food is _____, highly _____,
and easy to obtain.

40. (p. 287)   Even the time of day can influence eating. In one experiment obese subjects ate
more crackers when a clock was set closer to mealtime than it actually was. Subjects
of normal weight _____ their eating when they thought it
was closer to mealtime.

41. (p. 288) People of all weights can be found who are unusually sensitive to external eating cues, so this is not strictly a problem of the _____. Eating cues are a factor in some overeating, but they are not the sole cause.

42. (p. 288) As examples, Judith Rodin found that externally responsive girls were most likely to gain weight at a two-month summer camp. However, _____ overweight persons are more likely to be external eaters than are the truly obese.

43. (p. 288) For many people, _____ also contributes to overeating. In general, sweetness, high fat content, and variety tend to encourage overeating.

44. (p. 288) In one experiment, rats given a junk food diet gained almost _____ times as much weight as controls who ate only standard laboratory "rat chow." It seems that our culture may provide the worst possible kinds of foods for those with a tendency toward obesity.

45. (p. 288) Fatness does not come from constant overeating. Studies by Albert Stunkard and Judith Rodin show that overeating occurs mainly when a person is gaining weight. Once excess weight is gained, it can be _____ with a normal diet.

46. (p. 288) As people gain weight, many reduce their _____ _____ and burn fewer calories. Consequently, some overweight persons may continue to gain weight while consuming _____ calories then their slimmer neighbors.

47. (p. 288) People with overweight problems are just as likely to eat when anxious, angry, bored, or distressed. Furthermore, _____ often accompanies obesity in our fat-conscious culture. This can set up a pattern of overeating that leads to emotional distress and still more overeating.

48. (p. 289) While dieters do lose weight, most regain it soon after the diet ends. Many people experience a _____ that can push weight higher than before the diet began.

49. (p. 289) Many theorists now believe that dieting alters the physiology of the body. In effect, dieting causes the body to become highly efficient at conserving _____ and storing them as _____.

50. (p. 289) Frequent weight cycling caused by dieting tends to slow the body's _____ _____ (the rate at which energy is used up). This makes it harder to lose weight each time a person diets and easier to regain weight when the diet ends.

51. (p. 289) Hunger is affected by a number of factors in addition to actual bodily needs for food. _____ values are certainly important since what our society thinks are desirable foods or revolting edibles has much to do with eating habits.

52. (p. 289) Another important factor is _____. It has been demonstrated that the hungrier a person is, the more "pleasant" a sweet-tasting food is judged to be.

53. (p. 289) If a food causes sickness or if it simply precedes sickness caused by something else, we quickly learn to avoid such foods. This process is referred to as _____ _____.

54. (p. 289) Taste aversions are a type of _____ _____. Since a long time delay normally prevents conditioning, it is theorized that there is a

_____ tendency to associate an upset stomach with food eaten earlier.

55. (p. 289)   While such learning is usually protective, many human cancer patients suffer taste aversions long after the _____ of the drug treatment has passed.

56. (p. 289)   This phenomenon is also seen in animals. In a pioneering experiment, coyotes given lamb treated with lithium chloride became nauseated and vomited. After one or two such treatments, they developed _____ _____, a lasting distaste for the tainted food.

57. (p. 289)   Taste aversions may also help people avoid severe _____ imbalances. If you overeat something until you feel ill, your discomfort could create an aversion and restore some balance to your diet.

58. (p. 289)   In one classic experiment on _____-_____ _____, infants selected a balanced diet, and their health and growth were normal. However, the babies could only select from _____ foods. If candy had been a choice, they might not have done so well.

59. (p. 289)   Humans seem to have an innate preference for _____ and _____ food. Thus, an appetite for candy and junk food can easily override the weaker tendency to eat a balanced diet.

60. (p. 290)   Thirst is only partially related to dryness of the mouth and throat. When drugs are given that produce constantly wet or dry mouths, thirst and water intake remain normal. Like hunger, thirst appears to be controlled through the _____ where separate thirst and thirst-satiety systems are found.

61. (p. 290)   There are actually two kinds of thirst. _____ thirst occurs when there is a loss of water from the fluids surrounding the cells of your body due to bleeding, vomiting, diarrhea, sweating, or drinking alcohol.

62. (p. 290)   When a person loses both water and minerals in any of these ways, especially by perspiration, a slightly _____ liquid may be more satisfying than plain water.

63. (p. 290)   Before the body can retain water, minerals lost through perspiration (mainly salt) must be replaced. Thus, research shows that animals greatly prefer _____ _____ when body salt levels are lowered. Similarly, some nomadic peoples of the Sahara Desert prize _____ as a beverage, probably because of its saltiness.

64. (p. 290)   A second type of thirst occurs when you eat a salty meal. In this case excess salt within the body causes fluid to be drawn out of the cells. This produces _____ thirst.

65. (p. 290)   Drives like hunger, thirst, and sleepiness come and go in a fairly consistent cycle each day. Pain, by contrast, is an _____ drive since it is aroused only when damage to the tissues of the body takes place.

66. (p. 290)   Most of the primary drives cause a person to actively seek a desired goal. Pain is different in this respect, because the pain drive has as its goal the _____ or _____ of pain.

67. (p. 290)   Surprisingly, avoiding pain appears to be partially _____. This fact was

demonstrated in an experiment in which dogs reared in isolation acted like they did not know the meaning of pain or how to avoid it.

68. (p. 290)   Human pain avoidance is also affected by learning. Persons who feel they must be "tough" and not show any discomfort have increased _____ _____.

69. (p. 291)   Sexual motivation is quite unusual by comparison to other biological motives. Many psychologists do not think of sex as a primary motive because it is not necessary for _____ _____.

70. (p. 291)   In lower animals the sex drive is directly related to the action of _____ in the body. For example, females are only interested in mating when their fertility cycle is in the stage of _____, or "heat," caused by secretion of _____ into the bloodstream.

71. (p. 291)   Hormones are important in the male animal as well. In most lower animals, _____ will abolish the sex drive.

72. (p. 291)   In contrast to the female, the normal male animal is always ready to mate. His sex drive is primarily aroused by the behavior of a receptive female. In animals, mating is therefore closely tied to the _____ _____ of the female.

73. (p. 291)   The link between hormones and the sex drive grows weaker as we ascend the biological scale. Hormones do affect the human sex drive, but only to a limited degree. For example, one study found no connection between female sexual activity and the monthly _____ _____.

74. (p. 291)   In humans, mental, cultural, and emotional factors determine sexual expression. However, hormones do affect human sex drive. Males show a loss of sex drive after _____, and some women lose sexual desire when using _____ _____ _____.

75. (p. 291)   Sex drive shows no clear relationship to deprivation. It is therefore considered to be largely _____.

76. (p. 291)   The sex drive is also unusual in that its _____ is as actively sought as its _____.

77. (p. 291)   The non-homeostatic quality of the sex drive is demonstrated by the _____ _____. An animal allowed to copulate until apparently satiated will immediately resume sexual activity when a new partner is provided.

78. (p. 292)   Stimulus needs encompass drives for exploration, manipulation, and curiosity. Curiosity drive was demonstrated in experiments showing that monkeys would learn tasks for stimulation when no external _____ was offered.

79. (p. 292)   Closely related to curiosity is the drive for sensory stimulation. The nervous system seems to require varied, patterned stimulation to respond normally. This fact is apparently why people who have undergone severe _____ _____ often report sensory distortions and disturbed thinking.

80. (p. 292)   The drive for stimulation can even be observed in infants. When babies are shown patterns of varying complexity, they spend more time looking at _____ patterns.

81. (p. 293) _____ refers to variations in activation of the body and nervous system. It is zero at death, low during sleep, moderate during normal daily activities, and high at times of excitement, emotion, or panic.

82. (p. 293) The position known as the _____ _____ of motivation assumes that there is an ideal level of arousal for various activities and that individuals behave in ways that keep arousal near this ideal level.

83. (p. 293) According to arousal theory, _____ and the drive to seek _____ can be interpreted as an attempt to raise the level of arousal when it is too low.

84. (p. 293) Marvin Zuckerman has devised a test called the _____-_____ _____ (SSS) to measure individual differences in preferred arousal levels.

85. (p. 293) People who score high on the SSS tend to be _____, _____, and to value change. They also report more _____ partners, are more likely to _____, and prefer spicy, sour, and crunchy foods over blander foods.

86. (p. 293) Low sensation seekers are _____, _____, _____, and like the company of others.

87. (p. 293) Performance of a task is usually best when arousal is _____. The relationship between arousal and efficiency of behavior can be expressed as an _____ ____ function.

88. (p. 293) The optimal level of arousal also depends on the complexity of the particular task. If a task is relatively simple, the optimal level of arousal will be _____. When difficult or complicated, the best performance occurs at _____ levels of arousal.

89. (p. 294) This relationship is called the _____-_____ law. It applies to a wide variety of tasks and to measures of motivtion other than arousal.

90. (p. 294) Studies of anxious students show that they are typically most anxious when they don't know the material. One of the best ways to overcome test anxiety is to be _____.

91. (p. 294) Guided by internal "biological clocks," the body undergoes a complex cycle of changes every 24 hours called _____ _____.

92. (p. 294) Throughout the day, large changes take place in body _____, _____ pressure, _____ volume, amino-acid level, and in activity of the liver, kidneys, and endocrine glands.

93. (p. 294) Especially important is the output of the hormone _____, which causes general arousal. It is often 3 to 5 times greater during the day.

94. (p. 294) Differences in such peaks are so basic that when a "day person" rooms with a "night person," both are more likely to give their relationship a _____ rating.

95. (p. 295) The effects of sleep-waking cycles become especially noticeable whenever there is a major shift in time schedules. For example, if you travel great distances east or

west, your circadian rhythms will be out of phase with the physical environment producing what is called _____ _____.

96. (p. 295) _____ work in which the time of working rotates across days, evenings, and nights, can have a significant effect causing a loss of efficiency, as well as _____, _____, upset stomach, nervousness, depression and a decline in mental agility.

97. (p. 295) For major time zone shifts (5 hours or more), it can take from several days to ___ weeks to resynchronize.

98. (p. 295) Adaptation to jet lag is _____ when you get outside where you must sleep, eat, and socialize on the new schedule. Staying in a hotel room (where sleeping and eating can be done on the old schedule) slows the process.

99. (p. 295) The direction of travel also affects adaptation. Westerly flights take an average of ___ to ___ days adaptation. Easterly flights take _____ longer.

100. (p. 295) When you fly west, the sun comes up _____. This combined with the fact that the circadian rhythm naturally runs _____ than 24 hours explains why adaptation is easier. It's more like staying up late and sleeping in.

101. (p. 295) Work shifts that "rotate" _____ are more disruptive than those that _____. If work shifts must change, those lasting only three days are less disruptive than week-long shifts.

102. (p. 295) Consistent work shifts are the best. Even continuous _____ work is less disruptive than changing shifts.

103. (p. 295) If you can anticipate an upcoming body rhythm change, it is best to _____ yourself to your new schedule beforehand. For instance, before traveling you should go to sleep one hour later (or earlier) each day until your sleep cycle matches the time at your destination.

104. (p. 295) If you cannot preadapt, it at least helps to fly early in the day when you fly _____. When you fly _____, it is better to fly late.

105. (p. 296) _____ _____ states that we all are subject to three separate cycles: a physical cycle lasting _____ days, an emotional or sensitivity cycle of _____ days, and a 33-day intellectual cycle.

106. (p. 296) The first half of each cycle is supposedly _____ and the second half _____. All three cycles begin at birth and flow in and out of synchronization throughout one's life.

107. (p. 296) When a cycle changes from positive to negative, it is termed a _____ _____. When all three cycles line up on such days, the chances for disaster or accident are supposedly quite high.

108. (p. 296) The strongest evidence against biorhythm theory comes from attempts to match cycles with outcomes. For instance, one researcher compared 100 no-hit baseball games pitched in the major leagues to biorhythm charts for the pitchers. He found _____ _____ between cycles and these performances.

109. (p. 296) The Workmen's Compensation Board of British Columbia studied over 13,000 occupational accidents. They found that accidents are no more likely to occur on _____ days than at any other time.

110. (p. 296) Other studies have found absolutely no correlation between aviation accidents and pilots' biorhythms, or between biorhythms and recovery from _____, time of _____, or scores of _____ pros.

111. (p. 296) Psychologist Richard Soloman has offered an intriguing explanation for drug addiction and other learned motives using his _____-_____ theory.

112. (p. 296) According to this theory, a stimulus that causes strong emotion, such as fear or pleasure, is often followed by an _____ emotion when the stimulus ends.

113. (p. 297) Soloman assumes that when a stimulus is repeated, our response to it _____. In contrast, emotional aftereffects get _____ with repetition.

114. (p. 297) _____ _____ or goals such as success, status, approval, power, and so forth are acquired in complex ways through socialization and cultural conditioning.

115. (p. 297) A dominant social motive in American culture is need for achievement (nAch), the desire to meet some _____ _____ of excellence. The person with high needs for achievement strives to do well in any situation where evaluation takes place.

116. (p. 297) The need for achievement differs from a need for _____, which is a desire to have impact or control over others.

117. (p. 297) In researching nAch, psychologist David McClelland found that 14 years after graduation, students shown high, versus low, in need for achievement, were found more often in careers involving an element of _____ and _____.

118. (p. 298) Scores for achievement motivation have _____ for students in recent years. Some psychologists believe this may help account for the dramatic decline in Scholastic Aptitude Test scores observed in the last decade.

119. (p. 298) Those high in nAch are _____ risk-takers. They avoid goals that are too easy because they offer no sense of satisfaction. They also avoid long shots because there is no hope of success, or success is more due to luck than skill.

120. (p. 298) Persons low in nAch select either sure things or impossible goals where there is no _____ _____ for failure.

121. (p. 298) People high in nAch do better on various laboratory tasks, are more likely to complete _____ tasks, make better _____ in school, and tend to excel in their _____.

122. (p. 298) College students high in nAch tend to attribute success to their _____, and failure to _____ _____. High nAch students are more likely to renew their efforts when faced with a poor performance.

123. (p. 298) Fear of success most often occurs because:
1) success can require a stressful shift in _____-_____;
2) many people fear _____ when they stand out in a group; and
3) some people fear the extra _____ of being a "successful person."

124. (p. 298) Both men and women appear to be equally subject to success fears. But in our culture there is often an extra conflict for women. By adulthood, many men and women have learned to consider it "unfeminine" for a woman to excel. Successful women, then, are most often those who define achievement as an _____ feminine quality.

125. (p. 299) Benjamin Bloom recently completed a study of America's top performers in six fields. He found that _____ and _____, not great natural talent, led to success in the lives of the high achievers studied.

126. (p. 299) The upshot of Bloom's work is that talent is nurtured through dedication and hard work. It appears that this is most likely to happen when parents give their wholehearted _____ to a child's special interest, and when they place emphasis on doing one's _____ at all times.

127. (p. 299) Abraham Maslow has proposed a _____ (or ordering) of needs in his attempt to place human motivation in perspective.

128. (p. 299) The bottom or first level needs are _____. They are necessary for survival and tend to be prepotent or dominant over the higher needs.

129. (p. 299) The higher needs are expressed only when the prepotent physiological needs are satisfied. This tendency is true of the next level of needs, those for _____ and _____.

130. (p. 300) Maslow described these first two levels of needs as _____ needs, with the next broad level known as _____ needs. These include needs for love and belonging, needs for _____ and _____-_____ (recognition and self-respect) and the need for _____-_____.

131. (p. 300) According to Maslow, there is a tendency to move up the hierarchy to the _____-_____, the less powerful, but humanly important motives.

132. (p. 300) When survival needs are met, but meta-needs are unfulfilled, a person falls into a "_____ of _____" and experiences despair, apathy, and alienation.

133. (p. 300) Maslow estimated that only one person in _____ is primarily motivated by self-actualization needs. Most are concerned with esteem, love, or security.

134. (p. 300) _____ _____ occurs when there is no obvious external reward or ulterior purpose behind your actions, while _____ _____ stems from obvious external factors like pay, grades, rewards, obligations, or approval.

135. (p. 301) Research with children shows that excessive rewards can undermine spontaneous interest. Children lavishly rewarded for drawing showed _____ interest on subsequent occasions when allowed to draw spontaneously.

136. (p. 301) On the job, the _____ of work may be increased by salaries and bonuses. However, the _____ of work is tied more to intrinsic factors, such as interest, freedom of action, and constructive feedback.

137. (p. 301) When a person is _____ motivated, a certain amount of challenge, surprise, and complexity makes a task rewarding. When

_____ motivation is stressed, complexity, surprise, and challenge just become barriers to reaching a goal.

138. (p. 301) Motivation can't always be intrinsic since every worthwhile activity is not intrinsically satisfying. Extrinsic motivation is often needed if we are to develop enough _____ or _____ for an activity to become intrinsically rewarding.

139. (p. 301) Greene and Lepper summarized their findings by pointing out that:
   1) If there is no _____ interest in an activity to begin with, there is nothing to lose by using extrinsic rewards;
   2) If needed skills are lacking, _____ rewards may be necessary to begin;
   3) Extrinsic rewards may focus _____ on an activity so that real interest can develop;
   4) If extrinsic rewards or incentives are to be used, they should be as _____ as possible, used only when absolutely necessary and faded out as soon as possible.

140. (p. 302) Many people think the basic approach to controlling weight is to diet. What is really needed to control weight is a complete overhaul of _____ _____ and control of _____ for eating.

141. (p. 302) This approach has been called _____ _____ and involves a number of techniques and suggestions. The first of these is to have a physical check-up since about ___ percent of all weight problems are physical.

142. (p. 302) Keeping a diet _____ can be useful as a means of learning your eating habits. Along with this, count _____.

143. (p. 302) Develop techniques to control the act of eating by taking smaller _____, carrying only what you plan to eat to the table, putting all food away before leaving the kitchen, eating slowly, leaving food on your plate, and avoid eating _____.

144. (p. 302) Learn to weaken your personal eating cues by _____ when and where you do the most eating. Require yourself to _____ what you are doing in order to eat and be aware of the "_____-_____ syndrome."

145. (p. 302) Avoid snacks by fixing only a single portion using low-calorie foods. _____ the impulse to eat using a timer or by filling up on raw carrots, bouillon, water, coffee, or tea.

146. (p. 302) Exercise burns calories. Contrary to popular opinion, regular exercise does not increase appetite, and may lower the body's _____ _____ for fat storage.

147. (p. 302) Many psychologists are now convinced that no diet can succeed for long without an increase in exercise. Burning as little as _____ extra calories a day can play a major role in preventing regain of weight.

148. (p. 302) Get yourself committed to weight loss by involving as many _____ in your program as you can. Formal programs such as Overeaters Anonymous or Take Off Pounds Sensibly can be a good source of social support.

149. (p. 302) Make a list of _____ you will receive if you change your eating habits and _____ that will occur if you don't.

150. (p. 302) _____ your progress daily. Record your weight, the number of calories eaten, and whether you met your daily goal.

151. (p. 302) Try to identify specific high risk situations in which you are likely to overeat. Then form a plan to help you cope with the risk of _____.

152. (p. 303) You should set a "threshold" for weight control. A study of Weight Watchers members found that those who successfully maintained their weight loss had a regain limit of ____ pounds or less which, if exceeded, alerted them to immediately begin making corrections in their diet and exercise.

153. (p. 304) Serious   cases   of   undereating   are   called   _____ _____. Victims of this condition are mostly adolescent females (5 percent are males) who suffer devastating weight loss from self-inflicted starvation.

154. (p. 304) Anorexia nervosa is not a simple loss of desire for food. Many anorexics continue to feel hunger and struggle to starve themselves. The problem can best be described as a relentless pursuit of _____ _____.

155. (p. 304) Persons who suffer from anorexia nervosa have an obsessive fear of gaining weight. Often the problem starts with normal _____ that gradually begins to dominate the person's life.

156. (p. 304) In time, anorexics suffer physical weakness, absence of _____ _____, and a dangerous risk of infection. Five to _____ percent die of malnutrition or related health problems.

157. (p. 304) _____, also known as the binge-purge syndrome, is a second major eating disorder. Victims gorge on food, then induce vomiting or take laxatives to avoid gaining weight.

158. (p. 304) Bulimia, too, is far more prevalent in women than in men. A recent study of college women found that ____ percent are bulimic.

159. (p. 304) Typical risks associated with bulimia include sore _____, _____ loss, _____ spasms, _____ damage, dehydration, tooth decay, swelling of the _____ _____, menstrual irregularity, loss of sex drive, and even heart attack.

160. (p. 304) Close to _____ percent of anorexics are also bulimic. However, they are separate problems. Anorexics suffer a weight loss of at least _____ percent of their original body weight. Bulimics may be from any weight group (most are only slightly below average weight).

161. (p. 304) Bulimia is indicated if any three of the following conditions are present: _____ eating; hiding the amount eaten during a binge; gorging on food, followed by self-induced vomiting or abdominal pain; repeated attempts to lose weight by severe dieting; use of vomiting, laxatives, or diuretics to lose weight; frequent weight changes of more than ____ pounds; awareness that one's eating is abnormal, coupled with an inability to change; _____ or _____ following binges.

162. (p. 304) Both anorexics and bulimics have exaggerated fears of becoming fat. Anorexics, especially, have distorted body images. Most overestimate their body size by _____ percent or more.

163. (p. 305) Anorexics are usually described as "perfect" daughters. Many are would-be high _____ who frantically try to be "perfect" in one area—to have complete control over their weight and to be perfectly slim.

164. (p. 305) Bulimics are obsessed with weight, food, etc., and feel guilt, shame, and anxiety after a binge. _____ reduces the anxiety triggered by a binge and thus is highly reinforcing.

165. (p. 305) Recent research suggests that _____ may actually encourage binging since most bulimics go through this phase before they begin to purge.

166. (p. 305) Janet Polivy and Peter Herman have found that dieters eat _____ after first eating a large meal than they do if they ate nothing beforehand. It's as if once they have "broken" their diet, the suppressed urge to eat is released and a binge follows. This effect can occur even when dieters are merely told they ate a high calorie meal.

167. (p. 305) Treatment for anorexia usually begins with admitting the person to a _____. As a second step, the client enters counseling to work on the personal conflicts and family issues that led to weight loss.

168. (p. 305) For bulimia, psychologists have had some success with behavioral counseling that includes careful _____-_____ of food intake and work on extinguishing the urge to vomit after eating.

169. (p. 305) Although much progress is being made in treating eating disorders, most _____ do not seek help, and many actively resist it. _____ will sometimes seek treatment, but usually not until their eating habits become intolerable.

SELF-TEST

1. (p. 283) The concept of motivation can be related to a sequence of activities. Which of the following shows the proper order of a model of motivation?
   a. need, drive, response, goal, need reduction
   b. need, need reduction, goal, drive, response
   c. need, response, drive, goal, need reduction
   d. drive, need, goal, response, need reduction

2. (p. 283) Motivated behavior can be energized by external stimuli as well as by the push of internal needs. The "pull" exerted by a goal is called its
   a. drive reductio..   c. incentive value
   b. goal attainment   d. primary motivation

3. (p. 284) Motives based on biological needs which must be met for survival are called
   a. primary   c. secondary
   b. stimulus   d. learned

4. (p. 285) Within the body there are ideal levels for body temperature, concentration of various chemicals in the blood, etc. When the body deviates from these ideal levels, automatic reactions restore equilibrium. This process is known as
   a. Yerkes-Dodson Law   c. thermostasis
   b. homeostasis   d. biological calibration

5. (p. 285) True-False. Stomach contractions are the main source of food regulation and control of hunger.

6. (p. 286) Food and water intake are primarily regulated by
    a. the hypothalamus
    b. glands in the mouth that detect dryness
    c. stomach contractions
    d. blood content

7. (p. 286) True-False. The drive to initiate eating and the desire to stop eating are regulated by separate centers located respectively in the right and left brains.

8. (p. 287) Which of the following is *not* true of body set points for fat?
    a. The set point may be lastingly altered when a child is overfed.
    b. The set point appears to be entirely inherited, being linked with feeding patterns of parents.
    c. The set point acts like a "thermostat" for body fat, maintaining a proportion of fat.
    d. When an overweight person loses weight, the body goes below the set point, and the person feels hungry most of the time.

9. (p. 287) Which of the following is *not* true of obesity?
    a. The overweight are unusually sensitive to external cues for eating.
    b. For many people, diet contributes to obesity.
    c. Overweight people are generally more emotionally reactive than normal-weight people.
    d. People with weight problems are just as likely to eat when emotionally aroused as when hungry.

10. (p. 289) Which of the following is *not* true of taste aversions?
    a. They are a type of classical conditioning.
    b. They can be learned if a food causes sickness or simply precedes sickness caused by something else.
    c. It has been theorized that there is a biological tendency to associate an upset stomach with food eaten earlier.
    d. Bait shyness is a related, but distinctly different phenomenon in which animals actively seek a bait laced with addictive drugs.

11. (p. 290) Extracellular thirst occurs when
    a. there is an increase in water levels surrounding body cells
    b. intracellular thirst has reached homeostasis
    c. bleeding, vomiting, diarrhea, sweating, or alcohol consumption occurs
    d. you eat a salty meal

12. (p. 290) True-False. Avoiding pain is an entirely unlearned motive basic to survival.

13. (p. 290) Pain is called a(n) _____ _____ since it is aroused only when damage to the tissues of the body takes place.
    a. primary drive   c. chronic drive
    b. episodic drive   d. secondary motive

14. (p. 291) Which of the following is *not* true of sexual motivation?
    a. In lower animals and humans the sex drive is exclusively related to the action of hormones in the body.
    b. Human males may show a loss of sex drive after castration.
    c. Some women show loss of sexual desire when using birth control pills.
    d. Sex is not necessary for individual survival, but is a necessity for group survival.

15. (p. 291) The drive which is non-homeostatic in nature is
    a. hunger   c. sex
    b. thirst   d. oxygen intake

16. (p. 291) In animal research, the Coolidge Effect refers to
    a. learned avoidance of pain
    b. maze exploration for curiosity
    c. the resumption of sexual activity following satiation when a new partner is introduced
    d. the inverted U function relating arousal level and performance

17. (p. 292) Motives which provide useful information about the environment and stimulation to the nervous system are called
    a. primary needs   c. secondary needs
    b. stimulus needs   d. learned needs

18. (p. 293) Zuckerman developed which of the following to measure differences in preferred stimulus arousal level?
    a. SSS   c. Yerkes-Dodson law
    b. SST   d. nAch

19. (p. 294) According to the Yerkes-Dodson law, when a task is relatively simple, the optimal level of arousal will be
    a. low   c. high
    b. moderate   d. unimportant

20. (p. 294) Circadian rhythms refer to
    a. the cycles of our bodies' internal clocks
    b. the body's ever-changing levels of blood sugar
    c. the female sexual cycle
    d. the need-drive-response-goal attainment cycle

21. (p. 296) Which of the following is *not* one of the cycles postulated by biorhythm theory?
    a. intellectual cycle lasting 33 days
    b. physical cycle lasting 23 days
    c. critical day cycle lasting 13 days
    d. sensitivity cycle lasting 28 days

22. (p. 296) Which of the following is *not* a true statement with regard to the merits of biorhythm theory?
    a. There is absolutely no correlation between aviation accidents and pilot biorhythms.
    b. There is no relationship between occupational accidents and biorhythm cycles.
    c. Biorhythm theory makes logical sense and is based on scientific evidence.
    d. There is no connection between biorhythms and recovery from surgery.

23. (p. 297) Which of the following is *not* true of Soloman's opponent-process theory?
    a. Emotional aftereffects get stronger with repetition.
    b. When a stimulus is repeated, our response to it habituates, or gets weaker.
    c. A stimulus that causes strong emotion is often followed by a similar emotion when the stimulus ends.
    d. The opponent-process theory has been used to explain the maintenance of drug addiction, and the reinforcing effects of skydiving, and other hazardous pursuits.

24. (p. 297) Which of the following is true of the need for achievement (nAch)?
    a. It is essentially the same as need for power.

b. Those high in nAch are more often found in careers involving very little risk.

c. College students high in nAch tend to view success as the result of forces outside themselves.

d. Those high in nAch are generally moderate risk-takers.

25. (p. 298) Which of the following is *not* true of fear of success?
a. Both men and women are prone to act as if there is a conflict between success and femininity.
b. Fear of success is more likely to occur among women than men.
c. Fear of success seems related to requirements to shift self-concept, fear of rejection, and fear of extra demands.
d. Successful women are most often those who define achievement as contradictory to femininity, but learn to live with the conflict.

26. (p. 299) True-False. Biological needs tend to be prepotent over psychological motives or needs.

27. (p. 300) Maslow's hierarchy of needs places the order of needs as
a. basic, growth, meta
b. meta, basic, growth
c. growth, basic, meta
d. basic, meta, growth

28. (p. 301) True-False. Research with children has demonstrated that excessive rewards can undermine spontaneous interest in an activity.

29. (p. 302) Which of the following is *not* a behavioral dieting technique?
a. observe your eating habits and keep a diet diary
b. eat snacks frequently rather than preparing long meals
c. weaken personal eating cues
d. make a list of rewards you will receive for change

30. (p. 304) Which of the following is *not* true of anorexics?
a. Most are adolescent females.
b. Five to 18 percent die of malnutrition or related health problems.
c. Close to 90 percent are also bulimics.
d. They suffer a weight loss of at least 15 percent of their original body weight.

31. (p. 304) Typical health risks for bulimics include all of the following *except*
a. loss of sex drive
b. swelling of the salivary glands
c. sore throat
d. added hair growth

32. (p. 305) The single most common personal issue involved in anorexia and bulimia is
a. feelings of unreality
b. desires to rebel against society
c. needs for complete control
d. overinflated self-worth

ANSWERS — PROGRAMMED REVIEW

1. Motivation
2. need
3. drive
4. response; goal
5. need reduction
6. strength
7. external stimuli
8. incentive value
9. need; goal
10. primary motives
11. thirst, pain; sleep; temperature
12. Stimulus motives; innate
13. curiosity, exploration, manipulation; contact
14. learned, secondary
15. approval, status, security
16. fear, aggression

17. homeostasis
18. thermostat
19. Cannon, Washburn
20. hunger pangs
21. distended; sensory nerves
22. central
23. sugar; hypoglycemia
24. liver
25. hypothalamus
26. liver, stomach
27. lateral
28. eating; die
29. ventromedial
30. 1,000
31. sensory; motor
32. fat
33. set point
34. inherited; early
35. parents
36. more; larger
37. larger
38. external cues
39. available; visible
40. decreased
41. obese
42. moderately
43. diet
44. three
45. maintained
46. activity level; fewer
47. unhappiness
48. rebound
49. calories; fat
50. metabolic rate
51. Cultural
52. taste
53. taste aversion
54. classical conditioning; biological
55. nausea
56. bait shyness
57. nutritional
58. self-selection feeding; nutritious
59. sweet; fatty
60. hypothalamus
61. extracellular
62. salty
63. salt water; blood
64. intracellular
65. episodic
66. avoidance, elimination
67. learned
68. pain tolerance
69. individual survival
70. hormones; estrus; estrogen
71. castration

72. fertility cycle
73. menstrual cycle
74. castration; birth control pills
75. non-homeostatic
76. arousal; reduction
77. Coolidge Effect
78. reward
79. sensory deprivation
80. complex
81. Arousal
82. arousal theory
83. curiosity; stimulation
84. Sensation-Seeking Scale
85. extroverted, independent; sexual; smoke
86. orderly, nurturant, giving
87. moderate; inverted U
88. high; low
89. Yerkes-Dodson
90. overprepared
91. circadian rhythms
92. temperature; blood; urine
93. adrenaline
94. negative
95. jet lag
96. Shift; fatigue; irritability
97. 2
98. faster
99. 4; 5; 50%
100. later; longer
101. backwards; advance
102. night
103. preadapt
104. east; west
105. Biorhythm theory; 23; 28
106. positive; negative
107. critical day
108. no connection
109. critical
110. surgery; death; golf
111. opponent-process
112. opposite
113. habituates; stronger
114. Social motives
115. internalized standard
116. power
117. risk, responsibility
118. declined
119. moderate
120. personal responsibility
121. difficult; grades; occupations
122. ability; insufficient effort
123. self-concept; rejection; demands
124. acceptable
125. drive, determination
126. support; best

127. hierarchy
128. physiological
129. safety, security
130. basic; growth; esteem; self-esteem; self-actualization
131. meta-needs
132. syndrome of decay
133. ten
134. Intrinsic motivation; extrinsic motivation
135. little
136. quantity; quality
137. intrinsically; extrinsic
138. skill, knowledge
139. intrinsic; extrinsic; attention; small
140. eating habits; cues
141. behavioral dieting; 5
142. diary; calories
143. portions; alone
144. avoiding; interrupt; night-eating
145. Delay
146. set point
147. 200

148. people
149. rewards; punishments
150. Chart
151. relapse
152. 3
153. anorexia nervosa
154. excessive thinness
155. dieting
156. menstrual cycles; 8
157. Bulimia
158. 5
159. throat; hair; muscle; kidney; salivary glands
160. 50; 15
161. binge; 3; anxiety, depression
162. 25
163. achievers
164. Vomiting
165. dieting
166. more
167. hospital
168. self-monitoring
169. anorexics; Bulimics

ANSWERS — SELF-TEST

1. a
2. c
3. a
4. b
5. False
6. a
7. False
8. b
9. a
10. d
11. c
12. False
13. b
14. a
15. c
16. c

17. b
18. a
19. c
20. a
21. c
22. c
23. c
24. d
25. d
26. True
27. a
28. True
29. b
30. c
31. d
32. c

Chapter 12

Emotion

CONTENTS

TERMS AND CONCEPTS

voodoo deaths
adaptive behaviors
physiological changes
adrenaline
emotional expressions
primary emotions
autonomic nervous system (ANS)
sympathetic branch
parasympathetic branch
parasympathetic rebound
polygraph (lie detector)
kinesics
illustrators
emblems
commonsense theory of emotion
James-Lange theory
Cannon-Bard theory
Schachter's cognitive theory
attribution

facial feedback hypothesis
contemporary model of emotion
primary appraisal
secondary appraisal
problem-focused coping
emotion-focused coping
anxiety
defense mechanism
denial
repression
reaction formation
regression
projection
rationalization
compensation
sublimation
learned helplessness
mastery training
triangular theory of love

IMPORTANT INDIVIDUALS

Walter Cannon
Robert Plutchik

Eckhard Hess
George Engel

David Lykken
Charles Darwin
Paul Ekman
William James
Carl Lange
Phillip Bard
Stanley Schachter

Stuart Valins
Carrol Izard
Richard Lazarus
Sigmund Freud
Bruno Bettelheim
Martin Seligman
Aaron Beck
Robert Sternberg

PROGRAMMED REVIEW

1.　(p. 308)　Voodoo deaths can partially be explained by the victim's strong belief in the power of the curse. Walter Cannon believes that the real cause lies in changes that occur in the body which accompany strong _____ .

2.　(p. 309)　More recent research indicates that such deaths are more likely the result of the body's reaction to strong emotion, rather than fear itself. The cursed person's emotional response is so intense that the _____ _____ system overreacts and eventually slows the heart to a stop.

3.　(p. 309)　Emotions have a powerful influence on everyday behavior. For example, it is easier to make decisions when you are in a _____ mood. Likewise, people who are feeling _____ are more likely to help others in need.

4.　(p. 309)　The root of the word emotion means "to _____," and indeed emotions do. First, the body is _____ aroused during emotion.

5.　(p. 309)　Second, we are often motivated by emotions such as fear, anger, or joy. Underlying this is the fact that emotions are linked to such basic _____ behaviors as attack, retreat, seeking comfort, helping others, reproduction, etc.

6.　(p. 309)　At times human emotions can be disruptive, but in general they aid in _____ . This fact seems to explain why emotional reactions were retained in evolution.

7.　(p. 309)　Physiological changes within the body are a major element of many emotions. These changes include alterations in heart _____, blood _____, perspiration, and other bodily stirrings.

8.　(p. 309)　Most such reactions are caused by release of _____ into the bloodstream. This hormone stimulates the sympathetic nervous system, which in turn activates the body.

9.　(p. 309)　_____ _____ , or outward signs of what a person is feeling, are a major element of emotion. These are particularly important because they communicate emotion from one person to another. A marked shift in voice tone or modulation is one familiar example.

10.　(p. 309)　A final major element of emotion consists of _____ _____ , or a person's private emotional experience. This is the part of emotion with which we are typically most familiar.

11.　(p. 310)　Based on his research, Robert Plutchik believes there are eight _____ emotions which include fear, surprise, sadness, disgust, anger, anticipation, joy, and acceptance (receptivity).

12. (p. 310) Each of these emotions can vary in _____ to produce a variety of other emotions.

13. (p. 310) According to Plutchik, primary emotions can also be _____ to yield another, more complex emotion. For example, joy and fear may combine to produce guilt.

14. (p. 310) To a large degree the physical aspects of emotion are _____, or built into the body.

15. (p. 311) Unpleasant emotions produce especially consistent reactions including pounding heart, muscular tension, irritability, and so forth. This consistency is tied to the fact that they are generated by the _____ _____ _____ (ANS).

16. (p. 311) The reactions of the ANS are automatic and not normally under voluntary control. There are two divisions to the ANS, the _____ branch and the _____ branch.

17. (p. 311) The _____ branch prepares the body for emergency action: for "_____ or _____" by arousing a number of bodily systems and inhibiting others.

18. (p. 311) Most of the sympathetic reactions increase the chances that an organism will survive an emergency. _____ is released into the bloodstream for quick energy, the heart beats faster to distribute blood to the _____, _____ is temporarily inhibited, and blood flow in the skin is restricted to reduce _____.

19. (p. 311) The actions of the _____ branch generally reverse emotional arousal and calm and relax the body. The heart is slowed, the pupils return to normal size, blood pressure drops, and so forth.

20. (p. 311) In addition to restoring balance, the parasympathetic system helps build up and conserve _____ _____.

21. (p. 311) The parasympathetic branch responds much more _____ than the sympathetic. This finding explains why emotions do not subside until _____ or _____ minutes after the threat has passed.

22. (p. 311) After a strong emotional shock, the parasympathetic system may overreact and lower _____ _____ too much. This is why people sometimes become dizzy or faint at the sight of blood and other such shocks.

23. (p. 311) The parasympathetic system may overreact during intense fear and in rare cases causes death. This reaction, called a _____ _____, has been noted in voodoo curses and under the pressures of combat during war.

24. (p. 311) Another example of such deaths is provided by the young woman admitted to a hospital because she felt she was going to die. She strongly believed in a midwife's prediction that she would die before her twenty-third birthday. Indeed, she did die two days before this birthday, an apparent victim of her own _____.

25. (p. 312) In the case of older individuals or people with heart problems, the direct effects of _____ _____ may be enough to

bring about heart attack and collapse. Such was the case with the widow of Louis Armstrong.

26. (p. 312) Psychiatrist George Engel has studied hundreds of similar deaths. He found that almost _____ were associated with the extremely traumatic disruption of a close human relationship.

27. (p. 312) For example, recently widowed men have a sudden death rate _____ percent higher than married men of the same age do.

28. (p. 312) Eckhard Hess has studied the relationship between emotion and the size of a person's _____. Emotional effects such as arousal, interest, or attention can activate the sympathetic nervous system and cause dilation (enlargement).

29. (p. 312) Dilation of the pupils can occur during both pleasant and unpleasant emotions. However, most people tend to interpret _____ pupils as a sign of pleasant feelings, and _____ pupils as a sign of negative feelings.

30. (p. 312) To illustrate this, Hess demonstrated that men describe photos of a woman with _____ pupils as "soft," "feminine," or "pretty." The same woman with _____ pupils was described as "hard," "selfish," and "cold."

31. (p. 312) This effect was shown in an experiment where subjects were introduced to two potential partners (one of whom used eye drops to enlarge their pupils) and asked to choose one. Subjects of both sexes tended to select the person with the _____ _____.

32. (p. 312) Because bodily changes caused by the autonomic nervous system are good indicators of emotion, a number of techniques for measuring them have been developed. One of these is the _____ or lie detector.

33. (p. 312) A polygraph is a portable device capable of drawing a record of changes in heart _____, blood _____, breathing _____, and the _____ _____ _____ (GSR).

34. (p. 313) To be more accurate, a polygraph is not a lie detector at all, it only records general _____ _____. There is no unique "lie response."

35. (p. 313) When attempting to detect a lie, the polygraph operator begins by asking a number of _____ (nonemotional) questions. This process establishes a "_____," or normal emotional responsiveness.

36. (p. 313) To minimize the problem of general subject nervousness, a polygraph examiner asks a series of questions with _____ questions mixed among them.

37. (p. 313) As an alternative, subjects may be asked _____ questions that can be compared to critical questions. Such questions are designed to make almost anyone anxious.

38. (p. 313) Even when questioning is done properly, lie detection may be _____. Such was the case with Floyd Fay convicted of murdering his friend Fred Ery. Psychologist David Lykken has documented three such cases like this in which innocent people were convicted and imprisoned based on a polygrapher's testimony.

39. (p. 314) Proponents of lie detection claim _____ to _____ percent accuracy, but in one laboratory experiment, accuracy was lowered to _____ percent by subjects who intentionally thought exciting or upsetting thoughts during questioning.

40. (p. 314) The polygraph can be thrown off by self-inflicted pain, or by people who can lie without anxiety. One experiment showed that _____ drugs can interfere with the detection of lies.

41. (p. 314) The test's most common error is to label an innocent person guilty, rather than a guilty person innocent. In field studies involving real crimes and criminal suspects, an average of approximately ___ innocent person in ___ was rated as guilty by the "lie detector." In some instances, the "false positives" reached _____ percent.

42. (p. 314) In 1988 the United States Congress passed a law strictly limiting the use of lie detector tests for _____ _____ and employees of _____. However, there are still certain circumstances in which a polygraph may be given. You should be familiar with these and if given a lie detector test remain clam, then challenge the outcome if the machine wrongly questions your honesty.

43. (p. 314) Even the basic reactions of anger, fear, and joy, which appear to be unlearned, take time to develop. General _____ is the only emotional response newborn infants clearly express.

44. (p. 314) Bridges observed a large number of babies and found that all of the basic human emotions (both learned and unlearned) appear before age _____.

45. (p. 314) Bridges found that there is a consistent order in which emotions appear, and that the first basic split is between _____ and _____ emotions.

46. (p. 314) More recent research suggests that by the end of year _____, babies can express happiness, surprise, fear, anger, sadness, disgust, and interest.

47. (p. 314) When new parents see and hear a crying baby they feel annoyed and unhappy and their blood _____ and _____ increase. Such reactions encourage parents to tend to a baby's needs, thus increasing its chances for survival.

48. (p. 315) Development of the ability to express emotion is probably related to maturation of the _____ since children of all cultures show a similar pattern.

49. (p. 315) _____ _____ believed that emotional expressions were a carryover from more primitive and animal-like stages of evolution retained because communicating one's feelings to others is an aid to survival.

50. (p. 315) The most basic expressions do appear to be fairly universal. Children born _____ and _____ use the same facial gestures as others to display joy, sadness, disgust, etc.

51. (p. 316) By adulthood, many facial gestures are unique to various cultures. For example, among the Chinese sticking out the tongue is a gesture of _____, not of disrespect or teasing.

52. (p. 316) Despite such cultural differences, facial expressions of fear, surprise, sadness, disgust, anger, and happiness are recognized by people of all cultures. A _____ is the most universal and easily recognized facial expression of emotion.

53. (p. 316) The study of communication through body movement, posture, gestures, and facial expressions is called _____ and informally referred to as body language.

54. (p. 316)   While popular books on body language tend to list particular meanings for various gestures, researchers in the field emphasize that gestures are rarely this fixed in meaning. Instead an overall _____ _____ is communicated.

55. (p. 316)   The most expressive and frequently noticed part of the body is the face, capable of producing some 20,000 different expressions. Most of these are _____ _____ involving a mixture of two or more basic expressions.

56. (p. 316)   Facial   expressions   can   be   boiled   down   to   three   basic   dimensions   of _____-_____, _____-_____, and _____ (or arousal).

57. (p. 316)   Other emotional qualities are transmitted with the body, the most general being _____ or _____, and _____ or _____.

58. (p. 316)   _____ is expressed by casual position of the arms and legs, leaning back (if sitting), and spreading the arms and legs. _____ is expressed mainly by leaning toward a person or object.

59. (p. 317)   Recent research suggests that overall posture can indicate one's emotional state. When a person is _____, his or her posture is likely to be more erect. It remains debatable whether this tendency is a product of emotion or is simply learned.

60. (p. 318)   Because most people learn to maintain careful control over their facial expressions, detecting deception may be difficult. Deception is best revealed by the _____ _____.

61. (p. 317)   There are at least four theories which have been used to explain emotions. The _____ theory of emotion suggests that we perceive a stimulus, become aroused, and then respond.

62. (p. 317)   The _____-_____ theory is much the reverse of the commonsense theory of emotion. It postulates that bodily changes precede emotion and only later are we aware of the emotional experience.

63. (p. 317)   Another theory, which opposes that of James and Lange, proposes that emotional feelings and bodily arousal occur at the same time. This theory is the _____-_____ theory.

64. (p. 317)   The Cannon-Bard theory proposed that the thalamus simultaneously activates both the _____ (responsible for emotional feelings and emotional behavior), and the _____ (responsible for arousing the body).

65. (p. 318)   Most people assume that _____ eyes and _____ are clear signs of lying. Not so according to Paul Ekman. Also _____ _____ that involve touching one's own body (rubbing, grooming, etc.) are not consistently related to lying.

66. (p. 318)   The gestures people use to illustrate what they are saying may reveal lying. These gestures, called _____, tend to decrease when a person is telling a lie.

67. (p. 318)   Other movements, called _____, can also reveal lying. These

gestures have clear meanings within a particular culture and tend to increase when a person is lying.

68. (p. 318) Among the best clues to lying are the signs of strong emotion produced by the ANS. These include _____, blushing, blanching, _____ dilation, rapid or irregular _____, perspiration, frequent swallowing, _____ errors, and a louder, higher-pitched voice.

69. (p. 318) While the previous theories are mostly concerned with emotion as a physical response, a fourth theory, _____ theory of emotion, stresses _____ (mental) factors as important to emotion.

70. (p. 318) According to Schachter, emotion occurs when a particular _____ is applied to general physical arousal.

71. (p. 318) In support of his theory, Schachter showed that subjects given _____ before viewing a slapstick movie, rated the movie funniest. Subjects given a _____ were least amused, while a placebo group fell in the middle.

72. (p. 319) Stuart Valins has added an interesting refinement to the cognitive theory. According to Valins, perception of emotion depends upon what you _____ your feelings of physical arousal to.

73. (p. 319) To demonstrate attribution, Valins showed male students a series of slides of nude females, some paired with an amplified artificial heartbeat subjects believed to be their own. Asked to rate which females they found most attractive, they consistently chose the ones associated with a "_____ _____."

74. (p. 319) Attribution theory predicts that adding fear, anger, frustration, or rejection to a relationship tends to _____ a couple's feelings for each other.

75. (p. 319) In support of this, one study found that men interviewed on a swaying suspension bridge 230 feet above ground were _____ likely to later contact their woman interviewer than men interviewed on a wooden bridge ten feet above ground.

76. (p. 320) According to psychologist Carrol Izard, emotional activity causes innately pro- grammed changes in facial expression. The face then provides cues to the brain that help us determine what emotion we are feeling. This idea is known as the _____ _____ hypothesis.

77. (p. 320) This hypothesis states that having facial expressions and becoming aware of them is what leads to emotional experience. _____, for instance, arouses the body, but this arousal is not experienced as emotion because it does not trigger emotional expressions.

78. (p. 320) Paul Ekman monitored bodily reactions while subjects arranged their faces, muscle by muscle, into expressions of surprise, disgust, sadness, anger, fear, and happiness. "Making faces" brought about changes in the _____ nervous system, as reflected by heart rate and skin temperature.

79. (p. 320) Each facial expression produced a different pattern of activity. An angry face, for instance, _____ heart rate and skin temperature, whereas disgust _____ heart rate and skin temperature.

80. (p. 320)   Emotions determine expressions, and expressions may determine emotions. This could explain why when you are feeling sad, forcing yourself to _____ will sometimes cause an actual improvement in your mood.

81. (p. 320)   Psychologists are increasingly aware that the _____ of a situation greatly affects the course of emotion. This refers to evaluating the personal meaning of a stimulus.

82. (p. 320)   As an example of the contemporary model of emotions, when you see a snarling dog (an emotional stimulus), it is _____ (judged) as a threat. Your emotional appraisal gives rise to _____ _____ (your heart pounds and your body becomes stirred up).

83. (p. 320)   The appraisal also releases _____ _____ expressions (your face twists into a mask of fear and your posture becomes tense).

84. (p. 321)   At the same time, the appraisal leads to _____ behavior (running from the dog). It also causes a change in consciousness that you recognize as the _____ experience of fear. (The intensity of this emotional feeling is directly related to the amount of ANS arousal.)

85. (p. 322)   The original emotional stimulus can be _____, like the attacking dog, or it can be _____, such as a memory of being chased by a dog.

86. (p. 322)   According to Richard Lazarus, there are two important steps in the process of coping with a threatening situation. The first is _____ _____, in which you decide if a situation is threatening or not. Then you make a _____ _____ during which you choose a means of meeting the threat.

87. (p. 322)   The emotional effects of appraisal have been demonstrated through an experiment using a graphic film called _____. The film shows a painful operation being performed on the penises of adolescent boys of a primitive Australian tribe.

88. (p. 322)   Viewers watched the film under one of _____ different versions, ranging from no sound track to an emphasis on the pain, etc.

89. (p. 323)   Recordings of heart rate and GSR showed that the film emphasizing _____ aspects of the operation produced an _____ in emotion over that caused by the silent film.

90. (p. 323)   In contrast, the intellectual and denial sound tracks _____ emotion.

91. (p. 323)   After a person makes a secondary appraisal, coping attempts can be one of two types. _____-_____ coping is aimed at managing or altering the distressing situation itself. In _____-_____ coping, the person tries instead to control emotional reactions.

92. (p. 323)   Sometimes problem- and emotion-focused coping aid one another. It is also possible for the two types to clash or impede one another. For example, when suffering emotional distress over an important decision, you may make a premature choice to end the distress. While this may allow you to cope with your emotions, it can short-change _____-_____ coping.

93. (p. 323)   Threatening situations are often accompanied by an unpleasant emotional state known as _____, characterized by tension, uneasiness, apprehension, and worry.

94. (p. 323)   Anxiety caused by stressful situations or by our own shortcomings and limitations, may be lessened by the use of psychological _____ _____.

95. (p. 323)   A defense mechanism is any technique used to avoid, deny, or distort sources of threat or anxiety. They are also used to maintain an idealized _____-_____ so that we can comfortably live with ourselves.

96. (p. 323)   Many of the defense mechanisms were first identified by Sigmund Freud, who assumed they operate _____ creating large "blind spots" in awareness.

97. (p. 324)   Test anxiety refers to a combination of heightened _____ _____ (uneasiness, tension, sweating, pounding heart, nervousness) plus excessive _____ during test taking.

98. (p. 324)   Worries arise when taking a test that is appraised as a _____. Worries are the real heart of test anxiety because they directly interfere with thinking about the test. Some test anxious students actually spend as much time worrying as they do working on the test.

99. (p. 324)   The most direct antidote for test anxiety is _____ _____. Many test anxious students simply study too little and too late for exams.

100. (p. 324)   One solution for test anxiety is to _____ by studying well in advance of the test day. Those who are well prepared score higher, worry less, and are less likely to become overly aroused.

101. (p. 324)   As in other stressful situations, learning to _____ can help lower test anxiety. Anxiety is also lowered by support for others—so discuss any problems with your professors.

102. (p. 324)   Nervousness during tests can often be lessened by carefully _____ in your imagination how you will cope with upsetting events.

103. (p. 324)   Because worries are such a major part of test anxiety, changing _____-_____ thinking patterns can be the best solution of all. Learn to counter worries with calming, rational replies (coping statements).

104. (p. 324)   One of the most basic defense mechanisms is _____, to protect oneself from an unpleasant reality by refusing to accept or believe it.

105. (p. 324)   Denial is closely associated with _____, _____, and similar painful and threatening experiences.

106. (p. 325)   Freud noticed that his patients had tremendous difficulty recalling shocking or traumatic events from childhood. It seemed that powerful forces were holding these painful memories from awareness. Freud called this _____.

107. (p. 325)   _____ _____ is a defense in which impulses are not only repressed, they are also held in check by exaggerated opposite behavior. For

example, a mother who unconsciously resents her children may become absurdly overprotective and overindulgent.

108. (p. 325) In its broadest meaning, _____ as a defense mechanism refers to any return to earlier, less demanding situations or habits. For example, parents who have a second child find that the older child, frustrated by a new rival for attention, may demonstrate childish _____, bed-_____, or infantile _____.

109. (p. 325) _____, another defense mechanism, is the unconscious process whereby an individual tends to see his or her own shortcomings or unacceptable impulses in others. By exaggerating these unacceptable traits in others, the individual lessens his or her own failings.

110. (p. 325) When the explanations offered for our behavior are reasonable and convincing, but not the real reasons, we say a person is _____. This defense mechanism unconsciously provides us with reasons for behavior we ourselves find somewhat questionable.

111. (p. 326) Overuse of defense mechanisms requires great amounts of _____ energy. However, they do have value since they may prevent a person from being overwhelmed by a temporary threat and give him or her time to learn to _____ with continuing frustrations.

112. (p. 326) There are two defense mechanisms that have a decidedly more positive quality to them than those previously described. One of these, _____, is a form of behavior whereby a person tries to make up for some personal defect or fault.

113. (p. 326) _____ reactions are defenses against feelings of inferiority. If directed at overcoming the deficiency itself, they may be constructive.

114. (p. 326) _____ is defined as working off frustrated desires in substitute activities that are constructive and accepted by society.

115. (p. 326) Freud believed that almost any strong desire can be sublimated, but that the most easily and widely sublimated motives are _____.

116. (p. 327) Bruno Bettelheim has described a reaction called "give-up-itis" which he observed among Nazi concentration camp prisoners who developed a "zombie-like" detachment from their situations. Martin Seligman has described a similar reaction in Vietnam prisoner of war camps. Recent attempts to understand such events have focused on the concept of _____ _____.

117. (p. 327) Learned helplessness has been demonstrated in the laboratory with animals. If placed in one side of a divided box, dogs will quickly learn to leap to the other to _____ an electric shock or to _____ the electric shock when given a warning in advance.

118. (p. 327) In learned helplessness, dogs first given several painful shocks which they were _____ to prevent, later would not escape or avoid shock when given the chance.

119. (p. 327) Similar effects occur when humans are made to fail or receive punishment they cannot predict or prevent. However, where humans are concerned,

_____ have a large effect on helplessness. Helplessness in one situation can produce helplessness in other situations if people attribute their failure to lasting, general factors.

120. (p. 328) Seligman has drawn attention to the similarities between learned helplessness and _____. Symptoms that occur in both include feelings of powerlessness and hopelessness, decreased _____, lowered _____, loss of _____ drive and appetite, and a tendency to see oneself as failing, even when this is not the case.

121. (p. 328) With dogs, the most effective technique for eliminating learned helplessness has been to forcibly drag them away from the _____ into the "safe" compartment. After this is done several times, the animals regain "hope" and feelings of control over the environment.

122. (p. 328) When animals are given _____ _____ they become more resistant to learned helplessness. For example, animals that first learn to successfully escape shock are more persistent later in trying to escape inescapable shock.

123. (p. 328) Perhaps programs such as the _____ _____ schools might help immunize people against helplessness by giving them experience at mastering seemingly impossible challenges.

124. (p. 329) Recent studies show that during the school year, up to _____ percent of the students enrolled at American colleges suffer some of the symptoms of depression.

125. (p. 329) At any given time, roughly _____-_____ of the student population is involved.

126. (p. 329) In a more recent survey, college students reported that they got depressed from one to two times a _____. These episodes lasted from a few hours to several days.

127. (p. 329) A variety of problems seem to be associated with this problem. Four common issues include: (1) stresses from increased difficulty of college work and pressures to make a _____ choice; (2) _____ and loneliness; (3) problems with studying and _____; and (4) breakups of intimate _____.

128. (p. 329) Aaron Beck points out five monitors of depression. These signals include: (1) a consistently _____ opinion of yourself; (2) frequent self-criticism and self-blame; (3) placing _____ interpretations on events; (4) the _____ looks bleak and negative; and (5) your _____ feel overwhelming.

129. (p. 329) As solutions for dealing with "college blues," Beck and Greenberg suggest that you start by making a _____ _____. Keeping busy often helps.

130. (p. 329) Also, try writing down self-critical and negative thoughts, especially those that immediately precede feelings of sadness. Then write a _____ answer to each.

131. (p. 329) Attacks of the college blues are common and should be distinguished from more serious cases of depression. The National Association for Mental Health lists

_____ "danger signals" which can help distinguish normal from severe depression. Be familiar with them.

132. (p. 331)   According to psychologist Robert Sternberg's triangular theory of love, love is made up of _____, _____, and commitment.

133. (p. 331)   A relationship has intimacy, or closeness, if _____, sharing, _____, and support are present.

134. (p. 331)   Intimacy grows _____ at first, but in time it _____ _____. After it does, people in long-term relationships may gradually lose sight of the fact that they are still very close and mutually dependent.

135. (p. 331)   Passion refers mainly to _____ _____. It may be sexual, but it includes other sources too. Passion is the primary source of love's intensity.

136. (p. 331)   Passionate love often occurs against a backdrop of danger, adversity, or frustration. Perhaps because of this, _____ inspires the strongest feelings of love, while love for _____ is least intense.

137. (p. 331)   The third side of the love triangle, commitment, starts at zero before you meet a person and grows steadily as you get acquainted. Like intimacy, commitment tends to level off. It _____ _____ when a relationship is in serious trouble.

138. (p. 332)   The presence or absence of each factor in love produces eight different triangles. The first defines _____, a total absence of all three elements.

139. (p. 332)   In _____, you feel close to a person and communicate well with her or him. However, you do not feel any passion or deep commitment to the person.

140. (p. 332)   _____ love mixes intimacy with passion. Despite its intensity, it does not involve much commitment at first.

141. (p. 332)   _____ love describes commitments made rapidly on the basis of physical attraction, but without much emotional intimacy. Relationships started this way risk failure because lovers make a commitment before they really get to know one another well.

142. (p. 332)   _____ is a very superficial form of love in which a person is inflamed with passion but shares no intimacy or commitment with the beloved. In time, it may lead to more lasting kinds of love.

143. (p. 332)   _____ love refers to affection and deep attachment that is built on respect, shared interests, and firm friendship. It is lower-key emotionally, steady, long-term, and tends to grow in time.

144. (p. 332)   Couples sometimes reach a point where there is little passion or intimacy left in their relationship. If they stay together merely out of commitment or habit, they experience _____ love.

145. (p. 332)   _____ love occurs when two people are passionate, committed to one another, and emotionally close. Complete, balanced love of this kind occurs only in very special relationships.

146. (p. 332)   Other theorists have noted that Sternberg's theory may place too much emphasis on
_____. In most relationships, intimacy and commitment are a
bigger part of love.

147. (p. 332)   Our culture also tends to place much emphasis on passion as the main basis for
"falling" in love. However, this overlooks the fact that the passionate, breathless
state of love typically lasts only about ___ to _____ months.

148. (p. 332)   Sternberg   and   Michael   Barnes   found   that   relationships   are   generally
_____ if you think the other person feels about you as
you would like for her or him to feel about you.

SELF-TEST

1. (p. 308)   Voodoo deaths are now thought to be caused by
a. witchcraft
b. sympathetic nervous system arousal
c. overreaction of the parasympathetic nervous system
d. peripheral nervous system reversals

2. (p. 309)   Emotions seem to have been retained in evolution because
a. they are simply residual behaviors transmitted from our animal heritage serving
little purpose
b. they underlie adaptive behaviors and generally are an aid to survival
c. they primarily serve as universal communication facilitating cross-cultural
interactions
d. they are a by-product of our nervous system and as such evolved along with our
neural structure

3. (p. 309)   Physiological changes which underlie fear, anger, joy, and other emotions are
primarily caused by
a. release of pituitary hormones into the bloodstream
b. parasympathetic nervous system arousal
c. the shutdown of the sympathetic nervous system
d. release of adrenaline into the bloodstream

4. (p. 310)   Which of the following is *not* true of Robert Plutchik's ideas concerning emotion?
a. Primary emotions are primitive, less desirable emotions which are combined with
more sophisticated elements in the higher species.
b. Primary emotions can blend to produce a different more complex emotion.
c. Each primary emotion can vary in intensity to produce other related emotions.
d. There are eight primary emotions including fear, surprise, sadness, etc.

5. (p. 310)   Unpleasant emotional reactions are all generated by the
a. peripheral nervous system   c. automatic nervous system
b. autonomic nervous system   d. voluntary nervous system

6. (p. 311)   True-False. The sympathetic branch of the ANS responds much more slowly than the
parasympathetic branch.

7. (p. 311)   Which of the following is *not* associated with the parasympathetic nervous system?
a. preparations for "fight or flight"
b. reverse emotional arousal
c. build up and conserve bodily energy
d. calm and relax the body

8. (p. 312) True-False. Not only is the notion that enlarged pupils occur with pleasant emotions untrue, people actually prefer the appearance of individuals with constricted pupils.

9. (p. 312) Which of the following is true of lie detectors?
      a. There are several unique lie responses they can measure.
      b. They are 90 to 95 percent accurate.
      c. The test's most common error is to label a guilty person innocent.
      d. Only a few states require polygraph operators to be licensed.

10. (p. 312) Of the following bodily changes, which is *not* usually measured by the polygraph?
      a. heart rate   c. blood pressure
      b. GSR   d. brain waves

11. (p. 314) Which of the following emotions appear to be unlearned?
      a. remorse, sadness, frustration   c. surprise, awe, excitement
      b. guilt, grief, greed   d. joy, rage, fear

12. (p. 314) Bridges has found that among human infants, all of the basic emotions appear before age
      a. 6 months   c. 24 months
      b. 12 months   d. 36 months

13. (p. 315) True-False. Charles Darwin felt that human emotional expression was a carry-over from more primitive and animal-like stages of human evolution.

14. (p. 316) True-False. The ability to express emotion is highly learned and culturally dependent. For example, infants in China stick out their tongue as a gesture of surprise.

15. (p. 316) The most universal facial expression of emotion is
      a. smiling   c. frowning
      b. grimacing   d. winking

16. (p. 316) Which of the following is *not* true of kinesics?
      a. It is the study of communication through body movement, posture, gestures, and facial expressions.
      b. Generally, it can be accurately used to predict particular meanings from particular gestures.
      c. An overall emotional tone is usually communicated by body language.
      d. It is informally referred to as "body language."

17. (p. 316) Of the following, which is *not* a basic dimension of emotion conveyed by facial expressions?
      a. activation   c. attention-rejection
      b. pleasantness-unpleasantness   d. hope-disappointment

18. (p. 317) True-False. Because most people learn to maintain careful control over their facial expressions, a deception is better revealed by the lower body.

19. (p. 317) Which theory of emotion first stressed that emotional feelings follow bodily arousal?
      a. James-Lange theory
      b. Schachter-Singer cognitive theory
      c. attribution theory
      d. Cannon-Bard theory

20. (p. 318) The Cannon-Bard theory of emotion states that
      a. emotional feelings follow bodily arousal

b. the thalamus simultaneously activates the cortex and the hypothalamus

c. perception of emotion depends on what feelings of physical arousal are attributed to

d. emotion occurs when a particular label is applied to general physical arousal

21. (p. 318) True-False. According to Schachter's view of emotion it is the interpretation of physical arousal that determines the emotion experienced.

22. (p. 318) True-False. According to the idea of attribution, adding fear, anger, or frustration to a relationship tends to diminish a couple's feelings for each other.

23. (p. 322) Recordings of heart rate and GSR showed that viewers watching a graphic film called *Subincision* demonstrated the greatest emotional response when the film's soundtrack
    a. was totally absent (silent)
    b. emphasized the painful and traumatic aspects of the operation
    c. treated the operation in an intellectual and distant way
    d. glossed over the threatening aspects of the operation and denied that it was painful

24. (p. 323) Which of the following is *not* true of psychological defense mechanisms?
    a. They prevent us from facing reality and should be actively avoided at all times.
    b. Many were first identified by Freud who assumed they operate unconsciously.
    c. They are used to avoid, deny, or distort sources of anxiety.
    d. They are commonly used to maintain an idealized self-image.

25. (p. 324) Test anxiety does *not* involve which of the following?
    a. overpreparation leading to superficial competency
    b. heightened physiological arousal
    c. excessive worry
    d. lowered test scores

26. (p. 324) Which of the following is a useful technique to use in lowering test anxiety?
    a. being overprepared
    b. changing self-defeating thinking patterns
    c. rehearsing how to cope with upsetting events
    d. all of the above

27. (p. 324) When you protect yourself from an unpleasant reality by refusing to perceive it, this process is called
    a. repression   c. denial
    b. fantasy   d. sour grapes

28. (p. 325) When painful and dangerous thoughts are prevented from entering consciousness, this process is called
    a. sublimation   c. delusion
    b. repression   d. projection

29. (p. 325) Reaction formation involves
    a. preventing dangerous impulses from being expressed by exaggerating opposite behaviors
    b. reacting to the formation of anxiety-producing mental images by denying they exist
    c. attempts to overcome a deficiency or weakness by excelling in other areas
    d. working off frustrated desires in substitute activities that are constructive and accepted by society

30. (p. 325) Retreating to an earlier level of development or to earlier, less demanding habits or situations is called
  a. suppression
  b. repression
  c. projection
  d. regression

31. (p. 325) _____ as a defense mechanism means attributing to others one's own shortcomings or unacceptable feelings.
  a. Projection
  b. Compensation
  c. Sublimation
  d. Rationalization

32. (p. 326) Counteracting a real or imagined weakness by emphasizing desirable traits or by seeking to excel in others defines the process of
  a. compensation
  b. rationalization
  c. reaction formation
  d. sublimation

33. (p. 326) _____ is defined as working off frustrated desires in substitute activities that are constructive or socially acceptable.
  a. Sublimation
  b. Compensation
  c. Rationalization
  d. Projection

34. (p. 327) Learned helplessness may result when unpleasant events frequently occur which
  a. cannot be controlled by the individual
  b. are attributed to the negative behaviors of the individual
  c. produce high fear levels in the individual
  d. are not adapted to by the individual

35. (p. 327) Which of the following is a reasonable example of learned helplessness?
  a. Concentration camp survivors suffering what Bettelheim called "give-up-itis."
  b. Laboratory animals which do not escape or avoid shocks when possible after first receiving unavoidable shocks.
  c. Depression in humans accompanied by feelings of powerlessness and marked by passive endurance of psychological shocks.
  d. All of the above.

36. (p. 328) True-False. Mild depression among college students is relatively common since roughly one-quarter of the student population is involved at any given time.

37. (p. 328) Which of the following is *not* a common reason for depression among college students?
  a. lack of financial resources and tight budgets
  b. breakup of an intimate relationship
  c. isolation and loneliness
  d. pressures to make career choices

38. (p. 331) Which of the following is *not* an element defined by Sternberg as part of his triangular theory of love?
  a. commitment
  b. passion
  c. arousal
  d. intimacy

39. (p. 332) Sternberg refers to _____ love as affection and deep attachment that is built on respect, shared interests, and firm friendship.
  a. consummate
  b. companionate
  c. romantic
  d. fatuous

40. (p. 332) Which of the following is *not* true of Sternberg's concept of passion?
  a. It refers mainly to physiological arousal and is the primary source of love's intensity.

b. It is the main element of infatuation where neither intimacy nor commitment is involved.
c. Couples who have only strong passion left in their relationships are said to experience empty love.
d. Other theorists have suggested that Sternberg's theory places too much emphasis on passion.

ANSWERS — PROGRAMMED REVIEW

1. emotion
2. parasympathetic nervous
3. good; happy
4. move; physically
5. adaptive
6. survival
7. rate; pressure
8. adrenaline
9. Emotional expressions
10. emotional feelings
11. primary
12. intensity
13. mixed
14. innate
15. autonomic nervous system
16. sympathetic; parasympathetic
17. sympathetic; fight, flight
18. Sugar; muscles; digestion; bleeding
19. parasympathetic
20. bodily energy
21. slowly; 20; 30
22. blood pressure
23. parasympathetic rebound
24. terror
25. sympathetic activation
26. half
27. 40
28. pupils
29. large; small
30. large; small
31. larger pupils
32. polygraph
33. rate; pressure; rate; galvanic skin response
34. emotional arousal
35. control; baseline
36. critical
37. control
38. inaccurate
39. 90; 95; 25
40. tranquilizing
41. 1; 5; 75
42. job applicants; private businesses
43. excitement
44. two
45. pleasant, unpleasant
46. one
47. pressure; perspiration
48. brain
49. Charles Darwin
50. deaf, blind
51. surprise
52. smile
53. kinesics
54. emotional tone
55. facial blends
56. pleasantness-unpleasantness; attention-rejection; activation
57. relaxation, tension; liking, disliking
58. Relaxation; Liking
59. successful
60. lower body
61. commonsense
62. James-Lange
63. Cannon-Bard
64. cortex; hypothalamus
65. shifty; squirming; nervous movements
66. illustrators
67. emblems
68. blinking; pupil; breathing; speech
69. Schachter's cognitive; cognitive
70. label
71. adrenaline; tranquilizer
72. attribute
73. pounding heart
74. increase
75. more
76. facial feedback
77. Exercise
78. autonomic
79. raised; lowered
80. smile
81. appraisal
82. appraised; ANS arousal
83. innate emotional
84. adaptive; subjective
85. external; internal
86. primary appraisal; secondary appraisal
87. Subincision
88. four
89. traumatic; increase

90. reduced
91. Problem-focused; Emotion-focused
92. problem-focused
93. anxiety
94. defense mechanisms
95. self-image
96. unconsciously
97. physiological arousal; worry
98. threat
99. hard work
100. overprepare
101. relax
102. rehearsing
103. self-defeating
104. denial
105. death, illness
106. repression
107. Reaction formation
108. regression; speech; wetting; play
109. Projection
110. rationalizing
111. emotional; cope
112. compensation
113. Compensatory
114. Sublimation
115. sexual
116. learned helplessness
117. escape; avoid
118. helpless
119. attributions
120. depression; activity; aggression; sexual
121. shock
122. mastery training
123. Outward Bound
124. 78
125. one-quarter
126. month
127. career; isolation; grades; relationships
128. negative; negative; future; responsibilities
129. daily schedule
130. rational
131. ten
132. intimacy; passion
133. affection; communication
134. steadily; levels off
135. physiological arousal
136. romance; siblings
137. drops rapidly
138. nonlove
139. liking
140. Romantic
141. Fatuous
142. Infatuation
143. Companionate
144. empty
145. Consummate
146. passion
147. 6; 30
148. satisfying

ANSWERS — SELF-TEST

1. c	15. a	28. b
2. b	16. b	29. a
3. d	17. d	30. d
4. a	18. True	31. a
5. b	19. a	32. a
6. False	20. b	33. a
7. a	21. True	34. a
8. False	22. False	35. d
9. d	23. b	36. True
10. d	24. a	37. a
11. d	25. a	38. c
12. c	26. d	39. b
13. True	27. c	40. c
14. False		

Chapter 13

Health, Stress, and Coping

CONTENTS

Stress—Thrill or Threat?
Frustration—Blind Alleys and Lead Balloons
Conflict—Yes-No-Yes-No-Yes-No-Yes-No-Yes-No . . . Well, Maybe
Stress and Health—Unmasking a Hidden Killer
Health Psychology—Here's to Your Good Health
Stress Management
Meditation—The Twenty-Minute Vacation

TERMS AND CONCEPTS

frustration
stress
stress reaction
pressure
burnout
external frustration
social obstacles
nonsocial obstacles
personal frustration
displaced aggression
scapegoating
conflict
approach-approach conflicts
avoidance-avoidance conflicts
approach-avoidance conflicts
ambivalence
partial approach
double approach-avoidance conflicts
Social Readjustment Rating Scale (SRRS)
life change unit (LCU)
hassles (microstressors)
psychosomatic disorders
hypochondria

Type A personality
Type B personality
hardy personality
general adaptation syndrome (G.A.S.)
alarm reaction
stage of resistance
stage of exhaustion
psychoneuroimmunology
health psychology
behavioral medicine
behavioral risk factors
community health campaigns
stress management
progressive relaxation
stress innoculation
coping statements
negative self-statements
stereotyped response
concentrative meditation
receptive meditation
mantra
relaxation response

IMPORTANT INDIVIDUALS

Christina Maslack	Salvatore Maddi
Thomas Holmes	Suzanne Kobasa
Richard Lazarus	Hans Selye
Meyer Friedman	Donald Meichenbaum
Ray Rosenman	Herbert Benson

PROGRAMMED REVIEW

1. (p. 335) _____ is defined as a negative emotional state that occurs when one is prevented from reaching a _____.

2. (p. 336) _____ occurs whenever a challenge or a threat forces a person to adjust or adapt. While it is a normal part of life, it can do tremendous damage to one's health when it is severe or prolonged.

3. (p. 336) It is common to assume that stress is always _____, or that a complete _____ of stress is ideal. While unpleasant events do produce stress, so do travel, sports, dating, and other pleasant activities. A healthy lifestyle may include a fair amount of stress.

4. (p. 336) Your body's stress _____ begins with the same autonomic nervous system arousal that occurs during emotions. ANS responses include a rapid surge in your heart rate, blood pressure, respiration, muscle tension, etc.

5. (p. 336) _____-term stresses can be uncomfortable, but they rarely do any damage. _____-term physical changes can accompany prolonged stress. These changes can do much harm.

6. (p. 336) A major factor in stress is _____. This factor was shown in a laboratory experiment in which rats given shocks without warning developed severe ulcers.

7. (p. 336) _____ is another element in stress. It occurs when activities must be speeded up, when deadlines must be met, when extra work is added unexpectedly, or when a person must work at, or near, capacity for long periods.

8. (p. 337) People generally feel more stress in situations over which they have little _____. For example, DeGood found that among students subjected to an unpleasant shock-avoidance learning task, those subjects allowed to select their own rest periods showed _____ stress levels (as measured by blood pressure) than those who could not.

9. (p. 337) At work, prolonged stress sometimes results in _____, a condition that exists when an employee is physically, mentally, and emotionally drained.

10. (p. 337) Christina Maslack has identified three aspects of this problem. First, burnout involves _____ _____. Affected persons are fatigued, tense, apathetic, and suffer from various physical complaints.

11. (p. 337) A second aspect of burnout is _____, or detachment from others. "Burned-out" workers coldly treat clients as if they were objects and find it difficult to care about them.

12. (p. 337) The third aspect of burnout is a feeling of reduced _____ _____. Workers who have burned out do poor work, their self-esteem suffers, and they yearn to change jobs or careers.

13. (p. 337) Burnout may occur in any job but is a marked problem in emotionally demanding _____ professions, such as nursing, teaching, social work, counseling, or police work.

14. (p. 337) To help prevent burnout, a good start might include redesigning jobs, workloads, and responsibilities to create a better balance between demands and satisfactions. Building stronger _____ _____ systems at work could also help.

15. (p. 337) A good example of social support systems is the growing use of _____ _____ by nurses and other caregivers. These allow workers to give and receive emotional support as they talk about feelings, problems, and stresses.

16. (p. 338) Ultimately, stress depends on how a situation is perceived. Whenever a stressor is appraised as a _____, a powerful stress reaction follows.

17. (p. 338) The concept of "threat" does not mean that you believe your life is in danger. Rather threat has more to do with the idea of control. _____ control is just as important as _____ control in causing us to feel threatened by events.

18. (p. 338) Your personal sense of control in any situation comes from believing that you have the power to reach desired goals. It is threatening for a person to feel that he or she lacks _____ to meet a particular demand.

19. (p. 338) The _____ of the body's stress reaction often depends on what we think and tell ourselves about stressors. This is why it can be valuable to train yourself to think in ways that avoid triggering the body's stress response.

20. (p. 338) _____ frustration is based on conditions outside of the individual which impede progress toward a goal. They are based upon delay, _____, _____, _____, and other direct blocking of motives.

21. (p. 338) External obstacles can be either _____ (in which case other people's behavior is the source) or _____ (in which case events or situations are the source).

22. (p. 338) The amount of frustration experienced usually increases as the _____, _____, or _____ of the blocked motive increases.

23. (p. 338) _____ becomes stronger as we near a goal. Therefore, frustration is more intense when a person encounters an obstacle very close to a goal.

24. (p. 338) _____ frustrations can accumulate in their effect until a small irritation unleashes an unexpectedly violent response.

25. (p. 338) _____ frustrations are based on an individual's personal characteristics. They are ultimately based on personal limitations, although the resulting failures may be perceived as externally caused frustrations.

26. (p. 339) Although aggression is a common response to frustration, there are several others. The first response is usually _____, characterized by more vigorous efforts and more variable responses.

27. (p. 339)   Increased persistence can be very adaptive. The same is true of aggression that removes or destroys a barrier. However, since aggression can be disruptive and is generally discouraged, it is frequently _____.

28. (p. 339)   Targets of displaced aggression tend to be "safer" or less likely to retaliate than the original source of frustration. Sometimes long _____ of displaced aggression, in which one person displaces aggression to the next, can be observed.

29. (p. 339)   Psychologists attribute much hostility and destructiveness in our society to displaced aggression. A disturbing example is the finding that when unemployment increases, so does _____ _____.

30. (p. 339)   A particulary damaging form of displaced aggression is _____, in which a person becomes a habitual target of redirected aggression. For example, between 1880 and 1930 there was a strong correlation between the price of _____ and the number of lynchings of _____ in the American South.

31. (p. 339)   Another major reaction to frustration is _____ or withdrawal, either physically or psychologically leaving the frustrating situation.

32. (p. 339)   Two common forms of psychological escape are _____ (pretending not to care) and the use of _____.

33. (p. 339)   _____ occurs whenever a person must choose between incompatible or contradictory needs, desires, motives, wishes, or external demands.

34. (p. 340)   The simplest conflict comes from having to choose between two positive or desirable alternatives and is called _____-_____ conflict.

35. (p. 340)   Approach-approach conflicts tend to be the _____ to resolve. When both options are positive, the scales of decision are _____ tipped in one direction or the other.

36. (p. 340)   When forced to choose between two negative or undesirable alternatives, an _____-_____ conflict develops.

37. (p. 340)   These conflicts can be defined only on the basis of a personal _____ and _____.

38. (p. 340)   When faced with severe avoidance-avoidance conflicts in which there is no escape, people often _____, finding it impossible to make a decision or to take action.

39. (p. 340)   In cases where escape is possible, people may react to avoidance-avoidance conflicts by _____ the _____ so as to pull out of avoidance situations entirely.

40. (p. 340)   In an _____-_____ conflict a person is attracted to, and repelled by, the same goal or activity.

41. (p. 342)   In these situations, a person will feel _____ (mixed positive and negative feelings) toward the goal. This experience is usually translated into _____ approach.

42. (p. 342)   The most typical of the choices we usually must make is known as _____

_____ - _____ conflicts because each alternative has both positive and negative qualities.

43. (p. 342) When faced with this situation, people tend to _____ or waiver between the alternatives.

44. (p. 343) Thomas Holmes has demonstrated that stressful events reduce the body's natural defenses against disease and increase the likelihood of _____. Disaster and sorrow often precede illness.

45. (p. 343) More surprising is the finding that almost any major _____ in one's life requires adjustment and increases susceptibility to accident and illness.

46. (p. 343) Holmes and his associates have developed the _____ _____ _____ _____ (SRRS) to help determine the health hazards faced when stresses accumulate.

47. (p. 343) The SRRS expresses the effect of life events in _____ _____ _____ (LCUs).

48. (p. 343) If the total LCUs for events experienced during the past year exceeds _____, there is a high chance of illness or accident in the near future. A more conservative rating can be obtained by totalling LCUs for just the past six months.

49. (p. 344) The SRRS tends to be more appropriate for _____, more established adults. However, recent research has shown that entering college, changing majors, or breaking up a steady relationship can affect the health of younger adults.

50. (p. 344) The SRRS is not a foolproof way to rate stress and does have limitations. Some studies have _____ to confirm the LCU-illness link. Also, it is debatable whether _____ life events are always stressful. Another very important criticism is that people differ greatly in their reactions to the same event.

51. (p. 344) Richard Lazarus has studied the impact of minor but frequent stresses referred to as _____.

52. (p. 344) In a year-long study involving _____ men and women, Lazarus found that frequent and severe hassles were better predictors of day-to-day psychological and physical health than were major life events.

53. (p. 344) Lazarus found that the personal importance of hassles affects the amount of stress they produce. Hassles that are _____ to one's self-worth (such as work, family, and relationships) are most likely to cause trouble.

54. (p. 344) Prolonged stress reactions are related to a large number of _____ _____ in which psychological and emotional factors are associated with actual damage to tissues of the body.

55. (p. 344) Psychosomatic problems, such as ulcers, are not the same as _____ where a person imagines that they suffer from diseases.

56. (p. 344) The most common psychosomatic problems are gastrointestinal and _____, but other major problems include _____ (skin rash), hives, migraine headaches, rheumatoid arthritis, _____

(high blood pressure), _____ (ulceration of the colon), and heart disease.

57. (p. 345) Lesser health complaints that may be stress-related include muscle _____, headaches, neckaches, backaches, _____, constipation, fatigue, insomnia, and sexual _____.

58. (p. 345) It is estimated that at least _____ of all patients who go to a doctor either have a psychosomatic problem, or have a problem complicated by psychosomatic symptoms.

59. (p. 345) Usually several other factors combine with stress to produce physical damage. These factors include _____ differences, specific _____ weaknesses, and _____ reactions to stress.

60. (p. 345) Two noted cardiologists, Meyer Friedman and Ray Rosenman, have conducted long-term studies of personality and _____ problems.

61. (p. 345) They classified people into two categories: _____ ___ personalities (those who run a high risk of heart attack), and _____ ___ personalities (those unlikely to have heart attacks).

62. (p. 345) After an eight year follow-up, they found that the rate of heart disease among Type A's was more than _____ that among Type B's.

63. (p. 345) Type A people are hard-driving, ambitious, highly competitive, achievement oriented, and striving. Type A's work closer to their actual limits of endurance (on a treadmill), but say they are _____ _____ than do Type B people.

64. (p. 345) Type A's are characterized by _____ _____. They seem unsatisfied with the normal pace of events. They race the clock in self-imposed urgency.

65. (p. 345) Another characteristic of Type A's is their chronic _____ or _____. These feelings are strongly related to increased risk of heart attack.

66. (p. 345) While it is true that some recent studies have failed to show a link between Type A behavior and heart attacks, _____ of studies have supported the validity of the Type A concept. Many researchers believe it is possible that those studies which failed may not have accurately classified people as Type As and Bs in the first place.

67. (p. 345) There is growing evidence that _____ or _____ may be more important than other aspects of Type A behavior. Whatever the factors, it seems that Type A's would be wise to take their increased health risks seriously.

68. (p. 345) A recent large-scale study of heart attack victims found that modifying Type A behavior significantly _____ the rate of repeat heart attacks.

69. (p. 345) Many of the destructive habits of Type A people are summarized in the self-identification test presented in the text. The best way to avoid the self-made stress caused by Type A personality is to adopt behavior that is the _____ of these destructive habits.

70. (p. 346) For the last 10 years, psychologists Salvatore Maddi and Suzanne Kobasa have studied

people with a _____ _____. Such people seem to be unusually resistant to stress.

71. (p. 346) People with hardy personalities seem to hold a world view that consists of the following:
    1) They have a personal _____ to self, work, family, and other stabilizing values.
    2) They feel they have _____ over their lives and their work.
    3) They have a tendency to see life as a series of _____, rather than as threats or problems.

72. (p. 346) The answer to how stress causes physical damage seems to lie in the body's defense against stress, a pattern of reactions known as the _____ _____ _____, abreviated _____.

73. (p. 346) Study of the G.A.S. began when physiologist Hans Selye noticed that the initial symptoms of almost any disease or trauma are almost _____.

74. (p. 347) The first stage of the G.A.S. is called the _____ _____. During this stage the body mobilizes its defenses against stress.

75. (p. 347) During this first phase, the pituitary gland secretes a hormone that causes the adrenal glands to increase their output of _____ and _____, which speed up some bodily processes and slow down others to concentrate resources where needed.

76. (p. 347) During the alarm reaction, people experience such symptoms as headache, fever, fatigue, sore _____, shortness of _____, diarrhea, upset _____, loss of _____ and lack of _____.

77. (p. 347) If stress continues, the second stage, called the _____ of _____, begins. At this point the body's defenses are stabilized and symptoms disappear, but resistance to other stresses may be lowered.

78. (p. 347) Research demonstrates that animals placed in an extremely cold environment become more resistant to the cold, but more susceptible to _____.

79. (p. 347) It is during this second stage that the first signs of _____ disorders begin to appear.

80. (p. 347) If stress continues, the _____ of _____ may be reached. In this stage, the body's resources are exhausted and a psychosomatic disorder, organ failure, or complete collapse results.

81. (p. 347) Animals examined by Selye during the latter stages of the G.A.S. showed enlargement and discoloration of their _____ _____, intense shrinkage of the _____, spleen and lymph nodes, and deep bleeding _____ _____.

82. (p. 347) In addition to such direct effects, there is growing evidence that stress can disrupt the body's _____ _____, making people more susceptible to illness.

83. (p. 347) The area of research called _____ is beginning to uncover evidence that the body and the brain work together as a kind of "health care system."

84. (p. 347)   The body's immune system is regulated, in part, by the brain. Stress, upsetting
_____, and _____ may affect this link in
ways that increase susceptibility to disease.

85. (p. 347)   _____ appears to be an important factor in how stress affects us.
For instance, one recent study found that immune system response was suppressed in
rats given inescapable shocks but not in rats given escapable shocks.

86. (p. 347)   Another study found that the immune system was _____ in
students during stressful major exam times. Such findings suggest that part of the
link between stress and illness may be traced to changes in the immune system.

87. (p. 348)   Almost one-half of all deaths in the United States are primarily due to unhealthy
behavior   or   lifestyles.   A   new   specialty   called   _____
_____ aims to do something about it by using psychological principles to promote health and prevent illness.

88. (p. 348)   Psychologists   working   in   the   allied   field   of   _____
_____ apply psychological knowledge to medical problems.
Their interests include the control of pain, adjustment to chronic illness, adherence to
doctors' instructions, psychosomatic disease, and similar topics.

89. (p. 348)   Around the turn of the century, people primarily died from infectious diseases and
accidents. Today, people generally suffer and die from "lifestyle" illnesses such as
_____ disease, stroke, _____ cancer, and similar problems.

90. (p. 348)   Health psychologists have identified a number of major _____
_____ factors such as stress, untreated high _____ pressure,
cigarette smoking, abuse of alcohol or other drugs, overeating, Type A behavior,
_____, and driving at excessive speeds.

91. (p. 348)   Unhealthy   lifestyles   almost   always   create   _____
_____. That is, people who smoke are also likely to drink excessively.
Those who overeat usually do not get enough exercise, and so on.

92. (p. 349)   To help prevent disease and promote well-being, health psychologists first try to
remove behavioral risk factors. They are also interested in _____
behaviors that actively promote health including such practices as getting regular
_____, maintaining a balanced _____, managing
stress, etc.

93. (p. 349)   In a major study, nearly 7000 people were given a detailed health questionnaire that
focused on seven basic health practices. The outcome showed that men who engaged
in all seven health practices had a death rate almost ___ times lower than that of
men who engaged in zero to three practices.

94. (p. 349)   The death rate for women who engaged in all seven practices was ___ times lower
than that for women who engaged in zero to three practices.

95. (p. 350)   Smoking provides a good example of the behavioral possibilities of preventing illness.
For example, in one health psychology program, junior-high students were given
"standard" information on the unhealthy effects of smoking. Then, the students role
played ways to resist pressures to smoke. These students were only _____ as
likely to begin smoking as were students in a control group.

96. (p. 350) Psychologists have had some success with _____ _____ campaigns—educational projects designed to lessen a combination of major risk factors.

97. (p. 350) A good example is the Stanford Heart Disease Prevention Program. A media campaign about risk factors in heart disease was combined with special group workshops for high-risk individuals. After two years, the number of smokers had decreased by _____ percent in the test community, compared with _____ percent increase observed in untreated communities.

98. (p. 350) While the progress of the Stanford program may seem modest, it is worthwhile, cost-effective, and highly promising. Overall, results of the project show a _____ percent reduction in risk of heart disease in the target cities.

99. (p. 352) Stress triggers _____ effects, upsetting _____, and _____ behavior. Each element worsens the others in a vicious cycle. This is why learning to manage stress is so important.

100. (p. 352) Much of the immediate discomfort of stress is caused by the body's fight/flight emotional response. When action is prevented, we merely remain "uptight." A sensible remedy is to learn a reliable, drug-free way of _____.

101. (p. 352) Relaxing might be accomplished through vigorous exercise, meditation, or a technique called _____ relaxation in which people learn to relax systematically, completely, and by choice.

102. (p. 352) Stress also triggers ineffective behavior. Suggestions which may help you deal with stress more effectively include slow down, _____, strike a _____, recognize and accept your _____ and seek _____ support.

103. (p. 354) One further effect stress has is to trigger upsetting thoughts. This problem can be treated using the technique developed by Donald Meichenbaum called _____ _____.

104. (p. 354) Meichenbaum's method helps clients first learn to identify and monitor negative _____-_____ and then to develop an internal monologue of positive _____ _____.

105. (p. 354) A psychologist studying frustration forced rats to jump off a platform toward two elevated doors, one of which was randomly locked and caused the animal to bounce off and fall into a net, the other of which led to safety. Most rats adopted a _____ _____ of choosing the same door every time, even when this door was later permanently locked.

106. (p. 354) Persistence is different from stereotyped responding, but all too often people are not persistent because they fear _____.

107. (p. 354) Persistence that is not _____ can lead to stereotyped responses. It is important to know when to quit and establish a new direction.

108. (p. 354) There are several suggestions to help avoid needless frustration:
    1) Try to identify the _____ of your frustration.
    2) Is it something that can be changed?
    3) If it can be changed, is the effort worth it?
    4) Is there a real or imagined _____?

109. (p. 355) There are four additional suggestions which apply to conflict:
     1) Don't be _____ when making important decisions.
     2) Try out important decisions _____ when possible.
     3) Look for workable _____.
     4) When all else fails, make a decision and live with it.

110. (p. 356) _____ refers to a family of mental exercises designed to focus attention in a way that interrupts the typical flow of thoughts, worries, and analysis. People who regularly use it as a stress-reduction technique often report less daily physical arousal and anxiety.

111. (p. 356) In _____ meditation, attention is given to a single focal point, such as an object, a thought, or one's own breathing.

112. (p. 356) More difficult to attain is _____ meditation, wherein attention is widened to include a nonjudgmental awareness of one's total subjective experience and presence in the world.

113. (p. 356) In one experiment, college students were instructed to concentrate on breathing. At the end of a two-week period, many reported experiences of deep _____, pleasant _____ sensations, and extreme detachment from outside worries and distractions.

114. (p. 356) An alternative approach involves the use of a _____—smooth, flowing words that are easily repeated. Like breathing, this approach is basically used as a focus for attention.

115. (p. 356) Herbert Benson believes that the benefits of meditation are the same no matter what word is used for a mantra. He believes that the core of meditation is production of the _____ _____, an innate physiological pattern that opposes the stressful activation of the body's fight-or-flight mechanisms.

116. (p. 357) Many extravagant claims have been made about meditation. For example, members of the Transcendental Meditation movement have stated that _____ minutes of meditation are as restful as a night's sleep. However, one recent study found that merely "_____" for 20 mintues produces the same bodily effects as meditation.

117. (p. 357) Long-term meditators have also claimed improvements in memory, alertness, creativity, and intuition. However, a recent study by Warrenburg and Pagano found no improvements in _____, _____, or _____ skills that could be linked to TM.

118. (p. 357) There is some evidence that those who meditate regularly react _____ _____ to stressful stimuli during laboratory testing. However, they recover faster than nonmeditators, and say they feel less stressed.

119. (p. 357) Benson believes that the key elements for producing the relaxation responses are: (1) a _____ environment; (2) decreased _____ tension; (3) a mental device that helps shift thoughts away from ordinary, rational concerns; (4) a _____ attitude toward whether you are "succeeding" at becoming relaxed.

SELF-TEST

1. (p. 336)   Which of the following is *not* true of stress?
   a. A healthy lifestyle may include a fair amount of stress.
   b. Stress occurs anytime we must adjust or adapt to the environment.
   c. Stress may become harmful in threatening situations that are unpredictable.
   d. Stress is almost always harmful; complete lack of stress is ideal.

2. (p. 336)   Which of the following can produce stress?
   a. pressure
   b. unpredictability
   c. lack of control
   d. all of the above

3. (p. 337)   Which of the following is not an aspect of burnout as identified by Christina Maslack?
   a. depersonalization
   b. stereotyped responding
   c. reduced personal accomplishment
   d. emotional exhaustion

4. (p. 338)   You have been preparing for an examination on very difficult material. You have wisely scheduled your time so as to have just enough and then your teacher moves up the date of the examination. You will probably suffer which type of frustration?
   a. external
   b. personal
   c. conflicted
   d. impersonal

5. (p. 338)   Which of the following is *not* true of factors affecting frustration?
   a. External obstacles that produce frustration may be either social or non-social.
   b. Repeated frustrations can accumulate in their effect until a small irritation produces a violent response.
   c. Frustration usually increases as the strength, urgency, or importance of a blocked motive increases.
   d. Frustration is usually less intense as we near a goal.

6. (p. 338)   Personal frustrations refer to
   a. specific frustrations you personally experience because of other people's behavior
   b. how you personally interpret an event—some people find certain situations frustrating, while others do not
   c. frustrations based on an individual's personal characteristics
   d. intense frustrations produced by those to whom you are closest—family, friends, etc.

7. (p. 339)   True-False. Aggression followed by persistence is usually how people react to frustration.

8. (p. 339)   When you get an "F" on a test and then insult the person sitting next to you, you are showing _____ aggression.
   a. repressed
   b. suppressed
   c. displaced
   d. replaced

9. (p. 339)   Minorities have often served as _____ for the aggressions of whole societies.
   a. examples
   b. scapegoats
   c. facilitators
   d. primers

10. (p. 340)   When you can't decide which movie or play to go see because they're all so good, you may experience
   a. approach-avoidance conflict
   b. approach-approach conflict
   c. avoidance-avoidance conflict
   d. double approach conflict

11. (p. 340) Which of the following is *not* true of avoidance-avoidance conflicts?
    a. They may occur when people are forced to choose between two negative alternatives.
    b. They tend to be the easiest conflicts to resolve even though they are usually stressful.
    c. When faced with such conflicts, people often freeze.
    d. People sometimes react to this situation by leaving the field.

12. (p. 342) Ambivalence expressed in partial approach is often seen in
    a. approach-approach conflicts
    b. approach-avoidance conflicts
    c. avoidance-avoidance conflicts
    d. double approach-avoidance conflicts

13. (p. 342) Faced with a double approach-avoidance conflict we would most likely observe that people
    a. partially approach   c. leave the field
    b. freeze   d. vacillate

14. (p. 343) A high number of LCUs on the _____ indicates increased chance of illness or accident.
    a. G.A.S.   c. S.R.R.S.
    b. S.S.S.   d. none of the above

15. (p. 344) Which of the following is *not* true of hassles as studied by Richard Lazarus?
    a. They are distressing, daily annoyances.
    b. Central hassles are most likely to cause significant stress.
    c. Hassles are better predictors of day-to-day psychological and physical health than are major life events.
    d. Hassles can produce a ripple effect—that is, countless daily frustrations and irritations can spring from an original hassle.

16. (p. 344) True-False. Psychological stress can cause psychological problems, but rarely causes physical illness.

17. (p. 344) Which of the following is *not* true of psychosomatic disorders?
    a. The most common are gastrointestinal and respiratory.
    b. About one-half or more of all medical patients either have a psychosomatic disorder or a condition complicated by them.
    c. Stress is not the sole cause of psychosomatic disease.
    d. Hypochondria is a form of psychosomatic illness.

18. (p. 345) True-False. Type A personalities frequently suffer from a sense of time urgency.

19. (p. 345) There is now growing evidence that which of the following may be the most important aspect of Type A behavior?
    a. The Type A's inability to slow down and accommodate to the normal pace of events.
    b. The Type A's constant state of anger and hostility.
    c. The fact that Type A's are overly competitive and achievement oriented.
    d. The fact that Type A's are hard-driving, ambitious, and push themselves to their limits of endurance.

20. (p. 346) The hardy personality as defined by Maddi and Kobasa is characterized by all of the following *except*

a. personal commitment to self, work, family, and other stabilizing values
b. tendency to see life as a series of challenges
c. lack of Type A personality characteristics
d. feelings of control over their lives and work

21. (p. 347) The three stages of the G.A.S. are
a. alarm reaction, psychosomatic stage, stage of exhaustion
b. burnout, alarm reaction, stage of exhaustion
c. alarm reaction, stage of resistance, stage of exhaustion
d. burnout, psychosomatic stage, stage of adaptation

22. (p. 347) Which of the following is *not* a correct association?
a. alarm reaction—secretion of pituitary hormone that increases adrenal gland output of adrenaline and noradrenaline
b. stage of exhaustion—stress hormones depleted, psychosomatic disease, organ failure, or serious loss of health may occur
c. stage of resistance—job burnout with chronic fatigue and apathy
d. stage of resistance—body coping with original stressor but more susceptible to effects of other stressors

23. (p. 347) True-False. Psychoneuroimmunology is a new field of research that seeks to discover how various personality characteristics associated with poor stress tolerance can be altered by neurological techniques or immunological alterations.

24. (p. 348) All of the following are associated with health psychology *except*
a. community health campaigns
b. identification of behavioral risk factors
c. use of behavioral methods to promote health and treat disease
d. facilitation of peak performances

25. (p. 349) Which of the following is *not* a factor that has been identified as a basic health promoting behavior associated with increased life expectancy?
a. Engaging in regular physical exercise.
b. Eating three meals a day.
c. Using alcohol moderately or not at all.
d. Sleeping seven to eight hours a night.

26. (p. 352) Which of the following is *not* an effective approach to coping with stress?
a. vigorous exercise
b. meditation
c. progressive relaxation
d. developing a Type A personality

27. (p. 354) Stress innoculation is a technique effective in treating
a. upsetting thoughts
b. disorganization
c. physical tension
d. poor time management

28. (p. 356) Meditation has been shown to produce which of the following?
a. decreased oxygen consumption, reduced respiration, increased alpha brain wave activity
b. increased heart rate, increased blook pressure, sense of euphoria
c. improved sexual response, increased alertness, and improved intellectual capacity
d. intensified concentration, pleasant bodily sensations, extreme detachment from outside worries

29. (p. 356) Herbert Benson supports which of the following statements?
a. Any individual practicing meditation should make use of a person-specific mantra.

b. Meditation elicits the relaxation response that opposes stressful activation of the body's fight-or-flight mechanisms.
c. Meditators should presume an aggressive role in seeking to become relaxed during meditation.
d. Meditation should involve a temporary increase in muscle tension indicative of enhanced mental concentration on the body.

ANSWERS — PROGRAMMED REVIEW

1. Frustration; goal
2. Stress
3. bad; lack
4. reaction
5. Short; Long
6. unpredictability
7. Pressure
8. control; lower
9. burnout
10. emotional exhaustion
11. depersonalization
12. personal accomplishment
13. helping
14. social support
15. support groups
16. threat
17. Perceived; actual
18. competence
19. intensity
20. External; failure, rejection, loss
21. social; nonsocial
22. strength, urgency, importance
23. Motivation
24. Repeated
25. Personal
26. persistence
27. displaced
28. chains
29. child abuse
30. scapegoating; cotton; blacks
31. escape
32. apathy; drugs
33. Conflict
34. approach-approach
35. easiest; easily
36. avoidance-avoidance
37. needs, values
38. freeze
39. leaving the field
40. approach-avoidance
41. ambivalence; partial
42. double approach-avoidance
43. vacillate
44. illness
45. change

46. Social Readjustment Rating Scale
47. life change units
48. 80
49. older
50. failed; positive
51. hassles
52. 100
53. central
54. psychosomatic disorders
55. hypochondria
56. respiratory; eczema; hypertension; colitis
57. tension; indigestion; dysfunction
58. half
59. hereditary; organ; learned
60. heart
61. Type A; Type B
62. twice
63. less fatigued
64. time urgency
65. anger, hostility
66. hundreds
67. anger; hostility
68. reduces
69. opposite
70. hardy personality
71. commitment; control; challenges
72. general adaptation syndrome; G.A.S.
73. identical
74. alarm reaction
75. adrenaline, noradrenaline
76. muscles; breath; stomach, appetite; energy
77. stage of resistance
78. infection
79. psychosomatic
80. stage of exhaustion
81. adrenal glands; thymus; stomach ulcers
82. immune system
83. psychoneuroimmunology
84. thoughts; emotions
85. Control
86. weakened
87. health psychology
88. behavioral medicine
89. heart; lung
90. behavioral risk; blood; underexercise

91. multiple risks
92. increasing; exercise; diet
93. 4
94. 2
95. half
96. community health
97. 17; 12
98. 15
99. bodily; thoughts; ineffective
100. relaxing
101. progressive
102. organize; balance; limitations; social
103. stress innoculation
104. self-statements; coping statements
105. stereotyped response
106. failure
107. flexible
108. source; barrier
109. hasty; partially; compromises
110. Meditation
111. concentrative
112. receptive
113. concentration; bodily
114. mantra
115. relaxation response
116. 20; resting
117. verbal, musical, spatial
118. more strongly
119. quiet; muscle; passive

ANSWERS — SELF-TEST

1. d
2. d
3. b
4. a
5. d
6. c
7. False
8. c
9. b
10. b
11. b
12. b
13. d
14. c
15. d
16. False
17. d
18. True
19. b
20. c
21. c
22. c
23. False
24. d
25. b
26. d
27. a
28. d
29. b

Chapter 14

Child Development

CONTENTS

TERMS AND CONCEPTS

developmental psychology
neonate
reflex
grasping reflex
rooting reflex
sucking reflex
Moro reflex
looking chamber
maturation
principle of motor primacy (principle of
    readiness)
nature versus nurture controversy
heredity
chromosomes
genes
Deoxyribonucleic acid (DNA)
polygenetic
dominant genes
recessive genes
X chromosome
Y chromosome
sex-linked traits
human growth sequence
intrauterine environment

congenital problems
fetal alcohol syndrome
medicated birth
natural (prepared) childbirth
Lamaze method
birthing rooms
gentle birth
maternal influences
paternal influences
self-awareness
social referencing
critical period
imprinting
emotional attachment
separation anxiety
emotional bond
motherless monkeys
affectional needs
cooing
babbling
single-word stage
single-word pairs
telegraphic speech
biological predisposition

psycholinguist
transformations
stages of intellectual development
assimilation
accommodation
sensorimotor stage
object permanence
preoperational stage
concrete operational stage
formal operations stage
conservation
moral dilemmas
preconventional level
conventional level
postconventional level

feral children
deprivation dwarfism
hospitalism
surrogate mother
contact comfort
colostrum
enriched environments
early childhood education programs
artificial insemination
in vitro fertilization
genetic counseling
amniocentesis
eugenics (selective breeding)
genetic engineering
cloning

IMPORTANT INDIVIDUALS

Andrew Meltzoff
Keith Moore
Jerome Bruner
Robert Fantz
Jerome Kagan
Ferdinand Lamaze
Frederick Leboyer
Konrad Lorenz
Harry Harlow
Marshall Klaus

John Kennel
Louis Sander
William Condon
Noam Chomsky
Jean Piaget
Charles Croll
Lawrence Kohlberg
Carol Gilligan
René Spitz
Paul Chance
Morris Holland

PROGRAMMED REVIEW

1. (p. 362) _____ _____ can be described
    as the study of progressive changes in behavior and abilities from conception to
    death.

2. (p. 363) At birth the human _____ is completely helpless and will die if not
    cared for. While their senses are less acute, babies are immediately responsive to
    their surroundings. In fact, they will follow a moving object with their eyes and will
    turn in the direction of sounds.

3. (p. 363) A number of adaptive reflexes can be observed in the newborn. For example, an
    object pressed to its palm will be grasped with surprising strength. This reflex is
    appropriately called the _____ reflex and enhances survival by
    helping to prevent falling.

4. (p. 363) The _____ reflex is demonstrated by touching the baby's cheek. The
    baby will immediately turn toward your finger as if searching for something. This
    reflex helps the infant find a bottle or breast.

5. (p. 363) When a nipple touches the infant's mouth, the _____ reflex helps it to
    obtain the food it needs.

6. (p. 363) Obtaining food rewards _____, which rapidly increases in vigor

during the first days after birth. Thus, we see that learning begins immediately in the newborn.

7. (p. 363)   Also of interest is the _____ reflex. If the baby's head is allowed to drop, or if it is startled by a loud noise or other frightening stimulus, it will make movements similar to an embrace.

8. (p. 363)   Andrew Meltzoff and Keith Moore have found that babies are born _____, that is, they consistently imitate adult facial features.

9. (p. 363)   As early as ___ months of age, infants can also imitate other actions and they can repeat them the next day. Such mimicry is obviously an aid to rapid learning in infancy.

10. (p. 363)   Jerome Bruner showed that ___ to ___-week old babies demonstrate signs of understanding that a person's voice and body are _____. If babies heard their mother's voice coming from where she was standing, they remained calm. If her voice came from a loudspeaker several feet away, the babies cried.

11. (p. 364)   To test infant vision, Robert Fantz invented a device called a _____ _____.

12. (p. 364)   Fantz places a child on its back inside the chamber and places two objects overhead. By observing the movements of the infant's eyes, and the images reflected from their surface, Fantz found that three-day-old babies preferred _____ patterns to _____ colored rectangles.

13. (p. 364)   Other researchers have determined that infants are more excited by _____ and _____ in figures, and that they will look longer at _____ and _____ than they will at other colors.

14. (p. 364)   Infants spend more time looking at a _____ face pattern than a scrambled one or a colored oval.

15. (p. 364)   When real human faces were used, Fantz found that _____ faces were preferred to _____ faces.

16. (p. 364)   This preference reverses at about age ___, when unusual objects begin to hold greater interest. For example, Jerome Kagan found that children at this age were fascinated by a face mask with eyes on the chin and a nose in the middle of the forehead.

17. (p. 364)   _____ refers to growth and development of the body— especially the nervous system. It underlies the orderly sequence observed in the unfolding of many basic abilities, particularly motor abilities.

18. (p. 364)   While the _____ of maturation varies from child to child, the _____ is virtually universal. For instance, the strength and coordination needed for sitting appears before that needed for crawling.

19. (p. 365)   Typically, infants sit before they crawl (and crawl before they stand, etc.). A few children substitute rolling, creeping, or shuffling for crawling. A very small percentage move directly from sitting to _____ and _____.

20. (p. 365)   In general, increased motor control usually proceeds from _____ to _____, and from the _____ of the body to the _____.

21. (p. 365) Maturation often creates a condition of readiness for learning. This principle, known as the _____ of _____ _____, states that until the necessary physical structures are mature, no amount of practice will be sufficient to establish a skill.

22. (p. 365) Readiness is not an all-or-nothing effect. Training that comes too early will be _____; training that is only a little early may succeed, but will be _____; and training when a child is maturationally ready produces rapid _____.

23. (p. 366) Much needless grief can be avoided by respecting a child's rate of growth. For instance, eager parents who toilet trained an 18-month-old child in 10 weeks might have done it in 3 weeks by waiting until the child was 24 months old to begin. Parents may control when toilet training starts, but maturation tends to determine when it will be completed. Around _____ months is average for completion.

24. (p. 366) For many years psychologists have debated the _____ versus _____ controversy, trying to determine the relative importance of heredity and environment in the development of human beings.

25. (p. 366) Heredity is certainly an important factor in development. It has been estimated that the _____ information carried in each human cell would fill thousands of 1000-page books if translated into words.

26. (p. 366) The nucleus of every cell in the body contains 46 threadlike structures called _____ which transmit coded instructions of heredity.

27. (p. 367) _____ are smaller units on chromosomes that affect a particular process or personal characteristic. There are at least 100,000 such areas in every human cell.

28. (p. 367) Genes are made up of _____ _____, abbreviated _____. It is a long ladder-like chemical molecule that is made up of smaller molecules. The order of these smaller molecules, or organic bases, acts as a code for genetic information.

29. (p. 367) In some cases a single gene is responsible for a particular inherited characteristic, but most characteristics are _____, or determined by many genes working in combination.

30. (p. 367) When a gene is _____, the trait it controls will be present every time the gene is present; when _____, it must be paired with an identical gene before its effect will be expressed.

31. (p. 367) We receive one-half of our chromosomes (and genes) from each parent. If each parent has two brown-eye genes, the couple's children will all be brown-eyed. But if each parent has one brown-eye gene and one blue-eye gene, the parents would both have brown eyes, but there is one chance in ___ that their children will have blue eyes.

32. (p. 367) The sex of a child is genetically determined. When two "___" chromosomes are inherited the child will be a female, but an "___" chromosome paired with a "___" chromosome yields a male.

33. (p. 367) Some traits are _____-_____, that is carried only by genes on either the X or Y chromosome. Color blindness, which is carried on the X chromosome, is a good example.

34. (p. 367) Heredity instructions carried by the chromosomes influence development throughout life by affecting the sequence of growth, the timing of puberty, and the course of aging. Thus, the broad outlines of the human _____ _____ are universal.

35. (p. 367) In addition, heredity determines _____ and _____ color, the order of _____ development, and susceptibility to some _____. Heredity also exerts considerable influence over body size and shape, height, intelligence, athletic potential, personality traits, and a host of other details.

36. (p. 367) _____ (or the nurture side of the learning vs. heredity controversy) by no means takes a back seat in development. As Aldous Huxley noted, humans today are physically very similar to cave-dwellers of 20 or 30 thousand years ago. However, today's baby could become almost anything, while the Upper Paleolithic baby could only grow into a hunter or food-gatherer.

37. (p. 368) While both heredity and environment are separately important in development, the recognition that both are important and, in fact, _____ represents a more realistic approach. There is a constant interplay or _____ between the forces of nature and nurture.

38. (p. 368) Children show individual differences almost immediately after birth. Jerome Kagan found that newborn babies differ in various aspects of _____ which appears at least partially due to variations in bodily chemistry that affects brain activity.

39. (p. 369) Kagan reliably separated babies into 3 major categories, including _____ children who are relaxed and agreeable (about _____ percent of those observed), _____ children who tend to overreact to most situations (about _____ percent), and _____-to-_____-_____ children who are restrained and unexpressive (about _____ percent).

40. (p. 369) Because of inborn differences in temperament, babies rapidly become _____ _____ in their own development—especially their social development. They change their environment at the same time they are changed by it.

41. (p. 369) Consistent differences in temperament can be detected for at least the first 2 years of life. Yet by age 10, children's personalities show little connection to _____, _____, or _____ observed in infancy.

42. (p. 369) Thus, there appear to be at least three factors which combine to determine a person's developmental level at any stage in life. These elements are _____, _____, and the individual's own _____.

43. (p. 369) In considering the effects of environment on behavior, we must go back as far as the _____ environment of the womb. If a mother's health or nutrition is poor, if she contracts certain diseases such as German measles or syphilis, uses drugs, or is exposed to x-rays or atomic radiation, the resultant damage to the fetus is referred to as a _____ _____.

44. (p. 369) Congenital problems, or "_____ _____" as they are sometimes called, are distinct from _____ problems which are difficulties inherited from one's parents.

45. (p. 370) Even though there is no direct intermingling of blood between mother and fetus, some substances still reach the fetus. Most common prescription drugs reach the fetus and if the mother is addicted to _____, _____, or _____ the infant may be born with a drug addiction.

46. (p. 370) Other potentially damaging substances which if ingested by the mother can adversely affect the fetus include: general anesthetics, _____, _____, excessive amounts of vitamins ___, ___, B$_6$, and K, cocaine, some barbiturates, opiates, tranquilizers, synthetic sex hormones, and possibly even caffeine and aspirin.

47. (p. 370) Repeated heavy drinking by a pregnant woman can produce a pattern known as the _____ _____ _____, characterized by miscarriage or premature birth, low birth weight, and a variety of bodily defects and facial deformations. Many affected infants are mentally retarded.

48. (p. 370) There is increasing evidence that even modest use of alcohol during pregnancy can be damaging. Alcohol appears to cause severe _____ loss to the rapidly developing fetus, producing irreversible brain damage.

49. (p. 370) The maximum amount a pregnant woman should drink on any one day is one _____ of hard liquor, one _____ of wine, or _____ glasses of beer. Even these amounts can be damaging.

50. (p. 370) Smoking can elevate or lower the _____ _____ of the unborn child, and the mother who smokes heavily is more likely to _____.

51. (p. 370) Also, heavy smokers run a higher risk of _____ _____ and tend to give birth to _____ babies, both of which increase the chances of infant sickness and death after birth.

52. (p. 370) The infant death rate immediately before, during, or after birth is _____ higher if a woman smokes during pregnancy. A pregnant woman who smokes two packs of cigarettes a day blocks off about _____ percent of the oxygen supply to the fetus.

53. (p. 370) Until recently, _____ _____ in hospital delivery rooms were the rule in Western nations. In such births, the mother is assisted by a physician and given drugs ranging from local analgesics (painkillers) to general anesthetics that cause a loss of consciousness.

54. (p. 370) Increasingly, doctors and parents have come to realize that general anesthesia during birth has major drawbacks. They can dull or block the mother's _____ of birth. Also, they reduce _____ flow to the fetus and can cause the infant to be born partially anesthetized.

55. (p. 370) Studies show that babies whose mothers were given heavy doses of anesthetic tend to lag in _____ and _____ development.

56. (p. 371) In the last five years there has been a marked move away from use of general anesthesia during birth. Nevertheless, some form of painkiller is used in _____ percent of all deliveries in the United States.

57. (p. 371) Many psychologists are convinced that _____ or _____ childbirth is an effective way to minimize the discomfort of birth while giving babies the best possible start in life.

58. (p. 371)   The most widely used approach to natural childbirth is the _____
_____ named after its French physician developer.

59. (p. 371)   The Lamaze method begins by teaching couples what will happen _____
during birth. This helps to reduce fears and lessen anxiety.

60. (p. 371)   Couples are also taught methods of _____ and _____
control to minimize pain. Further, the father or a friend is trained to give support to
the mother during birth.

61. (p. 371)   Natural childbirth typically shortens _____ and minimizes _____.
In addition, it treats birth as a celebration of life, rather than a medical problem or a
disease.

62. (p. 371)   The French obstetrician _____ _____
advocates a system of gentle birth that purportedly makes it pleasant for both mother
and baby. It involves delivery in a silent, dimly lit room. Immediately after birth the
baby is placed on its mother's stomach and gently massaged, then the umbilical cord
is cut and the baby bathed in warm water.

63. (p. 371)   Many obstetricians have been skeptical of Leboyer's methods. Doctors working in a
darkened delivery room have had trouble detecting a "_____ _____."

64. (p. 371)   Another point to consider is that stress during birth may be normal and perhaps even
desirable. There is some evidence that babies born by cesarean section (surgical
birth) have a _____ survival rate.

65. (p. 371)   Leboyer claims that gentle births produce children who are happier, healthier, more
relaxed, and more emotionally stable. However, evidence in support of this claim is
not very convincing. While Leboyer babies are more relaxed than other newborns
during the first _____ or _____ minutes after birth, from then on there is no
measurable difference.

66. (p. 371)   The emotional intensity of birth magnifies its impact.   Many fathers form
_____ at the time of birth that may make a difference later in
the father's willingness to care for the child, or his reaction when the child angers
him.

67. (p. 371)   Researchers have found that fathers generally make a better transition to parenthood
when they participate in preparing for childbirth. While participation may be
valuable, it is not essential. The father's _____ toward the
birth of his child is probably more important.

68. (p. 372)   A recent study found that fathers who wanted to be present during delivery showed
_____ interest in their infants during the first year and were
_____ likely to help care for the baby. This was true whether or not the
father was actually able to attend the birth.

69. (p. 372)   Many hospitals now have _____ _____ that allow the
father to room-in in a homelike atmosphere. This allows him to participate in the
birth and to share in caring for the newborn while still having access to prompt
medical attention if needed.

70. (p. 372)   Even traditional delivery rooms are allowing fathers to be present during birth. In
some cases the father cuts the _____ _____ and

gives the infant its first bath. In many hospitals the baby spends its first night with the parents in the _____ _____.

71. (p. 372) The quality of mothering during the first few years of life is very important. One study of maternal influences showed that whether children were unusually competent or had a low degree of competence was set by age _____.

72. (p. 372) To understand how this finding was possible, children and their mothers were observed at home. Five types of caregiving styles were identified. One of these, _____ _____, went out of their way to provide educational experiences for their children and allowed them to initiate some activities.

73. (p. 372) Super mothers produce an A child, _____ in most areas of development.

74. (p. 372) The _____-_____ mother gave her children good physical care, but interacted with them very little; her childcare routines were rigid and highly structured. Her children tended to be of below-average competence and to approach problems _____.

75. (p. 372) Optimal caregiving is also related to the _____ of _____ between parents and children. For instance, a slow-to-warm-up child who has impatient parents may have more difficulty adjusting than if the same child had easy-going parents.

76. (p. 372) Another recent study found that children's intellectual abilities at age 6 can be predicted, to some extent, by their mothers' _____ to them during infancy. Effective mothers are those who are sensitive to their children's needs.

77. (p. 372) Paternal influences also contribute to the infant's development, but in different ways. Generally, the father's main role tends to be that of a _____ for the infant. They spend _____ or _____ times as much time playing with their infants as they do in caretaking.

78. (p. 372) Fathers are more visually _____ to the child, are much more _____, more physically arousing, and more likely to engage in _____ _____. Mothers speak to the infant more, play more conventional games, and spend more time in caretaking activities.

79. (p. 373) Differences in mothers' and fathers' behavior continue until at least _____ childhood.

80. (p. 373) Infants can get very different views of males and females. Females, who offer comfort, nurturance, and _____ stimulation, also tend to be close at hand. Males come and go, and when they are present, action, _____, and risk-taking prevail.

81. (p. 374) The growth of _____-_____, the recognition of your own image, depends on maturation of the nervous system.

82. (p. 374) One experiment in which rouge was placed on children's noses before being brought in front of a mirror showed that the probability that children would touch their nose was very low at ___ months, but jumped dramatically through the _____ year.

83. (p. 374) Infants shown their own videotaped images usually had to be _____ months old before they could tell their own images from those of other children.

84. (p. 374) Adults sometimes glance at the facial expressions of others in order to decide how to respond. This sort of _____ _____ can also be observed in babies.

85. (p. 374) By _____ months of age, most babies reference (glance at) their mothers when placed in an unfamiliar situation. Such was the finding with tests involving the visual cliff.

86. (p. 374) When mothers posed faces of _____ or _____, most babies crossed the deep side of the cliff. When they posed _____ or _____, few babies crossed.

87. (p. 374) _____ _____ are times when susceptibiity to environ-mental influences (both positive and negative) are increased.

88. (p. 375) Often, certain events must occur during a critical period in order for organisms to develop normally. Konrad Lorenz has demonstrated this fact in his experiments with _____ where a permanent behavior pattern is rapidly learned early in development.

89. (p. 375) Lorenz found that infant geese learned to follow moving objects seen early in devel-opment. This imprinting process occurs during a very brief critical period. For instance, Hess found that if ducklings are not allowed to imprint on their mother or some other object within _____ hours after hatching, they never will.

90. (p. 375) While true cases of imprinting are limited to birds and other animals, human infants do form an _____ _____ to their primary caregivers (usually parents).

91. (p. 375) There is a critical period for this attachment (roughly the first year of life). Around 8 to 12 months of age, babies display _____ _____ (crying and signs of fear) when their parents leave them alone, or alone with strangers.

92. (p. 375) Infants who spend much time with their _____ show nearly as strong an attachment to them as they do to their mothers. For many children, such attachments may be part of the first step in broadening social relation-ships to others.

93. (p. 375) Infants who are securely attached to their parents later show more _____, curiosity, problem solving ability and _____ competence in preschool.

94. (p. 375) It seems that _____ for young children does not interfere with normal attachment. A recent survey concluded that high-quality nonmaternal care does not have harmful effects.

95. (p. 375) Daycare has no ill effects until it exceeds _____ or more hours a week. Then there often are signs of insecurity in children's relationships with their mothers.

96. (p. 375) Some insecurity is especially likely if the child is _____–born and under ____ year of age, and if the mother works full time.

97. (p. 375) The key ingredient for secure attachment is a mother who is accepting and sensitive to her baby's _____ and _____.

98. (p. 375) Research with rhesus monkeys suggests that infant attachments have lasting effects. Harry Harlow has shown that baby monkeys separated from their mothers and raised in isolation never develop normal _____ behaviors and make very poor mothers if mated.

99. (p. 375) These "motherless monkeys" are coldly _____ or _____ to their babies and may brutalize or injure them. It has been suggested that a similar pattern may exist among humans. Most abusive parents were themselves rejected or mistreated as children.

100. (p. 375) Some psychologists believe that _____ behavior can often be traced to a lack of attachment in infancy. Children with severe attachment problems do not learn to trust and care about others and are cruel, angry, and self-destructive.

101. (p. 375) Meeting a baby's affectional needs is an important factor in early development. An important task of the first year of life is creation of a bond of trust and affection between the infant and at least one other person. A later capacity to experience _____ and _____ relationships may depend on it.

102. (p. 376) Studies by Marshall Klaus and John Kennel suggest that mother-child pairs who spend extra time together form a stronger _____ to one another. This is especially true if skin-to-skin touching is part of early contact.

103. (p. 376) They have reported that "bonded" babies are more _____, healthier, brighter, and _____ than those who are denied extra contact. However, the majority of studies have failed to support the idea that extended, early contact is crucial to bonding.

104. (p. 376) Critics point out that _____ children, _____ babies, and babies born by _____ section all develop normal, affectionate bonds with their mothers.

105. (p. 376) The development of language is also closely tied to maturation. By ___ _____ of age, the infant can control crying enough to use it as an attention-getting device.

106. (p. 377) Around 6 to 8 weeks of age, babies begin _____—the repetition of vowel sounds like "oo" and "ah."

107. (p. 377) By age ___ months, the nervous system has matured enough to allow the child to grasp objects, to smile, laugh, sit up, and to babble.

108. (p. 377) In the babbling stage, _____ sounds are added to produce a continuous outpouring of repeated language sounds. It increases when parents talk to the child.

109. (p. 377) At about ___ _____ of age, the child can stand alone for a short time and can respond to words. Soon afterward, the first connection between words and objects is formed.

110. (p. 377) Between the ages of $1\frac{1}{2}$ and ___ years, the child becomes able to stand and walk alone. By this time, the child's vocabulary may include from 24 to _____ words.

111. (p. 377) At first there is a _____-_____ stage during which the child says only one word at a time. Next, the child links words in _____-_____

pairs such as "car/ride." Soon after, words are arranged in simple two-word sentences called _____ _____: "Want Teddy."

112. (p. 377) From this point on, growth of vocabulary and language skills proceeds at a phenomenal rate. By first grade the child can understand around _____ words and can use about _____.

113. (p. 377) Louis Sander and William Condon filmed newborn infants as they listened to various sounds. They found that infants as young as one day old move their arms and legs in synchrony to the rhythms of _____ _____.

114. (p. 377) Linguist Noam Chomsky has long claimed that humans have a _____ _____ to develop language; he believes language is inborn like a child's ability to coordinate walking.

115. (p. 377) If such inborn language recognition exists, it may explain why children universally use a limited number of _____ in their first sentences.

116. (p. 377) Many psychologists feel that Chomsky underestimates the importance of learning. _____ (specialists in the psychology of language) have recently shown that language learning involves imitation of adults, rewards for correctly using words, and early, shared communication.

117. (p. 377) From this point of view, infants' behavior reflects a readiness to interact _____ with parents, not innate language recognition.

118. (p. 377) To elicit smiles and vocalizations from babies, parents quickly learn to change their actions to keep the infant's attention, arousal, and activity at optimal levels. A system of shared _____ is created which helps lay a foundation for later language use and establishes a pattern of "conversational" turn taking.

119. (p. 378) A baby's vocalizations and attention provide a way of interacting emotionally with parents. Even infants as young as ___ months make more speechlike sounds when an adult engages them in a turn-taking pattern of interacting.

120. (p. 378) A child's thinking is less _____ than that of an adult; they use fewer generalizations, categories, or principles. They also tend to base their understanding of the world on particular examples, tangible sensations, and material objects.

121. (p. 378) An indication of the concrete nature of thinking in very young infants is their failure to recognize the _____ of objects. For a very young child (4 or 5-month-old infant), out of sight can literally mean out of mind.

122. (p. 379) Before age 6 or 7, "the age of reason," children are unable to make _____. If you show a child a full, short, wide glass and a full, tall, narrow glass, the child will consider the taller glass to contain more fluid.

123. (p. 379) Jean Piaget investigated the series of _____ that children progress through intellectually. He believed that intellect grows through _____, the use of existing patterns in new situations, and through _____, the modification of existing ideas to fit new requirements.

124. (p. 380) Piaget's first stage, known as the _____ stage, includes the first ___ years of life.

125. (p. 380) During the first stage, the child shows a gradual emergence of the concept of _____ _____. At about a year and a half the child begins to pursue disappearing objects. By age ___, the child can anticipate the movement of an object behind a screen. These developments indicate that the child's conceptions are becoming more stable.

126. (p. 380) During the _____ stage (ages 2-7), the child is developing an ability to think _____ and to use language.

127. (p. 380) During this stage, the child's thinking is still very intuitive and the use of language is still not as sophisticated as it might seem. Children have a tendency to confuse _____ with the _____ they represent.

128. (p. 380) During this stage, children are also quite _____, usually taking the perspective that everything revolves around them. This fact helps us understand why children of this stage can seem so selfish or uncooperative at times.

129. (p. 380) By ___ to ___ years of age, the child enters the _____ _____ stage. An important development here is the mastery of the concept of _____.

130. (p. 380) During this period, a child's thoughts begin to include the concepts of _____, _____, and number. Categories and principles are used, and the child can think _____ about concrete objects or situations.

131. (p. 380) Usually children at this stage stop believing in Santa Claus. Similarly, Charles Croll found that _____ percent of children aged 5 to 7 believe that the Tooth Fairy is real. Around the ages of 7 to 8, however, most children begin to realize that this is a fantasy.

132. (p. 380) Another important development during the concrete operational stage is the ability to _____ thoughts or operations. Older children recognize that if $4 \times 2 = 8$, then 2×4 does, too. Younger children must memorize each relationship separately.

133. (p. 381) The final stage, the _____ _____ stage, includes ages _____ years and up. Here, thinking is based more on _____ _____. The child in this stage has come to consider hypothetical possibilities also.

134. (p. 381) In this last stage, full adult intellectual ability is attained. The older adolescent is capable of inductive and deductive reasoning and can comprehend abstract systems. From this point on, improvements in intellectual ability are based on gaining _____, _____, and wisdom, rather than on a boost in basic thinking capacity.

135. (p. 381) Today, many psychologists are convinced that Piaget gave too little credit to the effects of _____. For example, children of pottery-making parents can correctly answer questions about the conservation of clay at an earlier age than Piaget would have predicted.

136. (p. 381) According to learning theorists, children continuously gain _____ _____; they do not undergo stagelike increases in general mental ability.

137. (p. 381) Numerous studies do show that children make _____ mental gains at about

the ages Piaget stated. In fact, researchers have recently found evidence that cycles of _____ growth occur at times that correspond with Piaget's stages.

138. (p. 382) To study moral development, Kohlberg posed _____ _____ to children of different ages. By classifying the reasons children gave for their answers he identified three levels and six stages of moral development.

139. (p. 383) The first level, _____, includes _____ (stage 1), where actions are evaluated in terms of possible punishment, not goodness or badness. Here, obedience to power is emphasized.

140. (p. 383) A second stage of the preconventional level involves a _____- _____ orientation. At this stage, right action is determined by one's own needs.

141. (p. 383) The second level of moral development, the _____ level, includes stage 3 development called good boy/girl orientation. Good behavior is that which brings approval or pleases others.

142. (p. 382) Stage 4 (conventional level), _____ orientation, involves an emphasis on upholding law, order, and authority, doing one's duty, and following social rules.

143. (p. 383) The third level is called the _____ level. It includes stage 5, _____-_____ orientation, where support of laws and rules is based on rational analysis and mutual agreement.

144. (p. 383) Also included is stage 6, _____ of _____ _____, where behavior is directed by self-chosen ethical principles that tend to be general, comprehensive, or universal.

145. (p. 382) Kohlberg found that people advance through the stages at different rates. Stages 1 and 2 are most characteristic of young _____ and _____. Conventional group-oriented morals of stages 3 and 4 are characteristic of older _____ and most of the _____ population.

146. (p. 382) Kohlberg estimated that postconventional morality, representing self-direction and higher principles, is characteristic of only about _____ percent of the adult population.

147. (p. 383) Psychologist Carol Gilligan has pointed out that Kohlberg's system is concerned mainly with the ethics of _____. But Gilligan argues that there is also an ethic of _____ and responsibility to be considered.

148. (p. 383) Gilligan has studied women who face real-life dilemmas. She has concluded that male psychologists have defined moral maturity in terms of justice and autonomy. From this perspective, women's concern with _____ can look like a weakness rather than a strength.

149. (p. 383) Gilligan believes that caring is also a major element of moral development and suggests that _____ may lag in achieving it.

150. (p. 383) While the existence of so-called _____ _____ (raised in the wild) have rarely been documented, there are numerous cases of children who have spent the first 5 or 6 years of life in closets, etc. These children demonstrate the

destructive effects of early _____, since they are usually mute, severely retarded, and emotionally damaged.

151. (p. 384) Some of these children suffer from _____ _____ —stunted growth associated with isolation, rejection, or general deprivation in the home environment.

152. (p. 384) Examples, such as these early deprived children, suggest that in many ways all of infancy is a relatively _____ _____ in development.

153. (p. 384) René Spitz investigated the damaging effects of deprivation in early childhood. He used the term _____ to refer to a group of foundling-home babies suffering from a pattern of deep depression marked by weeping and sadness, long periods of immobility or mechanical rocking, and a lack of normal response to other humans.

154. (p. 384) Spitz discovered that the foundling home had an unusually high rate of infant _____, and development of the living babies was severely _____. He considered this "wasting away" to be due to a lack of dependable "mother figures."

155. (p. 384) Recent work supports the idea that lack of _____ is a major element in early deprivation. For example, improving living conditions failed to reverse declining mental health at one Canadian institution. Children improved only when placed with caring foster or adoptive parents.

156. (p. 384) A second major factor in many cases of deprivation is a lack of _____ _____. Foundling-home babies studied by Spitz were kept in bare rooms, in cribs with white sheets hung on the sides.

157. (p. 385) Experiments with animals have confirmed the destructive effects of a lack of stimulation in infancy. Harry Harlow found that infant rhesus monkeys separated from their real mothers always preferred surrogate mothers with a soft terry cloth surface. Harlow concluded from this finding that an important dimension of early stimulation is _____ _____ supplied by touching, holding, and stroking an infant.

158. (p. 385) Researchers working with humans have found much the same thing. For instance, just _____ minutes of extra touching a day can affect the developmental rate of infants in an institution.

159. (p. 385) Many psychologists have advocated breast feeding of infants as a means of assuring contact comfort. In addition, the breast-feeding mother produces _____, a protein-rich fluid containing antibodies, for the first few days after birth. However, the advantages of breast feeding are not overriding.

160. (p. 385) Contact comfort may underlie the tendency of many children to become attached to _____ objects. This appears not to be a cause for alarm, however. A recent study of 2- to 3-year-old "blanket-attached" children found that they were no more _____ than others.

161. (p. 385) An _____ environment is one that has been deliberately made more novel, complex, and richly stimulating. Rats raised in such environments dramatically out perform those raised in stimulus-poor environments. Also, they have larger and heavier brains with a thicker cortex.

162. (p. 386) One study of its effects upon human development involved giving newborn infants several kinds of extra stimulation each day for several months. These conditions did cause _____ _____ reaching to occur an average of six weeks early.

163. (p. 386) One of the most encouraging examples of the benefits of enrichment is Program _____ _____. Such early childhood education programs produce real improvements in later school performance, especially for the most needy children.

164. (p. 387) In considering maturation rates, it is wise for parents to recognize the difference between the _____ child and the _____ child. Developmental norms specifying ages at which particular abilities appear are based on _____; there is always a wide range of normal variation around this figure.

165. (p. 387) Parents can do much to provide opportunities for varied sensory experience during infancy. Stimulation through contact is quite helpful. For instance, the more time babies spend interacting with parents, the faster they develop _____ and _____ abilities.

166. (p. 387) The concept of responsiveness applies to toys and objects, as well as to parents' behavior. Particularly effective are experiences like those pointed out by psychologist Paul Chance that allow children to see _____-_____ results from their own behavior.

167. (p. 387) Many authorities are concerned about parents who try to push their children's intellectual development. True enrichment is responsive to the child's _____ and _____. It does not make the child feel pressured to perform.

168. (p. 387) Kagan's studies of babies in an isolated Guatemalan village provide evidence that enriching the environment during later childhood is also worthwhile. Babies raised in darkened huts were severely retarded by age _____, but became beautiful, normal children by age _____ due to the rich stimulation of village life during later childhood.

169. (p. 387) Piaget's concept of accommodation suggests that the ideal way to stretch a child's intellect is to provide experiences that are only slightly _____, _____, or _____. This gradual expansion helps minimize the frustration and withdrawal that experiences too far beyond the familiar may cause.

170. (p. 388) Effective parents typically follow a sort of _____-_____-ahead strategy when adapting their instructions to their infants' current level of ability.

171. (p. 388) Parents can contribute greatly to intellectual growth with their attitudes toward a child's investigation of the world. The child who repeatedly hears, "Don't touch that" may become _____ and intellectually _____.

172. (p. 388) Morris Holland offers several suggestions on how to relate to children at different stages of intellectual development. He suggests that during the sensorimotor stage _____ play is most effective.

173. (p. 388) During the preoperational phase, the child should be encouraged to _____ things in different ways.

174. (p. 388) During the concrete operational stage the child is beginning to use generalizations, but expect a degree of _____ in the child's ability to apply concepts of time, space, quantity, and volume to new situations.

175. (p. 388) During the formal operations stage, it becomes more realistic to explain things verbally or symbolically. Encourage the child to create _____ and to imagine how things could be.

176. (p. 389) Couples now have an array of new options available to deal with infertility. With _____ _____ sperm from an anonymous donor is used to impregnate the woman. Donors are selected so that their eye and hair color, height, and so on, match the husband's as closely as possible.

177. (p. 389) To produce a "test-tube" baby using _____ _____ _____, egg cells are surgically collected from the mother's ovary. The egg cells are then placed in a petri dish of nutrients and the father's sperm cells are added. After the egg cell is fertilized and begins dividing, it is implanted in the mother's womb where it develops normally.

178. (p. 389) In a new variation, an _____ woman may donate an egg cell to the infertile couple. The egg cell is then fertilized with the husband's sperm and implanted in the wife's uterus.

179. (p. 389) Infertile couples who are considering this new technique should be warned. The average first-time success rate is only ____ percent and the cost ranges from $4000 to $6000.

180. (p. 389) Many donors for artificial insemination are used _____ (one clinic reported that a single donor fathered 50 babies). Should rules of testing and record-keeping be applied here? This is but one of many unanswered questions raised by the new biological procedures now available to couples.

181. (p. 389) The possibility of selecting an infant's sex prior to conception may have an impact on parenthood. The procedure involves separating X- and Y-bearing sperm and then _____ _____ the egg cell with all male-producing, or female-producing, sperm.

182. (p. 389) At present, sex selection techniques cannot _____ to produce a child of the desired sex. The procedure is also expensive and some couples dislike the need for artificial insemination.

183. (p. 390) It is now possible to identify a large number of genetic disorders. Prospective parents who suspect that they may be carriers of genetic disorders may seek _____ _____ to help calculate the risk of a genetic disorder.

184. (p. 390) Parents who are potential carriers of genetic disorders may elect to have a child but then have a test performed about the fifth week of pregnancy to detect the presence or absence of the genetic defect. Such prenatal testing is done by _____, which involves taking amniotic fluid from the mother's womb.

185. (p. 390) Plants and animals have been improved more in the past 50 years than in the previous 5000. This progress is primarily due to _____, or selective breeding for desirable characteristics.

186. (p. 390)   Through the use of _____ _____ it may someday become possible to remove defective genes and replace them with normal ones. This process will soon be possible with one or two genes, but tampering on a major scale is not likely in the near future.

187. (p. 390)   _____, the production of an entire organism from a single cell, is also unlikely, at least where humans are concerned.

188. (p. 390)   It has also been predicted that ultimately people will carry "gene identity cards" based on _____ _____ made during childhood. These cards would show what hereditary diseases a person is predisposed to, or which may be passed on in childbearing when combined with the gene pattern of a mate.

SELF-TEST

1. (p. 362)   Developmental psychology is the study of progressive changes in behavior and abilities
   a. during infancy   c. during old age
   b. during adolescence   d. throughout life

2. (p. 363)   Of the following, which is *not* an adaptive, human neonatal reflex?
   a. rooting   c. Moro
   b. imprinting   d. grasping

3. (p. 364)   The looking chamber was devised by Robert Fantz to study
   a. development of infant vision
   b. critical periods in monkey development
   c. the principle of motor primacy
   d. how infants establish preferences for certain auditory stimuli

4. (p. 364)   Of the following, which sequence represents the progression in infant visual interest?
   a. attraction to complex patterns—preference for the familiar—interest in the unusual
   b. preference for the unusual—interest in complex patterns—attraction to the unfamiliar
   c. indifference to complex patterns—preference for the unusual—attraction to the familiar
   d. preference for simple rectangles—attraction to scrambled faces—preference for novel stimuli

5. (p. 364)   True-False. In general, increased muscular control develops at an equal rate throughout the body as maturation proceeds.

6. (p. 365)   Of the following, which is *not* defined by the phrase, "until the necessary physical structures are mature, no amount of practice will be sufficient to establish a skill?"
   a. principle of readiness   c. principle of motor primacy
   b. maturation   d. principle of accommodation

7. (p. 366)   True-False. The nature versus nurture debate refers to controversy regarding proper parenting styles (letting the child develop naturally at its own pace versus pushing or nurturing the child to succeed through special and early practice).

8. (p. 367)   Traits that are carried only by genes on either the X or Y chromosome are referred to as

a. polygenetic   c. sex-linked
b. recessive genes   d. monogenetic

9. (p. 367) True-False. Recessive genes determine particular traits only when paired with dominant genes.

10. (p. 369) Kagan's research with easy, difficult, and slow-to-warm-up children indicated that
    a. different mothering styles can produce children with varying personalities
    b. children move through various stages of personality development of which these three classes are representative
    c. newborn babies differ in temperament and thus are active participants in determining the course of their own development
    d. children from foster homes where emotional attachments are encouraged tend to be easy children while children from foundling-homes tend to be difficult or slow-to-warm-up

11. (p. 369) True-False. Environmental effects on development do not occur until after birth.

12. (p. 369) True-False. Congenital problems are those which result from the transmission of abnormal genes during conception.

13. (p. 370) Repeated heavy drinking by a pregnant woman can produce a pattern known as the fetal alcohol syndrome. It includes all of the following *except*
    a. miscarriage or premature birth
    b. infants with low birth weight and a variety of bodily defects and deformations
    c. children with mental retardation, poor coordination, or learning disabilities
    d. adolescents and adults who are prone to alcoholism

14. (p. 371) Which of the following statements is *not* true of the Lamaze method?
    a. It teaches couples what will happen physically during birth.
    b. The mother is taught methods of breathing and muscle control.
    c. The father is trained to give support to and coach the mother.
    d. Painkillers are regularly used to help reduce anxiety.

15. (p. 372) Which of the following is *not* true of fathers' involvement with birth?
    a. Fathers generally make a better transition to parenthood when they participate in preparing for childbirth.
    b. Many hospitals now have birthing rooms that allow the father to room-in, participate in the birth and share in caring for the newborn.
    c. While more hospitals now provide birthing rooms, traditional delivery rooms still exclude fathers.
    d. A recent study found that fathers who wanted to be present during delivery showed greater interest in their infants during the first year.

16. (p. 372) Which of the following is *not* usually a paternal influence in child development?
    a. being a playmate for the infant
    b. being an equal to the mother in caretaking responsibilities
    c. being tactile and physically arousing
    d. engaging in unusual play

17. (p. 374) True-False. Children tested for self-awareness show low probability of self-recognition at nine months. The probability increases through the second year.

18. (p. 375) True-False. Imprinting is an instinctive, innate ability that can take place at any time the appropriate environmental stimuli are present.

19. (p. 375)   Separation anxiety indicates the existence of
    a. human imprinting   c. biological predispositions
    b. acquired fears   d. emotional attachments

20. (p. 375)   Which of the following is *not* true of "motherless monkeys?"
    a. They develop abnormal sexual behaviors.
    b. The effects of their early deprivation can be partially reversed through pairing with younger animals.
    c. They make excellent mothers because of their own needs for increased physical contact.
    d. They are infant monkeys separated from their mothers and raised in isolation.

21. (p. 377)   True-False. Telegraphic speech refers to the period of language development marked by a continous outpouring of connected and repeated language sounds.

22. (p. 377)   Which of the following is *not* true of the roots of language?
    a. Sander and Condon found that even day-old infants move their limbs in synchrony to human speech.
    b. Children universally use a limited number of patterns in their first sentences.
    c. Children and parents develop a system of shared signals which establishes a "conversational" turn-taking pattern even prior to the child's first words.
    d. Infants quickly display a pattern of mutual monitoring with each other that facilitates social readiness for language between peers.

23. (p. 377)   True-False. Noam Chomsky believes that humans have a biological predisposition to develop language.

24. (p. 379)   According to Piaget, _____ refers to using existing patterns in new situations, while _____ involves modifying existing ideas to fit new requirements.
    a. conversation, transformation   c. concreteness, abstractness
    b. assimilation, accommodation   d. accommodation, assimilation

25. (p. 380)   According to Piaget, the development of the concept of object permanence takes place during the
    a. sensorimotor stage   c. concrete operational stage
    b. preoperational stage   d. formal operations stage

26. (p. 380)   Mastery of the concept of conservation usually occurs during the
    a. sensorimotor stage   c. concrete operational stage
    b. preoperational stage   d. formal operations stage

27. (p. 380)   True-False. Reversibility of thoughts or operations is usually an ability acquired during the preoperational stage.

28. (p. 382)   Which of the following is *not* a correct association according to Kohlberg's study of moral development?
    a. preconventional level—moral thinking determined by the consequences of actions
    b. anticonventional level—moral thinking is directed by self-chosen ethical principles
    c. postconventional level—advanced moral development directed by self-accepted moral principles
    d. conventional level—moral actions are directed by desire to conform to the expectations of others or to uphold socially accepted rules and values

29. (p. 382)   True-False. Kohlberg found that everyone goes through six stages of moral development, but not necessarily at the same rate.

30. (p. 384) Children raised in extremely isolated or restricted environments often suffer
    a. telegraphic speech   c. deprivation dwarfism
    b. congenital problems   d. stranger anxiety

31. (p. 384) René Spitz found that foundling-home infants who lacked emotional attachments suffered from all of the following *except*
    a. depression
    b. hospitalism
    c. overdependency resulting from too much mothering
    d. high mortality rate

32. (p. 385) True-False. Harlow's work with surrogate mothers has shown that contact comfort is an important dimension of early stimulation.

33. (p. 386) True-False. Experiments have shown that rats raised in stimulus-enriched environments have the same brain size as control subjects, but significantly better temperaments.

34. (p. 386) True-False. While sensory deprivation can seriously affect development, environmental richness seems to have little influence.

35. (p. 387) True-False. In most cases a child can be considered abnormal if he or she has not demonstrated a certain ability during the developmental norm established for children in general.

36. (p. 389) Which of the following is *not* true of the present state of sex selection techniques?
    a. The procedure can guarantee to produce a child of the desired sex.
    b. It involves separating X- and Y-bearing sperm.
    c. It involves artificially inseminating the mother.
    d. The procedure is relatively expensive, costing about $300.

37. (p. 390) True-False. Amniocentesis is the process of genetic engineering responsible for sex selection prior to conception.

38. (p. 390) Selective breeding for desirable characteristics is called
    a. eugenics   c. cloning
    b. genetic engineering   d. DNA control

ANSWERS — PROGRAMMED REVIEW

1. Developmental psychology
2. neonate
3. grasping
4. rooting
5. sucking
6. nursing
7. Moro
8. mimics
9. 9
10. 3; 8; connected
11. looking chamber
12. complex; simpler
13. circularity, curves; red, blue
14. human

15. familiar; unfamiliar
16. 2
17. Maturation
18. rate; order
19. standing, walking
20. head, toe; center, extremities
21. principle of motor primacy
22. unsuccessful; inefficient; learning
23. 30
24. nature; nurture
25. genetic
26. chromosomes
27. Genes
28. deoxyribonucleic acid; DNA

29. polygenetic
30. dominant; recessive
31. 4
32. X; X, Y
33. sex-linked
34. growth sequence
35. eye, skin; motor; diseases
36. Environment
37. inseparable; interaction
38. temperament
39. easy; 40; difficult; 10; slow-to-warm-up; 15
40. active participants
41. irritability; activity; attentiveness
42. heredity, environment; behavior
43. intrauterine; congenital problem
44. birth defects; genetic
45. morphine, heroin, methadone
46. cortisone, tetracycline; A, D
47. fetal alcohol syndrome
48. oxygen
49. ounce; glass; two
50. heart rate; miscarry
51. premature birth; underweight
52. 27; 25
53. medicated births
54. awareness; oxygen
55. muscular, neural
56. 95
57. natural, prepared
58. Lamaze method
59. physically
60. breathing; muscular
61. labor; pain
62. Frederick Leboyer
63. blue baby
64. lower
65. 15; 20
66. memories
67. attitude
68. greater; more
69. birthing rooms
70. umbilical cord; birthing room
71. 3
72. super mothers
73. competent
74. zoo-keeper; inflexibly
75. goodness of fit
76. responsiveness
77. playmate; four, five
78. attentive; tactile; unusual play
79. middle
80. verbal; exploration
81. self-awareness
82. 9; second
83. 15

84. social referencing
85. 12
86. joy, interest; fear, anger
87. Critical periods
88. imprinting
89. 30
90. emotional attachment
91. separation anxiety
92. grandmothers
93. resiliency; social
94. daycare
95. 20
96. first; 1
97. signals, rhythms
98. sexual
99. rejecting; indifferent
100. antisocial
101. warm, loving
102. emotional bond
103. alert; responsive
104. adopted; premature; cesarean
105. 1 month
106. cooing
107. 6
108. consonant
109. 1 year
110. 2; 200
111. single-word; single-word; telegraphic speech
112. 8,000; 4,000
113. human speech
114. biological predisposition
115. patterns
116. Psycholinguists
117. socially
118. signals
119. 3
120. abstract
121. permanence
122. transformations
123. stages; assimilation; accommodation
124. sensorimotor; 2
125. object permanence; 2
126. preoperational; symbolically
127. words; objects
128. egocentric
129. 7, 11; concrete operational; conservation
130. time, space; logically
131. 65
132. reverse
133. formal operations; 11; abstract principles
134. knowledge; experience
135. learning
136. specific knowledge
137. swift; brain

138. moral dilemmas
139. preconventional; punishment orientation
140. pleasure-seeking
141. conventional
142. authority
143. postconventional; social-contract
144. morality of individual principles
145. children; delinquents; children; adult
146. 20
147. justice; caring
148. relationships
149. males
150. feral children; deprivation
151 deprivation dwarfism
152. critical period
153. hospitalism
154. deaths; retarded
155. attachment
156. perceptual stimulation
157. contact comfort
158. 20
159. colostrum
160. inanimate; insecure
161. enriched
162. visually directed
163. Head Start

164. statistical; particular; averages
165. language; thinking
166. cause-effect
167. curiosity, interests
168. 2; 11
169. novel, unusual, challenging
170. one-step-ahead
171. passive; dulled
172. active
173. classify
174. inconsistency
175. hypotheses
176. artificial insemination
177. in vitro fertilization
178. unrelated
179. 6
180. repeatedly
181. artificially fertilizing
182. guarantee
183. genetic counseling
184. amniocentesis
185. eugenics
186. genetic engineering
187. Cloning
188. blood tests

ANSWERS — SELF-TEST

1. d
2. b
3. a
4. a
5. False
6. d
7. False
8. c
9. False
10. c
11. False
12. False
13. d
14. d
15. c
16. b
17. True
18. False
19. d

20. c
21. False
22. d
23. True
24. b
25. a
26. c
27. False
28. b
29. False
30. c
31. c
32. True
33. False
34. False
35. False
36. a
37. False
38. a

Chapter 15

From Birth to Death: Life-Span Development

CONTENTS

TERMS AND CONCEPTS

life-span psychologist
life stages
developmental tasks
psychosocial dilemma
authoritarian parents
overly permissive parents
effective parents
overprotection (smother love)
sibling rivalry
enuresis
encopresis
anorexia nervosa
pica
delayed speech
stuttering
learning disabilities
dyslexia
hyperactivity
minimal brain dysfunction (MBD)
behavior modification
autism
echolalia
sensory blocking

sensory "spin-out"
operant shaping
adolescence
puberty
social markers
imaginary audiences
transition period
menopause
climacteric
biological aging
gerontologist
fluid abilities
crystallized abilities
maximum lifespan
life expectancy
disengagement theory
activity theory
ageism
thanatologist
power assertion
withdrawal of love
child management
Parent Effectiveness Training (PET)

child abuse
Parents Anonymous
hospice
living will

passive euthanasia
active euthanasia
cryonics

IMPORTANT INDIVIDUALS

Erik Erickson
Diana Baumrind
Ivar Lovaas
David Elkind
Roger Gould
Daniel Levinson

Alex Comfort
Bernice Neugarten
Elizabeth Kübler-Ross
Stanley Coopersmith
Haim Ginott
Thomas Gordon

PROGRAMMED REVIEW

1. (p. 393) The challenges of development extend from beyond childhood and into old age. _____-_____ psychologists study both continuity and change in behavior during a lifetime.

2. (p. 394) There are six universal life stages which share certain broad similarities. These phases include _____, _____, _____, _____ _____, _____ _____, and _____ _____.

3. (p. 394) Each stage confronts a person with a new set of _____ _____ to be mastered. These tasks are skills that must be acquired or personal changes that must take place for optimal development.

4. (p. 394) Personality theorist Erik Erikson suggests that we face a specific _____ dilemma at each stage of life. Resolving these crises creates a new balance between a person and the social world. An unfavorable outcome makes it harder to deal with later crises.

5. (p. 394) During stage one, the first year of life, _____ is established by regular satisfaction of a baby's needs so that the world is seen as a safe and predictable place. _____ is caused by inadequte or unpredictable care and may become the core of later insecurity, suspiciousness, or inability to relate to others.

6. (p. 394) During stage two (1-3 years), parents help their children develop a sense of _____ when they encourage them to try new skills and reassure them if they fail. Consistent overprotection may limit development, and teasing and ridicule may result in feelings of _____ and _____, the unfavorable outcome of this stage.

7. (p. 394) During stage three (3-5 years), the child moves from simple self-control to an ability to take initiative. Parents can reinforce _____ by giving freedom to play, to ask questions, to use imagination, and to choose activities. If children learn to feel that their play, ideas, or questions are silly or stupid, they also learn to feel ashamed and _____ about the activities they initiate.

8. (p. 394) During stage four (years 6-12), the major tasks surround introduction to school. The major crisis involves the development of _____ versus

_____. The first develops if the child is praised for building, painting, and other productive activities. The second develops if a child's accomplishments are regarded as messy, childish, or inadequate.

9. (p. 395) Adolescence is the next major life stage. During stage five (12-18 years), the adolescent must build a consistent _____ out of self-perceptions and relationships with others. Failure to do so causes _____ _____ which may cause the person to seek identity by emulating musicians, athletes, etc.

10. (p. 395) Stage six, young adulthood, involves the psychological crisis of developing _____ versus _____. The former refers to an ability to care about others and a willingness to share experiences with them, the latter makes a person feel alone and uncared for in life.

11. (p. 396) Successful adjustment during middle adulthood, stage seven, centers on the development of _____, interest in guiding the next generation, while unsuccessful resolution leads to _____ and concern only with one's own needs and comforts.

12. (p. 396) According to Erikson, the previous seven stages of life become the basis for successful aging during stage eight, late adulthood. The person who has lived richly and responsibly develops a sense of _____ which allows aging and death to be faced with dignity. However, if previous life events are viewed with regret, the elderly person falls into _____ with a feeling that life has been a series of missed opportunities.

13. (p. 397) Psychologist Diana Baumrind has studied the effects of three major styles of parenting. She describes _____ parents as those who view children as having few rights but adultlike responsibilities.

14. (p. 397) Children of authoritarian parents are expected to stay out of trouble and to accept without question the parents' word on right and wrong behavior. Such children are typically _____ and self-controlled, but they also tend to be emotionally stiff, _____, _____, and lacking in _____.

15. (p. 397) _____ _____ parents view children as having few responsibilities, but rights similar to adults. Such parents require little responsible behavior, and rules are not enforced.

16. (p. 397) Overly permissive parents tend to produce _____, _____ children who misbehave frequently. Such children tend to "run amok" and to be aimless in their approach to life.

17. (p. 397) _____ parents are seen as those who balance their own rights with those of their children. Such parents are authoritative, but not authoritarian.

18. (p. 398) Effective parents are firm and consistent, not harsh or rigid in discipline. They encourage children to act responsibly. This parenting style produces children who tend to be _____, self controlled, _____, _____, and inquiring.

19. (p. 398) It is important for parents to remember that stress is a normal part of life. There is no point in trying to completely shield children from stressful stimulation. In fact, _____ (sometimes called "smother love") can be as damaging as overstressing a child or being excessively strict or permissive.

20. (p. 398) Researchers Chess, Thomas, and Birch have discussed several normal problems which may occur during childhood as reactions to stress. One of these, _____ _____, is a common problem. All children experience occasional wakefulness, frightening dreams, or a desire to get into the parents' bed.

21. (p. 398) _____ _____ of the dark, dogs, school, or of a particular room or person are also common.

22. (p. 398) Most children will be _____ at times, allowing themselves to be bullied by other children. There may also be temporary periods of _____ _____ when nothing pleases the child.

23. (p. 398) Children also normally display periods of _____ _____ marked by tantrums or refusal to do anything requested. This trait is particularly characteristic of _____-year-olds and may be a sign of growing independence.

24. (p. 398) Another normal problem is _____, in which the child refuses to leave the side of his or her mother. This difficulty is especially common among _____-year-olds.

25. (p. 398) Development does not always advance smoothly. Every child will show occasional _____ or _____ to more infantile behavior.

26. (p. 398) An additional problem common to the elementary school years is _____ _____ where jealousy, competition, and even hostility may develop between brothers and sisters.

27. (p. 398) Some sibling conflict may be constructive. A limited amount of aggressive give-and-take between siblings provides an opportunity to learn emotional _____, self-_____, and being a good sport. Parents should be careful not to play favorites or compare one child with another.

28. (p. 398) Parents should also expect school-age children to _____ at times against the rules and limitations of the adult world. Being with peers can offer a chance to do some of the things the adult world forbids. It is normal for children to be messy, noisy, hostile, or destructive to a moderate degree.

29. (p. 399) Significant emotional difficulties may develop during _____ _____ or over bowel and bladder habits. The two most common problems are _____ (lack of bladder control) and _____ (lack of bowel control).

30. (p. 399) Enuresis is more common than encopresis and many times more common among _____ who develop muscular control more slowly than _____. They can both represent expression of frustration or pent-up hostility.

31. (p. 399) Delays in toilet training or a few "accidents" are no cause for alarm. The average age for completing toilet training is _____ months, and it is not unusual for some children to take ____ months longer.

32. (p. 399) Many bed wetters have difficulties because they become extremely _____ when asleep. Limiting fluids during the evening, encouraging and rewarding "dry" nights, and taking an understanding and sympathetic attitude can all help.

33. (p. 399) Feeding disturbances are another area of emotional difficulty. _____ may be encouraged by an overprotective mother who compensates for feeling unloved by showering the child with "love" in the form of food.

34. (p. 399) Serious cases of undereating, or self-starvation, are called _____ _____. The victims are mostly adolescent females experiencing conflicts about maturing sexually. By starving themselves, they limit figure development, prevent menstruation, and delay the time when they must face adult responsibilities.

35. (p. 399) Another childhood problem associated with eating difficulties is a condition called _____, during which children go through a period of intense appetite and eat or chew on all sorts of inedible substances.

36. (p. 399) Speech disturbances may be another source of emotional difficulties. One of two common speech problems is _____ _____. This difficulty may result from a general lack of stimulation, parents who discourage growing up, childhood stresses, mental retardation, or emotional disturbances.

37. (p. 399) The other common problem, _____, was once held to be primarily a psychological disturbance, but now believed to be more _____ in origin. For example, it is ___ times more common in males than females, and there seem to be hereditary factors underlying its occurrence. However, learned fears, anxieties, and speech patterns probably add to the problem as well.

38. (p. 399) Stuttering occurs most when a person _____ that he or she is going to stutter. Therefore, parents must be careful not to add to a child's anxiety and frustration by being angry or critical.

39. (p. 399) If a child begins speech therapy before _____, there is a chance that stuttering will disappear. In some cases it may even disappear on its own. But if it doesn't disappear, or isn't treated, stuttering can become a _____ problem.

40. (p. 399) _____ _____ include problems with thinking, perception, language ability, control of attention, or activity levels. For example, _____ is an inability to read with understanding.

41. (p. 399) The causes of dyslexia are not known at present. However, researchers suspect that it is related to brain dominance. It is known that people with _____ or _____ dominance seem to be more prone to language disorders, including dyslexia.

42. (p. 399) One of the most significant learning disorders is _____, a condition in which the child is constantly in motion and cannot concentrate. It occurs in 3 to 5 percent of American children, with 5 times as many boys as girls being affected.

43. (p. 400) The most widely accepted theory of hyperactivity states that it is the result of _____ _____ _____, abbreviated _____, involving a lag in brain maturation or to undetected damage to the brain.

44. (p. 400) Physicians typically use _____ drugs to control hyperactivity. While such drugs do appear to lessen activity, psychologists have objected to the blanket use of powerful drugs which can be dangerous and unnecessary.

45. (p. 400) Some researchers have found _____ _____ to be as effective as drug treatment in controlling hyperactivity. This technique is essentially the application of learning principles to human problems. The basic idea is to reward the child when he or she is calm and attentive. When children are taught self-control in this way, improvements are more lasting than they are with drug treatment alone.

46. (p. 400) Childhood autism is a problem which affects 1 in 2500 children, boys ___ times more often than girls. It is one of the most severe childhood problems.

47. (p. 400) In addition to being extremely _____, the autistic child may throw gigantic temper tantrums including self-destructive behavior. Many autistic children are _____.

48. (p. 400) If they speak at all, they often parrot back everything said, a reaction known as _____. Autistic children also engage in frequent repetitive actions like rocking, flapping their arms, or waving their fingers in front of their eyes.

49. (p. 400) Additionally, the child may show no response to an extremely loud noise (_____ _____) or may spend hours watching a water faucet drip (_____ _____-_____).

50. (p. 400) At one time, experts blamed autism on parents. It is now recognized that autism is caused by _____ defects in the _____ _____.

51. (p. 400) Even as babies, autistic children are aloof and do not cuddle or mold to their parents' arms. Recent research suggests that the defect may lie in the _____, which affects attention and motor activity.

52. (p. 400) Even with help, only about 1 autistic child in ___ approaches normalcy. Nevertheless, almost all autistic children can make progress with proper care. When treatment is begun early, behavior modification has been particularly successful.

53. (p. 401) Teaching Billy (the autistic child described in the chapter preview) to talk began with his learning to blow out a match. Next he was rewarded for babbling meaningless sounds, then for accidentally saying a word. Notice that this process is basically an example of _____ _____.

54. (p. 401) In a behavior modification program such as that pioneered by Ivar Lovaas, each of the autistic child's maladaptive behaviors is altered using combinations of reward and punishment. In addition to food, sensory stimulation, such as _____ or _____, is often very reinforcing.

55. (p. 401) Researchers have found that following actions such as head banging and hand biting by _____ can bring a swift end to self-destructive behavior.

56. (p. 401) _____ refers to the period during which we move from childhood to acceptance as an adult. This change in social status is so natural that it is recognized in almost all cultures.

57. (p. 401) The _____ of adolescence varies greatly from culture to culture. Most 14-year-old girls in America live at home and go to school. But in rural villages of the Near East many are married and have children.

58. (p. 402) _____ refers to rapid physical growth coupled with hormonal changes that bring sexual maturity. This phenomenon is a biological event, while adolescence is a culturally defined period.

59. (p. 402) The peak growth spurt during puberty occurs earlier for girls than for boys. This accounts for the 1 to 2 year period when girls tend to be taller than boys. For girls, the onset of puberty typically occurs between _____ and _____, while for boys the range is _____ to _____.

60. (p. 402) Puberty tends to dramatically increase body awareness and concerns about physical appearance. About one-_____ of all boys and one-_____ of all girls report being dissatisfied with their appearance during early adolescence.

61. (p. 402) When puberty comes unusually early or late, its impact may be magnified. For boys, early maturation typically enhances their self-image. They tend to be more _____, _____, _____, self-assured, and popular with their peers.

62. (p. 402) Many late maturing boys are anxious about being behind in development. However, after they catch up they tend to be more _____, _____, self-assertive, and _____ of themselves.

63. (p. 402) Developmentally advanced girls in elementary school tend to have _____ prestige among peers. By junior high, however, early development leads to _____ peer prestige and adult approval.

64. (p. 402) Later maturing girls have the possible advantage of usually growing _____ and _____ than early maturing girls.

65. (p. 402) Early maturing girls date _____, are more independent, and are more active in school. They are also more often in _____ at school.

66. (p. 402) One added cost of early maturation is that it may force premature _____ _____. When a teenager begins to look like an adult, he or she may be treated like an adult. If not emotionally ready for this, the search for identity may end too soon, leaving the person with a distorted, poorly formed sense of self.

67. (p. 403) Psychologist David Elkind believes that a large number of American parents are hurrying their children's development causing more children than ever to show serious _____ _____.

68. (p. 403) Elkind's main thesis is that adolescence was once a sort of _____ _____ during which teenagers could adjust to the remarkable changes taking place in their lives. Today, they have adulthood thrust on them prematurely.

69. (p. 403) According to Elkind, the traditional social _____ of adolescence have all but disappeared. These are signs that tell where a person stands socially.

70. (p. 403) Another interesting pattern Elkind has noted in adolescent thought is their preoccupation with _____ _____. They act like others are as aware of their thoughts and feelings as they are themselves.

71. (p. 403) This tendency can lead to painful _____-_____, as in everyone staring at you. It also seems to underlie attention-seeking "performances" involving outlandish _____ or _____.

72. (p. 403)   The adolescent search for identity often results in increased conflict with _____. Some of this is necessary for growth of a separate identity. A complete lack of conflict may mean that the adolescent is afraid to seek independence.

73. (p. 403)   Adolescents and their parents usually agree on most basic topics. The largest conflicts tend to be over more superficial differences in styles of _____, _____, social behavior, etc. In general, adolescents tend to overestimate differences between themselves and their parents.

74. (p. 403)   Increased identification with _____ groups is quite common during adolescence. This gives a measure of security and a sense of identity apart from the family. It also provides practice in belonging to a social network.

75. (p. 403)   Conformity to peer values peaks in _____ adolescence, but it remains strong at least through high school. For many who choose college, the effect may be more a matter of placing further changes in identity on hold. Typically, commitment to an emerging adult identity grows _____ in later college years.

76. (p. 404)   Recent research by Roger Gould has identified several important substages in adult development. According to Gould, the age group 16-18 is marked by a struggle to escape from _____ _____ which may cause anxiety about the future and conflict about dependency.

77. (p. 405)   By ages 18-22, leaving the _____ is usually associated with building new friendships with other adults who serve as substitutes.

78. (p. 405)   Building a workable life summarizes ages 22-28 during which the two dominant activities are striving for _____ and reaching out to _____.

79. (p. 405)   By age 30 many people experience a minor life crisis, questioning what life is all about. _____ are particularly vulnerable during this time of dissatisfaction. _____ _____ and _____ are common symptoms of this mid-life cycle.

80. (p. 405)   People in the age 35-43 stage of life are typically beginning to become more aware of the reality of _____. Attempts to succeed at a career, or to achieve one's life goals become more _____.

81. (p. 405)   The urgency of the previous stage gives way to a calmer acceptance of one's fate in the _____ to _____ year age range. The predominant feeling is that former decisions can be lived with.

82. (p. 405)   After age _____, a noticeable mellowing occurs. Emphasis is placed on sharing day-to-day joys and sorrows.

83. (p. 405)   Psychologist Daniel Levinson carried out an in-depth study of adult lives and identified five periods when people typically experience a _____ period when one life pattern ends and opens the door to new possibilities.

84. (p. 405)   He found that most men went through a period of instability, anxiety, and change between the ages of _____ and _____.

85. (p. 405)   Roughly _____-_____ of the men studied by Levinson defined the midlife period as a last chance to achieve their goals, often stated as a key event.

86. (p. 405) A second pattern involved serious _____, often based on having chosen a dead-end job or lifestyle.

87. (p. 405) Levinson characterized a third pattern as "_____ _____." In this case, the person had earlier established a seriously flawed life structure. The midlife decision to "start over" was typically followed by 8 to 10 years of rebuilding.

88. (p. 405) In the forties and fifties, declining strength, physical vigor, and youthfulness make it clear to individuals that more than half of their time is gone. But, there is a letting go of the "_____" and an increased attempt to be _____ with the direction one's life has taken.

89. (p. 406) For most women during this era, _____ represents the first real encounter with aging. This process ends monthly menstruation. Also, the level of the hormone estrogen drops, sometimes causing drastic changes in mood or appearance and the occurrence of physical symptoms such as "hot flashes."

90. (p. 406) While many women experience anxiety, irritability, or depression at this time, most postmenopausal women feel that menopause was not as bad as they expected and that their anxiety came from _____ _____ what to expect.

91. (p. 406) Males do not undergo any abrupt physical change directly comparable to menopause, but often experience _____, or significant physiological change, with symptoms similar to those experienced by women in menopause.

92. (p. 406) During the climacteric, decreases in male hormone output may cause psychological symptoms similar to those experienced by women in menopause. However, men remain _____ at this time, and many of their symptoms are more likely related to self-doubts caused by declining vigor and changing physical appearance.

93. (p. 407) Currently, there are an estimated _____ million Americans over the age of 65; by the year 2020, there will be some _____ million people 65 and older, or one out of every five people.

94. (p. 407) _____ _____ is a gradual process that begins early in life. Peak functioning in most physical capacities reaches a maximum by about _____ to _____ years of age and then gradually declines.

95. (p. 407) For those who are still young, the prospect of physical aging may be the largest threat of old age. However, only about ___ percent of the elderly are in nursing homes. Many misconceptions about elderly people still exist.

96. (p. 407) As a _____ (one who studies aging), Dr. Alex Comfort estimates that only ___ percent of the disabilities of old people are medical, the rest are social, political, and cultural.

97. (p. 407) Comfort's view of aging is backed up by the studies of the intellectual capacities of aging individuals. Although "_____" abilities (those requiring speed or rapid learning) may decline, "_____" abilities, such as vocabulary and accumulated knowledge, actually improve at least into the seventies.

98. (p. 407) The length of our lives is limited by a boundary called the _____ _____. Current estimates of the average human lifespan place it around 95 to 110 years.

99. (p. 407)   For most people, _____ _____ (the actual number
of years the average person lives) is shorter than a lifespan. In the 1800's the average
was 36. By 1900 it was 49. In 1951 it was 69. Currently, it is _____ for males and
_____ for females.

100. (p. 407)   While there is no known way to extend human lifespan, the following rules can help
increase life expectancy: (1) Do not _____; (2) Use _____
in moderation or not at all; (3) Avoid becoming _____;
(4) Have high blood pressure treated; (5) Remain socially and economically active in
retirement; (6) _____ regularly throughout life; (7) Get married;
(8) Learn to manage _____; and (9) Choose long-lived parents.

101. (p. 407)   Two principal theories have been proposed to explain successful adjustment to the
physical and social changes that accompany aging. The _____
_____ of aging assumes that it is normal and desirable that people will
withdraw from society as they age.

102. (p. 408)   The second view, _____ _____, predicts that people who
remain active physically, mentally, and socially will adjust better to aging.

103. (p. 408)   The majority of studies conducted on aging support the _____
_____, although successful aging probably requires a combination of
activity and disengagement. For example, one researcher has shown that the elderly
tend to disengage from activities that are no longer satisfying while maintaining
those that are.

104. (p. 408)   _____ refers to discrimination or prejudice on the basis of age. It can
be positive (as in Japan, where increased age brings increased status and respect), but
in most western nations it tends to have a negative impact on older individuals.

105. (p. 408)   Another facet of ageism is _____ of the aged. Popular
images, especially as seen in movies and television, help perpetrate the myths underlying ageism.

106. (p. 409)   One of the best ways to combat ageism is to counter stereotypes with facts. As one
example, studies show that in many occupations older workers perform better at jobs
requiring both _____ and _____.

107. (p. 409)   Gradual slowing with age is a reality, but it is often countered by experience, skill, or
expertise. For example, one study showed that while older typists responded
_____ on reaction time tests, there was _____ _____
in the actual typing speeds of younger and older typists.

108. (p. 409)   Bernice Neugarten conducted a study of 200 people between the ages of 70 and 79.
She found that _____ percent were satisfied with their lives after retirement. She
also found that most prefer to live apart from their children and few are placed in
mental hospitals because of mental senility or uncaring children.

109. (p. 409)   In a public opinion poll of 1500 adults, only about ___ percent showed evidence of
directly fearing their own deaths.

110. (p. 409)   A recent study of individuals ranging in age from 30 to 82 years found no overall
differences in death anxiety associated with age. However, another study found that
younger individuals fear the _____ of death, whereas
older people fear the _____ of death.

111. (p. 409)   While these findings seem to indicate a general lack of fear about death, it may be more accurate to say that they reflect a deeply ingrained tendency to _____ the reality of death.

112. (p. 409)   Support for this idea comes from another survey in which less than _____-_____ of the respondents reported growing up in families in which death was openly talked about.

113. (p. 409)   A more direct indication of emotional responses to death comes from the work of Elizabeth Kübler-Ross, a _____ (one who studies death) who has spent hundreds of hours at the bedsides of the terminally ill.

114. (p. 409)   She has found that dying people display at least five basic reactions as they prepare for death. These include: (1) _____ and _____; (2) _____; (3) _____; (4) _____ and finally (5) _____.

115. (p. 410)   Not all terminally ill individuals display all of these reactions, nor do they always occur in this order. The list is meant only to describe _____ and _____ reactions to impending death.

116. (p. 410)   Understanding the emotional reactions involved in the process of dying can help the dying individual cope. Also, it is helpful to realize that close friends or relatives of the dying person may feel many of the same _____ before or after the person's death because they, too, are facing a loss.

117. (p. 410)   Perhaps the most important thing to recognize is that the dying person may have a need to _____ _____ with others to to discuss death openly.

118. (p. 410)   _____ is a natural and normal reaction to loss and an essential part of adjusting to death. Grief tends to follow a predictable pattern beginning with a period of _____ or numbness when the bereaved may remain in a dazed state showing little emotion.

119. (p. 410)   This reaction is followed by _____ of _____, episodes of yearning for the dead person and sometimes anguished outbursts of anger.

120. (p. 410)   The first powerful reactions of grief gradually give way to weeks or months of _____, _____, and depression. Life seems futile.

121. (p. 410)   The mourner is usually able to resume work or other activities after ___ or ___ weeks, but insomnia, loss of energy and appetite, and similar signs of depression may continue.

122. (p. 411)   Slowly the bereaved person accepts what cannot be changed, makes a new beginning, and moves toward resolution. Generally, a _____ or _____typically passes before the more intense stages of grief run their course.

123. (p. 411)   It has long been assumed that suppressing grief may later lead to more severe and lasting _____. However, research shows that a lack of intense grief does _____ usually predict later problems.

124. (p. 412)   As a single problem area in development, the question of how to be a good parent has

probably attracted more attention than any other. Much of the answer can be found in _____ and _____.

125. (p. 412) Effective discipline is authoritative yet _____. The goal is to socialize a child without undue _____ and without destroying the _____ of love and trust between parent and child.

126. (p. 412) One 22-year-long study found that children whose parents are critical, harsh, or authoritarian often become _____-_____ adults. They also have a higher than average record of _____ and substance abuse.

127. (p. 412) Many experts are advocating a new style of childrearing that recognizes a child's _____ _____. The child has room to move about freely within well-defined limits consistently applied.

128. (p. 412) Parents tend to base discipline on one or more of three techniques. _____-_____ techniques are associated with fear, hatred of parents, and a lack of spontaneity and warmth. Severely punished children also tend to be defiant, rebellious and aggressive.

129. (p. 412) Some parents use _____ of _____ by refusing to speak to a child, by threatening to leave, or by rejecting the child. This tends to produce children who are self-disciplined, but also anxious, insecure, and dependent on adults for approval.

130. (p. 412) The third technique, child _____, combines praise, recognition, approval, etc. to encourage desirable behavior. However, younger children may not always see the connection between rules, explanations, and their own behavior.

131. (p. 413) Stanley Coopersmith has found that _____ self-esteem was related to the use of physical punishment or withholding of love. _____ self-esteem was related to management techniques which emphasized strict and consistent discipline coupled with high parental interest and concern for the child.

132. (p. 413) In using physical punishment and withdrawal of love the following guidelines should be observed:
    1) Separate disapproval of the _____ from disapproval of the _____.
    2) Punishment should never be harsh or injurious to a child.
    3) Punishment is most effective when it is administered _____.
    4) Physical punishment is not particularly effective with children under age _____ or older than age _____.
    5) Reserve physical punishment for situations that pose an immediate danger to the younger child.
    6) Remember too that it is usually more effective to reinforce children when they are being good than it is to punish them for misbehavior.

133. (p. 413) Haim Ginott has suggested that it is essential to make a distinction between a child's _____ and a child's _____. He encourages parents to teach their children that all _____ are appropriate, only actions are subject to disapproval.

134. (p. 413) Thomas Gordon, who has developed a program called _____ _____ (PET), believes that parents should send _____ messages instead of _____ messages.

135. (p. 414) Estimates on the number of children who are physically abused by parents range from _____ percent to _____ percent. At a minimum, 1.7 million children are physically battered each year in the U.S.

136. (p. 414) In about _____-_____ of all such cases, the child is seriously injured. Every hear hundreds of children are killed by their parents.

137. (p. 414) Abusive parents are usually young (under _____ years old) and more are from _____ income levels. They often have a high level of stress and frustration in their lives. Typical problems include loneliness, marital discord, unemployment, drug or alcohol abuse, divorce, family violence, and work anxieties.

138. (p. 414) Some parents are aware they are abusive, but can't _____; others may hate their child because the child's diapers, crying, or needs are unbearable to them. Often these parents expect the child to make them _____ or loved and respond with violence when these unrealistic demands are not met.

139. (p. 414) A recent study found that in addition to being highly reactive to stress, abusive mothers are more likely to believe that their children are acting _____ to annoy them.

140. (p. 414) The core of much child abuse is a _____ of _____ established when parents were themselves mistreated as children. As an estimate, roughly _____ percent of all parents who were abused as children will mistreat their own children.

141. (p. 414) In a recent study, abused children were observed as they interacted with playmates. In almost every instance, they responded to distress with _____, _____, or physical assault.

142. (p. 414) Legal "cures" for child abuse are not very satisfying. Parents need help such as that available through _____ _____, a national organization staffed by former child abusers who are determined to help each other stop abusing children.

143. (p. 415) Another way of preventing child abuse is by changing _____. One recent survey found that corporal punishment is widely accepted in this country, even punishment that hovers on the threshold of abuse.

144. (p. 416) A _____ is basically a hospital for the terminally ill, modeled after a pioneering English facility. The development of such facilities is one of the reactions to the fact that more than 70 percent of the people in our country die outside their homes, much the reverse of how things were at the beginning of this century.

145. (p. 416) A hospice is different from a hospital in several ways. For one, there are lots of _____ present. Secondly, the _____ is pleasant, informal, and has a sense of continued living. And thirdly, the patient is allowed _____ of _____.

146. (p. 417) The "right to die" concept has been most recently focused by the Karen Ann Quinlan case. In most states it is illegal to remove life-supporting equipment as was done in her case. One solution gaining support is the _____ _____ made out when the person is healthy, saying that should the person become irreversibly ill, they do not want life sustained by medical machines or heroic measures.

147. (p. 417) The right to die won for Karen Quinlan by her parents may be thought of as _____ _____ in which death is allowed to occur

but is not actively caused. In _____ _____, steps would be taken to administer drugs that induce death painlessly.

148. (p. 417) _____ involves freezing a person's body upon death. The idea is to keep them frozen until medical science perfects ways to thaw, restore, and revive the person. However, freezing does serious damage to the body and would severely cripple the brain.

SELF-TEST

1. (p. 394) There are certain broad similarities in the universal life stages of each individual. Each represents a milestone in physical maturation and psychological development, and each confronts a person with a new set of
    a. developmental tasks
    b. life enhancements
    c. developmental modifications
    d. psychosocial outcomes

2. (p. 394) Which of the following is *not* a correct association according to Erikson's life stages?
    a. stage 2—autonomy versus shame and doubt
    b. stage 6—intimacy versus isolation
    c. stage 4—industry versus inferiority
    d. stage 1—generativity versus stagnation

3. (p. 395) A favorable outcome to the life crisis of adolescence would include
    a. faith in the environment and others
    b. concern for family, society, and future generations
    c. an integrated image of oneself as a unique person
    d. confidence in productive skills, learning how to work

4. (p. 396) If the psychosocial dilemma of middle adulthood is favorably resolved, the outcome is a(n)
    a. concern for family, society, and/or future generations
    b. confidence in productive skills, learning how to work
    c. feelings of self-control and adequacy
    d. ability to form bonds of love and friendship with others

5. (p. 397) Which of these is a correct match according to Baumrind's studies?
    a. effective parents—inquiring, assertive, self-controlled children
    b. authoritarian parents—dependent, immature children who misbehave frequently
    c. overly permissive parents—obedient, emotionally stiff, apprehensive children
    d. all of the above

6. (p. 398) True-False. Stress during childhood should always be avoided since the infant has little ability to deal with it at that age.

7. (p. 398) Of the following, which is *not* considered a normal reaction to the unavoidable stress of growing up?
    a. sibling rivalry
    b. anorexia
    c. specific fears of the dark, school, etc.
    d. reversals to more infantile behaviors

8. (p. 399) Which of the following is *not* true of enuresis?
    a. It is more common than encopresis.
    b. It is many times more common in females due to slower muscular development.
    c. It may represent expression of frustration or pent-up hostility.
    d. It may simply result because children are extremely relaxed when they sleep.

9. (p. 399)   Which of the following is true of anorexia nervosa?
   a. Most victims are adolescent males.
   b. It is possibly related to distortions in body image or conflicts about maturing sexually.
   c. It is often associated with encopresis or enuresis.
   d. The condition refers to excessive overeating leading to significant overweight problems.

10. (p. 399)   Which of the following is a type of eating disorder in which inedible objects are chewed or eaten?
   a. anorexia nervosa   c. autism
   b. enuresis   d. pica

11. (p. 399)   True-False.   The two most common speech problems among children are stuttering and echolalia.

12. (p. 399)   Which of the following is a learning disability?
   a. dyslexia   c. climacteric change
   b. pica   d. crystallized intelligence

13. (p. 400)   The most widely accepted theory of hyperactivity states that it is the result of
   a. poor diet   c. minimal brain dysfunction
   b. lack of parental discipline   d. environmental factors such as lighting

14. (p. 400)   Which of the following does *not* characterize childhood autism?
   a. extreme isolation   c. retarded language development
   b. sensory spin-out   d. hyperactivity

15. (p. 400)   Which of the following is a behavior disturbance in which spoken words are simply repeated in a parroting, stereotyped manner?
   a. encopresis   c. echolalia
   b. stuttering   d. glossalalia

16. (p. 401)   Autism, hyperactivity, and other extreme behavioral problems of childhood can be effectively treated through
   a. severe and consistent punishment
   b. behavior modification techniques
   c. increased parental attention
   d. proper diet

17. (p. 402)   True-False.   While the onset of adolescence may vary from culture to culture, the length is fairly consistent—usually about five years.

18. (p. 402)   Which of the following is *not* true of puberty?
   a. It is a biological process that refers to rapid physical growth, coupled with hormonal changes that bring sexual maturity.
   b. The onset for girls typically occurs between 11 and 14.
   c. It tends to dramatically increase body image and concerns about physical appearance.
   d. The peak growth spurt during puberty occurs earlier for boys than for girls.

19. (p. 403)   True-False.   David Elkind has theorized that teenagers are preoccupied with imaginary audiences which can lead to painful self-consciousness or attention-seeking "performances."

20. (p. 405) True-False. In Roger Gould's analysis of personality changes and psychological developments during adulthood, he found that people 29-34 years of age experience a mellowing of desires and an emphasis on sharing day-to-day joys and sorrows.

21. (p. 405) Which of the following is *not* a pattern of response to the midlife crisis as discussed by Daniel Levinson?
    a. People mellow out, accept their recognition of inevitable death, and place strong emphasis on family and friends.
    b. A serious decline may occur related to obvious failure or feelings of pointlessness.
    c. People break out of seriously flawed life structures and may literally start over.
    d. It is seen as a last chance to achieve life goals and can be a period of stress.

22. (p. 407) True-False. Only about five percent of the elderly are placed in nursing homes.

23. (p. 407) An expert on the problems of aging and the aged is called a
    a. thanatologist   c. obstetrician
    b. gerontologist   d. pediatrician

24. (p. 407) It is estimated that only about _____ percent of the disability of old people is medical.
    a. 5   c. 20
    b. 10   d. 25

25. (p. 407) True-False. Although there may be declines in crystallized abilities with aging, there is an improvement in fluid abilities.

26. (p. 408) Which of the following postulates that people who remain psychologically, physically, and socially involved are better able to adjust to the aging process?
    a. activation-arousal theory c. disengagement theory
    b. engagement theory   d. activity theory

27. (p. 409) True-False. One researcher found that older people fear the occurrence of death, and young people fear the circumstances of death.

28. (p. 409) A person who studies death and dying is referred to as a
    a. thanatologist   c. cerebrologist
    b. gerontologist   d. mortician

29. (p. 410) Which of the following is *not* a basic stage in preparation for death as described by Kübler-Ross?
    a. positioning   c. anger
    b. depression   d. acceptance

30. (p. 410) After the period of shock or numbness, the next predictable pattern a mourner usually experiences is
    a. acceptance of what cannot be changed, and the start of a new beginning
    b. weeks or months of apathy, dejection, and depression
    c. the absence of emotion accompanied by difficulties accepting the reality of loss
    d. pangs of grief in which the mourner experiences painful yearnings for the dead person

31. (p. 410) Which of the following is *not* true of grief?
    a. It is a natural and normal reaction to loss.
    b. In general, a week or two typically passes before the more intense stages of grief have run their course.

c. A person who avoids grief by suppressing feelings may later experience a much more severe and lasting depression.

d. It is important for those around the mourner to support their grief and allow its expression.

32. (p. 412) Which of the following parental styles results in children who tend to be self-disciplined and frequently anxious, insecure, and dependent on adults for approval?
a. power assertion
b. child management
c. withdrawal of love
d. power-oriented

33. (p. 413) Which of the following is *not* true of punishment as a parenting technique?
a. Physical punishment should be reserved for situations that pose an immediate danger to the younger child.
b. Spanking is not particularly effective for children under age two.
c. Spanking is most effective for children over age five.
d. Punishment should involve separating disapproval of the act from disapproval of the child.

34. (p. 413) True-False. Haim Ginott encourages parents to teach their children that all feelings are appropriate, only actions are subject to disapproval.

35. (p. 413) True-False. Thomas Gordon recommends that parents learn to send "I" messages rather than "you" messages, to their children.

36. (p. 414) Which of the following is *not* a characteristic frequently seen among abusive parents?
a. most do not begin abusing their child until the child reaches the rebellious teen years
b. many were themselves abused as children
c. they often have a high level of stress and frustration in their lives
d. more come from lower income levels

37. (p. 414) Parents Anonymous seeks to
a. assist courts in supervising foster home placements of abused children
b. use volunteers and former child abusers to create a network of support in helping parents to stop abusing their children
c. promote legislation setting criteria for who can and cannot become parents
d. study abusive parents, collect statistical data, and make suggestions to professionals treating abusive parents

38. (p. 416) True-False. A hospice is a hospital for the terminally ill where the dying person receives specialized care to improve the quality of life in the person's final days.

39. (p. 417) True-False. Passive euthanasia involves passively freezing a body immediately after death.

ANSWERS — PROGRAMMED REVIEW

1. life-span
2. infancy; childhood, adolescence; young adulthood, middle adulthood; old age
3. developmental tasks
4. psychosocial
5. trust; Mistrust
6. autonomy; shame, doubt
7. initiative; guilty
8. industry; inferiority
9. identity; role confusion
10. intimacy; isolation
11. generativity; stagnation
12. integrity; despair
13. authoritarian

14. obedient; withdrawn, apprehensive; curiosity
15. Overly permissive
16. dependent, immature
17. Effective
18. competent, independent, assertive
19. overprotection
20. sleep disturbances
21. Specific fears
22. overly timid; general dissatisfaction
23. general negativism; two
24. clinging; three
25. reversals, regressions
26. sibling rivalry;
27. control; assertion
28. rebel
29. toilet training; enuresis; encopresis
30. males; females
31. 30; 6
32. relaxed
33. Overeating
34. anorexia nervosa
35. pica
36. delayed speech
37. stuttering; physical; 4
38. fears
39. adolescence; lifelong
40. Learning disabilities; dyslexia
41. shared, reversed
42. hyperactivity
43. minimal brain dysfunction; MBD
44. stimulant
45. behavior modification
46. 4
47. isolated; mute
48. echolalia
49. sensory blocking; sensory spin-out
50. congenital; nervous system
51. cerebellum
52. 4
53. operant shaping
54. tickling, music
55. punishment
56. Adolescence
57. length
58. Puberty
59. 11; 14; 13; 16
60. half; third
61. poised; relaxed; dominant
62. eager; talkative; tolerant
63. less; greater
64. taller, thinner
65. sooner; trouble
66. identity formation
67. stress symptoms
68. grace period
69. markers
70. imaginary audiences
71. self-consciousness; dress, behavior
72. parents
73. dress; manners
74. peer
75. early; stronger
76. parental dominance
77. family
78. accomplishment; others
79. Marriages; Extramarital affairs; divorces
80. death; urgent
81. 45, 50
82. 50
83. transition
84. 37; 41
85. one-half
86. decline
87. breaking out
88. impossible dream; satisfied
89. menopause
90. not knowing
91. climacteric
92. fertile
93. 30; 50
94. Biological aging; 25, 30
95. 5
96. gerontologist; 25
97. fluid; crystallized
98. maximum lifespan
99. life expectancy; 71; 78
100. smoke; alcohol; overweight; Exercise; stress
101. disengagement theory
102. activity theory
103. activity theory
104. Ageism
105. stereotyping
106. speed; skill
107. slower; no difference
108. 75
109. 4
110. occurrence; circumstances
111. deny
112. one-third
113. thanatologist
114. denial and isolation; anger; bargaining; depression; acceptance
115. typical, appropriate
116. emotions
117. share feelings
118. Grief; shock
119. pangs of grief
120. apathy, dejection
121. 2; 3

122. month; two
123. depression; not
124. communication, discipline
125. sensitive; frustration; bond
126. self-absorbed; violence
127. psychological needs
128. Power-oriented
129. withdrawal of love
130. management
131. low; High
132. act; child; immediately; two; five
133. feelings, behavior; feelings
134. Parent Effectiveness Training; I; you
135. 3.5; 17

136. one-third
137. 30; lower
138. stop; happy
139. intentionally
140. cycle of violence; 30
141. fear; threats
142. Parents Anonymous
143. attitudes
144. hospice
145. people; atmosphere; freedom of choice
146. living will
147. passive euthanasia; active euthanasia
148. Cryonics

ANSWERS — SELF-TEST

1. a
2. d
3. c
4. a
5. a
6. False
7. b
8. b
9. b
10. d
11. False
12. a
13. c
14. d
15. c
16. b
17. False
18. d
19. True
20. False

21. a
22. True
23. b
24. d
25. False
26. d
27. False
28. a
29. a
30. d
31. b
32. c
33. c
34. True
35. True
36. a
37. b
38. True
39. False

Chapter 16

Dimensions of Personality

CONTENTS

TERMS AND CONCEPTS

hypothetical construct
personality
character
temperament
traits
personality types
introvert
extrovert
self-concept
personality theory
trait theorist
common traits
individual traits
cardinal traits
central traits
secondary traits
surface traits
clusters
source traits
factor analysis
Sixteen Personality Factor Questionnaire
    (16 PF)
trait profile

trait-situation interactions
birth order (ordinal position)
androgyny
Bem Sex Role Inventory (BSRI)
interview
structured interview
unstructured interview
halo effect
direct observation
rating scales
behavioral assessment
situational testing
personality questionnaires
Minnesota Multiphasic Personality Inventory
    (MMPI)
hypochondriasis
psychasthenia
hypomania
MMPI profile
validity scales
projective tests
Rorschach Inkblot Test
Thematic Apperception Test (TAT)

test battery   mental bias
sudden murderers   private self-consciousness
shyness   public self-consciousness
social skills   behavioral genetics
social anxiety

IMPORTANT INDIVIDUALS

Carl Jung   Melvin Lee
Gordon Allport   Philip Zimbardo
Raymond Cattell   Minerva Bertholf
Sandra Bem   Jonathan Cheek
Hermann Rorschach   Arnold Buss
Henry Murray   Michel Girodo

PROGRAMMED REVIEW

1. (p. 421)   A _____ _____ is an explanatory con-
    cept that is not directly observable. Personality is such a concept.

2. (p. 421)   Most psychologists regard personality as one's unique and enduring _____
    _____.

3. (p. 421)   Personality, then, refers to the _____ in who a person
    is, has been, and will become. It also refers to the special blend of talents, attitudes,
    values, hopes, loves, hates, and habits that mark each person as a unique individual.

4. (p. 421)   Many people confuse personality with what is known as _____, a term
    that implies that a person has been evaluated, not just described.

5. (p. 421)   Personality can also be distinguished from _____, which is
    the raw material from which personality is formed. It refers to the hereditary
    aspects of one's emotional nature: sensitivity, prevailing mood, etc.

6. (p. 422)   In   general,   psychologists   think   of   traits   as   _____
    _____ within a person that are inferred from observed
    behavior. We often use traits to predict future behavior from past behavior, since
    they imply some consistency in behavior.

7. (p. 422)   A personality _____ represents a category of individuals who have a
    number of traits or characteristics in common.

8. (p. 422)   Over the years, psychologists have proposed various ways to categorize personalities.
    For example, Carl Jung proposed that a person is either an _____
    (shy, self-centered person) or an _____ (bold, outgoing person). In
    reality, people are usually both, to some degree, depending upon the situation.

9. (p. 422)   Even though types tend to _____ personality, they
    do have value. Most often, types are used by psychologists as a shorthand way of
    labeling people who share similar personality traits, for example Type A or Type B
    personalities.

10. (p. 422)   Another way of understanding personality is to focus on a person's _____-
    _____. That is, a person's perception of his or her own personality
    traits.

11. (p. 422)   Your self-concept consists of all your ideas and feelings about who you are. It tends to shape our subjective world by guiding what we _____ to, _____, and _____ about.

12. (p. 422)   An individual's self-concept can greatly affect personal adjustment—especially when the self-concept is _____ or _____. A negative self-concept can result in depression or anxiety no matter how well a person does.

13. (p. 422)   A personality _____ is a system of assumptions, ideas, and principles proposed to explain personality.

14. (p. 423)   There are over 18,000 English words which refer to personal characteristics. Many of these words describe personality _____ (relatively permanent and enduring qualities that a person shows in most situations).

15. (p. 423)   In general, the trait approach attempts to identify traits which best describe a particular individual. To understand personality, _____ attempt to classify traits and to discover which are most basic.

16. (p. 423)   Splitting people into introverted and extroverted types is an oversimplification. But many psychologists regard one's _____ of introversion/extroversion as one of several important personality traits.

17. (p. 423)   For example, one recent study found that students scoring high in _____ chose study locations that provided more chances for socializing, and higher noise levels.

18. (p. 424)   Gordon Allport has analyzed several kinds of traits. He identifies _____ traits (those shared by most members of a culture which help reveal the similarities among people) and _____ traits (those which define unique personal characteristics).

19. (p. 424)   Allport has also distinguished three other types of traits, including _____ traits (those so basic that all of a person's activities can be traced to the existence of the trait).

20. (p. 424)   _____ traits are the basic building blocks that make up the core of personality. A surprisingly small number of these are sufficient to capture the essence of a person. For example, college students asked to write a short description of someone they knew well mentioned an average of only _____ central traits.

21. (p. 424)   _____ traits are less consistent and less important aspects of a person. They include such things as food preferences, attitudes, political opinions, and reactions to particular situations.

22. (p. 424)   A second major approach to the study of personality traits is illustrated by the work of _____ _____, who was dissatisfied with merely classifying traits, but instead wanted to learn how traits are organized and interlinked.

23. (p. 424)   Through the use of questionnaires, direct observation, and life records, Cattell assembled data on _____ traits (those characteristics making up the visible portions of personality).

24. (p. 424) He then noted that surface traits often appear in _____, or group-ings. Some traits appeared together so often they seemed to represent a single more basic trait Cattell called _____ traits.

25. (p. 424) While Allport classified traits subjectively, Cattell used a statistical technique called _____ _____ to reduce surface traits to source traits. This procedure uses _____ to identify interrelated traits.

26. (p. 424) Cattell's list of source traits forms the basis of a personality test called the _____ _____ _____ (often referred to as the 16 PF).

27. (p. 424) Like many personality tests of its type, the 16 PF can be used to produce a _____ _____. This tool is a graphic representation of the scores obtained by an individual on each trait.

28. (p. 424) There is now little doubt that personality traits show a degree of _____ over long periods of time. And yet, _____ also exert a powerful influence on our behavior.

29. (p. 426) This is why most psychologists now agree that both factors are interrelated in deter-mining behavior. Therefore, trait-situation _____ must be examined in order to fully understand behavior.

30. (p. 426) Birth order, or _____ _____, in a family can leave a lasting imprint on adult personality, the clearest differences being between firstborn and later-born children.

31. (p. 426) The firstborn seem to have a higher chance of achieving _____ than later-born, but are also _____, more conforming, and more likely to be _____ or neurotic under stress than later-born persons.

32. (p. 426) Later-born persons tend to excel in _____ _____. They are affectionate, friendly, and at ease with others. They also tend to be more _____ and _____ than firstborns.

33. (p. 426) Later-borns are typically more popular with their _____. They also display better social skills when interacting with _____.

34. (p. 426) The reason for these differences seems to lie in the "_____ _____" parents bring to each child.

35. (p. 426) The firstborn often get more attention, praise, and concern, are talked to more, punished more, and get more stimulation. They also are more likely to be a planned child and are breast-fed longer. Higher parental expectations are translated into high _____-_____.

36. (p. 426) For example, women business executives who have excelled in traditional, male dominated occupations tend to be firstborn children. It may be that these firstborn women were especially encouraged to _____ by their parents.

37. (p. 426) However, the inexperienced parents of the firstborn are more _____ and _____, which results in higher levels of anxiety and a tendency to conform to adult values among firstborn children.

38. (p. 426) Parents consistently report that they used _____ discipline and were

more relaxed with second or later children. The youngest child is particularly prone to be _____ and to have fewer responsibilities than older siblings.

39. (p. 427) Sandra Bem has used the _____ _____ _____ _____ _____ (BSRI) to classify individuals as traditionally masculine, feminine, or _____ (literally meaning "man-woman").

40. (p. 427) She found that _____ percent of those surveyed fell into traditional masculine or feminine categories, _____ percent scored higher on traits characteristic of the opposite gender, and _____ percent were androgynous, getting roughly equal scores on the masculine and feminine items.

41. (p. 427) Androgynous individuals are less hindered by sex roles or images of what is appropriate "masculine" or "feminine" behavior. They are more _____.

42. (p. 427) For example, in one experiment Bem gave people the choice of performing either a "masculine" activity or a "feminine" activity. Masculine men and feminine women consistently chose sex-appropriate activities, even when the opposite choice _____ _____.

43. (p. 427) Bem's conclusion from a number of studies is that rigid sex roles can seriously restrict behavior, especially for _____. They have great difficulty expressing warmth, playfulness, and concern.

44. (p. 428) The overall picture which has emerged from research on androgyny is that having "masculine" traits primarily means a person is _____ and _____, which is related to high self-esteem and to success in many situations.

45. (p. 428) Having "feminine" traits primarily means a person is _____ and _____ - _____. Such people tend to experience greater social closeness with others and more happiness in marriage.

46. (p. 429) Psychologists use various tools to assess personality. A very direct way to learn about a person's personality is to engage in conversation. An interview is described as _____ if the conversation is informal and the interviewee allowed to determine what subjects are discussed.

47. (p. 429) In a _____ interview, information is obtained by asking a series of preplanned questions.

48. (p. 429) Interviews are used to select persons for employment, college, or special programs, and for research on the dynamics of personality, and to provide information for _____ or _____. An advantage is that they allow observation of a person's tone of voice, hand gestures, posture, and facial expressions.

49. (p. 429) They also have certain limitations. Interviewers can be swayed by _____. A person identified by a title (i.e., house-wife) may be misjudged because of an interviewer's attitudes toward a particular life-style.

50. (p. 429) Also, the interviewer's own _____ may cause him or her to accentuate or distort qualities of the interviewee. A third problem in interviewing is

the _____ _____, the tendency to generalize a favorable or unfavorable impression to unrelated details of personality.

51. (p. 429) When used as an assessment procedure, _____ _____ is a simple extension of the natural interest in "people watching." It is a useful technique but is subject to the same problems of misperception as an interview.

52. (p. 430) For this reason, _____ _____ are used which limit the chance of overlooking some traits while exaggerating others.

53. (p. 430) An alternative to rating scales is to do a _____ _____ in which observers record how often various actions occur, rather than what traits they think a person has.

54. (p. 430) Behavioral assessments are not strictly limited to _____ behavior. In one study, students high in math anxiety were asked to think aloud while doing math problems. Then their thoughts were analyzed to pinpoint the causes of their anxiety.

55. (p. 430) A specialized form of direct observation is called _____ _____. It is based on the premise that the best way to learn how a person would react to a certain situation is to simulate that situation.

56. (p. 430) An interesting example of situational testing is the "_____ - _____" training now done by many police departments. As various high-risk scenes are acted out live, or on videotape, officers must decide whether or not to fire their guns.

57. (p. 431) Most personality _____ are paper-and-pencil tests requiring people to answer questions about themselves. As measures of personality, they are more _____ than interviews or observation.

58. (p. 431) Many personality tests have been created, including tests such as the Guilford-Zimmerman Temperament Survey, the California Psychological Inventory, the Allport-Vernon Study of Values, and the 16 PF. One of the best known and most widely used objective tests of personality is the _____ _____ (usually referred to as the MMPI).

59. (p. 431) The MMPI is composed of _____ items to which a subject must respond _____ or _____ or cannot say.

60. (p. 431) The answer to a single item of the MMPI tells nothing about personality. It is only through _____ of responses that personality is revealed.

61. (p. 431) Items on the MMPI were selected for their ability to correctly identify persons with particular _____ problems. If items are consistently answered in a particular way by depressed patients, it is assumed that others who answer the same way are also prone to depression.

62. (p. 431) The MMPI was designed to measure 10 major aspects of personality. Each is represented by a separate subscale on the test. Examples include:
1) the _____ subscale reflects exaggerated concern about one's physical health;
2) the _____ _____ subscale shows a disregard to social and moral standards and emotional shallowness in relationships;

3) _____ which suggests the presence of irrational fears (phobias) and compulsive (ritualistic) actions; and

4) _____ which suggests emotional excitability, manic moods or behavior, and excessive activity.

Other scales include depression, hysteria, masculinity/femininity, etc.

63. (p. 431) After the MMPI is scored, results are charted as an _____ _____.
This procedure allows comparison of a person's scores to those produced by normal adults, thus pinpointing various personality disorders.

64. (p. 432) Because truthful answers are important, the MMPI has additional _____ _____ to detect attempts of subjects to "fake good" (make themselves look good) or "fake bad" (make it look like they have problems).

65. (p. 432) Other scales within the MMPI help adjust final scores that are affected by personal _____ or by tendencies to _____ shortcomings and troubles.

66. (p. 433) It is necessary to consider information from interviews and other sources in connection with classifying people using the MMPI. If the test alone were used large numbers of _____ people would be classified as neurotic, severely depressed, or schizophrenic.

67. (p. 433) Most psychologists are well aware of the limitations of psychological tests, but many other organizations routinely use them, and errors or abuses sometimes occur. As a result, the U.S. Supreme Court handed down a decision limiting the use of tests as conditions of _____ or _____.

68. (p. 433) In contrast to personality assessments that provide information on observable traits, _____ tests attempt to uncover deep-seated or _____ wishes, thoughts, and needs.

69. (p. 433) A projective test provides an _____ _____ which subjects must describe, or about which they must make up a story. You must organize and interpret what you see in terms of your own life experiences.

70. (p. 433) Since projective tests have no _____ or _____ answers, the ability of subjects to fake or "see through" the test is greatly reduced. Projective tests can be a rich source of information, since responses are not restricted to simple true/false or yes/no answers.

71. (p. 433) One of the oldest and most widely used projective tests is the _____ _____ _____. It consists of a set of 10 standardized inkblots which vary in color, shading, form, and complexity.

72. (p. 433) The Rorschach is administered by first showing subjects each blot and asking them to _____ what they see in it. Later, subjects may be asked to identify specific _____ of a blot, to elaborate on previous descriptions, or to suggest a completely new story about a blot.

73. (p. 433) Obvious differences in content are important for identifying a subject's conflicts and fantasies. However, content is considered less important than what _____ of the inkblot are used to form an image and how the image is _____.

74. (p. 434) Another popular projective test is the _____ _____
_____ (TAT) developed by Henry Murray.

75. (p. 434) The TAT consists of _____ sketches depicting various scenes and life situations. The
subject is shown each sketch and is asked to make up a story about the people in it.
This procedure may be repeated several times.

76. (p. 434) Scoring of the TAT is restricted to analyzing the _____ of the stories.
Interpretation focuses on how people feel, how they interact, what events led up to
the incidents depicted in the sketch, and how the story will end.

77. (p. 434) Although projective tests have been popular with clinical psychologists, their
_____ (their ability to measure what they claim to measure) is
considered lowest among tests of personality.

78. (p. 434) Because of the subjectivity involved in scoring, _____ (consistency) of judgments among different users of the TAT and Rorschach is also low.

79. (p. 434) Despite the drawbacks of projective tests, many psychologists attest to their value,
especially as part of a _____ of tests and interviews.

80. (p. 435) Researchers like Melvin Lee, Philip Zimbardo, and Minerva Bertholf have investigated
the personalities of "_____ _____"—those who ex-
plode and commit violent crimes without warning.

81. (p. 435) Prison inmate studies showed that sudden murderers were passive, shy, and
_____ (restrained) individuals. Their attacks are
usually triggered by a minor irritation or frustration, but based on years of unex-
pressed feelings of anger and belittlement.

82. (p. 435) When sudden murderers finally release the strict controls they maintain on their
behavior, a furious attack ensues, usually out of proportion to the offense against
them. Often, such individuals experience _____ for some or all of
their violent acts.

83. (p. 435) In contrast, those previously violent murderers studied tended to be "masculine"
(aggressive), _____ (impulsive), and _____
likely to view themselves as shyer than the average person. Their violence was
_____ and they typically felt they had been cheated or betrayed and
were doing what was necessary to remedy the situation or to maintain their manhood.

84. (p. 436) _____ percent of American college students consider themselves to be shy.
Among those who are, three-fourths say they don't like it.

85. (p. 436) As a personality trait, _____ refers to an avoidance of others, plus
feelings of social inhibition (uneasiness and strain when socializing).

86. (p. 436) There are at least three basic elements of shyness. The first involves an under-
development of _____ _____. Many shy persons simply have
not learned how to meet others or how to start, maintain, and/or end conversation
and social endeavors.

87. (p. 436) _____ _____ is a second common element. For the shy,
nervousness in social situations is more frequent or intense. It is based on
_____ fears (fears of being embarrassed, ridiculed, rejected,
etc.).

88. (p. 436) A third problem for shy persons is a _____-_____ bias in their thinking. They almost always blame themselves when a social encounter doesn't go well.

89. (p. 436) Shyness is most often triggered by _____ or unfamiliar social situations. It may be magnified by formality, meeting someone of _____ status, being noticeably _____ from others, or being the focus of attention.

90. (p. 436) Jonathan Cheek and Arnold Buss found no connection between shyness and _____ self-consciousness (attention to inner feelings, thoughts, and fantasies).

91. (p. 436) Persons who rate high in _____ self-consciousness are intensely aware of themselves as social objects. They think that they are being rejected even when they are not. Such feelings trigger anxiety or outright fear during social encounters, leading to awkwardness and inhibition.

92. (p. 436) Shy persons tend to label their social anxiety a _____ _____ _____, while nonshy persons believe that _____ _____ cause their occasional feelings of shyness.

93. (p. 436) In general, nonshy persons tend to have higher _____-_____ than shy persons. This is because nonshy persons give themselves credit for their social successes and they recognize that failures are often due to circumstances.

94. (p. 436) In America, many children seem to "outgrow" shyness as they gain social skills and wider social experience. Some adults overcome shyness with the aid of a shyness _____ or similar program.

95. (p. 437) Psychologist Michel Girodo directs such a shyness clinic. She observed that shyness is often maintained by _____ or _____- _____ beliefs. Be familiar with the examples discussed.

96. (p. 437) There is nothing "innate" about learning social skills. They can be directly practiced in a variety of ways to help people learn to put more animation and skill into their self-presentation. As one example, get a _____ _____ and listen to several of your conversations.

97. (p. 437) A recent study of 200 men and women found that _____ agreed that whether you're a man or a woman you have the option of beginning a conversation.

98. (p. 437) Psychologist Chris Kleinke reported a study of 1,000 men and women rating a collection of typical "opening lines." An analysis revealed that the statements fell into three categories: cute-flippant, _____, and _____ (mild or harmless).

99. (p. 437) By a large margin, both men and women preferred opening lines that were direct or innocuous. Cute or flippant statements were least liked, especially by _____.

100. (p. 438) One of the simplest ways of becoming a better conversationalist is by learning to ask questions. The best questions are often _____-_____; they require more than one or two words to answer and often give you "free information" that will help further stimulate conversation.

101. (p. 439) _____ _____ is the study of inherited behavioral traits. This is the basis for selectively breeding animals, leading to striking differences in social behavior, emotionality, learning ability, aggression, activity, and other behaviors.

102. (p. 439) Genetic studies of humans rely mainly on comparisons of _____ _____ and other close relatives. Such studies show that intelligence, some mental disorders, temperament, and other complex qualities are influenced by heredity.

103. (p. 439) Psychologists at the University of Minnesota have studied twins who grew up in separate homes. Extensive testing indicates that when identical twins are reunited, they are astonishingly similar in _____ and _____ quality.

104. (p. 439) Observers are also struck by how often the twins display identical _____ gestures, _____ movements, and nervous _____, such as nail biting or finger tapping.

105. (p. 439) Reunited twins are quite similar on many physical tests, have highly correlated IQ scores, and tend to share similar talents. However, where personality is concerned, similarities exist, but are not as strong. For instance, identical twins frequently differ in _____ and _____.

106. (p. 440) The "Jim twins" are a good example of similarities found in twin studies that seem to go beyond what one would expect on the basis of heredity. However, much of the seemingly "astounding" coincidences shared by such reunited twins may be a special case of the _____ of _____ _____: similarities blaze brightly in the memories of reunited twins, while differences are ignored.

107. (p. 440) Strong, albeit coincidental, similarities can exist between nontwins. In fact, one recent study compared twins with unrelated pairs of students of the same age and sex. The unrelated pairs were almost as alike as twins are with respect to _____ beliefs, _____ interests, religious preferences, jobs held, hobbies, favorite _____, and so on.

108. (p. 440) A variety of studies suggest that heredity may be responsible for as much as _____ to _____ percent of the variation in some personality traits. Even so, there is danger in overstating the role of heredity in human behavior.

109. (p. 441) It is wise to remember that we do not inherit specific behavioral traits. Rather, we inherit certain _____ and _____ ways of reacting to the environment. These, in turn, can be greatly altered by experience.

SELF-TEST

1. (p. 421) One's enduring and unique behavior patterns defines which of the following?
   a. disposition   c. personality
   b. character   d. temperament

2. (p. 421) True-False. Personality is a hypothetical construct and is thus not directly observable.

3. (p. 421) Of the following, which is personality evaluated?
    a. disposition   c. temperament
    b. character   d. trait

4. (p. 422) Of the following, who first proposed that people are either introvert or extrovert types?
    a. Carl Jung   c. Raymond Cattell
    b. Gordon Allport   d. Henry Murray

5. (p. 422) Which of the following is *not* true of a person's self-concept?
    a. It is a person's perception of his or her own personality traits and consists of all their ideas and feelings about who they are.
    b. An inaccurate or inadequate self-concept can greatly affect personal adjustment in a negative manner.
    c. We creatively build our self-concepts out of daily experience, then we slowly revise them as we have new experiences.
    d. It is most important in early stages. Once a stable self-concept exists, it tends to have little ability to shape our subjective world.

6. (p. 424) Of the following, which traits are defined by Allport as ones that are so basic that all of a person's activities can be traced to the existence of that trait?
    a. common   c. central
    b. secondary   d. cardinal

7. (p. 424) True-False. Central traits are defined as those shared by most members of a given society.

8. (p. 424) Traits such as food preference, political opinions, and reactions to particular situations are classified by Allport as which of the following types?
    a. cardinal   c. secondary
    b. central   d. unique

9. (p. 424) True-False. Cattell formed his surface traits from certain core traits of the individual known as source traits.

10. (p. 424) The 16 PF was developed by which of the following?
    a. Allport   c. Cattell
    b. Sheldon   d. Jung

11. (p. 426) Which of the ordinal positions of birth is most likely to produce a child with high self-expectations, anxiety, and conformity?
    a. first   c. last
    b. middle   d. they are all about equal

12. (p. 427) The Bem Sex Role Inventory is used to
    a. classify individuals into feminine, masculine, and androgynous sex-role categories
    b. assess unconscious sexual desires through use of ambiguous stimuli
    c. classify direct observations; it is a type of behavioral assessment
    d. measure sex-role competence under situational testing conditions

13. (p. 427) True-False. Androgynous individuals score high in both masculine and feminine traits.

14. (p. 427) True-False. Androgynous individuals are usually less adaptable because they do not know how to implement sex-role appropriate behaviors.

15. (p. 429) Of the following, which is *not* a disadvantage associated with the interview technique of assessing personality?
    a. interviewer can be swayed by preconceptions
    b. interviewee may be influenced by actions of the interviewer
    c. halo effect
    d. technique is rigid and inhibits feelings

16. (p. 429) Of the following, which make use of rating scales and behavioral assessments to limit bias?
    a. interviews   c. direct observations
    b. projective tests   d. personality questionnaires

17. (p. 430) Situational testing is a special form of
    a. interviews   c. personality inventories
    b. projective tests   d. direct observations

18. (p. 431) One of the best known and most widely used objective tests of personality is the
    a. 16 PF   c. Rorschach Inkblot Test
    b. MMPI   d. TAT

19. (p. 432) Which of the following is *not* true of the MMPI?
    a. It is composed of 550 items to be answered true, false, or cannot say.
    b. Items were selected for their ability to correctly identify persons with particular psychiatric problems.
    c. It was designed to measure ten major areas of personality.
    d. It contains a "Lie Scale" which can be used to judge a person's character and determine his or her tendencies to disregard social and moral standards.

20. (p. 433) Which of the following is *not* true of the Rorschach Inkblot Test?
    a. It consists of 10 standardized blots varying in color, shading, form, and complexity.
    b. It is administered by showing each card to subjects and recording their response to a standardized list of questions.
    c. Responses are scored according to content, determinants, and location.
    d. It was developed by Swiss psychologist Hermann Rorschach in the 1920s.

21. (p. 433) True-False. The location and organization of responses to the Rorschach are considered less important than content.

22. (p. 434) Which of the following is *not* true of the TAT?
    a. Scoring is done objectively by simply counting the total number of responses to each card and dividing by the number of cards.
    b. It was developed by Henry Murray.
    c. It consists of 20 sketches depicting various scenes and life situations.
    d. Test administration usually involves asking subjects to make up a story about the people depicted in the card pictures.

23. (p. 434) Which of the following is *not* true of projective tests?
    a. They are usually scored with a high degree of objectivity among different test users.
    b. They provide ambiguous stimuli which subjects must describe or incorporate in a story.
    c. Their validity is lowest among tests of personality.
    d. They attempt to uncover deep-seated or unconscious wishes, thoughts, and needs.

24. (p. 435) True-False. "Sudden murderers" are more likely to be habitually violent individuals who feel cheated or betrayed and are very impulsive.

25. (p. 436) Which of the following is *not* a basic element of shyness?
    a. underdevelopment of social skills
    b. awkwardness and inhibition with friends and family
    c. social anxiety
    d. confidence-lowering mental bias in thinking

26. (p. 436) Which of the following is *not* true of shyness?
    a. As a personality trait it combines social inhibition with a tendency to avoid others.
    b. It can be magnified by formality, meeting someone of higher status, or being the focus of attention.
    c. It should be considered a major problem since it affects 40 percent of American college students.
    d. It is most often triggered by unfamiliar or novel social situations.

27. (p. 436) True-False. Cheek and Buss found that shy people have a tendency to be wrapped up in their own feelings and thoughts. They demonstrate heightened private self-consciousness.

28. (p. 437) Which of the following is *not* a good suggestion for overcoming shyness?
    a. Learn to use open-ended questions in engaging others in conversations.
    b. Become involved in social situations where better social skills can be learned.
    c. Practice with a tape recorder or mirror to learn how you come across to other people.
    d. Take responsibility for all social failures and recognize that social successes may just result from the situation.

29. (p. 437) True-False. Recent studies show that when men initiate conversations, women prefer that they begin with cute or flippant opening lines.

30. (p. 439) Behavioral genetics is
    a. an effort on the part of behaviorists to downplay the role of genetics in determining behavior.
    b. the study of acquired behavioral traits.
    c. the study of inherited behavioral traits.
    d. the study of how behavior affects genetic transmission.

31. (p. 439) Which of the following is *not* true of identical twins?
    a. Their appearance and voice quality are astonishingly similar.
    b. They have high correlated IQs.
    c. Their personalities are as similar as their physical features.
    d. They tend to share similar talents.

32. (p. 440) True-False. Striking similarities which appear to go beyond what one would expect on the basis of heredity are probably best understood as examples of how powerful genes really are in determining even very specific traits.

ANSWERS — PROGRAMMED REVIEW

1. hypothetical construct
2. behavior patterns
3. consistency
4. character
5. temperament
6. lasting qualities

7. type
8. introvert; extrovert
9. oversimplify
10. self-concept
11. attend; remember; think
12. inaccurate; inadequate
13. theory
14. traits
15. trait theorists
16. degree
17. extroversion
18. common; individual
19. cardinal
20. Central; 7.2
21. Secondary
22. Raymond Cattell
23. surface
24. clusters; source
25. factor analysis; correlations
26. Sixteen Personality Factor Questionnaire
27. trait profile
28. consistency; situations
29. interactions
30. ordinal position
31. eminence; shyer; anxious
32. social relationships; original, creative
33. peers; strangers
34. emotional set
35. self-expectations
36. achieve
37. anxious, inconsistent
38. lighter; pampered
39. Bem Sex Role Inventory; androgynous
40. 50; 15; 35
41. adaptable
42. paid more
43. men
44. independent, assertive
45. nurturant; interpersonally-oriented
46. unstructured
47. structured
48. counseling, therapy
49. preconceptions
50. personality; halo effect
51. direct observation
52. rating scales
53. behavioral assessment
54. visible
55. situational testing
56. Shoot-Don't Shoot
57. questionnaires; objective
58. Minnesota Multiphasic Personality Inventory

59. 550; true, false
60. patterns
61. psychological
62. hypochondriasis; psychopathic deviancy; Psychasthenia; Hypomania
63. MMPI profile
64. validity scales
65. defensiveness; exaggerate
66. normal
67. employment, promotion
68. projective; unconscious
69. ambiguous stimulus
70. right, wrong
71. Rorschach Inkblot Test
72. describe; sections
73. parts; organized
74. Thematic Apperception Test
75. 20
76. content
77. validity
78. objectivity
79. battery
80. sudden murderers
81. overcontrolled
82. amnesia
83. undercontrolled; less; moderate
84. Forty
85. shyness
86. social skills
87. Social anxiety; evaluation
88. self-defeating
89. novel; higher; different
90. private
91. public
92. lasting personality trait; external events
93. self-esteem
94. clinic
95. unrealistic; self-defeating
96. tape recorder
97. 90
98. direct; innocuous
99. women
100. open-ended
101. Behavioral genetics
102. identical twins
103. appearance; voice
104. facial; hand; tics
105. dominance, extroversion
106. fallacy of positive instances
107. political; musical; foods
108. 40; 50
109. potentials; general

ANSWERS — SELF-TEST

1.	c	17.	d
2.	True	18.	b
3.	b	19.	d
4.	a	20.	b
5.	d	21.	False
6.	d	22.	a
7.	False	23.	a
8.	c	24.	False
9.	False	25.	b
10.	c	26.	c
11.	a	27.	False
12.	a	28.	d
13.	True	29.	False
14.	False	30.	c
15.	d	31.	c
16.	c	32.	False

Chapter 17

Theories of Personality

CONTENTS

TERMS AND CONCEPTS

psychoanalytic theory
id
ego
superego
pleasure principle
psyche
libido
life instincts (Eros)
death instinct (Thanatos)
primary process thinking
reality principle
conscience
ego ideal
displacement
sublimation
neurotic anxiety
ego-defense mechanisms
unconscious
conscious
preconscious
socialization
psychosexual stages
oral stage
anal stage
phallic stage
genital stage

erogenous zone
fixations
oral-dependent personality
oral-aggressive personality
anal-retentive personality
anal-expulsive personality
phalic personality
Oedipus conflict
identification
Electra conflict
latency
neo-Freudians
striving for superiority
feelings of inferiority
style of life
creative self
basic anxiety
persona
introversion
extroversion
personal unconscious
collective unconscious
archetypes
anima
animus
self-archetype

mandalas
learning theories
situational determinants
habits
drive
cue
response
reward
social learning theorists
psychological situation
expectancy
reinforcement values
self-reinforcement
radical behaviorism
social reinforcement
imitation
humanistic theory
human nature

free choice
subjective experience
self-actualization
peak experience
fully functioning person
self
phenomenal field
self-image
symbolized
incongruent
congruence
ideal self
possible selves
conditions of worth
positive self-regard
organismic valuing
self-monitoring
Self-Monitoring Scale

IMPORTANT INDIVIDUALS

Sigmund Freud
Alfred Adler
Karen Horney
Carl Jung
John Dollard
Neal Miller
Julian Rotter
B. F. Skinner

Elaine Heiby
Lisa Serbin
Daniel O'Leary
Abraham Maslow
Carl Rogers
Hazel Markus
Paula Nurius
Mark Snyder

PROGRAMMED REVIEW

1. (p. 444) _____ theory, the best-known psychodynamic approach, grew out of Sigmund Freud's clinical study of disturbed individuals and evolved from 1890 until his death in 1939.

2. (p. 444) Freud became interested in the treatment of mental disorders when he determined that many of his patients' problems seemed to lack _____ _____.

3. (p. 444) Freud conceived of personality as a dynamic system of energies directed by three structures usually involved in any behavior. One structure, the _____, is made up of innate biological instincts and urges present at birth. It is self-serving, irrational, impulsive, and totally _____.

4. (p. 444) The id operates on a _____ _____, meaning that pleasure-seeking impulses of all kinds are freely expressed.

5. (p. 444) The energy for the entire psyche, or personality, was called the _____, derived from the _____ _____ (Eros) which promote survival and underlie sexual desires.

6. (p. 444) Freud also postulated a death instinct (_____) which he said is responsible for aggressive and destructive urges.

7. (p. 444) Most id energies are aimed at discharge of tensions related to _____ and _____.

8. (p. 444) The second structure, the _____ (sometimes described as the "executive"), draws energies supplied by the _____. It wins power to direct our behavior by matching the desires of the id with _____ _____.

9. (p. 444) The id can only produce mental images of things it desires (called _____ _____ _____). It must rely on others to carry out its orders.

10. (p. 444) Whereas the id operates on the pleasure principle, the ego is guided by the _____ _____, delaying action until it is practical or appropriate.

11. (p. 444) The ego is the system of thinking, planning, problem solving, and deciding. It is in _____ control of the personality.

12. (p. 444) The _____ acts as a judge or censor for the thoughts and actions of the ego. It is composed of a number of different aspects.

13. (p. 444) One part of the superego, called the _____, represents all actions for which a person has been punished.

14. (p. 444) If you act contrary to standards of the conscience, you are punished internally by _____ feelings.

15. (p. 444) The _____ _____ represents all behavior one's parents approved or rewarded. It is a source of goals and aspirations. When the standards of the ego-ideal are met, pride is felt.

16. (p. 444) In Freudian terms, a person with a _____ superego will be a delinquent, criminal, or antisocial personality. In contrast, an overly _____ superego may cause inhibition, rigidity, or unbearable guilt.

17. (p. 445) Freud did not picture the id, ego, and superego as parts of the brain, or as "little people" running the human psyche. Rather, they are separate and conflicting _____ _____ requiring a delicate balance of power.

18. (p. 445) To reduce tension, the ego could bring actions leading to friendship, romance, courtship, and marriage. If the id is unusually powerful, the ego may direct an attempted seduction. If the superego prevails, the ego may be forced to _____ or _____ sexual energies to other activities.

19. (p. 445) When the ego is threatened or overwhelmed, the person feels anxiety. Impulses from the id cause _____ _____ when the ego can barely keep them under control. Threats of punishment from the superego cause _____ _____.

20. (p. 445) Everyone develops habitual ways of reducing these anxieties and many resort to use of _____-_____ _____ to lessen internal conflicts.

21. (p. 446) A major principle of psychoanalytic theory is that behavior often expresses

_____ (or hidden) internal forces within the personality including repressed memories and emotions as well as the instinctual drives of the id.

22. (p. 446)   Modern scientists are beginning to identify brain areas that seem to have the kinds of unconscious effects Freud described. Especially important are areas linked with emotion and memory such as the _____ in the limbic system.

23. (p. 446)   The ego and superego may operate on two other levels besides the unconscious. The _____ level includes everything we are aware of at a given moment. The _____ contains material that can be easily brought to awareness.

24. (p. 446)   The operation of the superego gives another sign of the levels of awareness. At times a person may feel guilty without knowing why due to the _____ workings of the superego. Freudian psychology holds that such events cannot be easily brought to awareness or directly known by the individual.

25. (p. 446)   Every society must _____ its children by teaching them language, customs, rules, roles, and morals. While carrying out this process, parents leave traces of their own personality in their children.

26. (p. 446)   Freud theorized that the core of personality is formed before age six in a series of _____ _____.

27. (p. 446)   His account holds that childhood urges for erotic pleasure have lasting effects on development. While controversial, he used the term _____ very broadly to refer to several different physical sources of pleasure.

28. (p. 446)   At each stage a different part of the body becomes an _____ _____ (an area capable of producing pleasure). It serves as the principle source of pleasure, frustration, and self-expression.

29. (p. 446)   Freud believed that many adult personality traits can be traced to _____ (an unresolved conflict or emotional hang-up caused by overindulgence or by frustration) in one or more of the stages.

30. (p. 446)   During the first year of life, most of an infant's pleasure comes from stimulation of the mouth. If a child is overfed or frustrated, _____ traits may be created. Adult expressions of these needs include gum chewing, nail biting, smoking, kissing, overeating, and alcoholism.

31. (p. 446)   Fixation early in the oral stage produces an _____-_____ personality who is gullible, passive and needs lots of attention.

32. (p. 447)   Fixation later in the oral stage causes an _____-_____ adult who is argumentative, cynical, and exploitive of others.

33. (p. 447)   Fixation during the anal stage (age 1-3 years) can lead to the _____-_____ personality, who is obstinate, stingy, orderly, and compulsively clean. It may also lead to the _____-_____ personality who is disorderly, destructive, cruel, or messy.

34. (p. 447)   Adult traits of the _____ personality are vanity, exhibitionism, sensitive pride, and narcissism (self-love).

35. (p. 447) During the phallic stage (age 3-6 years), increased sexual interest causes the child to become physically attracted to the parent of the opposite sex. In males this generates the _____ _____, in which the boy feels rivalry with his father for the affection of the mother.

36. (p. 448) To ease his anxieties of the rival father (especially fear of _____), the boy must _____ with the father, and form a _____.

37. (p. 448) With girls, there is a competition for the father which produces the _____ _____. Freud believed that females already feel castrated and are, therefore, less driven to identify with their mothers than boys are with their fathers. The girl's identification with the mother is more gradual and less effective in creating a conscience.

38. (p. 448) According to Freud, there is a period of _____ from age six to puberty during which psychosexual development is temporarily interrupted.

39. (p. 448) At puberty an upswing in sexual energies activates all the unresolved conflicts of earlier years, the reason why adolescence can be filled with emotion and turmoil. During this _____ stage, personality is marked by a growing capacity for mature and responsible social-sexual relationships culminating in heterosexual love.

40. (p. 448) Freud's theory has been widely influential for a number of reasons:
1) it pioneered the idea that the first years of life help shape _____ _____;
2) it identified _____, _____ _____, and early _____ experiences as critical events in personality formation; and
3) Freud was among the first to propose that development proceeds through a series of _____.

41. (p. 448) Freud's theory remains controversial. His portrayal of the elementary school years, _____, as free from sexuality and unimportant for personality development is hard to believe.

42. (p. 448) Studies challenging Freud's view, show that an affectionate and accepting father is more likely than a stern one to create a strong _____ in a son.

43. (p. 448) Freud also overemphasized _____ in personality development; other motives and cognitive factors are of equal importance.

44. (p. 448) Freud's ideas quickly attracted a brilliant following. Those who stayed closest to the core of Freud's thought are now referred to as _____ - _____.

45. (p. 448) Alfred Adler broke away from Freud because he disagreed with Freud's emphasis on the _____, on instinctual drives, and on the importance of _____. Adler believed that we are social creatures governed by social urges—not by biological instincts.

46. (p. 448) In Adler's view, the main driving force in personality is a striving for _____—a struggle to overcome imperfections, an upward drive for competence, completion, and mastery of shortcomings.

47. (p. 449) Adler felt that everyone experiences _____ of _____ mainly because we begin life as small, weak and relatively powerless children surrounded by larger and more powerful adults.

They may also come from our personal limitations. The struggle for superiority arises from such feelings.

48. (p. 449)   While everyone strives for superiority, each person tries to _____ for different limitations and each chooses a different pathway to superiority.

49. (p. 449)   Adler believed that this process creates a unique _____ of _____, or personality pattern, for each individual.

50. (p. 449)   According to Adler, the core of each person's style of life is formed by age ___. He later emphasized the existence of a _____ _____, the ability of humans to create personality through choice and experience.

51. (p. 449)   According to Adler, valuable clues to a person's style of life are revealed by the _____ _____ that can be recalled.

52. (p. 449)   Karen Horney remained faithful to most of Freud's ideas, but rejected the claim that "_____ is destiny." She was among the first to counter the obvious male bias in Freud's thinking.

53. (p. 449)   She also disagreed with Freud about the causes of _____. Horney's view was that a core of _____ _____ occurs when people feel isolated and helpless in a hostile world. This dilemma causes troubled individuals to exaggerate a single mode of interacting with others.

54. (p. 449)   According to Horney, each of us can move _____ others, _____ from others, or _____ others. Emotional health requires a balance of each. Emotional problems lock people into overuse of only one of the three modes.

55. (p. 449)   Carl Jung was a student of Freud's, but the two parted ways as Jung began to develop his own ideas. Like Freud, Jung called the conscious part of the personality the _____, but noted that between the ego and the outside world we often find a _____, or mask: the "public self" presented to others when we adopt particular roles.

56. (p. 449)   Actions of the ego may reflect attitudes of _____ (in which energy is mainly directed inward) or _____ (in which energy is mainly directed outward).

57. (p. 449)   Jung used the term _____ _____ to refer to what Freud simply called the unconscious. It is a storehouse for personal experiences, feelings, and memories that are not directly knowable.

58. (p. 449)   Jung also proposed a deeper _____ _____, shared by all humans. It is at this level that _____ (original ideas, patterns or prototypes) exist. They are unconscious images that cause us to respond emotionally to symbols of birth, death, energy, animals, evil, and the like.

59. (p. 449)   Two particularly important archetypes are the _____ (representing the female principle) and the _____ (representing the male principle). Each person has both.

60. (p. 450)   Jung considered the _____ _____ the most important because it represents unity. He believed it is symbolized in every culture by _____ (magic circles).

61. (p. 450) Jung was the first to use the term "_____-_____" to describe a striving for completion and unity.

62. (p. 451) Learning theories of personality and the behaviorist position stress that personality is no more (or less) than a collection of _____ _____ _____ acquired through conditioning principles.

63. (p. 451) In general, learning theorists reject the idea that personality is made up of consistent traits. Instead they draw attention to the importance of _____ _____.

64. (p. 451) Thus, learning theorists have not entirely removed the "person" from personality. They agree that external events _____ with each person's unique learning history to produce behavior in any given situation.

65. (p. 451) Trait theorists also believe that situations affect behavior. But in their view, situations interact with traits. Learning theorists favor replacing the concept of "traits" with "_____ _____" in order to explain behavior.

66. (p. 451) Learning theorists John Dollard and Neal Miller consider _____ the basic structure of personality.

67. (p. 451) As for the dynamics of personality, they believe habits are governed by four elements of the learning process: (1) _____, any stimulus strong enough to goad a person to action; (2) _____, signals from the environment that guide response so they are most likely to bring about reinforcement; (3) response; and (4) reward.

68. (p. 452) The new breed of behavioral psychologists—who include perception, thinking, and other "mental" events in their view of personality—are called _____ _____ theorists (because they also emphasize social relationships and modeling).

69. (p. 452) The "cognitive behaviorism" of social learning theory is illustrated by three concepts proposed by Julian Rotter. Rotter points out that it is not enough to know the setting in which a person responds, we must also know the person's _____ _____ (how the person interprets or defines the situation).

70. (p. 452) Rotter's term _____ refers to anticipation that will produce reinforcement. To predict a response, we must know if the person expects their efforts to pay off. Expected reinforcement may be more important than actual past reinforcement.

71. (p. 452) Rotter's third concept, _____ _____ states that humans attach different values to various activities or rewards which must be considered in understanding personality.

72. (p. 452) Social learning theory adds to the behavioristic viewpoint the concept of _____-_____, personal reward we give ourselves in response to a positive evaluation of our actions.

73. (p. 452) The most extreme view of personality is held by _____ behaviorist B.F. Skinner who believes "personality" is a convenient fiction we invent to pretend we have explained behavior that is actually controlled by the environment.

74. (p. 453) Skinner believes that everything a person does is ultimately based on past and present _____ and _____.

75. (p. 453)   Elaine Heiby has developed a scale to evaluate self-reinforcement. Work in this area shows that high rates of self-reinforcement are related to high _____-_____.

76. (p. 453)   Numerous studies have shown that mildly _____ college students tend to have low rates of self-reinforcement. Learning to be more self-reinforcing appears to lessen _____.

77. (p. 454)   Rather than thinking in terms of psychosexual urges and fixations, modern learning theory emphasizes that childhood is a time of urgent and tearing drives, powerful rewards and punishments, and crushing frustrations. Also important is _____ _____ based on the effects of attention and approval from others.

78. (p. 454)   Dollard and Miller consider four developmental situations to be of critical importance: _____, _____ or _____ training; _____ training; and learning to express _____ or _____.

79. (p. 454)   A basic _____ or _____ orientation toward the world may be established by early feeding experiences. Feeding can also affect later social relationships because a child learns to associate people with satisfaction and pleasure, or frustration and discomfort.

80. (p. 454)   Many attitudes toward cleanliness, conformity, and bodily functions are formed during toilet and cleanliness training. Studies show that severe, _____, or _____ toilet training can have undesirable effects on personality development.

81. (p. 454)   When, where, and how a child learns to express anger and sexuality can leave an imprint on personality. Specifically, permissiveness for sexual and aggressive behavior in childhood is linked to adult needs for _____ probably because permitting such behaviors allows children to get pleasure from asserting themselves.

82. (p. 454)   Behaviorists tend to stress two processes that contribute greatly to personality development in general, and particularly to sex training. _____ refers to the child's emotional attachment to admired adults, especially to those the child depends on for love and care.

83. (p. 454)   Identification typically encourages _____, a desire to be like the valued and admired adult. Many of a child's "male" or "female" traits come from conscious or unconscious attempts to imitate the behavior of a same-sex parent with whom they identify.

84. (p. 454)   Psychologist Albert Bandura and others have shown that learning takes place _____ as well as directly. This fact means we can learn without direct reward by observing and remembering the actions of others.

85. (p. 455)   An example of differential sex role learning is provided by the study of Lisa Serbin and Daniel O'Leary. They found that teachers were _____ times more likely to pay attention to boys who were aggressive or disruptive than to girls acting the same way.

86. (p. 455)   Boys who hit other students or broke things typically got attention through loud scoldings, while girls got more attention when they were clinging to the teacher

(therefore being reinforced for submissive, _____, and _____ behavior).

87. (p. 455) Similar differences in reinforcement probably explain why males are responsible for much more aggression in society than females are. _____ rates and _____, for example, are consistently higher for men.

88. (p. 455) Humanists reject the pessimism of psychoanalytic theory and the Freudian view that personality is a battleground for biological instincts and unconscious forces. Instead, they view _____ _____ as inherently good and they seek ways to allow our positive potentials to emerge.

89. (p. 455) Humanists also oppose the mechanism of learning theory. They say we are creative beings capable of _____ _____.

90. (p. 455) The humanistic viewpoint also places greater emphasis on immediate _____ _____, rather than on prior learning. To understand behavior we must learn what is "real" for her or him.

91. (p. 456) Abraham Maslow studied the lives of people who seemed to be using almost all of their talents and potentials. He referred to this tendency as _____-_____.

92. (p. 456) Maslow found that such persons shared a number of similarities. These included:
    1) _____ perceptions of reality;
    2) comfortable _____ of self, others, and nature;
    3) spontaneity;
    4) _____-centering;
    5) autonomy;
    6) continued freshness of appreciation;
    7) fellowship with _____;
    8) profound _____ relationships;
    9) unhostile sense of _____.

93. (p. 456) Also, all of Maslow's subjects reported the frequent occurrence of _____ _____, occasions marked by feelings of ecstasy, harmony, and deep meaning.

94. (p. 456) Maslow's primary contribution was to draw attention to the _____ of continued personal growth. He considered self-actualization an _____ process, not a simple end point to be attained only once.

95. (p. 456) _____ _____ is a contemporary psychotherapist who, like Freud, based his theory on clinical experience. Unlike Freud, who portrayed the normal personality as "adjusted" to internal conflict, he sees greater possibility for inner harmony.

96. (p. 457) Rogers sees the _____ _____ person as one who has achieved an openness to feelings and experiences, and who has learned to trust inner urges and intuitions.

97. (p. 457) Rogers' theory of personality centers on the concept of the _____, a flexible and changing perception of personal identity that emerges from the _____ _____.

98. (p. 457) The phenomenal field is a person's total subjective experience of _____.
The _____-_____ is made up of those experiences identified as "I" or "me" which are separated from "not me" experiences.

99. (p. 457) According to Rogers, experiences that match the self-image are _____ (admitted into consciousness) and contribute to gradual changes in the self.

100. (p. 457) Information or feelings inconsistent with the self-image are said to be _____.

101. (p. 457) Experiences seriously incongruent with the self-image can be threatening, and they are often distorted or denied conscious recognition. This prevents the self from changing and creates a gulf between the self-image and reality. As the self-image grows more unrealistic, the _____ _____ becomes confused, vulnerable, dissatisfied, or seriously maladjusted.

102. (p. 457) When your self-image is consistent with what you really think, feel, do, and experience, you are best able to actualize your potentials. Rogers also considers it essential to have congruence between the self-image and the _____ _____—the image of the person you would most like to be.

103. (p. 458) In accord with Roger's thinking, researchers have found that people with a close match between their self-image and ideal self tend to be socially _____, _____, and _____. Those with a poor match tend to be _____, insecure, and lacking in social skills.

104. (p. 458) Psychologists Hazel Markus and Paula Nurius believe that each of us harbors images of many _____ _____ including the ideal self, as well as other selves we could become, or are afraid of becoming.

105. (p. 458) Possible selves translate our hopes, fears, fantasies, and goals into specific images of who we _____ be. They also give meaning to _____ behavior and help us evaluate it.

106. (p. 459) From the humanists' viewpoint, the development of one's self-image is highly dependent on information from the environment and contributes to later personality functioning. Rogers holds that positive and negative evaluations by others cause a child to develop internal standards of evaluation called _____ of _____.

107. (p. 459) By this term he means that we learn that some actions win our parents' love and approval while others are rejected. This process is directly related to a later capacity for self-esteem, positive self-evaluation, or _____ _____-_____.

108. (p. 459) He believes congruence and self-actualization are encouraged by substituting _____ _____ (direct, gut-level response to life experiences that avoids the filtering and distortion of incongruence) for conditions of worth.

109. (p. 459) None of the major theories can be fully proved or disproved. While they are neither true nor false, their implications or predictions may be. The best way to judge a theory is in terms of its _____.

110. (p. 459) In evaluating the different theories of personality, psychoanalytic theory seems to over-emphasize _____ and biological _____. These distortions were corrected somewhat by the neo-Freudians, but problems remain.

111. (p. 459) One of the most telling criticisms of Freudian theory is that it can be used to explain any psychological event _____ it has occurred, but offers little help in predicting _____ behavior.

112. (p. 460) Of the three major perspectives, the _____ have made the best effort to rigorously test and verify their ideas.

113. (p. 460) However, behavioristic theories tend to _____ the importance of temperamental, emotional, cognitive, and subjective factors in person-ality. Social Learning theory is an attempt to answer such criticisms.

114. (p. 460) A great strength of the humanists is the light they have shed on _____ dimensions of personality. However, they can be criticized for using imprecise con-cepts that are difficult to _____ or study _____.

115. (p. 461) While self-actualization offers the promise of personal growth, creativity, and fullness of life, it requires hard work, patience, and commitment. It is primarily a _____, not a goal or an end point.

116. (p. 461) Several points can be gleaned from the writings of Abraham Maslow as suggestions on how to achieve self-actualization. One is to be willing to _____.

117. (p. 461) You must learn to _____ _____. You can become an architect of self by acting as if you are personally responsible for every aspect of your life.

118. (p. 461) Another point is to examine your _____. Use self-discovery to try to make each life decision a choice for growth, not a response to fear or anxiety.

119. (p. 461) Try to see things as they are, not as you would like them to be. In other words, experience things _____ and _____.

120. (p. 461) Make use of positive experiences to promote growth. You might actively repeat activities that cause "_____ _____" (temporary moments of self-actualization).

121. (p. 461) Actualizing potentials may place you at odds with cultural expectations. This situation may produce fear which keeps many people from becoming what they might. You must be prepared to be _____.

122. (p. 462) Maslow found that self-actualizers tend to have a _____ or "_____" in life. Therefore, get involved and committed to problems outside yourself.

123. (p. 462) Self-awareness takes time to develop. Slow down and avoid _____ or over-_____ your time.

124. (p. 462) A valuable means of promoting self-awareness is to start a _____. Keeping records of experiences, daily thoughts, feelings, and attitudes can help make growth-oriented life changes.

125. (p. 462) As a final note, _____ your progress. It is important to gauge your progress and to renew your efforts. _____ is a good sign you are in need of further growth and change.

126. (p. 463) _____-_____ refers to differences in how people monitor (observe, regulate, and control) the image of themselves they display to others in public.

127. (p. 463) Some of us are _____ self-monitors, who are very sensitive to situations and expectations. In contrast, _____ self-monitors are less interested in controlling the impression they make.

128. (p. 463) Persons _____ in self-monitoring take a flexible approach to defining them-selves. They are very interested in their public "image." _____ self-monitors try to accurately present their beliefs and principles no matter what the situation is.

129. (p. 463) Psychologist Mark Snyder has studied self-monitoring extensively. He found that in social settings _____ self-monitors preferred to join clearly defined groups.

130. (p. 463) Snyder developed the _____-_____ _____ to measure high and low self-monitors. You should be familiar with the comparisons that have come from the use of this test.

131. (p. 464) In general, _____ self-monitors are adaptable and present themselves well in social situations. However, they tend to reveal little about their private feelings, beliefs, and intentions.

132. (p. 464) The primary drawback to being _____ in self-monitoring is a tendency to be unresponsive to the demands of different situations. Such individuals want to "just be themselves" even when adjustments in self-presentation would make them more effective.

133. (p. 464) Studies of self-monitoring raise questions about the idea that each person has a "_____ _____." High self-monitors, in particular, act as if they have many selves.

SELF-TEST

1. (p. 444) Which of the following is *not* a structure which directs the dynamic system of energies composing personality as proposed by Freud?
    a. superego   c. id
    b. self   d. ego

2. (p. 444) Which of the following is *not* true of the id?
    a. It is totally unconscious.
    b. It operates on the pleasure principle.
    c. It is associated with secondary process thinking.
    d. Most id energies are directed toward discharge of tensions associated with sex and aggression.

3. (p. 444) Of the following, which is in conscious control of the personality and acts as an executive for action?
    a. id   c. ego
    b. libido   d. superego

4. (p. 444) The conscience and the ego-ideal are parts of the
   a. id
   b. superego
   c. ego
   d. libido

5. (p. 445) Neurotic anxiety is caused by
   a. threats of punishment from the superego
   b. a breakdown of the ego's functions
   c. impulses from the id that threaten a loss of control
   d. overuse of ego-defense mechanisms

6. (p. 446) True-False. According to Freud, the preconscious is a level of awareness in which repressed memories and emotions are stored along with instinctual drives.

7. (p. 446) According to Freud, a personality characterized as argumentative, cynical, and exploitive of others is
   a. anal-retentive
   b. oral-aggressive
   c. oral-dependent
   d. anal-expulsive

8. (p. 447) According to Freud, a person whose personality is characterized as obstinate, stingy, orderly, and compulsively clean would be classified as
   a. oral-aggressive
   b. anal-expulsive
   c. anal-compulsive
   d. anal-retentive

9. (p. 447) According to psychoanalysis, which of the following does *not* occur during the phallic stage of development?
   a. Electra conflict
   b. elimination fixation
   c. Oedipus conflict
   d. conscience formation

10. (p. 448) True-False. One of the reasons psychoanalysis has been most influential in later psychological theories is because it pioneered the idea that the first years of life shape adult personality.

11. (p. 448) In the view of Alfred Adler, the main force in personality is
    a. libido
    b. striving for superiority
    c. feelings of inferiority
    d. basic anxiety

12. (p. 449) According to Karen Horney, the result when people feel isolated and helpless in a hostile world is
    a. incongruence
    b. organismic devaluing
    c. basic anxiety
    d. feelings of inferiority

13. (p. 449) The view that emotional health requires a balance in moving toward, away from, and against others was first proposed by
    a. Sigmund Freud
    b. Carl Rogers
    c. Alfred Adler
    d. Karen Horney

14. (p. 449) Which of the following is *not* an important archetype in Jung's theory of personality?
    a. Eros
    b. self
    c. animus
    d. anima

15. (p. 451) True-False. Learning theorists reject the idea that personality is made up of consistent traits.

16. (p. 451) According to Dollard and Miller of the behaviorist camp, which of the following is the basic structure or component of personality?

a. response
b. needs

c. habits
d. self-image

17. (p. 452) Which of the following is *not* a concept developed by the "cognitive behaviorism" of social learning theory as illustrated in the work of Julian Rotter?
a. expectancy
b. reinforcement value

c. psychological situation
d. organismic valuing

18. (p. 454) According to Dollard and Miller, which of the following contribute greatly to personality development in general, and particularly to sex training?
a. identification, imitation
b. fixations, urges

c. life instincts, death instincts
d. self-image, ideal self

19. (p. 455) Of the following, which describes the emphasis of the humanistic approach to personality?
a. subjective experience
b. objective experience

c. previous learning
d. stages of psychosexual development

20. (p. 456) The humanists' term for fulfillment of potential is
a. self-actualization
b. growth fulfillment

c. condition of worth
d. congruence

21. (p. 456) Which of the following is *not* a characteristic of Maslow's self-actualizers?
a. task-centering
b. dependency

c. efficient perceptions of reality
d. profound interpersonal relationships

22. (p. 456) True-False. All of Maslow's self-actualized subjects reported the frequent occurrence of peak experiences, that is, occasions marked by strong feelings of confidence resulting from the fulfillment of some important task.

23. (p. 457) A person's total subjective experience of reality is called (the)
a. self-image
b. reality perception

c. conscious understanding
d. phenomenal field

24. (p. 457) When your self-image is consistent with what you really think, feel, do and experience, you are best able to actualize your potential. Rogers calls this
a. incongruence
b. congruence

c. a position of worth
d. the ideal self

25. (p. 459) According to Rogers, a direct, gut-level response to life experiences that avoids the filtering and distortion of incongruence is called
a. self-actualization
b. organismic valuing

c. conditions of worth
d. ideal self

26. (p. 459) Which of the following is *not* a criticism that has been directed at psychoanalytic theory?
a. preoccupied with sex and aggression
b. overemphasizes biological instincts
c. offers little help in predicting future behavior
d. suggests a treatment procedure for psychological disorders

27. (p. 460) Of the following approaches, which has done the best job to rigorously test and verify their concepts?
a. humanism
b. psychoanalysis

c. behaviorism
d. cognitivism

28. (p. 460) True-False. The chief criticism of humanistic theory is its overly optimistic view of humanity.

29. (p. 461) True-False. According to Abraham Maslow, self-actualization is more a process than a goal or endpoint.

30. (p. 461) Which of the following does *not* indicate that a person is moving toward greater self-actualization?
    a. better being able to live up to standards set by others
    b. greater acceptance of yourself and others
    c. greater confidence
    d. less strain or conflict in accomplishing daily routines

31. (p. 463) Which of the following is *not* true of high self-monitors?
    a. They are flexible, adaptable, and display different behavior from situation to situation.
    b. They believe it is possible to love two people at the same time.
    c. They choose friends who are skilled or knowledgeable in various areas.
    d. They identify themselves in terms of their beliefs, emotions, values, and personality.

32. (p. 463) Which of the following is *not* true of low self-monitors?
    a. They are keenly interested in the actions of others and in trying to "read" their motives, attitudes, and traits.
    b. They are more interested in a potential date's personality than appearance.
    c. They value a match between who they believe they are and what they do.
    d. They prefer jobs where they can "just be themselves."

33. (p. 464) True-False. Using the Self-Monitoring Scale, psychologist Mark Snyder found that the main drawback to being low in self-monitoring is a tendency to be unresponsive to the demands of different situations.

ANSWERS — PROGRAMMED REVIEW

1. Psychoanalytic
2. physical causes
3. id; unconscious
4. pleasure principle
5. libido; life instincts
6. Thanatos
7. sex, aggression
8. ego; id; external reality
9. primary process thinking
10. reality principle
11. conscious
12. superego
13. conscience
14. guilt
15. ego ideal
16. weak; strict
17. mental processes
18. displace, sublimate
19. neurotic anxiety; moral anxiety
20. ego-defense mechanisms

21. unconscious
22. hippocampus
23. conscious; preconscious
24. unconscious
25. socialize
26. psychosocial stages
27. sex
28. erogenous zone
29. fixations
30. oral
31. oral-dependent
32. oral-aggressive
33. anal-retentive; anal-expulsive
34. phallic
35. Oedipus conflict
36. castration; identify; conscience
37. Electra conflict
38. latency
39. genital
40. adult personality; feeding; toilet training; sexual; stages

41. latency
42. conscience
43. sexuality
44. neo-Freudians
45. unconscious; sexuality
46. superiority
47. feelings of inferiority
48. compensate
49. style of life
50. 5; creative self
51. earliest memory
52. anatomy
53. neurosis; basic anxiety
54. toward; away; against
55. ego; persona
56. introversion; extroversion
57. personal unconscious
58. collective unconscious; archetypes
59. anima; animus
60. self-archetype; mandalas
61. self-actualization
62. learned behavior patterns
63. situational determinants
64. interact
65. past learning
66. habits
67. drive; cue
68. social learning
69. psychological situation
70. expectancy
71. reinforcement value
72. self-reinforcement
73. radical
74. rewards; punishments
75. self-esteem
76. depressed; depression
77. social reinforcement
78. feeding; toilet, cleanliness; sex; anger,
      aggression
79. active, passive
80. punishing, frustrating
81. power
82. identification
83. imitation
84. vicariously
85. three
86. dependent, passive

87. Murder; assault
88. human nature
89. free choice
90. subjective experience
91. self-actualization
92. efficient; acceptance, task; humanity;
      interpersonal; humor
93. peak experiences
94. possibility; ongoing
95. Carl Rogers
96. fully functioning
97. self; phenomenal field
98. reality; self-image
99. symbolized
100. incongruent
101. incongruent person
102. ideal self
103. poised; confident; resourceful; anxious
104. possible selves
105. could; current
106. conditions of worth
107. positive self-regard
108. organismic valuing
109. usefulness
110. sexuality; instincts
111. after; future
112. behaviorists
113. underestimate
114. positive; measure; objectively
115. process
116. change
117. take responsibility
118. motives
119. honestly, directly
120. peak experiences
121. different
122. mission; calling
123. hurrying; over-scheduling
124. journal
125. assess; Boredom
126. Self-monitoring
127. high; low
128. high; Low
129. high
130. Self-Monitoring Scale
131. high
132. low
133. true self

ANSWERS — SELF-TEST

1. b	6. False	11. b	16. c	21. b	26. d	30. a
2. c	7. b	12. c	17. d	22. False	27. c	31. d
3. c	8. d	13. d	18. a	23. d	28. False	32. a
4. b	9. b	14. a	19. a	24. b	29. True	33. True
5. c	10. True	15. True	20. a	25. b		

Chapter 18

Intelligence

CONTENTS

TERMS AND CONCEPTS

savant syndrome
intelligence
operational definition
reliability
test-retest reliability
split-half reliability
equivalent forms reliability
validity
criterion validity
objective
standardization
Stanford-Binet Intelligence Scale
mental age (MA)
chronological age (CA)
intelligence quotient (IQ)
deviation IQ
Wechsler Adult Intelligence Scale—Revised
    (WAIS-R)
Wechsler Intelligence Scale for Children—
    Revised (WISC-R)
performance intelligence
verbal intelligence
individual intelligence tests

group intelligence tests
Army Alpha
normal curve
GATE programs
g-factor
mental retardation (developmentally disabled)
levels of mental retardation
organic mental retardation
familial retardation
phenylketonuria (PKU)
microcephaly
hydrocephaly
cretinism
Down's Syndrome (mongolism)
eugenics
fraternal twins
identical twins
confluence model
Instrumental Enrichment
culture-fair tests
educable mentally retarded (EMR)
System of Multicultural Pluralistic Assessment
    (SOMPA)

IMPORTANT INDIVIDUALS

Alfred Binet   Adrian Dove
David Wechsler   Arthur Jensen
Lewis Terman   David McClelland
Howard Gardner   Robert Glaser
Robert Zajonc   Jane Mercer
Reuven Feuerstein   June Lewis

PROGRAMMED REVIEW

1. (p. 467) The _____ _____, in which "an island of brillance
    is found in a sea of retardation," occurs when a person of subnormal intelligence
    shows highly developed mental abilities in one or more very limited areas.

2. (p. 468) The first "intelligence" test was developed by _____ _____ who
    established questions an "average" child could answer which could then be used to
    distinguish slower students from the more capable.

3. (p. 468) A general description of intelligence given by David Wechsler defines it as the global
    capacity of the individual to act _____, to think
    _____, and to deal effectively with the _____.

4. (p. 468) A recent survey of 1,020 experts on intelligence shows that at least three-quarters of
    this group agree that the following elements are important parts of intelligence:
    _____ thinking or reasoning; problem-solving ability; capacity to
    acquire _____; memory; and adaptation to one's
    _____.

5. (p. 468) Beyond this, intelligence is usually defined using an _____
    _____, that is the procedures used to measure it have been specified.
    In this case, intelligence is what an _____ _____
    measures.

6. (p. 468) For a test to be _____ it must yield the same score, or close to the
    same score, each time it is given to the same individual. In other words, the scores
    should be consistent and highly correlated.

7. (p. 469) One way to assess reliability is to administer the test to a large group of people and
    then test them again at a later date. This method is known as _____-
    _____ reliability.

8. (p. 469) Reliability is sometimes determined by comparing the score on one-half of the test
    items to the score on the other half. This method is known as _____-
    _____ reliability.

9. (p. 469) Also, if two versions of the test were given, we could compare scores on one to scores
    on the other for each person. This method is known as _____
    _____ reliability.

10. (p. 469) A test has _____ when it measures what it claims to measure. This
    capacity can be established in various ways.

11. (p. 469) Validity is usually demonstrated by comparing test scores to actual performance.
    This procedure is known as _____ validity.

12. (p. 469) For example, a test of legal aptitude might be validated by comparing scores on the test to grades in law school. If high scores _____ with high grades or some other standard of success, the test may be considered valid.

13. (p. 469) A test is said to be _____ if it gives the same score when different people correct it.

14. (p. 469) Test _____ means that the same procedures are used in giving the test to all people and that the norm or average score is determined for a large group of people like those for whom the test is designed.

15. (p. 470) In 1916, Lewis Terman and others at Stanford University revised Binet's original test for use in this country. It is still widely in use today after several more revisions and is known as the _____-_____ Intelligence _____.

16. (p. 470) Since the Stanford-Binet assumes that intellectual ability in childhood improves with increasing _____, it is really a graded set of more difficult tests, one for each _____ _____.

17. (p. 470) The age-ranked questions of the Stanford-Binet allow a person's _____ _____ to be determined. This capacity gives a good indication of one's actual abilities but says nothing about whether overall intelligence is high or low. To know this, one must also consider _____ _____ (age in years).

18. (p. 470) Using these two age values, an IQ or _____ _____ can be determined. It is defined as _____ _____ divided by _____ _____ multiplied by 100.

19. (p. 470) An advantage of the IQ is that it allows comparison of intelligence among children with different combinations of _____ and _____ ages.

20. (p. 471) The IQ equals 100 when MA = CA, thus 100 is defined as _____ intelligence. While 100 is the mathematical average (or mean) for such scores, average intelligence is usually defined as any score from _____ to _____.

21. (p. 471) It is no longer actually necessary to calculate IQs for many modern tests. Instead, a _____ IQ score is used.

22. (p. 471) Finding a deviation IQ is determined by how far above or below _____ a person's score is, relative to others taking the test.

23. (p. 471) Tables supplied with the test are then used to convert a person's _____ _____ in the group to an IQ score. This approach avoids certain troublesome errors that occur when IQ is calculated directly.

24. (p. 471) IQ scores are not very dependable until about age ____. The correlation obtained at age 2 and those obtained at age 18 is only _____.

25. (p. 471) The average change in IQ on retesting is approximately ____ points in either direction, however changes of 15 points or more are not uncommon during intellectual development.

26. (p. 472) Studies of IQ have shown a gradual increase in intellectual capacity until about age _____. In general, persons who showed the largest IQ increases had been exposed to

stimulating intellectual experiences during early adulthood. Those who declined most typically suffered from chronic illness, drinking problems, or unstimulating life-styles.

27. (p. 472) After middle age, some studies of IQ have recorded _____ declines, while others indicate little or no change due to aging.

28. (p. 472) More recent findings have clarified this contradiction by showing that only certain abilities are affected by aging. When _____ _____ or _____ is emphasized, there is little decline until advanced age. But test items requiring _____, rapid _____, or perceptual _____ show earlier losses and a rapid decline after middle age.

29. (p. 472) An intriguing link between IQ and aging centers around the observation that _____ _____ may be signalled as much as five years in advance by significant changes in brain function. This terminal decline in IQ can be measured even when the person appears to be in good health.

30. (p. 472) A widely used alternative to the Stanford-Binet is the _____ _____ Intelligence Scale—Revised, abbreviated _____. The form adopted for children is called the _____ Intelligence Scale for _____—Revised, abbreviated _____.

31. (p. 473) The Wechsler tests are generally similar to the Stanford-Binet, but differ in some important ways. The WAIS-R is specifically designed to test _____ intelligence.

32. (p. 473) The Stanford-Binet only gives an overall IQ, whereas both the WISC-R and WAIS-R rate _____ intelligence in addition to _____ intelligence.

33. (p. 473) Both the Stanford-Binet and the Wechsler tests are _____ intelligence tests which must be administered by a trained specialist.

34. (p. 473) Other tests of intelligence have been designed for use with large groups of people. Group intelligence tests are usually in paper-and-pencil form and require test-takers to read, to follow instructions, and to solve problems of logic, mathematics, or spatial skills. The first group intelligence test was the _____ _____ developed for use in rating World War I military inductees.

35. (p. 473) Other examples of group intelligence tests include the _____ _____ _____ (or SAT), the _____ _____ _____ (or ACT), and the _____ _____ _____ (or CQT).

36. (p. 474) The distribution of IQs in the population approximates a _____ (bell-shaped) curve in which the majority of scores fall close to the _____, and relatively few at the _____.

37. (p. 474) It seems safe to assume that men and women do not differ in overall intelligence. However, on the WAIS-R women do better on _____ ability, _____, and _____ learning, whereas men are best in _____ of _____ relationships and _____ _____.

38. (p. 474) It is important to realize that such gender differences are small and based on _____. It is impossible to predict if any one individual will be good or bad at math or language simply from knowing his or her gender.

39. (p. 474) There are meaningful relationships between IQ scores and school "success." The correlation between IQ and school grades is _____ —a sizable association. However, it is wise to remember that many factors influence school grades and success.

40. (p. 474) IQ is not as good a predictor of out-of-school achievements such as art, music, creative writing, dramatics, science, and leadership. Tests related to _____, such as tests of ideational fluency, are much more strongly related to such achievements.

41. (p. 474) There is also a relationship between IQ and job classification. Persons holding white-collar professional positions average _____ IQs than those in blue-collar occupational settings. However, there is a range of IQ scores in all occupations.

42. (p. 475) It is tempting to conclude that professional jobs require more intelligence. However, higher status jobs often demand an academic degree which requires much the same type of intelligence as that measured by IQ tests. Therefore, selection procedures for professional jobs appear to be _____ in favor of a particular type of intelligence.

43. (p. 475) When variations in IQ are extreme, below 70 or above 140, influences on adjustment become unmistakable. Only _____ percent of the population falls in these ranges.

44. (p. 475) Only about ___ percent of the population scores above 140 on IQ tests. A person scoring this high is at least "gifted" and depending on the standards used, he or she may be considered a "genius."

45. (p. 476) Lewis Terman investigated some 1500 "gifted" children with IQs of 140 or higher. Terman's study makes it clear that the very bright tend to be gifted in many ways. He found the following results:
    1) Gifted subjects were socially well adjusted and showed above average _____ capacity.
    2) Children with high IQs also had high IQs when tested as adults.
    3) As a group, the gifted were above average in _____, _____, and physical appearance.
    4) The gifted have better than average mental health records, indicating a greater resistance to mental illness.
    5) As a group, the gifted were considered to be very professionally _____ as adults.

46. (p. 476) Terman found that the gifted have greater resistance to mental illness. The very intelligent (IQ of over _____) may have social and behavioral adjustment problems as children.

47. (p. 476) Not all of the gifted children Terman studied were superior as adults. Some had committed crimes, were unemployable, or were poorly adjusted. A recent follow-up study found that the highly successful subjects differed mainly in their greater _____ and _____ to succeed.

48. (p. 477) Early signs frequently observed in gifted children include: a tendency to seek out and identify with older children and adults; an early fascination with explanations and

problem solving; talking complete sentences as early as ___ or ___ years of age; an unusually good _____; precocious talent in art, music, or number skills; an early interest in books, early reading (often by age ___); showing of kindness, understanding, and cooperation towards others.

49. (p. 477) An unusually bright child may be gifted in ways other than that reflected by a high IQ score. If artistic talent, mechanical aptitude, etc. are considered, _____ out of 20 children could be considered "gifted" in some respect.

50. (p. 477) Having a high IQ is not without its problems. Boredom with classes and classmates can lead to behavioral problems. In recognition of these difficulties, many school systems now provide special classes under _____ and _____ _____ (GATE) programs, which combine classroom enrichment with fast-paced instruction.

51. (p. 477) Psychologist Howard Gardner has theorized that there are actually several different kinds of intelligence. These include abilities in: _____, logic and math, _____ and _____ thinking, music, bodily-kinesthetic skills (such as dance or athletics), _____ skills (self-knowledge), and _____ skills (leadership, social abilities).

52. (p. 477) If Gardner's theory is correct, traditional IQ tests measure only a part of real world intelligence. An implication is that our _____ may be wasting human potential. Some children might learn math or reading more easily if these topics were tied into art, music, dance, drama, etc.

53. (p. 477) Gardner's view is at odds with studies which suggest that scores on IQ tests mainly reflect an underlying "general intelligence" factor. This ___-_____ is said to explain the high correlations found among scores on various tests of intellectual ability and achievement.

54. (p. 477) An individual with intellectual abilities significantly below average is termed _____ or _____ _____. An IQ of _____ or below is regarded as the dividing line for retardation.

55. (p. 477) A person's ability to perform _____ _____, such as dressing, eating, communicating, shopping, and working also figures into evaluating retardation.

56. (p. 478) The severity of retardation is classified into one of four degrees along with a general educational classification. For example, an individual with an IQ ranging on the low end from roughly 50-55 to a high of 70 would be considered to have a _____ degree of retardation and to be educable. You should be familiar with the other categories.

57. (p. 478) Total care is only necessary for the _____. The _____ and _____ retarded are capable of mastering basic language skills and routine self-help skills. Many become self-supporting by working in _____ _____ (special simplified work environments).

58. (p. 478) The _____ retarded (about 85 percent of all those affected) benefit from carefully structured and supervised education. As adults, they are capable of

living alone and may marry (although they tend to have difficulties with many of the demands of adult life).

59. (p. 478)   About 50 percent of all cases of mental retardation are _____, or related to known physical disorders including:
    1) _____ injuries, such as lack of oxygen;
    2) _____ damage caused by maternal drug abuse, disease or infection contracted by the mother before birth, or by the child after birth;
    3) _____ disorders, such as cretinism or phenylketonuria; and
    4) _____ abnormalities.

60. (p. 478)   In 30 to 40 percent of cases, no known biological problem can be identified. In such cases the degree of retardation is usually mild, in the _____ to _____ IQ range, and quite often other family members are also mildly retarded.

61. (p. 478)   _____ _____, as it is called, occurs most often in very poor households. In some such homes nutrition, early stimulation, medical care, intellectual stimulation, and emotional support are inadequate.

62. (p. 479)   There are several distinctive forms of organic retardation, including _____, abbreviated _____, which results from the build-up of phenylpyruvic acid. This condition can now be detected by medical testing during the first _____ of life and can be controlled by special _____.

63. (p. 479)   PKU is genetically induced lack of an important enzyme. If PKU goes untreated, severe retardation typically occurs by age ___.

64. (p. 479)   The _____ suffers a rare abnormality in which the skull is extremely small or fails to grow, thus forcing the brain to develop in a severely limited space.

65. (p. 479)   Microcephaly causes severe retardation that usually requires the individual to be in an institution. They are typically _____, _____ behaved, and easy to work with.

66. (p. 479)   _____ is caused by excess production of cerebrospinal fluid within the brain which forces the brain against the skull, grossly enlarging the head and damaging brain tissue. It affects about 8000 babies every year in the U.S.

67. (p. 479)   A new medical treatment in which a tube is surgically implanted to drain fluid from the brain to the abdomen can now be used to avoid retardation if performed within the first _____ months of life.

68. (p. 479)   _____ develops in infancy due to insufficient secretion of thyroid hormone. In some parts of the world it is caused by too little _____ in the diet.

69. (p. 479)   Cretinism causes stunted physical and intellectual growth that cannot be corrected unless detected early. However, it is easily and routinely detected in infancy and may be treated by thyroid hormone _____.

70. (p. 479)   _____ _____ (once known as mongolism) causes moderate to severe retardation and a shortened life expectancy in 1 out of 800 babies. Distinctive features include almond-shaped eyes, a slightly protruding tongue, stubby hands, a stocky build, and sometimes a deep crease on the palm of the hand.

71. (p. 479) It is now known that the Down's child has an extra chromosome resulting from flaws in the parent's egg or sperm cells. Thus, the syndrome is _____, but not usually _____ (it does not "run" in the family).

72. (p. 479) Mothers in their early twenties have about one chance in _____ of giving birth to a Down's syndrome baby. After age _____, the odds increase to about one in 105. By age 48 the risk reaches one in _____.

73. (p. 479) Recent research has also linked age of the father to an increased risk of Down's syndrome. In about _____ percent of cases, the father is the source of the extra chromosome.

74. (p. 479) Down's syndrome children are usually _____ and _____, and they can do most of the things that other children can do, only slower. There is evidence that they continue to learn and make slow mental progress well into _____. While there is no "cure" for Down's syndrome, specially tailored educational programs can enable them to lead fuller lives.

75. (p. 480) In a classic study of genetic factors in learning, Tryon managed to breed separate strains of "_____-_____" and "_____-_____" rats.

76. (p. 480) This experiment and other studies of _____ (selective breeding for desirable characteristics) suggest that some traits are highly influenced by heredity.

77. (p. 480) The Tryon study seemed to show that intelligence is inherited, but later researchers found "maze-bright" rats weren't actually smarter, just more motivated by _____ and less easily _____ during testing.

78. (p. 480) In assessing the relative importance of heredity and environment on the development of intelligence, studies have looked at the similarity in IQ between relatives of varying closeness in genetic association. It is typically found that the similarity grows in _____ to the closeness in genetic association.

79. (p. 480) But relatives often share similar environments as well as heredity, so some select comparisons must be made. For example, _____ _____ come from two separate eggs fertilized at the same time; they are no more genetically alike than ordinary siblings, but their IQ scores tend to be more similar.

80. (p. 480) The reason for this increased similarity must be _____: Parents treat twins more alike than ordinary siblings, which results in a closer match in IQs.

81. (p. 480) More striking similarities are observed with _____ _____ who develop from a single egg and therefore have identical heredity. When reared in the same home environment, virtually identical IQs result. But when reared apart, the correlation drops from _____ to _____ showing the effects of less similar environments.

82. (p. 480) Psychologists who emphasize genetics believe these figures show that intelligence is _____ to _____ percent hereditary.

83. (p. 481) Environmentalists point out that some separated twins differ by as much as _____ IQ points. Also, separated twins are almost always placed in homes socially and educationally similar to their biological parents. This fact tends to _____ the apparent genetic effects.

84. (p. 481) Strong evidence for an environmental view of intelligence comes from families having one _____ child and one _____ child. Recent studies show that children reared by the same mother resemble her in IQ to the same degree, in spite of differences in heredity.

85. (p. 481) Trans-racially adopted children are as _____ similar in IQ to their adoptive brothers and sisters as biologically related siblings are.

86. (p. 481) Further support for the role of environment in intelligence is seen in one study where 25 children considered mentally retarded were transferred to a more stimulating environment. The result was an average gain of _____ IQ points. A second group of initially less retarded children who remained in the orphanage lost an average of _____ IQ points.

87. (p. 481) Data from 14 nations have shown average IQ gains of from ____ to _____ points during a single generation (the last 30 years). These IQ boosts, averaging 15 points, have occurred in far too short a time for genetics to explain them.

88. (p. 482) Robert Zajonc believe that IQ _____ as family size grows. That is, the brightest children come from the _____ families. In addition, the brightest children are, on the average, those who are born _____ in a family.

89. (p. 482) Zajonc has pointed out that average SAT scores declined in the United States during a period when family size _____.

90. (p. 482) Zajonc has developed the _____ to explain these findings. According to this theory, each arriving baby temporarily lowers the "average intellectual level" in the family, thus making it a less stimulating environment.

91. (p. 482) Critics of the confluence model believe that Zajonc's findings may be more related to the fact that, nationwide, large families are more common among couples with _____ social and educational advantages.

92. (p. 482) Even if Zajonc is right, the average IQ score for the older of two children is only _____ points higher than the average for the last of nine children. Such differences may mean little in terms of what a person can actually do.

93. (p. 482) Later-born children may excel in other ways. In any event, there is evidence that birth order differences in IQ may disappear by age _____.

94. (p. 482) _____ has little positive effect on aptitude and intelligence test scores. But there is increasing evidence that _____, in-depth training in thinking skills can increase tested intelligence.

95. (p. 482) Reuven Feuerstein has developed a program called "_____" which involves hundreds of hours of guided problem solving. Research has shown that such training can raise IQ scores.

96. (p. 482) Similarly, over 400 seventh grade students in _____ have taken special classes over the last six years under a program designed by American psychologists. Results have shown that the course had sizable, beneficial effects on students.

97. (p. 482) The problem with such training, however, is that it is very time consuming. Psychologists are now developing _____ _____ to teach problem solving, effective thinking, and other elements of intelligence.

98. (p. 482) There is probably no limit to how far _____ intelligence can go in a poor environment, but heredity may impose some limits on how far _____ IQ can go, even under ideal conditions.

99. (p. 482) Interestingly, _____ children tend to come from homes where parents encourage intellectual exploration, answer their children's questions, and spend time with their children.

100. (p. 485) There are many problems involved in the use and interpretation of IQ tests. One such problem is the language that is used. It tends to be biased in favor of white, middle-class backgrounds. In recognition of this problem, some psychologists are trying to develop _____-_____ tests that will not disadvantage certain groups.

101. (p. 485) The issue of environmental versus genetic factors involved in IQ has been strongly raised regarding the IQs of blacks. Most psychologists do not support the genetic emphasis espoused by Arthur Jensen. Instead, psychologists have responded with several counter-arguments:
    1) blacks are more likely than whites to live in intellectually _____ environments;
    2) even if the gap in IQ between blacks and whites is hereditary, it is small enough to be corrected by _____;
    3) assumptions, biases, and content of IQ _____ do not allow meaningful comparisons between ethnic, cultural, or racial groups; and
    4) the logic Jensen used in reaching his conclusions is faulty.

102. (p. 486) Only when black children are raised in exactly the same conditions as white children can hereditary factors be clearly assessed. Along this line, one study investigated the IQs of black children raised in white families. These children had IQ scores averaging _____, which is comparable to the national average for white children.

103. (p. 486) Criticism of intelligence tests used in public schools has also become an issue. Recent court decisions have led some states to _____ use of IQ tests in public schools.

104. (p. 486) Criticism of intelligence testing has also come from the academic community. David McClelland believes IQ is of little value in predicting real _____ to deal effectively with the world.

105. (p. 486) McClelland concedes that IQ predicts school performance, but when he compared a group of college students with straight As to another group with poor grades he found no differences in later _____ _____.

106. (p. 486) In considering the positive and negative aspects of standardized tests such as the Scholastic Aptitude Test, Robert Glaser points out that they are now used primarily to _____ people rather than to _____ instruction to the strengths, weaknesses, and needs of each student.

107. (p. 486) In considering the use of IQ tests, it is wise for the individual to remember that IQ is not intelligence—it is only an _____ of intelligence as defined by a particular test. If you change the test, you change the score.

108. (p. 487) Some psychologists are seeking ways to teach necessary intellectual skills to all children. For example, one experiment divided 40 children from extremely disadvantaged families into two groups. Experimental subjects received a wide

variety of stimulation and special attention, while control subjects did not. When tested at age $5\frac{1}{2}$, the average IQ for the control group was _____, but the experimental group showed an encouraging average of _____.

109. (p. 488) In the case of *Larry P. vs. the California State Superintendent of Education* it was ruled that IQ test scores alone can no longer be used for _____ _____ _____ (EMR) placement.

110. (p. 488) Jane Mercer, a sociologist who gave key testimony in the case, believes that schools often label children retarded, when they really lack _____ tied knowledge.

111. (p. 488) A child who does poorly in the classroom or on an IQ test may function perfectly well at home and in the community. Mercer refers to such children as "_____- _____ _____"—youngsters who are "retarded" only during the school day.

112. (p. 488) Mercer and her associate June Lewis believe that the _____ of _____ _____ _____ (SOMPA) can be effectively used in place of IQ testing to assess intellectual functioning.

113. (p. 489) SOMPA combines three ways of assessing a child:
    1) It looks for any _____ problems that may be causing low school performance.
    2) The child's behavior _____ the classroom is evaluated to avoid the mistake of creating a "six-hour retardate" on the basis of a test score.
    3) It assumes that when everything else is held constant the child who has learned the most probably has the most "learning potential."

114. (p. 489) SOMPA assumes that true potential can be masked by a child's cultural background. To avoid this problem, SOMPA compares each child's WISC-R score with that of children from _____ _____.

115. (p. 489) In December 1986, Judge Robert Peckham reiterated the California IQ test ban with a directive that appears to _____ even the use of alternatives like SOMPA.

116. (p. 489) Understandably, some psychologists object to the courts making educational decisions. Others point out that they must now resort to _____- _____ measures which may be subjective and open to potential abuse.

117. (p. 489) Critics of IQ testing reply that IQ gives little information about the _____ of a low score. It tells little about what corrective action should be taken.

SELF-TEST

1. (p. 468) Alfred Binet was responsible for
    a. developing SOMPA for testing minority youngsters
    b. developing the Army Alpha group intelligence test
    c. key testimony in the California court case involving the use of IQ tests in EMR placement
    d. developing the first "intelligence" test in which age-related items could be used to distinguish intellectually slower students from the more capable

2. (p. 468) Intelligence is usually defined using a(n) _____ definition.
    a. subjective   c. mathematical
    b. physiological   d. operational

3. (p. 469) When we administer a test to a large group of people, retest them at a later date and then compare the scores for similarity, we are investigating
    a. split-half reliability   c. test-retest reliability
    b. equivalent forms reliability d. construct validity

4. (p. 469) Which of the following is *not* a test of reliability?
    a. test-retest   c. split-half
    b. face   d. equivalent forms

5. (p. 469) A test has _____ when it measures what it claims to measure.
    a. split-half reliability   c. equivalent form reliability
    b. validity   d. culture fairness

6. (p. 469) When we compare test scores to actual performance, we are measuring
    a. face validity   c. split-half reliability
    b. test-retest reliability   d. criterion validity

7. (p. 469) A test is said to be _____ when it gives the same score when corrected by different people.
    a. objective   c. reliable
    b. standardized   d. valid

8. (p. 469) When norms are used in interpreting test scores and the test is administered the same way to everyone taking it, we say the test is
    a. objective   c. reliable
    b. standardized   d. valid

9. (p. 470) Of the following, which is *not* associated with the Stanford-Binet Intelligence Scale?
    a. chronological age   c. separate subscales
    b. mental age   d. intelligence quotient

10. (p. 471) According to the Stanford-Binet Intelligence Scale, if Jill is 15 years old and her MA is 18, her intelligence quotient is
    a. 78   c. 120
    b. 100   d. 16.5

11. (p. 471) True-False. IQ scores are not very dependable until about age six. After middle childhood, changes in IQ are usually quite small.

12. (p. 472) Which of the following is *not* associated with the WAIS-R?
    a. It is specifically designed to test adult intelligence.
    b. It can be administered as either a group test or an individual test.
    c. Test scores can be broken down into various areas to reveal strengths and weaknesses.
    d. It rates both verbal and performance intelligence.

13. (p. 474) Which of the following is *not* true of IQ scores?
    a. When graphically displayed the distribution approximates a normal curve.
    b. IQ is positively correlated with educational level.
    c. IQ differences of even a few points can tell much about intellectual potential.
    d. IQ is positively correlated with job classification.

14. (p. 474)   True-False. Women tend to excel on IQ test items that require arithmetic reasoning, verbal ability, and rote learning.

15. (p. 476)   According to Terman's work with mentally gifted children, which of the following is *not* correct?
    a. Gifted children were more susceptible to mental health problems.
    b. The gifted were considered quite successful in their later educational and professional endeavors.
    c. Gifted children were above average in height, weight, and physical appearance.
    d. The gifted tend to be especially well adjusted and above average in leadership capacity.

16. (p. 476)   True-False. The difference between gifted individuals who succeed and those who do not seems strongly tied to persistence and motivation to succeed.

17. (p. 478)   Which of the following is *not* an organic cause of mental retardation?
    a. fetal damage   c. metabolic disorders
    b. familial retardation   d. birth injuries

18. (p. 479)   The genetically inherited lack of an important bodily enzyme which causes the build-up of a destructive chemical defines the condition known as
    a. PKU   c. cretinism
    b. microcephaly   d. mongolism

19. (p. 479)   True-False. Microcephaly can now be effectively treated by surgically implanting a tube that drains excess cerebrospinal fluid into the abdomen.

20. (p. 479)   _____ is a form of retardation that develops in infancy due to the insufficient secretion of thyroid hormone.
    a. PKU   c. Cretinism
    b. Microcephaly   d. Mongolism

21. (p. 479)   Which of the following is *not* true of Down's syndrome?
    a. Victims of this disorder have one less chromosome than normal.
    b. The condition has been linked to the age of the mother.
    c. The condition has been linked to the age of the father.
    d. It was once known as mongolism and is characterized by almond-shaped eyes and an overly large, protruding tongue.

22. (p. 480)   Selective breeding for desirable characteristics is referred to as
    a. euthanasia   c. genetics
    b. eugenics   d. Army Alpha

23. (p. 480)   Which of the following is *not* evidence for environmental influence in IQ?
    a. Fraternal twins reared together have IQs more similar than those of ordinary siblings.
    b. Separated twins with large differences in IQs have been exposed to large educational and environmental differences.
    c. Apparent genetic effects in separated twin studies may be inflated because the twins are almost always placed in homes socially and educationally similar to their biological parents.
    d. Identical twins have IQs more similar than any other comparison of relatives, regardless of whether they are raised apart or together.

24. (p. 481)   Which of the following *cannot* be counted as evidence that environment can alter intelligence?

a. Arthur Jensen's claim that the lower IQ scores of blacks can be primarily attributed to "genetic heritage."

b. Children reared by the same mother resemble her in IQ to the same degree regardless of whether they are biological or adopted children.

c. One study found that children considered mentally retarded showed an average gain of 29 points when placed in more stimulating environments.

d. One study found that adopted children reared by more highly educated, professionally employed parents had higher IQs than siblings who remained with their biological parents.

25. (p. 482)   True-False.   Robert Zajonc believes that IQ decreases as family size grows and has developed the confluence model to explain this effect.

26. (p. 485)   True-False.   Psychological tests that disadvantage minority groups are called culture-free tests.

27. (p. 485)   Which of the following is *not* a criticism that psychologists have leveled at the extreme hereditarian view of Arthur Jensen?

a. Black children in the U.S. do not score significantly below white on standard IQ tests.

b. Blacks are more likely to live in intellectually impoverished environments that may affect intelligence.

c. The assumptions, biases, and content of standard IQ tests do not allow meaningful comparisons between ethnic groups.

d. The logic of their argument is faulty.

28. (p. 486)   True-False.   David McClelland believes IQ is of little value in predicting real competence to deal effectively with the environment.

29. (p. 487)   True-False.   Providing extra stimulation and special teaching attention can raise the IQ of young children above that of children not receiving such special treatment.

30. (p. 488)   The case of *Larry P. vs. the California State Superintendent of Education* revolved around

a. the use of standardized tests to determine whether a person is admitted to college

b. the use of IQ tests alone to determine EMR placement

c. the validity of IQ tests to assess racial differences

d. whether culture-fair IQ tests are as valid and reliable as more commonly used standard IQ tests

31. (p. 489)   True-False.   The idea of SOMPA is to keep average kids out of classes for the mentally retarded, and to identify gifted children who might otherwise be passed over as average.

ANSWERS — PROGRAMMED REVIEW

1. savant syndrome
2. Alfred Binet
3. purposefully; rationally; environment
4. abstract; knowledge; environment
5. operational definition
6. reliable
7. test-retest
8. split-half

9. equivalent forms
10. validity
11. criterion
12. correlate
13. objective
14. standardization
15. Stanford-Binet Intelligence Scale
16. age; age group

17. mental age; chronological age
18. intelligence quotient; mental age; chronological age
19. chronological, mental
20. average; 90, 109
21. deviation
22. average
23. relative standing
24. six; 31
25. 5
26. 40
27. slow
28. general information; comprehension; speed; insight; flexibility
29. impending death
30. Wechsler Adult Intelligence Scale—Revised; WAIS-R: Wechsler Intelligence Scale for Children—Revised; WISC-R
31. adult
32. performance; verbal
33. individual
34. Army Alpha
35. Scholastic Aptitude Test; American College Test; College Qualification Test
36. normal; average; extremes
37. verbal; vocabulary; rote; visualization; spatial; arithmetic reasoning
38. averages
39. .50
40. creativity
41. higher
42. biased
43. 3
44. 1
45. leadership; height, weight; successful
46. 180
47. persistence; motivation
48. 2; 3; memory; 3
49. 19
50. Gifted and Talented Education
51. language; visual, spatial; intrapersonal; interpersonal
52. schools
53. g-factor
54. mentally retarded; developmentally disabled; 70
55. adaptive behaviors
56. mild
57. profoundly; severely, moderately; sheltered workshops
58. mildly
59. organic; birth; fetal; metabolic; genetic
60. 50; 70
61. Familial retardation
62. phenylketonuria; PKU; month, diet
63. 3
64. microcephalic
65. affectionate; well
66. Hydrocephaly
67. 3
68. Cretinism; iodine
69. replacement
70. Down's syndrome
71. genetic; inherited
72. 2,000; 40; 12
73. 25
74. loving, responsive; adulthood
75. maze-bright, maze-dull
76. eugenics
77. food; distracted
78. proportion
79. fraternal twins
80. environmental
81. identical twins; .86; .72
82. 55; 75
83. 20; inflate
84. adopted, biological
85. similar
86. 29; 26
87. 5; 25
88. decreases; smallest; first
89. increased
90. confidence
91. low
92. 10
93. 17
94. Coaching; extended
95. Instrumental Enrichment
96. Venezuela
97. computer programs
98. down; up
99. gifted
100. culture-fair
101. impoverished; environment; tests
102. 106
103. outlaw
104. competency
105. career success
106. select; adapt
107. index
108. 95; 124
109. educable mentally retarded
110. culturally
111. six-hour retardates
112. System of Multicultural Pluralistic Assessment
113. medical; outside
114. similar backgrounds
115. eliminates
116. non-standard
117. cause

ANSWERS — SELF-TEST

1.	d	17.	b
2.	d	18.	a
3.	c	19.	False
4.	b	20.	c
5.	b	21.	a
6.	d	22.	b
7.	a	23.	d
8.	b	24.	a
9.	c	25.	True
10.	c	26.	False
11.	True	27.	a
12.	b	28.	True
13.	c	29.	True
14.	False	30.	b
15.	a	31.	True
16.	True		

Chapter 19

Maladaptive Behavior: Deviance and Disorder

CONTENTS

TERMS AND CONCEPTS

psychopathology
Diagnostic and Statistical Manual of Mental
    Disorders (DSM)
psychotic disorders
organic mental disorders
psychoactive substance use disorders
mood disorders
    mania
    depression
anxiety disorders
    phobic disorders
    panic disorder
    generalized anxiety disorder
    post-traumatic stress disorder
    obsessive-compulsive disorder
somatoform disorders
    hypochondriasis
    somatoform pain
    conversion reaction
        glove anesthesia

dissociative disorders
    amnesia
    fugue
    multiple personalities
    depersonalization
personality disorders
    paranoid personality
    narcissistic personality
    dependent personality
    compulsive personality
    borderline personality
    antisocial personality
sexual disorders
    gender identity
    transsexualism
    paraphilias
    psychosexual dysfunctions
neurosis
psychosis
insanity

expert witness
subjective discomfort
statistical definitions
normal curve
social nonconformity
cultural relativity
sociopathy, psychopathy (antisocial personality)
pedophilia
incest
fetishism
exhibitionism
voyeurism
transvestic fetishism
sexual sadism
sexual masochism
frotteurism
rape
anxiety
adjustment disorders
free floating anxiety
anxiety attack

phobias
  simple (or specific) phobia
  social phobia
  agoraphobia
obsessions
compulsions
belle indifference
avoidance learning
anxiety reduction hypothesis
dysthymia
cyclothymia
reactive depression
lithium carbonate
maternity blues
postpartum depression
insanity defense
M'Naghten rule
irresistible impulses
diminished capacity
Twinkie Defense
expert witness

IMPORTANT INDIVIDUALS

Marcie Kaplan
James Check
Neil Malamuth
Sigmund Freud

Carl Rogers
Edwin Shneidman
David Lester

PROGRAMMED REVIEW

1. (p. 495) Some of the facts of psychopathology are startling:
    1) One out of every _____ persons will become so severely disturbed as to require hospitalization at some point in his or her lifetime.
    2) Some 3 to 6 percent of the aged suffer from organic psychoses.
    3) Each year, some _____ percent of the population experiences an anxiety-related disorder.
    4) One out of every ____ school-age children is seriously maladjusted.
    5) Ten to 20 percent or more of all adults will suffer a major depression in their lifetime.
    6) Each year over _____ persons are admitted or readmitted to out-patient services or psychiatric treatment in general hospitals.

2. (p. 495) _____ may be defined as the inability to behave in ways that foster the well-being of the individual and ultimately of society. This definition covers not only obviously maladaptive behavior such as drug addiction, compulsive gambling, or loss of contact with reality, but also any behavior that interferes with personal growth and self-fulfillment.

3. (p. 496) Psychological problems are grouped into broad categories of maladaptive behavior. The most widely accepted system of classification is found in the _____ and _____ _____ of _____ _____, abbreviated _____.

4. (p. 497) The purpose of DSM-III-R is to provide a common _____ for various professionals. It helps _____ and classify problems and aids in the selection of appropriate therapies.

5. (p. 497) _____ disorders are among the most severe type of psychopathology, often requiring hospitalization. Here there is a loss of contact with reality with a major loss of ability to control thoughts and actions.

6. (p. 497) _____ mental disorders are problems caused by known and verifiable brain pathology; that is, by senility, drug damage, drug withdrawal, diseases of the brain, injuries, the toxic effects of poisons, and so on.

7. (p. 497) These disorders are often accompanied by severe emotional disturbances, impairment of _____, _____ loss, _____ changes, and delirium.

8. (p. 497) _____ _____ disorders are defined as psychological dependence on mood or behavior altering drugs: alcohol, barbiturates, opiates, cocaine, amphetamines, hallucinogens, cannabis, tobacco, and others.

9. (p. 497) Problems in this category usually center on impairment of _____ or _____ functioning and inability to _____ use of the drug.

10. (p. 497) _____ disorders involve significant disturbances in mood or emotion. Individuals with this disorder may be _____, meaning agitated, euphoric, and hyperactive, or they may be _____, running a high risk of suicide.

11. (p. 497) _____ disorders may take the form of _____ (irrational fears of objects, activities, or situations), panic (in which the person suffers unexplainable feelings of total panic), _____ _____ (chronic and persistent anxiety), or post-traumatic stress disorder (high anxiety that surfaces after an extremely distressing event). Also associated with this disorder is a pattern known as _____-_____ behavior.

12. (p. 497) _____ disorders are indicated when a person has physical symptoms suggesting physical disease or injury (paralysis, blindness, chronic pain, etc.) for which there is no identifiable cause.

13. (p. 497) _____ disorders include cases of temporary amnesia and instances of _____ _____, like that displayed by Ohio State "university rapist" William Milligan.

14. (p. 498) Also included are frightening episodes of _____ — feelings of being outside one's body, of behaving like a robot, or of being in a dream world.

15. (p. 498) _____ disorders are deeply ingrained, maladaptive personality patterns usually apparent by adolescence and continued throughout most of the individual's adult life.

16. (p. 498) They include _____ (overly suspicious), narcissistic (self-loving), dependent, _____, and antisocial and other personality types.

17. (p. 498) _____ disorders include _____ _____ disorders (where sexual identity does not match physical gender),

_____ (a persistent discomfort about one's sex and a desire to change to the opposite sex), and a wide range of deviations in sexual behavior known as _____ (fetishism, voyeurism, etc.).

18. (p. 498) Also found in this category are a variety of sexual _____ (problems in sexual desire or sexual response).

19. (p. 498) The former DSM-II listed _____ as a disorder. But the new, revised version (DSM-III-R) omits it because the term lumps together too many separate problems. Such behavior is now listed as anxiety disorders, somatoform disorders, and dissociative disorders.

20. (p. 498) Many professionals continue to use the term to loosely refer to problems associated with excessive anxiety. It still makes sense to separate these milder problems from _____, because they do not involve a major loss of contact with reality.

21. (p. 498) Insanity refers to legal responsibility for one's _____ or to the legal designation required for _____ commitment to a mental institution. It is usually established through the testimony of psychologists and psychiatrists who serve as expert witnesses in a court of law.

22. (p. 498) Defining normality is difficult. We can begin by saying that _____ _____ is characteristic of psychopathology. That is, the unhealthy personality will be marked by unhappiness, anxiety, depression, or other signs of emotional upset.

23. (p. 498) A problem with this definition of abnormality is that in some cases a person's behavior may be quite maladaptive without producing subjective discomfort. Additionally, in some cases a _____ of discomfort may indicate a problem.

24. (p. 498) Some psychologists have tried to define normality more objectively by using _____ definitions. For example, we could develop a test to learn how many people show low, medium, or high levels of anxiety. Usually this type of measurement will produce a _____ (bell-shaped) _____.

25. (p. 498) Unfortunately, a statistical definition of abnormality tells us nothing about the meaning of a _____ from the norm and does not help us draw the line between _____ and _____.

26. (p. 498) _____ _____ may also serve as a basis for judgments of normality. Abnormal behavior can sometimes be viewed as a failure in _____. Here we refer to the person who has not adopted the usual minimum rules for social conduct or who has learned to engage in socially destructive behavior.

27. (p. 499) Before any behavior can be defined as normal or abnormal, we must consider the _____ in which it occurs. Almost any imaginable behavior can be considered normal in some situation.

28. (p. 500) One of the most influential contexts in which any behavior is judged is that of culture. There is a high degree of _____ _____ in perceptions of normality and abnormality. Still, all known cultures classify people as abnormal if they either fail to communicate with others or are consistently unpredictable in their actions.

29. (p. 500) All definitions of abnormality are _____. In practice, the judgment that a person needs help usually occurs when the person does something that annoys or gains the attention of a person in a position of power who then does something about it.

30. (p. 500) There are several possibilities as to why more women than men are treated for psychological problems: (1) Due to _____ _____ training, women may be more willing to reveal distress and to seek help. (2) Because women are often denied power, responsibility, and independence in our society, they may more often feel depressed, anxious, or hopeless. (3) There may be a male _____ to traditional conceptions of normality.

31. (p. 500) This last possibility has been explored by psychologist Marcie Kaplan. She believes that women are penalized both for conforming to female _____ and for ignoring them.

32. (p. 501) Personality disorders involve deeply ingrained maladaptive personality patterns. For example, the _____ personality is overly suspicious, mistrusting, hypersensitive, guarded, and unsure of the loyalty and honesty of others.

33. (p. 501) _____ personalities are preoccupied with their own self-importance, need constant attention and admiration, and are absorbed in fantasies of power, wealth, brilliance, etc.

34. (p. 501) The _____ personality involves an extreme lack of self-confidence in which others are allowed to assume responsibility for major areas of the person's life, and the person places his or her own needs second to others.

35. (p. 501) Persons with a _____ personality disorder are capable of working, but repeatedly lose jobs because of turbulent relationships. They can be friendly and charming, but also extremely unpredictable, moody, and even suicidal.

36. (p. 501) The individual possessing an antisocial personality, known as a _____ or _____, is irresponsible, impulsive, selfish, lacking in judgment, unable to feel guilt, emotionally shallow, unable to learn from experience, lacking in moral values, and has a long history of conflict with society.

37. (p. 501) Many sociopaths are delinquents or criminals who may pose a threat to the general public. Studies show that more than _____ percent of all antisocial personalities have been arrested, usually for crimes such as robbery, vandalism, and rape.

38. (p. 502) Sociopaths are _____ the crazed murders that have been portrayed on TV and in movies. Many create a good impression and are frequently described as "charming." Their lying, self-serving manipulation, and lack of dependability only gradually become evident to their "friends."

39. (p. 502) People with antisocial personalities usually have a childhood history of emotional _____ and _____. Some psychologists believe that infants who fail to form a healthy emotional attachment to a caregiver later may be prone to antisocial behavior.

40. (p. 502) Adult sociopaths display some subtle physical differences. For example, they produce unusual _____ patterns suggesting _____ of the brain. This may explain why many are thrill seekers—they are searching for stimulation strong enough to overcome their "boredom."

41. (p. 502)   Interestingly, sociopaths tested in situations where they must learn to avoid an electric shock show much less _____ than normal. They might therefore be described as emotionally cold.

42. (p. 502)   Antisocial personality disorders are _____ treated with success since sociopaths manipulate therapy as they might any other situation. There is, however, some evidence that antisocial behavior declines somewhat after age _____.

43. (p. 502)   From a psychological point of view, the mark of true sexual deviations is that they are _____, _____, _____, or cause guilt, anxiety, or discomfort for one or both participants.

44. (p. 502)   Deviations fitting this definition are related to a wide variety of behaviors including: _____, sex with children; _____, sex with blood relatives; _____, sexual arousal associated with inanimate objects; _____, displaying the genitals to unwilling viewers; _____, viewing the genitals of others; _____ _____, achieving sexual arousal by wearing clothing of the opposite sex; sexual _____, deriving sexual pleasure from inflicting pain; sexual _____, desiring pain as part of the sex act; and _____, sexually touching or rubbing against a non-consenting person, usually in a public place such as a subway.

45. (p. 502)   Roughly _____ percent of all sexual arrests are for exhibitionism. These individuals are typically male, married, and most come from strict and repressive backgrounds.

46. (p. 502)   Exhibitionists have the _____ repeat rate among sexual offenders. Most of them feel a deep sense of _____, which produces a compulsive need to prove their "manhood" by frightening women. While they are usually harmless, those who approach closer than arm's reach may be dangerous.

47. (p. 502)   In general, a woman confronted by an exhibitionist can assume that his goal is to _____ and _____. By becoming visibly upset she actual encourages him.

48. (p. 502)   Child molesters are typically _____ and two-thirds are _____. Many are rigid, passive, puritanical, or religious. In one-half to two-thirds of all cases of molestation, the offender is a friend, acquaintance, or relative of the child. Most molestations rarely exceed fondling.

49. (p. 503)   Many authorities feel that a _____ incident of molestation is unlikely to cause severe psychological harm to a child. For most children the event is frightening, but not a lasting trauma. This is why parents are urged not to overreact. Doing so only further frightens the child.

50. (p. 503)   There are a number of hints of trouble that parents should watch for when there is suspicion of molestation; one is when the child fears being seen _____ (for instance during bathing). You should be familiar with the others as well.

51. (p. 503)   Repeated molestations, those that involve force or threats, incidents that exceed fondling, and especially victimization that involves a molester the child deeply trusts can leave lasting emotional scars. As adults, many molest victims develop

_____ _____ where lovemaking may evoke vivid and terrifying memories.

52. (p. 503) Most authorities no longer think of _____ as a sexual act; rather it is an act of brutality or aggression based on the need to debase others.

53. (p. 503) Many rapists are _____ _____ who impulsively take what they want without concern for others or who harbor deep-seated resentment or outright hatred toward women. Their goal is not sexual intercourse, but to attack, subordinate, humiliate, and degrade the victim.

54. (p. 503) Typical aftereffects for the victim include rage, _____, _____, loss of _____-_____, shame, and in many cases, a lasting mistrust of male-female relationships.

55. (p. 503) A number of writers have suggested that rape is in some ways related to sex role _____. That is, many people learn to believe that women should not show direct interest in sex. Men on the other hand are taught to take the initiative and to persist in attempts at sexual intimacy even when the woman says no.

56. (p. 503) Psychologists James Check and Neil Malamuth believe that such attitudes create a "_____-_____ _____." In their view, rape is only an extreme expression of a system that condones coercive sexual intimacy.

57. (p. 503) To test the hypothesis that _____ _____ contribute to rape, male college students were classified as either high or low in sex-role stereotyping. Each student then read one of three stories.

58. (p. 503) College males high in sex-role stereotyping were more aroused by the rape stories. Their arousal patterns, in fact, were similar to those found among actual rapists. Moreover, _____ percent of those tested indicated they would consider rape, especially if they could be sure of not being caught.

59. (p. 503) In another study of rape, over _____ of a sample of adults agreed with the statement, "A woman who goes to the home or apartment of a man on the first date implies she is willing to have sex."

60. (p. 504) The impact of rape is so great that most women who successfully avoid a rape attempt are just as _____ as rape survivors.

61. (p. 504) Anxiety is similar to fear, except that anxiety is a response to an unclear or _____ threat. Compared to anxiety, fear is more _____ and _____. Typically it is the result of a specific, identifiable threat.

62. (p. 504) Problems once called neuroses are now classified separately as anxiety disorders, dissociative disorders, and somatoform disorders. In general, these problems include: (1) high levels of _____ and/or restrictive, self-defeating behavior patterns; (2) a tendency to use elaborate _____ _____ or avoidance responses to maintain minimal functioning; and (3) pervasive feelings of stress, insecurity, inferiority, unhappiness, and dissatisfaction with life.

63. (p. 505) Anxiety, fears, and phobias are probably the most common psychological disturbances today. More than _____ percent of the adult population is so affected by these emotions that they could be diagnosed as having an anxiety disorder.

64. (p. 505) The term "nervous breakdown" has no formal meaning. It seems to imply some sort of disease of the nervous system, but there is nothing physically wrong with the nerves of an anxious or emotionally troubled individual. What many people have in mind when they use the term is properly called an _____ _____.

65. (p. 505) The presence of an adjustment disorder is signaled by extreme _____, _____ disturbances, loss of _____, physical complaints, and apathy, anxiety, or depression. Often, these problems are successfully treated with rest, sedation, supportive _____, and a chance to "talk through" fears and anxieties.

66. (p. 505) The outward symptoms of adjustment disorders and anxiety disorders can be similar. However, adjustment disorders typically disappear when life circumstances _____. This demonstrates their link to stressful events.

67. (p. 505) At least 6 months of unrealistic or excessive anxiety and worry is the essential feature of the anxiety disorder known as _____ _____.

68. (p. 505) The discomfort felt in this disorder is sometimes described as _____ _____ anxiety, because the anxiety is so general and related to many different worries. The individual is continually preoccupied by worries, which makes them irritable and unable to concentrate.

69. (p. 505) Affected individuals typically complain of _____, racing heart, _____ hands, dizziness, upset stomach, rapid breathing, and other symptoms of _____ nervous system activity.

70. (p. 505) The presence of _____ _____ differentiates what is known as panic disorder. This disorder is characterized by continuous tension that occasionally explodes into sudden, unexpected episodes of intense panic.

71. (p. 505) During an anxiety attack, affected individuals experience _____ palpitations or _____ pain, choking or smothering sensations, vertigo, feelings of _____, trembling, and fear of dying, going crazy, or losing control during the attack.

72. (p. 506) _____ are irrational fears that persist even when there is no real danger to a person.

73. (p. 506) In phobic disorders, persistent fears, anxiety, and avoidance are focused on various objects, activities, or situations. Affected persons recognize that their fear is unreasonable and excessive, but they cannot _____ it. For a phobic disorder to exist, the person's fear must _____ his or her daily life.

74. (p. 506) Phobias fall into three main categories. Some examples of simple phobias (those that may be attached to nearly any object or situation) are:
_____—fear of lightning
_____—fear of spiders
_____—fear of heights

_____ —fear of closed spaces
_____ —fear of blood
_____ —fear of darkness
_____ —fear of disease
_____ —fear of animals

75. (p. 506) A phobic disorder differs from ordinary fears in that it produces overwhelming anxiety that may cause _____, wild climbing and running, or _____. Such individuals are so threatened that they will go to almost any length to avoid the feared object or situation.

76. (p. 506) _____ phobias involve fear of situations in which one can be observed, evaluated, embarrassed, or humiliated by others. There is an avoidance of certain social situations, such as eating, writing, blushing, or speaking in public.

77. (p. 506) The most common and disruptive phobic disorder is agoraphobia. One expert estimates one out of every _____ people has this problem to a degree serious enough to restrict his or her life. They may have an intense fear of leaving the familiar setting of the home, becoming literally "housebound."

78. (p. 507) _____ are thoughts or images that intrude into consciousness against a person's will. In some cases they may be so disturbing that they cause anxiety or extreme discomfort.

79. (p. 507) The common obsessions are about _____ (such as poisoning one's spouse or stabbing a child), about being "dirty" or "unclear," about whether one has performed some action (such as turning off the stove), and about committing _____ acts.

80. (p. 507) Obsessions usually give rise to _____, irrational acts a person feels driven to repeat. Typically, these acts help control or block out anxiety caused by obsessions.

81. (p. 507) Not all obsessive-compulsive disorders are dramatic. Many simply involve extreme _____ and rigid _____. This focus helps the highly anxious person feel more secure by keeping activities totally structured and under control.

82. (p. 507) Most anxiety disorders are relatively lasting patterns. A notable exception is found in _____ - _____ _____ disorders. These problems occur when stresses outside the range of normal human experience cause a significant psychological and emotional disturbance.

83. (p. 507) PTSD reactions frequently follow sudden _____, such as floods, tornadoes, earthquakes, or serious accidents. Research shows that it also affects many political _____, _____ veterans, prisoners of war, and victims of terrorism, violent crime, child _____, or rape.

84. (p. 507) Characteristic symptoms of PTSD include repeatedly reliving the traumatic event, _____ of stimuli associated with the event, and a numbing of _____.

85. (p. 507) Also common are _____, nightmares, guardedness, an inability to _____, irritability, and explosions of anger or aggression, all of which may surface long after the stress has passed.

86. (p. 508) A dissociative reaction is marked by striking episodes of _____ (the inability to recall one's name, address, or past) or _____ (fleeing to escape threat or conflict). These phenomena are often triggered by highly traumatic events.

87. (p. 508) Dissociative disorders may also involve _____ _____, a rare condition in which two or more separate personalities exist in an individual. Such was the case with Sybil, a woman who had 16 complete and totally different personalities.

88. (p. 508) Sybil's alternate personalities developed during childhood when she was regularly beaten, locked in closets, perversely tortured, sexually abused and almost killed. Sybil's first dissociations allowed her to _____ by creating another person who would suffer torture in her place. Multiple personality often begins with similar unbearable childhood experiences.

89. (p. 508) Therapy for multiple personality is often aided by _____, which allows contact with the various personalities. The goal of therapy is integration and fusing of the various personalities into a single, balanced entity.

90. (p. 508) Somatoform disorders are noted in individuals who are continually distracted by fears of having a serious _____. Such individuals are preoccupied with bodily functions or minor physical problems.

91. (p. 508) Such individuals often have a complicated medical history and have consulted numerous doctors. Their unwarranted fear of having a disease persists despite the fact that there is no _____ basis for their complaints.

92. (p. 509) The person who has multiple physical complaints for which medical attention is sought, but for which no clear physical cause can be found, suffers from a somatoform disorder called _____.

93. (p. 509) _____ pain is a related problem in which the person is disabled by pain that has no identifiable physical basis.

94. (p. 509) A rarer form of somatoform disorder (or "body-form" disorder) is called a _____ _____, said to occur when anxiety or severe emotional conflicts are converted into physical symptoms resembling disease or disability.

95. (p. 509) An example of a conversion reaction is _____ _____, a loss of sensitivity in the areas of skin that would normally be covered by a glove.

96. (p. 509) Glove anesthesia shows that conversion symptoms often contradict known _____ facts. The system of nerves in the hands does not form a glovelike pattern and could not cause the observed symptoms.

97. (p. 509) Conversion disorders usually serve to excuse the person from a _____ situation. They may be revealed by a _____ of symptoms when the "victim" is asleep, hypnotized, or anesthetized.

98. (p. 509) Victims of conversion disorders usually show a lack of concern for their disability. This sign is referred to as _____ _____.

99. (p. 509) Conversion reactions probably account for many of the so-called miracle cures attributed to faith _____ or medical _____. Though "cured," new symptoms usually develop later.

100. (p. 510) At least three major psychological perspectives on the causes of dissociative, anxiety, and somatoform disorders can be identified. The first comprehensive explanation of neurosis was proposed by _____ _____ and is called the _____ approach.

101. (p. 510) According to Freud, neurosis (as it was called then) represents a raging conflict between the three subparts of the personality. The _____ becomes overwhelmed by anxiety caused by forbidden _____ impulses and guilt generated by the _____ in response to these impulses, resulting in rigid defense mechanisms and inflexible behavior.

102. (p. 510) Psychologist Carl Rogers, exemplifying the humanistic-existential approach, interprets emotional disorders as the end-product of a faulty _____-_____. He feels that anxious individuals build up an unrealistic picture of themselves which leaves them vulnerable to contradictory information.

103. (p. 510) Some psychologists take a more existential point of view, emphasizing that unhealthy anxiety reflects a loss of _____ in one's life.

104. (p. 510) According to this view, humans must show _____ and _____ in their choices if life is to have meaning, but too often we back away from life-enhancing choices.

105. (p. 510) This hesitancy occurs because we experience"_____ _____," the anguish that comes from knowing that we are personally responsible for our lives, hence, that we have a crushing responsibility to choose wisely and courageously.

106. (p. 511) Behaviorists assume that the "symptoms" of these disorders are _____ just as other behaviors are. For example, phobias can be acquired through classical conditioning. Anxiety attacks may reflect the generalization of conditioned emotional responses to new situations. The hypochondriac's "sickness behavior" may be reinforced by the sympathy and attention he or she gets.

107. (p. 511) One point that all theorists agree upon is that it is ultimately self-defeating and _____ (contradictory): it makes people more miserable in the long run, but its immediate effect is to temporarily lower anxiety.

108. (p. 511) The behavioristic explanation of the origins of this paradox is that self-defeating behavior begins with _____ _____. The powerful reward of immediate relief from anxiety keeps self-defeating avoidance behavior alive. This view is known as the _____ _____ _____.

109. (p. 511) Mood disorders are among the most serious of all. Studies show that in Europe and in this country between _____ and _____ percent of the adult population has had a major depressive episode at some time.

110. (p. 511) Depressive disorders are one of the most frequently occurring problems, accounting for approximately _____ percent of all cases treated by private clinicians.

111. (p. 511) Although manic behavior is included in the affective disorders, the most common problem is depression in which _____ and _____ are exaggerated, prolonged, or unreasonable.

112. (p. 511) Indications of a depressive disorder are sadness, hopelessness, inability to feel _____ or to take interest in anything, fatigue, limited _____, sleep and eating disturbances, feelings of worthlessness, an extremely negative self-image, and recurrent thoughts of _____.

113. (p. 511) If a person is depressed more days than not, for at least 2 years, the problem is termed _____.

114. (p. 511) If depression alternates with periods when the person's mood is elevated, expansive, or irritable, the problem is called _____.

115. (p. 511) If a loved one dies or a person suffers a major failure or setback, a period of mourning or depression is to be expected. But in _____ depression the person is unprepared to cope with a major loss because of a long series of former disappointments, or because the person is emotionally dependent or immature.

116. (p. 512) Depression and other affective disorders have resisted adequate explanation and treatment. Some researchers are focusing on the biology of mood changes with some success. For example, the chemical _____ _____ can be effective in treatment of some cases of depression, particularly those also showing manic behavior.

117. (p. 512) Others have sought psychological explanations. Psychoanalytic theory, for instance, holds that depression is caused by _____ _____ that is displaced and turned inward as self-blame and self-hate.

118. (p. 512) Many women are surprised to learn that they run an increased risk of depression after giving birth. The two most common forms of the problem are _____ _____ and _____ depression (which refers to the time period following childbirth).

119. (p. 512) An estimated _____ to _____ percent of all women undergo a temporary disturbance in mood, usually lasting from 24 to 48 hours after childbirth.

120. (p. 512) These "third-day" maternity blues are marked by _____, fitful _____, tension, _____, and irritability. For most women, this reaction is a normal part of adjusting to childbirth.

121. (p. 512) However, the maternity blues can be the beginning of a more lasting depression. As many as _____ percent of all women who give birth may develop a mild to moderate depressive disorder.

122. (p. 512) Typical signs of postpartum depression are _____, _____, despondency, feeling _____, and feeling unable to cope with the new baby. Depression of this kind may last anywhere from ___ months to about a year.

123. (p. 512) Predicting postpartum depression is difficult. However, the risk is increased by high levels of _____ during pregnancy and _____, attitudes toward childrearing. The occurrence of stressful life events before birth is also a major concern. Also, the amount of social support a woman receives seems to be an important facet of the problem.

124. (p. 514) Suicide ranks as the _____ cause of death in the United States with approximately 1 person out of _____ attempting suicide at some time in their life.

125. (p. 514) Several factors appear related to suicide; other popular beliefs appear untrue. For example, rates are lower on major holidays such as Christmas. The peak actually occurs in _____.

126. (p. 514) _____ times as many men as women complete suicide, but women make more attempts, the difference being due to the type of technique selected (men typically use guns, women typically attempt a drug overdose).

127. (p. 514) Suicide rates gradually rise during adolescence. They then sharply _____ during young adulthood (ages 20-24). From then until age 84, the rate continues to gradually _____ with advancing age.

128. (p. 514) More than half of all suicides are committed by individuals over _____ years old, although there has been a steady increase in the total number of suicides by adolescents and young adults.

129. (p. 514) Part of this increase comes from the ranks of college students where suicide is the _____ cause of death, the most dangerous period being the beginning of a semester, not during final exams.

130. (p. 514) Factors important in student suicide appear to include a sense of not living up to extremely high self-imposed standards, chronic _____ problems, and _____ difficulties.

131. (p. 514) There has been a recent dramatic increase in adolescent suicides. At present, about 5000 teenagers and young adults commit suicide each year in the U.S. This total is _____ the number reported 10 years ago.

132. (p. 514) Some professions, particularly _____ and _____, show higher than average suicide rates, but generally suicide is not related to income.

133. (p. 514) The highest suicide rates are found among the _____; the next highest rates occur among the _____; lower rates are recorded for single persons; and _____ individuals have the lowest rate of all.

134. (p. 514) The best explanation for suicide may simply come from a look at conditions which precede it. Usually there is a history of interpersonal troubles with family, in-laws, or a lover or spouse. Often there is a _____ problem, _____ adjustment problem, or _____ difficulties. Under such conditions anyone may reach a state of depression severe enough to attempt suicide; it is not limited just to the mentally ill.

135. (p. 515) The causes of increased adolescent suicide remain unclear. As with adults, there is often a backdrop of problems with drugs, depression, school, peers, family, divorced parents, or the break-up of a romance. Many cases seem to result from _____ expectations and an unusual sensitivity to hurt and disappointment.

136. (p. 515) It is a major fallacy to believe that people who talk about or threaten suicide are rarely the ones who try it. Of every 10 potential suicides, _____ give warning beforehand.

137. (p. 515) It is also not true that suicide cannot be prevented. It is estimated that about _____-_____ of all suicide attempts fall into the "to be" category, with another third characterized by a "to be or not to be" attitude. Only about ____ to ____ percent of cases represent individuals who definitely want to die.

138. (p. 515) As Edwin Schneidman points out, suicidal behavior is often a form of _____, a cry for help born out of pain, with clues and messages of suffering and anguish and pleas for response.

139. (p. 515) Schneidman has identified several common characteristics of suicidal thoughts and feelings. They include (1) escape, (2) unbearable psychological _____, (3) frustrated psychological _____, and (4) constriction of _____.

140. (p. 515) Suicide expert David Lester believes that in helping potential attempters the most important task is to establish _____ with the person; they need acceptance, not reassurance.

141. (p. 516) You can help by getting the person to commit themselves to daily schedules, even on a small scale. Also, don't end your efforts too soon. One of the most dangerous times is when a person suddenly seems to get better after a severe _____.

142. (p. 516) There are over _____ centers for suicide prevention in the U.S., and most sizable cities have mental health crisis intervention teams. Urge a suicidal person to call one of these resources if he or she becomes frightened or impulsive.

143. (p. 516) If a person actually threatens suicide, has a concrete, workable plan, and has the means to carry it out, you should ask that person to accompany you to a _____.

144. (p. 516) If a person seems on the verge of attempting suicide, don't worry about _____. Call the police, crisis intervention, or a rescue unit.

145. (p. 517) The insanity defense entered western law as the _____ _____ based on an 1843 ruling by the English House of Lords. This decision indicated that persons suffering from mental disease or other defects that prevent them from knowing right from wrong are insane.

146. (p. 517) Defendants may also claim they knew their act was wrong, but they had an _____ _____ they could not control.

147. (p. 517) A related defense claims _____ _____ to control actions or to know right from wrong. A person who commits a crime while under the influence of drugs might make this plea.

148. (p. 517) In Dan White's case the defense pleaded diminished capacity claiming, among other things, that White was deranged from eating too much "junk food." This argument became known as the _____ _____.

149. (p. 517) Criminal trials involving insanity have a typical pattern. Psychiatrists serving as _____ _____ for defense and prosecution present conflicting views leaving the jury to decide who is right.

150. (p. 517) More often, this "battle of the experts" never takes place. In ___ out of 5 cases, prosecutors, defense attorneys, medical experts, and judges agree before trial that the defendant is mentally ill.

151. (p. 517) The states of _____, _____, and _____ have banned the insanity plea, but in most states it remains intact. Several other states now allow only a "guilty, but mentally ill" plea.

152. (p. 518) Pleas of insanity are used in only about 1 out of every _____ court cases and succeed as a defense in only about _____ percent of those cases.

153. (p. 518) Verdicts of innocence by reason of insanity do not set defendants free. Rather they are committed to a _____ _____ and thereafter must prove they are no longer a danger in order to be released.

154. (p. 518) In some cases, persons declared "insane" have been hospitalized longer than they would have been imprisoned for a criminal conviction. Then again, on the average insane offenders are now held for about ____ years.

155. (p. 518) At present there is no way to accurately predict which individuals are likely to be dangerous. Follow-ups of arrests and mental hospital records show that from _____-_____ to _____-_____ of the time, experts are wrong in predicting violent behavior.

SELF-TEST

1. (p. 495) What percent of the U.S. population will become so severely disturbed as to require hospitalization at some point in time?
    a. 1   c. 8
    b. 5   d. 10

2. (p. 497) Which of the following would *not* be a possible cause of organic mental disorders?
    a. toxic effects of poisons   c. diseases of the brain
    b. senility   d. chronic depression

3. (p. 497) Which of the following is *not* a type of anxiety disorder?
    a. conversion reactions   c. panic disorder
    b. obsessive-compulsive disorder   d. phobias

4. (p. 497) _____ disorders are indicated when a person has physical symptoms suggesting disease or injury for which there is no identifiable cause.
    a. Organic   c. Anxiety
    b. Dissociative   d. Somatoform

5. (p. 498) Which of the following is *not* a type of personality disorder?
    a. paranoid personality   c. antisocial personality
    b. senile personality   d. narcissistic personality

6. (p. 498) True-False. Psychosis is the same as insanity.

7. (p. 498) Of the following, which has been used in attempts to define abnormality?
    a. subjective discomfort   c. social nonconformity
    b. statistical definitions   d. all of the above

8. (p. 501) People who are selfish, impulsive, unable to feel guilt, manipulative, and lacking in moral values are classified as
    a. psychotic   c. traumatized
    b. sociopathic   d. schizophrenic

9. (p. 502) The early history of sociopaths is usually marked by
    a. parental double-bind communication
    b. tension and stress

    c. emotional deprivation and disregard
    d. sexual perversion and obscenity

10. (p. 502)   Which of the following is *not* a correct match?
    a. pedophilia—sex with children
    b. voyeurism—displaying the genitals
    c. frotteurism—sexually touching a non-consenting person, usually in a public place
    d. sadism—inflicting pain as part of the sex act

11. (p. 502)   Which of the following is *not* true of child molesters?
    a. They are typically married and two-thirds are fathers.
    b. Many are rigid, passive, puritanical, or religious.
    c. Their acts rarely exceed fondling.
    d. In almost every case, force or threats are used.

12. (p. 503)   Which of the following is *not* true of rape?
    a. Psychologists no longer think of it as a sexual act.
    b. It is in some ways related to sex role socialization.
    c. Aftereffects can include rage, guilt, depression, and loss of self-esteem.
    d. Many rapists are psychotics who do not recognize the seriousness of their behavior.

13. (p. 505)   True-False. The term nervous breakdown has no formal meaning.

14. (p. 505)   Which of the following characterizes panic disorders?
    a. anxiety attacks   c. hallucinations
    b. amnesia   d. obsessions

15. (p. 506)   Which of the following is *not* a correct match?
    a. arastraphobia—fear of lightning
    b. zoophobia—fear of animals
    c. claustrophobia—fear of darkness
    d. acrophobia—fear of heights

16. (p. 506)   True-False.   Agoraphobia is the most common and debilitating of the phobic reactions. Persons suffering this disorder may literally become "housebound."

17. (p. 507)   Thoughts or images that intrude into consciousness against a person's will which may cause anxiety or extreme discomfort are called
    a. phobias   c. compulsions
    b. obsessions   d. hallucinations

18. (p. 507)   Irrational acts a person feels driven to repeat are called
    a. phobias   c. compulsions
    b. obsessions   d. hallucinations

19. (p. 507)   _____ disorders can occur when stresses outside the range of normal human experience cause a significant psychological and emotional disturbance.
    a. Affective   c. Phobic
    b. Post-traumatic stress   d. Adjustment

20. (p. 508)   Amnesia, fugue, and multiple personality are examples of
    a. conversion reactions   c. traumatic disorders
    b. dissociative disorders   d. anxiety disorders

21. (p. 509) Which of the following is *not* true of conversion reactions?
    a. They occur when anxiety or severe emotional conflicts are converted into physical symptoms resembling disease or disability.
    b. An example is multiple personality development in which a pathological splitting of the person's basic personality occurs.
    c. They usually serve to excuse a person from a threatening situation.
    d. They probably account for many so-called miracle cures attributed to faith healers and medical quacks.

22. (p. 510) Which of the following produces neurosis according to Freud?
    a. anxiety caused by id impulses for sex or aggression which threaten to break through into behavior
    b. guilt generated by the superego in response to id impulses
    c. the development of rigid defense mechanisms by the ego in response to conflicting demands of the id and superego
    d. all of the above

23. (p. 510) Humanist Carl Rogers believes that emotional disorders are the end product of a faulty
    a. childhood   c. self-image
    b. communication skill   d. id

24. (p. 511) Depressive reactions are the most frequently occurring affective disorder, accounting for approximately _____ percent of all cases treated by private clinicians.
    a. 25   c. 75
    b. 50   d. 90

25. (p. 511) In _____ depression, the person is unable to cope with a major loss because of a long series of former disappointments, or because the person is emotionally dependent or immature.
    a. incongruent   c. reactive
    b. affective   d. phobic

26. (p. 512) Crying, fitful sleep, tension, anger, and irritability following childbirth are characteristics which mark
    a. postpartum depression   c. psychogenic pain
    b. reactive depression   d. maternity blues

27. (p. 514) Which of the following is true of suicide?
    a. More men attempt suicide, but more women complete suicide.
    b. More than half of all suicides are committed by individuals under 30 years of age.
    c. The highest suicide rates are found among single, never married persons.
    d. At present, the number of adolescent suicides is double the number reported ten years ago.

28. (p. 515) Which of the following is *not* a useful suggestion in helping prevent suicide?
    a. Tell suicidal persons they really don't want to kill themselves; list reasons why they shouldn't.
    b. Talk about suicide directly; don't avoid the issue or the use of the term suicide.
    c. Continue your efforts even when the person suddenly seems better after a severe depression.
    d. Give the person a sense of acceptance not reassurance.

29. (p. 517) The M'Naghten rule refers to
    a. the court case decision that introduced the insanity defense into Western law

  b. the psychological law relating degree of anxiety to degree of pathology
  c. the legal statute which prevents use of the insanity plea in Montana and Idaho
  d. the standard procedures psychiatrists use as expert witnesses in reporting to the courts

30. (p. 517) Which of the following is *not* a court pleading in which the person claims psychological constraints precluded normal behavior or reasoning?
  a. insanity   c. diminished capacity
  b. irresistible impulse   d. cultural relativity

ANSWERS — PROGRAMMED REVIEW

1. 100; 12; 8; 2 million
2. Psychopathology
3. Diagnostic and Statistical Manual of Mental Disorders; DSM-III-R
4. language; diagnose
5. Psychotic
6. Organic
7. thinking; memory; personality
8. Substance use
9. social, occupational; stop
10. Mood; manic; depressed
11. Anxiety; phobias; generalized anxiety; obsessive-compulsive
12. Somatoform
13. Dissociative; multiple personalities
14. depersonalization
15. Personality
16. paranoid; compulsive
17. Sexual; gender identity; transsexualism; paraphilias
18. dysfunctions
19. neurosis
20. psychosis
21. actions; involuntary
22. subjective discomfort
23. lack
24. statistical; normal curve
25. deviation; normality; abnormality
26. Social nonconformity; socialization
27. context
28. cultural relativity
29. relative
30. cultural training; bias
31. stereotypes
32. paranoid
33. Narcissistic
34. dependent
35. borderline
36. sociopath, psychopath
37. 65
38. rarely
39. deprivation; neglect
40. brainwave; underarousal
41. anxiety
42. rarely; 30
43. compulsive, destructive, bizarre
44. pedophilia; incest; fetishism; exhibitionism; voyeurism; transvestic fetishism; sadism; masochism; frotteurism
45. 35
46. highest; inadequacy
47. shock; alarm
48. married; fathers
49. single
50. nude
51. sexual phobias
52. rape
53. antisocial personalities
54. guilt, depression; self-esteem
55. socialization
56. rape-supportive culture
57. stereotyped images
58. 44
59. half
60. depressed
61. ambiguous; focused; intense
62. anxiety; defense mechanisms
63. 10
64. adjustment disorder
65. irritability; sleep; appetite; counseling
66. improve
67. generalized anxiety
68. free floating
69. sweating; clammy; autonomic
70. anxiety attacks
71. heart; chest; unreality
72. Phobias
73. control; disrupt
74. Arastraphobia; Arachnephobia; Acrophobia; Claustrophobia; Hemophobia; Nyctophobia; Pathophobia; Zoophobia
75. vomiting; fainting
76. Social
77. 100

78. Obsessions
79. violence; immoral
80. compulsions
81. orderliness; routine
82. post-traumatic stress
83. disasters; hostages; combat; molestation
84. avoidance; emotions
85. insomnia; concentrate
86. amnesia; fugue
87. multiple personalities
88. escape
89. hypnosis
90. disease
91. medical
92. hypochondriasis
93. Somatoform
94. conversion reaction
95. glove anesthesia
96. medical
97. threatening; disappearance
98. belle indifference
99. healers; quacks
100. Sigmund Freud; psychodynamic
101. ego; id; superego
102. self-image
103. meaning
104. courage, responsibility
105. existential anxiety
106. learned
107. paradoxical
108. avoidance learning; anxiety reduction hypothesis
109. 10; 20
110. 25
111. sadness, despondency
112. pleasure; movement; suicide
113. dysthymia
114. cyclothymia
115. reactive
116. lithium carbonate

117. repressed anger
118. maternity blues; postpartum
119. 50; 80
120. crying; sleep; anger
121. 20
122. mood swings; inadequate; 2
123. anxiety; negative
124. seventh; 100
125. May
126. Three
127. increase; rise
128. 45
129. leading
130. health; interpersonal
131. double
132. medicine, psychiatry
133. divorced; widowed; married
134. drinking; sexual; job
135. unrealistic
136. 8
137. two-thirds; 3, 5
138. communication
139. pain; needs; options
140. rapport
141. depression
142. 300
143. hospital
144. over-reacting
145. M'Naghten rule
146. irresistible impulse
147. diminished capacity
148. Twinkie Defense
149. expert witnesses
150. 4
151. Montana, Idaho, Utah
152. 500; two
153. mental hospital
154. 2
155. two-thirds; nine-tenths

ANSWERS — SELF-TEST

1. a
2. d
3. a
4. d
5. d
6. False
7. d
8. b
9. c
10. b

11. d
12. d
13. True
14. a
15. c
16. True
17. b
18. c
19. b
20. b

21. b
22. d
23. c
24. a
25. c
26. d
27. d
28. a
29. a
30. d

Chapter 20

Major Mental Disorders

CONTENTS

TERMS AND CONCEPTS

delusions
    depressive
    somatic
    grandeur
    influence
    persecution
    reference
hallucinations
anesthesia
flat affect
organic psychosis
    general paresis
    senile dementia
    Alzheimer's disease
functional psychosis
delusional disorders
    erotomanic type
    grandiose type
    jealous type
    persecutory type
    somatic type
paranoid psychosis

major mood disorders
    bipolar disorders
        mixed type
        manic type
        depressed type
    unipolar disorder
    depressive disorders
        major depression
affective psychosis
schizophrenia
        disorganized (hebephrenic)
        catatonic
        paranoid
        undifferentiated
    schizotypal personality disorder
endogenous
seasonal affective disorder
phototherapy
waxy flexibility
mutism
double-bind communication
phenothiazine

dopamine
CT (computed tomography) scan
PET (positron emission tomography) scan
psychotherapy
somatic (bodily) therapy
   chemotherapy
      minor tranquilizers
      major tranquilizers (anti-psychotics)
      energizers

electoconvulsive therapy (ECT)
psychosurgery
   prefrontal lobotomy
   deep lesioning
tardive dyskinesia
hospitalization
community mental health center
paraprofessional
medical model

IMPORTANT INDIVIDUALS

Normal Rosenthal
R. D. Laing

David Rosenhan
Thomas Szasz

PROGRAMMED REVIEW

1. (p. 522) _____—a major loss of contact with shared views of reality—is among the most serious of all mental problems.

2. (p. 522) One of the major characteristics of psychosis is the presence of _____, false beliefs that are held even when the facts contradict them.

3. (p. 522) Some common types of delusion are:
   1) _____ delusions in which people feel they have committed some horrible crime or sinful deed;
   2) _____ delusions, such as belief that one's body is "rotting" away or emitting foul odors;
   3) delusions of _____ in which individuals think they are extremely important persons;
   4) delusions of _____ in which people feel that they are being controlled by other persons or unseen forces;
   5) delusions of _____, in which people feel others are "out to get" them; and
   6) delusions of _____, in which unrelated events are given personal significance (as when it is assumed that a newspaper article or a TV program is giving a special personal message to the person).

4. (p. 522) _____ are sensory experiences that occur in the absence of a stimulus. The most common psychotic hallucination is _____, but people may also feel "insects crawling under their skin," taste "poison" in their food or smell "gas" their "enemies" are using to "get" them.

5. (p. 522) Sensory changes may bring about extreme sensitivity to heat, cold, pain, or touch, or _____, a loss of normal sensitivity.

6. (p. 522) _____ emotions also accompany psychosis. Emotions may swing violently between extremes, or the person may be chronically hyperemotional, depressed, or emotionally "flat" or apathetic. In _____ affect, there are virtually no signs of emotion.

7. (p. 522) These major disturbances coupled with additional problems in thought, speech, memory, actions, and attention bring about _____ _____ and a break with reality.

8. (p. 523)   It is rare to find all these changes occurring at once; usually psychotic behavior occurs in brief _____.

9. (p. 523)   Psychosis does not usually occur without warning. A recent study found that for most psychotic patients, symptoms such as _____, _____ changes, or feeling "high" signaled a coming crisis.

10. (p. 523)   Psychotics are not necessarily totally unresponsive to their surroundings. One experiment found that psychotics who liked the hospital acted very _____ and _____ when interviewed under pretext of possible discharge, while a second group became amazingly free of _____ when interviewed regarding possible open ward privileges.

11. (p. 523)   This experiment shows that psychotic symptoms can be considered a primitive form of _____, the message being "I need help." This explanation becomes particularly evident in view of the universal difficulties psychotics have in _____ verbally with others.

12. (p. 523)   A psychosis based on known brain pathology caused by disease, gunshot wound, accident, etc., is termed an _____ _____, while a psychosis based on unknown or psychological factors is called a _____ _____.

13. (p. 523)   One example of organic psychosis is _____ _____, which occurs in some cases of untreated syphilis. In advanced stages, syphilis attacks brain cells and gradually brings about a deterioration in behavior.

14. (p. 523)   One characteristic of general paresis is a loss of _____, occasionally leading to inappropriate comments, shocking profanity, and obscenity.

15. (p. 524)   A second source of organic psychosis is _____ and _____ poisoning. This problem is of special concern since children who eat old-style paint may become psychotic or retarded.

16. (p. 524)   More subtle sources of lead can also be a problem. Children who live near congested streets may absorb lead from breathing automobile exhaust. Testing shows that this can lead to difficulties in _____ and _____ at school.

17. (p. 524)   Another hidden source of lead is old _____ _____ in schools. Many are contaminated by lead solder or lead-lined coolers.

18. (p. 524)   Probably the greatest cause of organic problems is _____ dementia, caused by premature deterioration of the brain due to circulatory problems, repeated strokes, or general shrinkage and atrophy of the brain.

19. (p. 524)   This problem is typically marked by disturbances in memory, abstract _____, judgment, _____ control, and personality, leaving the individual confused, suspicious, apathetic, or withdrawn.

20. (p. 524)   The most common cause of senile dementia is _____ disease. Other common causes are circulatory problems, repeated strokes, or general shrinkage and atrophy of the brain.

21. (p. 524)   Three major types of functional psychoses are _____

disorders, psychotic _____ disorders, and schizophrenia. There is also a general category called psychotic disorders not elsewhere classified.

22. (p. 524) Alzheimer's disease afflicts about 5 to 10 percent (or about 2 million) Americans over age 65. Its victims at first have difficulty _____ recent events. They slowly become more disoriented, _____, and confused. As their condition worsens, they become unable to read, write, and calculate. Eventually they are _____, _____, and unable to walk, sit up, or smile.

23. (p. 524) It is now known that highly selective damage to nerve cells in the brain is probably the cause of Alzheimer's disease. Especially important is the presence of unusual webs and tangles in nerve cells leading to and from the _____.

24. (p. 524) Important changes also take place in an area called the _____ _____ and in _____ necessary for carrying messages within the brain.

25. (p. 524) By the year 2000, it is estimated that 1 of every _____ adults over 65 will be a victim of Alzheimer's disease. Yet, there is no established treatment.

26. (p. 524) People with _____ disorders usually do not suffer from hallucinations, emotional excesses, or personality disintegration. The main feature of this problem is the presence of deeply held false beliefs.

27. (p. 525) The content of delusions may involve the following types:
1) _____—marked by erotic delusions that one is loved by another, especially by someone famous or of higher status;
2) _____—feeling that one has some great, unrecognized talent, knowledge, or insight or a special relationship with an important person or with God or that one is a prominent person;
3) _____—an all-consuming, unfounded belief that one's spouse or lover is unfaithful;
4) _____—feeling that one is being conspired against, cheated, spied on, followed, poisoned, maligned, or harassed;
5) _____—belief that one's body is diseased or infested with insects or parasites, or that it is emitting foul orders, or that parts of the body are misshapen or defective.

28. (p. 524) The most common delusional disorder, often called _____ _____, centers on delusions of persecution. The evidence such people find to support their beliefs is usually unconvincing to others.

29. (p. 525) Persons suffering paranoid delusions are _____ treated, because it is almost impossible for them to accept that they need help. Anyone who suggests that they have a problem simply becomes part of the "conspiracy" to "persecute" them.

30. (p. 525) Paranoids frequently lead lonely, isolated, and humorless lives marked by constant _____ and _____ towards others. Paranoids are not necessarily dangerous to others, but they can be.

31. (p. 525) Another major type of functional psychosis is _____ _____ disorders marked by persistent and excessive changes in mood or emotion. This problem accounts for about 14 percent of the patients admitted to mental hospitals.

32. (p. 525) In bipolar disorders, persons go "up" or "down" emotionally. The individual may be continuously loud, elated, hyperactive, and energetic (called _____ type) or may swing between this and deep depression (called _____ type).

33. (p. 525) Even when a person is sad and guilt-ridden, the problem is considered a bipolar disorder (_____ type) if the person has ever been manic in the past.

34. (p. 526) The person who only goes "down" emotionally suffers from a _____ _____. If severe depression occurs without any history of mania, it is called a _____ _____.

35. (p. 526) Major mood disorders can be limited primarily to emotional extremes. When persons with major mood disorders also have psychotic symptoms, it is called an _____ _____.

36. (p. 526) Manic individuals throw themselves into fits of activity characterized by extreme distractability, "_____ of ideas," constant _____, and restless _____. Eating or sleeping may be ignored, leading to states of total delirium.

37. (p. 526) Depressive reactions show a reverse pattern in which feelings of failure, sinfulness, worthlessness, and total despair predominate. Such reactions pose a serious threat since _____ attempted during a psychotic depression is rarely a "plea for help."

38. (p. 526) Manic and depressive reactions often appear to be related in bipolar disorders. Manic behavior may be considered an attempt to escape feelings of worthlessness and _____ through frenzied activity.

39. (p. 526) Major mood disorders and affective psychosis usually involve more severe mood distortions than other affective disorders and also involve psychotic delusions and hallucinations. In addition, they appear to be _____ (produced from within), rather than a reaction to external events.

40. (p. 527) Genetics has a role in the causation of major mood disorders, especially bipolar disorders. For example, among children of depressed parents, the rate of depression is _____ even if the children are adopted.

41. (p. 527) Researcher Norman Rosenthal has recently found that some people suffer depression only during the fall and winter months. When these symptoms are lasting and disabling, the problem is called _____ _____ disorder (abbreviated _____).

42. (p. 527) Starting in the fall, people with SAD sleep _____ but more poorly. They feel tired and drowsy and tend to _____. They become more sad, anxious, irritable, and socially withdrawn.

43. (p. 527) Although their depressions are usually only moderately severe, many victims of SAD face winter with foreboding. SAD affects ____ times more women than men, and most victims show signs of suffering from a bipolar disorder.

44. (p. 527) Experts believe that SAD may be related to an increased release of _____ during the winter. This hormone is secreted by the pineal gland to regulate the body's response to changing light conditions.

45. (p. 527)   SAD patients can be helped by exposure to very bright, full-spectrum fluorescent light, a treatment called _____. This has relieved depression with 3 to 7 days for 80 percent of those treated.

46. (p. 527)   _____ accounts for approximately half of all admissions to mental hospitals. One person in 100 will develop this psychosis. Most are young adults, but it can occur at any age.

47. (p. 527)   Schizophrenia does not refer to having more than one personality. Rather, schizophrenia can be interpreted to mean _____-_____, referring to a split between _____ and _____.

48. (p. 527)   Schizophrenia is often confused with a personality disorder that somewhat resembles it. The _____ _____ develops gradually, usually starting in adolescence. The individual becomes ever more withdrawn and isolated from his or her surroundings, displaying dulled emotions and peculiar behavior.

49. (p. 528)   In schizophrenia, emotions may become blunted or _____, or they may be very _____.

50. (p. 528)   In addition, schizophrenia is characterized by _____ from contact with others and a loss of interest in _____ activities; a breakdown of personal _____ and ability to deal with daily events; and delusions, hallucinations, and thought abnormalities.

51. (p. 528)   Schizophrenic delusions can be particularly bizarre. They often include the idea that the person's thoughts and actions are being _____, that his or her thoughts are being _____ so others can hear them, that thoughts have been "_____" into the person's mind, or that thoughts have been _____.

52. (p. 528)   In _____ schizophrenia (also called hebephrenic schizophrenia) the individual's personality disintegrates almost completely, resulting in silliness, laughter, bizarre and often obscene behavior. It typically develops in early adolescence or young adulthood, often preceded by serious personality disorganization in earlier years. Chances of improvement are limited and social impairment is usually extreme.

53. (p. 529)   In _____ _____ the person seems to be in a state of total panic. This situation brings about a stuporous condition in which odd positions may be held for hours or days.

54. (p. 529)   In catatonic schizophrenia, _____ _____ may occur in which the person can be arranged into any position like a mannequin. This immobility suggests that catatonic individuals are struggling desperately to control their inner turmoil because stupor occasionally gives way to a _____ _____, outbursts of agitated and sometimes violent behavior.

55. (p. 529)   _____ plus a marked decrease in responsiveness to the environment makes the catatonic patient difficult to "reach."

56. (p. 529)   The most common form of schizophrenic disorder is _____ _____. Like a paranoid delusional disorder, this condition centers around delusions of grandeur and persecution, but there is a major

_____ _____ not evident in
paranoid psychosis.

57. (p. 529) The paranoid schizophrenic also experiences _____
and has _____ that are more bizarre, fragmented, and uncon-
vincing than those of the paranoid. Such individuals may sometimes feel forced into
violence to protect themselves.

58. (p. 529) There is considerable overlap among the types of schizophrenia, with patients often
shifting from one pattern of behavior to another at different times during the course
of the psychosis. Many are simply classified as suffering from
_____ _____.

59. (p. 529) Some experts suspect that early _____
_____ may contribute to the later development of schizophrenia. Case
studies have found a greater than average degree of childhood stress among schizophrenics.

60. (p. 529) Many psychologists theorize that a _____ _____
environment is another risk factor in schizophrenia. For example, R.D. Laing
suggests that schizophrenia is an escape from unsolvable emotional conflicts.

61. (p. 529) Laing has claimed that the families of schizophrenics frequently engage in
_____-_____ communication where the listener is in a "no-win"
situation.

62. (p. 530) Support for this comes from a recent 15-year follow-up study of disturbed adolescents
which found that the families of persons most likely to become disturbed interacted
in ways that were laden with _____, conflict, _____,
prying, criticism, negativity, and emotional _____.

63. (p. 530) Although attractive, environmental explanations of schizophrenia are incomplete.
When the children of schizophrenic parents are raised away from their home environment, they are just as likely to become psychotic. Thus, children may inherit a
_____ for schizophrenia.

64. (p. 530) The _____ quadruplets are an interesting example of how heredity and
environment can influence the chances of schizophrenia. All four girls became ill
before age 25 and have since been in and out of mental hospitals. A nightmarish
family life and possible susceptibility to schizophrenia both seem to have been
present.

65. (p. 531) This tendency is shown by studies with identical twins. If one twin becomes schizophrenic, there is a _____ percent chance the other will also.

66. (p. 531) If both parents are schizophrenic, a child has a _____ percent chance of developing
the disorder; persons with a brother or sister and one parent who are schizophrenic
run a _____ percent risk themselves; with a brother or sister the risk is _____
percent, and for fraternal twins the chances of mutual schizophrenia is about _____
percent.

67. (p. 531) These figures can be compared to the risk of developing schizophrenia for the population in general, which is ___ percent.

68. (p. 531) The fact that LSD, PCP and similar drugs produce effects that mimic the symptoms
of psychosis has led many scientists to believe that psychosis may be based on

_____ _____ which cause the
body to produce some substance similar to a psychedelic drug.

69. (p. 531) This notion is further supported by the fact that _____
which are effective in treating an LSD overdose are effective in treatment of
schizophrenia.

70. (p. 531) Many researchers now believe that schizophrenia is directly related to overactivity in
brain systems involving _____, an important chemical messenger.

71. (p. 531) In support of this link, it is known that large doses of _____
which raise dopamine levels produce symptoms almost identical to paranoid schizophrenia. Also, all major _____ drugs block the action
of dopamine at receptor areas in the brain.

72. (p. 533) No extra or abnormal amounts of dopamine exist in the brains of schizophrenics, but
they do have nearly _____ the normal number of dopamine
_____. Many are found in the limbic system (a major emotional
system of the brain).

73. (p. 533) Many scientists now believe that dopamine activation triggers a flood of unrelated
thoughts, feelings, and perceptions, and directly accounts for the _____,
_____, _____ and
other disturbances of schizophrenia. Because of the extra receptors, schizophrenics
may get psychedelic effects from normal levels of dopamine in the brain.

74. (p. 533) Two new medical techniques are making it possible to directly observe the schizophrenic brain. The CT (_____ _____) scan
provides an x-ray picture of the brain.

75. (p. 533) In about one out of 10 young schizophrenics, the brain shows wider surface
_____ and enlarged _____ (fluid-filled spaces
within the brain). The meaning of such changes is still in doubt.

76. (p. 533) A second new technique, a PET (_____ _____
_____) scan, provides an image of brain activity by measuring
how much of a radioactive sugar solution is used in each area of the brain.

77. (p. 534) These measurements are translated into a colored map, or _____, of brain
activity. Distinct patterns linked with schizophrenia, mood disorders, and other
problems have been found using this technique.

78. (p. 535) Two basic forms of treatment for psychosis can be distinguished. The first, called
_____, can be described as two people talking about
one person's problems. A second major approach to treatment is _____
(or _____) therapy.

79. (p. 535) One of the main somatic treatments is _____, the use of
drugs to control or alleviate the symptoms of emotional disturbance.

80. (p. 535) Chemotherapy is more frequently used to combat _____, but may
also be used to relieve the anxiety attacks and other discomforts of nonpsychotic
disorders.

81. (p. 535) The three major classes of drugs include _____ _____
used to calm anxious or agitated persons, _____ used to improve the

mood of those who are depressed, and _____ used to control the hallucinations and other symptoms of psychosis.

82. (p. 535)　While drugs have improved the chances of recovery from a psychiatric disorder, there are some drawbacks. First of all, drugs generally do not _____ mental illness. Patients may separate temporary improvement caused by a drug from improvement they consider genuine.

83. (p. 536)　Also, there is the problem of side effects. For example, as many as _____ percent of patients taking major tranquilizers for extended periods develop _____ _____, a neurological condition where patients develop rhythmical facial and mouth movements, as well as unusual movements of the limbs and other parts of the body.

84. (p. 536)　Perhaps the most valid criticism of chemotherapy is the simple observation that it is _____. Many critics feel that the locks that came off the doors of old-style asylums have simply been replaced by "chemical locks."

85. (p. 536)　Another principal somatic treatment is _____ _____, abbreviated _____, a rather drastic medical treatment used mainly for depression, in which convulsions are produced by electric current.

86. (p. 536)　About _____ volts of electrical current are passed through the brain for slightly less than a second over a series of 6 to ___ sessions spread over 3 to ___ weeks.

87. (p. 536)　Proponents of ECT claim that shock-induced seizures alter the _____ balance in the brain, bringing an end to severe depression and suicidal behavior.

88. (p. 536)　Others have charged that ECT works only by _____ patients so they can't remember why they were depressed.

89. (p. 536)　Critics claim that ECT causes permanent _____ losses and occasional _____ damage. Proponents argue that detailed brain scans show no evidence of damage.

90. (p. 536)　It has been reported recently that if electrodes are applied to only _____ _____ of the head, memory loss is greatly reduced. However, this may not end depression.

91. (p. 536)　As is true of chemotherapy, the major problem with ECT seems to lie in _____ and _____. ECT is still considered by many to be a valid treatment for selected cases of depression.

92. (p. 536)　Most experts seem to agree on the following:
　　1) At best, ECT produces only _____ improvement.
　　2) ECT does cause permanent _____ losses in many patients.
　　3) ECT should be used as a last resort after _____ therapy has failed.

93. (p. 536)　The most extreme type of somatic therapy is _____, a general term applied to any surgical alteration of the brain.

94. (p. 537)　The best known psychosurgery is the _____ _____, where the frontal lobes are surgically disconnected from other areas of the brain.

95. (p. 537)　The original goal of this procedure when introduced in the 1940s was to _____ a person who had not responded to any other type of treatment. But later studies

showed that the effects are quite inconsistent and that it produces a high rate of undesirable _____ _____, such as seizures, extreme lack of emotional response, and even stupor.

96. (p. 537) While the lobotomy has been abandoned, psychosurgery is still considered a valid treatment by many neurosurgeons. Most now use _____ _____ techniques in which small target areas are destroyed in the brain's interior.

97. (p. 537) The appeal of deep lesioning is that it can have fairly specific effects. For instance, a patient with uncontrollable _____ impulses may be calmed by psychosurgery.

98. (p. 537) It is worth remembering that all forms of psychosurgery are _____. Because of continued controversy over psychosurgery, it is perhaps most accurate, even after decades of use, to describe it as an "experimental" technique.

99. (p. 537) Somatic therapy, psychotherapy, and other techniques may require a special setting or special control for a period of time. Traditionally, this fact has meant _____, which may itself be considered a form of treatment since it removes a troubled individual from situations that may be provoking or maintaining the problem.

100. (p. 537) In the last 20 years, the resident population in large mental hospitals has been reduced by _____-_____. Hospital stays are now held to a minimum through use of _____-_____ policies in which patients are released as soon as possible and readmitted only if necessary.

101. (p. 537) Support for this policy comes from research showing that most psychiatric patients do as well with _____-_____ hospitalization as they do with _____.

102. (p. 538) Unfortunately, this policy has not been very successful. Many chronic patients are being discharged to a lonely existence in hostile communities without adequate care. A large percentage of homeless persons interviewed recently at an emergency shelter had _____ problems.

103. (p. 538) Large mental hospitals may no longer be warehouses for society's unwanted, but many former patients are no better off consigned to bleak lives in nursing homes, single-room hotels, and _____-and-_____ homes. As much as anything, a simple lack of sufficient _____ prevents large numbers of people from getting the care they need.

104. (p. 538) A bright spot in the area of mental health care has been the passage of federal legislation to encourage creation of _____ _____ _____ centers. They have two primary goals: to directly aid troubled citizens and to promote _____ through consultation, education, and crisis intervention.

105. (p. 538) These centers have made mental health services more accessible than ever before. Much of their work is made possible by _____, individuals who work under the supervision of more highly trained staff.

106. (p. 539) David Rosenhan gained entrance to mental hospitals by complaining of hearing voices. In _____ out of 12 tries, he and his colleagues were admitted with a diagnosis of _____. None of the researchers was ever recognized by hospital staff as a phony patient.

107. (p. 539) Rosenhan spent from one to seven weeks in hospitals before being discharged and found that contact between staff and patients was very limited. Attendants and staff only spent an average of _____ percent of their time out of the glassed-in central compartment in the ward; daily therapist contact averaged about _____ minutes.

108. (p. 539) In a follow-up study, the staff of another hospital was warned that one or more pseudo-patients were going to try to gain admission. Among 193 candidates, _____ were labeled "fakes" and _____ more "suspicious" despite the fact that Rosenhan never sent any patients.

109. (p. 539) All of the normal people who served as pseudo-patients in the original studies were discharged as schizophrenics "in _____" (temporarily free of symptoms). The label that prevented hospital staff from seeing the normality of the researchers stayed with them when they left.

110. (p. 540) These findings carry an important message: _____ can be dangerous. It is more productive to label _____ than to label people.

111. (p. 541) Thomas Szasz has charged that medical concepts of disease have been wrongly applied to emotional problems. The "_____ _____," as this is called, treats such problems as "diseases" with "symptoms" that can be "cured."

112. (p. 541) Szasz believes that "mental illness" is just an idea used when trying to deal with _____ _____. He thinks such labels are used mainly to transform people from being responsible for their actions to non-responsible "patients" who need pity and therapy.

113. (p. 541) Szasz points out that "mental illness" labels do not explain anything. They are merely used to deal with persons whose behavior creates a _____ _____ or violates social rules.

114. (p. 541) It follows that if a person acts in a way that "offends" society and a law exists against such acts, the person may be jailed. If no law exists, the person may be "treated." Thus the distinction between madness and badness is a _____ judgment, not a medical reality.

115. (p. 541) He prefers to view emotional disturbances as "_____ in _____," making the goal of therapy "change" and the individual a "client."

116. (p. 541) Szasz's views have led him to question the handling of the civil rights of psychiatric "patients." He estimates that _____ percent of all patients in mental hospitals are there involuntarily. He feels it is indefensible to commit people because they *might* be dangerous.

117. (p. 541) According to Szasz, the only legitimate reason for depriving a person of freedom is for being "_____ to _____," but then only if the person has broken the law by committing violence or by threatening to do so.

SELF-TEST

1. (p. 522) Which of the following is *not* a correct match?
    a. delusion of reference—individuals think they are extremely important
    b. somatic delusion—individuals feel their bodies are rotting away and emitting foul odors

c. depressive delusion—persons feel they have committed some horrible crime or sinful deed

d. delusion of influence—persons feel they are being controlled by other persons or unseen forces

2. (p. 522)   Among psychotics, the most common hallucination is
    a. hearing voices.
    b. seeing objects fly around the room.
    c. seeing places or people related to the source of the psychosis.
    d. feeling vibrations.

3. (p. 522)   A characteristic feature of psychosis, _____ _____, means that there are virtually no signs of emotion.
    a. personality disintegration   c. emotional anesthesia
    b. depressive episodes   d. flat affect

4. (p. 523)   True-False. Typically, pychotic behavior occurs in brief episodes rather than patients displaying bizarre behaviors nearly all the time.

5. (p. 523)   General paresis is an example of
    a. organic psychosis.   c. senile psychosis.
    b. functional psychosis.   d. paranoid psychosis.

6. (p. 524)   True-False. A psychosis produced by mercury poisoning would be classified as a functional disorder since it is produced by an environmental factor.

7. (p. 524)   Which of the following is *not* true of senile dementia?
    a. It is probably the most common form of organic psychosis.
    b. It is associated with a loss of inhibition leading to shocking profanity and obscenity.
    c. It is closely associated with brain deterioration due to circulatory problems or repeated strokes.
    d. The person is usually confused, suspicious, apathetic, or withdrawn.

8. (p. 525)   Which of the following is *not* true of persons suffering paranoid delusions?
    a. They are rarely treated or admitted to mental hospitals.
    b. They suffer from hallucinations, emotional excesses, or personality disintegration.
    c. Most often, paranoid delusions center on feelings of persecution.
    d. Paranoids are not necessarily dangerous to others, but they can be.

9. (p. 525)   Which of the following is *not* true of major mood disorders?
    a. They account for about 14 percent of patients admitted to mental hospitals.
    b. They are characterized by persistent and excessive changes in mood or emotion.
    c. They appear to be a reaction to external events rather than endogenous.
    d. Three types include manic, depressive, and mixed.

10. (p. 526)   Constant talking, flights of ideas, extreme distractibility, restless movements, failure to eat or sleep, and incoherent, agitated, out of control behavior characterizes
    a. manic type bipolar disorder.   c. schizotypal personality disorders.
    b. disorganized schizophrenia.   d. senile dementia.

11. (p. 526)   True-False. Manic behavior can be viewed as a reaction of individuals trying to escape depression and therefore produces symptoms commonly associated with depression.

12. (p. 527) Approximately _____ of all admissions to mental hospitals are diagnosed as
schizophrenic.
a. 1/3
b. 1/2
c. 2/3
d. 3/4

13. (p. 527) Which of the following is *not* true of the schizotypal personality?
a. It is often confused with schizophrenia.
b. Affected individuals gradually become withdrawn and isolated.
c. Such individuals are usually seen as colorful or exotic; they display an exaggerated
range of emotions.
d. This disorder develops slowly, usually starting in adolescence.

14. (p. 528) Which type of schizophrenia is marked by almost complete personality disintegration
resulting in silliness, laughter, bizarre and often obscene behavior?
a. simple
b. disorganized
c. catatonic
d. paranoid

15. (p. 529) In _____ schizophrenia, the person seems to be in a state of panic which
produces a stuporous condition.
a. simple
b. disorganized
c. catatonic
d. paranoid

16. (p. 529) True-False. Waxy flexibility refers to the glassy-eyed look of catatonic schizophrenia.

17. (p. 529) The most common form of schizophrenic disorder is
a. simple.
b. disorganized.
c. catatonic.
d. paranoid.

18. (p. 529) True-False. There are only minor differences between the symptoms of a paranoid
delusional disorder and paranoid schizophrenia.

19. (p. 529) True-False. Although difficult to treat, the symptoms used in classifying schizophrenic patients are very straightforward. Patients can be easily classified into one
or the other of the categories.

20. (p. 529) True-False. Schizophrenia is caused solely by psychological trauma at an early age.

21. (p. 531) If one identical twin becomes schizophrenic, the chances of the other twin becoming
schizophrenic are
a. 23%.
b. 46%.
c. 79%.
d. 10%.

22. (p. 531) Which of the following drugs are effective in the treatment of schizophrenia?
a. amphetamines
b. phenothiazines
c. adrenochromes
d. psychedelics

23. (p. 531) Evidence is mounting that the biochemical basis for schizophrenia may be linked with
which system?
a. noradrenaline-cortical
b. dopamine-limbic
c. tardive dyskinesia
d. prefrontal lobes

24. (p. 533) True-False. It now appears that schizophrenics may have an overabundance of dopamine in their limbic systems, thus accounting for their bizarre abnormal behavior.

25. (p. 533) True-False. Observations of the brain using a CT scan shows that one in 10 schizophrenic brains has wider surface fissures and enlarged ventricles.

26. (p. 533) The PET scan is
    a. a technique which produces an x-ray picture of the brain.
    b. a type of psychosurgery considered far more effective and reliable than a prefrontal lobotomy.
    c. a term used by Laing to describe the dysfunctional family systems of many schizophrenics.
    d. a technique which produces a colored map illustrating brain activity.

27. (p. 535) Which of the following is *not* a major class of drugs used in chemotherapy?
    a. psychedelics   c. antipsychotics
    b. minor tranquilizers   d. energizers

28. (p. 536) Which of the following is a neurological side effect of extended major tranquilizer usage?
    a. deep lesioning   c. senility
    b. mutism   d. tardive dyskinesia

29. (p. 536) Which of the following is not a criticism that has been directed at chemotherapy?
    a. does not "cure," only temporarily relieves symptoms
    b. adverse drug side-effects
    c. overuse
    d. has no advantages over long-term hospitalization

30. (p. 536) ECT is used primarily in treating
    a. mania.   c. paranoia.
    b. depression.   d. psychosis.

31. (p. 537) True-False. Prefrontal lobotomies are still widely performed in cases of chronic, agitated schizophrenia.

32. (p. 537) True-False. Studies have shown that patients do as well with 3-4 weeks of hospitalization as they do with 3-4 month periods.

33. (p. 538) True-False. The aim of community mental health centers is to provide direct treatment services and prevention programs.

34. (p. 539) True-False. David Rosenhan and his associates found it very difficult to gain admission to mental hospitals by faking symptoms.

35. (p. 541) Which of the following is *not* true of the position taken by Thomas Szasz?
    a. He believes emotional disturbances should be viewed as problems in living.
    b. Involuntary commitment involves a serious loss of civil rights.
    c. A medical model should be applied to our treatment of the mentally ill.
    d. People should not be hospitalized just because they might be dangerous to themselves.

ANSWERS — PROGRAMMED REVIEW

1. Psychosis
2. delusions
3. depressive; somatic; grandeur; influence; persecution; reference
4. Hallucinations; hearing voices
5. anesthesia
6. Disturbed; flat
7. personality disintegration

8. episodes
9. insomnia; emotional
10. bizarre, disturbed; symptoms
11. communication; communicating
12. organic psychosis; functional psychosis
13. general paresis
14. inhibition
15. lead, mercury
16. thinking, attention
17. drinking fountains
18. senile
19. reasoning; impulse
20. Alzheimer's
21. delusional; mood
22. remembering; suspicious; mute; bedridden
23. hippocampus
24. nucleus basilis; chemicals
25. 10
26. delusional
27. erotomanic; grandiose; jealous; persecutory; somatic
28. paranoid psychosis
29. rarely
30. suspicion; hostility
31. major mood
32. manic; mixed
33. depressive
34. unipolar disorder; major depression
35. affective psychosis
36. flights; talking; movement
37. suicide
38. depression
39. endogenous
40. higher
41. seasonal affective
42. longer; overeat
43. 4
44. melatonin
45. phototherapy
46. Schizophrenia
47. split-mind; thought; emotion
48. schizotypal personality
49. flat; inappropriate
50. withdrawal; external; habits
51. controlled; broadcast; inserted; removed
52. disorganized
53. catatonic schizophrenia
54. waxy flexibility; catatonic episode
55. Mutism
56. paranoid schizophrenia; personality disintegration
57. hallucinations; delusions
58. undifferentiated psychosis
59. psychological trauma
60. disturbed family

61. double-bind
62. confusion; guilt; attacks
63. potential
64. Genain
65. 46
66. 46; 17; 10; 14
67. 1
68. biological abnormalities
69. phenothiazines
70. dopamine
71. amphetamines; antipsychotic
72. double; receptors
73. voices, hallucinations, delusions
74. computed tomography
75. fissures; ventricles
76. positron emission tomography
77. scan
78. psychotherapy; somatic; bodily
79. chemotherapy
80. psychosis
81. minor tranquilizers; energizers; antipsychotics
82. cure
83. 10; tardive dyskinesia
84. overused
85. electroconvulsive therapy; ECT
86. 150; 8; 4
87. biochemical
88. confusing
89. memory; brain
90. one side
91. overuse; misuse
92. temporary; memory; drug
93. psychosurgery
94. prefrontal lobotomy
95. calm; side effects
96. deep lesioning
97. aggressive
98. irreversible
99. hospitalization
100. two-thirds; revolving-door
101. short-term; longer
102. psychiatric
103. board-and-care; funding
104. community mental health; prevention
105. paraprofessionals
106. 11; schizophrenia
107. 11.3; seven
108. 43; 19
109. remission
110. labels; problems
111. medical model
112. disturbing behavior
113. social disturbance
114. moral

115. problems in living
116. 90
117. dangerous to others

ANSWERS — SELF-TEST

1. a		19. False
2. a		20. False
3. d		21. b
4. True		22. b
5. a		23. b
6. False		24. False
7. b		25. True
8. b		26. d
9. c		27. a
10. a		28. d
11. False		29. d
12. b		30. b
13. c		31. False
14. b		32. True
15. c		33. True
16. False		34. False
17. d		35. c
18. False		

Chapter 21

Insight Therapy

CONTENTS

Psychotherapy—Getting Better by the Hour
Origins of Therapy—Bored Skulls and Hysteria on the Couch
Psychoanalysis—Expedition into the Unconscious
Humanistic Therapies—Restoring Human Potential
Group Therapy—People Who Need People
Transactional Analysis—Different Strokes for Different Folks
Psychotherapy—An Overview
Seeking Professional Help—When, Where, and How?
Becoming a Community Mental Health Resource—How to Help
A Therapist Named Eliza

TERMS AND CONCEPTS

psychotherapy
individual therapy
group therapy
insight therapy
action therapy
directive therapy
non-directive therapy
time-limited therapy
trepanning
demonology
exorcism
ergotism
hysteria
psychoanalysis
free association
dream analysis
manifest content
latent content
dream symbols
analysis of resistance
analysis of transference
short-term dynamic therapy

spontaneous remission
humanistic therapies
client-centered therapy
non-directive approach
unconditional positive regard
empathy
authenticity
reflection
existential therapy
logotherapy
confrontation
Gestalt theory
directive approach
psychodrama
role playing
role reversals
family therapy
sensitivity groups
encounter groups
large group awareness training
therapy placebo effect
transactional analysis (TA)

ego-states
Child
Parent
Adult
crossed transactions

ulterior transactions
games
emotional rapport
catharsis

IMPORTANT INDIVIDUALS

Philippe Pinel
Sigmund Freud
H. J. Eysenck
Carl Rogers
Victor Frankl

Frederick (Fritz) Perls
Jacob L. Moreno
Eric Berne
Joseph Weizenbaum

PROGRAMMED REVIEW

1. (p. 545) _____ is any psychological technique designed
    to facilitate positive changes in a person's personality, behavior, or adjustment. The
    term most often refers to verbal interaction between trained mental health
    professionals and their clients.

2. (p. 545) Popular accounts tend to depict psychotherapy as a complete personal transforma-
    tion. But as Bernie Zilbergeld points out, therapy is not equally effective for all
    problems. Chances of improvement are fairly good for _____, low
    self-esteem, some _____ problems, and _____,
    conflicts.

3. (p. 545) More complex problems can be difficult to treat. Therapy usually does not bring
    about dramatic changes in behavior or an end to personal problems. For many people,
    therapy's major benefit is that it provides _____, _____,
    and a way to make positive changes.

4. (p. 545) Psychotherapy need not be undertaken only as a means of solving a deep psychological
    problem or an immediate crisis; some therapies are designed to encourage
    _____ _____ and enrichment for people who are already
    functioning effectively.

5. (p. 546) _____ therapy is defined by therapy sessions involving
    only one client and one therapist.

6. (p. 546) _____ therapy involves therapy sessions in which several clients partici-
    pate at one time with one or more therapists.

7. (p. 546) _____ therapy is any psychotherapy whose goal is to lead clients to
    a deeper understanding of their thoughts, emotions, and behavior.

8. (p. 546) _____ therapy is any therapy designed to bring about direct changes in
    troublesome thoughts, habits, feelings, or behavior.

9. (p. 546) _____ therapy is any approach in which the therapist
    provides strong guidance during therapy sessions.

10. (p. 546) _____-_____ therapy is a style of therapy in which

clients assume responsibility for solving their own problems; the therapist assists but does not guide or give advice.

11. (p. 546) _____-_____ therapy is any therapy begun with the expectation that it will last only a certain limited number of sessions.

12. (p. 546) Attempts to cure psychological problems have occurred throughout history. During the Stone Age, spirits were released from the head by a process called _____, where a hole was bored, chipped, or bashed into the skull.

13. (p. 546) During the Middle Ages, treatment for the mentally ill in Europe focused on _____. Abnormal behavior was attributed to supernatural forces. As treatment, _____ was used to drive out such evil.

14. (p. 546) One explanation for the rise of demonology may lie in a condition called _____. Eating bread made from tainted rye containing ergot fungus may have produced pinching sensations, convulsions, muscle twitches, facial spasms, delirium and hallucinations which made people appear "possessed."

15. (p. 546) Finally, a more compassionate view of the mentally ill emerged after 1793 when _____ _____ changed the Bicetre Asylum in Paris from a "mad house" to a mental hospital by personally unchaining the inmates.

16. (p. 546) The first true psychotherapy was developed around the turn of the century by _____ _____. He called it _____.

17. (p. 546) Freud sought to understand and treat cases of _____, where physical symptoms like paralysis or numbness occur without known physical cause. Such problems are now called somatoform disorders.

18. (p. 547) Freud's patients usually reclined on a couch during therapy as a means of encouraging _____ and a free flow of thoughts and images from the _____. This procedure is the least important characteristic of psychoanalysis and one that has been abandoned by many modern analysts.

19. (p. 548) Freud's theory stressed that _____ memories, motives, and conflicts—especially instinctual drives for sex and aggression—are the cause of neurosis. These factors force a person to develop rigid defense mechanisms and to devote excessive amounts of time and energy to compulsive and self-defeating behavior.

20. (p. 548) Freud relied on four basic techniques to uncover the unconscious roots of neurosis. One of these, _____ _____, required the patient to say whatever came to mind without regard for whether it made sense, or was painful or embarrassing.

21. (p. 548) Freud considered a second technique, _____ _____, to be especially helpful because supposedly forbidden desires and unconscious feelings are more freely expressed in dreams.

22. (p. 548) In analyzing dreams, Freud distinguished between the _____ (obvious, visible) content and the _____ (hidden) content. The latter he sought to reveal by interpreting dream _____.

23. (p. 548)   When associating or describing dreams, the patient may _____ talking or thinking about certain topics. Such _____ are said to reveal particularly important unconscious conflicts.

24. (p. 548)   The individual undergoing psychoanalysis may _____ feelings to the therapist that relate to important past relationships with others. This process is considered a prime opportunity to help the patient undergo an emotional _____, where repressed emotions can be recognized and understood.

25. (p. 548)   Psychoanalysts have become relatively rare since most people cannot afford ____ to ____ therapy sessions a week for up to ____ years.

26. (p. 549)   Today, most psychoanalytic therapists have switched to doing short-term _____ therapy. They rely on _____ _____ to more rapidly uncover unconscious conflicts. They also seek to actively provoke emotional reactions that lower defenses and provide insights.

27. (p. 549)   The development of newer, more streamlined dynamic therapies is in part due to questions about the _____ of traditional psychoanalysis.

28. (p. 549)   Psychologist H. J. Eysenck has suggested that psychoanalysis takes so long that patients improve due to the mere passage of time. This improvement is called _____ _____.

29. (p. 549)   To support his argument, Eysenck cites research showing that people placed on waiting lists _____ at the same rate as those who begin therapy. However, more recent work affirms that psychoanalysis is usually _____ than no treatment at all.

30. (p. 549)   The goal of Freudian therapy is _____. The humanistic therapies seek to help people make full use of their _____.

31. (p. 549)   Psychoanalysts delve into childhood, dreams, and the unconscious. Humanistic psychologist Carl Rogers, creator of _____-_____ therapy, has found it more productive to explore _____ thoughts and feelings.

32. (p. 550)   Rogers believes that the psychoanalyst tends to take a position of authority about what is wrong with the patient that may not be right or valuable to the client. Thus, Rogers uses a _____-_____ approach in that the client determines what will be discussed during each session.

33. (p. 550)   The therapist's job is to create an "atmosphere of growth" by maintaining four basic conditions. First, the therapist offers the client _____ _____—the client is accepted totally.

34. (p. 550)   Second, the therapist attempts to achieve genuine _____ for the client by trying to view the world through the client's eyes.

35. (p. 550)   As a third condition, the therapist strives to be _____ in his or her relationship with clients.

36. (p. 550)   Fourth, rather than making interpretations, posing solutions, or offering advice, the

therapist _____ the client's thoughts and feelings and serves as a psychological "mirror."

37. (p. 550) _____ therapy focuses on problems of existence or "being in the world." Its goals are self-knowledge and self-actualization.

38. (p. 551) While client-centered therapy seeks to uncover a "true self," existential therapy emphasizes the idea of _____ _____. Through choices one can become the person he or she wants to be.

39. (p. 551) Existential therapy attempts to restore meaning and vitality to life so that the individual has the _____ to make rewarding and socially constructive choices.

40. (p. 551) Typically, existential therapy focuses on the "ultimate concerns" of human existence: death, _____, _____, and _____.

41. (p. 551) One example of existential therapy is Victor Frankl's _____, developed on the basis of experiences in a _____ _____ camp. Frankl felt that those who survived with their sanity did so because they had managed to hold on to a sense of _____ (logos).

42. (p. 551) Like most existential therapists, Frankl uses a very flexible approach centered around _____ in which the person is challenged to examine the quality of his or her existence and choices, and to _____ the unique and intense here-and-now interaction of two human beings.

43. (p. 551) _____ therapy, which is most often associated with Frederick (Fritz) Perls, is built around the idea that perception or awareness becomes disjointed and incomplete in the maladjusted individual.

44. (p. 551) The Gestalt approach is more _____ than either client-centered therapy or existential therapy, and it places a special emphasis on immediate experience.

45. (p. 551) The German word Gestalt means _____, or complete. The Gestalt therapist seeks to help the individual rebuild thinking, feeling, and acting into connected wholes. This is achieved by expanding personal awareness, by accepting responsibility for one's thoughts, feelings, and actions, and by filling in gaps in experience.

46. (p. 551) Gestalt therapists believe that we often shy away from expressing or "owning" upsetting feelings. This creates a _____ in self-awareness that may become a barrier to personal growth. The Gestalt therapist encourages the individual to become more aware of his or her _____ _____.

47. (p. 551) In all his work, Perls emphasized that emotional health comes from getting in touch with what you _____ to do, not what you _____ do, _____ to do, or should want to do.

48. (p. 552) Above all else, Gestalt therapy emphasizes _____ experience. Clients are urged to focus on immediate reactions with the goal being to live now, live here.

49. (p. 552) In _____ _____, a person can act out, or directly experience, problems in addition to talking about them. Also, support is provided by other members who share similar problems.

50. (p. 552)   Groups also help form a bridge between _____ and _____-
               _____ problems by providing a situation that is more realistic than the
               protected atmosphere of individual therapy. A number of specialized group
               techniques have emerged.

51. (p. 552)   One of the first group approaches was developed by Jacob L. Moreno, who called his
               technique _____. Through this technique, an individual
               _____ _____ (acts out) dramatic incidents resembling those that cause
               problems in real life.

52. (p. 552)   Therapists using the role-playing technique of psychodrama often find _____
               _____ especially helpful. For example, a teenage boy could be asked to
               role play his father or mother in order to better understand their feelings.

53. (p. 552)   In _____ therapy, husband, wife, and children work as a group to
               resolve the problems of each family member. This approach tends to be brief and
               focused on specific problems.

54. (p. 553)   Family therapists believe that problems are rarely limited to a _____
               family member: a problem for one is considered a problem for all. Thus, everyone
               works together to solve the problems.

55. (p. 553)   Talk-radio psychology raises some important questions. In defense of themselves,
               such psychologists point out that listeners may learn solutions to their own problems
               by hearing others talk. Many also stress that their work is
               _____, not _____.

56. (p. 553)   The American Psychological Association has taken the position that media psycholo-
               gists should discuss only problems of a _____ _____,
               instead of actually _____ a person.

57. (p. 554)   Sensitivity groups tend to be less _____ than encounter
               groups; the focus is more on extending sensitivity to oneself and others. As one
               example, the "_____ _____," in which blindfolded participants are led
               about by "guides," is a typical exercise used to develop trust and confidence in others.

58. (p. 554)   In _____ groups, more intense emotion and communication
               may take place. Here, the emphasis is on tearing down defenses and false fronts
               through discussion that can be brutally honest.

59. (p. 554)   Because there is a danger of hostile confrontation and psychological damage,
               encounter group participation is safest when members are carefully
               _____ and a _____ leader guides the group.

60. (p. 554)   The basic principles of sensitivity and encounter groups are still used by many
               _____ to improve employee morale and relationships. Spe-
               cially designed encounter groups for _____ couples are also widely
               held.

61. (p. 554)   Lifespring, Actualizations, and est are examples of _____
               awareness training. They combine psychological exercises, confrontation, new
               viewpoints, and group dynamics to promote personal change.

62. (p. 554)   While such groups may fill some need not met by society or traditional psychotherapy,
               there is little evidence that these experiences are truly _____.

63. (p. 554) Many of the claimed benefits may simply result from a kind of _____ _____ effect related to positive expectations, a break in daily routine, and an excuse to act differently.

64. (p. 554) _____ _____ (TA) is a therapy that blends humanistic thought with some updated elements of psychoanalysis.

65. (p. 554) TA teaches people a model of behavior to use in becoming more aware of themselves and their interactions with others — especially those involving various "_____." Because TA emphasizes relationships, it is often conducted as a _____ therapy.

66. (p. 554) The personality scheme of TA proposed by Eric Berne postulates three basic parts or _____-_____ that can be distinguished from each other by distinct behaviors, words, tones, gestures, attitudes, and expressions.

67. (p. 554) The _____ is a carry-over from youth that can be primitive, impulsive, demanding, creative, playful, or manipulative.

68. (p. 554) The _____ ego-state is an internal record of all the messages received from one's parents or other authority figures as personality developed. It can be evaluative and restrictive, or nurturing and allowing.

69. (p. 554) The _____ is a mature and rational decision-making part of the personality that, when in charge, allows an individual to explore alternatives and their consequences and decide which ego-state is needed.

70. (p. 555) Using this ego-state system, troubled relationships are seen as _____ transactions, where a message sent from one ego-state is answered by statements from another ego-state.

71. (p. 555) Also, in an _____ transaction, the exchange appears to take place on one level, but actually takes place on another.

72. (p. 555) Ulterior transactions form the basis of _____, indirect ways of communicating such as the "if it weren't for you" game that is very common in marriage.

73. (p. 555) In surveys of hundreds of studies of psychotherapy and counseling, a modest but consistent _____ for therapy was found to exist. Though based on averages, overall it was effective for more people than not.

74. (p. 555) A recent analysis of over 2400 patients found that about _____ felt better after only 8 therapy sessions (or in about 2 months of weekly one hour sessions). After 26 sessions (or about 6 months), roughly _____ had improved.

75. (p. 556) One author writing in 1959 counted at least 36 major systems of psychotherapy. The count could easily exceed _____ today.

76. (p. 556) All of the psychotherapies discussed include some combination of the following goals: insight, resolution of _____, an improved sense of _____, a change in unacceptable patterns of _____, better _____ relationships, and an improved picture of oneself and the world.

77. (p. 556) All psychotherapies include some combination of several important goals. To accomplish these goals, all psychotherapists offer:

1) a _____ _____, sometimes called the therapeutic alliance, between client and therapist based on emotional rapport;
2) a protected setting in which emotional _____ (release) can take place;
3) some _____ or _____ for the suffering the client has experienced, and proposed action which if followed will end this suffering;
4) a new perspective for clients about themselves and their situations.

78. (p. 558)   In determining when you should seek professional help, several guidelines can be suggested. The first is: if your level of psychological discomfort becomes comparable to a level of _____ discomfort that would cause you to see a dentist or physician.

79. (p. 558)   Another sign is the occurrence of significant _____ in observable behavior like the quality of your work, your rate of absenteeism, your use of drugs, or your relationships with others who are important to you.

80. (p. 558)   If you find friends or relatives making suggestions that you seek professional help, they may be seeing things more _____ than you.

81. (p. 558)   Definitely seek help if you have persistent or disturbing _____ thoughts or impulses.

82. (p. 558)   There are several ways of seeking professional help. One of these avenues is to look in the "_____ _____." These listings will put you in touch with individuals in private practice.

83. (p. 558)   Most counties and many cities offer services through community or county _____ _____ _____ listed in the phone book.

84. (p. 558)   Many cities have _____ _____ _____ organized to keep listings of therapists and services.

85. (p. 558)   If you are a student, many schools have special counseling facilities. Also, some psychologists and low-cost "outreach" clinics make their presence known to the public through _____ _____.

86. (p. 558)   The choice between a psychiatrist and a psychologist is somewhat arbitrary. Both are trained to do psychotherapy. Fees for _____ are usually higher.

87. (p. 558)   If fees are a problem, consider that many individual therapists and almost all community mental health centers charge on a _____ _____, or ability-to-pay basis.

88. (p. 559)   A balanced look at psychotherapies suggests that all _____ are about equally successful, but all _____ are not. The most successful psychotherapists are those who use whatever method seems most helpful and whose personal characteristics include _____, integrity, sincerity, and _____.

89. (p. 559)   Since the relationship between a client and therapist is the therapist's basic tool, you must trust and easily relate to a therapist for therapy to be effective. Clients who _____ their therapist are generally more successful in therapy.

90. (p. 559) In trying to help someone in constructive personality change, there appear to be two essential conditions:
    1) an _____ _____ of the person and an unshakable positive regard for him or her as a human; and
    2) a capacity to communicate your understanding of the discomfort the person feels; we may call this second quality _____.

91. (p. 559) Several points may help you when a friend wants to talk about a problem. First, you should practice _____ _____; a person with a problem needs to be heard.

92. (p. 560) Try to understand the problem from the person's point of view. As you do, check your understanding often. This may help to _____ the problem and provide the person with a better position to discover solutions.

93. (p. 560) By focusing on the person's _____ you can avoid making him or her defensive. This process helps permit the free outpouring of emotion that is the basis for catharsis.

94. (p. 560) Avoid giving _____. It is not unreasonable to do so when asked, but beware of the trap described by Eric Berne, "Why don't you? Yes, but . . ."

95. (p. 560) Accept the person's frame of _____ and avoid contradicting the person with your point of view. If individuals feel that their point of view is understood, they will feel freer to examine it objectively and to question their perspective.

96. (p. 560) One of the most productive things you can do is to give _____ by simply reflecting (restating) thoughts and feelings said by the person.

97. (p. 560) To encourage the person to feel unhurried and to speak freely, be sure to listen patiently. Studies of counselors show that pauses of ___ seconds or more are not unusual, and interrupting is rare.

98. (p. 560) Because your goal is to encourage free expression, use _____ questions (those that call for an open-ended reply) rather than _____ (those which can be answered yes or no).

99. (p. 560) Your efforts to help should include maintaining _____. Avoid the temptation to gossip.

100. (p. 562) Joseph Weizenbaum has developed a _____ _____ named "ELIZA" that can respond like a nondirective therapist with patients.

101. (p. 562) While many critics claim that the use of such a technique would be dehumanizing or that important nonverbal information would be omitted, supporters believe it would have the advantages of low _____, convenience, _____, and dependability.

102. (p. 562) Critics view experimentation with computerized therapy as "dehumanizing technology." They also point out that computers would miss _____ messages contained in a glance, a gesture, laughter, or tears.

103. (p. 562) On the other hand, there is evidence that tape recording your thoughts on a problem and then listening to the tape can contribute to self-awareness. In similar fashion, a computer "therapist" might provide a helpful _____ _____.

SELF-TEST

1. (p. 546) Which of the following is *not* a correct match?
   a. insight therapies—foster a deeper understanding of the assumptions, beliefs, emotions, and conflicts underlying a problem
   b. directive therapies—places responsibility for the course of therapy on the client
   c. action therapies—focus on directly changing troublesome habits and behavior
   d. individual therapies—proceed on a one-to-one basis between client and therapist

2. (p. 546) True-False. Trepanning was used in the Stone Ages to treat ergotism.

3. (p. 546) During the Middle Ages, treatment for the mentally ill in Europe focused on
   a. demonology   c. unconscious motives
   b. ego-states   d. physiological abnormalities

4. (p. 546) A compassionate view of the mentally ill slowly emerged after 1793, facilitated by the work of _____ at the Bicêtre Asylum in Paris.
   a. Freud   c. Charcot
   b. Pinel   d. Frankl

5. (p. 548) Which of the following techniques was *not* used by Freud as part of psychoanalysis?
   a. analysis of transference   c. analysis of resistance
   b. analysis of irrational beliefs   d. dream analysis

6. (p. 549) True-False. Psychoanalysis as originally conducted by Freud is still in widespread use today.

7. (p. 549) True-False. When psychotherapy has been effective in changing human thinking or behavior, we speak of spontaneous remission.

8. (p. 549) The goal of psychoanalysis is
   a. adjustment   c. self-actualization
   b. self-knowledge   d. to rebuild connected wholes

9. (p. 550) Which of the following is *not* true of client-centered therapy?
   a. It focuses on conscious thoughts and feelings.
   b. The client determines what will be discussed during each session.
   c. The therapist's job is to create an "atmosphere of growth."
   d. It was developed by humanistic psychologist H. J. Eysenck.

10. (p. 550) Which of the following is *not* a basic condition for effective therapists as outlined by Carl Rogers?
    a. The therapist makes positive regard conditional upon therapeutic progress.
    b. The therapist strives to be authentic in his or her relationship with clients.
    c. The therapist attempts to achieve genuine empathy for the client.
    d. The therapist does not make interpretations, but instead reflects thoughts and feelings.

11. (p. 551) Which of the following is *not* true of existential therapy?
    a. It tries to promote self-knowledge and self-actualization.
    b. It seeks to uncover a "true self" hidden behind an artificial screen of defenses.
    c. It emphasizes the idea of free will.
    d. It focuses on ultimate human concerns such as death, isolation, and meaningfulness.

12. (p. 551) Which of the following is *not* true of logotherapy?
     a. It was developed by Victor Frankl on the basis of experiences in a Nazi concentration camp.
     b. It uses a flexible approach centered around confrontation.
     c. When it is successful, it brings about a reappraisal of what's important in life.
     d. It attempts to restore meaning and vitality to life through such experiences as the "trust walk" and the "blind mill."

13. (p. 551) According to Fritz Perls, emotional health comes from getting in touch with what you
     a. should do   c. want to do
     b. ought to do   d. should want to do

14. (p. 552) An advantage to group therapy is that
     a. it permits a therapist to provide a greater depth of empathy to clients
     b. it allows clients to experience the here-and-now more directly
     c. it provides a more realistic situation than the protected atmosphere of individual therapy
     d. it doesn't really provide any special advantages, but it does allow psychologists to work with more people at one time

15. (p. 552) A teenager would most likely act out a typical family fight in
     a. psychodrama   c. client-centered therapy
     b. Gestalt therapy   d. logotherapy

16. (p. 552) A primary technique in psychodrama is
     a. dream analysis   c. crossing transactions
     b. role playing   d. large group awareness training

17. (p. 553) True-False. Family therapists believe that problems within a family can usually be traced to a single individual who must be helped through therapy to "own" his or her problems.

18. (p. 554) Which of the following is *not* true of sensitivity groups?
     a. Participants take part in exercises that gently enlarge awareness of oneself and others.
     b. While different from traditional psychotherapy, they have been shown to be therapeutic.
     c. They are less confrontive than encounter groups.
     d. Their principles are used by many businesses to improve employee morale and relationships.

19. (p. 554) Encounter groups are designed to
     a. enhance adjustment through nondirective therapeutic techniques
     b. bolster the ego through group unconditional positive regard
     c. enhance self-awareness through "trust walks" and "blind mills"
     d. tear down defenses and facades in order to facilitate greater self-awareness

20. (p. 554) True-False. There are no dangers involved in participating in an encounter group.

21. (p. 554) True-False. Encounter and sensitivity groups may comfort, but they do not cure anything.

22. (p. 554) Of the following therapies, which focuses on the analysis of personality ego-states?
     a. Gestalt therapy   c. logotherapy
     b. transactional analysis   d. client-centered therapy

23. (p. 554) True-False. The Parent is a mature and rational decision-making part of the personality according to TA.

24. (p. 555) According to TA, when communication exchange appears to take place on one level but actually takes place on another, this is called a(n)
    a. ulterior transaction   c. role reversal
    b. crossed transaction   d. life script alteration

25. (p. 555) True-False. According to Berne, one way to overcome destructive transactions is to develop new ways of communicating called "games."

26. (p. 556) All psychotherapies have as their goals which of the following?
    a. an improved sense of self   c. resolution of conflicts
    b. better interpersonal relations d. all of the above

27. (p. 558) Which of the following is *not* a sign that you should seek professional help?
    a. You find friends or relatives making the suggestion that you seek professional help.
    b. You have persistent or disturbing suicidal thoughts or impulses.
    c. Your psychological discomfort is comparable to a level of physical discomfort that would make you seek medical treatment.
    d. There have been no significant negative changes in your observable behavior for some time.

28. (p. 559) True-False. A balanced look at psychotherapies suggests that all techniques are about equally successful.

29. (p. 559) Which of the following is *not* true of successful therapists and effective therapy?
    a. Clients who dislike their therapists do better because they are forced to consider a strongly opposing point of view.
    b. Successful therapists are distinguished by warmth, integrity, sincerity, and empathy.
    c. Successful therapists are willing to use whatever method seems most helpful for a client.
    d. Since the relationship between a client and therapist is the therapist's most basic tool, clients must trust and easily relate to a therapist.

30. (p. 559) True-False. Psychotherapy is an art, not a science.

31. (p. 560) Which of the following is *not* a useful guideline to consider when "counseling" a friend?
    a. maintain confidentiality
    b. challenge the person's frame of reference
    c. reflect thoughts and feelings
    d. avoid giving advice

32. (p. 562) Joseph Weizenbaum has developed a computer program called ELIZA that
    a. simulates non-directive psychotherapy
    b. can analyze a therapist's technique and provide suggestions for improvements
    c. can record group interactions and provide feedback when crossed or ulterior transactions occur
    d. analyzes and synthesizes psychological data and creates plausible "life scripts"

ANSWERS — PROGRAMMED REVIEW

1. Psychotherapy
2. phobias; sexual; marital
3. comfort, support
4. personal growth
5. Individual
6. Group
7. Insight
8. Action
9. Directive
10. Non-directive
11. Time-limited
12. trepanning
13. demonology; exorcism
14. ergotism
15. Philippe Pinel
16. Sigmund Freud; psychoanalysis
17. hysteria
18. relaxation; unconscious
19. repressed
20. free association
21. dream analysis
22. manifest; latent; symbols
23. resist; resistances
24. transfer; reeducation
25. 3; 5; 7
26. dynamic; direct interviewing
27. effectiveness
28. spontaneous remission
29. improve; better
30. adjustment; potentials
31. client-centered; conscious
32. non-directive
33. unconditional positive regard
34. empathy
35. authentic
36. reflects
37. Existential
38. free will
39. courage
40. freedom, isolation, meaningfulness
41. logotherapy; Nazi concentration; meaning
42. confrontation; encounter
43. Gestalt
44. directive
45. whole
46. gap; immediate experience
47. want; should; ought
48. present
49. group therapy
50. therapy; real-life
51. psychodrama; role plays
52. role reversals
53. family
54. single
55. educational; therapeutic
56. general nature; counseling
57. confrontive; trust walk
58. encounter
59. screened; trained
60. businesses; married
61. large group
62. therapeutic
63. therapy placebo
64. Transactional analysis
65. games; group
66. ego-states
67. Child
68. Parent
69. Adult
70. crossed
71. ulterior
72. games
73. positive effect
74. 50; 75
75. 200
76. conflicts; self; behavior; interpersonal
77. caring relationship; catharsis; explanation, rationale
78. physical
79. changes
80. objectively
81. suicidal
82. yellow pages
83. mental health centers
84. mental health associations
85. newspaper advertisements
86. psychiatrists
87. sliding scale
88. techniques; therapists; warmth; empathy
89. like
90. unconditional acceptance; empathy
91. active listening
92. clarify
93. feelings
94. advice
95. reference
96. feedback
97. 5
98. open; closed
99. confidentiality
100. computer program
101. cost; consistency
102. nonverbal
103. sounding board

ANSWERS — SELF-TEST

1. b		17. False	
2. False		18. b	
3. a		19. d	
4. b		20. False	
5. b		21. True	
6. False		22. b	
7. False		23. False	
8. a		24. a	
9. d		25. False	
10. a		26. d	
11. b		27. d	
12. d		28. True	
13. c		29. a	
14. c		30. True	
15. a		31. b	
16. b		32. a	

Chapter 22

Behavior Therapy

CONTENTS

TERMS AND CONCEPTS

behavior therapists
classical conditioning
conditioned stimulus (CS)
unconditioned stimulus (US)
unconditioned response (UR)
conditioned response (CR)
aversion
aversion therapy
conditioned aversion
rapid smoking
Antabuse
response-contingent
transfer
generalization
desensitization
hierarchy

reciprocal inhibition
counterconditioning
vicarious desensitization
operant conditioning
positive reinforcement
nonreinforcement
extinction
punishment
shaping
stimulus control
time out
tokens
target behaviors
token economy
cognitive behavior therapists
rational-emotive therapy
covert sensitization

IMPORTANT INDIVIDUALS

Ivan Pavlov
Roger Vogler
Joseph Wolpe
B. F. Skinner

Aaron Beck
Albert Ellis
Scott Hamilton
David Waldman

PROGRAMMED REVIEW

1. (p. 566) Psychologists called _____ _____, who use behavior modification and cognitive behavior therapy, feel that insight or understanding of one's problems is unnecessary. Instead these therapists try to directly alter troublesome thoughts and change _____.

2. (p. 566) Behavior modification is based on the principal assumption that people have _____ responses that cause problems and that they can change them or _____ more appropriate habits.

3. (p. 566) Broadly speaking, behavior modification refers to any attempt to use the learning principles of _____ or _____ conditioning to change human behavior.

4. (p. 566) Classical conditioning is the process of learning originally studied by Russian psychologist _____ _____.

5. (p. 566) Through this process a previously neutral stimulus, the _____ _____, is followed by a stimulus, the _____ _____, which always produces a response, the _____ _____.

6. (p. 566) Eventually the conditioned stimulus begins to produce the response directly. The response is then called a _____ _____.

7. (p. 567) Classical conditioning can be used to associate discomfort, called an _____, with a bad habit. This procedure is called _____ _____.

8. (p. 567) When an aversion (or negative emotional response) is paired with a bad habit such that the habit no longer occurs or is replaced by a competing response, a _____ _____ has developed.

9. (p. 567) Aversion therapy has been used to treat drinking, overeating, and gambling, as well as hiccups, _____, _____, vomiting, bed-wetting, and maladaptive sexual behaviors such as _____ and _____.

10. (p. 567) Aversion therapy can be an aid to persons who want to quit smoking. _____ smoking is the most widely used method. Subjects smoke continuously, taking a puff every 6 to 8 seconds.

11. (p. 567) A number of studies suggest that rapid smoking is the most _____ behavior therapy for smoking. Also, health risks of rapid smoking are _____. However, without the help of a therapist, most people quit too soon for the procedure to succeed.

12. (p. 567) The most basic problem with rapid smoking is that about _____ - _____ of those who quit smoking begin again. But, former smokers who get encouragement from others are much more likely to stay smoke free. In contrast, former smokers whose social groups include many smokers are more likely to begin smoking again.

13. (p. 567) Psychologist Roger Vogler uses aversion therapy with alcoholics who have tried almost everything to stop drinking, including therapy with _____, a drug that causes an alcoholic to become violently nauseated after drinking.

14. (p. 567)   Vogler associates painful, but noninjurious _____ _____ with the intake of alcohol. This condition takes the pleasure out of drinking and causes the patient to develop a conditioned aversion to drinking.

15. (p. 567)   The shock is presented most of the time when the patient is beginning to take a drink. This _____ _____ (or response connected) association helps develop a conditioned aversion to alcohol.

16. (p. 568)   One problem with successful treatment is getting aversive conditioning to _____ or _____ from the therapy situation to the "real world."

17. (p. 568)   One way to improve transfer is to make the therapy situation resemble the normal site of drinking as much as possible. Vogler has accomplished this feat by having patients undergo aversion therapy in a simulated _____ or in other simulated sites.

18. (p. 568)   Aversion therapy is used as a last resort. Vogler also trains alcoholics to discriminate _____ _____ levels (so clients can tell how drunk they are), teaches them alternatives to drinking, and offers alcohol education and general counseling.

19. (p. 568)   Also, alcohol abusers are _____ as they go from sober to drunk; later they are shown the tape. Apparently, few people have any idea of how unattractive they are when drunk.

20. (p. 568)   Commercial aversion programs for _____, _____, and alcohol abuse have attracted large numbers of willing customers.

21. (p. 568)   When psychologists use aversion therapy, they often back it up with _____ _____.

22. (p. 568)   For mild problems, it is not always necessary that a person receive shocks. For example, merely _____ a trained actor who appears to get _____ while biting his nails can effectively curb the problem.

23. (p. 569)   _____, a reduction in fear, is usually brought about by gradually approaching a feared stimulus while maintaining complete relaxation.

24. (p. 569)   An ordered set of steps called a _____ is used to allow the individual to _____ to gradual approximations of the end, desired behavior.

25. (p. 569)   Desensitization is also based on a principle, developed by Joseph Wolpe, called _____ _____, which means that one emotional state can prevent the occurrence of another.

26. (p. 569)   Desensitization is primarily used to help people unlearn or countercondition strong anxieties or _____ such as fear of heights, water, snakes, and so forth.

27. (p. 569)   Desensitization usually involves three steps:
    1) the client and therapist _____ a _____, a list of fear-provoking situations involving the phobia, and ranging from the least disturbing to the most;
    2) the client is taught exercises that produce total _____; and

3) the client performs the least disturbing item on the list until no _____ is felt, then moves on to the next most fearful item, and so on through the hierarchy.

28. (p. 570) In situations where it is impractical for the client to act out the steps, clients can observe models performing the feared behavior. This process is known as _____ _____.

29. (p. 570) Desensitization also works well when a person vividly _____ each step in the hierarchy. If the steps can be visualized without anxiety, fear in the actual situation is reduced.

30. (p. 571) The principles of _____ conditioning have been developed by _____ _____ and his associates mostly through laboratory research with animals.

31. (p. 571) There are several principles used to deal with human behavior. One of these principles is _____ _____, the process whereby an action that is followed by reward will occur more frequently.

32. (p. 571) The principle of _____ means that an action not followed by reward will occur less frequently.

33. (p. 571) If the response is not followed by reward after it has been repeated many times, it will go away. This phenomenon defines the process of _____.

34. (p. 571) If a response is followed by discomfort, or an undesirable effect, the response will be suppressed (but not necessarily extinguished). This phenomenon defines the process of _____.

35. (p. 571) _____ means rewarding actions that are closer and closer approximations to a desired response.

36. (p. 571) Responses tend to come under the control of the situation in which they occur. When they do we speak of _____ _____.

37. (p. 571) A _____ _____ procedure usually involves removing the individual from a situation in which reinforcement occurs, thus preventing reward from following an undesirable response.

38. (p. 571) Most frequently occurring human behaviors lead to some form of reward. An undesirable response can be eliminated by _____ and _____ the rewards which maintain it.

39. (p. 571) Most of the rewards which maintain human behavior are more subtle than food, money, etc. Rather they include _____, _____, and concern.

40. (p. 572) Examples of these reinforcers are often seen in classrooms. Frequently, misbehaving children are surrounded by others who giggle and pay attention to them. If seating is rearranged so that the disruptive children are surrounded by less responsive students, misbehavior _____.

41. (p. 572) Attention from a teacher can also be a reinforcer. An experiment showed that when teachers paid extra attention to classroom behavior, it _____.

42. (p. 572) Also, misbehavior _____ when attention took the form of scolding such as the teacher saying, "Sit down!"

43. (p. 572) Nonreward and extinction can eliminate many of these problem behaviors. For example, in the classroom example when misbehaving children were _____ and attention was given to children not misbehaving, misbehavior _____.

44. (p. 572) A typical strategy used in institutions to deal with a particular disturbing response is _____ _____, refusing to reward maladaptive responses by refusing to play the attention game.

45. (p. 572) Another form of time out is to _____ an individual immediately from the setting in which an undesirable response occurs so that the response will not be rewarded.

46. (p. 572) An approach that has been used is based on _____, symbolic rewards that can be exchanged for real rewards. They are being used in mental hospitals, halfway houses for drug addicts, schools for the retarded, programs for delinquents, and ordinary classrooms.

47. (p. 573) Using tokens, a therapist can immediately reward a _____ response. This token allows a therapist to use _____ _____ to influence behavior directly, instead of vaguely urging patients to "get themselves together."

48. (p. 573) For maximum impact, the therapist selects specific _____ _____ and then reinforces them with tokens. Gradually, patients are required to do more or better responses in order to receive rewards.

49. (p. 573) Full-scale use of tokens in an institutional setting produces _____ _____. In such programs, patients are rewarded with tokens for a wide range of socially desirable or productive activities. They must pay tokens for privileges and for engaging in problem behavior.

50. (p. 574) Generalization to the outside world can be a problem in token economies. The most effective token economies are those that gradually switch from tokens to _____ _____ such as recognition and approval.

51. (p. 574) In recent years a new breed of behavior therapists has appeared. _____ behavior therapists, as they are called, are interested in thoughts, as well as visible behavior.

52. (p. 574) Rather than looking only at maladaptive actions, cognitive therapists try to learn what people think, believe, and feel. They then help clients change _____ _____ that lead to trouble.

53. (p. 574) Cognitive therapy has been especially effective in the treatment of _____ which Aaron Beck believes is a result of negative, self-defeating thoughts.

54. (p. 574) Depressed persons see themselves, the world, and the future in negative terms. According to Beck this situation occurs because of several major distortions in thinking. The first is _____ _____. For example, if five good things happen during the day and three bad, the depressed person will focus only on the bad.

55. (p. 574)   _____ is another thinking error under-
lying depression.   An example would be considering yourself a total failure, or
worthless, if you were to lose a job or fail a class.

56. (p. 574)   Also, Beck says that depressed persons tend to _____ the importance
of undesirable events, and they engage in _____ - _____ - _____
thinking (seeing events, or themselves, as completely good or bad, right or wrong,
successful or a failure).

57. (p. 574)   Cognitive therapists make a step-by-step effort to correct negative thoughts that
underlie depression or similar problems.   At first, clients are taught to
_____ and keep _____ of their own thoughts (especially
those linked to depression).

58. (p. 574)   Next, clients are asked to collect information to _____ their beliefs.   For
instance, a depressed person's weekly list of activities might be used to challenge the
all-or-nothing thought, "I had a terrible week."

59. (p. 574)   In an alternative approach, the cognitive therapist looks for an absence of effective
_____ skills and thought patterns, not for the presence of self-defeating
_____.   The aim in this case is to teach clients how to _____ with
anger, depression, and similar problems.

60. (p. 574)   One widely used form of cognitive therapy is that which Albert Ellis calls
_____-_____ therapy, abbreviated _____.

61. (p. 574)   Ellis assumes that people become unhappy and develop self-defeating habits because
of _____ beliefs.

62. (p. 574)   Ellis analyzes the situation using the letters "A-B-C."   The person assumes the cause
of   the   emotional   _____ (C)   to   be   the
_____ experience (A).   Rational-emotive therapy shows
the client the true cause of the difficulty is the client's irrational and unrealistic
belief (B).

63. (p. 574)   RET holds that events cannot _____ us to have feelings.   We feel as we do
because of our beliefs and expectations.

64. (p. 574)   Ellis believes that most irrational beliefs come from three core ideas, each of which
is unrealistic:
1) I must _____ well and be _____ of by
significant others.
2) You must treat me _____.
3) Conditions must be the way I want them to be.

65. (p. 575)   Rational-emotive therapy takes a very _____ approach,
since the therapist may directly attack clients' logic, challenge their thinking, or
confront them with evidence contrary to their beliefs.

66. (p. 575)   RET has been criticized by some as superficial and argumentative, but Ellis' basic
insight has merit.   For instance, one recent study found that having irrational beliefs,
like those discussed by Ellis, is related to feelings of _____ and
_____.

67. (p. 576)   The technique of _____ _____ can be
applied by writing a series of disturbing or disgusting scenes related to the problem
and then frequently imagining those scenes during the day.

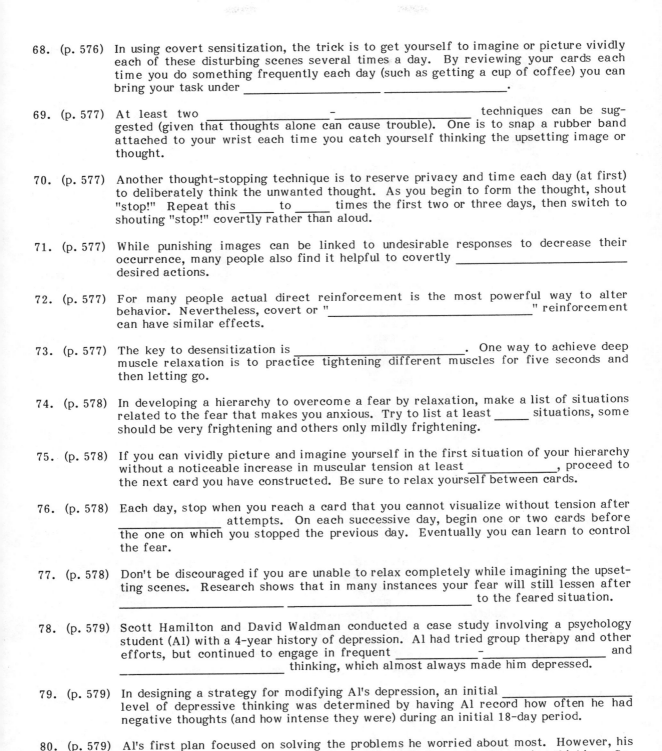

68. (p. 576) In using covert sensitization, the trick is to get yourself to imagine or picture vividly each of these disturbing scenes several times a day. By reviewing your cards each time you do something frequently each day (such as getting a cup of coffee) you can bring your task under _____ _____.

69. (p. 577) At least two _____-_____ techniques can be suggested (given that thoughts alone can cause trouble). One is to snap a rubber band attached to your wrist each time you catch yourself thinking the upsetting image or thought.

70. (p. 577) Another thought-stopping technique is to reserve privacy and time each day (at first) to deliberately think the unwanted thought. As you begin to form the thought, shout "stop!" Repeat this _____ to _____ times the first two or three days, then switch to shouting "stop!" covertly rather than aloud.

71. (p. 577) While punishing images can be linked to undesirable responses to decrease their occurrence, many people also find it helpful to covertly _____ desired actions.

72. (p. 577) For many people actual direct reinforcement is the most powerful way to alter behavior. Nevertheless, covert or "_____" reinforcement can have similar effects.

73. (p. 577) The key to desensitization is _____. One way to achieve deep muscle relaxation is to practice tightening different muscles for five seconds and then letting go.

74. (p. 578) In developing a hierarchy to overcome a fear by relaxation, make a list of situations related to the fear that makes you anxious. Try to list at least _____ situations, some should be very frightening and others only mildly frightening.

75. (p. 578) If you can vividly picture and imagine yourself in the first situation of your hierarchy without a noticeable increase in muscular tension at least _____, proceed to the next card you have constructed. Be sure to relax yourself between cards.

76. (p. 578) Each day, stop when you reach a card that you cannot visualize without tension after _____ attempts. On each successive day, begin one or two cards before the one on which you stopped the previous day. Eventually you can learn to control the fear.

77. (p. 578) Don't be discouraged if you are unable to relax completely while imagining the upsetting scenes. Research shows that in many instances your fear will still lessen after _____ _____ to the feared situation.

78. (p. 579) Scott Hamilton and David Waldman conducted a case study involving a psychology student (Al) with a 4-year history of depression. Al had tried group therapy and other efforts, but continued to engage in frequent _____-_____ and _____ thinking, which almost always made him depressed.

79. (p. 579) In designing a strategy for modifying Al's depression, an initial _____ level of depressive thinking was determined by having Al record how often he had negative thoughts (and how intense they were) during an initial 18-day period.

80. (p. 579) Al's first plan focused on solving the problems he worried about most. However, his use of a reinforcement system did not consistently lessen his depressive thinking. So,

Al dropped the reinforcement system after 2 weeks and concentrated on directly changing his _____ _____.

81. (p. 579) Al's cognitive program had three elements. First, he kept a _____ of events and thoughts that immediately preceded his becoming depressed. He then reevaluated the event and restated his thoughts about it in a more rational form.

82. (p. 579) Second, he administered daily covert _____ to himself. This took the form of reading written, positive statements about himself while engaging in pleasant activities.

83. (p. 579) The third element involved setting aside times each day when he would relax and mentally rehearse coping with _____ situations. He tried to imagine the worst possible turn of events and to picture himself dealing with the situation _____.

84. (p. 579) Hamilton and Waldman report that Al's original reinforcement system did eliminate many of the sources of his self-critical thoughts, but new depressive thoughts began to replace the old worries. In Al's case it proved more effective to _____ _____ his depressive thinking.

85. (p. 580) When behavior therapy was first developed, many observers feared that it would be used to control people against their _____. By now, most fears of behavior therapy have faded. For one thing, it is clear that _____ psychotherapies modify behavior in one way or another.

86. (p. 580) A second reason is that studies show that behavior therapists are rated just as _____ and _____ as traditional therapists.

87. (p. 580) Some critics still object to the use of behavior modification with "_____" groups, such as in schools, prisons, mental institutions, etc. Proponents of behavior modification consider it _____ to withhold treatment from such individuals.

SELF-TEST

1. (p. 566) Behavior modification is based upon which of the following assumptions?
   a. Conflicts between the conscious and unconscious produce maladaptive behaviors.
   b. Responses that cause problems are learned and can therefore be unlearned.
   c. The thwarting of self-actualization produces abnormal ego-states.
   d. Insight is the key to normal adjustment.

In aversion therapy, an aversive event such as an electric shock is presented when an undesirable behavior such as drinking alcohol occurs. Refer to this example in answering Questions 2-6.

2. (p. 566) The electric shock could be called a(n)
   a. conditioned stimulus   c. conditioned response
   b. unconditioned stimulus   d. unconditioned response

3. (p. 566) The pain of the shock and its physiological consequences could be called a(n)
   a. conditioned stimulus   c. conditioned response
   b. unconditioned stimulus   d. unconditioned response

4. (p. 566) In this example, alcohol could be called a(n)
   a. conditioned stimulus   c. conditioned response
   b. unconditioned stimulus   d. unconditioned response

5. (p. 566) When a conditioned aversion to alcohol develops, discomfort in drinking the alcohol could be called a(n)
     a. conditioned stimulus   c. conditioned response
     b. unconditioned stimulus   d. unconditioned response

6. (p. 567) The above example exemplifies the work of which of the following?
     a. Roger Vogler   c. Ivar Lovaas
     b. Joseph Wolpe   d. B. F. Skinner

7. (p. 567) The most widely used aversion therapy for smoking is
     a. use of Antabuse which makes smokers vomit whenever they inhale a cigarette
     b. electric shock paired with videotapes of cancerous lungs
     c. rapid smoking method
     d. overgeneralization technique

8. (p. 567) Aversion therapy is usually arranged so that the aversion is _____ contingent.
     a. response   c. solution
     b. problem   d. stimulus

9. (p. 568) Which of the following can be a problem in aversion therapy?
     a. getting the aversion to be response contingent
     b. finding effective aversions
     c. getting patients to overcome their aversions so that therapy can proceed
     d. generalization of aversion conditioning to the "real world"

10. (p. 569) True-False. Desensitization allows patients to adapt to a hierarchy of feared stimuli.

11. (p. 569) Desensitization is based partly on the principle of
     a. retroactive inhibition   c. reactive inhibition
     b. proactive inhibition   d. reciprocal inhibition

12. (p. 570) When acting out feared responses is impractical, clients can observe models who are performing the feared behavior. This procedure is called
     a. counterconditioning   c. vicarious desensitization
     b. implosive therapy   d. generalized desensitization

13. (p. 570) True-False. Desensitization in which the patient imagines each of the steps in the hierarchy is almost as effective as actually experiencing each step.

14. (p. 571) True-False. Punishment extinguishes behavior.

15. (p. 571) True-False. The process of gradually rewarding closer approximations to a final desired response is called sensitization.

16. (p. 571) When responses come under the control of the situation in which they occur, we speak of
     a. stimulus dominance   c. stimulus cueing
     b. response control   d. stimulus control

17. (p. 571) True-False. A variation of nonreinforcement is the time out procedure whereby an individual is removed from a situation in which reinforcement occurs.

18. (p. 571) True-False. Most human behavior is maintained by primary reinforcers like food and water.

19. (p. 572) When children misbehave in order to gain attention, an effective way of decreasing this misbehavior is to
    a. ignore children when they misbehave
    b. be reinforcing and kind to children when they misbehave
    c. direct negative statements at children when they misbehave
    d. give children what they want so they will no longer misbehave

20. (p. 572) One behavioral approach to therapy is based on the use of _____, symbolic rewards that can be exchanged for real rewards.
    a. tokens   c. points
    b. symbolia   d. chips

21. (p. 573) Tokens are used in reward and punishment procedures to change specific actions called
    a. sequential acts   c. contingent responses
    b. target behaviors   d. unconditioned responses

22. (p. 573) When full-scale use of tokens is employed in an institutional setting, the program is called a
    a. behavioral community   c. reinforcer program
    b. token economy   d. secondary reward setting

23. (p. 573) Of the following, which is a challenging problem in the use of behavior modification techniques?
    a. ineffectiveness with some personality types
    b. lack of sound theoretical base
    c. poorly defined connections between applications and basic research
    d. difficulties of generalization of results from the therapy setting to the real world

24. (p. 574) Cognitive behavior therapists are interested in
    a. understanding the dynamics of schizophrenia
    b. applying traditional psychotherapies to cognitive problems
    c. helping clients change thinking patterns
    d. using cognitive tokens to enhance personal sensitivity

25. (p. 574) According to cognitive behavior therapists, which of the following is not associated with depression?
    a. Depressed clients tend to minimize the importance of undesirable events.
    b. The depressed demonstrate selective perception of unpleasant events or situations.
    c. The depressed engage in all-or-nothing thinking, seeing events or themselves as completely good or bad, right or wrong, successful or a failure.
    d. Depression is associated with overgeneralization in which the person feels a total failure, or worthless, due to a single loss or failure.

26. (p. 574) According to Albert Ellis, RET seeks to identify and alter
    a. emotional consequences   c. rational assumptions
    b. activating experiences   d. unrealistic beliefs

27. (p. 575) True-False. Rational-emotive therapists are very directive and may directly attack clients' logic, challenge their thinking, and confront them with evidence contrary to their beliefs.

28. (p. 576) When you systematically imagine a series of disturbing or disgusting scenes in order to reduce undesirable behaviors associated with the scenes, you are using

    a. counterconditioning   c. covert sensitization
    b. vicarious desensitization   d. implosive therapy

29. (p. 577) True-False. Snapping a rubber band worn on the wrist can be an effective thought-stopping technique when applied each time an upsetting or undesirable thought or image occurs.

30. (p. 579) Hamilton and Waldman reported a case study of a change in depressive thinking accomplished through behavior modification. Which of the following was *not* an element of the effective system used by the subject Al?
    a. He set aside times each day when he would relax and mentally rehearse coping with stressful situations.
    b. He kept a record of events and thoughts that immediately preceded his becoming depressed—then he reevaluated the event and restated his thoughts about it in a more rational form.
    c. He focused on solving the problems he worried about most; he earned points for accomplishments and reinforced himself for constructive behavior.
    d. He administered daily covert reinforcement to himself by reading written, positive statements about himself while engaging in pleasant activities.

31. (p. 580) True-False. While many observers feared that behavior therapy would be used to control people against their will, everyone has always agreed that it is the ideal therapy for "captive" groups.

ANSWERS — PROGRAMMED REVIEW

1. behavior therapists; behavior
2. learned; relearn
3. classical, operant
4. Ivan Pavlov
5. conditioned stimulus; unconditioned stimulus; unconditioned response
6. conditioned response
7. aversion; aversion therapy
8. conditioned aversion
9. sneezing, stuttering; fetishims, transvestism
10. Rapid
11. effective; small
12. one-half
13. Antabuse
14. electric shock
15. response contingent
16. transfer, generalize
17. tavern
18. blood alcohol
19. videotaped
20. overeating, smoking
21. supportive counseling
22. watching; shocks
23. Desensitization
24. hierarchy; adapt
25. reciprocal inhibition
26. phobias
27. construct a hierarchy; relaxation; anxiety

28. vicarious desensitization
29. imagines
30. operant; B. F. Skinner
31. positive reinforcement
32. nonreinforcement
33. extinction
34. punishment
35. Shaping
36. stimulus control
37. time out
38. identifying; removing
39. attention, approval
40. decreases
41. increased
42. increased
43. ignored; decreased
44. time out
45. remove
46. tokens
47. positive; operant shaping
48. target behaviors
49. token economy
50. social rewards
51. Cognitive
52. thinking patterns
53. depression
54. selective perception
55. Overgeneralization

56. magnify; all-or-nothing
57. recognize; track
58. test
59. coping; thinking; cope
60. rational-emotive; RET
61. faulty
62. consequence; activating
63. cause
64. perform; approved; fairly
65. directive
66. anger; unhappiness
67. covert sensitization
68. stimulus control
69. thought-stopping
70. 10; 20
71. reinforce

72. visualized
73. relaxation
74. 10
75. twice
76. three
77. repeated exposures
78. self-criticism; negative
79. baseline
80. depressive thoughts
81. record
82. reinforcement
83. stressful; calmly
84. directly attack
85. will; all
86. warm, caring
87. captive; unethical

ANSWERS — SELF-TEST

 1. b
 2. b
 3. d
 4. a
 5. c
 6. a
 7. c
 8. a
 9. d
10. True
11. d
12. c
13. True
14. False
15. False
16. d

17. True
18. False
19. a
20. a
21. b
22. b
23. d
24. c
25. a
26. d
27. True
28. c
29. True
30. c
31. False

Chapter 23

Social Psychology I

CONTENTS

TERMS AND CONCEPTS

social psychology
culture
roles
ascribed roles
achieved roles
role conflict
status
group structure
group cohesiveness
norms
autokinetic effect
personal space
proxemics
intimate distance
personal distance
social distance
public distance
attribution
attribution theory
situational demands
self-handicapping

fundamental attribution error
need to affiliate
social comparisons
social comparison theory
interpersonal attraction
self-disclosure
reciprocity
overdisclosure
social exchange theory
romantic attraction
mutual absorption
social influence
conformity
groupthink
group sanctions
social power
reward power
coercive power
legitimate power
referent power
expert power

authority
obedience
passivity
compliance
foot-in-the-door effect

door-in-the-face effect
low-ball technique
assertiveness training
social trap
tragedy of the commons

IMPORTANT INDIVIDUALS

Stanley Milgram
Philip Zimbardo
Muzafer Sherif
Steven Berglas
Leon Festinger
Elliot Aronson
Zick Rubin
Soloman Asch

Irving Janis
Robert Cialdini
Thomas Moriarty
Joseph Wolpe
Robert Alberti
Michael Emmons
Garrett Hardin

PROGRAMMED REVIEW

1. (p. 584) Stanley Milgram conducted an interesting social psychology experiment to see how many messages could be delivered through the mail from one side of the continent to the other if each "link" had to be a first-name acquaintance. Amazingly, about one message in ___ made it with the number of intermediary "links" averaging about _____.

2. (p. 585) _____ _____ is the study of how people behave in the presence (actual or implied) of others.

3. (p. 585) _____ is an ongoing pattern of life that is passed from one generation to the next.

4. (p. 585) In each group an individual belongs to, they occupy a _____ in the structure of the group. _____ are expected behavior patterns linked with various social positions.

5. (p. 585) Roles that are not under the individual's control—male or female, etc.—are called _____ roles, while _____ roles are those which are attained voluntarily, or by special effort—wife, teacher, scientist, bandleader, etc.

6. (p. 585) Roles can be useful because they streamline many of our daily interactions. However, it is not unusual for a person to occupy two or more opposing roles which results in _____ _____, an uncomfortable or frustrating situation.

7. (p. 585) The impact of roles is dramatically illustrated by Philip Zimbardo's "prison" experiment. Male college students paid to serve as "inmates" or "guards" assumed their roles so quickly that the experiment was halted after _____ days due to brutality by the "guards" and problems of hysterical crying, confusion, and severe depression among "inmates."

8. (p. 585) Zimbardo's interpretation of the prison experiment is that the roles assigned were so powerful that in just a matter of days the experiment had become "_____" for those involved.

9. (p. 586) After the experiment, many guards found it hard to believe their own behavior. It would seem that the source of many destructive human relationships can be found in _____ _____.

10. (p. 586) Position in a group also determines one's _____. This factor can operate very subtly to influence behavior in many situations.

11. (p. 586) For example, in one experiment, subjects approached by a well-dressed researcher, and asked to return a dime left in a phone booth, did so in _____ percent of the cases, while only _____ percent returned it when the researcher was poorly dressed.

12. (p. 586) Groups are made up of people who are in some way interrelated. There are two very important dimensions of any group. Group _____ is the organization of roles, communication pathways, and power in the group.

13. (p. 586) _____ groups have a high degree of structure. _____ groups may or may not be highly structured.

14. (p. 586) Group _____ is basically an indication of the degree of attraction between group members. It is the basis for much of the power groups exert over their members.

15. (p. 586) A very important aspect of the functioning of any group is its _____, standards of conduct which prescribe appropriate behavior in a given situation.

16. (p. 586) One early study of how group norms are formed made use of a striking illusion called the _____ _____. Here a stationary pinpoint of light appears to move in a completely darkened room.

17. (p. 586) Using this effect, psychologist Muzafer Sherif found that when two or more people give estimates of the amount of drift, their judgments rapidly _____.

18. (p. 587) There is a similar convergence of attitudes, beliefs, and behavior among members of most groups. A good example can be found in norms governing the use of _____ space, the "spatial envelope" that extends "I" or "me" boundaries past the skin.

19. (p. 587) There are unspoken rules covering the interpersonal distance considered appropriate for formal business, casual conversation, waiting in line with strangers, etc. The study of rules for the personal use of space is called _____.

20. (p. 587) Hall identifies four basic zones related to personal space. One of these is called _____ _____ which extends about 18 inches out from the skin. Entry here is reserved for special people or circumstances.

21. (p. 587) _____ _____ is the distance maintained in comfortable interaction with friends. It extends from about $1\frac{1}{2}$ to 4 feet from the body.

22. (p. 587) _____ _____ involves separation of about 4 to 12 feet. This distance is used in conducting impersonal business and at casual social gatherings.

23. (p. 587) _____ _____ involves separation by more than 12 feet. Here interactions take on a decidedly formal quality.

24. (p. 588) Attribution is the process of making inferences about behavior. For example, if a person tastes food, then salts it, you might assume the food needed salt. You have attributed the person's actions to an _____ cause. If a person salts food before tasting it, you might assume the person really likes salt. You have attributed the person's actions to an _____ cause.

25. (p. 588) Several factors greatly influence attribution, for example _____.
If a person always avoids you, coincidence is ruled out and you may attribute that person's actions to a dislike for you.

26. (p. 588) However, the individual's avoidance of you may simply reflect shyness if that person avoids others too. Here is where _____ enters the picture. If the person only avoids you, you will probably assume that the individual dislikes you.

27. (p. 588) To infer cause, we typically have to take into account the behavior of the _____, the _____ of the action, and the _____ in which the action occurs. For example, how you interpret a compliment will depend on each of these factors.

28. (p. 588) In making attributions, we are very sensitive to _____ demands. When a person is quiet and polite in church, it tells us little about the individual's personality because the environment demands such behavior.

29. (p. 588) When situational demands are quite strong, we tend to _____ claims that a person's actions are internally caused. For example, you may question the sincerity of professional athletes who endorse commercial products.

30. (p. 588) _____ (or agreement) is another factor affecting attribution. When many people engage in the same behavior, it implies that behavior has an external cause.

31. (p. 589) We tend to infer causes for behavior from circumstantial evidence. In doing so we often make mistakes. The most common error, called the _____ _____ error, is to attribute the actions of others to _____ causes, while attributing our own behavior to _____ causes.

32. (p. 589) Steven Berglas has done studies showing that _____-_____ occurs when a person does not feel very confident about succeeding. In order to protect a fragile self-image, people sometimes arrange to be evaluated while "handicapped" so that they can attribute failure to the handicap.

33. (p. 589) If they succeed, their self-image gets a boost because they succeeded under conditions that everyone knows hinder performance. Thus, self-handicappers try to arrange a _____-_____ situation.

34. (p. 589) There are many ways to arrange self-handicapping. Procrastination on school assignments may be one. However, drinking _____ is among the most popular—and dangerous.

35. (p. 589) Most of us have used self-handicapping at times when we faced a difficult challenge and were doubtful about success. It becomes a problem when it turns into a _____, rather than a way of coping with life's harshest demands.

36. (p. 590) Attribution research has uncovered an interesting double standard for men and women. In a study by Deaux and Emswiller, male and female subjects were asked to rate the cause of success for a male or female whom they overheard perform extremely well on a perception task. Both men and women attributed male success to _____ and female performances mainly to _____.

37. (p. 590) We have already observed that the need to _____ appears to be a basic human characteristic. This fact is probably true because it helps us meet needs for approval, support, friendship and information. We also seek company to alleviate fear or anxiety.

38. (p. 590) This notion was experimentally demonstrated in a study of subjects waiting to participate in an experiment using painful electric shock. Most subjects chose to wait with other people in circumstances similar to their own. Here, as with other threatening or unfamiliar situations, _____ _____ serve as a guide for behavior.

39. (p. 591) Social psychologist Leon Festinger was among the first to point out that _____ _____ fills needs for social comparison and that when there are no objective standards, we turn to others to evaluate our feelings, actions, opinions, or abilities.

40. (p. 591) Festinger emphasizes that social comparisons are not made randomly, or on some ultimate scale. Useful personal evaluation requires comparison with people of _____ _____.

41. (p. 591) _____ _____ theory holds that a desire for self-evaluation determines what groups are joined, and provides a general motive for associating with others.

42. (p. 591) _____ _____ are the basis for most voluntary social relationships.

43. (p. 591) Social psychologist Elliot Aronson lists several things that determine with whom you are likely to become friends. One of these factors is simple _____ _____. Our friends are selected more on the basis of opportunity.

44. (p. 591) A main reason for proximity's effect is that it increases _____ of _____ between people. Laboratory studies show that we are generally attracted to people with whom we have had frequent contact.

45. (p. 591) Another important factor is _____ _____. Beautiful people are consistently rated more attractive than those of average appearance. This is an example of the halo effect.

46. (p. 592) This factor seems to be more an influence for women than men. For example, one study of dating patterns among college dormitory residents found a strong relationship between _____ _____ and dating frequency for women, but not for men. Beauty is a factor mainly in initial acquaintance. Later, more substantial personal qualities become important.

47. (p. 592) _____ is another quality which leads to interpersonal attraction. We are attracted to those who are talented, but human.

48. (p. 592) A fourth important factor is _____. People with common backgrounds, interests, attitudes or beliefs are attracted to each other.

49. (p. 592) _____ percent of all people in Western societies marry at some point. We tend to marry someone who is like us in almost every way.

50. (p. 592) A variety of studies show that people who marry are highly similar in _____, _____, race, religion, and _____ background.

51. (p. 592) In addition, the correlation of attitudes and opinions for married couples is ___. For mental abilities it is ___. And for socioeconomic status, height, weight, and eye color it is ___.

52. (p. 592) In the United States both men and women agree that the following qualities are most important when looking for a mate: kindness and understanding, _____, _____ personality, good _____, adaptability, and _____ attractiveness.

53. (p. 592) Men rank physical attractiveness as the _____ most important feature, whereas women rank it _____. Men rank good earning capacity _____, while women rank it _____.

54. (p. 592) A major step toward friendship usually involves _____-_____, sharing private thoughts and feelings and revelation of your "true self." Experimental work confirms that we more often reveal ourselves to people we like than to those we find less attractive.

55. (p. 592) There are definite norms about when self-disclosure is acceptable and when it is not. Moderate self-disclosure leads to _____ (a return in kind) while _____ gives rise to suspicion and reduced attraction.

56. (p. 593) As relationships progress, quite often they can be understood in terms of maximizing rewards while minimizing "costs." According to _____ theory, we unconsciously weigh such rewards and costs. For a relationship to last, it must be profitable for both parties.

57. (p. 593) Zick Rubin has provided some answers to the similarities and differences between love and liking. He found that scores for love of partner and love of friend _____ more than those for liking.

58. (p. 593) Dating couples liked and loved their partners, but most liked their friends. Women, however, were a little more "_____" of their friends than were men.

59. (p. 593) Romantic love, in contrast to simple liking, usually involves deep _____ _____ of the lovers. In other words, lovers (unlike friends) attend almost exclusively to one another.

60. (p. 593) Consistent with this idea, Rubin found that couples scoring high, compared to low, on the love scale spend _____ time gazing into each other's eyes.

61. (p. 594) One of the most heavily researched topics in social psychology concerns the effects of _____ _____. When people interact, they almost always affect one another's behavior.

62. (p. 594) As one example of social influence, consider the street-corner experiment in which either a well-dressed man or one dressed in shabby clothes crossed against the light. _____ people followed the well-dressed man than the other.

63. (p. 594) In another sidewalk experiment, groups of various sizes all looked at a sixth-floor window across the street on cue. A camera recorded the number of passersby who also stopped to stare. The _____ the influencing group, the more people were swayed to join in staring at the window.

64. (p. 594) Social influence ranges from simple suggestions to intensive indoctrination (brainwashing). Everyday behavior is probably most influenced by group pressures for _____.

65. (p. 594) Conformity situations develop when individuals become aware of differences between themselves and group actions, norms, or values. One of the better known experiments on group pressures for conformity was staged by _____ _____ in the early 1950s.

66. (p. 595) In Asch's experiment, subjects were asked to select a comparison line that was closest in length to a standard. Six other people gave their answers prior to the subject. It was found that subjects conformed to the answers of the accomplices on about _____-_____ of the critical trials.

67. (p. 595) Furthermore, _____ percent of those tested yielded at least once. This result is underscored by the fact that other people tested alone erred in less than ___ percent of their judgments.

68. (p. 595) A variety of experiments have shown that people with high needs for _____ or certainty are more likely to be influenced. People who are _____, low in self-_____, or who are concerned with the opinions or _____ of others are also more susceptible.

69. (p. 595) In most of our experiences with groups, we have been rewarded with acceptance and approval for conformity, and threatened with rejection or ridicule for nonconformity. These reactions are called _____ _____.

70. (p. 595) This notion is illustrated by later experiments in which Asch made up groups of six real subjects and one trained dissenter. When "Mr. Odd" announced his wrong answers, he was greeted with _____ and sidelong _____.

71. (p. 596) Several factors besides importance of the group can affect the degree of conformity. In Asch's experiment, the _____ of the majority made a difference. The number of conforming subjects increased dramatically as the majority increased from 2 to ___ people, but beyond this, an increase in numbers produced little effect.

72. (p. 596) Even more important than the size of the majority is its _____. Having at least one person in your corner can greatly reduce pressures to conform. In terms of numbers, a unanimous majority of 3 is _____ powerful than 8 with 1 dissenting.

73. (p. 596) Psychologist Irving Janis blames the Bay of Pigs and similar fiascoes on _____—a compulsion by decision makers to maintain each other's approval, even at the cost of critical thinking.

74. (p. 596) The core of groupthink is misguided group _____, which prevents members from "rocking the boat" or questioning weak arguments and sloppy thinking. The resulting _____ _____ and

self-censorship causes members to believe that there is a greater agreement and unanimity than actually exists.

75. (p. 596)   To prevent groupthink fiascoes Janis suggests that group leaders should
   1) define each group member's role as that of _____ _____ ;
   2) avoid stating their _____ in the beginning;
   3) state the problem _____ , and without bias;
   4) invite outside colleagues or different members each meeting to play _____ _____ .

76. (p. 596)   In addition, Janis suggests that there should be a "_____ - _____ " meeting to reevaluate important decisions. That is, each decision should be reached twice.

77. (p. 597)   In understanding the ways in which people are able to influence each other, it is helpful to distinguish among five types of social power:
   1) _____ power lies in the ability to reward a person for complying with desired behavior;
   2) _____ power is based on the ability to punish a person for failure to comply;
   3) _____ power comes from acceptance of a person as an agent of an established social order;
   4) _____ power is based on respect for, or identification with, a person or a group; and
   5) _____ power is based upon recognition that another person has knowledge or expertise necessary for achieving a goal.

78. (p. 597)   A person who has power in one situation may have very little in another. In those situations where a person has power, he or she is described as an _____ .

79. (p. 597)   Psychologist Stanley Milgram has conducted a provocative series of studies on _____ . The experiment involved "teachers" who gave "learners" progressively more intense shocks for errors in list memorization.

80. (p. 597)   "Teachers" thought that "learners" were actually being shocked using voltage ranging from 15 to 450 volts. In the first experiment, Milgram found that ____ percent of those tested obeyed his instructions to continue shocking learners up to 450 volts. No one stopped short of 300 volts.

81. (p. 598)   In a follow-up experiment, Milgram conducted the same study in a shabby office building to control for the prestige of Yale University. Here ____ percent of the "teachers" obeyed his instructions.

82. (p. 598)   Milgram found that distance between the "teacher" and the "learner" was important. When subjects were in the same room as the "learner," only ____ percent were fully obedient.

83. (p. 598)   When they were face-to-face with the "learner" and required to force his hand down on a shock plate, only ____ percent obeyed.

84. (p. 598)   Milgram also found that distance from the authority had an effect. When the experimenter delivered his orders over the phone, only ____ percent obeyed.

85. (p. 599)   On a more positive note, when real subjects saw two other "teachers" (both actors) resist orders and walk out of the experiment, only ____ percent continued to obey.

86. (p. 599) In conformity situations the pressure to "get in line" is usually indirect. When an authority commands obedience, the pressure is direct and difficult to resist. A third possibility involves the term _____ which has been used to describe situations in which a person with little or no authority makes a direct request to another person.

87. (p. 599) A person who agrees to a small request is later more likely to comply with a larger demand.   This is the formal definition of the _____-_____-_____ _____ effect.

88. (p. 599) As an example of this principle, if someone asked you to put a large, ugly sign in your front yard you would refuse. If, however, you had first agreed to put a small sign in your window, you would later be much _____ _____ to allow the big sign to be placed in your yard.

89. (p. 600) Robert Cialdini and his associates coined the term _____-_____-_____- _____ effect to describe the reverse of the foot-in-the-door effect. On some occasions the best way to get a person to agree to a small request is to first make a major request.

90. (p. 600) The _____-_____ technique consists of getting a person committed to act and then making the terms of acting less desirable. Automobile dealers are notorious for using this method. They get the customer to agree to buy at an attractively low price, then use various techniques to bump the price up before the sale is concluded.

91. (p. 600) Thomas Moriarty has demonstrated excessive, passive compliance under realistic conditions. Two subjects (one an accomplice) were placed in a small room and given a difficult task to complete. The accomplice turned on a tape-player at full volume for 17 minutes and would turn it off only after a third request. In this experiment, _____ percent of the subjects said nothing.

92. (p. 601) It is possible that passive compliance in Moriarty's study is limited to artificial experiments. However, when Moriarty and his students staged loud conversations in theaters or libraries, few people _____.

93. (p. 601) In other _____ experiments, people were accosted in phone booths. The experimenter explained that he had left a ring in the booth and asked if the subject had found it. When the subject said "no," the experimenter demanded that the subject empty his pockets. Most did.

94. (p. 602) Joseph Wolpe, and others, have pioneered a therapeutic technique called _____ _____ using group exercises, videotapes, mirrors, and staged conflicts.

95. (p. 602) The first step to becoming more assertive is to convince yourself of three basic rights: the right to _____, to _____, and to right a wrong.

96. (p. 602) A basic distinction can be made between _____-_____ and _____ behavior. Aggression is an attempt to get one's own way no matter what. Assertion techniques emphasize firmness, not attack.

97. (p. 603) To improve your assertiveness, begin by _____ how you would confront a situation. Practice is the key.

98. (p. 603) Working in front of a mirror or _____ _____ the scene with a

friend (where they take the part of the person or situation you wish to confront) can help.

99. (p. 603)   Another important principle is _____; continue practice until your responses become almost automatic. Such practice will help prevent becoming flustered in the actual situation.

100. (p. 603)   One more technique is the _____ _____. Simple persistence through repeating a request as many times and as many ways as necessary is often all that is needed for successful self-assertion.

101. (p. 603)   Responding assertively to verbal aggression (a "put-down") is a real challenge. A good way to respond is offered by psychologists Robert Alberti and Michael Emmons:
    1) if you are wrong _____ it;
    2) acknowledge the other person's _____;
    3) assert yourself about the other person's _____; and
    4) briskly end the interchange.

102. (p. 604)   A _____ _____ is any social situation that rewards actions that have undesired effects in the long run. For instance, many people are enticed into drinking too much at parties because their pleasure is immediate and their discomfort comes later.

103. (p. 604)   Psychologists have been especially interested in _____ social traps. Here, no one individual acts against the group interest, but if many people act alike, collective harm is done.

104. (p. 604)   Social traps are especially damaging when we are enticed into overuse of _____ resources. This is what happened a few years ago to crab fishermen in Alaska.

105. (p. 604)   Garrett Hardin calls situations like the one involving the Alaskan crab fishermen the _____ of the _____: each person acts in his or her self-interest, which causes the resource to be used up so that everyone suffers.

106. (p. 605)   In some situations it might be possible to dismantle social traps by rearranging rewards and costs. There is evidence that in real social traps people are _____ _____ to restrain themselves when they believe others will too.

SELF-TEST

1. (p. 585)   Social psychology is
    a. the study of how people behave in the presence (actual or implied) of others
    b. the study of how intrapsychic factors affect social organization
    c. a branch of psychology primarily interested in cross-cultural social studies
    d. a division of psychology closely aligned with economics that seeks to understand how the economy affects social behavior

2. (p. 585)   True-False. Ascribed roles are those which are attained voluntarily, such as wife, teacher, scientist, etc.

3. (p. 585)   Which of the following was *not* true of Philip Zimbardo's simulated "prison" experiment?

    a. Normal, healthy, male college students were paid to serve as "inmates" and "guards" in a simulated prison.

    b. Each day the guards tormented the prisoners with more frequent commands, insults, and demeaning tasks.

    c. After a month the experiment had to be halted, so the final results were never known.

    d. Zimbardo interpreted problems during the experiment to be a result of the powerful roles prisoners and guards assumed.

4. (p. 586) Which of the following is *not* true of groups and their members?

    a. Position in a group determines a member's status.

    b. Group structure is the organization of roles, communication pathways, and power in the group.

    c. Group norms are standards of conduct that prescribe appropriate behavior in a given situation.

    d. Group cohesiveness refers to ongoing patterns of group life where such representations as language, marriage customs, and sex roles are passed from one generation to another.

5. (p. 586) True-False. In an experiment on group norms, Sherif found that when two or more people were asked to observe the autokinetic effect and give judgments on the degree of light drift, their answers tended to rapidly converge.

6. (p. 587) The study of the interpersonal use of space is called

    a. spacology   c. proxemics

    b. kinesthetics   d. distances

7. (p. 587) Which of the following is *not* a correct match?

    a. public distance—formal interactions such as speeches, lectures, and business meetings

    b. social distance—maintained in comfortable interactions with friends

    c. intimate distance—the most private personal space reserved for special people or circumstances

    d. personal distance—extends from about $1\frac{1}{2}$ to 4 feet from the body; basically keeps people within "arm's reach" of each other

8. (p. 588) Which of the following is *not* true of attribution?

    a. When situational demands are quite strong we tend to more easily accept that a person's actions are internally caused.

    b. Attributions can be either external or internal.

    c. Distinctiveness and consistency are two factors that greatly influence attribution.

    d. To infer causes, we typically take into account the behavior of the actor, the object of the action, and the setting in which the action occurs.

9. (p. 588) True-False. Psychologists have found that we consistently attribute the behavior of others to internal causes, while attributing our own behavior to external causes.

10. (p. 590) In a study by Deaux and Emswiller, subjects who overheard a man or a woman perform extremely well on a perception task

    a. attributed male success to luck and female success to skill

    b. attributed success for both sexes to luck when they themselves were female

    c. attributed success for both sexes to skill when they themselves were male

    d. attributed male success to skill and female success to luck

11. (p. 590) True-False. When a situation is threatening or unfamiliar, we tend to rely more upon our own judgment rather than making social comparisons.

12. (p. 592)   Which of the following is *not* a factor in interpersonal attraction?
       a. physical reciprocity   c. physical proximity
       b. similarity   d. physical attractiveness

13. (p. 592)   True-False. In an experiment studying the role of competency in degree of inter-personal attraction, Aronson found that superior but clumsy individuals were more attractive than individuals who were only superior.

14. (p. 592)   Which of the following is *not* true of self-disclosure?
       a. Moderate self-disclosure leads to reciprocity and is a major step toward friendship.
       b. Rapid and unexpected self-disclosure produces immediate trust and intimacy.
       c. Overdisclosure gives rise to suspicion and reduced attraction.
       d. We more often reveal ourselves to persons we like than to those we find less attractive.

15. (p. 593)   According to social exchange theory, a relationship must be _____ to endure.
       a. meaningful   c. profitable
       b. reasonable   d. positive

16. (p. 593)   True-False. Dating couples like and love their partners, but mostly like their friends, according to the research of Zick Rubin.

17. (p. 593)   True-False. Men tend to rate their friends higher on the love scale than do women.

18. (p. 595)   Which of the following is *not* true of Soloman Asch's experiments on conformity?
       a. It was found that 75 percent of all subjects yielded to group judgment at least once.
       b. The tendency to agree with the group's judgment continued to increase as the size of the group increased, even up to as many as 8 people.
       c. It showed that even more important than the size of the group was the unanimity.
       d. Punishment for conformity as seen in the experiment are referred to as negative sanctions.

19. (p. 596)   When decision making compulsively maintains personal status and conformity at the expense of critical thinking, we speak of
       a. proxemics   c. role conflict
       b. obedience   d. groupthink

20. (p. 597)   Of the following, which is *not* a type of social power?
       a. coercive   c. referent
       b. legitimate   d. adaptive

21. (p. 598)   Milgram's original study of obedience to authority found that _____ percent of those tested obeyed by going all the way up to the 450 volt shock level.
       a. 25   c. 65
       b. 50   d. 75

22. (p. 598)   True-False. Milgram found in the obedience experiment that distance from the "learner" and the experimenter had less effect on subjects' tendency to obey than did the setting where the experiment was conducted.

23. (p. 599)   Which of the following is *not* a factor that helps explain whether a person will comply with a request?
       a. the door-in-the-face effect   c. the passivity effect
       b. the low-ball technique   d. the foot-in-the-door effect

24. (p. 600) When the best way to get a person to agree to a small request is to first make a major request, this situation involves
    a. the door-in-the-face effect
    b. obedience through authority
    c. external cause attribution
    d. the foot-in-the-door effect

25. (p. 600) True-False. Investigators such as Thomas Moriarty have discovered that passivity is a relatively minor problem in our society today.

26. (p. 602) Convincing yourself that you have the right to refuse, to request, and to right a wrong is a basic principle of
    a. conformity
    b. assertiveness training
    c. groupthink
    d. proxemics

27. (p. 602) True-False. Assertion is a direct, honest expression of feelings and desires that is not exclusively self-serving. Aggression is an attempt to get one's own way no matter what and does not take into account the feelings or rights of others.

28. (p. 603) You simply restate your request as many times and as many ways as necessary in an assertiveness technique called
    a. the broken record
    b. redundant rehearsal
    c. overlearning
    d. the perpetual motion machine

29. (p. 604) A _____ _____ is any situation that rewards actions that have undesired effects in the long run.
    a. role conflict
    b. coercive power
    c. social trap
    d. situational demand

30. (p. 604) When people share a scarce resource, each person may act in his or her self-interest, which causes the resource to be used up so that everyone suffers. Garrett Hardin has called such situations
    a. groupthink
    b. tragedy of the commons
    c. overdisclosure
    d. polarized cooperation

ANSWERS — PROGRAMMED REVIEW

1. 5; seven
2. Social psychology
3. Culture
4. position; Roles
5. ascribed; achieved
6. role conflict
7. six
8. reality
9. destructive roles
10. status
11. 77; 38
12. structure
13. Organized; Informal
14. cohesiveness
15. norms
16. autokinetic effect
17. converge
18. personal
19. proxemics
20. intimate distance
21. Personal distance
22. Social distance
23. Public distance
24. external; internal
25. consistency
26. distinctiveness
27. actor; object; setting
28. situational
29. discount
30. Consensus
31. fundamental attribution; internal; external
32. self-handicapping
33. no-lose
34. alcohol
35. habit
36. skill; luck
37. affiliate
38. social comparisons

39. group membership
40. similar backgrounds
41. Social comparison
42. Interpersonal attractions
43. physical proximity
44. frequency of contact
45. physical attractiveness
46. physical beauty
47. Competence
48. similarity
49. Ninety
50. age, education; ethnic
51. .5; .4; .3
52. intelligence; exciting; health; physical
53. third; sixth; eleventh; eighth
54. self-disclosure
55. reciprocity; overdisclosure
56. social exchange
57. differed
58. loving
59. mutual absorption
60. more
61. social influence
62. More
63. larger
64. conformity
65. Soloman Asch
66. one-third
67. 75; 1
68. structure; anxious; confidence; approval
69. group sanctions
70. laughter; glances
71. size; 3
72. unanimity; more
73. groupthink

74. loyalty; conformity pressures
75. critical evaluator; preferences; factually; devil's advocate
76. second-chance
77. reward; coercive; legitimate; referent; expert
78. authority
79. obedience
80. 65
81. 48
82. 40
83. 30
84. 22
85. 10
86. compliance
87. foot-in-the-door
88. more likely
89. door-in-the-face
90. low-ball
91. 80
92. protested
93. naturalistic
94. assertiveness training
95. refuse; request
96. self-assertion; aggressive
97. rehearsing
98. role playing
99. overlearning
100. broken record
101. admit; feelings; aggression
102. social trap
103. collective
104. scarce
105. tragedy of the commons
106. more likely

ANSWERS — SELF-TEST

1. a
2. False
3. c
4. d
5. True
6. c
7. b
8. a
9. True
10. d
11. False
12. a
13. True
14. b
15. c

16. True
17. False
18. b
19. d
20. d
21. c
22. False
23. c
24. a
25. False
26. b
27. True
28. a
29. c
30. b

Chapter 24

Social Psychology II

CONTENTS

TERMS AND CONCEPTS

attitude
misdirected letter technique
"mean" world view
conviction
open-ended interview
social distance scale
attitude scales
reference group
persuasion
role playing
cognitive dissonance
brainwashing
cults
love bombing
prejudice
discrimination
racism
scapegoating
personal prejudice
group prejudice
authoritarian personality

ethnocentric
F scale
dogmatism
social stereotypes
symbolic prejudice (modern prejudice)
status inequalities
equal-status contact
superordinate goals
nuclear winter
jigsaw classroom
aggression
frustration-aggression hypothesis
aggression cues
weapons effect
social learning theory
aggressive pornography
anger control
prosocial behavior
bystander apathy
empathic arousal
sociobiology

IMPORTANT INDIVIDUALS

Theodore Newcomb	Elliot Aronson
James McConnell	Konrad Lorenz
Margaret Singer	Neil Malamuth
Gordon Allport	Ed Donnerstein
Theodore Adorno	Leonard Eron
Milton Rokeach	Bibb Latané
Jane Elliot	John Darley
Gerald Clore	John Dovido
Muzafer Sherif	Edward Wilson

PROGRAMMED REVIEW

1. (p. 609) An _____ is a mixture of belief and emotion that predisposes a person to respond to other people, objects, or institutions in a positive or negative way. They summarize past experience and predict or direct future actions.

2. (p. 609) For example, wrongly-addressed mails have been sent to households in an approach known as the _____ _____ technique; the number of letters returned to the post office demonstrates that actions are closely connected to attitudes.

3. (p. 609) There are three ways in which attitudes are expressed. Most attitudes have a _____ component, an _____ component, and an _____ component.

4. (p. 609) Attitudes are acquired in several basic ways. Sometimes through _____ _____ with the object of the attitude. Attitudes are also learned through _____ with others holding the attitude. Attitudes are also acquired through the effects of _____ _____.

5. (p. 609) Group membership certainly influences attitudes. In one classic study, discussion groups were formed to discuss the case of a juvenile delinquent. As a test of group pressures on attitudes, a person was introduced into the group who advocated extreme punishment. At first the group directed _____ of the comments to him.

6. (p. 610) If the deviate stuck to his position, he was almost completely _____ from further conversation. And later, the deviate was strongly _____ in ratings made by other group members.

7. (p. 610) Attitudes are also influenced by the _____ _____. Ninety-eight percent of American homes have a television set, which is on an average of almost 7 hours a day.

8. (p. 610) The values and information thus channeled into homes exerts a powerful influence on attitudes. For instance, the heavy dose of violence on television may lead viewers to develop a "mean" world view. That is, frequent viewers _____ their chances of being involved in a violent incident. Also, heavy viewers are _____ likely to feel that most people can be trusted.

9. (p. 610) Some attitudes are formed quite inadvertently through _____ _____. If you have limited contact with an event and it is negative, you will tend to take an unduly dim view of all such events.

10. (p. 610) Attitudes are only one of the many determinants of actions in a particular situation. The _____ _____ of one's actions weigh heavily on the choices that are made.

11. (p. 610) Also important is our expectation of how others will _____ our actions. By taking this factor into account, researchers have been able to predict family planning choices, adolescent alcohol use, reenlistment in the National Guard, voting on a nuclear power plant initiative, and so forth.

12. (p. 610) Finally, we must consider the effect that long-standing _____ have on action. There are often large differences between attitudes and behavior— particularly between privately held attitudes and public behavior.

13. (p. 611) Barriers to action typically fall when a person holds an attitude with _____ —meaning that an attitude is of central importance to a person.

14. (p. 611) The issues about which you have conviction are those that you feel strongly about (emotionally), that you believe are important, that you frequently think about and discuss, and that you feel knowledgeable about. Such attitudes often lead to major changes in _____ _____.

15. (p. 611) Attitudes can be measured in several different ways. For example, a person might be asked in an _____-_____ _____ some question that requires the statement of an attitude.

16. (p. 611) Another approach which has been bery useful as a measure of attitudes towards groups is a _____ _____ _____. This tool measures the degree to which a person would be willing to have contact with another person.

17. (p. 611) Use of _____ _____ is one of the most common approaches to attitude measurement. These scales consist of statements expressing various possible attitudes on an issue. By computing scores on all items, people can be rated for overall acceptance or rejection of a particular issue.

18. (p. 611) Although attitudes are relatively stable, they are subject to change. Some attitude change can be understood in terms of the concept of _____ _____ whose values and attitudes are seen by individuals as being relevant to their own.

19. (p. 611) In the 1930s, Theodore Newcomb studied real life attitude change among students at Bennington College. While all students could count the college and their families as membership groups, only one or the other tended to become their _____ group.

20. (p. 611) _____ refers to any deliberate attempt to change attitudes by imparting information. An example is TV advertising which costs business corporations, politicians, and others over $5 billion yearly in attempts to change attitudes.

21. (p. 611) In most cases the success or failure of attempted persuasion can be understood by considering the characteristics of the _____, the _____, and the _____.

22. (p. 611) Research on persuasion suggests that attitude change is encouraged when:
1) the communicator is likable, trustworthy, an expert on the topic, and similar to the audience in some respect;

2) the message appeals to emotions, particularly to _____ or _____;

3) the message also provides a clear course of action that will, if followed, reduce fear or anxiety;

4) the message states clear-cut _____;

5) ____ sides of the argument are presented (for a well-informed audience);

6) only one side of the argument is presented (for a poorly informed audience);

7) the persuader appears to have nothing to _____ if the audience accepts the message; and

8) the message is repeated as frequently as possible.

23. (p. 612)   Emotional experiences can drastically alter attitudes. To actively bring about attitude change, psychologists have experimented with creating similar experiences through _____ _____.

24. (p. 612)   For example, women who were known smokers and asked to play the role of a cancer patient drastically _____ their smoking. Control subjects who listened to a tape recording of similar information showed _____ change.

25. (p. 612)   The influential theory of _____ _____ states that contradicting or clashing thoughts cause discomfort. If individuals can be made to act in a way that is inconsistent with their attitudes, they may change their thoughts to bring them into agreement with their actions.

26. (p. 612)   Cognitive dissonance theory suggests that people _____ information contradictory to their attitudes and _____ new information that contradicts ideas they already hold.

27. (p. 612)   The amount of _____ or _____ for acting contrary to one's attitudes and beliefs can influence the amount of dissonance created.

28. (p. 613)   An example is shown in the now classic study where college students performed an extremely boring task. Students paid $20.00 for lying to others about the experiment rated the experiment as boring. But those paid only $1.00 actually rated the experience as being _____ and _____.

29. (p. 613)   More recent studies indicate that we are especially likely to experience dissonance when we _____ an event to occur that we would rather hadn't.

30. (p. 614)   Many people associate brainwashing with techniques used by the Chinese on American prisoners during the Korean War. Through various types of "thought reform," the Chinese were able to coerce approximately _____ of these prisoners to sign false confessions.

31. (p. 614)   James McConnell has studied brainwashing and notes that it requires a _____ audience. Complete control over the environment allows a degree of psychological manipulation that would be impossible in a normal setting.

32. (p. 614)   Furthermore, McConnell has identified three techniques used for brainwashing: (1) the target person is _____ from other people who would support his original attitudes; (2) the target person is made completely _____ on his or her captors for satisfaction of needs; (3) the indoctrinating agent is in a position to _____ the target person for changes in attitude or behavior.

33. (p. 614) Brainwashing typically begins with an attempt to make the target feel completely helpless. Physical and psychological abuse serve to _____ former values and beliefs. _____ comes about when exhaustion, etc., become unbearable. When prisoners break, they are suddenly rewarded with praise, food, etc. This condition serves to _____ new attitudes.

34. (p. 614) In most cases, the dramatic shift in attitudes brought about by brainwashing is _____. Most "converted" prisoners of the Korean War eventually reverted to their original beliefs and repudiated their indoctrinators.

35. (p. 615) Psychologist Margaret Singer has studied and aided hundreds of former _____ members. Her interviews reveal that, in recruiting new members, such groups make use of a powerful blend of guilt, manipulation, isolation, deception, fear, and escalating commitment.

36. (p. 615) She found that some of those interviewed were suffering from marked psychological distress when they joined a cult, but most were simply undergoing a period of mild _____, indecision, or _____ from family and friends.

37. (p. 615) Cult members try to catch potential converts at a time of need, especially when a sense of _____ will be attractive to the convert.

38. (p. 615) Conversion is achieved through various steps. Often it begins with intense displays of affection and understanding called "_____ _____."

39. (p. 615) Next comes _____ from non-cult members along with drills, _____, and _____ to wear down physical and emotional resistance and to generate commitment.

40. (p. 615) At first recruits make small commitments, then larger commitments are encouraged, with making a major commitment usually the final step. Such major public commitments create such a powerful _____ _____ effect it becomes virtually impossible for converts to admit that they have made a mistake.

41. (p. 615) Once in the group, members are cut off from former _____ groups, kept physically and psychologically _____, and the cult can control the flow and interpretation of _____ members receive.

42. (p. 615) Cult members remain in cults partially out of a desire for social acceptance and approval, but more often former members mention _____ and _____ as the main reasons for not leaving even when they wished they could.

43. (p. 616) _____ is a negative attitude or a prejudgment tinged with unreasonable suspicion, fear, or hatred.

44. (p. 616) Prejudice that is institutionalized and backed by social power structures is referred to as _____, _____, or _____ depending on the group affected.

45. (p. 616) Both racial prejudice and institutionalized racism may lead to _____, behavior that prevents individuals from doing things they might reasonably expect to be able to do.

46. (p. 616)   Discrimination is often deeply woven into society. For instance, in one study 15 college students who had received no traffic citations in the previous year attached bumper stickers supporting a militant black organization to their cars. During the next 17 days the group received a total of _____ traffic citations.

47. (p. 616)   One theory suggests that prejudice is a form of _____, a type of displaced aggression in which hostilities generated by frustration are redirected to other targets.

48. (p. 616)   This notion was demonstrated in a study in which subjects at a summer camp were asked to rate Mexicans and Japanese before and after a frustrating test. Subjects in this study consistently rated members of these two groups _____ after being frustrated.

49. (p. 616)   Like other attitudes, the development of prejudice sometimes can be traced to _____ _____ with members of the rejected group. The tragedy in such cases is that once such antipathy is established, it prevents accepting additional, more positive experiences which could reverse the damage.

50. (p. 616)   Psychologist Gordon Allport has concluded that there are two important sources of prejudice. _____ _____ occurs when members of another racial or ethnic group represent a threat to the individual's security or comfort.

51. (p. 616)   Another type of prejudice occurs simply through the individual's adherence to _____ _____. You may have no personal reason for disliking out-group members but do so because you are expected to.

52. (p. 616)   Theodore Adorno has conducted extensive research on what he calls the _____ _____.

53. (p. 616)   Originally this work was directed at studying anti-Semitism as a means of understanding the social climate of World War II Germany. In the process, Adorno discovered that people who are prejudiced against one group tend to be prejudiced against all _____-_____.

54. (p. 616)   This personality has a collection of personal attitudes and values marked by rigidity, inhibition, and oversimplification. Authoritarians tend to be very _____, considering their own national, ethnic, or religious group to be superior to others.

55. (p. 616)   To measure these qualities, the "___" scale was created. (F stands for facism.) It is made up of statements concerning power, authority, and obedience with which the person can agree or disagree.

56. (p. 617)   As children, authoritarians were usually severely _____ and learned to fear _____ (and to covet it) at an early age.

57. (p. 617)   The "F" scale tends to list statements slanted toward politically conservative authoritarians, but as noted by psychologist Milton Rokeach, rigid and authoritarian personalities can be found at both ends of the political spectrum. For this reason, Rokeach prefers to describe rigid and intolerant thinking as _____—an unwarranted positiveness or certainty in matters of belief or opinion.

58. (p. 617)   It is still true that racial prejudice runs deep in many nations. For example, one experiment showed that liberal white male college students were _____

_____ to give shocks (under laboratory conditions) to a black victim than to a white victim.

59. (p. 617) An unfortunate by-product of group membership is that it often limits contact with people in other groups. Also, groups themselves may come into conflict. In many cases, intergroup conflict is accompanied by _____ images of out-group members and by bitter prejudice.

60. (p. 617) A social stereotype is an oversimplified image of people who fall into a particular category. They may be either _____ or _____ images.

61. (p. 618) Today's racism often takes the form of _____ _____ (also sometimes called "modern prejudice"). That is, many people realize that crude and obvious racism is socially unacceptable. However, this may not stop them from expressing prejudice in disguised forms.

62. (p. 618) Stereotypes held by the prejudiced tend to be unusually _____. When given a list of negative statements about other groups, prejudiced individuals agree with most of them, even though they are often _____ statements.

63. (p. 618) In one study, prejudiced subjects even expressed negative attitudes towards two _____ groups, the "Piraneans" and the "Danirians."

64. (p. 618) When a prejudiced person meets a pleasant or likable member of a rejected group, the out-group member tends to be perceived as "an _____ to the _____," not as a denial of the stereotype.

65. (p. 619) In a unique experiment, teacher Jane Elliot sought to give pupils a direct experience with prejudice. Brown-eyed children were discriminated against while blue-eyed children received special rewards. Within two days there was a very clear effect. It was possible to get children to hate each other because of their eye color and _____ _____—differences in the power, prestige, or privileges of two or more persons or groups.

66. (p. 619) Several lines of thought have been presented on how to combat prejudice. One approach suggests that more frequent _____-_____ contact between groups in conflict reduces prejudice and stereotypes.

67. (p. 619) Much evidence suggests it does. For example, in one early study white women living in integrated and segregated housing projects were compared for changes in attitude toward their black neighbors. In the integrated project, whites showed a _____ change in attitude toward members of the other racial group. Those in the segregated project showed no change or actually became _____ prejudiced than before.

68. (p. 619) Gerald Clore and his associates set up a unique children's summer camp to further test this idea. Blacks and whites were equally divided in number, power, privileges, and duties. Testing showed that the children had significantly more _____ attitudes toward opposite-race children after the camp than they did before.

69. (p. 619) Psychologist _____ _____ and his associates conducted an ingenious experiment with 11-year-old boys at a summer camp to study prejudice and how to overcome it.

70. (p. 619)   After strong intragroup loyalties had been established, it was found that having leaders from each group meet did nothing to reduce hostilities. Also, just getting the groups together did little. It was only when the boys had to work together that hostilities subsided. This result indicates that the creation of _____ _____ serves to help restore relations between groups.

71. (p. 620)   A superordinate goal exceeds or overrides all others. One such example on a global scale might be desire to avoid nuclear holocaust and _____ _____—the devastating drop in global temperature that would follow the fire storms, dust, and smoke of a nuclear strike and result in global crop failure, famine, and death on a large scale.

72. (p. 620)   Contrary to the hopes of many, _____ public schools often has little positive effect on racial prejudice. In fact, prejudice may be made worse, and the self-esteem of minority students frequently decreases.

73. (p. 620)   Minority group children often enter newly integrated schools unprepared to compete on an equal footing. This fact, plus the intense competition in classrooms, almost guarantees that children will _____ learn to like and understand each other.

74. (p. 620)   Elliot Aronson has pioneered a way to apply the concept of superordinate goals to ordinary classrooms by making people mutually _____.

75. (p. 620)   Aronson has successfully created "_____" classrooms that emphasize cooperation rather than competition. Each child is given a "piece" of the information needed to prepare for a test which he or she must teach to the other members of five and six children groups.

76. (p. 621)   Compared to children in traditional classrooms, children in jigsaw groups were _____ prejudiced, they liked their classmates _____, they had _____ positive attitudes toward school, their _____ improved, and their self-esteem increased.

77. (p. 621)   Also, brighter students are not sacrificed by this method. High achievers working in cooperative groups never do _____ than they do when learning alone, and often they do _____.

78. (p. 621)   The human capacity for aggression is staggering. It has been estimated that during the 125-year period ending with World War II, _____ million humans were killed by other humans (an average of nearly one person per minute).

79. (p. 621)   Furthermore, _____ now ranks as a major cause of death in the United States. Also, more than 1.7 million American children are subjected to physical _____ by parents each year.

80. (p. 621)   Ethologists such as Konrad Lorenz feel that humans are naturally aggressive, having inherited a "_____ _____" from our animal ancestors.

81. (p. 621)   Lorenz believes that aggression is a _____ rooted behavior observed in all animals, including humans. Also, he feels that humans lack certain innate patterns that in other animal species _____ aggression.

82. (p. 621)   Despite problems with this instinctive view, there is evidence that a biological basis for aggression may exist. Physiological studies have shown that there are brain areas capable of triggering or ending aggressive behavior. Also, there is a relationship

between aggression and such physical factors as _____ (low blood sugar), _____, and specific _____ injuries and disorders.

83. (p. 622) None of the above conditions can be considered a direct cause of aggression. Instead they probably lower the _____ for aggression, making hostile behavior more likely to occur.

84. (p. 622) The effects of alcohol and other drugs provide another indication of the role of the brain and biology in violence and aggression. A variety of studies show that alcohol is involved in large percentages of _____ and _____ crimes.

85. (p. 622) The fact that we are biologically _____ of aggression does not mean that aggression is _____, or "part of human nature." This point was made in 1986 by a group of 20 eminent scientists.

86. (p. 622) The _____ - _____ hypothesis states that frustration is closely associated with aggression. However, frustration does not always lead to aggression.

87. (p. 622) Frustration may lead to _____ responding, or perhaps to a state of "learned helplessness." Also, aggression can occur in the _____ of frustration.

88. (p. 622) Frustration probably encourages aggression because it is _____ (uncomfortable). Many experiments have shown that unpleasant stimuli tend to increase aggression.

89. (p. 622) Aversive stimuli probably raise overall arousal levels so that we become more sensitive to _____ _____. Such signals may be internal (angry thoughts for instance) or external (for example, a raised middle finger).

90. (p. 622) One study showed that even inanimate objects may serve as cues for aggression. Subjects were ridiculed and shocked by another person. Just before they got a chance to "return the favor," they saw either a couple of badminton rackets, or a shotgun and a revolver. The latter subjects gave _____ shocks to the person who had angered them.

91. (p. 622) The implication of this _____ _____ seems to be that the symbols and trappings of aggression encourage aggression.

92. (p. 622) The simplest and one of the most widely accepted explanations of aggression comes from _____ _____ theory which holds that we learn to be aggressive by observing aggression in others.

93. (p. 622) Considered in such terms, it is no wonder there is so much violence in America. A _____ crime occurs every 54 seconds, 40 percent of the population own _____, ____ percent agree that "when a boy is growing up, it is very important for him to have a few fist-fights," and ____ percent of the population admit to having slapped or kicked another person.

94. (p. 623) Until recently, most evidence regarding the effects of pornography suggested it has no major adverse effects when stimuli involved are merely erotic or sexual in content. However, in the last 10 years there has been an increase in

_____ pornography in the mass media (referring to depictions in which violence, threats, or obvious power differences are used to force someone to engage in sex).

95. (p. 623) Researchers Neil Malamuth and Ed Donnerstein have concluded that a principal finding of such studies is that aggressive-pornographic stimuli do _____ aggression by males against females.

96. (p. 623) Social learning theory implies that watching violence may _____ increase aggression, rather than _____ _____ aggressive urges. This is supported by Leonard Eron's finding that one of the best predictors of how aggressive a young man would be at age 19 was the violence of the TV programs he preferred when he was 8 years old.

97. (p. 623) Some psychologists have succeeded in teaching people to control their anger and aggressive impulses. The key to _____ _____ is the fact that people who respond calmly to upsetting situations tend to see them as problems to be solved.

98. (p. 623) To limit anger, people are taught to:
    1) define the problem as _____ as possible.
    2) make a _____ of possible solutions.
    3) _____ the likely success of each solution.
    4) choose a solution and try it.
    5) assess how successful the solution was and make adjustments if necessary.

99. (p. 625) In studying the Kitty Genovese case, psychologists Bibb Latané and John Darley reached several conclusions. Failure to help (bystander apathy) was related to the _____ of people present.

100. (p. 625) Everyone thought someone else would help. Personal responsibility was spread so thin that no one took action. This result indicates that the more potential helpers present, the _____ the chances that help will be given.

101. (p. 625) There are four "decision points" individuals must pass through before giving help. First, they must _____ that something is happening. Next, they must _____ the event as an emergency. Then they must take _____, and finally they must select a course of _____.

102. (p. 626) Latané and Darley suggest that if a sidewalk is crowded and you are in trouble, few people will even see you because of widely accepted norms to carefully "keep their eyes to themselves." Laboratory experiments show that _____ students working in groups exposed to a thick cloud of smoke actually noticed it, while _____ students working alone noticed it immediately.

103. (p. 626) After subjects in groups noticed the smoke, they coolly surveyed the reactions of others while being surveyed themselves. Until someone acts _____ _____ acts.

104. (p. 626) Groups limit assuming responsibility by causing a _____ of _____. They produce a feeling that no one is personally responsible for helping.

105. (p. 626) This idea was demonstrated in an experiment in which students took part in a group discussion from separate rooms over an intercom system. Actually there was only

one real subject, the others were confederates. During the discussion one of the confederates simulated an epileptic-like seizure and called out for help. In the six-person groups, over one-_____ of the subjects took no action at all. Some subjects in the three-person groups failed to respond, but those who were alone took action immediately.

106. (p. 626) It is not always clear how all the group factors combine in emergency situations, however. In one naturalistic experiment, when a "victim" "passed out" in a subway, he received _____ help when carrying a cane than a liquor bottle. However, most people were willing to help in either case.

107. (p. 626) Psychologist John Dovido has summarized some of the major factors that affect helping behavior. Many studies suggest that when we see a person in trouble, this tends to cause heightened _____.

108. (p. 626) This aroused, keyed-up feeling can motivate us to give aid, but only if the rewards of helping outweigh the costs. Higher costs almost always _____ helping.

109. (p. 626) Potential helpers may also feel _____ arousal. This means that they empathize with the person in need or feel some of the person's pain, fear, or anguish.

110. (p. 626) Empathic arousal also motivates helping. In fact, feeling a connection to the victim may be one of the most important factors in helping. This, perhaps, is why being in a good mood also increases helping. When we are feeling successful, happy, or fortunate, we may also feel more _____ to others.

111. (p. 626) There is also evidence that people who see others helping are more likely to offer help themselves. For example, motorists were much _____ _____ to stop to help a woman fix a tire when they had just passed another woman being helped by someone.

112. (p. 627) Also, persons who give help in one situation tend to perceive themselves as _____ people. This change in self-image encourages them to help in other situations.

113. (p. 627) One more point is that norms of _____ encourage us to help others who have helped us. For all these reasons, helping others not only assists them directly, it encourages others to help too.

114. (p. 628) Sociobiologists such as Edward Wilson believe that competition, war, territoriality, aggression, sibling rivalry, conformity, male-female differences, fear of strangers, altruism, and many other behaviors are "in our _____."

115. (p. 628) The core idea in _____ is that social behavior evolves in ways that maximize the fitness of a species for survival. For instance, animals that compete successfully for food, territory, mates, and so forth are more likely to survive and reproduce. Thus, competitiveness gradually becomes a trait of following generations.

116. (p. 628) Sociobiologists explain altruistic actions like the selfless heroism of a soldier by pointing out that such actions help improve chances that an individual's _____ will survive.

117. (p. 628) Sociobiology seems to say that genes manipulate our behavior to ensure their survival. It's major strength is that it helps relate human _____ to _____ . Its major weakness is that it probably overstates its case. The degree of _____ _____ assumed by sociobiologists is so extreme that even most biologists question it.

118. (p. 629) The danger inherent in sociobiology is that it can be used to support the social _____ _____. By defining human nature as relatively fixed and unchanging, sociobiology discourages attempts to change current cultural practices.

SELF-TEST

1. (p. 609) A(n) _____ is a mixture of belief and emotion that predisposes a person to respond to other people, objects, or institutions in a positive or negative way.
   a. role
   b. attitude
   c. belief
   d. emotion

2. (p. 609) Of the following, which is *not* a component of attitudes?
   a. emotional
   b. residual
   c. belief
   d. action

3. (p. 609) Of the following, which is *not* a factor that influences attitude formation?
   a. group membership
   b. order of birth
   c. chance happenings
   d. child rearing

4. (p. 610) Which of the following is *not* true of mass media such as television?
   a. Images of male and female roles, and racial or ethnic minorities are fairly and accurately represented.
   b. Heavy doses of violence may lead viewers to develop a "mean" world view.
   c. Heavy viewers are less likely to feel that most people can be trusted.
   d. Frequent viewers overestimate their chances of being involved in a violent accident.

5. (p. 610) Which of the following is a reason why some attitudes are acted upon and others are not?
   a. immediate consequences
   b. habits
   c. evaluation by others
   d. all of the above

6. (p. 611) Of the following, which is *not* a method for measuring attitudes?
   a. open-ended interviews
   b. social distance scales
   c. attitude scales
   d. rank order measurements

7. (p. 611) True-False.   Reference groups are control groups used in social psychology experiments.

8. (p. 611) Which of the following would *not* be expected to encourage attitude change through persuasion?
   a. The communicator is dissimilar to the audience.
   b. The persuader appears to have nothing to gain if the audience accepts the message.
   c. The message is repeated as frequently as possible.
   d. The message appeals to emotions, particularly anxiety and fear.

9. (p. 612) True-False.   Role playing can be an effective technique for bringing about attitude changes.

10. (p. 612) Which of the following defines the position of cognitive dissonance theory?
    a. Tensions between groups in conflict can be reduced through cognitive mediation.
    b. Cognitive attitudes can best be understood by understanding dissonance between the communicator, message, and audience.
    c. If behavior is inconsistent with attitudes it will produce discomfort that may change thoughts to bring them into agreement with actions.
    d. Frustration produces increased arousal which may result in heightened tendencies toward aggression.

11. (p. 612) True-False. Cognitive dissonance theory holds that people tend to seek out new information that contradicts ideas they already possess.

12. (p. 612) True-False. Cognitive dissonance theory states that the amount of reward or justification for acting contrary to one's beliefs determines the amount of dissonance created.

13. (p. 614) Which of the following is *not* a brainwashing technique identified by McConnell?
    a. The indoctrinating agent is in a position to reward the "target" for changes in attitudes or behavior.
    b. The "target" person is isolated from other people who would support his or her original attitudes.
    c. The "target" is made completely dependent on his or her captors for satisfaction of needs.
    d. The captors try to reason with the "target" rather than using psychology or physical abuse.

14. (p. 614) True-False. One of the most frightening aspects of brainwashing is that it is often permanent because of the intensity of indoctrination.

15. (p. 615) In her work with cult members, Margaret Singer found that most converts joined
    a. when they were suffering marked psychological distress
    b. because they enjoyed the initiation process
    c. when they were undergoing a period of mild depression, indecision, or alienation from family and friends
    d. because they were kidnapped and literally forced to join

16. (p. 615) True-False. Love bombing is a brainwashing technique often used by various cults.

17. (p. 615) True-False. Previous cult members most often mention guilt and fear as the main reasons for remaining with the group.

18. (p. 616) Which of the following is *not* true of the authoritarian personality?
    a. Authoritarians were usually severely punished as children and learned to fear and covet authority.
    b. Authoritarians tend to focus their rejection on only one group rather than on all out-groups.
    c. Authoritarians tend to be very ethnocentric.
    d. It can be described as a collection of personal attitudes and values marked by rigidity, inhibition, and oversimplification.

19. (p. 616) The "F" scale is used to measure
    a. qualities of the authoritarian personality
    b. susceptibility to brainwashing
    c. social status
    d. aggression

20. (p. 617)   Which of the following is *not* true of social stereotypes and the individuals who hold them?
    a. Social stereotypes are oversimplified images of people who fall into a particular category.
    b. Stereotypes are always negative.
    c. Stereotypes held by the prejudiced tend to be unusually irrational.
    d. Pleasant or likeable members of a rejected group are seen as "an exception to the rule," not a disconfirmation of the stereotype.

21. (p. 619)   Jane Elliot's experiment with blue- and brown-eyed children showed the importance of _____ in the development of prejudice.
    a. status inequalities   c. racism
    b. social stereotypes   d. insubordinate goals

22. (p. 619)   True-False.   Research on racism indicates that more frequent equal-status interaction between groups in conflict helps reduce stereotypes and prejudice.

23. (p. 619)   True-False.   One technique for minimizing hostilities between conflicting groups is to create superordinate goals for the groups to work on together.

24. (p. 620)   Which of the following is *not* true of "jigsaw" classrooms developed by Aronson?
    a. They facilitate individual effort and independence.
    b. They involve giving students individual pieces of information they must teach to other students.
    c. Children in such classrooms are less prejudiced and like their classmates more than in traditional classrooms.
    d. Students in such classrooms do not have to compete against each other for attention and grades in the same way they do in traditional classrooms.

25. (p. 621)   True-False.   Some ethologists, such as Konrad Lorenz, feel that human aggression is an innate predisposition.

26. (p. 622)   True-False.   When frustration encourages aggression it probably does so by raising overall arousal levels so that we become more sensitive to cues for aggression.

27. (p. 622)   The idea that aggression is learned is an explanation offered by
    a. the frustration-aggression hypothesis
    b. cognitive dissonance theory
    c. social learning theory
    d. Lorenz's ethological theory

28. (p. 623)   True-False.   Most recent evidence suggests that viewing aggressive pornography has no major adverse effects.

29. (p. 623)   The key to anger control is
    a. the principle of fairness—if you keep your temper so will the other person
    b. the fact that people who respond calmly to upsetting situations tend to see them as problems to be solved
    c. letting hostilities out all at once so that less control is necessary for day-to-day frustrations
    d. suppressing anger until it is appropriate to release it in safe or nonviolent situations

30. (p. 625)   True-False.   According to Latané and Darley, one reason for bystander apathy is that bystanders are inhibited from taking action by the presence of others.

31. (p. 625) Which of the following is *not* a "decision point" individuals must pass through before giving help?
    a. They must define the event as an emergency.
    b. They must notice that something is happening.
    c. They must diffuse responsibility for action.
    d. They must select a course of action.

32. (p. 626) True-False. Groups are often less likely than individuals to offer help in an emergency due to the problem of diffusion of responsibility.

33. (p. 628) Which of the following is *not* true of sociobiology?
    a. It states that social behavior evolves in ways that maximize the fitness of a species for survival.
    b. Its danger lies in the fact that it can be used to support the social status quo.
    c. Its major strength is that it takes a strong position of biological determinism.
    d. It postulates that altruistic actions occur because this helps improve chances that an organism's kin will survive.

ANSWERS — PROGRAMMED REVIEW

1. attitude
2. misdirected letter
3. belief, emotional, action
4. direct contact; interaction, child rearing
5. all
6. excluded; rejected
7. mass media
8. overestimate; less
9. chance conditioning
10. immediate consequences
11. evaluate
12. habits
13. conviction
14. personal behavior
15. open-ended interview
16. social distance scale
17. attitude scales
18. reference groups
19. reference
20. Persuasion
21. communicator; message; audience
22. fear, anxiety; conclusions; both; gain
23. role playing
24. reduced; little
25. cognitive dissonance
26. avoid; reject
27. reward; justification
28. pleasant, interesting
29. cause
30. 16
31. captive
32. isolated; dependent; reward
33. unfreeze; Change; refreeze
34. temporary

35. cult
36. depression, alienation
37. belonging
38. love bombing
39. isolation; disciplines, rituals
40. cognitive dissonance
41. reference; isolated; information
42. fear, guilt
43. Prejudice
44. racism, sexism, ageism
45. discrimination
46. 33
47. scapegoating
48. lower
49. direct experiences
50. Personal prejudice
51. group norms
52. authoritarian personality
53. out-groups
54. ethnocentric
55. F
56. punished; authority
57. dogmatism
58. more willing
59. stereotyped
60. positive, negative
61. symbolic prejudice
62. irrational; conflicting
63. nonexistent
64. exception to the rule
65. status inequalities
66. equal-status
67. favorable; more
68. positive

69. Muzafer Sherif
70. superordinate goals
71. nuclear winter
72. integrating
73. not
74. interdependent
75. jigsaw
76. less; more; more; grades
77. worse; better
78. 58
79. murder; abuse
80. killer instinct
81. biologically; inhibit
82. hypoglycemia; allergy; brain
83. threshold
84. murders; violent
85. capable; inevitable
86. frustration-aggression
87. stereotyped; absence
88. aversive
89. aggression cues
90. stronger
91. weapons effect
92. social learning
93. violent; firearms; 70; 18

94. aggressive
95. increase
96. increase; drain off
97. anger control
98. precisely; list; Rank
99. number
100. lower
101. notice; define; responsibility; action
102. few; most
103. no one
104. diffusion of responsibility
105. third
106. more
107. arousal
108. decrease
109. empathic
110. connected
111. more likely
112. helpful
113. fairness
114. genes
115. sociobiology
116. kin
117. behavior; biology; biological determinism
118. status quo

ANSWERS — SELF-TEST

1. b
2. b
3. b
4. a
5. d
6. d
7. False
8. a
9. True
10. c
11. False
12. True
13. d
14. False
15. c
16. True
17. True

18. b
19. a
20. b
21. a
22. True
23. True
24. a
25. True
26. True
27. c
28. False
29. b
30. True
31. c
32. True
33. c

Chapter 25

Sexuality and Gender

CONTENTS

TERMS AND CONCEPTS

primary sexual characteristics
secondary sexual characteristics
menarche
ovulation
menopause
sex hormones
gonads
estrogens
androgens
testes
ovaries
adrenal glands
testosterone
hermaphroditism
progestin
androgenital syndrome
biological biasing effect
gender identity
sex role socialization
sex roles
instrumental behaviors
expressive behaviors
sexual scripts
erogenous zones
nocturnal emissions
castration

sterilization
masturbation
homosexuality
lesbianism
ego-dystonic homosexuality
homophobia
sexual response phases
    excitement
    plateau
    orgasm
    resolution
ejaculation
refractory period
acquaintance (date) rape
sexually transmitted disease (STD)
acquired immune deficiency syndrome (AIDS)
erectile dysfunction
primary impotence
secondary impotence
sensate focus
premature ejaculation
squeeze technique
retarded ejaculation
general sexual dysfunction (frigidity)
orgasmic dysfunction
vaginismus

IMPORTANT INDIVIDUALS

John Money
Ethel Albert
Margaret Mead
Alfred Kinsey
John Gagnon
Morton Hunt
William Masters

Virginia Johnson
Shere Hite
Helen Kaplan
Bryan Strong
Christine DeVault
Sidney Jourard

PROGRAMMED REVIEW

1. (p. 633) _____ _____ characteristics refer to the sexual and reproductive organs themselves: the penis; _____, and _____ in
   males; and the ovaries, _____, and _____ in females.

2. (p. 633) _____ _____ characteristics appear at puberty in
   response to hormonal signals from the pituitary gland.

3. (p. 633) In females, they include development of the _____, the broadening of
   the _____, and other changes in body shape; for males, they include development of facial and body _____, and deepening of the _____.

4. (p. 633) These changes signal physical readiness for reproduction. This maturity is especially
   evident in the female _____ (the onset of menstruation).

5. (p. 633) Soon after menarche, monthly _____ begins. This refers to
   the release of ova (eggs) from the ovaries. From this time until
   _____ (the end of regular monthly fertility cycles), women
   can bear children.

6. (p. 633) Both primary and secondary sexual characteristics are closely related to the action of
   _____ _____ (chemical substances secreted by glands of the
   endocrine system).

7. (p. 633) The _____, or sex glands, affect sexual development by secreting female
   hormones called _____ and male hormones called _____.

8. (p. 633) The gonads in the male are the _____, and in the female, the
   _____.

9. (p. 633) The _____ glands, located above the kidneys, also supply sex hormones
   in both males and females and add to the development of secondary sexual characteristics at puberty.

10. (p. 633) All individuals normally produce both estrogens and androgens, the proportion of
    which influences sexual differences. The development of male or female genitals
    before birth is largely due to the presence or absence—before birth—of
    _____, one of the androgens.

11. (p. 634) _____ _____ is determined at the instant of conception: two X
    chromosomes initiate development of a female; an X chromosome plus a Y chromo-
    some produces a male.

12. (p. 634) For the first _____ weeks of prenatal development, there is no difference between

genetically male and female embryos. However, if a Y chromosome is present, testes develop and supply testosterone, stimulating male development.

13. (p. 634) In the absence of testosterone, the embryo will develop female reproductive organs and genitals, regardless of _____ _____. Nature's primary impulse, then, is to make a female.

14. (p. 634) A genetic male will fail to develop male _____ if too little testosterone is formed during prenatal growth.

15. (p. 634) Even if testosterone is present, an inherited _____ _____ may exist, again resulting in female development.

16. (p. 634) Hormonal problems during early development may lead to _____ where dual or ambiguous sexual anatomy frequently occurs.

17. (p. 635) For instance, a developing female may be masculinized by _____ (a drug given to prevent miscarriage).

18. (p. 635) Masculinization can also result when normal amounts of estrogen are produced, but a genetic abnormality causes the adrenal glands to release too much androgen. This condition is called the _____ _____ and can produce a female child with male genitals.

19. (p. 635) Some of these children are reared as male. Usually, however, the condition is detected and corrected by _____. If necessary, extra estrogen may be given after birth.

20. (p. 635) In addition to determining genital development, the interplay of sex hormones before birth may also permanently "sex-type" the _____ which is thought to alter later chances of developing masculine or feminine characteristics.

21. (p. 635) Although hormonal action is important in human sexual development, evidence suggests that most sex-linked behavior is _____.

22. (p. 635) Still, some researchers feel that prenatal exposure to androgens or estrogens exerts a biological _____ _____ on later psychosexual development in humans.

23. (p. 635) Support for this comes from the work of John Money who has shown that women exposed to androgens before birth are typically "_____" during childhood. However, after adolescence, the girls evidence traditional interests in marriage and motherhood.

24. (p. 636) Some researchers feel that biology underlies male-female differences in thinking abilities. They claim that women are more often "_____-brained" and thus are better at _____ skills and rote learning, while men are more "_____-brained" and thus do better on _____ tasks.

25. (p. 636) Others strongly reject this theory. To them, such claims are based on shaky evidence and sexist thinking. After all, they point out, men (as a group) do only _____ better on spatial tasks and women are only _____ better at language skills.

26. (p. 636) The most telling recent evidence may be the fact that differences between male and female scores on the _____ _____

Test are rapidly declining. This is probably best explained by the growing similarity of male and female interests, experiences, and educational goals.

27. (p. 636) The one thing that is certain in the gender debate is that males and females are more _____ than they are _____. There is no biological basis for the unequal treatment women have often faced at work, school, and elsewhere.

28. (p. 636) One's personal, private sense of maleness or femaleness is referred to as _____ _____. This term can be distinguished from _____ _____ which are observable traits, mannerisms, interests, and behaviors defined by one's culture as "male" or "female."

29. (p. 636) Gender identity appears to be a _____ self-perception. Cases of hermaphroditism emphasize this point. Those individuals raised as boys will act like and consider themselves boys; those raised as girls will act like and consider themselves girls.

30. (p. 636) Gender identity is essentially formed by ___ or ___ years of age and few problems occur with hermaphroditic individuals as long as a final decision concerning their sex is made by the age of _____ months.

31. (p. 636) Gender identity begins with male-female labels and is then influenced by _____ _____ _____, that is, by subtle pressure exerted by parents, peers, and cultural institutions that urge boys to "act like boys" and girls to "act like girls."

32. (p. 636) In determining adult sexual behavior and sex-linked personality traits, _____ _____ are probably as important as chromosomal, genital or hormonal sex. This term refers to the favored pattern of behavior expected of individuals on the basis of their gender.

33. (p. 636) The naturalness of sex roles is certainly questionable based on cross-cultural observations. For example, Ethel Albert has identified numerous cultures in which women do the heavy work because men are considered too _____ for it.

34. (p. 636) Also, in the Soviet Union, roughly _____ percent of the medical doctors and a large proportion of the work force are women.

35. (p. 636) Margaret Mead's observations of the _____ people of New Guinea offer another good example. She found that sex roles in that culture are a nearly perfect _____ of the American stereotypes. That is, women do the fishing and manufacturing, are expected to control the power and economic life of the community, and take the initiative in courting and sexual relations. Men are expected to be dependent, flirtatious, and concerned with their appearance.

36. (p. 637) A side effect of sex role socialization is the imprint left on activities having nothing to do with gender. For example, there is also evidence that boys are more _____ than girls, and that girls are more _____ than boys.

37. (p. 637) Learning sex roles begins immediately after birth. Infant girls are held more _____ and treated more _____ than boys. Both parents play more _____ with their sons than with their daughters.

38. (p. 637) Later, _____ are allowed to roam over a wider area without special permission and are expected to run errands earlier.

39. (p. 637) Daughters are told that they are _____ and that "nice girls don't fight." Boys are told to be _____ and that "boys don't cry." Sons are more often urged to control _____, while parents tolerate aggression toward other children more in _____ than _____.

40. (p. 637) Overall, parents tend to encourage their sons to engage in _____ (goal-directed) behaviors, to control their emotions, and to prepare for the world of work. Daughters are encouraged in _____ (emotion-oriented) behaviors, and to a lesser degree, are socialized for the maternal role.

41. (p. 637) It appears that in our culture, male seems to be defined by many people as "_____ _____." There is a vague fear of expressive and emotional behavior in male children, because it seems to imply _____.

42. (p. 638) A capacity for sexual arousal is apparent at _____ or soon after. This fact has been verified by sexual researcher Alfred Kinsey who found instances of _____ (sexual climax) in boys as young as five months old and in girls as young as four months.

43. (p. 638) Kinsey also found that children aged ___ to ___ spontaneously engage in manipulation and exhibition of their genitals.

44. (p. 638) Fifty percent of males and twenty-five percent of females report having engaged in preadolescent _____ _____.

45. (p. 638) Sexual arousal is a complex phenomenon. It may be produced by direct stimulation of the body's _____ _____: genitals, mouth, breasts, ears, anus, and to a lesser degree the surface of the body in general.

46. (p. 638) John Gagnon believes that we learn a variety of _____ _____ that determine when and where we are likely to express sexual feelings, and with whom.

47. (p. 638) When two people follow markedly different scripts, misunderstandings are almost sure to occur. In such cases considerable "_____" of scripts is often needed for sexual compatibility.

48. (p. 638) To study gender differences in sexual arousal, one study used medical recording devices to measure sexual arousal in males and females as they listened to erotic tape recordings. The material was _____ arousing for both sexes.

49. (p. 638) This and similar findings suggest that women are no less physically aroused by erotic stimuli than are men. However, compared with men, women more often have a negative _____ response to explicit pictures of sex. That is, women more often report feeling upset and disgusted by these stimuli.

50. (p. 638) If capacity for sexual arousal is measured by frequency of orgasm (brought about by masturbation or intercourse), the peak of male sexual activity is at age _____.

51. (p. 638) Kinsey's studies (done in the early 1950s) placed the peak of female sexual activity at about _____ years of age.

52. (p. 638) However, in recent years women have participated more fully in sexual activities, and

at an earlier age. The peak rate of female sexual activity is still _____ than that of males but is becoming more comparable.

53. (p. 638)   In males, the strength of the sex drive is related to the amount of _____ secreted by the testes. When it dramatically increases at puberty, so does the sex drive.

54. (p. 639)   In addition to estrogen, androgens may also be important to the female sex drive. One study found that frequency of intercourse for married women was _____ when their androgen levels were at a peak.

55. (p. 639)   Furthermore, when women are given androgens for medical reasons, some report _____ sexual desire.

56. (p. 639)   Some women also report variations in arousal at various times during their monthly cycle. If such a relationship does exist, its effects are probably _____, since women may engage in sexual activity at any time during their monthly cycles (including during menstruation).

57. (p. 639)   According to Kinsey, about 85 percent of males and 35 percent of females have had sexual _____ that resulted in orgasm. These experiences typically begin during adolescence and may continue throughout adulthood.

58. (p. 639)   Kinsey found some _____ in the number of men who have nocturnal orgasm after marriage, but _____ _____ among women.

59. (p. 639)   Alcohol is a _____. As such, it may, in small doses, stimulate erotic desire by lowering inhibitions. However, in larger doses alcohol suppresses _____ in women and _____ in men.

60. (p. 639)   In lower animals, _____ (surgical removal of the testicles) or removal of the ovaries usually completely abolishes sexual activity in _____ animals. However, sexually _____ animals (particularly higher animals) may show little immediate change in sexual behavior.

61. (p. 639)   In humans, the effects of castration _____; initially, some individuals show a sex drive decline, others do not. However, after several years have passed almost all subjects report a _____ in sex drive.

62. (p. 639)   _____ (surgically based birth control such as a vasectomy or a tubal ligation) has nothing to do with castration. Men and women who undergo this procedure experience no loss of sex drive. If anything, they may become more sexually active when pregnancy is no longer a concern.

63. (p. 639)   Aging does not unavoidably end sexual activity. The crucial factor appears to be _____ and opportunity. Individuals who fairly regularly engage in intercourse after age _____ to _____ have little difficulty in later years.

64. (p. 639)   _____ may be defined as deliberate self-stimulation which causes sexual gratification or orgasm. Rhythmic self-stimulation has been observed in infants under one year of age.

65. (p. 639)   Masturbation in the male usually takes the form of _____ or other manipulation of the penis. Female masturbation most often centers on stimulation of the _____ or the areas immediately surrounding it.

66. (p. 639)   Kinsey reports that _____ percent of the women he surveyed had masturbated at some time, and _____ percent of the males reported having masturbated.

67. (p. 639)   Morton Hunt's more recent survey showed almost identical rates. But he believes that a liberalization of attitudes toward masturbation has taken place as reflected in the fact that _____ now begin masturbatory experiences earlier.

68. (p. 639)   Through masturbation people discover what is pleasing sexually and what their natural rhythms and preferences are. It is therefore an important part of the _____ development of most adolescents.

69. (p. 640)   Among other things, it provides a healthy _____ for sexual intercourse during a period when sexual activity is discouraged and young people are maturing emotionally.

70. (p. 640)   Morton Hunt found that a sizable number of married people masturbate at least occasionally—approximately _____ percent.

71. (p. 640)   "Self-abuse," as masturbation was once called, has enjoyed a long and unfortunate history of religious and medical condemnation. For example, 50 years ago a child might be told that masturbation would cause _____, _____, sterility, or other such nonsense.

72. (p. 640)   The contemporary view is that masturbation is a normal and acceptable sexual outlet. There is no harm caused by masturbation itself. Typically, the only negative effects of masturbation are the _____, _____, or _____ that occur when an individual has learned negative attitudes toward it.

73. (p. 640)   It is estimated that about ___ to _____ percent of all adult men in Western societies are predominantly homosexual. Adult women who are lesbians represent ___ to ___ percent of all women. This means there may be 22 million gay people in the United States.

74. (p. 640)   A major survey of 76 cultures found that almost _____-_____ accept some form of homosexuality.

75. (p. 640)   Many people mistakenly believe that homosexuality is caused by a _____ imbalance. However, this is highly unlikely since measured levels for most gay men and lesbians are within the normal range.

76. (p. 640)   Research suggests that a combination of _____, biological, and social and _____ influences combine to produce one's sexual orientation.

77. (p. 640)   Apart from sexual orientation, testing consistently shows no difference in _____ or adjustment between heterosexuals and homosexuals.

78. (p. 640)   Emotional adjustment, then, appears to be independent of sexual preference. Therefore, homosexuality cannot be considered a sexual _____.

79. (p. 640)   Psychologically, homosexuality is regarded as a problem only if a person feels lasting guilt, self-hate, or similar negative emotions. This condition is referred to as _____-_____ homosexuality.

80. (p. 640) This problem is probably rare because the majority of adult homosexuals display _____ patterns and _____ histories similar to those of heterosexuals.

81. (p. 640) The problems faced by homosexuals are more often related to rejection by family, discrimination in employment and housing, and to the undercurrent of _____ (referring to prejudice, fear, and dislike aimed at homosexuals) in American society.

82. (p. 641) In a series of experiments, interviews, and controlled observations, William Masters and Virginia Johnson directly studied sexual intercourse and masterbation in nearly 700 males and females. They have classified sexual response in both males and females into four phases: _____, _____, _____, and _____.

83. (p. 642) Sexual arousal in the male is signaled by _____ of the _____ during the excitement phase.

84. (p. 642) There is also a rise in _____ rate, increased _____ flow to the genitals, enlargement of the _____, erection of the _____, and numerous other bodily changes.

85. (p. 642) If sexual stimulation ends, the excitement phase will gradually subside. Continued stimulation moves the individual into the _____ phase, in which physical changes and subjective feelings of arousal become more intense.

86. (p. 642) If stimulation ends during this phase, sexual arousal will subside more slowly and may produce considerable _____. Further stimulation during the plateau phase brings about a reflex release of tension resulting in sexual climax, or _____.

87. (p. 642) In the mature male, orgasm is usually accompanied by _____ (release of seminal fluid) and is followed by a short _____ period during which a second orgasm is impossible.

88. (p. 642) Only rarely is the male refractory period immediately followed by a second orgasm. Orgasm is usually followed by _____, a return to lower levels of sexual tension and arousal.

89. (p. 642) Although the timing and intensity of the phases vary for individual women, the basic pattern of response is the same as that for men. During the excitement phase, a complex pattern of changes prepares the vagina for intercourse. Also, the _____ become erect, _____ rate rises, and the skin may become _____.

90. (p. 642) During orgasm, from _____ to _____ muscular contractions of the vagina, uterus, and related structures serve to discharge accumulated sexual tension. No form of _____ accompanies female orgasm.

91. (p. 642) Both _____ and _____ in the female usually last longer than they do in the male. After orgasm, about _____ percent of all women return to the plateau phase, after which orgasm may occur again.

92. (p. 642) Masters and Johnson exploded the Freudian myth that clitoral orgasm is an immature form of female response. They showed there is no difference in _____ _____ no matter what form of stimulation produces orgasm.

93. (p. 642)   As a matter of fact, the _____ is quite lacking in nerve endings for touch. Most sensations during intercourse, therefore, come from stimulation of the clitoris and other external tissues.

94. (p. 642)   Women in one study said they would rather not choose between vaginal or clitoral stimulation, but if forced, _____-_____ preferred clitoral sensations.

95. (p. 642)   Also, Shere Hite found that, among 3000 women surveyed, only _____ percent regularly achieved orgasm during intercourse without separate massaging of the clitoris.

96. (p. 642)   During lovemaking, _____ to _____ minutes are usually required for a woman to go from excitement to orgasm. Males may experience all four stages in as little as ___ minutes.

97. (p. 642)   In a study of 1000 married women, _____ percent reached orgasm if intercourse lasted 1 to 11 minutes, and _____ percent climaxed if intercourse lasted 15 minutes or more. _____-_____ percent said that orgasm occurred within 1 minute of the start of intercourse.

98. (p. 642)   At one time the concept of _____ _____ was considered the goal of lovemaking. More recently, this notion has been rejected as an artificial concern that may reduce enjoyment.

99. (p. 643)   During _____, 70 percent of females reach orgasm in four minutes or less. Slower female response during intercourse probably occurs because stimulation to the _____ is less direct.

100. (p. 643)   Masters and Johnson found that for women, subjective feelings of pleasure and intensity of orgasm are not related to penis _____. Also, while individual differences exist in flaccid penis size, there is much less variation in size during _____.

101. (p. 643)   It is true that about 1 woman in ___ does not experience orgasm during the first year of marriage, and only about _____ percent regularly reach orgasm through intercourse alone.

102. (p. 643)   However, this does not imply lack of physical responsiveness, since approximately _____ of all women reach orgasm when masturbating.

103. (p. 643)   Only about ___ percent of the male population is capable of multiple orgasm (and then only after an unavoidable refractory period). Most males are limited to a second orgasm at best.

104. (p. 643)   Most women who regularly experience orgasm are capable of multiple orgasm, although only about _____ percent do. A woman should not assume that something is wrong if she isn't orgasmic or multiorgasmic. Undoubtedly, many women have satisfying sexual experiences even when orgasm is not involved.

105. (p. 643)   Compared with earlier decades, the gap between sexual values and actual behavior has narrowed. For example, traditional morality called for female virginity before marriage. Yet, in the 1940s and 50s, as many as _____ percent of women who married had engaged in premarital sexual relations.

106. (p. 643)   Changing attitudes toward sex are illustrated by the result of national polls concerning the acceptability of premarital intercourse. In a 1959 poll _____ percent thought

it was wrong; in 1969 only _____ percent rejected it; while by 1973 only _____ percent felt likewise.

107. (p. 643)   In a more recent survey, only _____ percent of those between ages 18 and 29 believed that premarital sex is unacceptable. Similar changes have been observed in attitudes toward extramarital sex, homosexuality, sex education, and a variety of related issues.

108. (p. 643)   Changes in sexual attitudes are still larger than changes in actual behavior. Largely, there is greater tolerance for sexual behavior, especially that engaged in by others. For example, a poll of *Psychology Today* readers found that _____ percent accepted extramarital sex under some circumstances. But in practice only _____ percent of its married readers had actually had extramarital sexual experience.

109. (p. 644)   A recent *Redbook* magazine survey showed about the same results: _____-_____ percent of respondents of all ages had engaged in at least one extramarital affair. These percentages have not changed greatly in the last 40 years.

110. (p. 644)   Significant behavioral changes can be seen in premarital intercourse rates. In the early 1950s, Kinsey found that _____ percent of males and _____ percent of females had engaged in premarital intercourse by age 25. In the 1970s, Hunt obtained _____ percent for males and about _____ percent for females.

111. (p. 644)   Another study found that _____ percent of women married after 1973 had engaged in premarital relations. A variety of additional studies support the idea that premarital intercourse rates have increased.

112. (p. 644)   To some extent these changes are related to a tendency to postpone marriage. In the U.S. alone, _____ million unmarried couples are living together.

113. (p. 644)   Another major element of the "sexual revolution" is earlier participation in sexual behavior by both sexes. A Louis Harris poll conducted in 1986 found that _____ percent of the nation's 17-year-olds were sexually experienced.

114. (p. 644)   For 16-year-olds, the figure was _____ percent, for 15-year-olds it was _____ percent, and for 14-year-olds, _____ percent.

115. (p. 644)   This particular aspect of increased sexual behavior remains troubling. Today, the U.S. has one of the highest teenage _____ rates among all industrialized nations.

116. (p. 644)   Although sexual intercourse by unmarried couples is more common today, most couples emphasize mutual commitment and a loving relationship. Most women have only _____ premarital sexual partner(s) whom they eventually marry, while men typically have about _____ premarital partners.

117. (p. 644)   The association between sexuality and love or affection remains strong for the _____ of the population. Both premarital sex and cohabitation are still widely viewed as preludes to marriage or as temporary substitutes for it.

118. (p. 644)   A good summary of the changes that have occurred in sexual behavior is found in the phrase, "the slow death of the _____ _____." The gap between male and female sexual patterns has continued to close.

119. (p. 645)   The importance of respecting the right to say no is underscored by the recent dramatic increase in cases of acquaintance (or date) rape. One recent study found

that _____ percent of all female college students had been raped. Roughly _____ of these rapes were by first dates, casual dates, or romantic acquaintances.

120. (p. 645)   Men who commit date rape often believe they have done nothing _____. But the effects of acquaintance rape are no less devastating than rape committed by a stranger.

121. (p. 645)   The incidence of _____ _____ diseases (abbreviated _____) has been rising in the U.S. for the last 20 years. Today, sexually active individuals run an elevated risk of getting chlamydia, gonorrhea, hepatitis B, herpes, syphilis, and the like.

122. (p. 645)   For many people, _____ _____ _____ (AIDS) has added a new fear. Whereas most other STDs are treatable, AIDS is almost always fatal once symptoms appear.

123. (p. 645)   AIDS is caused by a _____ that disables the immune system. This allows various other "opportunistic" diseases to invade the body without resistance and victims eventually die, usually of multiple infections.

124. (p. 645)   The first symptoms of AIDS may show up as little as ___ months after infection, or they may not appear for up to ___ years. Because of this long incubation period, infected persons often pass AIDS on to others without knowing it.

125. (p. 645)   AIDS is spread by direct contact with _____ _____—especially blood, semen, and vaginal secretions. The AIDS virus cannot be transmitted by casual contact—shaking hands, social kissing, sharing drinking glasses, etc.

126. (p. 645)   AIDS has been called the _____ _____because male homosexuals were its first highly visible victims. However, this label is in error, because AIDS can be spread by all forms of sexual intercourse and has affected persons of all sexual orientations.

127. (p. 645)   Those who are at greatest risk include men who have had sex with other men, people who have shared _____, blood transfusion recipients (between 1977 and spring 1985), _____ (because they may require frequent blood transfusions), sexual partners of people in the above groups, and _____ with a history of multiple partners.

128. (p. 645)   AIDS is having a strong impact on sexual behavior in some groups. Among gay men there has been a sharp _____ in monogamous relationships and in abstaining from sex. Gay men have also significantly _____ participation in high-risk sexual behaviors.

129. (p. 645)   Evidence is growing that the risk of AIDS infection is _____ for hetero-sexuals than once predicted. Nevertheless, the total number of heterosexual cases is growing.

130. (p. 646)   Impotence (also known as _____ _____) is the inability to maintain an erection for sexual intercourse. It may be an occasional or continuous problem.

131. (p. 647)   Males suffering from _____ impotence have never been able to produce or maintain an erection. Those who have previously performed successfully,

but then have become impotent, are said to suffer from _____
impotence.

132. (p. 647) Sex therapists Masters and Johnson feel that a problem of impotence exists when failure occurs on _____ percent or more of a man's lovemaking attempts and should therefore be distinguished from an occasional inability. True impotence typically persists for months or years.

133. (p. 647) Occasional impotence is _____. Overreaction to it may generate fears and doubts that can contribute to further impotence. At such times, it is particularly important for the man's partner to practice patient reassurance to help prevent the establishment of a vicious cycle.

134. (p. 647) It is now recognized that roughly _____ percent of impotence cases are organic, or physically caused. Even then, it is almost always made worse by anxiety and other emotional reactions.

135. (p. 647) If a man can have an erection at times other than lovemaking (during sleep, for instance), the problem probably is not physical but rather _____ (a result of emotional factors).

136. (p. 647) Organic impotence may result from alcohol or drug abuse, diabetes, _____ disease, _____ and urological disorders, neurological problems, and reactions to _____ for high blood pressure, heart disease, or stomach ulcers.

137. (p. 647) According to Masters and Johnson, primary psychogenic impotence is often related to harsh _____ training, early sexual experience with a seductive _____, or other experiences leading to guilt, fear, and sexual inhibition. In a few instances, unrecognized _____ feelings may also be a source of conflicts.

138. (p. 647) Secondary psychogenic impotence may be related to anxiety, guilt or fear. It often starts with excessive consumption of alcohol or the presence of _____ ejaculation leading to repeated sexual failures. Initial doubts become severe fears of failure which serve to further inhibit sexual response.

139. (p. 647) Medical treatment for organic impotence may employ _____ or _____. Treatment for both organic and psychogenic impotence also usually includes _____ to remove fears and psychological blocks.

140. (p. 647) In _____ _____, a technique used in treating impotence and other sexual disorders, the couple is initially told to take turns stroking various parts of each other's bodies. Genital contact is avoided at first, with emphasis placed on giving pleasure and on signaling what is most gratifying.

141. (p. 648) Masters and Johnson define the problem of _____ _____ as one in which a man is unable to delay sexual climax long enough to satisfy his partner in at least one-half of their lovemaking attempts.

142. (p. 648) Helen Kaplan says that prematurity exists when ejaculation occurs _____ or when there is an inability to tolerate high levels of excitement at the plateau stage of arousal.

143. (p. 648) Theories advanced to explain this common problem in male sexual adjustment have ranged from the idea that it may represent _____ toward the man's sexual partner to the suggestion that most early male sexual experiences tend to encourage rapid _____.

144. (p. 648) Kaplan adds that excessive _____ and _____ over performance are usually present, and that some men simply engage in techniques that maximize sensation and make rapid orgasm inevitable.

145. (p. 648) The most common treatment for premature ejaculation is the _____ _____. Here the man's sexual partner stimulates him manually until he signals that ejaculation is about to occur. The man's partner then firmly squeezes the tip of the penis to inhibit orgasm. When the man feels he has control, stimulation is repeated.

146. (p. 648) Among males, _____ _____ (an inability to reach orgasm) was once considered a rare problem. But milder forms of this dysfunction have recently accounted for increasing numbers of clients seeking therapy.

147. (p. 648) Typical background factors are strict _____ training, fear of _____, lack of interest in the sexual partner, symbolic inability to give of oneself, unacknowledged homosexuality, or the recent occurrence of _____ life events.

148. (p. 648) Treatment for retarded ejaculation consists of sensate focus, _____ by the man's partner, and stimulation to the point of orgasm followed by immediate intromission and ejaculation. Work also focuses on resolving personal _____ and _____ difficulties.

149. (p. 648) Women who show little or no physical arousal to sexual stimulation and persistently derive no pleasure from sexual stimulation suffer from _____ _____ commonly referred to as _____.

150. (p. 648) Female general sexual dysfunction is similar to male impotence; it may be either primary or secondary. Also, it has similar causes. Treatment includes sensate focus, genital stimulation by the woman's partner, and "_____" intercourse controlled by the woman.

151. (p. 648) The most prevalent sexual complaint among women is _____ _____, an inability to reach orgasm during intercourse.

152. (p. 648) Often it is clear in such cases that the woman is not completely unresponsive; rather, she is unresponsive in the context of a _____.

153. (p. 649) While sex therapists try to avoid placing blame, some instances of "orgasmic dysfunction" can be traced to inadequate _____ or faulty _____ on the part of the woman's partner. The male partner must be sexually adequate and must have a commitment to ensuring gratification of the woman.

154. (p. 649) If we focus only on the woman, the most common source of orgasmic difficulties is _____ of sexual response.

155. (p. 649) Female orgasm requires a degree of abandonment to erotic feelings that may be inhibited by ambivalence or hostility toward the relationship, by _____, fears of expressing _____ _____, and by tendencies to control and intellectualize erotic feelings.

156. (p. 649) In Kaplan's treatment program, anorgasmic women are first trained to focus on their sexual responsiveness through _____ or vigorous stimulation by a partner. As the woman becomes consistently _____ in these circumstances, her responsiveness is gradually transferred to intercourse.

157. (p. 649) In the condition known as _____, muscle spasms make intercourse impossible. It is often accompanied by obvious fears of intercourse or at least high levels of anxiety.

158. (p. 649) Treatment of vaginismus is similar to what might be done for a nonsexual _____, including desensitization, progressive relaxation, and hypnosis.

159. (p. 649) It is best to view sexual adjustment within the broader context of a _____. It is a form of communication. Couples with strong and caring relationships can probably survive most sexual problems. A couple with a satisfactory sex life but a poor relationship _____ lasts.

160. (p. 649) Masters and Johnson believe that when there are disagreements about sex, the rule should be "each partner must accept the other as the final authority on his or her own feelings." Partners are urged to give feedback by following the "_____ and _____" rule.

161. (p. 649) When problems do arise, partners are urged to be responsive to each other's needs at an _____ level and to recognize that all sexual problems are _____. It is particularly important to avoid the "numbers game."

162. (p. 650) In a study that compared happily married couples with unhappily married couples, Navran found that in almost every regard the happily married couples showed superior _____ skills.

163. (p. 650) Several guidelines can be suggested to help facilitate communication. One of them is to avoid "_____," that is saving up feelings and complaints.

164. (p. 650) Another suggestion is to be open about _____. Happy couples not only talk more, they convey more personal feelings and show greater sensitivity to their partner's feelings.

165. (p. 650) Don't attack the other person's _____. Expressions of negative feelings should be given as statements of one's own feelings, not as statements of _____.

166. (p. 650) Don't try to _____ a fight; instead, try to resolve the differences without focusing on who is right or wrong.

167. (p. 650) Recognize that _____ is appropriate. However, constructive fights require that couples fight fair by sticking to the real issues and not "hitting below the belt."

168. (p. 650) Bryan Strong and Christine DeVault suggest that if you really want to mess up a relationship, follow "Ten Ways to Avoid Intimacy." One of these ways is "Don't talk

about anything meaningful, especially about _____." You should be familiar with the others.

169. (p. 652) Sidney Jourard has conducted some intriguing studies in human touching, not only in our country, but cross-culturally. He discovered that, in American society, most regions of a young adult's body remain untouched unless one has a close friend of the _____ _____, and even that depends upon their relationship. This was not the case in such countries as France or Puerto Rico.

170. (p. 652) Jourard also found interesting sex differences. Daughters are touched more right into their twenties. Mothers are allowed to touch a girl's hair frequently. One-half the parents get to touch their daughter's _____, and one-half manage a literal pat on the _____. Sons, on the other hand, receive considerably less touching. Also, parents stop touching boys much earlier.

171. (p. 652) However, taboos do exist. Only _____ percent of the girls studied received a paternal pat on the bottom and _____ were touched by their fathers in the genital areas. The same restrictions did not necessarily hold true with male students and their mothers.

SELF-TEST

1. (p. 633) The penis, testes, and scrotum in the male and the ovaries, uterus, and vagina in females are
   a. gonads
   b. secondary sexual characteristics
   c. erogenous zones
   d. primary sexual characteristics

2. (p. 633) True-False. Secondary sexual characteristics refer to the lesser physical differences between males and females such as the position of sexual and reproductive organs.

3. (p. 633) True-False. Menarche marks the end of a female's ability to reproduce.

4. (p. 633) Female hormones, _____, and male hormones, _____, secreted by the gonads affect sexual development and behaviors.
   a. estrogens, androgens   c. testosterones, progesterones
   b. androgens, estrogens   d. adrenalins, noradrenalins

5. (p. 633) The gonad(s) in the male is (are) the
   a. penis   c. testes
   b. scrotum   d. prostate

6. (p. 633) The gonad(s) in the female is (are) the
   a. ovaries   c. vagina
   b. clitoris   d. uterus

7. (p. 633) Development of male or female anatomy is largely due to _____ before birth.
   a. genetic sex
   b. the presence or absence of testosterone
   c. secondary sexual characteristics
   d. gonadal sex

8. (p. 634) Which of the following is *not* associated with sexual abnormalities in prenatal development?

    a. androgen insensitivity among genetic males
    b. exposure to progestin among genetic females
    c. the XY chromosome combination where testosterone is produced
    d. the androgenital syndrome

9. (p. 635) When a genetic abnormality causes the adrenal glands to secrete excess amounts of androgen, it can produce a condition known as _____ where a female child has male genitals.
    a. gender misidentity   c. vaginismus
    b. androgenital syndrome   d. impotence

10. (p. 635) Some researchers feel that prenatal exposure to androgens or estrogens exerts a biological biasing effect on later psychosexual development. Which of the following suggests this idea?
    a. The fact that transsexuals such as Dr. Renee Richards become genetically different following hormonal treatments.
    b. Research conducted by John Money demonstrating that women exposed to androgens before birth were typically "tomboys" during childhood.
    c. The fact that women are more often "right-brained" and thus better at math and visual-spatial skills.
    d. The fact that men are more often "right-brained" and thus better at language skills.

11. (p. 636) A learned self-perception of one's maleness or femaleness is referred to as
    a. expressive behavior   c. sex role socialization
    b. instrumental behavior   d. gender identity

12. (p. 636) Which of the following is of primary importance in the acquisition of gender identity?
    a. primary sexual expression   c. sex role socialization
    b. erogenous zones   d. gender instrumentation development

13. (p. 636) The _____ reported by Mead have a nearly perfect reversal of American sex role stereotypes.
    a. Zulu culture   c. people of the Soviet Union
    b. Tchambuli people   d. Tsari society

14. (p. 637) Overall, parents tend to encourage their sons to engage in _____ _____, while daughters are encouraged in _____ _____.
    a. expressive behaviors, nonexpressive behaviors
    b. sex roles, orgasmic functioning
    c. gender identity, instrumental responsiveness
    d. instrumental behaviors, expressive behaviors

15. (p. 638) Which of the following is *not* true of early sexual behavior?
    a. Kinsey found that females are more likely to be sexually aroused during infancy than males.
    b. Kinsey has verified instances of orgasm in boys as young as 5 months old and in girls as young as 4 months.
    c. Fifty percent of males and 25 percent of females report having engaged in pre-adolescent sex play.
    d. Children aged 2 to 5 spontaneously engage in manipulation and exhibition of their genitals.

16. (p. 638) True-False. Women are more inclined, when measured physiologically, to respond negatively to explicit pictures of sex than men.

17. (p. 638) In males, the strength of the sex drive is related to
    a. various times of the month in male cycles
    b. the degree of sperm available
    c. the amount of androgens secreted by the testes
    d. only cognitive factors, since males are physically always prepared for intercourse

18. (p. 639) Which of the following is *not* true of erotic dreams accompanied by orgasm?
    a. They typically begin in adolescence.
    b. According to Kinsey, about 85 percent of males and 35 percent of females have experienced them.
    c. They are an indication of possible sexual disorder if they occur beyond the late 20s.
    d. They are also known as noctural emissions.

19. (p. 639) True-False. In humans, the effects of male and female castration include increased sex drive related to freedom from anxieties regarding pregnancy.

20. (p. 639) True-False. A critical factor for an extended sex life appears to be regularity of sexual activity.

21. (p. 639) Which of the following is *not* true of masturbation?
    a. Approximately 90 percent of all women reach orgasm when masturbating.
    b. Hunt found that approximately 70 percent of married men and women masturbate at least occasionally.
    c. Adolescents now begin masturbation at a later age because intercourse occurs earlier.
    d. Hunt found that 94 percent of males and 63 percent of females have masturbated.

22. (p. 642) Which of the following is *not* true of male sexual response?
    a. Only 50 percent of males are capable of multiple orgasms.
    b. Males may experience all four sexual stages in as little as 4 minutes.
    c. Sexual arousal is signaled by erection of the penis and other bodily changes.
    d. In the mature male, orgasm is accompanied by ejaculation.

23. (p. 642) All of the following statements about female sexual response are true *except*
    a. no form of ejaculation accompanies female orgasm
    b. both orgasm and resolution last longer in females than they do in males
    c. there is no relationship between penis size and level of female sexual gratification
    d. vaginal orgasms are more intense than clitoral orgasms

24. (p. 642) True-False. Simultaneous male and female orgasm should be the ultimate goal of sexual intercourse.

25. (p. 643) True-False. Slower female sexual response during intercourse probably occurs because stimulation of the clitoris is less direct. During masturbation, 70 percent of females reach orgasm in 4 minutes or less.

26. (p. 643) Which of the following is *not* true of the "sexual revolution"?
    a. Generally attitudes about sexual behavior have changed more radically than actual sexual behavior.
    b. Comparing Kinsey's and Hunt's results, it seems that there has been a significant increase in the extent of extramarital sex.
    c. Results from several surveys support the idea that premarital intercourse rates have definitely increased in the last 20 years.
    d. Currently, most women have only one premarital sex partner while men have about six.

27. (p. 644) True-False. Recent surveys of sexual behavior indicate that a major element of the "sexual revolution" is a marked increase in sexual expression among females.

28. (p. 646) True-False. Secondary impotence refers to frigidity in females.

29. (p. 647) A major sexual adjustment technique which involves nongenital physical contact is
    a. sensate focus   c. sex role socialization
    b. squeeze technique   d. orgasmic relearning

30. (p. 648) The technique most often used in treating premature ejaculation is
    a. sensate focus   c. sex role socialization
    b. the squeeze technique   d. orgasmic relearning

31. (p. 648) Retarded ejaculation refers to an inability to
    a. sustain erection   c. achieve orgasm
    b. feel physical pleasure   d. achieve erection promptly

32. (p. 648) Which of the following is *not* true of female general sexual dysfunction?
    a. It is usually defined as a persistent inability to derive pleasure from sexual stimulation.
    b. As in male impotence, it may be primary or secondary.
    c. The causes bear general similarity to those seen in male impotence.
    d. Treatment usually includes the "squeeze technique."

33. (p. 648) True-False. The most prevalent sexual complaint among women is orgasmic dysfunction.

34. (p. 649) A condition in which muscle spasms make intercourse impossible for the female is known as
    a. frigidity   c. orgasmic dysfunction
    b. androgenital syndrome   d. vaginismus

35. (p. 650) Which of the following is *not* a useful guideline in improving and maintaining a healthy emotional relationship?
    a. recognize that anger is inappropriate
    b. avoid gunnysacking
    c. don't try to win a fight
    d. be open with feelings

36. (p. 652) True-False. Compared with countries such as France and Puerto Rico, there is very little touching between individuals in our culture.

37. (p. 652) Which of the following is *not* true of familial contact as reported by Jourard?
    a. Girls are touched by both parents much more frequently than boys.
    b. Touching of boys ends much earlier than for girls.
    c. Most fathers pat their daughters on the bottom.
    d. One-half the parents touch their daughters on the lips, and half manage a pat on the back.

ANSWERS — PROGRAMMED REVIEW

1. Primary sexual; testes, scrotum; uterus, vagina
2. Secondary sexual
3. breasts; hips; hair; voice
4. menarche
5. ovulation; menopause
6. sex hormones
7. gonads; estrogens; androgens

8. testes; ovaries
9. adrenal
10. testosterone
11. Genetic sex
12 6
13. genetic sex
14. genitals
15. androgen insensitivity
16. hermaphroditism
17. progestin
18. androgenital syndrome
19. surgery
20. brain
21. learned
22. biasing effect
23. tomboys
24. left; language; right; spatial
25. slightly; slightly
26. Scholastic Aptitude
27. alike; different
28. gender identity; sex roles
29. learned
30. 3; 4; 18
31. sex role socialization
32. sex roles
33. weak
34. 75
35. Tchambuli; reversal
36. aggressive; empathetic
37. gently; tenderly; roughly
38. boys
39. pretty; strong; emotions; boys; girls
40. instrumental; expressive
41. not female; effeminancy
42. birth; orgasm
43. 2; 5
44. sex play
45. erogenous zones
46. sexual scripts
47. rewriting
48. equally
49. emotional
50. 18
51. 30
52. later
53. androgens
54. highest
55. increased
56. small
57. dreams
58. reduction; no change
59. depressant; orgasm; erection
60. castration; inexperienced; experienced
61. vary; decrease
62. Sterilization

63. regularity; 45; 50
64. Masturbation
65. stroking; clitoris
66. 60; 95
67. adolescents
68. psychosexual
69. substitute
70. 70
71. insanity; acne
72. fear, guilt, anxiety
73. 5; 10; 3; 5
74. two-thirds
75. hormone
76. hereditary; psychological
77. personality
78. disorder
79. ego-dystonic
80. adjustment; occupational
81. homophobia
82. excitement; plateau; orgasm; resolution
83. erection; penis
84. heart; blood; testicles; nipples
85. plateau
86. frustration; orgasm
87. ejaculation; refractory
88. resolution
89. nipples; pulse; flushed
90. 3; 10; ejaculation
91. orgasm, resolution; 15
92. physical response
93. vagina
94. two-thirds
95. 26
96. 10; 20; 4
97. 50; 66; Twenty-five
98. simultaneous orgasm
99. masturbation; clitoris
100. size; erection
101. 3; 30
102. 90
103. 5
104. 15
105. 75
106. 88; 68; 48
107. 22
108. 80; 30
109. Twenty-six
110. 70; 33; 97; 70
111. 93
112. 2.3
113. 57
114. 46; 29; 19
115. pregnancy
116. one; six
117. majority

118. double standard
119. 15; one-half
120. wrong
121. sexually transmitted; STD
122. acquired immune deficiency syndrome
123. virus
124. 2; 7
125. body fluids
126. gay plague
127. needles; hemophiliacs; heterosexuals
128. increase; reduced
129. lower
130. erectile dysfunction
131. primary; secondary
132. 25
133. normal
134. 40
135. psychogenic
136. vascular; prostate; medication
137. religious; mother; homosexual
138. premature
139. drugs; surgery; counseling
140. sensate focus
141. premature ejaculation
142. reflexively
143. hostility; climax
144. arousal; anxiety

145. squeeze technique
146. retarded ejaculation
147. religious; impregnating; traumatic
148. manual stimulation; conflicts; marital
149. general sexual dysfunction; frigidity
150. nondemanding
151. orgasmic dysfunction
152. relationship
153. stimulation; technique
154. overcontrol
155. guilt; sexual needs
156. masturbation; orgasmic
157. vaginismus
158. phobia
159. relationship; rarely
160. touch and ask
161. emotional; mutual
162. communication
163. gunnysacking
164. feelings
165. character; blame
166. win
167. anger
168. feelings
169. opposite sex
170. lips; back
171. 13; none

ANSWERS — SELF-TEST

1. d
2. False
3. False
4. a
5. c
6. a
7. b
8. c
9. b
10. b
11. d
12. c
13. b
14. d
15. a
16. False
17. c
18. c
19. False

20. True
21. c
22. a
23. d
24. False
25. True
26. b
27. True
28. False
29. a
30. b
31. c
32. d
33. True
34. d
35. a
36. True
37. c

Chapter 26

Applied Psychology

CONTENTS

TERMS AND CONCEPTS

applied psychology
industrial/organizational psychology
personnel psychology
flexitime
engineering psychologist (human factors
    engineer)
natural design
feedback
job analysis
critical incidents
biodata
personal interview
vocational interest tests
aptitude tests
assessment center
scientific management (Theory X)
Theory Y
work efficiency
psychological efficiency
participative management
management by objectives
quality circles
job satisfaction
job enrichment
environmental psychology
physical environments

social environments
behavioral settings
territoriality
territorial markers
crowding
density
attentional overload
environmental assessment
architectural psychology
educational psychology
teaching strategy
direct instruction
open teaching
consumer psychology
consumer behavior
marketing research
brand images
consumerism
mock juries
demographic information
community survey
sports psychology
task analysis
peak performance (flow)
career development
    exploration phase

fantasy stage   later career phase
tentative stage   vocational aspiration
realistic stage   vocational counselor
establishment phase   career centers
midcareer phase

IMPORTANT INDIVIDUALS

Jack Keating   Terry Daniel
Elizabeth Loftus   John Calhoun
Donald Norman   Garvin McCain
Robert Baron   Irving Janis
Frederick Taylor   Dan Wheeler
Douglas McGregor

PROGRAMMED REVIEW

1. (p. 656) _____ psychology refers to the use of psychological principles and
    research methods to solve practical problems. Increasingly psychology is being used
    to enhance the quality of life and to improve human performance.

2. (p. 656) Applied psychology can make a life-or-death difference. For example, psychologists
    Jack Keating and Elizabeth Loftus created a life-saving "_____ _____"
    that tells people exactly what to do.

3. (p. 657) This unusual voice alarm has a simple message that contains three key elements:
    (1) Research has shown that switching from a female to a male voice (or the reverse)
    is very _____ _____. (2) During emergen-
    cies, people like to feel that some _____ is in control.
    (3) The crucial reminder to avoid the _____ is repeated, so it
    will be remembered.

4. (p. 657) The largest areas of applied psychology are _____ and counsel-
    ing psychology. A closely related speciality is _____
    psychology which treats whole neighborhoods or communities as "clients."

5. (p. 657) Community psychologists typically emphasize _____,
    _____, and _____. Often,
    they target drug abuse, child _____, unemployment, prejudice, and
    similar problems for solution.

6. (p. 657) From the 1920s until the present, _____/organizational
    psychologists have studied the problems people face at work. Their efforts will likely
    affect how you are selected for a job and how you are tested, trained, and evaluated
    for promotions. They may even help design your work environment or the machines
    you use at work.

7. (p. 657) I/O psychologists are employed mostly by government, industry, and business.
    Typically, they work in: _____ and _____
    (personnel psychology), human _____ at work, and industrial
    _____ (the design of machines and work
    environments).

8. (p. 658) To improve worker morale, industrial psychologists have proposed the use of flexible
    working hours or _____. The basic idea is that starting and

quitting times are made flexible, as long as employees are present during a core work period.

9. (p. 658) Recent studies of two groups of clerical workers suggest that flexitime did improve morale. A switch to this schedule brought a number of benefits, including more job _____, better work-group _____, better relations with supervisors, and less _____.

10. (p. 658) To adapt machines for human use, the engineering psychologist (or _____ _____ engineer) must make them compatible with our sensory and motor capacities. For example, displays must be easy to perceive, controls easy to use, and the tendency to make errors must be minimized.

11. (p. 658) Donald Norman refers to effective human factors engineering as _____ _____. Effective design makes use of signals that are naturally understood by people without any need to learn them.

12. (p. 658) Another major point that Norman emphasizes is that effective design supplies clear _____. In good design each control produces an immediate and obvious effect.

13. (p. 659) Since employed adults spend an average of over _____ hours a year at their jobs, and since the odds are ___ out of 10 that you are or will be employed in business or industry, there is value in knowing how selection for hiring and promotion is done.

14. (p. 659) Personnel selection begins with a _____ _____ to find out exactly what workers do and what skills or knowledge they need for success in a job.

15. (p. 659) A job analysis may be done by interviewing workers or supervisors, by giving them questionnaires, by observing work, or by identifying _____ _____—situations that an employee must be able to cope with if he or she is going to succeed in a particular job.

16. (p. 659) After desirable skills and characteristics are identified, the next step is to learn which job applicants possess them. Currently, the methods most often used for evaluating job candidates are: gathering _____, _____, giving _____ psychological tests, and the _____ center approach.

17. (p. 659) The premise behind biodata (detailed biographical information) is that past behavior tends to predict future behavior. Some of the most useful items are: past _____ interest, _____ achievement, _____ interest, extracurricular activities, _____ activities, social popularity, friction with brothers and sisters, attitudes toward school, and parents' socioeconomic status.

18. (p. 659) The traditional personal interview is still one of the most popular ways of selecting candidates for jobs or promotions. However, interviews are subject to the _____ effect and similar problems. For this reason, psychologists continue to investigate factors that affect interviews.

19. (p. 660) In addition to general intelligence and personality tests, personnel psychologists often use _____ _____ tests, such as Kuder Occupational Interest Survey and the Strong-Campbell Interest Inventory.

20. (p. 660) If you take an interest test and your choices match those of people who are

_____ in a given occupation, it is assumed that you, too, would be comfortable doing the work they do.

21. (p. 660) _____ tests are another mainstay of personnel psychology. Such tests rate a person's potential to learn tasks or skills used in various occupations. As an example, clerical tests emphasize the capacity to do rapid, precise, and accurate office work.

22. (p. 661) _____ _____ programs are set up by many large organizations to do in-depth evaluations of job candidates. They are used primarily to fill management and executive positions.

23. (p. 661) After applicants have been tested and interviewed at an assessment center, they are placed in simulated work situations for observation and evaluation. For example, in the _____-_____ test, the applicant is asked to quickly read a basket full of memos, requests, and problems typical of those faced by executives, and take appropriate action.

24. (p. 661) In another, more stressful test, applicants take part in a _____ _____ discussion in which they try to solve a realistic business problem. By observing applicants, it is possible to evaluate leadership skills and, especially, how job candidates cope with stress.

25. (p. 661) Assessment centers have had success in predicting performance in a variety of jobs. For instance, one recent study of women found that assessment center predictions of management potential were strongly related to career progress ___ years later.

26. (p. 661) On the basis of long-range studies, it appears that future success is most clearly predicted by _____ _____ skills, leader-ship, energy, _____ to stress, tolerance for _____, need for advancement, and planning skills.

27. (p. 661) One "problem" with interviews is that physically _____ individuals are often given more positive evaluations even on traits that have no connection to appearance. Robert Baron tested whether this effect might even extend to the effects of wearing a pleasant perfume or cologne.

28. (p. 661) Baron found that _____ interviewers did, in fact, give higher ratings to job applicants who wore pleasant scents. But _____ gave lower ratings to persons who wore perfume or cologne. He speculates that the lowered ratings were due to greater awareness of the scents by the interviewers and resentment of the implied attempt to influence ratings.

29. (p. 662) One of the earliest attempts to improve worker efficiency was made in 1923 by Frederick _____. He standardized work procedures and emphasized careful planning, control, and orderliness.

30. (p. 662) Modern versions of Taylor's approach are called _____ _____ (also known as Theory X). Emphasis is placed on time-and-motion studies, task analysis, job specialization, assembly lines, pay schedules, and increased productivity.

31. (p. 662) Managers who follow Theory X tend to assume that workers must be goaded or guided into being productive. The term Theory X was coined by Douglas McGregor as a way to distinguish scientific management from a style that emphasizes human relations at work—_____ ___.

32. (p. 662) Many psychologists working in business are concerned with improving _____ efficiency—maximum output at lowest cost. As a result, they alter conditions they believe will affect workers (time schedules, work quotas, bonuses, etc.).

33. (p. 662) However, _____ efficiency is just as important as work efficiency. Businesses must be able to retain workers, minimize absenteeism, sustain good morale and labor relations, etc., if they are to prosper.

34. (p. 662) McGregor's Theory Y approach focuses on the human element. Theory Y managers assume that workers enjoy _____ and are willing to accept _____. They assume that worker needs and goals can be meshed with the company's, and that people are not naturally passive or lazy.

35. (p. 662) Theory Y assumes that people are industrious, creative, and rewarded by challenging _____. Given the proper conditions of freedom and responsibliity, people will work hard to gain competence and to use their talents fully.

36. (p. 662) Many features of Theory Y are illustrated by the Honda plant at Marysville, Ohio. Two elements that stand out as effective methods are _____ management and management by _____.

37. (p. 662) In participative management, employees at all levels are included in decision making. Such employees come to see work as a cooperative effort. Resulting benefits include greater productivity, greater job _____, and less job-related _____.

38. (p. 662) In management by objectives, workers are given specific _____ to meet (for instance, reaching a certain sales figure, making a certain number of items, etc.) so they can tell if they are doing a good job.

39. (p. 662) Workers are free to choose (within limits) how they will achieve their goals. As a result they experience a greater sense of _____ and personal meaning in their work.

40. (p. 662) One popular answer as to how workers below management level can be involved more in their work is the use of _____ _____. These are voluntary discussion groups that meet regularly, with or without supervision, to try to find ways to solve business problems or improve efficiency.

41. (p. 662) Quality circles and similar worker involvement programs have many limitations. Usually such groups do not have the _____ to put their suggestions into practice directly. Nevertheless, studies verify that greater involvement can have a _____ impact on organizations and employees.

42. (p. 662) Applying Theory X methods to work without taking worker needs into account can produce an immediate rise in productivity while job _____ declines. When job _____ is low, morale falls, absenteeism skyrockets, and there is a high rate of employee turnover leading to high training costs and inefficiency.

43. (p. 663) Job satisfaction comes from a good fit between a person's interests, abilities, needs, and expectations, and his or her work. Eight of the most important aspects of work are: (1) _____ work; (2) enough help and equipment to get the job done; (3) enough _____ to get the job

done; (4) enough _____ to get the job done; (5) good pay; (6) opportunity to develop special abilities; (7) job _____; (8) seeing the results of one's work.

44. (p. 663) A second survey done in the U.S. in the early 1980s again found that satisfying, rewarding work ranked first in worker preference. High _____ rose to second place.

45. (p. 663) These findings trouble some observers who worry that a swing toward greater _____ has occurred in the last 10 to 15 years. Even so, intrinsically interesting work still tops the list.

46. (p. 663) To summarize much research, we can say that job satisfaction is highest when workers are: (1) allowed ordinary _____ contacts with others; (2) allowed to use their own _____ and intelligence; (3) recognized for doing well; (4) given a chance to apply their skills; (5) given relative freedom from close _____; and (6) given opportunities for promotion and advancement.

47. (p. 663) There is now ample evidence that incentives such as bonuses, earned time off, and profit sharing can _____ productivity. However, in recent years far too many jobs have become routine, _____, _____, and unfulfilling.

48. (p. 663) To combat the discontent this can breed, many psychologists recommend a strategy called _____ _____. This usually involves removing some of the controls and restrictions on employees and giving them greater responsibility, freedom, choice, and authority.

49. (p. 664) Also, instead of performing an _____ part of a larger process, employees may switch to doing a complete _____ of work or completing an entire item or project.

50. (p. 664) Whenever possible, workers are given _____ about their work or progress. This _____ comes to them directly instead of to a supervisor. Workers are encouraged to learn new and more difficult tasks and to learn a broad range of skills.

51. (p. 664) Job enrichment has been used with great success by large corporations. It usually leads to lower production _____, increased job _____, reduced _____, and less _____.

52. (p. 664) By doing an analysis of scenic beauty, Terry Daniel and his colleagues have helped guide harvesting plans for the U.S. Forest Service. Apparently, the ideal forest, in the public eye, consists of a green _____, a few _____, healthy pine trees, and one or two picturesque, old fallen _____.

53. (p. 664) Daniel's work falls into an area known as _____ psychology, a specialty concerned with how environments influence our behavior.

54. (p. 664) Environmental psychologists are interested both in _____ environments (natural or constructed) and in _____ environments (such as a dance, business meeting, or party). They also give special attention to _____ settings (for example, an office, locker room, church, casino, or classroom).

55. (p. 665) As we move farther from the body, it becomes apparent that personal space also extends to adjacent areas that we claim as our "territory." For example, in the library _____ _____ might include protecting your space with a book, coat, notebook, or other personal belonging.

56. (p. 665) Researchers have found that the more attached you are to an area, the more likely you are to signal your "ownership" with obvious _____ _____, such as decorations, plants, photographs, posters, etc.

57. (p. 665) A major finding of environmental research is that much of our behavior is controlled, in part, by the environment. For example, psychologists have found that a variety of factors influence the amount of _____ that occurs in public places.

58. (p. 666) Many architects now "harden" and "de-opportunize" public settings to discourage vandalism and graffiti. Some such efforts _____ opportunities (doorless toilet stalls, tiled walls). Others _____ the lure of potential targets (a raised flower bed around signs helps protect them).

59. (p. 666) Urban stress involves many factors in our country today; one of them is overcrowding. The world's population is now well over ___ billion, and it will more than double in the next 40 years.

60. (p. 666) One way to assess the effect crowding has on people is to study the effects of overcrowding among animals. As one example, consider the work of John Calhoun. He let a group of laboratory rats breed without limit in a confined space. At its peak, the colony numbered _____ rats, yet was housed in a cage designed to comfortably hold about 50.

61. (p. 666) Overcrowding was further exaggerated, since the two dominant males staked out private territory leaving the remaining space to the rest of the colony. Overcrowding resulted in a high incidence of pathological behavior. For example, females abandoned _____ _____ and _____ for their young. Pregnancies _____ and infant _____ ran extremely high.

62. (p. 666) Many of the animals became indiscriminately _____ and went on rampaging attacks against others.

63. (p. 666) Also, abnormal sexual behavior was rampant, with some animals displaying _____, _____, _____, or total sexual _____.

64. (p. 666) Many of the animals died, apparently from _____-_____ diseases. The link between these problems and overcrowding is unmistakable.

65. (p. 666) While many of these behaviors can be observed in crowded inner-city ghettos, factors such as _____, _____, _____, and health care disadvantages may also be to blame.

66. (p. 666) In fact, most laboratory studies of crowding in humans have failed to show any serious ill effects. This result may occur because crowding is a _____ condition that is separate from _____ (the number of people in a given space).

67. (p. 666) Crowding refers to subjective feelings of being _____ by social inputs or by a loss of _____.

68. (p. 666) Crowding may interact with the type of situation in which it occurs to intensify existing stresses or pleasures. For example, Garvin McCain has reported that there are substantial increases in _____ _____ among prison inmates and mental hospital patients living in crowded conditions.

69. (p. 667) One result of high densities and crowding is a condition psychologist Stanley Milgram called attentional _____, stress induced by continuous sensory stimulation, information, and contact with others.

70. (p. 667) Milgram believes city dwellers learn to prevent overload by engaging in only brief, superficial _____ _____, by ignoring _____ events and by adopting _____ and _____ expressions.

71. (p. 667) A recent study of the effects of daily exposure to noise showed that children attending schools near Los Angeles International Airport had higher _____ _____ than those from quieter schools.

72. (p. 667) Children attending the noisy schools were more likely to give up attempts to solve a difficult puzzle and they were poorer at proofreading a printed paragraph. These effects may resemble a state of "learned _____."

73. (p. 667) Support for this hypothesis comes from recent studies in several large and smaller nearby towns. Of persons approached in _____ _____ by a child asking for help, about 72 percent obliged, while in _____ they offered help only about 46 percent of the time. In some cities (Boston and Philadelphia) only about _____ - _____ were willing to help.

74. (p. 667) A more recent analysis of _____ studies confirmed that "country people are more likely to help than city people." Thus, a blunting of sensitivity to the needs of others may be one of the more serious costs of urban stresses and crowding.

75. (p. 667) The way people think about the environment greatly affects behavior. Mental "maps" of various areas often guide actions and alter decisions. For instance, in a study recently done in Philadelphia researchers found that an existing school bus route contributed to _____, because many of its stops were at corners where children were afraid of being attacked and beaten.

76. (p. 668) This problem was approached by first doing an _____ _____ through which psychologists could develop a picture of environments as they are perceived by people using them.

77. (p. 668) An assessment often includes such things as charting areas of _____ use in buildings, using _____ scales to measure reactions to various environments, and even having people draw a version of their "cognitive map" of a building, campus, or city.

78. (p. 668) In the Philadelphia experiment, residents of the neighborhood were asked to rate how much stress they felt when walking in various areas. The result was a _____ map that showed the areas of highest perceived stress. School buses could then be rerouted to "low pressure" areas.

79. (p. 668) In one well-known experiment, Baum and Valins found that students housed in long, narrow, corridor-designed dormitories often feel _____ and _____. Such students tended to withdraw from other residents

and even made more trips to the same campus health center than did those living in other buildings.

80. (p. 668) By studying the effects of existing buildings, psychologists specializing in _____ psychology are often able to suggest design changes that solve or avoid problems.

81. (p. 668) Baum and Valins found that residents living in rooms clustered in threes, with each suite sharing a small bathroom, were more satisfied than those living in dorms with a long corridor and one central bathroom. The latter students made fewer _____ in their dorm and showed greater signs of _____ from social contact.

82. (p. 668) Baum and Davis also compared students living in a long-corridor dorm to those living in a long-corridor dorm where the hallway was divided into half with unlocked doors and the three center bedrooms converted into a lounge area. Residents of the latter building reported less stress from _____, formed more _____, and were more open to social contacts.

83. (p. 668) A major problem in the conservation of energy on a personal level is that _____ concerning energy use (the monthly bill) arrives long after the temptation to consume energy. Psychologists have shown that moderately lower energy bills result from simply giving families daily _____ about their use of gas or electricity.

84. (p. 669) Even more effective are programs that give _____ rewards for energy conservation. This is especially true for _____-_____ apartment complexes where families do not receive individual bills for their utilities.

85. (p. 669) In such apartments, families have no reason to save gas and electricity. Often, they consume about _____ more energy than they would in an individually metered apartment.

86. (p. 669) _____ psychology seeks to understand how people learn and how teachers instruct. Specialists in this field design aptitude and achievement tests, evaluate educational programs, and help train teachers at colleges and universities.

87. (p. 670) One good way to become more effective in sharing your knowledge with others is to use a specific _____ _____. One example involves using the following steps: (1) learner preparation, (2) stimulus presentation, (3) learner response, (4) reinforcement, (5) evaluation, and (6) spaced review.

88. (p. 670) There is little doubt that teaching styles can greatly affect student interest, motivation, and creativity. Two of the most basic types are _____ _____ and _____ _____.

89. (p. 670) In direct instruction, factual information is presented by _____, demonstration, and _____ practice. In open teaching, active teacher-student _____ is emphasized. Both have advantages.

90. (p. 670) Students of direct instruction do slightly better on _____ tests than do those in open classrooms. However, students of open teaching do somewhat better on tests of _____ thinking, creativity, and problem solving. They also tend to be more _____, curious, and _____ in their attitudes toward school.

91. (p. 670) _____ psychology is an applied field that focuses on how and why consumers act as they do.

92. (p. 671) Actually, _____ _____ can be separated into several steps. These include: deciding to spend, selecting a brand, shopping, making the purchase, and evaluating the product in use.

93. (p. 671) At each step, advertising, packaging, and a host of other factors affect our behavior. To pinpoint such factors, a type of public opinion polling called _____ _____ is often done.

94. (p. 671) In marketing research, people in a representative sample are asked to give their personal impressions of products, services, and advertising. In this way researchers have learned, among other things, that powerful, widely held _____ _____ often develop. This helps us understand why many people purchase products for their labels as much as for their performance.

95. (p. 671) In addition to marketing research, consumer psychologists do _____ testing of products; they try to match products to consumer _____; they test public acceptance of new products, brand names, and packaging; and they devise plans to change buying _____.

96. (p. 671) Image-conscious advertising campaigns do affect our beliefs about products even when wrong. For example, in one recent test, three nationally advertised brands of beer were compared. When taste was the only cue available, there was _____ evidence of any noticeable difference in brands.

97. (p. 671) Not all consumer psychology is profit oriented. For instance, principles of consumer behavior may be used to encourage the _____ of water or fuels. Also, many consumer psychologists are interested in protecting and enhancing consumer _____ by persuading people to act in their own best interest.

98. (p. 671) It was consumer psychologists who documented the large number of commericals on "_____." Each year the average child sees over _____ commercials, most of which are for highly sugared cereals and overpriced toys.

99. (p. 671) Related research showed that children under age ____ are easily victimized because they often cannot distinguish commercials from the program itself.

100. (p. 671) Such findings have helped advance the cause of _____ —attempts to enhance consumer knowledge, rights, and welfare for both children and adults.

101. (p. 672) Psychologists use _____ _____ made up of volunteers to probe how jurors reach decisions about the guilt or innocence of defendants. Some are simply given written evidence and arguments to read while others are shown videotaped trials staged by actors.

102. (p. 672) Studies show that jurors are rarely able to put aside their biases, attitudes, and values while making a decision. For example, jurors are less likely to find _____ defendants guilty (on the basis of the same evidence) than _____ defendants.

103. (p. 672) It appears, however, that if being attractive helped a person _____ a

crime, it can work _____ her or him in court. An example would be a handsome man on trial for swindling money from an unmarried middle-aged woman.

104. (p. 672) A second major problem is that jurors are not very good at separating _____ from other information, such as their perceptions of the defendant, attorneys, witnesses, and what they think the judge wants. Jurors find it hard to _____ information that slips out in court.

105. (p. 672) A related problem occurs when jurors take into account the severity of the _____ a defendant faces. Jurors are not supposed to let this affect their verdict, but many do.

106. (p. 672) A third area of difficulty arises because jurors usually cannot _____ _____ until all the evidence is in. Typically, jurors form an opinion _____ in the trial, making it hard for them to fairly judge later evidence that contradicts what they think.

107. (p. 672) Problems like these are troubling in our legal system. However, each of these factors has much less effect as a crime becomes more _____ or the evidence becomes more _____-_____.

108. (p. 673) Before a trial begins, opposing attorneys are allowed to disqualify a limited number of potential jurors who may be biased. Psychologists help identify people who will favor or harm an attorney's efforts using several techniques. As a first step, _____ _____ (e.g., age, sex, race, occupation, etc.) is frequently collected for each juror.

109. (p. 673) To supplement demographic information, a _____ _____ may be done to find out how local citizens feel about the case. The assumption is that jurors probably have attitudes similar to people with backgrounds like their own.

110. (p. 673) Although talking with potential jurors outside the courtroom is _____ _____, other information networks are available. If possible, a psychologist may interview _____, acquaintances, _____, and co-workers of potential jurors.

111. (p. 673) Psychologists often watch for _____ personality traits in potential jurors. Such individuals tend to believe that punishment is effective, and they are more likely to vote for conviction.

112. (p. 673) At the same time, the psychologist typically observes potential jurors' _____ behavior. The idea is to try to learn from body language which side the person favors.

113. (p. 673) Cases where wealthy clients have the advantage of psychological jury selection raise ethical questions. But since both sides help select jurors, the net effect in most instances is a more _____ jury.

114. (p. 673) _____ psychologists seek to understand and improve sports performance and to enhance the benefits of sports participation.

115. (p. 673) Some sports psychologists might teach an athlete how to _____, ignore distractions, or cope with emotions. They might also provide personal counseling for performance-lowering _____ and _____.

Others are interested in studying factors that affect athletic _____, such as skill learning, the personality profiles of champion athletes, the effects of spectators, etc.

116. (p. 673)   Before the advent of sports psychology, it was debatable whether "homespun" coaching methods helped or hurt. For example, in early studies of volleyball and gymnastics, it became clear that people teaching these sports had very little _____ or crucial, underlying _____.

117. (p. 674)   A major contribution by psychologists in this field has been their ability to do detailed studies of complex skills. In such a _____ _____, sports skills are broken into subparts, so that key elements can be identified and taught.

118. (p. 674)   Sports psychologists have found that top marksmen consistently squeeze the trigger _____ heartbeats. As a result of careful study leading to this finding, competitors have begun to use various techniques to steady and control their heartbeat.

119. (p. 674)   Sports often provide valuable information on human behavior in general. For example, a recent study found that children's _____ - _____ improved significantly after a season of Little League baseball.

120. (p. 674)   Such benefits are most likely to occur when competition, rejection, criticism, and the "one-winner mentality" are minimized. Psychologists emphasize _____ play, _____ rewards, _____ - _____ of emotions, independence, and self-reliance.

121. (p. 674)   Adults also benefit from sports. For instance, researchers have reported that distance running is associated with lower levels of _____, _____, fatigue, and _____ than are found in the nonrunning population.

122. (p. 674)   Many athletes report episodes during which they experience intense concentration, detachment from surroundings, a lack of fatigue and pain, a subjective slowing of time, and feelings of unusual power and control. This phenomenon is called _____ _____ and is when "personal bests" tend to occur.

123. (p. 674)   This experience has also been called "_____" because the athlete feels as if he or she were in a trance. They become one with performance and flow with it.

124. (p. 675)   A curious aspect of flow is that it cannot be _____ to happen. In fact, if a person stops to think about it, the flow state goes away.

125. (p. 676)   Needs for _____ and challenge, the desire to do something worthwhile, opportunities to _____, and needs to use skills and abilities are all ranked higher than money by workers.

126. (p. 676)   Usually, by the time a person has selected a career path, it takes a large amount of effort and possibly major risk to change course. This fact is illustrated by a survey in which _____ percent of those polled said that, for better or worse, they felt "locked into" their current jobs.

127. (p. 676)   For most people who enter professions, career development tends to flow through four broad phases. These are: (1) the _____ phase,

during which an initial search for career possibilities is made; (2) the _____ phase, during which the person finds a job, enters a career, develops competence, and gains status; (3) the _____ phase, which is a time of high productivity and acceptance by co-workers; and (4) the _____ career phase, when the individual serves as a respected expert, and often, as a "mentor" for younger workers.

128. (p. 676) During the exploration phase, most people go through a series of stages as they choose a vocation. In the _____ stage children under age 10 simply imagine what they want to be when they grow up.

129. (p. 676) During the _____ stage (roughly ages 10 to 18), adolescents begin to form more realistic, if somewhat general, ideas about what they want to do. Their plans may shift several times during this period.

130. (p. 676) During the _____ stage (usually after high school), the first steps are taken to find out what particular jobs are like and to prepare for them.

131. (p. 677) There is evidence that vocational choice is often rather haphazard. It is not unusual for students to allow a tentative choice of _____ to determine school coursework. They find themselves channeled into a career path without really having made a clear decision.

132. (p. 677) The best single predictor of the job category you will enter is your _____ _____—what you tell yourself you would like to do.

133. (p. 677) The easiest way to improve occupational choice is to consult a _____—counseling psychologists who have specialized in the skills and knowledge needed to match people with jobs.

134. (p. 677) Many colleges now offer vocational counseling at campus _____ _____. They can provide a wealth of information about various jobs and careers.

135. (p. 677) A useful library resource is the _____ _____ published yearly by the U.S. Department of Labor. It provides job descriptions, information on necessary training, average earnings, and the number of jobs likely to be available in coming years.

136. (p. 677) Many businesses are now trying to reduce stresses at work. For instance, one recent study found that teaching employees stress inoculation techniques and progressive relaxation lowered _____ levels and _____ ratings at work.

137. (p. 677) Another way of improving work adjustment is to examine your approach to making career decisions. Irving Janis and Dan Wheeler have described four basic _____ styles by which people typically deal with work dilemmas.

138. (p. 677) The _____ style is the most effective of the four. It describes individuals who evaluate information objectively and make decisions with a clear understanding of the alternatives.

139. (p. 677) Persons with the _____ style drift along with a nonchalant attitude toward job decisions. They tend to let chance direct their careers and to take whatever comes along without really making plans.

140. (p. 678)   People with the _____-_____ style are
fully aware of the risks and opportunities presented by career choices and dilemmas.
However, they are uncomfortable making decisions. This leads them to procrastinate,
rationalize, and to make excuses for their inaction and indecision.

141. (p. 678)   People with the _____ style more or less panic
when forced to make career decisions. They may collect hundreds of job
announcements and brochures, but they become so frantic that making logical
decisions is nearly impossible.

142. (p. 679)   Long-term space inhabitants will face confinement and other trying conditions,
including: _____ movement, _____
from loved ones, _____ monotony, noise, and many other stresses.

143. (p. 679)   The Skylab-3 "space _____" was brief, but showed how important the
human element will be in space. Psychologists have focused on understanding
expected problems and possible solutions.

144. (p. 679)   Space habitats must be designed with human behavior in mind. To begin, the
_____ environment, or "micro-society," on a space station will need to
operate as smoothly as possible.

145. (p. 679)   For this reason many problems may be avoided by carefully _____
and _____ future space residents before they go aloft.

146. (p. 679)   Design of a space station as a living environment must take many human factors into
account. For instance, researchers have learned that astronauts prefer rooms with
clearly defined "_____" and "_____"—even in the weightlessness of space.

147. (p. 679)   Provisions must be made for regular exercise. Also full-body _____
are necessary since a lack of this provision was a major complaint among subjects in
earlier confinement experiments.

148. (p. 679)   Behavior patterns will change over time within a space station, and control of one's
environment can help lower stress. At the same time people need stability. Eating at
least one meal together each day can help keep a crew working as a
_____ unit.

149. (p. 680)   _____ _____ will need to be carefully controlled in space to
avoid disrupting bodily rhythms. At best, a space station will be at least as noisy as
the typical office. Researchers are experimenting with various earmuffs, eye shades,
and sleeping arrangements to alleviate such difficulties.

150. (p. 680)   Privacy in the first permanent space stations will have to be based mainly on
temporarily blocking out _____ and _____
contact with others; there will be too little room for separate quarters.

151. (p. 680)   Forced togetherness is stressful mainly because temporary retreat from contact with
the group is difficult or impossible. Thus, control over the _____ of
contact one has with others is more important than having a _____
room.

152. (p. 680)   Space habitat designers recognize the need to define private
_____. It will be important to identify small areas
that can be personalized and "owned" by each individual.

153. (p. 680) _____ monotony will be a problem in space. Researchers are developing stimulus environments that will use music, videotapes, and other diversions to combat monotony and boredom.

154. (p. 680) Most people in restricted environments find that they prefer _____-_____ pastimes such as reading, listening to music (with individual earphones), looking out windows, writing, and watching films or television. This preference may show again the need for privacy and psychological withdrawal from the group.

155. (p. 680) Separation from family, friends, and one's home community is a major stressor. Abundant opportunities to communicate with associates and loved ones on earth will be the best antidote for _____ _____. Some psychologists also believe that there should be a psychological support group on earth with whom a space station crew would talk to prevent emotional problems.

156. (p. 680) Many studies of long-term isolation show steady declines in _____. Most inhabitants intend to use their free time for creative pursuits. But in reality they end up marking time and many become apathetic.

157. (p. 680) As many as ___ percent of space inhabitants may experience some psychological disturbance. Most often the problem has been _____. However, in rare instances people could become paranoid, psychotic, etc. It will be important to teach crew members basic counseling skills.

SELF-TEST

1. (p. 657) The largest area of applied psychology is
   a. industrial/organizational psychology
   b. behavioral medicine
   c. clinical/counseling psychology
   d. engineering psychology

2. (p. 658) Which of the following types of psychologist would be most likely to be involved in developing user-friendly computers, push-button telephones, and easy to perceive traffic signals?
   a. sports psychologist   c. consumer psychologist
   b. environmental psychologist   d. human factors engineer

3. (p. 658) The development of flexitime at a particular business would most likely be instituted with the help of a
   a. personnel psychologist   c. human factors engineer
   b. architectural psychologist   d. vocational counselor

4. (p. 659) Critical incidents are
   a. situations that an employee must be able to cope with if he or she is going to succeed in a particular job
   b. simulated test situations used by assessment centers to gauge the leadership qualities of potential executives
   c. potential dangerous situations caused by design flaws as determined by an industrial psychologist
   d. industrial accidents caused by conflicts between Theory X and Theory Y management styles

5.   (p. 659)   Which of the following would *not* be used by a personnel psychologist in making employee selections?
     a. biodata   c. standardized psychological tests
     b. biomedical data   d. job analysis

6.   (p. 660)   True-False.   Two examples of vocational interest tests include the Kuder Occupational Interest Survey and the Strong-Campbell Interest Inventory.

7.   (p. 660)   _____ tests are used to rate a person's potential to learn tasks or skills used in various occupations.
     a. Job analysis   c. Vocational interest
     b. Standardized   d. Aptitude

8.   (p. 661)   Which of the following is *not* true of the assessment center approach to personnel selection?
     a. It is used primarily to fill management and executive positions.
     b. Exercises such as the "in-basket test" and the "leaderless group" are typical of the type of situations used to monitor candidates' abilities.
     c. One recent study found that assessment center predictions of management potential among a group of women were only weakly related to career progress 7 years later.
     d. Assessment centers have had success in predicting performance in a variety of jobs, careers, and advanced positions in the military.

9.   (p. 662)   Which of the following is *not* true of Theory X?
     a. It is also known as scientific management.
     b. The term was coined by Douglas McGregor.
     c. It uses time-and-motion studies, task analysis, job specialization, assembly lines, pay schedules, etc. to increase productivity.
     d. It assumes that workers enjoy independence and are willing to accept responsibility.

10.   (p. 662)   Which of the following are elements that make Theory Y methods effective?
     a. management by objectives   c. work efficiency scheduling
     b. coercive management   d. psychological efficiency minimalization

11.   (p. 663)   True-False.   While interesting work, adequate help, information, and authority are important features of any job, good pay is the main determinant of job satisfaction among workers.

12.   (p. 664)   Environmental psychologists are interested in each of the following except
     a. behavioral settings   c. physical environments
     b. social environments   d. interactive settings

13.   (p. 665)   Topics such as territoriality, vandalism, behavioral settings, architectural design, natural environment, pollution, etc. would be of special interest to
     a. environmental psychologists   c. human factors engineers
     b. educational psychologists   d. health psychologists

14.   (p. 666)   The term _____ refers to the number of people in a given space.
     a. crowding   c. overload
     b. discrimination   d. density

15.   (p. 667)   True-False.   Attentional overload refers to subjective feelings of being overstimulated by social inputs or by a loss of privacy.

16. (p. 667) Milgram believes city dwellers learn to prevent overload by engaging in all of the following, *except*
    a. adopting cold and unfriendly expressions
    b. disregarding nonessential events
    c. engaging in only brief, superficial interpersonal contacts
    d. being more willing than people who live in small towns to help people in distress

17. (p. 667) True-False. The greater tendency of children from noisy schools to give up or become distracted is a serious handicap. It may even indicate a state of "learned helplessness."

18. (p. 668) An environmental assessment might be expected to include any of the following *except*
    a. having people draw a version of their "cognitive map" of a certain environment
    b. measuring all of the job-related components that define success within a certain business environment
    c. using attitude scales to measure reactions of schools, businesses, parks, etc.
    d. charting areas of highest or lowest use in buildings

19. (p. 669) True-False. Environmental psychologists have shown that programs which give monetary rewards for energy conservation are very effective, especially in master-metered apartment complexes.

20. (p. 670) Which of the following is true of teaching styles as studied by educational psychologists?
    a. In open teaching, factual information is presented by lecture, demonstration, and rote practice.
    b. Students of direct instruction do slightly better on achievement tests than do those in open classrooms.
    c. In direct instruction, active teacher-student discussion is emphasized.
    d. Students of open teaching do slightly poorer on tests of abstract thinking, creativity, and problem solving than do those receiving direct instruction.

21. (p. 671) Special interest topics such as brand loyalty, effects of advertising, package design, and shopping behavior would be of particular concern to which applied field?
    a. behavioral medicine   c. consumer psychology
    b. marketing psychology   d. human factors engineering

22. (p. 671) True-False. Not all consumer psychology is profit oriented. Principles of consumer behavior may be used to encourage the conservation of gasoline, water, or electricity.

23. (p. 672) Which of the following is *not* an area which might be investigated by psychologists interested in law?
    a. expert testimony   c. jury selection
    b. bail setting   d. peak performance

24. (p. 674) In a psychological task analysis
    a. sports skills are broken into subparts so that key elements can be identified and taught
    b. the individual components of a particular industrial job are identified for later integration with human factor considerations
    c. candidates for executive positions are given ambiguous roles to play to assess their ability to empathize
    d. athletes are required to perform at peak level in order to analyze those factors of greatest importance to the individual sportsman

25. (p. 674) Which of the following is a research finding that has been reported by sports psychologists?
    a. Distance running is associated with lower levels of tension, anxiety, fatigue, and depression.
    b. Children's self-esteem decreases following a losing season of play, especially when the "one-winner mentality" is minimized.
    c. During "flow" athletes experience reduced concentration, but heightened awareness of surroundings.
    d. Top marksmen consistently squeeze the trigger during heartbeats.

26. (p. 676) Which of the following is *not* a correct definition/match?
    a. later career phase—individual serves as a respected expert
    b. exploration phase—initial search for career possibilities is made
    c. tentative phase—individual finds a job, develops competence, and gains status
    d. fantasy stage—children under age 10 simply imagine what they want to be when they grow up

27. (p. 677) True-False. The best single predictor of the job category you will enter is your family background—many times the phrase "like father like son" is true.

28. (p. 677) Which of the following is a good way to improve occupational choice?
    a. consult a vocational counselor
    b. become familiar with the *Occupational Outlook Handbook*
    c. use a career center if available at your campus
    d. all of the above

29. (p. 677) Which of the following is considered to be a constructive coping style by Janis and Wheeler?
    a. hypervigilant style   c. defensive-avoidant style
    b. vigilant style   d. complacent style

30. (p. 679) True-False. Researchers studying psychological adjustment to long-term space travel have found that astronauts prefer rooms with clearly defined "up" and "down"—even in the weightlessness of space.

31. (p. 680) Which of the following would *not* be a pastime frequently used by space crews?
    a. watching films or television   c. competitive contact sports
    b. reading   d. listening to music

32. (p. 680) True-False. Many studies of long-term isolation show steady increases in motivation. As recreational pastimes become more routine, workers focus more effort and energy into mission tasks.

ANSWERS — PROGRAMMED REVIEW

1. Applied
2. fire alarm
3. attention getting; authority; elevators
4. clinical; community
5. prevention; education; consultation; neglect
6. industrial
7. testing, placement; relations; engineering
8. flexitime
9. satisfaction; relations; absenteeism
10. human factors
11. natural design
12. feedback
13. 2000; 9
14. job analysis
15. critical incidents
16. biodata; interviewing; standardized; assessment
17. athletic; academic; scientific; religious

18. halo
19. vocational interest
20. successful
21. Aptitude
22. Assessment center
23. in-basket
24. leaderless group
25. 7
26. oral communication; resistance; uncertainty
27. attractive
28. female; males
29. Taylor
30. scientific management
31. Theory Y
32. work
33. psychological
34. independence; responsibility
35. work
36. participative; objectives
37. satisfaction; stress
38. goals
39. independence
40. quality circles
41. power; positive
42. satisfaction; satisfaction
43. interesting; information; authority; security
44. income
45. materialism
46. social; judgment; supervision
47. increase; repetitive; boring
48. job enrichment
49. isolated; cycle
50. feedback; feedback
51. costs; satisfaction; boredom; absenteeism
52. meadow; young; logs
53. environmental
54. physical; social; behavioral
55. territorial behavior
56. territorial markers
57. vandalism
58. limit; weaken
59. 5
60. 80
61. nest building; caring; decreased; mortality
62. aggressive
63. hypersexuality, bisexuality, homosexuality; passivity
64. stress-caused
65. nutrition; education; income
66. psychological; density
67. overstimulated; privacy
68. death rates
69. overload
70. social contacts; nonessential; cold, unfriendly
71. blood pressure
72. helplessness
73. small towns; cities; one-third
74. 65
75. truancy
76. environmental assessment
77. highest; attitude
78. contour
79. crowded, stressed
80. architectural
81. friends; withdrawing
82. crowding; friendships
83. feedback; feedback
84. monetary; master-metered
85. 20
86. Educational
87. teaching strategy
88. direct instruction, open teaching
89. lecture; rote; discussion
90. achievement; abstract; independent; positive
91. Consumer
92. consumer behavior
93. marketing research
94. brand images
95. laboratory; needs; habits
96. no
97. conservation; welfare
98. kidvid; 20,000
99. 6
100. consumerism
101. mock juries
102. attractive; unattractive
103. commit; against
104. evidence; ignore
105. punishment
106. suspend judgment; early
107. severe; clear-cut
108. demographic information
109. community survey
110. not permitted; relatives; neighbors
111. authoritarian
112. nonverbal
113. balanced
114. Sports
115. relax; stresses, conflicts; achievement
116. knowledge; skills
117. task analysis
118. between
119. self-esteem
120. fair; intrinsic; self-control
121. tension, anxiety, depression
122. peak performance
123. flow
124. forced

125. recognition; learn
126. 44
127. exploration; establishment; midcareer; later
128. fantasy
129. tentative
130. realistic
131. major
132. vocational aspiration
133. vocational counselor
134. career centers
135. Occupational Outlook Handbook
136. adrenaline; depression
137. coping
138. vigilant
139. complacent
140. defensive-avoidant
141. hypervigilant
142. restricted; separation; sensory
143. strike
144. social
145. selecting; training
146. up, down
147. showers
148. social
149. Sleep cycles
150. visual, auditory
151. amount; private
152. territories
153. Sensory
154. non-interactive
155. social isolation
156. motivation
157. 5; depression

ANSWERS — SELF-TEST

1. c
2. d
3. a
4. a
5. b
6. True
7. d
8. c
9. d
10. a
11. False
12. d
13. a
14. d
15. True
16. d
17. True
18. b
19. True
20. b
21. c
22. True
23. d
24. a
25. a
26. c
27. False
28. d
29. b
30. True
31. c
32. False

Appendix A

Careers in Psychology

CONTENTS

Majoring in Psychology
Employment Outlook
Additional Sources of Information

PROGRAMMED REVIEW

1. (p. 683) The majority of students studying introductory psychology are not psychology
   _____.

2. (p. 683) About half of all undergraduate psychology majors do not plan to work as
   _____. Nearly 50 percent of all psychology
   majors seek full-time jobs immediately after they graduate.

3. (p. 683) If you think you would like to major in psychology, but you are not interested in
   graduate training, here are some points to consider:
   1) _____ workers hold one job forever, or even remain in a single line of work
      for life.
   2) The nature of work is likely to _____ greatly in your lifetime, and
      adaptability will be important.
   3) A _____ education that develops many skills makes a person more
      vocationally adaptable.
   4) It is a major myth that every job requires a precise set of _____.
   5) Specific undergraduate programs do not exist for many mental health professions.
   6) Psychology can make a good undergraduate major leading to later specialized
      training.
   7) Job recruiters look primarily for general competence in verbal and written
      communication, plus social skills and facility in meeting the public.

4. (p. 683) A brief list of "marketable" abilities provided by a psychology degree includes the
   following: clear, analytic _____, objectivity and keen observa-
   tion; an ability to handle _____, recognize _____, and
   draw conclusions; ability to plan and organize complex activities; ability to
   _____ clearly, both verbally and in writing; the
   capacity to comprehend abstract principles and the subtleties of human behavior;
   ability to critically evaluate evidence; interpersonal skills; and
   _____ knowledge relevant to success in many settings.

459

5. (p. 684) Training in psychology at the _____ degree level tends to yield fewer choices than those available to graduates with bachelor's degrees or more advanced training. People with this degree in psychology are qualified to do interviewing, to give and score specific psychological tests, and to communicate the needs of clients to psychologists and other professionals.

6. (p. 684) In general, a person with an associate degree can expect to work directly with clients, but under the _____ of more highly trained professionals.

7. (p. 684) Some specific training programs exist where a year or two of training can lead directly to a job in a local mental health facility. Provisions have been made for "_____-_____" trainees to combine classroom study with on-the-job training.

8. (p. 684) A bachelor's degree in psychology can be considered preparation for a _____ of jobs or occupations. It is also a good prelude to _____ training in several related professions. Furthermore, it is a first step toward a master's or doctoral degree in psychology.

9. (p. 684) Some jobs for which an individual with a bachelor's degree in psychology might wish to apply require _____ training (becoming a high school teacher, for example).

10. (p. 684) Also, you may be more competitive for some types of positions if you were to _____ a psychology major with a minor in another area, such as business.

11. (p. 684) In other cases it would be better to make psychology your _____, in combination with a major in a related area (law enforcement and nursing are examples).

12. (p. 684) A _____ degree in psychology usually requires from 1 to 2 years of graduate-level training beyond the bachelor's degree. It usually requires completion of a research thesis and/or a certain number of hours of supervised practical experience in an applied setting.

13. (p. 685) At present the most popular master's-level specialty is _____ psychology—undoubtedly because this is one of the most direct routes to a career as a mental health professional.

14. (p. 685) Those with a master's degree in counseling psychology may further specialize in _____ and _____ counseling, vocational or educational counseling, _____ counseling, or _____ counseling.

15. (p. 685) Many counselors are _____-_____, but some work for human service agencies, at mental health clinics, and occasionally for the military or large businesses.

16. (p. 685) Recently, employment opportunities have become more limited for new master's-level psychologists. When positions open in noncounseling areas, they are often filled by _____-_____ psychologists.

17. (p. 685) On the other hand, a master's degree could make you more competitive for jobs at the bachelor's level. It might also help you qualify for higher _____.

18. (p. 685)   It usually takes at least 3 years of education beyond a bachelor's degree to attain a _____ (Ph.D., Psy.D., or Ed.D.). More often, it takes 4 or more years to complete, and some specialties require at least 1 more year of _____.

19. (p. 685)   If you want to become a psychologist, a Ph.D. is a _____ degree. It requires completion of a dissertation (an original research contribution to the field).

20. (p. 685)   Psychologists who primarily want to work as therapists now earn a _____ degree. This newly created degree allows students to gain practical experience as a psychotherapist rather than doing a dissertation.

21. (p. 685)   The _____ is also typically more applied in orientation than the Ph.D. Coursework for this degree focuses on the psychology of learning and education.

22. (p. 685)   In most states a doctoral degree alone does not automatically allow a person to practice psychology. To be legally _____ or _____ as a psychologist, a person usually must have a doctorate in psychology, plus at least 1 year of internship, as well as having passed written and oral state licensing exams.

23. (p. 686)   If you wish to pursue a doctorate in psychology, you should begin planning now. Getting admitted to a doctoral program in psychology is as difficult as getting into _____ _____.

24. (p. 686)   To learn more about applying for graduate school, consult the book *Graduate Study in Psychology* published by the American Psychological Association. Appendix ___ in the book gives practical, step-by-step information on how to get accepted to graduate school.

25. (p. 686)   There is value in deciding early if you intend to seek employment or to enter graduate school. Businesspeople and faculty members differ _____ in what they believe is most important when considering students for employment or admission.

26. (p. 686)   _____ and ability to present oneself effectively is highly valued in the business world. Courses taken, grades, recommendations, writing ability, and other academic performance factors are much more important when considering graduate training.

27. (p. 686)   Jobs for people with psychology degrees are expected to grow _____ than average in coming years. However, professional-level jobs (master's and doctorate) will account for a relatively small percentage of total new positions.

28. (p. 686)   With projections for a decline in college enrollments, _____ positions will be in especially short supply. Even in industrial, clinical, and other applied areas there will be much competition for positions.

29. (p. 686)   To make yourself highly employable, you should:
     1) attend an _____ accredited graduate school.
     2) gain work experience while in school (by working as a research assistant, or even as a volunteer).
     3) specialize in additional skills that are in demand.

30. (p. 686) _____ areas of psychology are probably the best bet for employment in the near future. _____-related jobs also look good, especially
anything associated with senior citizens.

31. (p. 686) Two of the fastest growing jobs for the next decade are projected to be
_____ _____ and
_____. Both
positions are open to bachelor's and master's degree holders.

If you are interested in further study in psychology or in pursuing psychology as a career, you should
be familiar with the references provided in the main text. Note that all of the resources listed are
available through the American Psychological Association. Many of them are probably available
through your college library or career center.

SELF-TEST

1. (p. 683) Which of the following is a true statement?
   a. Learning psychology can provide a general knowledge of behavior that aids success
   in various occupations.
   b. Most undergraduate psychology majors will go on to pursue graduate studies in
   psychology.
   c. The majority of students studying introductory psychology are psychology majors.
   d. The majority of undergraduate psychology majors plan to work as psychologists.

2. (p. 683) Which of the following is *not* a "marketable" ability provided by a psychology degree?
   a. ability to critically evaluate evidence
   b. ability to handle data, recognize patterns, and draw conclusions
   c. subjectivity and ability to read other people's personalities
   d. clear, analytic thinking

3. (p. 684) Which of the following is probably *not* a job that would be open to an individual with
   an A.A. degree?
   a. youth supervisor   c. self-employed marriage counselor
   b. nursing home attendant   d. public survey worker

4. (p. 684) If you are interested in becoming a job analyst, drug counselor, child welfare agent,
   college admissions representative, biofeedback technician, or family services worker
   you should have, as a minimum, which of the following degrees?
   a. A.A.   c. M.A.
   b. Ph.D.   d. B.A.

5. (p. 685) True-False. The most popular master's-level specialty is counseling psychology.

6. (p. 685) Which of the following is *not* true of psychologists with a master's degree?
   a. They are almost entirely self-employed individuals.
   b. They have begun to move into areas such as hospices, child abuse clinics, rape
   counseling centers, stress clinics, etc.
   c. Recently, employment opportunities have become more limited for new master's-
   level psychologists.
   d. Those with a degree in counseling psychology may further specialize in marriage
   and family counseling, vocational or educational counseling, or child counseling to
   name a few.

7. (p. 685)   True-False.   It usually takes 4 years or more to complete a doctorate and some applied specialities may require at least 1 more year of internship.

8. (p. 685)   Which of the following is *not* a correct statement?
    a. The Ed.D. is applied in orientation and focuses on the psychology of learning and education.
    b. A Ph.D. is a research degree.
    c. A Psy.D. allows students in clinical psychology to gain practical experience as a psychotherapist rather than doing a dissertation.
    d. Psychologists holding Psy.D. degrees are active in all areas of psychology.

9. (p. 685)   True-False.   In most states a doctoral degree alone can automatically allow a person to practice psychology.

10. (p. 686)   True-False.   Getting admitted to a doctoral program in psychology is as difficult as getting into medical school.

11. (p. 686)   If you plan to pursue a doctoral-level career in psychology it is wise to follow all of the following suggestions *except*
    a. specialize in additional skills that are in demand
    b. seek the Psy.D. or Ed.D. degree rather than the Ph.D.
    c. attend an APA-accredited graduate school
    d. gain work experience while in school

12. (p. 686)   Which of the following is *not* an area of psychology with especially good job prospects for the immediate future?
    a. animal learning   c. clinical
    b. industrial/organizational   d. health

13. (p. 686)   True-False.   Two of the fastest growing jobs for the next decade are projected to be employment interviewers and occupational therapists.

14. (p. 686)   Which of the following can help you in deciding upon a major or career in psychology?
    a. your psychology teacher   c. the American Psychological Association
    b. the campus career center   d. all of the above

ANSWERS — PROGRAMMED REVIEW

1. majors
2. psychologists
3. Few; change; broad; skills
4. thinking; data; patterns; communicate; general
5. associate
6. supervision
7. psych-tech
8. variety; advanced
9. additional
10. combine
11. minor
12. master's
13. counseling
14. marriage; family; child; rehabilitation
15. self-employed
16. doctoral-level

17. pay
18. doctorate; internship
19. research
20. Psy.D.
21. Ed.D.
22. licensed, certified
23. medical school
24. D
25. greatly
26. Personality
27. faster
28. academic
29. APA
30. Applied; Health
31. employment interviewers, occupational therapists

ANSWERS — SELF-TEST

1. a
2. c
3. c
4. d
5. True
6. a
7. True
8. d
9. False
10. True
11. b
12. a
13. True
14. d

Appendix B

Statistics

CONTENTS

TERMS AND CONCEPTS

descriptive statistics
inferential statistics
graphical statistics
frequency distribution
histogram
abscissa
ordinate
frequency polygon
measures of central tendency
mean
median
mode
measures of variability
range

standard deviation
z-score
normal curve
population
sample
tests of statistical significance
correlation
scatter diagram
positive correlation
zero correlation
negative correlation
Pearson r
percent of variance

IMPORTANT FORMULAS

$$SD = \sqrt{\frac{\text{sum of } d^2}{n-1}}$$

$$Z = \frac{X - \bar{X}}{SD}$$

$$r = \frac{\Sigma XY - \frac{(\Sigma X)(\Sigma Y)}{N}}{\sqrt{(\Sigma X^2 - \frac{(\Sigma X)^2}{N})(\Sigma Y^2 - \frac{(\Sigma Y)^2}{N})}}$$

PROGRAMMED REVIEW

1. (p. 688) One of the two major divisions of statistical methods is _____
    _____. They are used to summarize numbers so they become more
    meaningful and more easily communicated to others.

2. (p. 688) The second type of statistics, known as _____
    statistics, is used for decision-making, for generalizing from small samples, and for
    drawing conclusions.

3. (p. 688) A _____ _____ is made by breaking
    down the entire range of possible scores into classes of equal size and then recording
    the number of scores falling in each class.

4. (p. 688) Frequency distributions can be used to demonstrate _____ statis-
    tics (a basic type of descriptive statistics that presents data in a "visual" format).

5. (p. 688) Frequency distributions are often expressed graphically using _____
    where the height of the bars drawn for each class interval indicates the number of
    scores in that class.

6. (p. 688) Histograms are made by labeling class intervals on the _____
    (horizontal line) and frequencies (the number of scores in each class) on the
    _____ (vertical line).

7. (p. 688) Next, _____ are drawn for each class interval. The height of each _____
    is determined by the number of scores in each class.

8. (p. 688) An alternative way of graphing a distribution of scores is the more familiar
    _____ _____. Here, points are placed at the
    center of each class interval to indicate the number of scores. Then, the dots are
    connected by straight lines.

9. (p. 689) A second category of descriptive statistic includes measures of _____
    _____. Such measures are simply numbers describing a "middle
    score" around which other scores fall.

10. (p. 689) One type of "average" is the _____, computed by adding all the scores for each
    group and dividing by the number of scores in the group.

11. (p. 689) The mean is sensitive to extremely _____ or _____ scores in a distribution
    and, consequently, is not always the best measure of central tendency.

12. (p. 689) In such cases, the "middle score" in a group of scores, called the _____, is
    used instead.

13. (p. 689) The median is found by _____ scores from the highest to the
    lowest and selecting the score that falls in the middle.

14. (p. 690) If there is no "middle score" (which occurs when there is an even number of scores),
    the two scores which share the middle position are _____ to get a
    single score.

15. (p. 690) A final measure of central tendency is the _____. It simply represents the most
    frequently occurring score in a distribution.

16. (p. 690)   Although the mode is easy to obtain, it can be an _____ measure, especially in a small group of scores.

17. (p. 690)   The advantage of the mode is that it gives the score actually obtained by the _____ number of people.

18. (p. 691)   When we want to know if scores are grouped closely together or scattered widely, we use measures of _____ to attach a numerical value to the "spread" of scores.

19. (p. 691)   The simplest way to describe variability is to use the _____, which is the spread between the highest and lowest scores.

20. (p. 691)   The better measure of variability is the _____ _____.

21. (p. 691)   SD is obtained by computing the _____ (or difference) of each score from the mean and then _____ it (multiplying it by itself). These squared deviations are then added and averaged (the total is divided by the number of deviations minus one). Taking the square root of this average yields the standard deviation.

22. (p. 691)   A particular advantage of the standard deviation is that it can be used to "standard-ize" scores in a way that gives them greater meaning. This process is done using the ___-_____.

23. (p. 691)   To convert original scores to z-scores, the mean is subtracted from the score and the resulting number is divided by the _____ for the group of scores from which the original score came.

24. (p. 692)   When chance events are recorded and graphed, they often resemble what is called a _____ _____. Measures of psychological variables tend to roughly match this.

25. (p. 692)   For example, _____, memory-span, and _____ are all known to be distributed approximately normally.

26. (p. 692)   A great deal is known about the mathematical properties of the normal curve. For example, there is a fixed relationship between the _____ _____ and the normal curve such that it measures off constant proportions of the curve above and below the mean.

27. (p. 692)   As an example of this principle, notice that _____ percent of all cases fall between one standard deviation above and below the mean and _____ of all cases fall between ± 2 SD. Between ± 3 SD, _____ percent of all cases can be found.

28. (p. 692)   Relationships between the standard deviation (or z-scores) and the normal curve do not change. This makes it possible to _____ various tests or groups of scores if they come from distributions that are approximately normal.

29. (p. 693)   _____ _____, the other major divi-sion of statistical methods, includes techniques that allow us to generalize from the behavior of small groups of subjects to that of the larger groups they represent.

30. (p. 693)   In any scientific investigation, we would like to observe the entire set or _____ of subjects, objects, or events being studied. However, this prospect is usually impossible or impractical.

31. (p. 693) Instead, _____ or smaller cross sections of a population are selected, and used to draw conclusions about the entire population.

32. (p. 693) The major necessity for any sample is that it be _____. It must truly reflect the membership and characteristics of the larger population.

33. (p. 693) A very important aspect of representative samples is that their members are chosen at _____. In other words, each member of the population must have an equal chance of being included in the sample.

34. (p. 693) When we compare results from different groups, we wish to know if they might have simply occurred by chance or if they represent a real difference. Tests of _____ _____ provide an estimate of how often experimental results could have occurred by chance alone.

35. (p. 693) The results of a test of statistical significance are stated as a probability giving the odds that the observed difference was due to chance. In psychology, any experimental condition attributable to chance ___ times or less out of 100 is considered significant.

36. (p. 694) If we know, in an experiment where a drug increased memory, that the _____ is .025 (p = .025) that this effect was due to chance, we can conclude with reasonable certainty that the drug really did affect memory.

37. (p. 694) Many of the statements that psychologists make about behavior do not result from the use of experimental methods and are usually not analyzed using tests of statistical significance. Instead, they deal with the fact that two variables are _____-_____ (varying together in some orderly fashion).

38. (p. 694) The simplest way of visualizing a correlation is to construct a _____ _____ where one measure is indicated by the X axis and the second by the Y axis. The intersection of each pair of measurements is plotted as a single point.

39. (p. 694) Scatter diagrams are useful in demonstrating the three basic kinds of relationships between variables or measures. When there is a _____ relationship, increases in scores for one variable are associated with increases in scores for the other.

40. (p. 694) A _____ correlation occurs when there is no relationship between two variables.

41. (p. 694) With a _____ correlation, increases in the scores of one variable are associated with decreases in the other.

42. (p. 694) Correlations can also be expressed as a _____ of correlation, a number falling between +1.00 and –1.00.

43. (p. 694) If the correlation is +1.00 a _____ _____ relationship exists; if it is –1.00 a _____ _____ relationship has been discovered.

44. (p. 694) The most commonly used correlation coefficient is called the _____ ___. Be sure you know how to calculate this value.

45. (p. 694) Correlations in psychology are rarely perfect. Most fall somewhere between

_____ and plus or minus one. Still, they help us to identify relationships that are worth knowing.

46. (p. 695) Correlations are particularly valuable for making _____. If we know two measures are correlated, and we know a person's score on one measure, then we can predict the person's score on the other.

47. (p. 695) For example, most colleges use some combination of high school GPA, teacher ratings, SAT scores, etc., in making admission selections. Although no single predictor is perfectly correlated with success in college, together they correlate _____ and provide a useful screening technique.

48. (p. 696) If you square the correlation coefficient (multiply r by itself) you get a number telling the percent of _____ accounted for by the correlation.

49. (p. 696) For example, if the correlation between IQ scores and college GPA is 0.5, _____ percent of the variation in college grades is accounted for by knowing IQ scores.

50. (p. 696) It is important to recognize that the existence of a correlation between two measures does not mean that one causes the other. This fact is expressed by the phrase, "_____ does not demonstrate _____." Often two correlated variables are related through the influence of a third variable.

SELF-TEST

1. (p. 688) _____ statistics summarize data so they become more easily communicated.
   a. Inferential
   b. Cognitive
   c. Deviation
   d. Descriptive

2. (p. 688) The graphical display of frequency distributions which uses bars to indicate the frequency of scores within class intervals is the
   a. frequency polygon
   b. histographic planing
   c. histogram
   d. scatter diagram

3. (p. 688) Graphical display of a frequency distribution using straight lines connecting dots representing the number of cases for each class interval is called a
   a. scatter diagram
   b. normal line
   b. histogram
   d. frequency polygon

4. (p. 689) True-False. When we speak of the average of a distribution of scores, we are automatically referring to the mean.

5. (p. 689) The measure of central tendency which ranks scores from the highest to the lowest and selects the middle score is the
   a. mode
   b. mean
   c. standard deviation
   d. median

6. (p. 690) The measure of central tendency which expresses the most frequently occurring score in a distribution is the
   a. mode
   b. mean
   c. standard deviation
   d. median

7. (p. 691) A statistical range refers to
   a. a type of averaging
   b. a measure of variability
   c. a test of statistical significance
   d. one of the axes of a graph

8. (p. 691) Which of the following is a measure of variability?
    a. Pearson *r*   c. standard deviation
    b. mode   d. correlation

9. (p. 692) True-False. In a normal curve exactly 68 percent of all cases fall between 3 SD above and below the mean.

10. (p. 693) True-False. The two major divisions of statistical methods are descriptive statistics and preferential statistics.

11. (p. 693) All members of a set compose the _____, while an individual member of that set is called a _____.
    a. norm, element   c. population, sample
    b. group, deviation   d. population, representative

12. (p. 693) True-False. The major requirement for any sample is that it be representative.

13. (p. 693) Differences in experimental results are considered significant when it is demonstrated that they could only have occurred _____ or fewer times out of 100 by chance alone.
    a. 5   c. 20
    b. 10   d. 50

14. (p. 694) The simplest way of visualizing a correlation is to construct a
    a. normal curve   c. frequency polygon
    b. scatter diagram   d. histogram

15. (p. 694) When two variables are not related, we speak of
    a. positive correlation   c. negative correlation
    b. zero correlation   d. statistical significance

16. (p. 694) A negative correlation exists when _____ in the value of one score are associated with _____ in the value of an associated score.
    a. increases, increases   c. increases, decreases
    b. decreases, decreases   d. changes, changes

17. (p. 694) The number +1.00 could represent all of the following except
    a. a coefficient of correlation
    b. the result of calculating Pearson's *r*
    c. a perfect positive relationship
    d. a perfect negative relationship

18. (p. 695) Correlations are particularly valuable for
    a. expressing central tendency   c. estimating a population
    b. expressing variability   d. making a prediction

19. (p. 696) If the correlation between two factors is .70, the number 49 represents _____ accounted for by the correlation.
    a. the standard deviation   c. the percent of variance
    b. the z-score   d. the range

20. (p. 696) True-False. Correlation proves causation.

ANSWERS — PROGRAMMED REVIEW

1. descriptive statistics
2. inferential
3. frequency distribution
4. graphical
5. histograms
6. abscissa; ordinate
7. bars; bar
8. frequency polygon
9. central tendency
10. mean
11. high, low
12. median
13. arranging
14. averaged
15. mode
16. unreliable
17. greatest
18. variability
19. range
20. standard deviation
21. deviation; squaring
22. z-score
23. standard deviation
24. normal curve
25. height, intelligence

26. standard deviation
27. 68; 95; 99
28. compare
29. Inferential statistics
30. population
31. samples
32. representative
33. random
34. statistical significance
35. 5
36. probability
37. co-relating
38. scatter diagram
39. positive
40. zero
41. negative
42. coefficient
43. perfect positive; perfect negative
44. Pearson *r*
45. zero
46. predictions
47. highly
48. variance
49. 25
50. Correlation; causation

ANSWERS — SELF-TEST

1. d
2. c
3. d
4. False
5. d
6. a
7. b
8. c
9. False
10. False

11. c
12. True
13. a
14. b
15. b
16. c
17. d
18. d
19. c
20. False

Crossword Puzzles
and Answer Keys

Prepared by:
David E. Cunningham,
IECC-Olney Central College

Chapter 1
"Psychology and Psychologists"

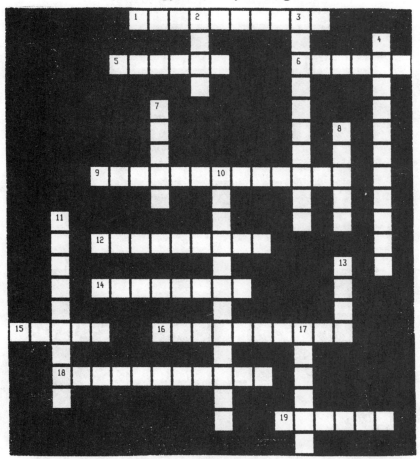

ACROSS

1. science studying organisms'
   behavior and mental processes
5. he considered introspection
   unscientific
6. psychologists concerned about
   learning disabilities of students
9. "looking inward"
12. evidence gained via observation
    and measurement
14. psychologists who study
    crime prevention
15. bearded psychoanalyst watched
    for slips of the tongue
16. he advanced gestaltism
18. psychologist concerned with
    design of machinery, autos
    and airplanes
19. psychologist studying attitudes
    and groups

DOWN

2. authored your <u>Introduction
   to Psychology</u> text
3. school of thought professing
   "whole exceeds sum of parts"
4. psychologist that "compares"
   behavior of different animals
7. visible, observable behavior
8. father of first psychology lab
10. M.D. specializing in abnormal
    behavior or psychotherapy
11. he is associated with
    structuralism
13. super technique to study and
    read by
17. self - actualization is his
    concept

Chapter 2
"Research Methods in Psychology"

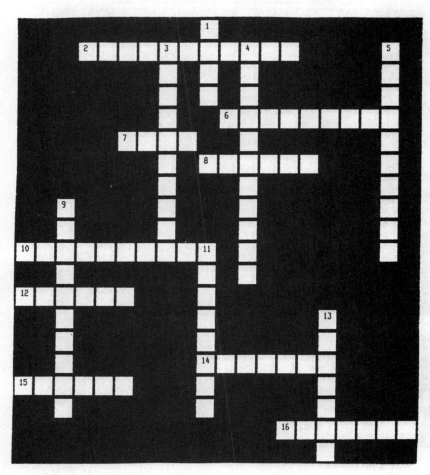

ACROSS

2. relation between two events
6. repeat
7. observer sees what he expects to see
8. summarizes existing data and predicts future observation
10. educated guess
12. method polling large groups of people
14. this group provides a basis for comparison
15. ____ assignment places subjects to control and experimental groups
16. fake pill

DOWN

1. a clever mathematical horse
3. outside variables
4. variables altered by the experimenter
5. the ____ Method has five steps and follows in a logical fashion
9. used to identify cause-effect relationship
11. participants in an experiment
13. researcher carried out "shocking" experiment

Chapter 3
"The Brain, Biology, and Behavior"

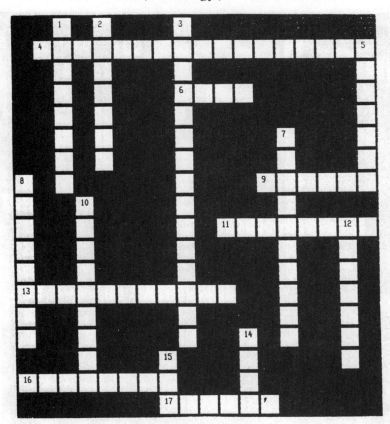

ACROSS

4. chemicals crossing synapse
6. usually carries messages away from soma
9. drug used as arrow poison by S. American Indians
11. lobe associated with touch, temperature and pressure
13. this branch prepares you for "fight or flight"
16. relay station to cortex for sensory information
17. damage to this area causes difficulty in speaking and writing

DOWN

1. lobe associated with hearing and language
2. damage to this lobe decreases ability to think, reason and plan
3. this branch calms the body to a lower level of arousal
5. tiny gap between neurons
7. "tunnel" by which damaged nerve fibers can repair themselves
8. corpus _____ connects the two brain hemispheres
10. tumors found in this lobe may cause visual problems
12. "mindblindness"
14. cell body of neuron
15. electrical stimulation of the brain (abbr.)

ACROSS

1. misshapen cornea or lens
   causes this condition
4. below the limen (limit or threshold)
5. receptor cells producing
   color sensations
8. farsightedness
9. sharpness of vision
11. receptor cells allow us
    to see at night
13. the sense of taste
15. _____ nerve fibers carry
    sharp pain very quickly
17. a color with a narrow band
    of wavelength is "pure" or _____
18. brain releases this chemical
    to combat pain

DOWN

2. _____ (3-color) theory
3. nearsightedness
6. the study of thresholds and
   other related topics
7. specific "color" of a stimulus
10. three tiny bones of middle ear
12. drug used to treat space
    sickness
14. the sense of smell
16. contains only cones--about
    50,000 of them

ACROSS

2. produces a powerful sensation of depth with vision
8. perceptions of stimuli that do not exist
12. how sensations are assembled into a meaningful "picture"
13. stimuli that allow more than one interpretation
14. information or events perceived by ESP

DOWN

1. ability to foretell future events
3. mind reading
4. Extra-Sensory Perception (abbr.)
5. distortions of stimuli that actually exist
6. _____ psychologists studied the "figure-ground" organization
7. this cliff was used to study depth perception
8. respond less to an unchanging stimulus
9. _____ perspective refers to apparent convergence of parallel lines in the environment
10. this "looks" larger when low in the sky
11. most important source of depth perception is _____ disparity

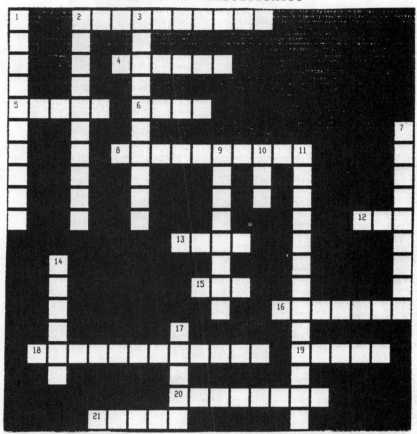

ACROSS

2. sleep attack disorder
4. these occur about 90 min. apart at night
5. brain waves that occur in Stage 4
6. Freud believed dreams represent _____ fulfillment
8. momentary shift in brain wave patterns to that of sleep
12. most active chemical in cannabis (short term)
13. Sudden Infant Death Syndrome (abbr.)
15. rapid eye movement (abbr.)
16. Freud analyzed dreams through these
18. sleepwalking
19. cannot breathe and sleep at same time
20. difficulty going or staying asleep
21. English surgeon who used hypnosis

DOWN

1. these symptoms may occur when a drug is withheld
2. bad dreams
3. she says emotional tone clues one to dream meaning
7. to be aware
9. short burst of electrical brain activity
10. electroencephalograph (abbr.)
11. Freudian Dream Theory is _____ Approach
14. explained dreaming via activation-synthesis hypothesis
17. type of dream in which dreamer "wakes" within dream

Chapter 7
"Conditioning and Learning I"

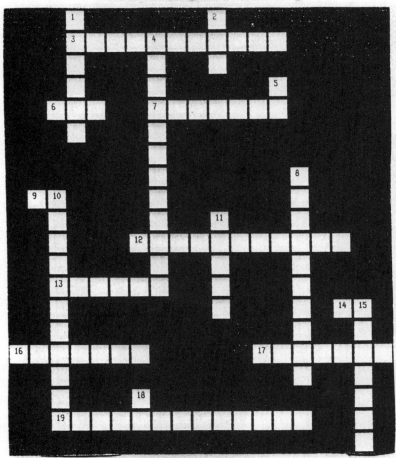

ACROSS

3. events before a response are called ____
6. this animal salivated a lot
7. Harvard psychologist B.F. ____
9. conditioned stimulus (abbr.)
12. training period used to make association between the CS and US
13. chimps were taught to work for these secondary reinforcers
14. unconditioned stimulus (abbr.)
16. this principle says a high frequency response can help reinforce a low frequency response
17. fears that persist when no real danger exists
19. avoiding black cats and walking under ladders exhibits this type of behavior

DOWN

1. his name should "ring" a bell
2. conditioned emotional response (abbr.)
4. events that follow a response are called ____
5. unconditioned response (abbr.)
8. removal of the reinforcement causes this to occur
10. sudden reappearance of learned response after apparent extinction describes ____ recovery
11. ____ ratio reinforcement is very easy to extinguish
15. gradual molding of desired response
18. conditional response (abbr.)

Chapter 8
"Conditioning and Learning II"

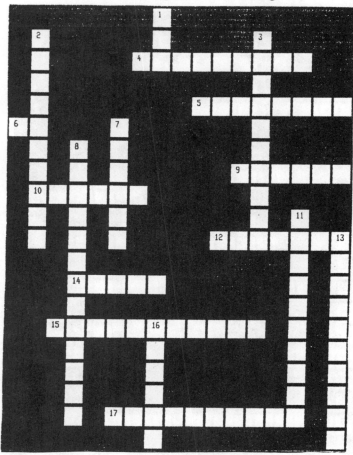

ACROSS

4. _____ learning is based on insight or understanding
5. observational learning
6. knowledge of results (abbr.)
9. punishment may cause this
10. opposite of spaced practice
12. he studied observational learning and imitating
14. brain waves denoting relaxation or heightened arousal
15. process of monitoring body processes
17. punishment should be intense, immediate, and _____

DOWN

1. Computer-Assisted Instruction (abbr.)
2. _____ instruction provides immediate feedback
3. it shows a lot of violence
7. learning remains hidden until reward is given
8. learning by watching
11. decreases likelihood of undesired response occurring again
13. common response to frustration
16. negative reinforcement increases responding by _____ discomfort

Chapter 9
"Memory"

ACROSS

5. the multiple choice question is a common test for ____
7. short-term memory (abbr.)
9. memory traces may fade or ____
10. prior learning inhibiting recall of later learning leads to ____ interference
11. long-term memory (abbr.)
12. memory ____ are changes in nerve cells or brain activity
13. he developed a "curve of forgetting"
14. marine snail used in memory studies
15. ____ attention determines what goes into STM
17. brain area acting as "switchboard" between STM and LTM
18. information one hears and is held in sensory memory two seconds or less
19. ____ memory serves as mental dictionary

DOWN

1. image last 1/2 second
2. tip-of-tongue (abbr.)
3. memories which are false
4. imagery yielding photographic memory
5. used to take an essay exam
6. much forgetting attributed to ____
8. any kind of memory system or aid
13. memory that records life events
16. to be remembered, information is ____, stored and retrieved

Chapter 10
"Cognition and Creativity"

ACROSS

2. going from specific facts or observations to general principles denotes _____ thinking
4. sudden mental reorganization of elements of problem in which solution becomes obvious
5. American sign language (abbr.)
7. Washoe was a talking _____ who used American sign language
10. problem-solving technique where participants are encouraged to produce ideas without criticism and evaluation
12. an idea that represents a class of objects or events
13. basic speech sounds are called _____
14. this stage of creative thought involves the "Aha" experience
15. first step of creative thought
16. creative thinking requires _____ thought

DOWN

1. tendency to get stuck on wrong solutions creates a barrier to solving problems
3. _____ meaning refers to emotional or personal meaning of a concept
6. rules for word order in sentences
8. with this stage of creative thought, problem solving proceeds at subconscious level
9. he challenged his chimp with a multiple-stick problem
11. going from general principles to specific situations exemplifies _____ thinking

CHAPTER 11
"Motivation"

ACROSS

1. ____ hypothalamus is "satiety" center of brain
3. brain area regulating hunger
6. aversion learned if food causes sickness
9. changing eating habits leads to behavioral ____
11. learned motives
12. may present major health risk and low self-esteem
15. pain avoidance is an ____ drive
16. organ that sends signals to brain to encourage eating
17. body equilibrium
18. sensation seeking scale (abbr.)
19. binge-purge syndrome

DOWN

2. ____ hypothalamus is "feeding" center of brain
4. motives based on biological survival needs
5. curiosity and exploration are examples of these motives
7. in humans, this drive is largely nonhomeostatic
8. ____ value is the "pull" exerted by a goal
10. he offered hierarchy of motives
11. prolonged ____ deprivation may cause disturbed thinking and sensory distortion
13. ____ motivation comes from within
14. serious eating disorder -- lose much body weight

Chapter 12
"Emotion"

ACROSS

1. American college students may suffer from symptoms of ____
4. justifying one's own behavior by giving reasonable, yet false reasons for it
6. branch of ANS prepares one for "fight or flight"
9. American functionalist believed one experiences an emotion after reacting
10. galvonic skin response (abbr.)
11. autonomic nervous system (abbr.)
14. "don't believe it" -- a defense mechanism
15. hormone that stimulates sympathetic nervous system

DOWN

2. working off frustrated desires in a socially acceptable manner
3. study of communication via body movements
4. return to an earlier behavior
5. attributing one's own feelings, shortcomings, or unacceptable impulses to others
7. gestures that have clear meanings within a particular culture
8. defense mechanism used to make up for personal defect or weakness
12. he described cognitive theory of emotions
13. lie detector

Chapter 13
"Health, Stress, and Coping"

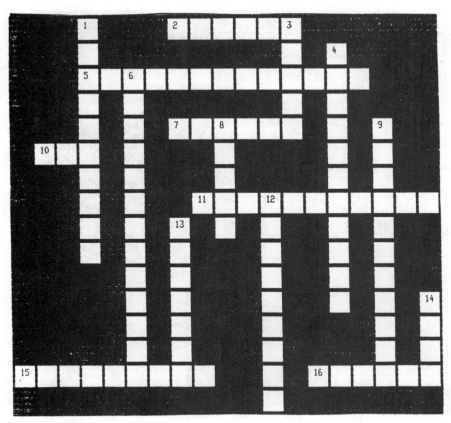

ACROSS

2. this specialty of psychology
   is concerned with improving
   one's well being
5. one who suffers from imaginary
   diseases
7. a psychological escape in which
   one pretends not to care
10. General Adaptation Syndrome (abbr.)
11. results when one is prevented from
    reaching a goal
15. it can be effective in combatting
    stress
16. this occurs when demands are
    placed on an organism to adjust

DOWN

1. in this stage the body's
   stress hormones are depleted
3. the ____ personality seems to
   be resistant to stress
4. a waivering between alternatives
6. these disorders are related to
   the "mind and body"
8. the ____ reaction mobilizes the
   body's resources to cope with
   added stress
9. mixed positive and negative
   feelings
12. target of displaced aggression
13. distressing daily annoyances
14. Social Readjustment Rating
    Scale (abbr.)

Chapter 14
"Child Development"

ACROSS

2. environment that is richly stimulating
5. he studied institutionalized babies
6. unable to take another's viewpoint
9. growth and development of the body -- especially the nervous system
11. environment
13. reflex which helps infant find bottle or breast
14. simple two-word sentences describe this speech
15. specialists in psychology who study language

DOWN

1. first stage of Piaget's Cognitive Theory
3. babies suffering from this condition are sad and depressed
4. Piaget's final stage of cognitive development
7. physical foundations of personality such as sensitivity, moodiness, etc.
8. in this stage consonant sounds are added to vowels
10. heredity
12. babies repeating vowel sounds like "oo" and "ah"

ACROSS

4. ____ parents are the most
   effective parents according to
   Diana Baumrind
5. form of euthanasia -- steps
   taken to speed up death
6. he felt we experienced
   psychosocial crisis
7. form of euthanasia -- no steps
   taken to hasten death
10. rapid physical growth and
    hormones cause this condition
    of sexual maturity
11. severe condition of undereating
13. one who studies aging
14. severe childhood problem -- child
    is locked into a private world
15. Minimal Brain Dysfunction (abbr.)

DOWN

1. freezing one's body at death
2. this theory says withdrawal
   from society is necessary and
   desirable in old age
3. lack of bowel control
4. Erikson's shame and doubt vs.____
8. lack of bladder control
9. inability to read with
   understanding
12. prejudice on basis of age

ACROSS

5. one's unique, enduring
   behavior patterns
7. Bem Sex-Role Inventory (abbr.)
8. Thematic Apperception Test (abbr.)
12. bold, outgoing person
13. he described introverts
    and extroverts
14. ____ position refers to one's
    birth order
15. shy, self-centered person

DOWN

1. test consisting of 10
   standardized ink blots
2. Minnesota Multiphasic
   Personality Inventory (abbr.)
3. these children often are
   high achievers
4. tests providing ambiguous
   stimuli for subjects to describe
6. these are relatively permanent
   and enduring qualities a person
   shows most of the time
9. he studied surface traits
   of personality
10. possessing both male and female
    traits
11. he identified "common traits"

ACROSS

2. Freudian theory of personality
4. he said strive to reach your potentials
5. he believed personality is a striving for superiority
7. he proposed an unconscious level exists and influences one's personality
9. energy derived from life instincts (EROS)
10. the "executive" component of one's personality - Freudian term
11. acts as a judge or censor for thoughts and actions of ego
13. principle by which ego functions
15. humanist who developed self theory
16. found in collective unconscious according to Jung

DOWN

1. he and Miller look at personality from behavioral viewpoint
2. at this stage oedipus or electra conflicts arise
3. death instinct proposed by Freud
6. principle under which the id operates
8. contents of mind beyond one's awareness
12. Freud's first stage of psychosexual theory
14. part of one's personality demanding immediate gratification

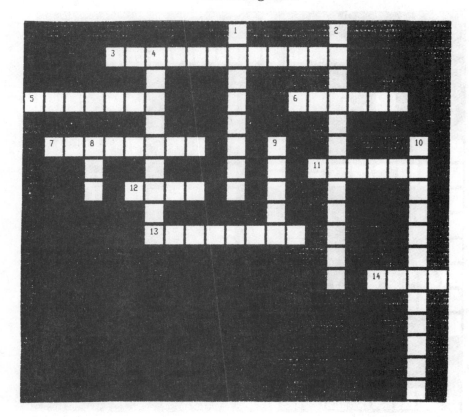

ACROSS

3. small headedness
5. classification of IQ
   from 90-109
6. portion of WAIS-R measures
   vocabulary, arithmetic etc.
7. classification of IQ
   from 120-129
11. he once said IQ's of blacks
    are lower due to genetics
12. degree of retardation for an
    IQ range 50-55 (educable)
13. degree of retardation for an
    IQ range 35-40 (trainable)
14. Weschler Adult Intelligence
    Scale (abbr.) - Revised

DOWN

1. test is ____ if it yields
   similar scores on retest
2. condition of water on the brain
4. retardation resulting from
   insufficient thyroid hormone
8. Phenylketonuria (abbr.)
9. he developed first successful
   IQ test
10. global capacity of person to
    act purposefully, think
    rationally and deal well with
    environment

Chapter 19
"Maladaptive Behavior: Deviance and Disorder"

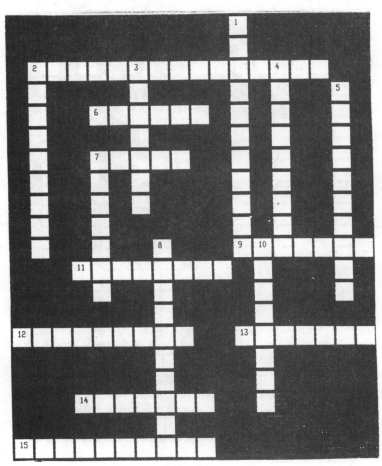

ACROSS

2. inability to behave in ways that foster the well being of an individual and society
6. billionaire with fear of contamination
7. with this disorder one has brief moments of intense anxiety
9. inability to recall one's name, address, or past events
11. this personality may consider actions of others as threatening
12. sexual arousal associated with inanimate objects
13. drug used to treat depression in some cases
14. it ranks as 7th cause of death in U.S.
15. sex with children

DOWN

1. most common phobia -- fear of losing control in public places
2. these psychopathological disorders often require hospitalization
3. _____ mental disorders are caused by brain pathology (i.e., senility, injuries)
4. persistent intrusion of unwelcome thoughts
5. irrational act a person feels driven to repeat
7. irrational fears that persist even when there's no real danger
8. this personality is sometimes referred to as a psychopath
10. Sybil had this personality condition

Chapter 20
"Major Mental Disorders"

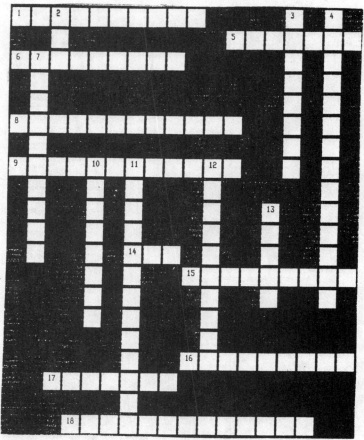

ACROSS

1. these drugs improve the mood of those who are depressed
5. with this disorder a person goes up or down emotionally
6. ___ schizophrenic characterized by body positions held for hours or days
8. use of drugs to alleviate symptoms of emotional disturbance
9. ___ schizophrenia characterized by silliness, laughter, and often obscene behavior
14. positron emission tomography (abbr.)
15. false beliefs held even when facts contradict them
16. a severe mental disturbance characterized by a break in contact with reality, delusions, etc.
17. ___ or bodily therapy (i.e., chemotherapy, ECT)
18. surgical alteration of the brain

DOWN

2. electroconvulsive therapy (abbr.)
3. chemical messenger in brain related to schizophrenia
4. sensory experiences that occur in absence of a stimulus
7. victims of this disease may not remember recent events and become confused
10. he and his colleagues had themselves committed to a mental hospital
11. drugs used to control hallucinations
12. affective psychoses appears to be ___ (produced from within)
13. he believes that mental illness is a myth

Chapter 21
"Insight Therapy"

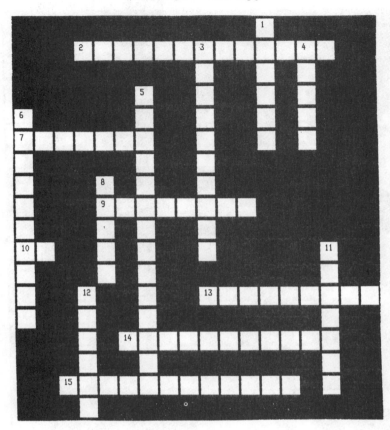

ACROSS

2. any psychological technique used
   to facilitate positive changes
   in a person's personality or
   behavior
7. capacity to feel and see what
   another is experiencing
9. practice of driving off an "evil
   spirit" of one who is "possessed"
10. Transactional analysis (abbr.)
13. emotional ____ (release) in a
    protected setting is useful in
    many psychotherapies
14. with this therapy individuals
    play roles resembling their
    real-life problems
15. in psychoanalysis, an emotional
    attachment to therapist by the
    patient

DOWN

1. he is connected with logotherapy
3. process of drilling or chipping
   holes in skull to release evil
   spirits
4. he unchained the "mentally ill"
5. this technique is "granddaddy"
   of most modern psychotherapies
6. repeating or restating what a
   client has said -- a psychological
   "mirror"
8. he proposed transactional analysis
   theory
11. ____ means whole
12. he is a client-centered therapist

ACROSS

4. in _____ therapy one associates
   a negative emotional response
   with undesirable habits
7. a reduction in fears
9. with this conditioning CS and
   US are paired
12. RET gets rid of this kind of
    beliefs
13. he is associated with Rational-
    Emotive Therapy
14. behavior _____ refers to changing
    one's behavior by learning
    principles of classical or
    operant conditioning
15. therapist selects specific _____
    behaviors that could or should
    be improved

DOWN

1. use of tokens in an institutional
   setting leads to development
   of a token _____
2. if shock is used to control
   drinking, it must be _____
   contingent
3. symbolic rewards that can be
   exchanged for real rewards
5. ordered set of steps forms this
6. Rational-Emotive Therapy (abbr.)
8. key to desensitization is _____
10. he and his dog are associated
    with classical conditioning
11. _____ means rewarding actions
    that are closer and closer
    approximations to a desired
    response

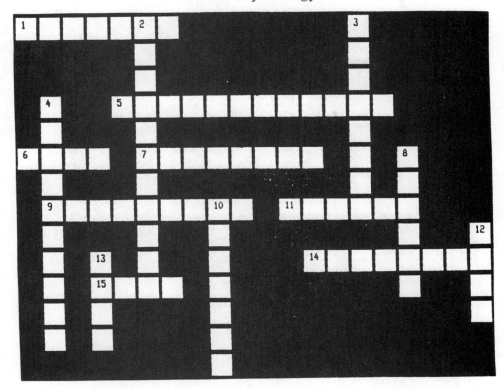

ACROSS

1. he was "shocked" by his findings on obedience
5. group ____ is the degree of attraction among group members
6. ____ -in-door effect used by sales people
7. in describing personal space one's ____ distance extends about 18" from skin
9. study of rules for personal use of space
11. people look "flat" -- lectures, formal speeches are made at ____ distance
14. he studied role playing in prison
15. he used lines in his conformity experiment

DOWN

2. this "effect" occurs with pinpoint of light in darkened room
3. distance maintained in interacting with friends
4. this conformity factor has been the blame for Susan B. Anthony dollar and Bay of Pigs invasion
8. "important people" keep ____ distance by using a desk in their offices
10. an ongoing pattern of life passed from one generation to the next
12. after slamming this in your face one may be more willing to agree to a lesser demand
13. assuming attractive people are intelligent, honest, etc., may exemplify this effect

Chapter 24
"Social Psychology II"

ACROSS

3. a negative attitude held toward members of various "out-groups"
4. viewpoint that social behaviors have roots in heredity
8. cognitive ____ means clashing thoughts
12. ____ goals restored relation between "Rattlers" and "Eagles"
13. this is strongly connected to frustration
14. Reverend Jim Jones was leader of one of these

DOWN

1. these classrooms emphasize cooperation rather than competition
2. she studied and helped cult members
3. deliberate attempt to change attitudes by imparting information
5. she was murdered in Queens, N.Y.
6. form of forced attitude change dependent on control of target person's environment
7. first step in brainwashing technique
9. ____ behavior is helping behavior
10. final step in brainwashing technique
11. the ____ learning theory holds we learn to be aggressive via observing others' aggressive acts

Chapter 25
"Sexuality and Gender"

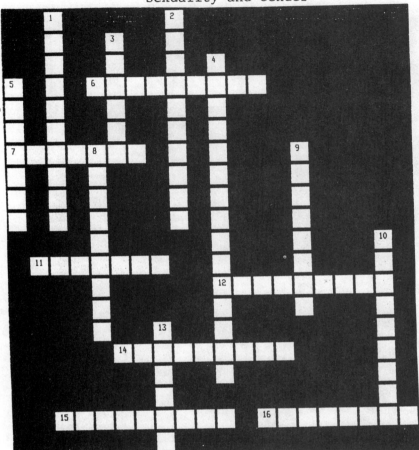

ACROSS

6. male hormones
7. gynecologist who studied human sexual response
11. Masters' research partner
12. inability to produce or maintain an erection
14. female may be masculinized by this drug
15. facial and body hair in males are examples of ____ sexual characteristics
16. among males an inability to reach orgasm is a condition known as ____ ejaculation

DOWN

1. spasm of muscles at entrance of vagina
2. prejudice, fear, and dislike aimed at homosexuals
3. one's private sense of maleness or femaleness is one's ____ identity
4. defects in sexual development resulting in dual or ambiguous sexual anatomy causes this condition
5. ____ sexual characteristics are the sexual and reproductive organs themselves
8. these ____ zones are productive of pleasure or erotic desire
9. gender ____ is essentially formed by 3 or 4 years of age
10. the squeeze technique is used to treat ____ ejaculation
13. sex glands

Chapter 26
"Applied Psychology"

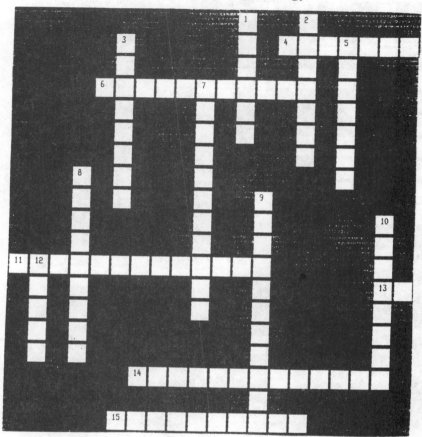

ACROSS

4. detailed biographical information
6. area of psychology concerned with design of machines and work environments for human use
11. specialty of psychology concerned with territorial behavior and personal space
13. industrial/organizational (abbr.) psychologist
14. this management procedure allows employees at all levels to help make decisions
15. work ____ (maximum output at lowest cost)

DOWN

1. these psychologists work with athletes
2. he described attentional overload
3. area of psychology focusing on how and why consumers act as they do
5. the number of people in a given space
7. these psychologists seek to understand how people learn and teachers instruct
8. flexible working hours
9. first phase of career development
10. ____ tests rate one's potential to learn
12. it can be very distracting

PUZZLE KEY

CHAPTER 1

```
          P S Y C H O L O G Y
          O               E           C
  W A T S O N       S C H O O L       O
          O         E               M
      O             S       W       P
      V             T       U       A
      E       I N T R O S P E C T I O N
  T   R       N     P   Y   N       A
  I   T       E     S   S   D       T
  T   E M P I R I C A L             I
  C   H       C   H       S Q       V
  H   F O R E N S I C     3         E
E N E R       G   A       R
F R E U D   W E R T H E I M E R
E N E       N   R   A   S
N G I N E E R I N G     L
E   N                   O
R   T             S O C I A L
```

CHAPTER 2

```
                  H                           S
    C O R R E L A T I O N                     C
              X   N                           I
              T   S     R E P L I C A T E     E
          B I A S   P     T H E O R Y         N
              N   I                           T
      E       E   N                           I
  H Y P O T H E S I S                         F
  S U R V E Y     U     B               M     I
              M   B     J               I     C
              E   J     E     C O N T R O L
  R A N D O M       C   T               G
                    T   S               R
                              P L A C E B O
                                        M
```

CHAPTER 3

```
      T   F           P
  N E U R O T R A N S M I T T E R S       S
      M   O         R   A X O N           Y
      P   N         A                     N
      O   T         S           N         A
      R   A         Y           E         P
      A   L         M       C U R A R E   S
  C   L       O     P   P A R I E T A L   E
  O           C     A   U   L   G
  L           C     T   R   E   N
  L           I     H   I   M   O
A S Y M P A T H E T I C   L   S   I
  O           I     I   C   E   O   A
  M           T     C   S   M   M
  T H A L A M U S       O
          E     B R O C A ' S
```

CHAPTER 4

```
      A S T I G M A T I S M
          R                   Y
  S U B L I M I N A L     C O N E S
          C               P   I   H         P
  H Y P E R O P I A       A C U I T Y       S
          M               H   E             Y
          A                           O   R O D S   S
  G U S T A T I O N                   S   O       C
          I               L           S   P       O
          C           L A R G E       I   H       P
      F       S A T U R A T E D       C   Y       O
      O                   I           L   S       L
      V   B E T A - E N D O R P H I N S   I       A
      A                   O               C       M
                                          S       I
                                                  N
                                                  E
```

PUZZLE KEY

CHAPTER 5

```
                                                    P
          S T E R E O S C O P I C        G          R
          E         S         L          E     V    E
          L         P         L          S     I    C
          E                   U          T     S    O
          P         H A L L U C I N A T I O N S U    G
          A         A         I          L     A    N
          T         B         N          T     L    I
          H         I         E                     T
          Y         T         A               M     I
                    U         R               O     O
                    A         R E T I O N      O     N
          P E R C E P T I O N                  N
                    E
                    A M B I G U O U S
          C L A I R V O Y A N C E
                    L
```

CHAPTER 6

```
     W      N A R C O L E P S Y
     I      I       A
     T      G       R        D R E A M S                     C
     H      H       T                                        O
     D E L T A      W I S H                                  N
     R      M       R                                        S
     A      A   M I C R O S L E E P          P               C
     W      R       G        P     S        S       T H      I
     A      E       H        I     Y        Y          C     O
     L      S       T        N  S I D S     C       O        U
                             G       L      H       D        S
            H                    R E M      O   S Y M B O L S
            O                       S       D   Y
            B                               Y   N
     S O M N A M B U L I S M   A P N E A    N   A
            S              L               A    M
            O              U   I N S O M N I A   C
            N              C
              B R A I D    I
                           D
```

CHAPTER 7

```
          P             C
          A N T E C E D E N T S
          V           O R       U
          L           N         U
     D O G            S K I N N E R
          V           E                    E
                      Q                     X
     C    S           U                     T
     P    P           E              F      I
     O    O       A C Q U I S I T I O N     N
     N    N           N         X     I     C
     T    O           C    T O K E N S      T
     A    N                     E     D     I
     N    E                           U  S  O
     E  P R E M A C K       P H O B I A S   N  S
     O    U           C                     N  H
     U  . S U P E R S T I T I O U S         A  P
     S                                         I
                                               N
                                               G
```

CHAPTER 8

```
                        C
          P             A                T
          R             L     D I S C O V E R Y
          O                             L
          G                             E  M O D E L I N G
     K    R       L                     V
          A       A                     I        E S C A P E
          M   O   T                     S              P
          M   B   E                     I        B A N D U R A
          E   S   N                     O             N      G
          D   E   T                              P    I      G
              R       A L P H A                  U    S      R
              V                                  N    H      E
            B I O F E E D B A C K                I    M      S
              A                  N               S    E      S
              T                  D               H    N      I
              I                  I               M    T      O
              O                  N               E           N
              N                  G               N
              A     C O N S I S T E N T
              L
```

PUZZLE KEY

CHAPTER 9

```
                  I           T                         E
P           R E C O G N I T I O N                       I
S           E     N           N                         D
E           C     STM         T M                       E
U   D E C A Y                 E   C                      T         M
O           L                 R                          I         N
            L T M             P R O A C T I V E         C         E
                              E                                   M
                              R                                   O
                      T R A C E S                                N
                      R                                          I
              E B B I N G H A U S                               C
              P     C
      A L Y P S I A   S E L E C T I V E                     E
              S                                             N
          H I P P O C A M P U S           E C H O          C
              D                                            O
      S E M A N T I C                                      D
              C                                            E
                                                          D
```

CHAPTER 10

```
                              F
                   I N D U C T I V E
           C                  X
           O                  A
           N   I N S I G H T   T               C H I M P
A S L      N                  I               I     N
  Y        N                  O       K       N     C
  N        O                          O       H     U
B R A I N S T O R M I N G             H     C B     A
  A        X                          L     O       T
  X        I          V   D   C O N C E P T R       I
P H O N E M E S                       R     I       O
           V                                O       N
           E   I L L U M I N A T I O N
           D
               O R I E N T A T I O N
                              I
                   D I V E R G E N T
                              E
```

CHAPTER 11

```
              V E N T R O M E D I A L
                                    A
          H Y P O T H A L A M U S    T
              R                  T A S T E
      I     D I E T I N G        I   E   R
      N     M                M   M   X   A
S E C O N D A R Y            A    U       L
N     E     R Y             S    L
S     N                A    L O B E S I T Y
O     T                N    W       T
R     I                O            R
Y   E P I S O D I C     R      L I V E R
      V     A          E       N
    H O M E O S T A S I S      S S
            X                  I
            I                  C
B U L I M I A
```

CHAPTER 12

```
              D E P R E S S I O N
                          U
              K           B
      R A T I O N A L I Z A T I O N
P     E       N           I
R     G       E   S Y M P A T H E T I C
O     R   E S I C           M       C
J A M E S S   I             B       O
E     S   G S R   S         L       M
C     I       I         A N S       P
T     O       O     P       C       E
I     N           P O       H       N
O                 O L       A       S
N               E P I S O D I C     A
    H O M E O S T A S I S   H   D E N I A L
          X       G         T       O
          I       R         E       N
A D R E N A L I N E
                  P
                  H
```

PUZZLE KEY

CHAPTER 13

```
E           H E A L T H
X                 A       V
H Y P O C H O N D R I A C
A         S       D       I
U         Y   A P A T H Y  L
S         C       L       L         A
G A S     H       A   F R U S T R A T I O N
T         O       R   M       C       I       M
I         S       M       A       T       B
O         O             H       A       I       I
N         M             A       P       O       V
          A             S       E       N       A
          T             S       G               L
          I             L       O               E
          C             E       A               N         S R
EXCERCISE               G   S T R E S S         R R
                        O
                        A
                        T
```

CHAPTER 14

```
S       E N R I C H E D
E               O
N       F       S P I T Z
S       O       P
O       R       I               E G O C E N T R I C
R       M       T       B
I       A T U R A T I O N       N               T
M       L       L   B A B B L I N G       E
O               I       B       N A T U R E   M
T               S       L       U R T U R E   E
O               M       I       R           C R A
R                       N       E       R O O T I N G
                        G           C           E
                        TELEGRAPHIC     O       N
                                        I       T
                        PSYCHOLINGUISTS
```

CHAPTER 15

```
          C           D           E
A U T H O R I T A T I V E       N C
A     Y           S E R I K S O N
ACTIVE N           E               P
O     I           G     P A S S I V E
N     C           E               E
O     S           M               S
M                 E               I
Y                 N               S
    E             T
    N         D
P U B E R T Y   A N O R E X I A
    R         S               G
    E         L               E
    S     G E R E N T O L O G I S T
    I         X               S
    S   A U T I S M       M B D
              A
```

CHAPTER 16

```
R   M   F   P
O   M   I   R
R   P E R S O N A L I T Y
B S R I   S J       T
S R I     T E       A T
C H       B C       A I
H A       O T       I T     A
A L       R I       C S     N
C L       N V       A       D
H A       S E X T R O V E R T
  L           A T E L   J U N G
  P O R D I N A L           G
  O                         Y
INTROVERT                   N
  R
```

PUZZLE KEY

CHAPTER 17

```
              D
  P S Y C H O A N A L Y T I C
  H       L           H
  A   M A S L O W     A D L E R
  L       A           N
P L I B I D O   F R E U D   A
L C                   N     T
E         D           C   E G O
A                     O     S
S               S U P E R E G O
U                     C       R
R E A L I T Y         S       A
E       D             C       L
              R O G E R S   L
                      U
  A R C H E T Y P E S
```

CHAPTER 18

```
                    R           H
      M I C R O C E P H A L Y   Y
      I             E           D
A V E R A G E       L I     V E R B A L
      R             I           O
    S U P E R I O R   B   B     C     I
      K       N   I   L   I   J E N S E N
      U   M I L D   E   N     P     N   T
              M O D E R A T E A     S   E
                            L       E   L
                            Y   W A I S   L
                                        I
                                        G
                                        E
                                        N
                                        C
                                        E
```

CHAPTER 19

```
                A
                G
P S Y C H O P A T H O L O G Y
P       R       R       B       C
S   H U G H E S A       S       O
Y   A       P   P       E       M
C   P A N I C   H       S       P
H   H       I   O       S       U
O   O       C   B       I       L
T   B           I       O       S
I   I       A   A M N E S I A   I
C   P A R A N O I D U           O
    S       N   A   L           N
            T   A   T
F E T I S H I S M   L I T H I U M
            O       P
            C       L
      S U I C I D E E
            A
P E D O P H I L I A
```

CHAPTER 20

```
E N E R G I Z E R S         D   H
      C               B I P O L A R
C A T A T O N I C           P   L
      L                     A   L
      Z                     M   U
C H E M O T H E R A P Y     I   C
      H                     N   I
D I S O R G A N I Z E D     E   N
I M   O       N     N         S A
M E   S       T     D         Z T
E R   E       I P E T   D E L U S I O N S
R S   N       P   G         Z   O
      H       S   E                 N
      A       Y   N     P S Y C H O S I S
      N       C   O
              H   U
              O S O M A T I C
              T
    P S Y C H O S U R G E R Y
```

PUZZLE KEY

CHAPTER 21

```
                           F
        P S Y C H O T H E R A P Y
              P       R A N       E
  R       E   P   A N N     L     E L
  E M P A T H Y C H A N N I N G
  F       B E R N A     A L   C   I S M
  L       E R N E   A L   G
  E       R           Y       C A T H A R S I S   G
  C     T A                                         E
  T   I N G                                         S
  G     R O G E R S   P S Y C H O D R A M A         T
                I                                   A
        T R A N S F E R E N C E                     L
              S
```

EMPATHY · PSYCHOTHERAPY · FRANKL · REPANNING · PSYCHOANALYTICALLY · EXORCISM · BERNE · ROGERS · CATHARSIS · GESTALT · PSYCHODRAMA · TRANSFERENCE · REFLECTING

CHAPTER 22

```
                                            E
                          R       A V E R S I O N   C O N O M Y
        T       R E       E       P
        H I K   R E       S       O M Y
D E S E N S I T I Z A T I O N     N S E
        R N S       R
        R A   R E L A X   R
        C L A S S I C A L
        H Y   S   1 R R A T I O N A L   P
        A P   H   A T       V L
        T O   A   E L L I S   L O
M O D I F I C A T I O N       V
        N
T A R G E T
```

AVERSION · ECONOMY · RESPONSE · DESENSITIZATION · HIKRRARHY · CLASSICAL · RELAX · IRRATIONAL · ELLIS · SHAPING · MODIFICATION · TARGET · PAVLOV

CHAPTER 23

```
M I L G R A M
          A U T
  G       O K   C O H E S I V E N E S S     P
F O O T   I N T I M A T E       S           E
  R   P R O X E M I C S   P U B L I C       R
  U   H   N       I           O             S
  P   A S C H     T           C             O   D
  T   L     H     U       Z I M B A R D O   N   O
  H   O           L           I             A   O
  I               T           A                 R
  N               U           L
  K               R
                  E
```

MILGRAM · GROUPTHINK · FOOT · COHESIVENESS · INTIMATE · AUTOKINETIC · PROXEMICS · PUBLIC · ASCH · HALO · CULTURE · ZIMBARDO · PERSONA · SOCIAL · DOOR

CHAPTER 24

```
                  J                               S
    P R E J U D I C E                             I
    E             J       S O C I O B I O L O G Y N
    R             S A W                           G
    S           G I                               E
    U         B R                       U         R
    A       I N O                       N
    S I O N A D I S S O N A N C E       F
    I       N I N G           P R O S   R E E Z I N G   R
    O       V N W             R   O             E       E
    N       E A S H       S U P E R O R D I N A T E     F
    S       S I H I N G       R   C                     R
    O       E N G             O   I                     E
    C A G G R E S S I O N     C   A                     E
    I       G                 I                         Z
    A                         A                         I
    L                 C U L T                           N
                                                        G
```

PREJUDICE · JIGSAW · SOCIOBIOLOGY · SINGER · PERSUASION · DISSONANCE · BRAINWASHING · SUPERORDINATE · PROSOCIAL · UNFREEZING · REFREEZING · AGGRESSION · SOCIAL · CULT

PUZZLE KEY

CHAPTER 25

```
        V               H
        A       G       O
        G       E       M       H
P       I   A N D R O G E N S
R       N       D   R   P   R
I   M A S T E R S   O   H   M           I
A   R           O   B   P   A   D       D
R   U           G   I   H   P   E   D   P
Y   S           E   A   R   T   N   R   E
    J O H N S O N       D   A   I   T   M
    O           O U     I M P O T E N C E
                S       T   D   Y   I   R
                    G   I       G   M   E
            P R O G E S T I N    E   A   T
                    N   M             T   U
    S E C O N D A R Y   R E T A R D E D
                    A
                    D
                    S
```

CHAPTER 26

```
                            S       M
                    C       P       B I O D A T A
                    O       O       L       E
        E N G I N E E R I N G       R       N
                    S       T       A       S
                    U       S       M       I
            F       M               M       T
            L       E       R               Y
            E               E
            X               X               A
    E N V I R O N M E N T A L               P
            O               L               T
            I       I       O               I O
            S       I       R               T U
            E       M       A       P A R T I C I P A T I V E
                    E               O
                    E F F I C I E N C Y
```